Bibliographic
Control of
Nonprint Media

Bibliographic Control of Nonprint Media

edited by
Pearce S. Grove
and
Evelyn G. Clement

American Library Association
Chicago 1972

Library of Congress Cataloging in Publication Data
Main entry under title:

Bibliographic control of nonprint media.

   Bibliography: p.
   1. Cataloging of audio-visual materials—Congresses.
I. Grove, Pearce S., 1930–   ed. II. Clement,
Evelyn G., 1926–   ed.
Z695.66.B52   025.3′4′7   70-183706
ISBN 0-8389-0109-3

International Standard Book Number 0-8389-0109-3 (1972)

Library of Congress Catalog Card Number 70-183706
Copyright © 1972 by the American Library Association

Printed in the United States of America

Dedication

The editors dedicate this work to the memory of Galen Pearce, Louis Brown, and Edwin Hatch.

Galen L. Pearce exemplified the spirit of the scholarly quest so vital to discovery and innovation. His life and death during the media institute, upon which this publication is based, had a profound effect on his colleagues who came to love him early in August 1969.

Louis H. Brown's expenditure of energy and dedication to professional commitments was unequaled. Through his tireless devotion to centralized bibliographic control, the Library of Congress now has funds to enlarge its staff and begin a Machine-Readable Cataloging (MARC) program for nonprint media. Dr. Brown's sudden death leaves a void that can never be adequately filled.

Memorial scholarships at the Association for Educational Communications and Technology have been established in the names of both Dr. Pearce and Dr. Brown by their colleagues.

Edwin Lewis Hatch, son of Orin and Frances Hatch, was a very happy little boy as part of the institute family in Norman, Oklahoma. Although an accident claimed his life just prior to his fourth birthday, which would have been December 25, 1970, he lives on in many hearts.

Contents

Contents

Preface

Sixty-eight papers by forty-nine contributors from the United States, Canada, and Great Britain are presented here as a consequence of the United States Office of Education media institute, Systems and Standards for the Bibliographic Control of Media. While these papers do not represent a verbatim transcription of the institute proceedings, the taped transactions of this group's meetings provide, nevertheless, the basic content of this volume. Formal lecture sessions, group discussions, and committee meetings were taped when the institute met in Norman, Oklahoma, August 1969, in concentrated isolation. Other sessions were recorded when the same group of some forty specialists from a variety of academic disciplines met in planned integration and interaction with the American Library Association Midwinter meeting in Chicago, January 1970, and with the Association for Educational Communications and Technology conference in Detroit, April 1970.

Transcriptions made from these recordings were reworked by the editors, who were also the director and assistant director of the institute, and sent to speakers, discussion leaders, and committee chairmen or reporters for a further revision of the spoken word for printed copy. Written committee reports, participant summaries, and speakers' outlines or notes were then requested for those sessions not recorded or for which transcriptions were not possible. The editors again reworked and integrated the materials, revising, rewording, and rewriting the presentations several times. The papers were then typed, read, corrected, and sent to the contributors for final corrections of fact.

The process of reducing evolutionary presentations and discussions into logical and coherent papers is the burden accepted by the editors in preparing this book. They also accept responsibility for the accuracy of expression and interpretation of the thoughts and ideas of all the contributors.

Acknowledgments

Those to whom the editors are indebted number several hundred. In addition to the institute participants, speakers, and special guests, there were many consultants who contributed to the institute in its formative stage. Among them were Dr. Anna Hyer, Dr. Frank Bertalan, Dr. William Fulton, and Dr. Harry Skelly. The influence of two institute staff members, Dr. Herman L. Totten and Mr. William Quinly, is felt throughout the volume, as indeed it was during the institute sessions.

The editors are also grateful to Dr. James B. Sublette, Dean of Graduate Studies at Eastern New Mexico University, and other members of the university's faculty research committee who extended assistance through a modest but essential grant.

A staff of thirty persons—including transcribers, typists, assemblers, indexers, revisers, readers, and an illustrator—gave extensive support to the manuscript preparation. The transcribers and typists were June Rankin, Rhonda Evans, Penny Carrasco, Miller Malone, Mabel Aragon, Pauline Vicenti, Jackie Rankin, Cheri Mankin, Barbara Aragon, Bea Cano, Linda Delaney, Rita Balencia, Emelina Duran, Nancy Mitchell, Mickey Paden, Jan Edwards, Doris Mahan, Becky Barnett, Winifred White and Crystal Ainsworth. Those who read and offered literary criticism were Dr. James Penrod, Lino deSousa, Pat Fitzner, Ed Richter, Elaine Grove, and Brenda Grove. Mrs. Laurie Sundborg assisted with the preparation of the bibliography and the supervision of some transcription work. Darrel Jenkins and Mike Garcia helped assemble the pages. and Travis Mitchell drew figures for the publication.

In addition to the editors, one person, Mrs. June Rankin, saw the manuscript through every stage of its development. Her patience and skill matched their determination to bring this sourcebook for the organization of nonprint media into print. Therefore, she is the one to whom they owe the most for joining them in this endeavor.

Institute Participants

George L. Abbott, Media Librarian, Syracuse University Library, Syracuse, New York

Ovid L. Bayless, Directorate of Instructional Technology, U.S. Air Force Academy, Colorado Springs, Colorado

Mary R. Boyvey, Program Director, Texas Education Agency, Austin

Paul Brawley, Editor, Nonprint Materials, *The Booklist,* American Library Association, Chicago

Helen H. Britton, Senior Catalog Librarian and Assistant Catalog Reviser, Ohio State University Libraries, Columbus (now Catalog Librarian, Texas A&M University, College Station)

Gerald R. Brong, Assistant Director, Audio-Visual Center, Washington State University, Pullman

Louis H. Brown, Supervisor, Educational Media Distribution, Bureau of Audiovisual Instruction, University of Colorado, Boulder (now deceased)

Mary B. Cassata, Head, Reference Department, University Library, State University of New York at Buffalo (now Associate Director for Public Services)

Bernard Chibnall, Head of Media Services, Media Service Unit, University of Sussex, Brighton

Margaret Chisholm, Associate Professor, School of Library and Information Science, University of Maryland, College Park (now Dean)

Harlow W. Clarke, Director, Instructional Material Center, Sacramento County Office of Education, Sacramento, California

Robert L. Claussen, Instructional Media Coordinator, Visual Instructional Bureau, University of Texas, Austin

Antony Croghan, Lecturer, School of Librar-ianship, Northwestern Polytechnic, London

James A. Fee, Coordinator of Audiovisual and Television Education, Contra Costa County Schools Department, Pleasant Hill, California (now Director of Media Services, San Mateo County Schools, Redwood City, California)

Malcolm S. Ferguson, Audiovisual Specialist, Special Projects Office, National Library of Medicine, Bethesda, Maryland

Gilbert Fites, Director, Division of Library Science, Northeastern State College, Tahlequah, Oklahoma

Eugene B. Fleischer, Director of Audio-Visual Resources, Brevard Junior College, Cocoa, Florida (now Director of Learning Resources, Ocean County College, Tom River, New Jersey)

Catheryne S. Franklin, Assistant Professor, Graduate School of Library Science, University of Texas, Austin

Orin W. Hatch, Librarian and Director of Instructional Resources, New Mexico Junior College, Hobbs

Sister James Ellen Huff, Director of Library, Spalding College, Louisville, Kentucky (now retired and a consultant)

Ann M. Jenkins Assistant Professor of Library Science, North Carolina Central University, Durham

B. Eugene Koskey, Assistant Professor, School of Library and Information Science, University of Wisconsin, Milwaukee (now Director, Instructional Materials Center, College of Education, University of New Mexico, Albuquerque)

Jules Leni, Vice-President, Comprehensive Service Corp., New York

Shirley Lewis, Head, Cataloging Department,

Canadian Book Wholesale Co., Ltd., Scarboro, Ontario

Janet E. Macdonald, Chief Cataloger, Cooperative Book Centre of Canada, Ltd., Toronto (now Audiovisual Librarian, North York Public Library, Willowdale, Ontario)

Roger B. McFarland, Media Specialist, Bro-Dart Industries, City of Industry, California (now Librarian, Mount San Antonio College, Walnut, California)

Glenn D. McMurry, Chief, Distribution Branch, National Audiovisual Center, Washington

Robert G. Murray, Assistant Librarian for Cataloging, Northeastern University Library, Boston

David G. Nevin, Director, Audio-Visual Department, Washington University Libraries, St. Louis, Missouri

Edward F. Newren, Lecturer, Division of Education Media, and Program Supervisor, AV Center, Indiana University, Bloomington (now Assistant Professor, Graduate School of Library Science, University of Michigan, Ann Arbor)

Elizabeth F. Pasternak, Cataloging Manager, Xerox Professional Library Service, Santa Ana, California (now Librarian, Los Alimitos-Rossmoor Branch, Orange County Library, Santa Ana, California)

Galen L. Pearce, Assistant Professor, College of Education, University of Nevada, Reno (now deceased)

Catherine Ann Peer, Communications Librarian, Communications Center, University of Pittsburgh (now Director of Nonprint Services, Richard Stockton State College, Pomona, New Jersey)

Jean Riddle, Head, Library Technical Services, Borough of East York Board of Education, Toronto (now Jean Riddle Weihs, Course Director, Library Techniques, Seneca College of Applied Arts and Technology, Willowdale, Ontario)

Wanda K. Sivells, Director, Learning Center, Wharton County Junior College, Wharton, Texas

Jeanette H. Swickard, Senior Editor, Publishing Services, American Library Association, Chicago (now Librarian, Evanston Public Schools, Evanston, Illinois)

Alma M. Tillin, Technical Services Librarian, Berkeley Unified School District, Berkeley, California

Carolyn I. Whitenack, Professor and Chairman, Educational Media, Purdue University, Lafayette, Indiana

T. M. Williams, Assistant Professor of Communication, Brigham Young University, Provo, Utah (now Director of Continuing Education and Community Services, Utah State System of Higher Education, Salt Lake City)

Lynn Zelmer, Director, International Communications Institute, University of Alberta, Edmonton (now Assistant Supervisor, Programming, Educational Media Division, Department of Extension, University of Alberta, Edmonton)

Staff

Evelyn G. Clement, Doctoral candidate, Graduate Library School, Indiana University, Bloomington, formerly Learning Resources librarian, Oral Roberts University, Tulsa, Oklahoma. Institute Assistant Director (now Chairman, Department of Library Service, Memphis State University, Memphis, Tennessee)

Pearce S. Grove, Library Director, Eastern New Mexico University, Portales. Institute Director

William J. Quinly, Director, Media Center, Florida State University, Tallahassee. Institute Instructor

Herman L. Totten, Librarian, Wiley College, Marshall, Texas. Institute Instructor (now Assistant Dean, Graduate School of Library Science, University of Kentucky, Lexington)

Introduction

It seems that man has always faced the task of maintaining a pictorial record of his accomplishments and his follies. The care and organization of maps and drawings have been of concern throughout history. In recent times photography has provided another way of recording man's activities—and another document to catalog and file.

Fred Ott's celebrated sneeze before a motion picture camera in 1894 was copyrighted as our first paper-print photoreproduction. A provision in the act establishing the United States National Archives in 1934 recognized that "unique ability of the motion picture camera to record events of historical purposes." Ten years later the Library of Congress established a Motion Picture Division. This step led to the cataloging of films in 1946 and to a general acceptance of newer media as invaluable records of the present and past. Nevertheless, nonprint media has yet to receive the attention given print material.

On March 10, 1971, United States Senator Howard M. Baker introduced Senate Bill 1169 in the 92nd Congress "to preserve, for purposes of study and research, nationally televised news and public interest programs." Under the provisions of this bill

The Librarian of Congress shall:
(1) obtain, preserve, and index videotapes or films of—
   (A) nationally televised evening news programs; and
   (B) such other nationally televised programs as the Librarian of Congress determines to be of substantial public interest, including, but not limited to, public affairs programs and other programs dealing with current events;

(2) produce subject matter tapes or films which shall present a collection of or portions of programs obtained under clause (1) of this section, in the order in which such programs or portions were broadcast, dealing with a particular subject during a given period of time, without any alteration or change in such programs or portions of programs; and
(3) make available for purposes of study or research copies of videotapes of films obtained or produced under this section.

Educational systems specialists lament the deplorable lack of organization of nonprint media for utilization in the learning process. Audiovisual personnel have, out of despair, made a painful entry into the world of bibliography while librarians, long experienced in the bibliographic control of printed matter, still appear preoccupied with more conventional forms of information and reluctant to turn their expertise to the organization of nonprint media.

The executive secretary of the American Historical Association is assisting the work of several committees within his organization to establish new patterns for the learning of history through the scholar-oriented integration of print and nonprint media. In an appearance before librarians, Paul Ward concluded that the success of AHA's undertaking rests, in large part, with the willingness of librarians to accept multimedia materials as equally important as print, and he requested that librarians and audiovisual and other information specialists join in this endeavor.

Even in our electronic era which is characterized by rapid change, the rate of growth and expansion exhibited in what is called media is phenomenal. New terms are coined before others are understood and accepted. The terms *audiovisual materials, software, educational media,* and *nonbook material* are all used synonymously with *media, nonprint media,* and even *multimedia.* The increased rate of their production, public acceptance, and demand without an equal concern for bibliographic control—selection tools, acquisition procedures, cataloging, classification, storage, retrieval, effective use, and potential reuse— has driven those responsible for their care, access, and use to the point of despair.

Professional committees and groups have adopted a variety of locally developed organizational schemes. Commercial producers and distributors are attempting to assist with various methods of service, only to find inevitable frustration with the lack of accepted standards. Although private government grants have provided opportunities for study, research and experimentation are uncoordinated and isolated. The result leads to duplication (the perpetual reinvention of the wheel) and to even greater confusion for the individual user.

Against this background the United States Office of Education media institute entitled Systems and Standards for the Bibliographic Control of Media was organized. It was convened to facilitate: (1) the systematic evaluation of existing bibliographic sources for nonprint material; (2) a critical review of published and unpublished guides, manuals, handbooks, schedules, and suggested standards by librarians, audiovisual specialists, and commercial firms; (3) the consideration of user needs and their implications for systems of retrieval; (4) an examination of current research and the identification of conflict, duplication, and trends in the control of audiovisual software; (5) an evaluation of commercial firms' concerns, needs, and proposed solutions; (6) the consideration of systems and standards for the location, evaluation, selection, storage, and retrieval of nonbook material; (7) the establishment of an international perspective in the consideration of controls for media; and (8) the establishment of structured dialogue between members of the various professions mutually concerned with the control and use of media.

To accomplish these objectives, nonprint-media specialists in the United States, Canada, and Great Britain were brought together in participant-speaker-consultant roles through an institute structured with intervals between three sessions over a one-year period. The initial three-week session, in August 1969 in Norman, Oklahoma, was designed to integrate the various disciplines through the selection of thirty-seven participants and some twenty speaker-consultants from library science, audiovisual, information science, communications, and education.

Each speaker's itinerary and institute schedule were purposely planned whereby he would spend one-half day as a participant-observer in the presence of the preceding speaker from a different discipline who was concerned with the same topic or one closely related. The speakers then had one-half day without other speakers followed by one-half day as a speaker-consultant with a speaker-observer present. Speakers were then required to shift to a participant-observer-consultant role for the last half day when the next speaker-consultant began his presentation. The mixture of disciplines and changing roles of the speakers encouraged involvement and brought about the camaraderie with participants sought by the institute staff. To increase the feeling of give-and-take, speakers were encouraged not to rely on formally prepared speeches and participants were encouraged to interrupt the speakers with comments and questions. Naturally the structure of the sessions and the emphasis on the interaction between participants and speaker-consultants has had an effect on the papers contained in this volume. The discussions sometimes occur mid-speech and not after it as is usual. Because speaker-consultants were present during the presentations of others, they too contributed to the discussions. Since their comments have a special authority, they have been identified. The identity of participants was difficult to arrive at from the transcripts, and so none is given. Because the institute was convened on three occasions, it will be apparent that all presentations were not made at the same time. When necessary the introductions to each of the ten parts explain the time and setting.

Succeeding sessions of the institute, with the same participants, focused on the specific roles of professional associations, national service centers, commercial organizations, and government in national and international plans for the bibliographic control of nonprint media. Following the initial three-week session in Oklahoma, a fourth week was held in conjunction with the American Library Association Midwinter Conference in Chicago during January 1970. The third session, with the same participants and some speakers returning as participants or observers, was planned for those present to interrelate with the annual convention of the Association for Educational Communications and Technology in Detroit during April of 1970.

Interim periods were utilized for committee work, institute planning, specific research and study, and interaction with professional associations. This activity has led to major changes in commitments and structure of national organizations. New committees, divisions, and interest groups were formed in the American Library Association, Association for Educational Communications and Technology, American Society for Information Science, and the Library of Congress. Other organizations such as the National Audio Visual Association, Educational Film Library Association, National Center for Educational Statistics, National Library of Medicine, Canadian Library Association, and the Library Association (Great Britain) have strengthened their commitment to the organization of nonprint media. Books and articles have appeared in at least three countries as a result of the institute. Three monographs already in print have been revised and a three-nation committee established to maintain another, the *Anglo-American Cataloging Rules*. The publication entitled *Films, a MARC Format* (1970) resulted in part from the determination of institute participants and speakers.

Standards, statistics, bibliographic format, the application of automation techniques, packaging, selection tools, storage facilities, and retrieval devices for nonprint media are a continuing interest of those participating in the institute. What has occurred to stimulate interest in the bibliographic control of nonprint media for quick and proper utilization is shown in some measure through the contents of this volume.

The sixty-eight papers, reports, and discussions by forty-nine specialists in the organization and use of media present research activity and current practices in the United States, Canada, and Great Britain with some aspects of the problem in France, Italy, and the Scandinavian countries. They conclude that nonprint media is not presently organized for its intelligent selection and utilization, and that professional bibliographers in the Association for Educational Communications and Technology, the Educational Film Library Association, the American Society for Information Science, and the American Library Association have failed to establish standards, while commercial companies, less constrained by tradition, are answering the cries of collectors and users with incompatible schemes, codes, and forms of bibliographic entry.

Through the interest of these writers and the contributions of their media centers and professional organizations, the bibliographic control of nonprint media is beginning to receive the attention essential to effective communications and learning. Nonprint media is no longer viewed solely as an enrichment of print, but rather as a basic aspect of communication among a world population confronted with numerous languages, customs, slang, idioms, writing skills, and unprecedented demands for speed in the exchange of concepts, emotions, and expectations.

Professional organizations and national centers are rethinking their commitments and reevaluating their responsibilities. In January of 1970 the presidents of three national associations, with a combined membership in excess of 60,000, were asked to assess the relationship of their organizations to the control of nonprint media. Strong opinions were expressed by all, favoring a major commitment of each profession—library, audiovisual, and information science—to the development of systems and standards for the bibliographic control of nonprint media.

Part 1

Instructional Technology and Media Utilization

American educators have extolled the virtues and potential benefits of instructional technology so successfully that it is now commonly advocated by many prominent leaders in our society. Although it is viewed as enrichment by some and a panacea by others, the use of technological innovation in education at all levels has been accepted, even expected, in the United States.

Specialists in the fields of the educational process, instructional technology, learning theory, information networks, and media systems were brought together to interact with each other and with institute participants with similar backgrounds in audiovisual, library, and information science disciplines.

Joseph Becker has been a pioneer in the application of data-processing techniques to information storage and distribution. His advocation of local, regional, national, and international networks for communication supports Robert Heinich's and Robert Snider's thesis that our current state of technological development makes available an unrealized potential for the improvement of instruction and learning.

Eugene Koskey has suggested a new set of descriptors for the objectives stressed by Louis Brown in his concern for increased utilization of nonprint media in the educational process. Margaret Chisholm was particularly concerned with its most effective utilization, while James Doyle and George Grimes reported experimental studies on the flow of educational information from source to receiver and the results of a federally funded project to effect a statewide information network.

Interlibrary Communications and Networks

Joseph Becker

In 1945 the computer was just coming into its own. As a matter of fact, it was the Manhattan Project and some of our jet fighter production needs that led to the computer itself becoming a reality. The first computer appeared in 1943 or 1944 on the University of Pennsylvania campus in Philadelphia. It was called the ENIAC, which is an acronym for Electronic Numerical Integrater and Computer; there are many acronyms in the computer field.

Many professions are now finding meaningful and sensible ways of applying technology to a wide variety of processes in various aspects of our society. In contrast to the single computer in the world only twenty-five years ago, we now have seventy-five or eighty thousand computers in the United States alone. In the early 1970s that number is expected to double.

As librarians, we have been dedicated to the principle of sharing information all of our professional lives. We have been sharing information from our collections and the collections of others with our constituents, requiring them to come to us and engage in this type of interaction, and then depart. The traditional way has been to establish a central collection within four walls and invite the library's constituents to come in and use it. We have operated very successfully in the past with this passive

approach to interaction. However, because of the advent of several different factors, the least of which is technology, the suggestion is now being made that maybe instead of being passive collectors and requiring people to come to us, we can, as a profession, consider ourselves active disseminators and essentially broadcast our information to others, no matter where they may be.

Where they may be is suddenly important. Thirty or forty years ago we could rely on the communities surrounding our libraries to be fairly stable. This is no longer true in the United States. Mobility of population, as indicated by our last census, is such that we can no longer rely on serving our fixed community.

The second thing we must consider is the question of economy. Can many university libraries, for example, strive to become another Harvard, attempting to build buildings as large as those at Harvard and to house collections the size of Harvard's? It is unrealistic and could not be achieved, even if it were desired. The notion of sharing resources among different institutional organizations looms as a possible answer to this question. How do you get information, no matter where it is located, into the hands of those who use it? Economy is a factor, while another one is certainly the form of information.

This is no longer only a world of print but now a world of both print and nonprint media. Librarians, I hope, are ready to accept the new

President, Becker and Hayes, Inc., Bethesda, Maryland (library automation consultants)

media as an additional responsibility. There are some who have not thus far made the transition, but it is anticipated that within the profession the rate of acceptance will be accelerated. The fact remains, however, that we no longer talk of sharing information from books, but of sharing information in all its forms, whether they be visual, audio, or a combination of both. Mixed media, mobile population, and economy are factors, even pressures, that are urging us to find some new means of interlibrary cooperation.

There is another factor, that of time. The tempo of modern living is such that the requirements on us from business, industry, national growth, et cetera, make time an extremely precious commodity. Consequently, if information is one of the mainstays of progress, then response time required to satisfy the need for information becomes terribly important and critical. As a matter of fact, we continue to compress that time into the shortest possible period.

The interdisciplinary nature of modern life and our professions compounds the problem further. No longer is man interested in one particular thing but rather in many related things. The resources which at one time served him well on a local basis are no longer adequate to serve his diverse interests. The general practitioner leaves medical school, equipped during his educational life with a well-rounded background on medical practice and procedures, and then enters practice. While he is doing this, a whole series of specialties has evolved in medicine, such as cardiology and orthopedics. Not every general practitioner can be a cardiologist but he must find some way to keep abreast of the results of research, not just in general, but in various specific fields which happen to be extremely important to him. Continuing education, in terms of satisfying his diverse professional interest, becomes critical to him and his patients. This is but one example of the continuing-education requirements of other professions. Lawyers have this same problem. Almost every field of endeavor is beginning to expand its scope of interest in order to satisfy these interdisciplinary requirements.

So all of these factors—mixed media, mobile population, economy, time, and interdisciplinary interests—are encouraging librarians to look for new ways of cooperating. We already have a good record, with many valuable programs of interlibrary cooperation. Perhaps the most prominent is that of interlibrary loan, a reasonably active system for getting the physical book from one point to another. However, in terms of frequency of use and traffic across the country, it is not particularly impressive. I do not wish to lessen its importance, but in terms of communication traffic, our present procedures do not carry a heavy load.

Although some emphasis has been placed on library cooperation in the past, increasing importance will be given to interlibrary communications in the future. Cooperative endeavors will have to be more formally organized, perhaps even by contract, to achieve the results needed. They are also going to require a willingness on the part of those well endowed to serve the less fortunate. Those to whom the service is extended should not be too greedy about what they get, for it will mean sharing in the fullest sense of the word.

Where we in the United States have designed our libraries and their programs to be reasonably self-sufficient, that has not been the case, for example, in Europe. There libraries have built specialized collections primarily; a kind of Farmington Plan for Europe whereby a particular library, although it obtains the basic materials that its local constituents require, specializes in one field. A review of European libraries will indicate very little overlap in these specialized areas. There is more uniteletypewriter communication among European libraries than that found among American libraries, a fact which may partially explain the development of more specialized collections there.

The distributing of information in all its forms, to those who need it, when they need it, is what networks are all about, in terms of our professional interests at the present time. We must begin to think of networks because the term *interlibrary communications* today implies networking of information. In its simplest definition, a network is an interconnection of systems, things, or people. When one thinks of an information network, he must think in terms of two or more participants engaged in a common pattern of information exchange through communications for some functional purpose, an information network.

Information networks are found in the world of education, seen in governments, utilized in industry, and beginning to emerge in libraries. The notion of networking information is not restricted to the United States even though we are the custodians and distributors of the lion's share of recorded information in every field of endeavor.

An expanding population and greater number of interdisciplinary interests result in the increased production of knowledge and information. The latter has a tendency to expand not linearly but exponentially, because of the combined growth of population and the geometric growth of individual interests within that expanding population. Companies like International Business Machines, Weyerhaeuser, or General Electric, with worldwide business interests and facilities, have begun to provide for themselves built-in telephone companies for the transmission of information at different points, mainly in support of management. In many segments of society more than a budding interest is evident in finding new methods of distribution; that is, the transmission and receipt of information in forms acceptable to libraries.

This interest has not gone unnoticed in government. President Johnson, at the signing of the Public Broadcasting Act, made several comments about the importance of communication and its relationship to libraries. Very seldom has a United States president used the word *library* in any of his utterances. And there was President Johnson, talking about modern communications and libraries, the relationship of communications to libraries, the relationship of communications and libraries to education, and the ability to bridge individual interests, wherever the resources are, wherever the man is. He said he was not just speaking of a broadcast system, but also of a means of sending and receiving information wherever individual interests may be. Two-way communications for voice information over the telephone has been present for forty years, but in terms of other kinds of information, it has been one-way communication, with the possible exception of the postal service. Mr. Johnson was speaking of two-way communication, and when we think in terms of real information interest, in education particularly, we refer to two-way communications, with all forms of data, not just voice.

After President Johnson made his statement, several events occurred. The Networks for Knowledge Act was passed by Congress, who also considered an education technology bill with important aspects of communications. Another important development was the establishment of a task force on telecommunications policy. Its report, like that of the National Advisory Commission on Libraries, was published just about the time the administrations were changing. A commission created by one president is often not favored by his successor. The National Commission on Libraries and Information Sciences faced this same dilemma. The commission has not been unaware of the requirements of media for two-way communication; in fact, it highlights the awareness of commercial carriers such as the American Telephone and Telegraph and Western Union. These companies are aware of changes in communications requirements, and they realize that in 1970 more than half the traffic that flows over their telephone lines is not voiced; it is data. It is the language of the television camera, the facsimile scanner, the teletypewriter, or hundreds of other devices that have emerged for the transmission of data.

This is a staggering statistic, but it is even more meaningful when you realize that the telephone line is a very inefficient carrier of this form of data. It was never designed for this purpose; it was designed to carry human speech and recorded information. Consequently, the current channels of communication are being used in an inefficient manner. For example, to send a picture on a picture phone requires one hundred times the capacity of the telephone lines required to send a voice. If 1 percent of the 100,000,000 telephones in the United States were picture phones, we would exhaust our supply of telephone carrying capacity. The picture requires a broader band width for transmission; it needs something more than just a single telephone line to get it efficiently from one point to another.

There are two divisions in the world of technology which bear on the preceding matters. The first has to do with computers, and the second with communication. Since the middle forties computers have proceeded through three generations. (Seven or eight years stands for one generation as far as the computer man is concerned.) Third-generation computers are in operation, while the fourth-generation computers are on the drawing boards, with some possibly in the stage of hardware development.

The first machines were slow compared to those today, but very fast in terms of human calculation. They could only process one job at a time. They took a lot of space and required considerable air conditioning to keep them going. The second-generation machines were more efficient than their antecedents. They were smaller in size, since the manufacturers were able to use microminiaturization. They were able to replace the vacuum tube with a transistor. Third-generation machines employ electronic microscopy for the manufacture of their circuits, and the requirements for air conditioning were greatly reduced because there is now very little heat generated. Each of these engineering developments led to a smaller size machine.

A third-generation machine is able to accommodate several problems at once. As it is reading out the solutions to problem 1, it is already bringing in and beginning to process problem 2. Unlike computers of the first two generations, those of the third are very, very fast in terms of their internal speeds, which are measured in nanoseconds. A nanosecond is a billionth of a second, or, more graphically, a nonasecond is to a second what a second is to thirty years.

These computers, regardless of their generation, are able to store information, in either numerical or alphabetic form, by using the binary system, which is a mathematical system for representing information by combinations of zeros and ones. The decimal system can represent information from 0 through 9, that is, ten different ways, but in the binary system the information can be represented

only by 0 and 1. By combining 0s and 1s, you can pose the machine to represent the letter A; it can be 0-1, 0-1, 0-1; forevermore, that combination of bits means the letter A. If you have 0-1, 0-1, 1-0 in binary language, you have increased the one just by one, and if that represents the letter B, then you have sequenced the A and B in binary representation, and you can begin to alphabetize or manipulate. The fact remains that a digital computer can handle language; it does not just handle numbers. If you had a little man who could look around inside the machine, he would find that it was using numerical techniques for handling alphabetical information.

The wonderful thing about third-generation computers, however, is the interface; the joining of computers with communications is facilitated with third-generation equipment. This was not the case in either the first or second generation without a lot of elaborate intermediate equipment. It is now possible to plug a computer into a telephone line and let it "zap" its information over that line, inefficiently, but nonetheless over that line to a distant point. Technological development has been very important, not only for the internal housekeeping functions that automation will effect within the library, but also because more and more information is emerging in the form of magnetic tape. Within the library community we are generating our own information. Each week, all of the bibliographic information prepared for the 1,000 or 1,200 American imprints that the Library of Congress processes is available on magnetic tape to subscribers. With one's own computer it is possible to generate any number of products. This is what is known as the MARC program, MA for Machine, R for Readable, and C for Cataloging.

The MARC II format was the one accepted by the professional library community for recording bibliographic information in machine-readable form. The MARC II record and technical chartings have a communications format, which means that it can be transmitted from place to place, machine to machine. It also means that it contains certain kinds of information, which any computer operator will be able to understand, giving directions about how to proceed with the processing of the data which follows. However, the data which follow can be any kind of data. It need not be just bibliographic information on monographs; it can be bibliographic information about audiovisual materials; it can be citation information on journal articles; it can be from maps; it can be from music. You make up your own codes for this, but the basic format remains the same. This is a very important fact which is not widely understood. The Washington State Library had a MARC II experimental program in which catalogs, three-by-five-inch cards, and labels for books were generated by MARC record. Indiana University developed selective bibliographies utilizing the tracing information. The computing center developed a program that would search the subject headings indicated by faculty members and then would print out the bibliographic information. There are a number of different ways of treating MARC, but the bibliographic information is in magnetic tape form.

Chemists are putting *Chemical Abstracts* on magnetic tape; *Biological Abstracts* are on magnetic tape. In fact, some forty to fifty different magnetic tape files are beginning to emerge from different secondary and primary indexing activities, a fascinating development. This means that information, the kind we are interested in, will begin to appear in greater abundance in magnetic tape form. Publishers are beginning to develop manuscripts in machine-readable format, producing magnetic tapes which will drive electronic photocomposition machines to produce a book more cheaply than using hot lead. As publishers begin to face text in machine-readable form, I suspect that they will also make available digital tapes that may be of use to the library in the future. The digital language of the computer will probably become a primary manner of sharing information between one institution and another, or between one institution and a group of individuals.

The maze of wires that cross this country for the voice transmission of our telephone messages is a system which was designed forty years ago. Interestingly enough, it was established on a highly decentralized basis at first. A great many problems had to be resolved in

order to reach the sophistication and incredible accuracy which we have today for talking between distant points. The problem of interconnecting local telephone systems is very similar to the problem that we will face if we try to connect local library networks. Almost every state now has some kind of an information network. Within some of the states there are localized network programs interconnecting universities, some interconnecting libraries in one way or another. There is great danger that if this mushrooming occurs throughout the country, we will have a very tough problem of interconnection, much like the telephone company faced thirty to thirty-five years ago.

We do not have wires connecting every telephone to every other telephone, but rather a series of pump stations, or central stations, a hierarchical system that is dedicated to moving the voice traffic with as much facility as possible. The telephone company maintains a statistical analysis, measuring the traffic between and among points throughout the United States on a continuous basis. Computer programs analyze this data and are able to predict trends in new requirements for increased lines.

Human speech, no matter how fast one talks, is very slow. The telephone system converts human speech into tones, and the tones are carried over the line to a distant point. When you try to use the same system for sending data from the teletypewriter or the computer from one point to another, the data have to be converted from the zeroes and ones, which constitute the letters, to a series of tones, which then can be carried over the wires and be reconverted at the other end to operate another computer or teletypewriter. We have even sent television pictures over telephone lines. However, a television picture, if you were to break it down, consists of a lot of black and white dots that constitute every single line of the 500 or 800 that make up one particular frame picture. There could be tens of thousands of these tiny dots just to constitute one frame, with each dot having a different 0-1 pattern to take care of the gray scale. When you try to push all this data through a telephone line, it takes a long time to reconstitute the data if you must go through this tonal conversion for the entire transmission. When we hear people speak of slow-scan television, they are referring to the transmission of television information over a narrow-band carrier.

In addition to the telephone line, there is the coaxial cable, which is so named because the small copper wires and the sheathing in which they are kept essentially have the same longitudinal axis. These wires can carry many times the capacity of a single telephone wire, thereby making it a wide-band transmission channel of communication. Coaxial cables transmit picture and voice efficiently on a local basis. They may carry a thousand feet, and then an amplifier must be introduced before the next segment so that the fidelity and strength of the signal can be repeated. As long as there is a sufficient number of amplifier repeaters in the line at appropriate intervals, any distance can be covered.

Coaxial cable is undoubtedly the form by which picture information of Community Antenna Television (CATV) systems will eventually reach the home. These are essentially rebroadcasting commercial facilties capturing, with a very high-fidelity antenna, signals coming from many different points, television signals from different cities beyond the receiving capability of rooftop antennas.

In a communications engineer's terms, the coaxial cable, which is 300 megacycles wide, represents an efficient carrier for picture information. Between and among libraries and institutions, this is the wire to be most concerned about, because it is the most efficient carrier of the graphic information which is so much a part of the newer media. In addition to telephone lines and coaxial cable, there are microwave stations capable of providing broad-band communication highways many times the capacity of a single coaxial cable. These are being set up for the Bell System and Western Union throughout the United States for rapid transmission of large quantities of information. The telephone lines, coaxial cable, and microwave stations are interconnected and interrelated channels. Your voice may go by microwave from New York to San Francisco and then coaxial cable from San Francisco to Sausalito. Microwave stations must

be placed thirty miles apart and have to be within sight of each other. Most of them are built on the tops of mountains for the necessary height. Many are being established as part of the program which commercial carriers have for bulk, broad-band, data-transmission facilities to increase the capacity of the telephone-line network.

A fourth and very exciting carrier of communications is the satellite. Round and only a few feet in diameter, with an antenna on top, it is coated with solar batteries in order to take the energy from the sun and convert it into electrical energy inside the satellite. The communications satellite can carry many times the capacity of the microwave relay station. As an example, to transmit a message from New York to London by microwave relay stations, towers about 410 miles above the top of the Empire State Building and the top of St. Paul's Cathedral in London are needed. It is possible to beam information to the satellite, which in turn relays it to the ground.

The Apollo pictures were distributed to the world by a communications satellite which beamed the images from the moon to ground stations, which, in turn, transmitted them to video sets. This was the first intercontinental use of all the satellite facilities for a single incident.

The satellite has a receiver, an amplifier, a frequency changer, and a transmitter. It will convey voice, picture, or combinations of voices and pictures; it has a great capacity that has not yet been used to its fullest. Some intelligent experiments are needed in order to begin to use it for other than a routine station for broadcasting. Educational implications here are recognized, and we are eager to use it for two-way communications.

The optical scanner, the television camera, and the digital computer are all devices which require broad-band transmission facilities for efficient communication. The satellite has such facilities and will operate even better where laser is used. Light Amplification by Stimulated Emission of Radiation (LASER) comes from the high-energy physics field. What it means is that you can take low-energy particles and excite them to a point where they can be released as a narrow beam of coherent light. This light can then be focused from a ground to a satellite; it is coherent. It is as if it were a pipe. If you sent signals through that pipe, there would be no discursion of the signals; they would be carried as water is carried along a pipe from point to point. The laser is an efficient pipe for the transmission of data. The capacity of the laser for accurate measurement is terribly important for astro-physical and orbital purposes, but for communication the laser beam is the next technological step for improving the efficiency of transmission of broad-band communication.

Even though they may be named differently, I have found that networks invariably have been grouped under one of three headings: by type of equipment, by form of the signal, or by function or purpose. Type of equipment used might mean a teletypewriter network, a facsimile network, a radio network, or a telephone network. By form of signal you may have the analog network or the digital network, or a combination of them. By function or purpose, there is the library network, biomedicine information network, agricultural network, financial network, and airplane reservations network.

Let me now proceed to some of the devices that are used to develop these networks. The third-generation computers interface well with communications equipment, a development which has led to the very exciting notion of communicating with the computer from a distance. It flies under the banner of time sharing, since you can have many different users of one computer, sharing the computer processing time and yet not interfering with other subscribers' use of the computer. A device in my office is connected by my telephone line to a computer located in downtown Washington. For a monthly charge (it is charged as a local call), I am able to communicate with the computer whenever I choose. The fact that the computer can operate in nanoseconds means that customers using the computer would not know that others were on the line because they would be sharing with each others' use of the computer. Think of having bibliographic information at a central location or a regional location, with a device such as this that you might use for

interrogating that bibliographic data base and getting selections from it.

In an article written two years ago for the *Wilson Library Bulletin,* mention was made of the possibility that MARC information, instead of being distributed on tapes as it currently is to facilitate processing in a local situation, might someday line up in a direct-access memory. If this were the case, then it would be possible to browse through certain elements of the bibliographic file until you locate the pertinent information. There are a number of experiments in the country underway now that are testing this thesis. For our purpose in understanding communications, it is a question of being able to use a terminal device remote from the computer, geared or linked in some way to the telephone, and over the telephone lines to communicate with the computer and get a human-readable response from it.

The Data-Phone converts the digital language of the terminal device into tones which then can be transmitted over the telephone lines and reconverted at the other end. If one wants to use the computer, he must pick up the telephone and dial the computer, which emits a beep signal indicating it is ready for service. The telephone receiver is then placed into some sort of a cradle, a part of the device, and a dial out on-line with the computer is made. The Data-Phone device is absolutely essential in linking up with the computer when one is remote from it and using a terminal.

An interesting device which has been in use by some librarians is known as Electrowriter, a trade name of Victor Comptometer. Here again, some kind of conversion device is required to use it in combination with telephone lines. With a stylus, you simply write in longhand on a paper anything you wish. Beneath the paper is a metal grid which has a control matrix of X and Y coordinates; the machine translates what is written into X and Y coordinates over the telephone line system to another device just like it, except that the device has an ink pen attached to it. The pen mechanically draws a graph of the coordinates you send, and the receiver at the distant location has a longhand message. This is a way of transmitting interlibrary loan requests or all-points bulletins to library branches. It is a very inexpensive device.

There are also ways of transmitting punched information from point to point. During the day, wherever you happen to be, you can send punched card information through the telephone system, and a keypunch machine will automatically punch the data that it receives. If you have some circulation control systems or bibliographic control systems which utilize punched cards, and you want a central location to build up a system of transactions during the day, you can do it without the keypunch machine at the receiving end having an individual attendant. The Touch-tone telephone with all twelve buttons will permit you to communicate with the computer. It is different from the rotary system. When you dial the rotary phone, the person at the other end hears nothing but your voice. With the Touch-tone telephone if one continues to depress the buttons, the receiving party will hear the tones that emanate as a result of the depression of the buttons. The fact that this can be done means that while the connection is open, tonal information can be transmitted from point to point, and if one's ears are tuned to the differences, messages can be sent between humans. Of course, since tones can be converted to digital information, a computer can process this data.

Question: Where has the computer gotten with visual recognition of type? I do not mean specially designed computer type—you know, check stuff—but a generalized, visualized scanner.

Mr. Becker: You are talking about optical scanning? Where the type font is described, there is no problem, because the reference memory used is finite and has been wired for this particular type font. The problem is the intermixed type fonts, which produce an almost infinite variety of combinations and permutations and signals, and we do not have the technology to handle them. But there are new techniques for getting a "best fit" rather than an exact match, in which you accept a certain tolerance of error in the process of electronic scanning. We will come to it gradually, but it does not exist today. There is a machine that will accept handwriting, provided you write the letters in capital letters within boxes that have been imposed on the page.

Comment: You have not mentioned a very important aspect of our problem; this type of equipment can send information very fast. One can spend all week looking over the information received in two minutes.

Mr. Becker: A very good point indeed. There is a word that I have heard used among communications people (not an acronym): it is *zap*. We can zap information from one point to the next. You can sit at a teletypewriter and type out a message a key at a time, based on how fast you can depress the key; or you can store the message on punchpaper tape, then at night you can zap it to another location. It goes much faster than if you depress it a key at a time. The use of our telephone systems for data transmission has a severe constraint in that we pay the telephone rate. If you sit and communicate from one teletypewriter to another, taking your time about depressing those keys, you are paying just as you would for a long distance call; in effect, it is more costly. The machine can keypunch machine-readable information much faster than you can type. You can save up your interlibrary loan requests on punchpaper tape and zap them at night, using the lower night rates for the telephone.

Question: Mr. Becker, I wonder if you know where the first formal statement of the 24-hour communications satellite was made and by whom? This is very interesting. The first formal statement of the 24-hour communications system, complete with orbits worked out, was published in *Wales,* in Britain in April 1945 by Arthur C. Clarke who is a science fiction writer. In 1945, well within memory, Arthur Clarke could not patent it because it was beyond the bounds of technology at the time; therefore no patent could be granted to him. He has wistfully remarked if it could have been, he would have owned Communications Satellite Corporation. The statement was published in *Wales,* where it was noticed, and, in fact, the theory from then on was picked up by other people. If, as a science fiction writer he had published it as a fact article in *Astounding,* it probably would be lost. This is another of the problems of bibliographic control. We index *Wales,* but we do not index *Astounding* or *Galaxy.* Less than twenty-five years ago, Clarke's communications system was not within the bounds of possibility; Mr. Becker now is passing over it quite casually. It is remarkable that the first formal statement of it was in 1945 by a science fiction writer in a respectable journal. Do you know why it got into a respectable journal? He sent it in with "B.Sc." typed after his name and hoped the editors would not recognize him as being the same Arthur C. Clarke who was writing books about space flight.

Question: What part are libraries playing in these communications developments?

Mr. Becker: The library community has not employed a communications satellite for any experimental purpose that I know of, and there have in fact been very few educational uses of the satellites. The satellite has been used in the field of biomedicine for doctors consulting between London and New York on a case involving electrocardiography (EKG). The patient has an EKG taken in London; then both the EKG squiggles as well as voice are relayed to New York where groups of physicians are present to interpret the test. Libraries have not done anything to demonstrate the concept of information transmission distribution in all of its forms, print and nonprint media, on any intercontinental basis.

There are a number of plans by various agencies and commissions to place the next satellite up over the four time zones. They are planning to provide facilities for educational, rather than commercial purposes, to reach the school and the home for that matter. Hughes Aircraft Company has put together a satellite for the National Aeronautics and Space Administration which is called a direct communications satellite. Instead of the satellite's having to reach ground stations which redistribute the information, the plans are for it to reach the individual home or building on the ground without any intervening wires. In this way a particular antenna at a particular home can be read directly by the satellite, and the satellite becomes a switchboard in the sky. This is a whole new concept in terms of organizing communications resources for the most efficient distribution of matter. The picture-phone arrangement is ideal, since the satellite offers the broad-band facilities.

Question: You spoke of the transmission of data in nanoseconds, but somewhere between what is currently practical in time and the ideal when I get this kind of service, I have to talk in terms of funds. Somewhere along the way, there is a whole network of feeders and retrievers and program systems with classified input and output which demands a bank of people in a network. What kind of network can adequately feed such a system, and yet set some perimeter of reason, not only in terms of the machinery or technology, but also in terms of the human capacity to think? Now what kind of staffing or network is necessary to supply such a system?

Mr. Becker: I am not sure that it is correct to interpret what I said as being the beginning of the development of a system which will require significantly larger staff or resources. What I am describing is simply increasing our capacity to do essentially what we have been doing all along, but do it faster, if necessary. Now I do not see that the communications satellite is replacing the United States mails, for example, nor do I see it replacing the library reference desk. This is a new level of capacity that is available for mass and selective distribution of mixed messages. The messages are mixed in terms of type—picture messages or voice messages—and they are mixed in terms of their length. If you care to use the system, it is entirely up to you and dependent on your needs. At the present time, you do not decide how your telephone call will go from Oklahoma City to Washington, D.C. You are never aware whether it goes by way of San Francisco, or whether it goes on a direct line to Chicago and down to Washington. That decision is made by someone else, based on the capacity which is available at that particular instant. The same thing applies to communications satellites and other broad-band channels of communication. You select, as the originator, the response time you need, and you can rely on higher-level capacities to do the job for you.

Question: Do you think that it would be better to develop a national network system and then subsystems, rather than developing state systems as some of us are beginning to do?

Mr. Becker: Theoretically that is the desirable way to go, but practically speaking, I do not see an emergency blueprint on a national scale that everything and everyone will follow. Eventually, we are going to find that electronics is establishing a different kind of territory, probably national more than state. In fact, the countries that have an advantage at this time, ironically enough, are those that do not have intermediate units of government such as we do.

EDUCOM, an acronym that does not scan right, stands for Interuniversity Communications Council. EDUCOM was started five years ago by interest on the part of six medical schools that were eager to increase the access to medical resources and continuing education to physicians through communications technology. They persuaded the Kellogg Foundation to provide a grant for developing an organization that would promote discussion and also perhaps implement plans. The sum of $450,000 was approved for a four- or five-year period. The presidents of various universities became interested in the program, and the scope was expanded from the improvement of modern medicine to the improvement of communications, interconnecting needs, of universities in general. Today we have 108 different institutions of higher learning that are members of EDUCOM.

A meeting was held at the University of Colorado in 1966, to which were invited librarians, computer specialists, communicators, and university administrators. A plan called Edunet was developed there for the redistribution of multimedia materials among universities in support of scholarship, curriculum, and university aims and objectives in general.[1] The idea was that human resources at one institution can be made available to students at another. It was also suggested that

graphic information, textual files, or specialized computer files can be shared. This general plan, while not funded by anyone, does provide the rough outline of a very interesting concept.

EDUCOM has since dedicated its interest to educating faculty and students with respect to the new communications technology. It has one operating program which is being investigated to find the reciprocal advantage of the computer capacity at different institutions. The Educational Information Network consists of twenty-four universities, each committing, contractually, to make available a certain percentage of the capacity of its computer power to a central pool. In addition, each university contributes to the pool (EDUCOM) a copy of the specifications of its computer program, of its computer files, and of its computer configuration. Thus, if a university has a particular type of problem, we will acquaint them with the specifications of how to present their data and will put them in touch with the university that will actually process the job. This avoids every university's repeating a program and file organization: it is a community approach to the sharing of computer power and resources.

EDUCOM has had two research projects. With the National Library of Medicine we continue to investigate ways and means by which medical information can be distributed directly to commissions of research, educators, and other fields of medicine. Another project is with the National Agricultural Library, investigating ways and means by which NAL can have more direct relationships with the land-grant universities and their libraries.

If networking information were to come about, it would happen first in the fields of medicine and agriculture, which represent health care and food, and, perhaps, in the area of urban affairs as well. These areas are very much a part of the top priority of the federal government, so that the dollar resources needed for backup systems in each of these areas could be made available if the problem is seriously tackled.

Question: You have described an information network among educational institutions

---

[1]George W. Brown, James G. Miller, and Howes A. Keenan, *Edunet* (New York: Wiley, 1967).

for the purpose of using technology. What other cooperative groups among educational institutions exist in the United States? Is there any equivalent to a standing conference of national and university libraries in Britain, where representatives of our university libraries, the British Museum, and the others talk to each other?

Mr. Becker: The Association of Research Libraries is an organization dedicated to cooperation among university libraries; there is also the Joint Council of Educational Television in Washington and the Associated University, Inc., which takes in the ten Ivy League schools. Harvard and Massachusetts Institute of Technology are not members of EDUCOM, since they have their own association. There is no planned approach to the introduction of networking activity even within a state. The Texas State Coordinating Board developed a plan several years ago called the Knowledge Network, which has given rise to a number of programs in the state, within education at the university level and at the secondary level. This general plan has also been used as a point of departure for building a telecommunications system for state activity such as connecting the license bureau to the census bureau.

Question: Which comes first, the chicken or the egg? Do you link things together because it is easy to run cable between certain institutions? Or do you link things together because an organization already exists, and cable enables you to link them more efficiently? I am using *cable* as sort of a generic term for physical linking.

Mr. Heinich: Whatever the political and administrative divisions are, they tend to form the links first. Would you agree, Mr. Becker?

Mr. Becker: Yes. However, it seems these patterns will have to change one way or another. The plan for Washington State was a very interesting experience. It meant understanding the kinds of libraries that provide services to the state of Washington. There are major state resources such as the University of Washington Library, which is an impressive collection, the Seattle Public Library, which is the largest public library in the state, and the Boeing Aircraft Company library, which has extensive facilities in Washington. Then there

are other kinds of libraries within geographic areas. The EDUCOM study suggested that the state of Washington be divided into twelve areas on political, geographic, and economic lines.

The object is, first, to develop a new administrative plan for the state and, second, to have that plan made viable through contractual relationships between and among libraries and affiliates. It is not cooperation, but a contractual arrangement, a financial commitment, with each unit representing a building block in the pyramid. We cannot withdraw from this system and expect the pyramid to remain intact. The organizational side of it precedes everything else. It takes an agreement on the part of the library community and the political structure of the state to accept this plan and to implement it in such a way that there is a smooth transition from the old to the new. It is extremely important to have grass-roots support, because the success of the plan is eventually determined by the willingness of librarians to change.

Question: Can I take advantage of my English status at this point to put a very tactless question? I have just appointed you, Mr. Becker, not merely president of the United States, but dictator. You have absolute and total power and you want to construct a national system. Would you start at the bottom and work up, or would you start from the top and work down?

Mr. Becker: It is best to proceed from both sides. I would encourage the development of a communications blueprint for the nation, capable of providing communications capacity for integrated mixed media distribution of information in the United States. Then I would go all the way down to the grass roots and face the public with the plan.

Question: Suppose that the grass roots have said, "No, we do not want it; it costs too much; we do not like the way you are doing this." What would you do?

Mr. Becker: I think there would be some of that, especially at the beginning. First, I should continue to educate them so that they understand the implications. The second thing is money. I do not see how informational organizations, libraries, can continue to grow in an unrestricted manner. There will have to be some brakes applied sooner or later. As the money becomes more precious and we begin to establish national priorities, I am hopeful that information distribution will become extremely important to our national growth.

Mr. Heinich: A very real conflict exists in U.S. education at the present time, between certain traditional forces, political operations, and what is economically feasible. For example, in terms of schools, a proposal has been advanced to have all financing of the public schools at the state rather than the local level, although control would reside at the local level. No one really believes that if all financing came from the state level, we could have local control. We need this kind of shared responsibility between these two levels, but we have traditional political control which is at variance now with the requirements of the country and economic feasibility of certain systems. The Constitution makes a national responsibility of defense, but a state responsibility of education. Another interesting thing about this, and it may be difficult to understand, is that we have rulings by the Supreme Court which establish telecommunications as interstate commerce. In the commercial field, electronics communication is interstate commerce and therefore of national concern; but this does not apply to educational television. That is a state concern.

Comment: One of the problems that we have had in the United States is that in trying to help underprivileged countries, we have tended to suggest that they adopt an educational system which is very much like our own, one which we can scarcely afford and they really cannot. Universities in the United States have been trying to assist university systems in underdeveloped countries to be exactly like themselves, which is not appropriate.

The copyright law was developed, I think, fifty-four years ago and has never been changed, but about ten years ago the register and publisher of copyright at the Library of Congress began to draft a proposed amendment to the law in order to accommodate each period for the previous fifty years. Unfortunately, or fortunately, I am not sure which,

the whole question of technology was ignored at the very beginning, and people were concerned largely with printed material. But, as you know, the copyright law also refers to motion pictures and, more recently, to community antenna television. Then we began to get involved in the copyright implications of using computers. Do you extract a toll when you enter textual information into a computer? Do you extract a toll on output when you use the computer? What constitutes copyright infringement when you use machines? Is community antenna television a violation of copyright? Or does retransmission have nothing to do with the content of the material; is it simply an extension of communication? Well, this latter question was solved by the Supreme Court when it said that CATV would not constitute a violation of copyright. The technological implications of copyright are poorly understood, analytically or any other way, in Washington at the present time. While there has been some pressure to change the revised copyright law, it seems more likely that we will see another commission being established in Washington on the technological implications of copyright. This commission, it is hoped, will have attached to it librarians, communicators, and audiovisual specialists who will try to develop some sensible approach to the handling of the newer media in terms of communication.

Comment: It is worth remembering that copyright itself was a response to a technological invention, cheap and easy printing, but there is nothing inherent in copyright that is against technology.

Mr. Heinich: The publishers, of course, are considerably concerned about what direction the copyright law will take. I just want to make one comment about this, in terms of audiovisual materials. Unrestricted duplication of materials is much more of a threat to nonprint materials than it is to print, due to the nature of the technology that is available. It is very easy for the technology that we have at the present time to eliminate sources of certain kinds of materials.

Comment: It is said that authors are starving to death while public libraries are overusing their books. We want to ensure that authors do not starve. This brings in a very new and very dangerous principle, which bases payment on use rather than purchase. We must cope with the inequity, but I do not think copyright is the answer. Ford's saying to Hertz, or even the second-best people: "Look, you bought our car. A car owned by a car rental firm gets much more intensive use than one owned by an individual, those customers for which the price was established. Therefore, we expect a royalty from car rental firms." Now, in England we have a statement, a dictum, that books are different. This is one of the instances in which we are prepared to subsidize, on the grounds that books are different and should not affect the general principle of copyright.

Mr. Heinich: On the general principle of technology, in the terms of a facilitating apparatus that encourages technological solutions to problems, the copyright law as it exists is out of joint. We must seek an appropriate solution.

Comment: We have not stopped to ask why was copyright established in the first place. It was not put in to help the librarians; it was put in as a device for rewarding the producer. If we ignore this basic assumption and talk of copyright in terms of how we can get around it, or how we can bend this principle of rewarding the producer, we are not going to get very far. The producer has got a much stronger inducement. We are only going to get somewhere if we accommodate the two viewpoints, and you cannot accommodate a viewpoint you do not recognize.

Application of Technology to Instruction

Robert Heinich

It is important to remember that the use of technology in education today is about at the point where it was for the greater part of our society a hundred years ago. The problems we are experiencing in terms of relationships between people, relationships of people to instruments, and organizational restructuring, are the result of the impact of technology on education similar to its impact on society a hundred years ago. It is interesting to go back into the literature of technology and see certain parallels. For example, in *Das Kapital* you will find that Marx's analysis of the guild shows a striking similarity to the positions of the National Education Association (NEA) and the American Federation of Teachers at the present time in relation to technology.

I would like to put technology in a certain perspective. First, I want to give a definition of what I mean by technology. Galbraith defines technology in *The New Industrial State* as the "systematic application of scientific and other organized knowledge to practical tasks." It means the division and subdivision of the component parts of tasks, because only then can knowledge be brought to bear on them. This definition implies that technology is a way of going about solving problems, with or without machinery. It is an historical fact that technology preceded science, although we frequently think that it was the other way around.

It is only recently that science itself became the basis of technological development.

There are three aspects of technology. The first refers to Galbraith's definition, which is the technological process. This is the analysis of specific tasks and the development of solutions to the problems. The second is what might be called the residue of technology, the invention, or what is sometimes referred to in the literature as the technical product. These are the things that technology develops that are used in the solution of problems. Unfortunately, we generally define technology by its residue, by the things it leaves behind. Now in this sense the technical product consists not only of machinery, but all of the software, too. For example, a transparency is just as much a technical product as the machine that displays it. Remember this well, because when we get into areas such as programmed instruction, we have a hard time justifying the use of the word *machine*.

It is interesting to note that as technology advances, both kinds of technical products tend to become more closely associated. The development of software in advanced technology becomes much more closely related to the hardware than it was in previous stages. For example, in computer operations the program for the computer and the computer itself are much more closely related, in the sense of interaction, than the relation between a motion-picture projector and a film. So the second part of technology is the residue, the invention.

Professor, Educational Research Center, Indiana University, Bloomington

The third part of technology is what I would refer to as a social structure that permits, encourages, and facilitates technological solutions to problems. Our society today is structured so that it rewards, encourages, and facilitates technological solutions to certain problems. Education at the present time is structured in exactly the opposite way; it discourages technological solutions to problems. It does not facilitate them; it does not encourage them; rather, it tends to hamper them. This means we have to examine the structure of education to find out what it is that stands in the way.

These are the three phases of technology: the technological process, the things of technology or the technological products, and the technological setting or milieu or facilitating apparatus which encourages technological solutions to problems. Without the last, the first two are rather unimportant and become luxury items. It is interesting that in early history technology was used to produce luxury items. It was not until a shift occurred in the application of technology to mass production that we really had any progress at all.

At the present time, with the way that we can now apply technology, we have reached the point where we are in disjuncture with the tradition of education. Disjunctures have occurred before, and education has had to change before. We tend to think that education in its present form is God-given and has always been the same. In the history of the United States we have seen the Latin grammar school fall to the academy and the old hilltop college fall to the state university because they could not respond to the needs of society. You will find presently a number of alternate responses to the public education system occurring in various ways and for various reasons. Alternate systems are starting to appear.

We have talked in terms of a systems approach in instructional technology for some time, and yet many of us do not even agree on what a systems approach is. More interesting is the fact we *are* talking about it and that we even dare to think about instruction in terms of a systems approach. There have been forces that have tended to push us towards a systems approach, and I would like to identify several.

Only twenty years ago, you could design a school building almost entirely without reference to audiovisual materials. The main problem would be room darkening, but that was about the only architectural problem involved. As a matter of fact, audiovisual equipment was put entirely in the furniture and fixtures category.

They were not included in the building itself, not in the construction, but in furniture and fixtures, or in other words, the things that can be taken care of after you build the building. With the advent of television, language laboratories, dial access and retrieval systems, and computer-assisted instruction (CAI), you have to plan the building at the same time you plan the program. How space is broken down for instructional purposes depends on how instruction is to be carried out. Technology breaks the thirty-students-to-a-box concept. However, the main force pushing us into a systems approach to instruction is the changing nature of media. Television was the first start-to-finish instructional system to break with the traditional use of media as *aids*.

Systems technology makes instruction visible, and this principle really applies to all technology. Language laboratories first made me really become aware of this as a principle, which I generalized and applied to other comprehensive media systems.

The steps for developing programmed instruction are very similar to the steps for planning television. They are cast in different terminology, but in many respects they are very similar. For example, we begin by converting the content into behavioral objectives. This is similar to the development in television where you first decide what it is that you can teach with television. Once having specified what the behavioral objectives are, then it is necessary to devise steps to achieve the objectives. What may well be the major contribution of programming instruction is the tryout and revision process. If the target population cannot go through the program successfully, the *program* is at fault, not the target population. The program is revised until the target population can go through it successfully.

This is an attempt to get feedback from the student into the actual construction of instruction itself and make changes accordingly.

We view programmed instruction as self-contained instruction. Traditional audiovisual materials are not conceived in this way; they are devised with the idea that at some later time in their use, a classroom teacher will complete the instructional loop. Programmed materials are not conceived in those terms. They are conceived as self-contained instruction, and we have a validation process to make sure that the program teaches what we intended to teach. It is the application of the technological process to the task of instruction. We have the analysis of the task into its component parts, and then the solution of that task by devising the steps to achieve it. In this sense, it is a technology, specifically a technology of instruction.

The introduction of these materials created a *Zeitgeist* that made us look at traditional materials differently. We began to think of traditional materials as being able to incorporate more and more the direct instructional job into their design. We started putting packages of materials together in a much more comprehensive fashion. For example, the Planet Earth series represented one of the early attempts in the reemergence of a discipline as a curriculum force. The Planet Earth series was a series of thirteen films based on the projects of the International Geophysical Year and, as such, became a basis for earth science classes in some places. It was a comprehensive package of materials.

We have a number of curriculum projects. Many people think that the Physical Science Study Committee (PSSC) started the whole business, but the math people preceded them by at least two years. The basic revisions in mathematics were started at the University of Illinois in 1954 and PSSC started in 1956. I mention these years specifically because I want to emphasize that both of these projects were well underway before Sputnik. PSSC was initiated in 1956 by Gerald Zacharias at the Massachusetts Institute of Technology (MIT), with a letter to the president of MIT, James Killian, who was then the scientific adviser to the president of the United States. From the

National Science Foundation, Zacharias obtained about $8 million to change high school physics. His first idea was to do a course in physics on film, but a lot of things changed his mind. By the design of PSSC, the physicists attempted to reestablish direct contact with physics teachers in the high schools. This is what I mean when I speak of the emergence of the desciplines as a force in curriculum in the public schools. There is an old struggle over who actually is in direct line with high school teachers. The physicists used PSSC as a means to reestablish that.

Now the discipline groups like the Biological Sciences Curriculum Study are talking about establishing an undergraduate teacher-education program in their disciplines. Language study lends itself to this kind of thing, and it is not surprising to find some of the most sophisticated packages of materials in this field. For example, Encyclopaedia Britannica's *La Familia Fernandez* is a very intricate package of films, filmstrips, tapes, workbooks, and manuals. The package is so highly integrated and so carefully articulated that you cannot simply use this part or that part; use it all or it collapses.

We found that curriculum innovations accompanied by well-developed sets of materials succeed much better than those that are not. The PSSC physicists said their main concern was not what teachers would do with PSSC materials, but what the PSSC materials would do with students. This is a very interesting statement, because they ran head on into the problem that anyone runs into in massive, technologically based instruction. There is a fundamental base of operation in education that resists this application of technology. The materials need to be treated as part of curriculum planning rather than as classroom implementation. The plan to use the materials must be incorporated into the assignment structure, into curriculum planning itself. I am not talking about getting together in curriculum meetings and saying, "Oh yes, let's list this film and that filmstrip." Definite assignments are made that involve technology. With the introduction of technology in this form, segments of instruction can be assigned directly to technology, with no intervening people. At this level, rather than on the classroom implementation level, we can assign large segments of instruction either to mediated instruction—that is, instruction incorporated in media forms—or to classroom instruction. We know from the research in media that we can do complete instructional jobs, or modules, depending solely on how we decide to design instruction.

There is something that confused media specialists for a long time and still does to some extent. Many media people developed during a time when research done in the field was to find out how much certain audiovisual materials would add to classroom procedures. When they started getting "no statistically significant difference" results from television and programmed instruction, they did not realize that it was an answer to a different question. The question now is, "Can you use mediated instruction instead of classroom instruction?" Because of the research that we have in media, we are in a position now to reverse the usual research question. The research question had been, "What can media bring to the classroom?" We now should ask, "When we teach a course with media, with television, with programmed instruction, language labs, what do people themselves add to this procedure that helps the situation? What do classroom teachers bring to a teaching situation that makes a difference?"

At a curriculum-planning level we can assign instructional responsibility in three broad categories. First, we can design assignments in the traditional way, making all instructional assignments through classroom teachers. All decisions about the use of the materials go through the person who has been assigned to do this. Another choice, supported by research in the field, is that we can make assignments to mediated teachers. This would be teaching by television, programmed instruction, or language laboratory, and the entire course can be taught this way.

We should remember, because we are so thoroughly and historically rooted in the classroom-teacher concept, that television does not teach, the computer does not teach, the language laboratory does not teach. People teach, but they teach through these instruments. We

seldom think of it that way. For example, if a child is going through a set of materials, with no live teacher present in the classroom, we say he is engaged in self-instruction. It is instruction in mediated form by a mediated teacher, not self-instruction. We are so rooted to tradition that when there is no live teacher present, we call it self-instruction.

We can use a design which combines instructional assignments made through mediated teachers and specific instructional assignments to classroom teachers. Individually Prescribed Instruction (IPI) as carried out in Pittsburgh, for example, follows this format. Neither one of these types of teachers, during the tactical part of instruction, can eliminate the instruction of the other. In a traditional arrangement the final decision is made by the classroom teacher. The assignments have been made in two different ways. For example, in IPI, the student goes through a unit once he has begun it because he is assigned to it for specific objectives.

When we use film, the concept of shared responsibility is a source of many problems. The curriculum is not structured to manage instruction in this fashion. For example, the Harvey White series demonstrated that it could teach physics in any high school. In fact, a problem arose *because* it taught physics. In Wisconsin, where the series was used, a statewide study was made, related to the attitudes of students and teachers toward the Harvey White films. The study showed that teachers resented sharing their classroom with another teacher. The basic fallacy is that the curriculum planners did not realize that when a film course is part of the curriculum, there are really two separate assignments made. They made the false assumption that the assignment for the entire course was still to the classroom teacher. Under those conditions conflict was inevitable.

There is another way of doing this, which I think would have different results. Suppose the Harvey White series was available in 8mm-film cartridges. Half of the time that the student is taking physics, he goes to some place where he puts the film in a projector and watches it. This is part of his assignment. The other half of his time is spent in a class with a physics teacher. In the class they optimize the use of the films and go through the rest of the lessons. Notice that the student's time is split. The trouble with the previous arrangement was that the curriculum planners assumed that the classroom teacher still had charge of all the student time, and a conflict resulted. If you keep making the assumption that the student's entire time is assigned to a classroom teacher, you are going inevitably to run into problems when you take half of that student's time to view films. That structure does not encourage or facilitate the use of technology. IPI is more successful because it tends to hide this, to mask what is actually going on. The students are being assigned for a good part of their time directly to mediated instruction, but it is pursued independently. They go through it on their own, without coming into conflict.

Suppose that Carolyn Whitenack and I are both teaching U.S. history and decide we want to go into team teaching. We examine the course and decide which topics can be taken care of in large group instruction and which should be taken care of in group discussion We decide, because of preference, talent, and other things, that Carolyn will take the large group sessions and I will take the small group sessions. Normally, I do not go into the room where Carolyn is holding forth before these large group sessions; I can do something else useful with my time. One day, I go in to see what is happening in the large group session. Carolyn gets into an area and a way of treating the topic that I do not like, but because of tradition in the profession, I do not go up to the front of the room and yell "stop!" After the session is over, we will get together on the strategy planning level. We may go through the topic and perhaps change something, but I do not interrupt her while she has the students that are assigned to her.

Suppose we had decided instead that we would have the large group sessions by television. Because of the ridiculous way we generally arrange these things, Carolyn is on the television in my classroom, and I am with the students. Now, when she gets into a topic that I disagree with, all of the tradition and all the force of the profession will encourage me to go

up and turn off the set. Nothing has changed but the mode of presentation. Because of our basic orientation, I could not interrupt her when she is standing in front of the group in person, but I can eliminate her if she is coming through a television set—even though, technically, those students are still assigned to her. Mediated instruction should never come into a classroom with the classroom teacher being used as a monitor, a disciplinarian. Conflict is inevitable if you arrange the situation that way. If your students are to be assigned mediated instruction for any large segment of time, you have to arrange the instructional management procedure so that it is separated from their normal classroom orientation.

On the university and college level, the choices have tended to be that either you give the entire assignment to the classroom teacher or you give the entire assignment to a mediated teacher. It is very difficult to get a combination unless the people are identical, as is the case with Sam Postlethwaite at Purdue.

There are two fundamental ways you can organize an instructional system. You can organize a very complex apparatus to serve the needs of the classroom teacher, with the assumption that all instructional assignments are still given to classroom teachers. That is a perfectly viable way of doing it. Or you can organize it so that instructional assignments are made at a planning level. You have to determine ahead of time whether or not a particular piece of equipment or material fits into this or that configuration. What is the intended use? Is it intended to take over a large part of the instructional burden, or is it intended to be a tool for use at some later time? You have to make that kind of decision. You have to decide at what level you will use the materials. Because we tend to be rooted in the traditional classroom, we still tend to assume that all the decisions reside there. We are going to have to change.

Question: A clarification of terms. Does media faculty mean people who assist . . . ?
Mr. Heinich: No, when I say media faculty, I mean people whose instructional assignment is to incorporate instruction in a

mediated form with which students then interface. I am not talking about people who are helping some other faculty member use an overhead projector or film. When I use the term *mediated teacher*, I am referring to someone whose entire instructional effort is presented to students in a mediated form. I am not talking about a teacher with media. For example, if I am teaching an entire calculus course with a program, or with television, that course would be taught by mediated teachers.

Comment: But whether you produced this or whether another specialist from Purdue or some place produced it, of course, doesn't matter.

Mr. Heinich: That is right.

Comment: Another thing is that you bypass the teacher. I think all of us recognize the need for mediated teaching, but you will never win by bypassing the teacher.

Mr. Heinich: Well, let me approach the question two ways. You are not limited to what you have at your own institution, even though we are afflicted all the time with that NIH phenomenon—Not Invented Here. As you move into this area, you are in a position to use the efforts of a much broader group of people. If we get to the point where we can certify instruction, rather than people, it allows instruction in any form to be inspected, approved, and used for students.

Comment: You are using media in a very narrow sense. You mean nonprint media, when all of us know that this applies just as much to the print technology. I have not heard you mention that this whole morning!

Mr. Heinich: Programmed instruction, 99 percent of it is print.

Comment: Programmed instruction is a completely different technique altogether. Print technology is the linear presentation of concepts with print on paper, and programmed technology does not necessarily encompass that in a number of ways.

Mr. Heinich: Let me give you an illustration of this. About seven or eight years ago, Sidney Pressey took the first section of Skinner's *Analysis of Behavior*, which is programmed, took advantage of the organization of the material, recast it into a narrative form,

and presented it to students, with opportunities at certain places to give them advance organizers. The students did just as well as they did with Skinner's *Analysis of Behavior* in a constructed response form. You could not distinguish Pressey's version from what you call print technology. Normally, print technology is not produced with the concept of self-instruction in mind, but there is no reason why it cannot be.

Let me mention another aspect of this that is extremely important, and why you run into problems here. The textbook, by and large, is not designed to take away any of the instructional duty of the classroom teacher. One of the evaluations you make of a textbook, if you evaluate it as a teacher, is precisely how much a textbook may do to help *you* organize instruction. The student may take the textbook home, and he may complete a number of assignments, but it does not affect how much of his time is assigned to the teacher during the school day. The administrative pattern of the classroom is not affected by the textbook in that fashion. We get into problems with television, programmed instruction, and language laboratories because these activities do affect how much of the student's time is assigned directly to the teacher. We are trying to shoehorn instructional technology into an administrative pattern that is not appropriate. I am not excluding print media; instruction can be incorporated in any form that can do the job.

Comment: In the United States, though, the textbook–classroom-teacher situation is sort of a crutch for poor instruction. Because of the marketing aspects in our country, it becomes a sort of a garbage-can approach to the curriculum.

Mr. Heinich: By and large, the textbook is used as a course of study. It lays out the scope and sequence. In the last survey of principals that I know about, as reported in NEA's publication *The Principals Look at the Schools*, the vast majority of teachers in the United States rely on the textbook to determine the scope and sequence of the course.

Comment: I would like to make some comments on this textbook-versus-program issue. I am not talking about bad programming or bad textbooks; I am talking about comparable qualities. One of the principles of programming is the redundancy or repetition, so that you learn the material regardless of how much *study* you devote to it. This is not true of a textbook. A textbook makes a statement, then goes on to the next statement, and there is very little redundancy. That is a basic difference. Even where there is redundancy in a textbook, it is not necessarily the best type. There is another distinction, too. The principle of a program is that it is tested and validated before it gets into the hands of the student. How many textbooks go through this process?

Mr. Heinich: I was involved in the publishing business for several years. The technique of putting together a textbook is different from putting together a programmed book. The textbook is organized fundamentally with the idea of what makes it most helpful to the teacher, rather than what makes it most helpful to the student. I am not saying that it excludes the student, but the primary focus is on the teacher. The people in correspondence instruction had a tremendous amount of valuable experience using standard texts. These people adapted, reorganized, and generated auxiliary material to standard print materials to make them much more self-instructional. We could learn a lot from them. As a matter of fact, when programming first came out, the people who were most interested were the people in correspondence instruction, but they found that programmed instruction could help them less than it helped the rest of education, since they had been doing precisely that for a long time with standard print materials.

Question: Are not textbooks, if they are designed for teachers, evaluated from that point of view just as much as programmed instruction is evaluated from the point of view of the student?

Mr. Heinich: The textbook is field-tested and evaluated on how well it fulfills its task of helping the teacher. The program is field-tested, tried out, and revised on the basis of whether or not the student can go through it himself. I will not agree to that.

I want to respond to Joe Becker's presentation in a few ways, not in terms of the techniques of information handling, about which I know little, but in terms of the way information can be handled, organized, or disseminated. This reinforces a good deal of what I have said about changing or altering the patterns of decision-making involved in the use of information, and particularly in education. By rearranging this information availability pattern, we also change, in the organization, the business of who decides what information to use at any given time. At the present time, we are still assuming certain broad patterns in decision making which are going to change in the future. I mentioned electronics earlier in an overarching technique which tends to be a decentralizing influence. It is certainly different from the overarching concept of mechanism which we have had in the past.

Several sociologists have commented that the metaphor of the past scientific era was mechanism, exemplified by a clock. Today it is organicism, exemplified by the computer. There are certain very interesting differences between the two. One is that, in the computer, once a button is pushed, things tend to operate in parallel rather than in a linear sequence. There is also a tendency to share control all the way up and down the line rather than utilizing the sequential aspect of control. This can be seen in certain patterns of development in terms of the organizational structure that Mr. Becker was talking about, such as EDUCOM.

The territorial aspect of electronics is quite different from mechanics, and we have not yet fully realized this. School consolidation is a good example. At the present time, school consolidation is machine-dependent upon the school bus. If the bus were to disappear overnight, consolidated districts would have to break apart again. We have not yet realized that another form of instructional consolidation is available to us now; that is electronic consolidation. In the future it may not be necessary to transport students to a building in order to carry on instruction. Electronics, in this sense, may destroy the school as we know it today. It will be broken apart and reorganized in different forms. When that occurs, we are going to have to include a different level of information about instructional materials than we now have.

There have been some struggling attempts in

the last several years to establish a nationally based organization which would serve as a central clearinghouse for instructional information on materials that goes beyond the simple description of things. The simple listings we have are primitive compared to the kinds of information decision makers need. The Educational Products Information Exchange (EPIE) is attempting to get field information on materials so that their instructional uses might be better defined for people in the field. As decision making, in terms of instruction, advances farther and farther into the operative information we have been talking about, this kind of information will be essential, even more essential than it is now. The responses of organizations like EPIE are initial attempts to deal with this.

Very recently, the Department of Audiovisual Instruction (DAVI), now Association for Educational Communications and Technology (AECT), sponsored a study by the American Institute of Research (AIR) on the possibility of establishing the same kind of information services nationally that EPIE represents. DAVI posed a general question, but AIR came up with a recommendation which is very close to what EPIE is, a central pooling agency to give information on the field-tested results of certain instructional materials. In the future you will have to provide for some way of cooperating with that kind of agency to provide that kind of information. Validation data will have to be available, particularly in large-scale innovations such as PSSC, BSCS, program instruction, and computer-assisted instruction. This conference has not been discussing that kind of information. As far as I can tell, we have been talking about purely bibliographic information, but I am suggesting that for certain classes of materials, the information will have to be much more detailed than that. We have a problem in education, closely related to this, in trying to disseminate innovations at a much more rapid rate than we have traditionally been able to do. It is possible that the information from this type of field testing will lead toward the means by which innovations are disseminated more rapidly.

Several interesting attempts have been started along this line. Educational Services, Inc., in Massachusetts—which is now the regional laboratory for New England, Educational Development Center—working with Jerome Bruner several years ago, developed a fifth-grade social studies course called Man: A Course of Studies. The center is in the process of working with the Kettering Foundation to introduce this across the country. Ten universities have been selected to be training centers for teachers who are going to use this innovation. Simulated field testing of the material involved, disseminated at various points, would help in giving the school the information it needs about how well this particular innovation works with what kind of children, in what kind of area. Some agency must handle centralized information, and I think it is really necessary for people like yourselves to find out what is going on in relation to curricular-connected, mass-oriented materials which are being produced by places like the Educational Development Center. We should probably develop certain standards along these lines by the formation of joint committees among the various professional associations.

As technology becomes more sophisticated, more comprehensive decision making has to be made at earlier stages in the development of the system by more people than we have been accustomed to in the past. This change also results in a tendency to share and transfer control up and down the line at the various points of the system. I say sharing, because many times we think of it as a transfer. If you start a state network of computer operations, it is more of a sharing back and forth of control rather than of transfer. This will become more typical in the future. Many of the responses that are being made in education at the present time are towards this end.

The Education Commission of the States, with a membership of about thirty-seven of the states, and with headquarters in Denver, is working toward some national policies in education that will certainly facilitate a number of things. One, for example, is a national certification procedure. Another very interesting project is a national pension plan for teachers, which will have an impact on the fluidity of the profession across the country, and is a plan very similar to the one which is in effect in most higher educational institutions. The Education Commission of the States itself is a response to the need for action across state lines in terms of the political units you were mentioning before, and I believe we are going to see much more of this. The National Assessment Program is another response. It requires little imagination to see that the logical outcome of national assessment is that commercial firms will produce packages of material guaranteeing that students will surpass national assessment standards, and they will market them on this basis.

This also means that you will not be serving the same kinds of people as you were before on the same basis. For example, at the present time school libraries or audiovisual centers are organized on the basis of making materials available to teachers. In the future, teachers may not be the main customers. Rather, they may be students who are allowed to go through certain curricular sequences on their own, or they may be curriculum directors, who also contract for certain sequences. The teacher, in some cases, may no longer be the main person involved. Many of the structures we have in education will be drastically altered in the process of getting this

achieved. One of the current goals of the National Education Association (NEA) in education is achieving a differentiated staff, where different kinds of assignments are made to different people within the school. This is going to come to the fore in the next several years, in clashes between militant teacher groups (whether union or NEA), school boards, and the administration within districts before these issues are finally settled.

Let me emphasize just one last thing. We are in a period, in information handling and in education, of discontinuity with the past. We are dealing with a change in kind, not just simply of degree, and the change is fundamental. It would be very difficult to predict in the future exactly what forms things are going to take or who is going to be handling what, but I think it is very safe to say that what we are capable of doing now is radically different from what we have done in the past. We get false assurance by saying that it is really in continuity with what we have been doing, just a more sophisticated way of doing things. I think it is much more than that; I think it will mean fundamental changes in our institutions.

Technology
and the School:
Promises, Promises

Robert C. Snider

A technological revolution has changed life and work for everyone in America during this century, with the exception of students and teachers whose lives and work in the class-room have changed very little. On the sur-face, the ills of education today are reflected in concerns that are largely limited to the constraints of the classroom: who is teaching what, to whom, in what way, and with what effect? The roots of the problem extend far beyond the classroom, but they are less obvi-ous than some of the more spectacular symp-toms of student unrest, teacher militancy, and growing lack of support from local elector-ates. In spite of considerable effort to improve the schools, John Goodlad points out that "Much of the so-called educational reform movement has been blunted on the classroom door."

There are a number of experimental pro-grams in the schools with machines, materials, methods, and people to improve this situation, but these are often only exceptions which fail to outlast their federal or foundation support. Such efforts also tend to be limited in scope, trying one thing at a time. There is no one place to see a complete demonstration of all available resources applied systematically and thoughtfully to solve the problems of educa-tion. "The pieces of the educational revolution are lying around unassembled," says John Gardner.

Assistant Director, Division of Educational Tech-nology, National Education Association, Washington

Effective assessment and communication of such innovations are almost nonexistent, and widespread application of positive results is further limited by an apparent lack of inter-est in any practice which was not developed locally. This malaise is especially common among curriculum workers, who live in fear of a national curriculum for anything, includ-ing spelling and algebra.

At a more basic level, the problems facing education today are related to the goals, pur-poses, and objectives of the school and to how the schools are organized to accomplish these objectives. Is today's school organized primar-ily to accomplish a clearly stated measurable set of objectives, which are firmly set in a framework of priorities? Is today's school able to marshal all available resources to accom-plish these objectives with maximum effective-ness? Is today's school able to measure its success and adjust its processes to ensure more individual success for everyone in the system? When these questions can be answered in each school district with a resounding and confi-dent yes, then the schools will be in a position to be a part of our contemporary, technolog-ical society. When this happens, technology will play a larger role in both the *what* and the *how* of learning.

Effort directed toward how one is going to do something without prior thought about what it is one wants to do may at first ap-pear to be putting the cart before the horse. Although the history of any technology ap-pears often to be the story of means without ends, a closer look at this phenomenon will show that technological extensions of man have not only made it possible to achieve existing goals but also have in the process made it possible to accomplish new and very desirable human objectives. When a new machine is introduced into a human system, its introduction is typically based on the question, "Can it do better and faster and cheaper the things we are already doing?" The more important, yet seldom asked, question is "Will this machine make it possible to do some of the things we should be doing now, but which have never before been possible?"

The term *technology* comes from the Greek *technologia*, which means the systematic treatment of an art. A technology of instruction, which has yet to be assembled in the schools, will be a systematic treatment of the art of teaching. At the same time it will embody a great deal from the emerging behavioral science of learning. It will include more than audiovisual aids, although the new communication machines, methods, and media will be a basic part of any forthcoming technology of instruction. This particular kind of technology had deep roots in the history of education.

Man has developed his communication systems with related technology for transmission. Signs and pictures, language and writing, clay tablets and paper, paint and ink, printing and photography, all are examples of man's penchant for learning, teaching, and toolmaking. In every case new communications media have been hailed as harbingers of a revolution in teaching methods, but in every case, they seem to have fallen far short of their promises.

With the pedagogic understatement of the nineteenth century, Thomas Edison predicted that the primary use of the motion picture would be made in the schools. The first national meeting on educational radio, with its great promise for the schools, was convened in 1930. In the fifties considerable resources supported a great effort to make a difference in the classroom with educational television. The pace goes on and on, with computers, communications satellites, teaching machines, language laboratories, electronic study carrels; all bring the same old promise to make a

real difference in the classroom. Promises. Promises.

Has all of this made any real difference in what teachers do in classrooms, in how instruction is managed, and in how children learn in classrooms today? One could be gentle and say that the answer, like the schools, is pluralistic, but anyone who knows teachers and teaching and who visits schools will report that communication technology has made very little difference. We have made little use of it in the teaching-learning process that persists today in the classroom. This relatively recent array of communications technology has been formidable in educational circles but has had little effect in the classroom.

Even today educators frequently view the product of the new technology as just another audiovisual aid, crutch, or superfluous frill to supplement the classroom teacher, who remains sovereign in the principality of the classroom. Each new medium of instruction has been applied to the corpus of the school as a bandage, until today the patient, covered all over with bandages, is very sick indeed. The application of technology to current methods and practices in the schools will only worsen the condition. It would be like giving a heart-lung machine to Molière's physician, with his total misunderstanding of blood circulation; it would simply kill the patient faster, more expensively.

If one takes seriously the lessons to be learned from the history of technology, there can be no doubt about the future technology of instruction. Once a technological product meets a responsive human need, it becomes pervasive and irreversible. The more important question for now has to do with the future of the school and how it will relate to the coming technology of instruction.

Public education may become more and more like public health, where an acceptable level of healthiness for everyone is assumed, and certain environmental safeguards are invoked by the government to ensure such goals as pure food, pure water, and generalized control of infectious disease. The special health problems of illness and injury are given individual diagnosis and treatment until the person involved can be returned to the generally healthy population. As learning becomes more and more a lifelong process and as the environment becomes increasingly saturated with information, a shift in this direction for education can already be noted. At a time when children are turning off because it is time to go to school—that is, turning off their transistor radios, record players, televison sets, and tape recorders—we must find ways to increase the relevance of the school. If we do not, education for the world of tomorrow will eclipse the schools of today.

The massive introduction of instructional technology at the wrong time, for the wrong reasons, and by the wrong groups may come as a result of increasing trade unionism among teachers. Convinced that schools can be improved only by higher staff salaries and lower student-teacher ratios, classroom teachers may find themselves sharing the Luddish featherbed with railroad firemen, while an ill-conceived version of instructional technology is hastily delivered on the doorstep of the school. Fortunately, increasing professionalism and concern for improved practice among teachers makes this dire contingency much less likely than it appeared to be two years ago.

The most desirable, and I hope the most likely, marriage of present educational practice and the forthcoming technology of instruction will be the result of careful study and thoughtfully coordinated action on the part of school boards, the teaching profession, students, and many other groups, including specialists in instructional technology and the federal government. The federal government will most likely play as important and unique a role in the development of instructional technology as it has in the space program, the National Institute of Health and, in an earlier era, the railroads.

The commissioner of education has received a report on the most comprehensive study ever made in this area from the Commission on Instructional Technology. This report should be required reading for school board members and superintendents, since it may be the important first step toward a comprehensive federal policy regarding instructional technology and the public interest.

We should anticipate some of the most often heard objections to the idea of an instructional technology. People equate technology to mechanization, while, in fact, one of the problems with technological society is that people tend to behave like machines. Most frequent is the idea that it will mechanize or dehumanize the school and the relationship between student and teacher. Consider the present and future degree of dehumanization and mechanization in the schools as they now exist. Some of our classrooms are very mechanistic. We must learn to individualize instruction and handle student movement on a more rational basis. To what degree have the wheel, the locomotive, and the jet engine dehumanized transportation? There are dangers, but they are inherent in the way humans apply technology, rather than in the technology itself. This is one of the great challenges of instructional technology.

Will machines replace teachers? Promising work in staff differentiation indicates that humans will be a very necessary part of any technology of instruction but that the teachers will be somewhat more specialized in a much greater variety of roles. Teachers will embrace technology in order to free themselves for work that only humans can do, much as doctors and lawyers have done.

Comment: You have said quite effectively that education is going to hell in a handcart, helped by the trade union practices of the teachers. You imply that this is to be corrected by bringing in information technology and that we ought to go forth as John the Baptist to spread the information technology!

Mr. Snider: That is not *information* technology, but *instructional* technology; there is a tremendous difference.

Question: Sorry, I am a librarian, and I instinctively drift over to my particular area, but what actually am I preaching? Am I just to go forth and say instructional technology is a good thing?

Mr. Snider: When Harold Wilson was campaigning to be elected prime minister of Great Britain some five or six years ago, someone asked him to characterize the difference between his foreign policy and that of his opponent, to which he replied, "Well, I should say the difference is about 25 years." This is the difference between audiovisual aids, or educational media availability, and instructional technology. I have made some assumptions here that may be debatable, but if you buy the assumptions, then the question is "What do we do?"

Comment: I am accepting your assumptions because I am English and because I do not know enough even to challenge them. To phrase my question a little more seriously, what in fact is the overall strategy that you would recommend for us to take away? You said the bits are there, and I've been hearing about the bits, and they are fascinating; I know of some of the bits. Now, how would you pull them together so that we can go forth and say, "Do this" or "This is what we ought to be working on."

Mr. Snider: First, I would follow the example of federal government involvement in large technological developments in the past and appoint a permanent continuing Commission on Instructional Technology. We had one that has been very good, although temporary and quite amateurish. We learned a great deal from it that will make a difference. While a continuing commission is needed, I would not want it dominated by the cults, the television people, the computer people, or the programmed instruction people. This federal commission should have funds to finance studies, to experiment, and to develop pilot programs.

One short block from my office, there is a District of Columbia school building which was dedicated by Abraham Lincoln. Classes are still being conducted there with an incredibly low level of technology utilization. Probably the best index we have of the level of technology in any society is the per capita power consumption. If the power fails in any modern office, all activity ceases. The air conditioning system, electric typewriters, and Stenorettes stop functioning. With a power failure the modern office building is helpless. This school near my office would not even know the power had failed, for it makes absolutely no difference. Nothing has changed in that building since the day Abraham Lincoln dedicated it, except that the teachers are getting more money. Our most acceptable and exportable product is educational expertise. We should capitalize on this and turn the schools of Washington, D.C., into an educational show place for the world.

Question: I am not certain what you mean by instructional technology, although I have a pretty good guess. I am interested to know your definition.

Mr. Snider: Instructional technology is basically the statable, measurable objectives to which all available resources are applied, although the resources are a big thing, human, nonhuman, man, machine, et cetera, with a measurable, self-adjusting feedback.

Comment: A defined series of aims with a measurable objective at the end, for a system designed to achieve things, with feedback to adjust qualitatively.

Mr. Snider: He answered his own question.

Instructional Objectives: A New Set of Descriptors

B. Eugene Koskey

In order to accomplish something in the area of instruction and learning, it is a good idea to know exactly what is to be accomplished. This involves, of course, objectives of the instructional endeavor. There are basically two ways of stating instructional objectives, either in terms of rather broad concepts or in quite specific terms. Although there are some instances in which broad concept objectives are desirable, in most cases the nitty-gritty of instruction and learning deals with more specifically stated objectives.

You may have heard the designations *specific objectives, behavioral objectives,* and *objectives* stated in operational terms. All of these designations are synonymous. They all refer to an objective stated in such a way as to indicate exactly what behavior or behaviors the learner will be able to perform after he has completed the instructional sequence, and under what conditions this behavior can be expected to be displayed.

Learning, as defined by psychologists, is a change in behavior, that is, being able to do something after experiencing a learning situation which could not have been done beforehand. The specific (or behavioral) objective, then, logically deals with this concept. The key to the behavioral objective is the statement of some specific behavior (something the

student will be able to do) which can be both observed and measured. These two criteria also apply to evaluation. If we cannot observe or measure something, it is rather difficult to evaluate it properly.

Looking at some of the objectives which have been used in education for many years, we commonly find statements such as wanting students "to gain an appreciation for classical music" or "to understand the principles of biology" or "to know the multiplication tables." Such statements of objectives are not necessarily bad or wrong. However, if we analyze these statements using the two criteria mentioned above—the ability to observe and measure the behavior implied in the objective —we find that some difficulty arises. In the first example, "to gain an appreciation for classical music," how does one observe appreciation? How does one measure it? It seems likely that we could agree that "gaining an appreciation" is a rather vague concept which presents some difficulty in determining exactly what specific elements would be involved in the instruction/learning process. The same would be true of understanding something or knowing something. The terms *understanding* and *knowing* represent internalized kinds of activity. Again, these are not wrong objectives, but they do present great difficulties when one is faced with the problem of evaluating them. If we were to give these statements of objectives to different instructors, each may well come up with a somewhat different set of cri-

Assistant Professor, School of Library and Information Science, University of Wisconsin, Milwaukee

teria for each objective. Therefore, these non-specific objectives could, and very likely do, present problems for students who have different instructors but who are required to take the same examination. If we are effectively and fairly to evaluate instruction and learning, the instructional objectives must be stated in terms which describe externalized behavior, in order that it may be observed and measured.

The term *measure* may need some qualification at this point. What is meant by measure in this context is not necessarily a precise mathematical measurement (although some objectives may dictate just such a measurement), but, in the main, the ability of the observer to determine precisely whether or not the objective in fact has been achieved as stated. Here, of course, we are not considering evaluation scales based upon the normal distribution curve, but an absolute standard for each objective which in effect tells the observer whether or not the student can actually perform the task described by the objective at or above a predetermined satisfactory level.

If we look at some examples of specific or behavioral objectives, we find statements such as "the student should be able to state the names of the capital cities of all fifty of the United States" or "to list the five main causes of the Civil War." Applying the criteria of observation and measurement, we can readily see that in both cases we could observe the behavior (stating and listing) and measure it, that is, determine quite easily whether or not the response was stated or listed correctly.

The key word in a statement of an objective is the verb. In the cases cited above, *to state* and *to list* are the verbs. Other verbs which may have been used are *to write* or *to recite*. The essence of behavioral objectives, then, is that they tell us exactly what is to be the outcome of an instructional situation in terms of some action on the part of the learner which can be interpreted by almost all concerned in the same manner. Only if this kind of situation exists can we justify a fair evaluation of student learning.

If we cannot evaluate an instructional endeavor with a rather high degree of competency, we may find it somewhat difficult to justify. It is important to understand that the educational community is coming under increasing pressure to justify its programs and to prove that they are worth the cost in terms of their effectiveness. This kind of pressure applied to the field of education, I predict, will not fade away, but will become a central issue in the effort of those persons, both inside and outside of education, to increase the efficiency and effectiveness of our schools.

At this point you may agree that specific statements of instructional objectives are valuable. However, you may also be asking, "What does this have to do with the bibliographic control of media?" The answer lies in the area of identifying instructional materials. If an educational system is to be based upon the achievement of specific objectives, instructors and students alike will be seeking information which will pertain to those objectives. What information do we now have for identifying the content of a particular film, filmstrip, audiodisc, or tape? Our primary identifiers are title, a rather broad subject matter classification, a brief and not always accurate synopsis, and sometimes an author. These entries hint at what the item is able to do, but do not necessarily indicate it specifically. However, if behavioral objectives were included in the description of an item and the items could be called by a computer or other retrieval system by these identifiers, each student and instructor would spend considerably less time in determining whether or not an item was suitable for his purpose. For example, in the case of the objective "to be able to list the five main causes of the Civil War," the selection of materials would be simplified if an identifier "list the main causes of the Civil War" were used.

Since a great deal of instructional material already exists on the market, the question arises about how such an identification can be added to the description of these already cataloged items. Although there may be other alternatives, I would like to propose a two-part plan in answer to the question.

The first part of the plan would be to have people at the local level assign behavioral objective designations to materials as they use them. These designations would then be forwarded to a central clearinghouse for processing into a master list, to be distributed on a national basis. This activity might be carried out in a similar manner to that of the Educational Film Library Association evaluation program. It would only be necessary to add an *objectives* category to the evaluation form. This method would not cover the entire inventory of material available, but, with good cooperation at the local level, would eventually involve those items which were in use.

The second part involves persuading producers of forthcoming materials and the distributors of materials already in existence to help. It would also be beneficial if producers could be persuaded to begin their productions with a statement of specific objectives and let this statement guide the entire production from beginning to end. This procedure would assure the producer of a product which would actually do what it set out to accomplish, as well as make the task of assigning objectives as descriptors a rather simple one. These two activities could, of course, be carried on simultaneously.

In summary, in order to accomplish the instruction/learning endeavor in a systematic, effective, and efficient way, it would seem wise to turn to specific statements of objectives as guides to that end. If this is to be the case, instructional materials described in terms of these specific objectives would make the tasks of both instructors and students much easier.

Comment: I have done that. While this may sound heretical, I am going to propose that I do not think it is the answer. There is a great deal of literature coming out that pooh-poohs the whole idea of specifying behavioral objectives. The people who are really hung up on this are the media people. The trend is going toward a cognitive approach, not a behavioral approach to learning. I recently read a paper in which the author really let the programmed-learning people have it. We should not really predetermine what the students should do. In fact, the thing that we cannot measure may be the important thing. We are narrowing the student's thinking to this programmed system, for instance. I am not proposing an alternative, I am saying there is another area of competency beginning to emerge.

Of course, I do not believe that the behavioral people are going to fade out of the picture. I am not going to shoot down your whole program, but there is another area that really is beginning to grow.

Mr. Koskey: I am glad you brought this up. This is an important point to make, and it is true. I have some colleagues in the curriculum area who will shoot this down, too. They say that if you are going to specify objectives, you cannot have just five objectives, you must have five hundred, because you have to be so specific. This is silly. I am not saying this is the only way to do it, but I am saying this is the way it works. I think we have had it in education with this old myth about, well, it is education and we really cannot measure it. We have the tools to measure things now, and I think we must realize that public institutions particularly are going to be in hot water. They are in hot water now, but the temperature is going to go up.

Comment: This does not necessarily have to be an either/or thing, you know, behavioral or cognitive. You can use the two practically running concurrently. I have no quarrel; you can certainly test. I would say we may not have sufficiently refined testing, but a seminar in itself can be a testing device. If, in fact, you are using a seminar based on a learning process in the student before he reaches the seminar, this in itself can be a testing device from which you take it farther. I am speaking, of course, as one unsullied by educational psychology or teacher training of any kind. Can a course be demonstrated to be totally erroneous? It is all so terribly black and white.

Media Communications and Instructional Systems

Louis H. Brown

Media and systems as part of education and educational organizations have their only justification in terms of what they contribute to learning. Research endeavors associated with education and based on the acquisition of new knowledge are worthwhile only when that knowledge has applicability.

The focus of this presentation is on the *learner* and *learning* since the use of media or any method of presentation is valid only to the extent that it enhances the learning process. To apply media to the learning process, we must recognize the factors involved and the procedures that will assure a high probability of success. To achieve learning we must understand how humans acquire and utilize knowledge, constantly improve their effectiveness and efficiency in learning, and organize procedures to achieve desired goals.

Therefore, the center of focus is a human being identified as the learner. This involves the student and fields of knowledge typically known as the psychology of learning, communications, and education. The process involves structural systems. Another area to be incorporated in the overall process is the actual process of learning. Although it will not be dealt with here, I have no intention of lessening the importance of what is learned, content transmission.

Educational Media Supervisor of Distribution, Bureau of Audiovisual Instruction, University of Colorado, Boulder

The media person who is and should be sincerely concerned with the learning process must draw upon the competencies represented by the behavioral scientists with particular concern for the field of educational psychology. The behavioral scientist is well aware of the derivation of individuality than can be traced back to a unique genetic composition which each person possesses. He is astute at recognizing that individual uniqueness is related to the process of interaction with the unique history of experiences to which each person has been exposed. This genetic-cultural interaction is manifest in such a manner that each individual reacts to a particular situation in a way that is personal to him and is like no other person's reaction.

Individual reaction is often unobservable, which accounts for a great deal of the uniqueness possessed by individual learners. Yet, there are observable characteristics unique to each individual such as age, sex, and ethnic origin. Other identifiable, if not observable, attributes of individual learners, are socioeconomic background, intelligence, creativity, history of success and failure, learning rate, basic needs, verbal facility, perceptual orientation, value scale, and interest.

The irony of our situation is that education is charged with the task of transmitting our culture to each individual. The teacher who has experienced the typical four-year teacher-education program finds the task of adapting to individual learner needs difficult indeed. The job requirement is for expertise in specific areas of competencies. The discussion of learning problems by subject-area teachers is probably enlightening but not productive when subjected to critical evaluation. All too often, the individualization of instruction is a rearrangement of presenting a similar, if not the same, sequence of learning material with the only discernible variable being that of time. Learning sequences for group situations is evident in textbooks, media production such as films or filmstrips, and television sequences. Branch programming techniques have undoubtedly come as close to accommodating the individual learner as any material we now have available. American education has been known to provide extensive remedial programs in an attempt to overcome limitations found within the organized system of presentation, to improve the system itself.

Concern for individual learners does not necessarily imply that a unique program is needed for every human being who enters the educational establishment. Behavioral scientists agree that patterns of similarity can be identified for a variety of groups. When the characteristics of learning for particular individuals have been noted, it is reasonable to assume that relevant instructional sequences can be developed for specific patterns.

Attendant with learner characteristics is the hierarchy of learning levels and their relevance for certain kinds of learners. In conjunction with the hierarchy of learning, we must also give attention to such factors as motivation, ability, and temperament in determining appropriate sequences of instruction. In these latter areas of concern one must recognize and deal with the basic needs of human beings. You may recall that human needs range from hunger, thirst, security, stability, love, personal worth, status, and self-actualization. As the term *hierarchy* implies, whether we deal with levels of learning or need, higher levels are predicated on the accomplishment of lower levels, which means the problem is even more complex. Psychologists have also identified individuals that are constructively motivated as opposed to those who are defensively motivated. Constructively motivated learners are

said to have high achievement needs and low anxiety, while defensively motivated learners are those with high anxiety and little need for achievement.

Behavioral scientists have also identified for us areas that have been described as cognitive domain, divergent or convergent thinking, and memory. They have identified relevant aspects of the nature of learners that are crucial to the design of instructional sequences. When a broad area of learning such as a cognitive domain is identified, one has to perceive the outcomes in terms of subsystems such as psychomotor, intellectual, or attitudinal. Often involved in subsystems are the identification of substantive areas as contrasted with those of process.

This cursory reference to factors inherent in learning is not meant to be exhaustive or even explanatory. The hope is that I have vividly illustrated the need for expertise in these areas when attempting to develop effective learning sequences. An analogy in the medical profession is the general practitioner who does not attempt, usually, to set himself up as an expert in brain surgery or psychiatry. In other words, the more complex the auto, the more specialized is the mechanic. When the needed expertise is utilized, we can develop efficient and effective means for dealing with the lower levels of learning that will allow later development of higher levels of achievement. Media can play a significant role in providing the techniques needed to accommodate learners. Although the content area concerned is not a subject of this paper, goals related to content and behavioral change also have a hierarchy. Broad goals are those objectives that deal with the propagation of our society, while the lower level of objectives are those that deal with precise and functional activities on which the broad goals are based. Preciseness in definition is required at this lower level of objectives. Some behavioral scientists have indicated that unmeasurable objectives do not meet the qualifications of a behavioral objective. They contend that only when the objective is defined in a specific behavior term can we hope to organize learning sequences that can be evaluated for effectiveness and efficiency. This precision of definition is required at all levels of the learning hierarchy.

An integral part of the development of learning sequences is that of evaluation. Again, the typical teacher-education background does not provide an adequate competency in this area for teachers to develop and evaluate instructional sequences. Evaluation has been improved appreciably in the last decade. We are now in a position to ascertain, with some degree of accuracy, learning accomplishments above the lower or content levels. Testing personnel now have the mechanisms whereby they can assess not only the content but also attitude and emotional outlook created or changed on the part of the learners. Evaluation expertise is needed in order to give direction for the achievement of objectives.

Learning sequences are critical to the work of the media specialist. These competencies must be brought to bear if technology is to affect learning. In deference to the existing vagueness of the functions served by media, it would be appropriate to identify the functions implied for the media specialist.

The supportive functions of media technicians are those involved with maintenance and repair of equipment, with the movement of equipment, with production such as television programming or photography production, or with library shelving activity such as cataloging items and maintenance of inventory. In terms of formal education the competencies identified with technicians can be derived from bachelor degree programs, technical programs, or vocational programs.

A higher order of function is performed by media professionals, sometimes referred to as media generalists, strategists, or specialists. They function in the areas of developing learning resources, research in media design and utilization, capabilities for programming, and the design of modalities of communication. Included in these generalists' functions are most certainly leadership functions including those dealing with teaching, demonstrations, workshops, and institutes. Usually attendant with these functions are administrative responsibilities that pertain to the overall organization or to a segment of the organization, such as the supervision of a film or tape library, budget considerations, personnel, and functions that pertain directly to the development and design of an instructional system. This level of media function requires a broad and in-depth background that can be directly related to the doctoral level of achievement in academic institutions.

Depending upon the size of the media collection or learning resources operation, the above functions at both levels may be carried on in their entirety by one person or, in the case of very large operations, may be divided among several people. In this paper I will focus on the functions that relate at the higher level and specifically those pertaining to the development and design of instructional systems. In the context of this presentation, *system* refers to mechanical or electronic arrangements while *systems* relates to the procedures involved in the development of a sequence of learning materials and the sequence of presentation.

In order to affect the conditions of learning and to use the best that is available in systems development, we should first consider technology and systems in terms of their capabilities within the educational environment. Doctors Eddling and Paulson have identified *media* as being both objects of inquiry and tools for inquiry. Media can be used as a microscope to gain better understanding of the nature of learning behavior. The studies application of media is concerned with deriving useful principles that describe relative relationships. For the behavioral scientist, media can be a very useful tool in his attempt to understand behavior.

Stimulus configurations are made available by technology and may be developed with the hope that various learner responses to different configurations can be established. This application of media is primarily concerned with particularization rather than generalization. It is in this area that the media generalist, who is concerned with predicting behavior or rendering it predictable, can be most effective. Specific instructional materials can be designed and created to develop specific kinds of behavior.

Behavior can be modified through instructional technology which can be an effective means of mediating human learning to obtain designated educational objectives. It is the practicing educator who has the greatest requirement for this kind of utilization of instructional technology. The application of technology in this situation is concerned with making general use of specific instructional tools developed by the media generalist.

In conjunction with these primary uses of media for instruction, they have three properties that render them particularly applicable for affecting behavior or learning. The fixative property enables one to capture, preserve, and reconstruct an event. The event, so captured, can be used without being consumed. This fixative property permits an event to be transported through time since it can be reconstituted.

A control or a manipulative property is possible since media enables the transformation of events in many ways. Events may be speeded up, slowed down, stopped, or reversed. Where the scope may be broader it may be brought to a very narrow focus. An event may be edited, resequenced, interspersed, or shown simultaneously with another event. This range of stimulus alternatives that may be presented is greatly expanded by technology. While the fixative property of media permits a transformation of events through time, the distributive property permits the transformation of events through space and at the same time presents a common experience for variable sized audiences. This particular characteristic of instructional technology is significant to the modification of behavior for broad social impact.

To take advantage of the uses that can be served by media and the properties offered by media requires the integrated efforts of a variety of competencies including those of the behavioral scientist, the educational media generalist, media technologist, and academic content specialist. The behavioral scientist is concerned with technology only as it enhances his understanding of behavior. The media professionalist is primarily concerned with technology as it permits the prediction of behavioral outcomes. The content specialist is primarily concerned with technology as it can modify behavior.

The fixative property of instructional technology can be used to study behavior and help us to establish learning principles. The ability to capture, preserve, and reconstitute an event can have great significance to the behavioral scientist. This is particularly true in the case of photographic and electronic media which require no translation or decoding. Media can serve the development of instructional principles by controlling the number of modalities employed, thus changing the form of the configuration, or by changing the sequence in which configurations are presented, or by varying the rate of the presentation.

The way materials are presented can be varied with the distributive property of media. To determine utilization principles a study can be made of any fixed configuration of media for specific settings or specific types of learners regardless of their physical location. The fixative property of media also permits the replication of the same specific stimulus configuration for a variety of settings. Thus, predictions can be made for the effects of a given learning sequence under different instructional conditions. A variety of materials and strategy may be utilized to gain predictions of specific stimulus configurations for precise kinds of behavior.

The distinctive property of media enables specific prepackaged learning experiences to instruct all learners regardless of ability and background. Media permits the extension of instruction to a wide audience of learners, either individually or in groups.

Even under deprived conditions, instructional technology permits availability of materials to learners who otherwise would have to be denied these materials. Often instructional objectives can be obtained even when teachers do not possess the required knowledge or skill, or when specific resources and facilities are not available. Under certain conditions, the fixative property of media makes it possible for one expert teacher to be replicated and used in a variety of learning situations to provide required learning sequences. The manipulative property of technology offers the educator an opportunity for obtaining the most effective means of reaching educational objectives, for it can be controlled to provide the optimum learning experience.

The distributive property of technology can permit educators to achieve more learning per dollar expended. For example, it is estimated that the cost per student hour of instruction in a traditional school classroom has risen from a cost of forty cents in 1950 to ninety cents in 1968. It is predicted that even expensive computer-assisted instruction will range in the neighborhood of thirty-five to fifty cents per student hour, which is contrary to the popular notion that computers are too expensive to be considered for instructional purposes.

Media professionals have a complex task to perform in the development of learning sequences. Media specialists who are thought of as producers—such as television directors, photographers, librarians, projectionists, and engineers—do not possess the required competencies for the higher-level functions of the media professional needed. To be able to work in the area of instructional systems, the media professional must work closely with behavioral scientists and develop applications of media that can be directly evaluated for learning outcomes. Competency or expertise is not effective unless it can be organized with purpose. Organization with purpose is the role of instructional systems development. If it is not apparent at this point, let me reemphasize that the process is only as good as the competencies and expertise that are brought to bear in the procedures. It is relatively simple to outline the sequence of steps in this presentation, but the true effectiveness of the procedure is determined by those involved in the process.

Many flow charts for systems development have been presented. Most are rather complex and even cumbersome to use as a guideline in the process of developing instructional sequences. A relatively simple instructional systems development scheme that this author has utilized and found most effective is based on a team approach. The team represents prime areas of expertise involved in systems devel-

opment, those of behavioral scientists or specialists in learning, professionals who are specialists in evaluation, and academic subject or content area specialists.

The learning specialist has a working knowledge of the principles of learning and learning psychology, while the evaluation expert possesses the ability to test short- and long-range objectives. Educational media specialists have a wide background and capability in educational technology and its application as well as being knowledgeable in curriculum design and physical plant requirements. The content specialist determines the content material and instructional objectives associated with them. These people operate as a team. As the content or subject area of material changes, content specialist members of the team may change. This team, with the expertise assembled, makes the process operable.

The steps involved in the systems approach may be related to those involved in a scientific method. Such an analogy may also be helpful for individuals who desire to associate activities in physical sciences with those in the area of behavioral science and education. The scientific method, in a simple version, consists of (1) clearly identifying the problem; (2) becoming as familiar as possible with the problem, including prior attempts to solve it; (3) making selection of the course of action that holds the highest probability of success; (4) putting the plan of action into effect and adding new knowledge encountered to the sum total of information; (5) obtaining as precise a measurement and record as possible in the process; (6) testing and retesting to verify; and (7) modifying or changing as indicated by the results.

Application of the systems approach to educational problems is scientific in nature and tends to follow the broad guides provided in a scientific method. The problem educators have is to secure the most effective and efficient learning possible. Keep in mind that the systems approach is an organized procedure to achieve desired goals. In order to achieve objectives, our first step in the systems approach is to determine as far as possible the kind of learner with which we are dealing.

The input phase (1) adds to our fund of knowledge consisting of such information as the number of students involved, abilities of the students by categories, prior grades, and perhaps testing profiles from standardized tests. The team becomes as knowledgeable as possible about the learners involved and, if necessary, particularly where specific competencies are required from an earlier level of involvement, should develop new evaluation techniques to gain further data on students.

Equally as important are the circumstantial factors associated with the learner. These include information concerning the number of faculty available to teach, faculty attitudes toward teaching a course, prior problems encountered by the faculty in teaching the course, and problems encountered by students. A brief résumé of the course by the content specialist or faculty member often provides insights into their problems and attitudes. Consideration must be given to physical facilities, such as classrooms and instruction materials available.

The next phase (2) is a very precise one. In terms of the scientific method, the problem must be clearly defined. In terms of the behavioral scientist working with an instructional system, we also need very specific behavioral objectives. Setting such goals is not an easy task, but one requiring considerable time. Usually instructors define objectives in rather general and somewhat vague terms. Instructional systems, however, require precise definitions of what is actually expected of the learner as a result of his learning experience; for example, objectives for programmed instruction. If we anticipate the instructor's following through on the implementation of the learning experience, then the interpretation must be that of the instructor. The instructor must arrive at the behavioral objective and be willing to accept this definition of the objective. For typical classes it is somewhat ironic to find general objectives in vague terms for a course, while the testing to determine the success or failure of the learner is done in very precise segments. The objectives are exposed and scrutinized by the entire team without identifying those with particular expertise. Information is brought to bear on learning principles, possible evaluations, and appropriate methods of presentation. This expertise is never made an issue at this point but is reflected in the kinds of questions that are asked in the evolving definition of objectives.

The concern of the team at phase 3 is the development of an organized approach that offers the best arrangement to achieve the objectives of the course. This phase is again similar to the scientific method, as a course of action is chosen and then pursued. Although the emphasis is on individual students, consideration has to be given for large group arrangements, small group arrangements, remedial programs, preparation laboratories, number of sessions per week, length of sessions, and many other possible combinations. Techniques for presenting the material are involved in this step. A vast array of educational technology has very often provided the very means of implementing a desired organizational pattern.

Obviously, planning at this phase (4) is conditioned by the number and kinds of students; the physical plant available for classrooms and laboratories; the overall schedule of student classes; the outlook, motivation, and capability of the personnel; and the equipment available to make the strategy work.

Measurement for determining the achievement of objectives, phase 5, is designed in precise modes. The development of examinations is probably one of the most readily accepted aspects of the systems approach since most instructors have very little background in this area. Tests are not restricted to content knowledge, but in some instances, attempt to determine the attitude of the student. The level of expertise brought to bear determines the limits that the team is able to achieve at this point.

In order to put the strategy into effect, materials to do so must be made available, phase 6. The educational-media specialist who has the entire background of the systems approach from the input stage has a wide variety of presentations to be considered—each in terms of its capability to achieve the objectives within the strategy that has been organized. All forms of media have to be considered, such as films, audiotape, television, single-concept programs, programmed materials, models, field trips, resource people, telelectures, and combinations of these media in a variety of presentation formats.

The term *instructional systems* does not refer to mechanical marvels such as dial access, or an audio system, or a television system. These are hardware combinations, not the process that is the systems approach.

It is also important to emphasize that selection of media depends upon the purpose that it is supposed to serve. Although we do not have empirical evidence that a given media will produce a specific kind of result for a specified learner, this instructional systems approach provides a very real opportunity to evaluate the effectiveness of media for given types of learners. I would suggest in this respect that the purposes and uses of media can be brought to bear and evaluated at this point. Simple guides, however, are by no means proven for effectiveness.

Very often faculty members or administrators are carried away with the novelty of hardware. Our experience with teaching machines, language laboratories, and—probably the most infamous of all—television equipment serves to remind us of this danger. As media professionals, we must insist on adapting equipment to meet a behavioral objective with a fierceness that would make Attila the Hun proud. One must avoid utilizing hardware for the sake of justifying its existence; for example, utilizing a closed-circuit television system to distribute films is ridiculous, but utilizing a closed-circuit distribution system for access to especially designed sequences by individual students is another matter. As many experienced media persons know, the techniques employed with one set of hardware are usually possible to use with another. Thus, camera techniques used with television can and are used in the production of film. The point is simply that the sofeware employed to communicate with the learner is the critical element, not the gadgets.

As we develop software materials, the principles of programming become very evident. This is especially true when we are gearing learning sequences for a variety of learner abilities. In this respect, we had several programs to reach a given behavioral objective for several kinds of listeners. Hardware does allow us many means of presenting the software without detracting from it. Phase 7 of the system is to evaluate the materials with a limited number of students and the faculty involved. In its simplest form, the faculty member or content expert reviews the content materials for accuracy with a view of the mode of presentation.

The high point, phase 8, in the instructional systems is the actual employment of the material by the strategy developed. The purpose, of course, is to evaluate constantly the effectiveness and the cost effectiveness of the material. Thus, at any point in the process, recycling is always possible. As we learn more about the application of a given instructional sequence, we are able to better refine it. Very often new insights are gained into the abilities and backgrounds of students which can be brought to bear on the learning sequence. As with scientific endeavors, we must continuously test. Outcomes must be weighed against the objectives.

This eight-step model, with all the implications that we have made for expertise, will work when employed as a team operation. There are implications inherent in the system that may or may not be obvious, such as the constant concerns of administrators for time, people, and money.

Another implication for educators is that this systems approach is as scientific as any method employed in the physical sciences. Very often educators tend to think of scientific approaches when inanimate materials are involved as being very different from those endeavors with people. However, one need only discuss the problems in science projects with a physicist or a chemist to find that there are many variables in their work as well and that they seldom achieve 100 percent success. The physical scientist will also tell you that many trials are required before any degree of probability is reached. We have the method, what we need is the courage to proceed.

The implication for using technology effectively in education is clear. If the media professional is viewed as a librarian dispensing material, or as a cart pusher, we will miss a real possibility to accommodate individual learners. Media and media professionals have to be involved at an effective level in our development of instructional materials and presentations if we are to benefit from technology. To be effective, the media professional works at the policy and design level and, with researchers, in the area of behavioral science and evaluation. Kids can push carts, technicians can produce films or videotapes. Media professionals should have the opportunity and the capacity to develop learning sequences as part of an instructional team. Those unwilling to provide themselves with the required background, degrees and competencies, are of little value in this regard. Technology is here and it behooves all of us to find the means to take advantage of it. The systems approach offers one possibility.

Effective
Utilization
of Media

Margaret Chisholm

Previous presentations have been primarily identified with higher education, but I intend to draw your attention to the other end of the educational spectrum, toward kindergartens and elementary education. Others were concerned with the problems of control, storage, and dissemination of media, and I would like to add another dimension, that of effective utilization of media.

One of my major areas of interest is the exemplary utilization of media in the teaching-learning process. My thesis is that for real and pervasive change to take place in education it must be implemented at the elementary level. We have been considering this extensive continuum, and until now you have been led to think in somewhat philosophic concepts about standards and systems which are necessary to provide foundations for future developments in the media field. I would like to explore another aspect of the continuum, the idea that in order to effect pervasive change we will have to consider the utilization of media as it relates to the total teaching-learning process.

There must be a focus of attention on elementary education as well as secondary and higher education, as it is imperative to incorporate all that is known about behavioral objectives, learning theories, and instructional systems into elementary teaching as well as

into instruction on a higher level. I contend that one of the greatest areas of potential for achieving relevancy is in the education of younger learners. An opportunity for real change in education could come through encouraging creative educators to become involved in the cooperative development of instructional systems to make the teaching-learning process for young students a truly exciting adventure. Our ultimate goal is not only the control of media, not only the storage, not just the dissemination of media, but eventually total accessibility and effective utilization so that the learner will have opportunity for creative inquiry. So it is a challenge for the leaders in the media field to do what they can to motivate and encourage creative, innovative teachers to utilize media and to become involved in the development of instructional systems made possible through educational technology. This is an initial step which can be taken to bring about changes in education that everyone agrees we desperately need.

Historically, the rationale presented to support the use of media in instruction was Dale's "cone of experience." This concept has often been used in basic audiovisual courses, but it still has value in presenting basic theory. Dale states that direct purposeful experiences are the most lasting and meaningful, and when one moves from the concrete to the more abstract, from real and contrived experiences to dramatic presentations, demonstrations, field

Associate Professor, School of Library and Information Sciences, University of Maryland, College Park trips, exhibits, motion pictures, radio, pictures, and recordings, learning becomes more difficult. As one reaches the top of the cone, the visual and verbal symbols are least effective in teaching. In *The History of Instructional Technology*, Saettler proposes that even within the part of Dale's cone representing verbal symbols there is a hierarchy, as within the verbal realm there is a range from concrete to abstract. All educators may not know the rationale of Dale's cone of experience, so it could be helpful to present this idea to them. This may help convince teachers that the theory behind the utilization of media is that they move away from the top of the cone.

Research in the media field shows that we learn about 1 percent through taste, about 2 percent through touch, 3 percent through smell, about 11 percent through hearing, and about 83 percent through sight. But what do we retain? Learners retain about 10 percent of what they read, about 20 percent of what they hear, about 30 percent of what they see, about 50 percent of what they see and hear, about 70 percent of what they see as they speak, but about 90 percent of what they say as they participate in activities. An unsophisticated way to state this idea is through an old Chinese proverb: "I hear and I forget; I see and I remember; I do and I understand." During the past forty years, research in the field of audiovisual or media education has shown that there are positive increases in learning effectiveness when media is used.

Francis Keppel, former United States commissioner of education, has said that the first revolution in American education was the revolution in quantity. Of course, that means that educational institutions had to accommodate large numbers of students with great diversity in abilities. This revolution in quantity needed support through the use of audiovisual materials. However, Keppel also pointed out that the next turn of the wheel must be a revolution in quality. This revolution will demand that a utilization of the total spectrum of technology be brought to bear on the problems of education.

Current innovative programs, whether they are in the area of curriculum development or in organizational pattern—such as ungraded classrooms, individualized instruction, multi-aged grouping, or flexible scheduling—cannot be successful without having a tremendous range of materials made accessible to every student and teacher. Leaders in the field of educational technology have the responsibility of informing educators about current experimental programs being conducted. For example, in Palo Alto a program is under way that is sponsored by the Institute for Individual Educational Development. This program could have significance for educators all over the country, as it is based on one form of utilization of technology. It is based on Teaching-Learning Units managed through computerization. As children come into the program, an assessment is made of their educational level; then Teaching-Learning Units are devised in two-week segments which provide flexibility and variety. A specifically designed program is developed for each student matching the curriculum to his individual needs. Each student's progress as determined through evaluation tests is transmitted to the computer. The tests are scored, and printouts of the resulting data are provided to the school the following day. Further instructional plans are determined by this data. Through the use of technology, individualized instruction is becoming a reality. Creative teachers can adapt ideas from these highly sophisticated programs and use aspects of the program to fit the needs of their students. Experimental patterns of teaching must be evaluated, and we must play a role in disseminating this information to those who are actively engaged in teaching.

Authorities in various parts of the country have been making predictions about the future of education. Harold Gore of the Educational Laboratories, speaking at the University of Southern Florida in Tampa, claimed that the trend is toward having the media center become the main part of the school and having all teaching-learning activities centered there, or emanating from that point. He also pointed out that the school facility of tomorrow will be flexible and will lend itself to innovation and experimentation. Various arrangements of space will make it possible for students to work singly, in small groups, or in large groups. Educational technology will determine building plans. The only real danger to education is rigidity. Persons in the field of media and technology, above all others, must be flexible and innovative.

Teachers and school administrators are concerned about their roles in the future. Instead of the traditional classroom teacher, there will be a person called a "stimulator," or a person who can motivate intellectual curiosity and start the learning process. Another will be the "personalizer," one who will help students with individual problems. There will be a "facilitator," one who is in charge of selecting and applying the proper materials to meet the needs of the students. The group "presenter" will utilize television or other technology to reach large groups of students. The researcher will be one who synthesizes research results and conducts additional research to improve the teaching-learning operation.

As an ultimate goal educators must be able to guide the learner toward developing individual creative inquiry. This ultimate goal appears to be to develop within a student the motivation and the skill to inquire, to seek knowledge for himself in a creative way. Through effective use of educational technology we must lead the student to the point where he can competently seek out new knowledge. One vital component is that after the student has been involved in individual creative inquiry, the student must be able to convey his knowledge to others, and we must provide the means for the transmission of information in whatever form is most appropriate. We do not have the final product of education until the result of the creative inquiry can be conveyed to others for their utilization.

We must today be prepared to educate people in what nobody knew yesterday and to prepare students in our schools for what no one yet knows but what someone must know tomorrow. We find ourselves involved in a highly complex task in attempting to solve the problems of education for the future. One immediate task is to approach the problem of the control and organization of media for accessibility and retrieval. Educational technology requires that ideas, men, and machines be combined in the most effective way to meet the individual educational needs of each student. The control and organization of media provide access to ideas, one of these essential components.

Question: We appear to have the challenge of conveying this message to administrators and to teachers throughout the whole educational field. In addition, we have responsibility for informing persons in the public library field. Now do you think this can be accomplished? How can their attitudes be changed?

Mrs. Chisholm: It will surely require an effective public relations program besides formal and informal educational programs. For example, this institute is an example of an educational exchange of information, as it is made up of many types of people with different backgrounds, representing many different fields dealing with media. We are addressing ourselves to a problem that can be solved only through the exchange of information among many disciplines and areas of interest.

Question: What do you believe must be the basic consideration underlying the organization of media?

Mrs. Chisholm: Whether the field is public libraries, academic libraries, or education, the needs of the user must be considered in determining the organization of media.

Question: There is currently a great deal of confusion over the organization of media. Marshall McLuhan said, "The level of information in the informal educational system is higher than it is in the formal educational system." Does this mean that formal education is going out of existence?

Mrs. Chisholm: The difference is that most of the information persons receive from outside formal education is not structured or directed toward a particular end. It is random, and so therefore does not meet structured goals.

Question: Can people structure their own information? A computer expert at the University of Colorado says that within twenty years everyone will have a computer the size of a transistor radio to carry with him, and all kinds of information will be available. Could a person then structure his own education?

Comment: In England people have had access to computers two blocks away for the past sixty to seventy-five years. A computer takes information, stores it, processes it, and then ultimately retrieves it. In the case I am describing, the "computer" happens to be books. I have not noticed any crowd of people going in madly structuring their own education from this, but nonetheless, they have had access to the world's knowledge.

Mrs. Chisholm: It seems that the conclusion of the discussion might be that all of the organizations and institutions we represent have similar problems in dealing with in-service education of the personnel, changing the attitudes of the personnel, financing the program, and meeting the needs of the clients or users. We do not have the complete answers but hope that a meaningful solution may evolve from this institute.

The Progression of Educational Information

James Doyle
George H. Grimes

The process through which an item of information progresses as it moves from its creation within a person's mind to its potential resting place within an encyclopedic summary of a given subject field has been characterized as the "bibliographic chain." The progressive links in this chain (fig. 1) are:

Information residing in human resources
Information being created by institutions
Work in progress
Unpublished studies
Periodicals
Reports and monographs
Indexing and abstracting services
Annual reviews and state-of-the-art reports
Bibliographic reviews
Books
Encyclopedic summaries.

Not all newly created items of information complete the entire bibliographic-chain sequence. Many are subsumed under other topics en route and many simply exhaust their usefulness and disappear from view. Those which have the necessary validity, significance, and appeal travel the full distance.

Mr. Doyle is Head of Reference, University of Detroit Library.

Mr. Grimes is Director, Curriculum Laboratories, Department of Instructional Services, Detroit Public Schools.

The progression of the bibliographic chain is tied to time. That is, newly created information which is sufficiently useful moves chronologically from a distinct idea through the other stages of the bibliographic chain to its ultimate destination in the generalized knowledge mass represented by an encyclopedic summary.

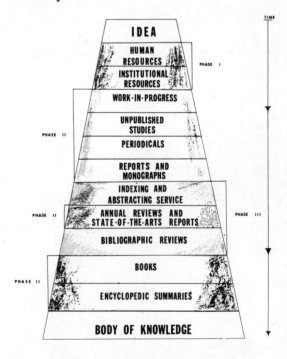

Fig. 1. A bibliographic chain

In its initial concept a piece of information is perceived as a rather distinct entity whose full implications and interrelationships with other knowledge are only partially realized, if at all. As this piece of information becomes progressively integrated with other new bits of knowledge and with preexisting knowledge, it loses its unique identity and becomes enmeshed in the fabric of our intellectual heritage. It may spawn its own unique progeny, but it usually emerges as another dimension of some previously existing concept. If this newly integrated bit of information duplicates but does not improve the previously existing concept, it will, it is hoped, sink into oblivion. This is, unfortunately, not always the case.

Each stage in the bibliographic chain represents a further integration of distinct information into the general knowledge mass. There are three separate but interrelated phases represented by the links in the chain.

Human and institutional resources (phase 1) are packages of information only in the most general sense. At this stage the information basically resides within the minds of people, either individually (as with consultants) or in groups (as with the staff of a project). These resources include individual and collective thoughts, observations, deductions, investigations, assumptions, and unplanned discoveries.

Printed materials with intellectual content (phase 2) begin with a human idea which has reached the point where it can be committed to print or another information form. This act produces, in general chronological sequence, work-in-progress reports, unpublished studies, periodical articles, reports and monographs, annual reviews and state-of-the-art reports, books, and eventually encyclopedic summaries of the resulting body of knowledge.

Printed materials which have no intellectual content of their own (phase 3), but which help locate actual information include indexing and abstracting services, as well as bibliographic reviews. Annual reviews and state-of-the-art reports may also provide some actual content in addition to performing identification functions and are, therefore, included in both phases 2 and 3. Phase 3 materials lead to information but do not normally contain

information themselves. They are basically location tools.

It should be noted that the relationship of phases 2 and 3 has no direct bearing on the time lag inherent in the bibliographic chain. This is because the printed items, with no intellectual content of their own, often parallel those materials with intellectual content, as the purpose of the former is to provide effective access to the latter. The time lag inherent in the bibliographic chain lies mainly in the movement of ideas through and between phases 1 and 2.

Taken in its broadest sense, the bibliographic chain can be applied to the creation and development in any field of intellectual endeavor. For the purposes of this paper, the authors have chosen to use the field of education as a context. A closer look at the links in the bibliographic chain for the field of education reveals some of the particular characteristics of each information format.

Human Resources

A human resource is an individual who can supply certain skills and competencies without necessarily speaking for any particular organizational structure. Generally, human resources are consultants who might be connected with universities, state departments of education, and intermediate or county school districts. While these organizations are indeed the principal sources of consultants, one should not limit consideration to that level. Significant resources can often be found in local school districts in the form of administrators, teachers, and project directors who are very close to the activities and details of their program. Personnel of service agencies connected to universities should not be overlooked. These agencies generally work in the areas of accreditation and educational surveys and have access to important educational information. With the advent of federal involvement, many federal projects, regional laboratories, and research and development centers have evolved and have on their staffs individuals with a wealth of experience.

Institutional Resources

There are two general subcategories of institutional resources, agencies and projects. Agencies are organizations which have an on-going administrative structure and staff, and both short- and long-range programs. The agency may have a profit or nonprofit orientation and single or varied interests. Due to the recent proliferation of federal and local school projects and exemplary programs, a whole new type of institutional resources has appeared. These projects, unlike the continuing agencies, can be identified by their relatively short and circumspect nature. They usually deal with a rather restricted focus and may be one aspect of a larger, more permanent pattern, especially at the local school-district level.

To date little has been done to help identify agencies and projects. One may contact the resources mentioned for human resources or consult *Research in Education*, the monthly abstracting journal of the Educational Resources Information Center (ERIC), which has a special institutional index and current projects section in each issue. Human and institutional resources need to be considered while an information search is under way. The steps taken will largely be determined by the searcher's familiarity with the resource potential in the area in question. The exploration of all available human and institutional resources should be attempted to assure maximum exposure to potential information sources.

Printed Resources

A complete listing of the specific inclusions in the entire bibliographic chain may be found in the booklet *Information Resources: A Searchers' Manual.*[1] Examples are given for each print category in the bibliographic chain.

Work in Progress: Work in progress refers to those resources which give access to the current work of educational researchers. This work could be at various stages, but not to the point where it is ready for publication within the next links in the bibliographic chain. This type of information often aids

people working in complementary areas and helps avoid unnecessary duplication of effort. *Research in Education* is the monthly abstracting journal that indexes the documents fed into the Educational Resources Information Center's microfiche collection by ERIC's nineteen clearinghouses. The publication also has a projects section which supplies abstracts of educational projects just funded by the U.S. Office of Education.

Unpublished Studies: Unpublished studies are research materials that have reached a completed state but which are not intended for formal publication, at least in their present form. This category includes an organization's internally produced reports, informally circulated items, graduate essays, theses, and dissertations.

The DATRIX (Direct Access to Reference Information, a Xerox service) is a method whereby one can, for a fee, search the complete file of doctoral dissertations maintained by University Microfilms in Ann Arbor, Michigan. Users should request a keyword booklet and a search form which allows one to structure the subject search of the computer, thus gaining efficient access to the largest body of unpublished studies in the United States.

Periodicals: Periodicals refer to magazines, journals, newsletters, and similar serial items which appear at regular intervals. These publications contain articles of various lengths and levels of interest. Journals may publish lengthy and sophisticated articles that are de facto reports. Magazines and newsletters may publish only descriptions, abstracts, and condensations. Periodical articles usually appear simultaneously with the unpublished materials or shortly thereafter. Please note that this category includes serial publications such as loose-leaf services and other frequently updated items which are periodical in nature. The *American Educational Research Journal* is an official journal of the American Educational Research Association, an affiliate of the National Educational Association. It publishes long, scholarly articles on current research topics of interest to educational researchers.

Reports and Monographs: Once unpublished studies have been evaluated and revised, they are often formally published as

---

[1] George H. Grimes and James Doyle, *Information Resources: A Searcher's Manual* (Detroit: Michigan-Ohio Regional Educational Laboratory, 1969).

reports or monographs. These are intended for public, rather than informal circulation, and they are frequently part of an irregular series published by professional associations, universities, or commercial publishers. The *NEA Research Reports* are an example. They are irregularly published, detailed research reports of studies conducted by the Research Division of the National Education Association.

Indexes and Abstracting Services: Indexing and abstracting services are the first of the secondary publications. That is, they have no actual intellectual content of their own but are location tools for the primary publications. Indexes usually appear within a few months of the serial literature they control, but the time lag is greater with abstracting services, where abstracts must be prepared. These publications usually give subject, author, and title control, but there are notable exceptions to this rule. *Vertical File Index* is a subject and title index to selected pamphlet materials necessary for vertical files.[2] Full order information is provided. The annual cumulation was discontinued in 1964 due to the ephemeral nature of the items indexed.

Annual Reviews and State-of-the-Art Reports: These are secondary publications which do have intellectual content. Their purpose is to collect all current published material (since the last review or report) in a given field or discipline and synthesize it into one objective report on the major accomplishments, problems, and trends in that field for the period of time covered. The *National Society for the Study of Education Yearbook* would be a good example of an annual review.[3] It is a compilation of scholarly papers on various topics currently important to education and its related fields. Two volumes are issued on different topics each year.

[2]*Vertical File Index* (New York: Wilson, 1923–
[3]*National Society for the Study of Education Yearbook* (Chicago: Univ. of Chicago Pr., 1895–).

Bibliographic Reviews: Bibliographic reviews are bibliographies in a given field, usually annotated and selective, which list all major publications in that field over a given span of time. These may be published irregularly in book form or at regular intervals in journals or annual reviews. An example is *The Teacher's Library: How to Organize It and What to Include.*[4] In addition to explaining the organization of professional teacher's library, this volume supplies a basic book list.

Books: The time lag is generally great in the area of scholarly books on research topics, especially in education. Books are usually a revised version of formal report literature which reflects further study, with additional background and historical data added. The book entitled *Readings in Nonbook Librarianship* is a compilation of articles by the editor on a specific subject area.[5]

Encyclopedic Summaries: This is the last major link in the bibliographic chain, and the one in which the time lag is greatest. Encyclopedic summaries are designed to give a broad overview of a whole field. Due to the infrequent publication and updating policies of encyclopedic works, the material is usually three or more years out of date. The *Encyclopedia of Educational Research* is an example of a encyclopedic summary, a basic encyclopedic work in the field of education with scholarly articles on all relevant topics in education and lengthy bibliographies.[6] It is published every ten years and updated by the *Review of Educational Research.*[7]

[4]National Education Association, *The Teacher's Library: How to Organize It and What to Include* (Washington, D.C.: The Association, 1968).
[5]Jean Spealman Kujoth, ed., *Readings in Nonbook Librarianship* (Metuchen, N.J.: Scarecrow, 1968).
[6]*Encyclopedia of Educational Research* (4th ed.; London: Macmillan, 1969).
[7]*Review of Education Research* (New York: American Educational Research Assn., 1931–).

A Proposed Educational Information System for the State of Michigan

George H. Grimes

The original impetus for an investigation of the feasibility, and subsequent specification, of the particulars for an educational information system for the state of Michigan stemmed from the internal information requirements of the state Department of Education staff and the expressed needs of educators in the field.

Concern on the part of the Curriculum Division and other Department of Education and intermediate school-district personnel for an effective means of locating information necessary for decision making and program development resulted in the convening of an ad hoc committee to discuss the possibility of a statewide educational information system in November 1968. Attending this meeting were representatives of the department, the Wayne County Intermediate School District and ASSIST (Activities to Stimulate and Support Innovation in Schools Today) Center, the State-wide Dissemination Project (STADIS), and the Michigan-Ohio Regional Educational Laboratory (MOREL). The particular interest of the ASSIST Center and MOREL was that both of these organizations operated educational information systems at different geographical and political levels of service. They, therefore, represented a community of interest and were also experienced in the dissemination of resources. Subsequent meetings in 1968

and the spring of 1969 led to the decision that a feasibility and design study should be undertaken. The author, an educational information specialist, was contracted to carry out such a study during the summer of 1969 with funding from Title III of the United States Federal Elementary and Secondary Education Act of 1965.

Design and Procedures

The overall design strategy for study stemmed from the logic of a paradigm of the nature and operations of information networks suggested by Jordan Baruch of EDUCOM (Interuniversity Communications Council).[1] Information networks are interconnected and interrelated systems of information producers, storage and retrieval facilities, and users. Baruch sees three types of communication networks: the needs-resources or natural network, the physical network, and the organizational network.

The procedure followed was to determine the current status of the needs for an existence of educational information resources in the state of Michigan. A literature search of information services resulted in a 204-item stratified bibliography developed within the bibliographic-chain approach as discussed by

Director, Curriculum Laboratories, Department of Instructional Services, Detroit Public Schools, Detroit.

[1]"Thoughts on Taking Office," *EDUCOM* 3:3 (Mar. 1968).

Grimes and Doyle.[2] Once it was determined— through the use of such information-gathering procedures as structured interviews, a questionnaire survey, small group feedback, a literature search, solicitation of expert opinion, and site visitations—that an actual need existed, a physical and organizational network was suggested for a statewide multilevel educational information system. The system envisioned includes a complementary and supporting system of information resource service centers located at intermediate and state levels, directly connected to local district information services as well as national resources. The emphasis is on user relevance and overall system economy through an appropriate placement of functions.

Theoretical Rationale

The theoretical rationale of the system is based on the assumption that the process basic to the operation of any information system is that of information transfer. The representation of the process of information transfer which was accepted as being most helpful for the purposes of the study was the Murdock-Liston model.[3] Murdock and Liston state that their general model of information transfer is based upon the classic sender-channel-receiver concept. The Osgood Model of Human Communication,[4] which builds from Shannon's more generalized mathematical conception, is related to the Murdock-Liston model as a viable and supportive explanation of the basic human communication process.

The model shown in figure 1 was originally created by Frederick Goodman of the University of Michigan for the Central Midwestern Regional Educational Laboratory (CEMREL) to show the parameters of educational

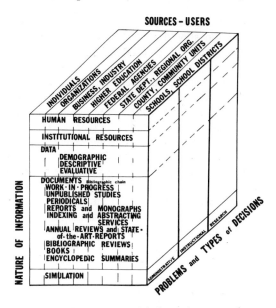

Fig. 1. Parameters of information control

information from its inception, through its nature and formats, to the types of decisions it is used for. Information finally flows back to the users who are, in a general sense, the same type of persons and agencies who created the information in the first place. The category of simulation was added to the original model for use in the MOREL Information System, and the bibliographic-chain document progression was added for the purposes of this study.

Recommendations

The basic recommendation of the report is that human, institutional, and print and other media resources should be the basic content of the system. The assumption basic to the system is that the system should be built on user requirements, with the end product of the system being user service. This assumes that the user is the best judge of the relevance of an item of information to his needs. An interface delegate (a warm, walking computer terminal) should stand at the intersection of user requirements and system's resources, for ease of access, currency of information, and rapidity of service. Of these factors, access to the human interface agent and information is the most important.

There should be two-way vertical articulation within the system from user needs to ma-

[2]George H. Grimes and James M. Doyle, *Information Resources: A Searcher's Manual* (Detroit: Michigan-Ohio Regional Educational Laboratory, 1969); idem, "The Bibliographic Chain in Education," *RQ* 9:298-302 (Summer, 1970).

[3]John W. Murdock and David M. Liston, Jr., "A General Model of Information Transfer: Theme Paper," *American Documentation* 18:707 (Oct. 1967).

[4]Charles E. Osgood, ed., "Psycholinguistic, a Survey of Theory and Research Problems," *Journal of Abnormal and Social Psychology*, Morton Prince Memorial Supplement, sec. 2 (Oct. 1964).

terials and from materials to user needs. This articulation should extend throughout the four natural levels of a total educational system (local, regional, state, and national). The Michigan system, however, should concentrate its efforts at the state and regional levels, while always taking into consideration national and local needs and resources. Existing resources should not be duplicated, but rather coordinated and supplemented. The state Department of Education should assume the responsibility of coordinating activities at all levels. The system should support and promote the development of local information-system efforts which are consistent with the purposes and structure of the statewide system, and internal reference and current awareness services should be provided to the state Department of Education and intermediate school district offices that house system components.

The informational content of the system is knowledge in all forms and formats, with each form of information assumed to have its own integrity. Each information format should be used when and where it can do the job better than any other form of information in relation to its particular strengths and weaknesses. Technical functions of the system should include materials, evaluation, acquisition, technical processing, storage for retrieval, access for use, and evaluation of system relevancy and performance. The acquisition and processing of local and state documents is another important service, as are query negotiation and formulation of search strategies. The program should also be designed to facilitate current awareness of new information resources and the availability of a variety of information products, from education and related areas, to meet varying user needs. The system would also package and reformulate information in areas of high request redundancy, analyze output where needed, and identify voids in the state information organization to point out areas of need and development potential. Service and activities of the system would be publicized to potential users.

Each regional center should specialize in areas of particular local concern for the benefit of the entire system. Management information and dissemination as well as production

and utilization of audiovisual materials are complementary and related areas which, although not direct concerns of the system, should be taken into account in the system's design and operation.

The major operational components of the system's central coordinating office are to: coordinate, evaluate, maintain, and publicize the system's human and institutional resources bank; maintain special collections of general value, a union catalog of all holdings, a comprehensive reference collection; and telephone and telefacsimile links with all parts of the system. The office should also provide system development leadership, carry out centralized technical processing where appropriate, repackage and synthesize information for areas of specific concern, identify and assess statewide needs, and coordinate with national systems and resources.

The departmental reference station would provide services through reference specialists (interface delegates); telephone, delivery, and telefacsimile link to the central office; a ready reference collection; a collection of departmental publications; and an information file on critical issues. It would also coordinate departmental current-awareness services and the identification of human and institutional resources by the department staff.

Regional centers are proposed to provide reference and current-awareness services to local districts and educators and a comprehensive educational reference collection. The regional staff would identify, gather, and process local materials for use by the center and the entire system, as well as human and institutional resources, and evaluate their relevance to regional and statewide needs. There would be a need to create and maintain special collections in areas of regional interest and information files on significant topics. Regional centers would also identify and assess regional needs, publicize the system, maintain close liaison with local districts, help establish local information services, train local personnel, and act as a referral agency for management information, dissemination activities, and audiovisual materials and equipment.

The central coordinating office should be located in the Bureau of Library Services, while the departmental reference station would be appropriately housed in the Curriculum Division. It is recommended that approximately seven centers be established, giving primary service to specified regional service areas. Where possible these centers should be associated with existing facilities such as ESEA Title III Regional Centers of intermediate school districts. In no case should a regional center serve only one intermediate school district. However, if the recommendations of the governor's Commission on Educational Reform regarding regional education areas are implemented, those areas should become the location of the regional information centers. The Wayne County ASSIST Center should be considered the prototype for the development of other regional centers.

The proposed Michigan Educational Information System should be closely coordinated with local and national information services to eliminate, as far as possible, unnecessary duplication and to promote a more effective information-services hierarchy at all levels.

Implementation

A realistic view of the development of a Michigan Educational Information System must assume that an immediate, fully developed installation would be very improbable, and probably unwise, and that it will be necessary to follow a phased series of implementation steps. The first component to be implemented should be the departmental reference station and its associated personnel at the state library (central coordinating office). This would allow the implementation of direct service to state Department of Education personnel, initiate the basic structure of the Lansing unit of the system, and provide a pilot activity for the total system. Personnel commitment for this step would be two professional information specialists, one at the state library and one at the department reference station, and two secretaries, one at each location. The space commitment would be at the state library for an expanded educational reference collection

and a standard-sized office at the curriculum division. Appropriations must also be provided for a departmental reference collection and the maintenance of an expanded educational reference collection at the state library. The anticipated date for the first phase to be in effect is January 1970.

The Wayne County Intermediate School District ASSIST Center should be continued beyond its present funding expiration date of June 30, 1969, to provide expanded service to all of southeastern Michigan and, on an interim basis, to as much of the rest of the state as feasible. This would entail appropriate augmentation of its budget to support this expanded responsibility. Expanded service should be possible by September 1970.

The Michigan Educational Information System director should plan the effective expansion and the full-scale implementation of the system and be responsible for the evaluation of the original design in light of the pilot activities and the redesign of the system as appropriate. The director would also investigate funding alternatives for the system, develop detailed specification of all remaining system components, and implement, coordinate, and direct the entire system. This position should begin September 1970. Under a master plan devised by the director and his advisers, expansion of the central coordinating office and the addition of the necessary regional centers would take place one year later, September 1971.

Conclusion

Legislation was introduced in the spring of 1970 which would enable the Michigan State Department of Education to set up a series of regional centers which would include the services recommended in the Michigan Educational Information System study. When and if this legislation becomes effective, a strong theoretical and practical base will already exist to bring statewide educational information services for the state of Michigan to early fruition.

Part 2

Access and Use Requirements

Those who use or need but fail to use the fruits of technological innovations are, it seems, seldom consulted as a distinct group for observation and study when commodities are designed for their use. This ironical phenomenon is particularly applicable to the field of information science. The designers of systems to ensure the most efficient and effective use of information fail to begin with a study of consumer needs, skills, and interests of potential consumers of these products. This concern resulted in the early consultation of user needs by authors of committee reports and papers in this section. They interviewed users, devised questionnaires, evaluated processes, observed consumers in action, and consulted with a variety of specialists concerned with the entire process of communication.

Committee members expressed their concern for individual and classroom-oriented accessibility to nonprint media which may at times appear in opposition to industry's conception of what should be produced. The lack of coordination between the producer and the professional disciplines responsible for effective and efficient utilization was recognized and steps toward long-range solutions sought. More specific attention was devoted to bibliographic organization and control of nonprint media by Antony Croghan, Orin Hatch, and Louis Brown.

These specific concerns are followed here by T. M. Williams' projection of requirements for change. He developed a "diffusion and adoption theory" and then applied this model to the actual process being attempted by him and his colleagues to bring about a realization of the need for bibliographic expertise for the proper organization of nonprint media.

In response to the paucity of information on the characteristics of user needs, five committees were formed to study specific aspects of nonprint-media use or barriers to it. Their findings reveal that a complex system of bibliographic control is essential to satisfy the diversity of persons to be served: a wide range in interest, language proficiency, and grasp of the framework.

One committee, chaired by Harlow Clarke, attempted to define the limits of the problem and to visualize the core elements needed to bring about adequate control for a broad level of users. The committee led by Gerald Brong utilized interview techniques to identify basic problems—terminology, components of the bibliographic citation, and the elements of a system for control of nonprint media.

Antony Croghan's committee members concentrated on a systems approach to the logical sequence involved in information transfer and its bibliographic control. The committee chaired by Orin Hatch examined the currently existing organization of nonprint media, raised various questions concerning it, and gave possible alternatives. Reference tools similar to those presently serving print media were suggested as aides to the user and those who seek to serve him.

The committee chaired by Louis H. Brown related media control to its educational use and value, stressing the expansion of existing facilities where expertise exists and the potential services to organizations and institutions throughout the world. Specific recommendations include development of national programs at the Library of Congress and, with adequate funding, a great variety of services offered to libraries and other information centers by the Library of Congress.

The members of all five committees reached an understanding of the urgent need for improved bibliographic control for the potential user of nonprint media. They urge the removal of all possible barriers to non-print media use and recommend that specific steps be taken to ensure a nationwide system of bibliographic control for nonprint media.

Tad Williams, institute participant and specialist in communications, presented the concept of diffusion and adoption theory as a plan for change in order that his fellow participants could see their many concerns for the effective organization and utilization of media in a broad perspective of societal needs, understanding, and acceptance. Mr. Williams continued his initial lecture to his colleagues in Oklahoma with a perspective of progress some

five months later in Chicago. He then made a final report of observations and recommendations to the same audience six months later in Detroit.

Through this twelve-month sequence of events Mr. Williams was both a fellow participant and an observer of participant activity. During this time numerous needs were recognized by the participants, analyzed, and studied; solutions were sought; and changes in professions and their organizations were attempted. The study of change at such a close range was strengthened by Mr. Williams' opportunity to withdraw entirely from institute activity between the three formal sessions. The results of Mr. Williams' research and observations afford one insight into the internal strivings of a mission-oriented group of professional persons, their plan for change, and the application of diffusion and adoption theory to accomplish their specific objectives and long-range goals.

Nonprint-Media
User Needs
Examined

Harlow Clarke, Committee Chairman

The initial considerations of our User Needs Committee were based on the paradigm of chaos in this field. The next decision was that there must be established a control point of some kind, which was interpreted in several different ways, either as a private institution, a federally funded institution, or a combination of institutions with communications data banks supporting a complete central communications system. From this control point the material or information necessary for the organization of data would be disseminated, and this would include classifying and cataloging in whatever form necessary for the user (fig. 1).

An attempt has been made to identify functions of proposed agencies that would allow the development of a system as well as to identify those institutions that provide the functions needed to establish such a system. It was found impossible in our deliberations to attach specific functions to specific institutions:

Functions	Institutions
Educational	Libraries
Research	Professional groups
Historical	Business
Archival	General public
Institutional	Museums
Informational	Foundations
Reference	Schools
Recreational	Universities (academic)
	Government agencies
	Private collections

Specific proposals from the committee include the identification of the audience and its needs. We did not make an effort to define the user's function, although Antony Croghan suggests we have this in his survey research.

Question: There are three types of data: information, reference, and recreation. Now, could one ask for consultation outside these three areas?

Mr. Croghan: You are asking for a further breakdown of what we have here. In other words, a function within one of these, a subfunction, is certainly a question. Reference in England simply refers to a part of a building where we retain a basic collection of books in the library. It is related to the storage of books and immediate reference service. When you speak of the library's reference function, are you using inaccurately two aspects of the library—the library that is used for entertainment in all of its recreational aspects, but as a purposeful tool to supply information which you can then break down into factual information, information about information, and services related to information?

Comment: You must be thinking in terms of reference service as information equipment.

Mr. Croghan: What we mean by reference is going into much greater depth, in fact, into

---

Committee members: Gerald Brong, Malcolm Ferguson, Eugene Koskey, and Janet Macdonald.

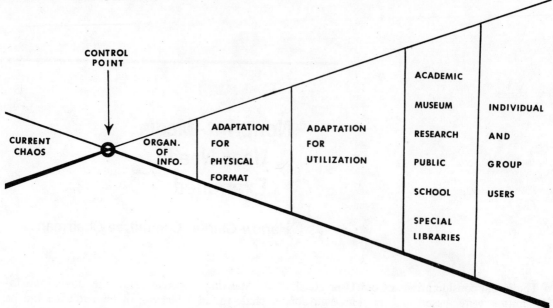

Fig. 1. Diagram showing dissemination of material from control point

research. Are you using reference as a very general term to cover everything except supplying books for fun?

Comment: Yes, in a sense, we are.

Mr. Croghan: You mean the advisory function may relate to anything, and the time may come when the adolescent, wanting information on etiquette, will be referred to reference, or the consulting service often found in public libraries?

Mr. Clarke: We did not think to include this kind of a function as we discussed this topic.

Mr. Croghan: Does the term *function* refer to the function of the library itself or to the function the media or material will have when put to use? Now if we accept the latter definition, then how this library operates does not apply. When we used, for example, the term *education* we were trying to define a particular area in which materials are used. Various steps leading to the proper utilization of these materials may require consultation, research, reference search; but we are not using these terms. This is a generalized report with a list of sample terms which are suggested to you for your consideration. We have identified our potential audience and now need to discover what they want. We must know their aims and

means. The need assessment task is one of the initial tasks that has to be undertaken to further work on the organization of bibliographic data.

Mr. Leni: I have been thinking about methods of implementation, not implementation of bibliographic control in general, but the specific task of defining the needs—the need of assessment or, as Arthur Brody calls it, performance standards. I think we can agree that discussion is not a very feasible or effective means of translating generalized concepts into specific definitions, for it is the goal of research. Considerable research has been done on the use of media. However, we do not really know what research, if any, has been done in the specific area of media assessment within the context of bibliographic controls. Therefore, one of the very first steps to be undertaken is a survey of what effort has already been made in this area.

At least one or two isolated efforts have been made to define performance standards of bibliographic control. But in a country as large as the United States, there is always a great deal of activity in progress of which other people are unaware. In fact, it is possible for two projects to be going on within the United States Office of Education without one program director knowing what the other program director is doing.

In addition, procedures should be developed for surveying media users in each of the functional and organizational categories to compile statistical data that could then be translated into performance standards. My own personal opinion is that we of the institute are not the ones to perform this task, for we already have full-time activities. If this task is to be achieved within a meaningful period of time, it is essential that a director and staff devote full time to the project.

Finally, some investigation should be made of the impact on bibliographic controls that will be made by the rapid changes in media utilization, such as those Robert Heinich refers to in his paper. Such a study could be conducted by an institution of higher learning, by the staff of professional organizations, or by a cooperative trade organization. It could also be done by private research or consulting firms. We should make proposals, although the disposition, of course, will be made by the organization supplying the funds.

While our committee has been trying to confine itself to the area of need assessment, it is encouraging to think in terms of the overall system study, all of the parts fitting within the scope of whatever finance study will become the outgrowth of the institute. We are thinking of need assessment as the first phase and the actual problems of finding information content a subsequent phase. The operating or research body may be able to present carefully researched and evaluated approaches to bibliographic resources. My specific recommendation is that a proposal be written for the funding of a professionally conducted study.

Comment: In the library world, we have had need assessment until we are boiling over with it. Right now, we want to generate some action. We have had a huge grant from the Council on Library Resources for need assessments and probably some twenty additional studies of need assessment. The National Advisory Commission on Libraries and the Commission on Instructional Technology have data on needs assessment. What we need is to get these operative.

Committee Recommendations

The group of people who composed the User Needs Committee plus other members of the institute propose that a task force be created to perform the following:

1. Articulate the need for a commonly acceptable group of items with accepted meanings that may be used by controllers, organizers, and other users of media as we create and manipulate bibliographic information about media.

2. Provide existing organizations, agencies, and interested groups with a statement of what is desired by users of media in the area of bibliographic control.

3. Prepare and disseminate throughout the media field a statement setting forth the many and varied attempts to identify and define terms related to the creation and manipulation of bibliographic information.

4. Prepare a list of terms to be defined and develop an interim list of definitions that may be used by those who create and manipulate bibliographic information about media.

The procedure would be for a group of participants not bound to the American Library Association, Department of Audiovisual Instruction, or any other interest group to operate as an independent agency attempting to pull together the various interested individuals and groups concerned with the tasks listed above.

User Needs and Bibliographic Control of Nonprint Media

Gerald R. Brong, Committee Chairman

The User Needs Committee was assigned the tasks of identifying (1) the needs of the users of bibliographic systems designed for media and (2) the requirements of a bibliographic control system. The committee interpreted the task to mean that it should identify and functionally define the essential components of a bibliographic entry (components are the parts that function to meet the stated needs of the user) and narrowed its focus to a single point. When a patron of a library seeks information about the holdings of that library from the data file representing the holdings, what data does he need to make an initial selection of items (informational units) and to locate and obtain the informational units, and what information is needed to employ the unit to provide the desired information? When the librarian, as opposed to the patron, needs to use the data file on holdings, what information does he need and for what functions? Is this information different from what the patron needs?

Procedure

Members of the committee received ideas from many people with an interest in media

control who were not attending the institute, such as school district instructional materials coordinators, audiovisual directors, and school librarians. For example, the total library staff of a medium-sized school district met with committee representatives. Public librarians, industrial librarians, personnel from state and county libraries, members of the developmental team responsible for MARC II, information scientists, and college and university librarians all became sources of information. Reports of the committee's efforts were presented at state and regional library and audiovisual meetings and responses sought from participants. Interaction with representatives from commercial firms producing nonprint resource materials and with other committees from professional organizations provided a most interesting exchange of ideas.

Opportunities for the committee to meet face-to-face were limited to one brief meeting on the last day of the institute's first phase. All committee communications were by correspondence and telephone, with several full committee meetings conducted by conference calls. To expedite the writing of the report, the committee was divided into three teams, each performing a specific set of assigned tasks; terminology, elements of data, and a system of control. The results of team activities were exchanged and then drafts of the report were circulated among all teams for corrections or content changes.

Committee members: Mary R. Boyvey, Mary B. Cassata, Harlow W. Clarke, Robert L. Claussen, Malcolm Ferguson, Eugene Koskey, Jules Leni, Janet Macdonald, Roger McFarland, and Galen Pearce.

Terminology

Two separate aspects of the terminology problem were identified. There were the larger problems of terminology associated with nonprint resources in general and the immediate problem of terminology needed by the group as its tasks were undertaken. The institute participants agreed that a terminology problem does exist in the area of nonprint resources. Many questions were discussed and efforts made to provide some definitions for a brief list of terms, but no real solutions were achieved during phase 1. The fact that terminology was not standard was a problem the committee had to live with during its efforts. The committee agreed that it could not and should not attempt to establish a glossary of terms relevant to nonprint resources. It provided only the necessary definitions of words or concepts to allow its members to communicate.

The committee recommends that the establishment of a workable system of terms for identifying things and functions in the nonprint resource field be assigned a high priority. After this system of terms is identified, a conscious effort should be made to communicate these terms to the full library-media field, and efforts toward education for their acceptance should be carried out. It is further recommended that the institute body compile a list of terms needing definition in the nonprint bibliographic-control field. This list could then be submitted to operating groups or committees of the American Library Association, Association for Educational Communications and Technology. Educational Film Library Association, American Society for Information Science, and others, with a request that the terms be operationally defined and the library-media field be made aware of the accepted definition of the terms in question.

The committee defined a number of terms as it proceeded with its tasks. These definitions reflect the frame of reference for this committee and should not be considered the only correct definitions of these terms:

1. A bibliographic element is a part or piece of information in a bibliographic entry.

2. A bibliographic entry or reference is a statement containing information which describes a published or unpublished work that provides the user with data to identify and locate the precise item listed. The entry in a library cataloging system will further allow the user to make judgments leading to the selection or rejection of the item as one to be sought and used.

3. The collation is the physical description of a work.

4. An essential element is an element without which the user of the entry would be unable to obtain all necessary data from that entry.

5. A subject analytic is a heading or catalog entry identifying the subject of a part of a work.

6. The user is any person, librarian or patron, using the information in the bibliographic system.

Members of the committee were convinced quite early that, except for the terms required to describe physical features of nonprint resources or patterns of use, the basic vocabulary dealing with bibliographic systems for the print field is applicable in working with nonprint materials. This fact was confirmed as the study continued.

Element Identification

A list of bibliographic elements with their definitions, considered by the committee to be *essential* to any bibliographic system employed with nonprint resources, was made. Most of the listed elements are now used in bibliographic-control systems for nonprint resources and print materials. The committee has reconfirmed the fact that these are essential to the user of a bibliographic system. Elements are not listed in any order of importance, nor does the listing of an element signify that it must be a separate entry rather than a part of some other element in the bibliographic data the user wishes to utilize.

Although the committee membership did not achieve agreement on elements, significant questions have been raised and further study of the elements is recommended. These elements are based on what the user of a biblographic-control system (the patron and not the librarian) identified as essential. There will be other essential elements added as the needs of the librarians, another major category of user, are identified. The essential elements for bibliographic control of nonprint media identified by users are:

1. *Title* (including all subtitles) provides means for exact identification of item in question. Titles, rather than call numbers, are often used as locators for nonprint resources.

2. *Creator* (author function, i.e., writer, compiler, corporate body, etc.) identifies who is responsible for intellectual content of the item. Often not a significant element unless the item presents a work (i.e., filmplay, recording of an opera, speech recording) with identifiable intellectual uniqueness. Most general educational films, for example, would not have a creator entry. The producer may also be the creator.

3. *Edition statement* indicates if item is other than first edition. Revision should be noted. Integrity of creater-producer is essential when establishing edition identification.

4. *Production date* indicates when content was written, photographed, recorded, edited, etc. It always precedes copyright or release date and is the most important of the dates associated with an item.

5. *Producer* (often combined with number 1 above) sponsors the item, and its creation and production place is usually the location of the producer but it may be the location of the setting. NOTE: Except when the producer was all or in part responsible for the intellectual content of the item or the place influenced intellectual content, this element was considered by some to be less than essential data.

6. *Release date* indicates date when item was released for use or sale. It provides indication of the physical age of the item and of the reproduction techniques that may have been used. The release date should not be used by producers to prove the currency of an item —this is the function of the production date. A difference between the release date and the production date indicates a time lapse between production and release.

7. *Distributor* is the source from which an item can be obtained by purchase, rental, or other means. Responsible to the producer for item's distribution, the distributor may also be the producer.

8. *Physical data or description* lists physical characteristics such as medium and format, length in minutes or frames or feet, visual properties, audio properties, number of items in a set, or other data that affect utilization. NOTE: Special equipment requirements, if not obvious from the foregoing, would be mentioned.

9. *Series statement* states that item is part of an identifiable group of items; series title listed. Integrity of producers and distributors is essential in identifying this element.

10. *Notes* provide additional amplifying data about the item, such as indications of intended uses or techniques of use, evaluative statements with reference to source of evaluation, mention of unique production techniques, and mention of additional articles included with the item (guides, scripts, etc.).

11. *Annotation-description* (an extension of notes) describes the content of the item if not clearly identified by the title or other elements in the bibliographic entry. Strong support was found for the inclusion of evaluative information by expert evaluators in resource center bibliographic-holdings files.

12. *Subject headings or subject tracings* are used in a bibliographic file with entries arranged by subject. They are handled exactly like any other bibliographic library file. Tracings give the user a further clue to content.

13. *Location indicator* is to be used if it provides a location address allowing the user to retrieve the specific item. It may be a classification number or symbol, accession number, or shelving address. As was indicated in number 1 above, the title may be the locating device.

14. *Intended audience* (may be part of notes) indicates the intellectual content, sophistication, or degree of readiness needed for a user to find the content of the item meaningful. It also indicates restriction of use. NOTE: This information was requested by educators more frequently than by others, such as resource librarians, who were also queried.

Organization for Bibliographic Control

A standardized bibliographic-control system is needed for all resource materials, including those in nonprint format. Although it has some limitations, the MARC system offers the greatest present potential for a control system, and work must now be expanded to include nonprint resources. The systems proposed and promoted not only should be sources for bibliographic data, with title or author entry, but also should have capabilities for searching out entries on specific subjects and should be designed to accommodate entries for all types of media.

1. It is suggested that the institute study and perhaps make a statement on the role of commercial library service organizations in the development of a standard bibliographic system.

2. It is further suggested that the institute encourage study and develop formal statements about copyright law, the uses of copyrighted materials in libraries, and the production of standards for identification of nonprint resources, such as title frames and production dates.

3. Electronic transmission of information is a rapidly expanding field; therefore, it is recommended that the institute review what has been presented about library networking and examine existing and proposed bibliographic-control systems for nonprint resources to see if they meet the needs of these new information and library systems.

4. Adequate exchange between the producers of nonprint resources and librarians has been lacking, and, therefore, the committee recommends that the institute issue a statement indicating its desire to establish a meaningful dialogue.

5. A task of high priority should be the establishment of a workable system of terms for identifying media and functions in the area of nonprint resources. After this system of terms has been developed, a conscious effort should be made to communicate it to the library-media field and to educate personnel in the field for the acceptance of these terms. It is further recommended that a list of terms needing definition in the nonprint-resources bibliographic-control field be compiled. These terms should be operationally defined and the library-media field made aware of them.

6. An operational bibliographic-control system, adaptable to machine manipulation, is of the utmost importance and should be established immediately. The Library of Congress is actively working to extend the MARC system to motion pictures and filmstrips. This institute should provide input to the Library of Congress in the nonprint realm and make known the identification of essential elements for any entry dealing with nonprint resources.

If nothing else was accomplished by the functioning of this committee, it can be said with certainty that the concern for bibliographic-control systems for nonprint media has been spread to others, who are now aware of the existence of the problem, appear eager to see the problem solved, and pledge their support to this end. The committee wishes to continue its awareness of current activities in the field of cataloging rules revision which affect nonprint media and report them to the institute membership.

A thorough examination of bibliographic elements for nonprint resources was undertaken and an attempt made to equate these elements with those for print materials. The elements defined are essential to any system that would meet the needs of the people with whom the committee worked and of the members of this committee. The majority of the committee felt that with further refinement, existing bibliographic-control systems used for print materials are applicable to nonprint resources.

Based on the functionally defined elements in this report, it is believed that a system incorporating these elements (and other elements deemed essential) can be designed, or an existing system meeting the requirements of nonprint resources can be identified and put into service on an international scale.

Systems
Approach to
Information Control

Antony Croghan, Committee Chairman

The key areas within which we need to define our problems have been identified (fig. 1). These are placed in an order of priority, based on the simple principle that the ones

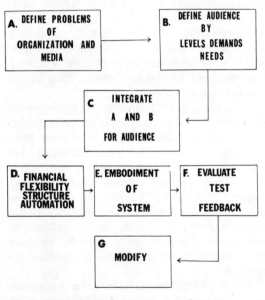

Fig. 1. Flow chart of systems control process

that needed information earliest came at the beginning. One can assume, therefore, that square E, embodiment of system, has appeared at that point because it was felt that

Committee members: Edward F. Newren and Galen L. Pearce

we needed to solve or define all earlier steps before we could reasonably start on square E.

This analysis is produced with the assumption that it is a disposable document. By disposable it is meant that although this may be an acceptable system for problem solving, the areas involved must be expanded. In doing so, the procedure will automatically check the order in which we have placed them, because in order to define the audience the enabling goals are needed first. Then the boxes must be arranged in an order. They are put forward here in some terms not to prejudge decisions, but simply to give something with which to start.

If we assume the adoption of systems analysis in some form or another, the statements and definitions of our own particular problems and personal solutions, must be the first thing we put down. Are they entirely local or do they apply for a national system as well? This would have to be the next question of each stage if we are going to end not with one single system but with a single reservoir from which to draw.

The development of the *California Manual* is an admirable illustration of this process (pages 340–42). Alma Tillin started from a local situation and generalized to a wider one serving California, which I am certain could be generalized even further. Perhaps not up to the national level, for if so, I would start quarreling with some things. However, she has given me a basis on which to quarrel with the national level. By this I mean, if you are working in a junior high school, is this what junior high schools are doing throughout the nation?

When we come down to the embodiment of system, we tend to say at that point, "Well, I haven't enough information." This is analysis, systems analysis, and the corollary to any analysis, if one is to eventually come up with something of value, must be a synthesis, a pooling together of what is decided. Within the English context, and I will narrow this down to my own experience, the problem is not that people do not have skills that they could use or do not know how to start, but that they need to be told the pathway down which to go. They need not be told their destination, but to be given a map of the area so that they can plan their own route. One of the things we might do, since we are using this as a pilot project for problem solving, is generalize this advice and, as it were, put out a little manual saying, "Think about these kinds of things in this order, and these are possible solutions." I am thinking now of the flow charts which have the *yes* and *no* decisions at various stages. These take a lot of time to prepare, but we can do the system analysis that would allow personnel of individual systems to set about preparing them. I would ask, Can we in fact evaluate this as a system of problem solving for people with similar problems?

When we come up with our system of problem solving, we might thrust it at the institute speakers when they arrive, not expecting them to rewrite their papers but warning them that almost the first question will be, "And how do you think what you are doing fits in with our system?" Agreement on this system will ensure that, within our own specialties, we are thinking in the same way. If we decide that we need a classification scheme, I hope that media people will leave that to librarians. When it comes to the physical requirements for the storage of film and how to describe it, media people should get together, make up their own minds, and tell the librarians. I am prepared to take over some of the

work, if this means that at a point I can leave it to the experts in another area. I promise to be an authoritarian about this. I do not mind for this committee has the image of George III in their minds, so why should I not reinforce it?

Mr. Pearce: There are several systems, and we tried to reduce the essential elements into a rather simple thing. They can get very complicated, although they all have about the same rationale. They are all behavioral objective oriented, so whatever system you come up with, it will probably have essentially the same elements. We certainly do not wish to spend two weeks developing an elaborate road map when only the essential elements will probably suffice. This is about the simplest one.

Mr. Newren: It was our joint decision that each of these boxes (circles originally because we did not want to get backed into a corner) has to be expanded considerably. We must now break down to very finite degrees just exactly what goes into each box, because there are subsystems for each, and the wording we have given conveys only the briefest hint of its operation.

Mr. Croghan: We have assumed that in fact we are designing the system for everyone, and thereby we have labeled box B "define audience." Designing something, a printed document, to be circulated over the whole of the United States, is a relatively simple definition. Oddly enough, in a very small organization such as a high school, the levels, demands, and needs are far more complex, because you know them in far more detail. You really cannot know the detailed needs of the possible 200 million Americans you are serving. On the copy of the system flow which I have there are feedback links. The other two members of the committee took one look and went white!

Question: If box A is to be accomplished first, do you see that the time schedule is really practical?

Mr. Croghan: "Organization and media" is the subject of this institute. By *organization*, are we thinking narrowly of cataloging, an integrated catalog or classification, a catalog for this material, or the information services that would be needed to use this catalog? If we have an integrated catalog, a library that is only interested in film will, for its own special needs, have to pull it out. Now this is, in my view, the function of information service; this is the use of bibliographical tools tailored towards a particular need. Any bibliographical organization I would plan would not stick solely to the physical machinery—the catalogs, printed cards, or computer—but take in the machinery needed to use these catalogs—the differing levels, the committees, and the objectives of these particular things.

We blindly talk of *nonbook media* or of *media*. What do we mean? At Oral Roberts University I asked if they catalog the models in the biology laboratory. Such a model is an information-bearing media, regardless of the fact that it happens to be polystyrene and several feet in size. The fact that it actually depicts a particularly revolting interior of a frog is just one of the nasty things about our job. Just what, in fact, do we mean by *media*? Perhaps we have a consensus, but we have never spelled out precisely what this consensus is. It is surprising how often in our discussions we start talking about media and end up talking about films or slides. What is media and does it include books? If so, does this widen our audience?

Comment: We wanted a road map, and I think, even though this is very broad and general, it is at least a road map. A definition of terms could very well be included in the process. If we are going to produce a document, we must define explicitly the terms to be used in the document. We should define not just *media*, but any term that might have a controversial nature so that we can have clear communication in this document. As far as implementation is concerned, we can get several committees started working concurrently. We are never going to get 100 percent consensus on anything, and so whatever definition of terms we agree on will have to be decided by majority vote.

Comment: I would hope we could come to a consensus instead of taking a majority vote. If it seems impossible, then of course we have to face that fact, but we should try to reach a consensus through discussion, both informally and formally.

Mr. Croghan: At this point we need diversity. A consensus does not mean a single system, for it can mean an agreement to disagree.

Comment: It looks like a fine system, but until I have an understanding of it, you have a fine system which is still not *my* system. The simplicity of it makes us assume falsely that we do understand it, but it is obviously not that simple. We may get so tied up with the system that the system becomes the end in itself. Let us try to make it a working tool and not quibble over definitions.

Mr. Croghan: Square A is the first step. We decided to accept the limitation set by the title of this institute, the two basic problems, organization and media. Square B refers to doing something for a certain kind of person. Although you can define these in a number of ways for bibliographical purposes, the basic ones are the levels appropriate to your situation. In an academic situation, these levels are formal academic ones. However, the situation could be a junior high, university, factory, or any other where one is using media as teaching aids. Levels may be defined in terms of work, or you may even choose to define them in terms of a formal structured organization within the factory. You will have the known demands of your clientele, and you have their unknown demands which you must anticipate: the things they need, but do not yet know they need. Audiovisual materials for a lot of teachers in England come under this category. They need the materials, but they do not yet know they need them.

Are the demands made by the differing levels different in themselves, or does it turn out that the levels are irrelevant because the demands made on the system are the same from each level? We know we have different kinds of people coming in, but perhaps we do not realize that they are asking for the same kind of things.

We might put the first two squares together. We are organizing the media for specific kinds of audiences, which is square C, one of the synthetic stages. We integrate these together, and now we put forward our enabling goals, square D. Of the four goals the first two are inherent in knowledge: flexibility and structure, a flexible system or a structured system. One decision is part of the organization of knowledge itself. *Automation* was thrown in to remind us of the physical embodiment of this. It is no use to work designing a beautiful, flexible system to meet all of your needs, if it requires a computer, and all we have is a blackboard and chalk. Which brings us to the last of the enabling goals, and a crass one, I fear: Can you get the money?

Librarians tend to think of enabling goals solely in technical terms, and administrators solely in financial ones; but they are all part of the system we are designing, the narrowly conceived machinery for implementing a program. This can be, for example, the cataloging card system run by the Library of Congress, which produces about 180,000,000 cards a year. That does not sound narrow, but it is a relatively limited way of disseminating information.

I personally feel that if we have done the jobs demanded in the first four parts, we will in square E be able to design systems that are compatible with each other, that will work on all levels we need. This is possible because in square B the levels, needs, and demands are defined.

Square F is where one evaluates, tests, and obtains feedback. Now this is certainly where the connections really become obvious, because of that splendid word *feedback*. A reader comes screaming into your library saying, "You give me thirty cards all telling me that you have so and so's history of England, and you know I am interested in American history!" That's feedback all right, of the most positive kind. At that point, square G, you modify and put in a loop. This must not be a closed finite system, such as the hieroglyphic language of the ancient Egyptians, which is not capable of any further modification at the moment. On the whole, no system is closed.

Problems of
Media and of Their
Organization

Orin Hatch, Committee Chairman

Some significant problems relating to implementation have been omitted from this preliminary report of this committee that was assigned to define the problems of media organization. Briefly, they come under the nice clear heading of finances. There must be an adequate financial structure before any implementation is possible. Although finance is not mentioned in our statement of the problems, it must certainly be considered at the time of instrumentation. Another problem is that of time. The committee has discussed the amount of time it might take to implement anything evolved from the decisions we make, as well as the sequence in which solutions to these problems are sought. These must be considered, but, because they are related to implementation, our particular committee did not include them.

We began with the media themselves, discussing the structures, the forms, and the actual physical objects. We chose to exclude any mention of machinery or equipment, since they belong in another dimension altogether. There is no mention of manuscripts either, nor of books, nor of any forms other than audiovisual materials. The first question to be answered before beginning to organize is, What

media are we talking about? The committee has not specified what the line of attack on the problem should be, but it recognizes that this is a crucial problem which has led to considerable misunderstanding. We need to decide which media should be included and what terms will be used to describe them. The terms selected should then be defined.

After considering these very preliminary problems, we go into a second group of problems. These may be designated as problems of media control, with several subcategories including the actual cataloging, classification, and storage. The crucial question here, I think, is the elementary one, What do we mean by bibliographic control? Is this the real problem, rather than the broader one of information retrieval or the still broader problem of education? The answer to this question is crucial to the definition of the problem.

Once we have defined bibliographic control, we are led necessarily to another group of questions. How will we use bibliographic control in relation to activities of some lesser problems? In our discussion we have asked what bibliographic elements should be included for a citation for evaluation or selection purposes, such as a citation listed in a review journal; a citation for acquisition purposes, such as a *Books in Print* for media; a citation for a bibliographic reference; and a citation for a sales, rental, or loan book catalog. There is another basic question: Should the main

---

Committee members: Ovid L. Bayless, Paul L. Brawley, Gilbert G. Fites, Sister James Ellen Huff, Ann M. Jenkins, Shirley E. Lewis, Robert G. Murray, Edward F. Newren, and Wanda Sivells.

catalog card entry or the machine-input entry be used as a master entry in which all the other elements are found and from which these other entries can be derived? There is the additional consideration of whether there should be a title page, or an equivalent. Should we demand of publishers that they find some format for giving us the information on every product in order to eliminate the disagreement about what is the title?

We came next to a consideration of subject indexing. Considering the needs of the user and the existing list of subject headings—that is, *Library of Congress* and *Sears*—what kind and how much subject indexing is required to make the catalog (whether manual or automated) a relevant bibliographical tool? Should still another subject-headings list be devised that would allow for in-depth subject indexing? Considering the needs of the user, the physical characteristics peculiar to each media, and the structure of existing classification schemes, should any or all media be classified?

We have not been concerned with archives, which are not individual items, but groups of documents such as publications or manuscripts. How do you integrate archival material into a library if you include them in lists of media? Is it necessary to have a classification system for media? Or is it necessary simply to revise some accession system which works very well for receiving archival and other types of material? Is it necessary to have more than half a dozen large film libraries? If so, is it essential to arrange them so that people can browse through the materials, or would it be more economical to have the materials cataloged and listed by a numerical system? When we really consider the cost of some of the materials, we might decide that the subject classification system for arrangement of materials is not necessary. We might decide that a subject indexing system, different from what we have devised, might be advisable for nonprint media.

Problems related to storage include the location of materials for use at the local level, such as provision for browsing among the audiovisual media, and use at the regional, national, and international levels. We must also consider the storage of these materials for automated retrieval purposes and preservation.

There are other considerations which one may feel are necessary for adequate bibliographic control but which are not really related to the primary problem assigned our committee. For example, is an index to the media literature (such as *Library Literature* and *Education Index*), which would include references to general articles, books, and reviews of media, necessary? We have in the library world very sophisticated indexes in which we have under subject and author entries the information about references to different articles, books, and reviews. Could we have something like this in the media field? Should there be other tools such as a *Publisher's Weekly*? Should we have *Books in Print*, or *Book Review Digest*, or *Book Review Index* for media? These would be indexes in which one could find evaluations and reviews of media for selection. Although the inadequacies of the *Educational Media Index* are known, nothing better is available at present. Should it be revised, expanded, and updated?

There are also some related problems which are even farther beyond our realm, except that we must in all cases take them into consideration. Should there be established minimum standards to determine the physical qualities of what goes into making the physical object? Should there be standards for the storage of the various types of media? How should they be protected from light, fire, humidity, and magnetic fields? What should the environmental temperatures be? Should there be a minimum standard for equipment to ensure proper use of the media? Should we have standards for evaluation? Should there be a study of the selected terms that should be considered in any evaluation?

To present a preliminary statement of the problems of media and their organization, we have taken a few liberties. We realize this. Perhaps the motto of this committee should be "Fools rush in where angels fear to tread."

Problems of
Media and of Their
Control

Louis H. Brown, Committee Chairman

Education has a long history of concern for the variables that exist among learners. This concern was carried forward into this century by John Dewey and has been explored within the last decade under the sponsorship of federal and foundation grants. Any serious investigator of the problems attendant to individual learning patterns has been forced to recognize the need for (1) the identification of information (existing and future productions) in all formats, and (2) the means of retrieving both descriptive information and physical material. Also attendant to these areas of concern is the basic need to correlate instructional materials with learner variables. The need for information retrieval is not restricted to the educational setting but, indeed, exists for all focal points of information sources such as public libraries, industrial libraries, film collections, audiotape libraries, videotape storage centers, archives, and research endeavors.

The process of retrieving, distributing, and evaluating learning materials is becoming more complex as information continues to expand at a very rapid rate. Systems of retrieval must be able to provide what is available not only now, but also in the future—more and more kinds of content. The task will not lessen with

time but will in fact be compounded as information and instructional materials in a variety of formats continue at the present rate of growth.

Technology applicable to retrieval systems has advanced to the degree that it offers us a very real means of dealing with the need for accessing information to accommodate the variety of user needs. Technology can effect the compilation and retrieval of pertinent information from data banks of a size not yet in existence with speed and relative economy. Technology can produce the traditional forms of information retrieval, such as indexes and catalogs, to handle great volumes according to content or other descriptors that may be desired by users.

In order to effect the usefulness of technology we must, as it has been reaffirmed by the expertise brought together by the education media institute, establish (1) a basic system for classification by content area, with appropriate identifiers and information sources of whatever mode or format, and (2) the mechanism for implementing the identification, classification, cataloging, and physical distribution of materials.

Topics of particular concern to this committee include usage and program classification, codes and logical schemes of organization, and the needs of users for access to nonprint media. We quickly became aware of the unique

Committee members: Harlow W. Clarke and Orin W. Hatch.

combination of professional persons on our committee and at this entire institute. It seems probable to us that such a mixture of non-print-media creators, organizers, and communicators have never before come together for direct confrontation on a problem of vital concern to all. We must, therefore take full advantage of this opportunity to make our maximum contribution on this special occasion.

The identification of media is itself a formidable task, as we have discovered. There appears to be no comprehensive listing of print and nonprint media. Both seem to defy agreed-upon definitions, possibly reflecting rapid technological innovations and also the difficulty that the somewhat insecure professional associations and their memberships have in working cooperatively for the anticipated benefit of a third party, their public. Specific terms with agreed-upon definitions are essential to progress toward the organization of nonprint media. Associations should be asked to initiate this research immediately.

Comment: The institute staff will seek an agreement from the American Library Association for the revision of its twenty-seven-year-old *A.L.A. Glossary of Library Terms* and a meeting of this institute with the National Education Association, Department of Audiovisual Instruction [name changed to Association for Educational Communications and Technology in 1970].

The problems of access to, cataloging of, classification for, and storage of nonprint media are central to our purpose. To accomplish bibliographic access we must identify the bibliographic elements essential to the following:

1. Citation for evaluation and selection purposes: e.g., a review published in a journal
2. Citation for acquisition purposes: e.g., a publication for all media similar to *Books In Print*
3. Citation for bibliographic reference: e.g., Maurice Tauber's United States of America Standards Institute (USASI) Standards Z39.4 1969
4. Citation for a sales, rental, or loan book catalog

5. Main catalog card or machine-input entry.

These elements should be considered in view of actual user needs and existing codes and rules; for example, the *Anglo-American Cataloging Rules* and Department of Audiovisual Instruction's *Standards for Cataloging, Coding and Scheduling Educational Media*. We might also ask if one entry serves as a master entry from which data for all others may be derived? Or should one entry serve for all types?

Another recurring question is whether or not there should be a title page equivalent for nonprint media. This attempt to utilize concepts established for print materials must be carefully examined, with an expected agreement by a broad representation of nonprint and print media specialists.

Subject headings or identifiers are required to make the catalog, whether manual or automated, a relevant bibliographic tool. Existing lists—such as, *Library of Congress* and *Sears* —need to be analyzed for user-need satisfaction and changed accordingly.

Physical characteristics peculiar to each medium should be examined and related to the existing classification schemes, *Dewey*, Library of Congress, and Universal Decimal. In addition, the question of whether or not any or all media need be classified should be considered.

The proper storage of each medium of communication is also important to the efficient utilization of nonprint resources. Projected use at the local, regional, and national levels is further complicated by the relationship of storage to automated retrieval purposes, when the basic purpose of preservation is often overlooked.

Bibliographic considerations for the control of nonprint media should include:

1. Is it necessary to have a separate index to the media literature, such as *Library Literature*, which would contain references to journal articles, books, and reviews of media?
2. Should reference tools simlar to those now available for print materials, e.g., *Books in Print, Book Review Digest,* and *Publisher's Trade List Annual,* be developed to serve the audiovisual profession?

3. Would it be advantageous to revise and expand the *Educational Media Index?*
4. Should current literature indexes and abstracts include references to all audiovisual media?

Related concerns of particular importance involve established standards for quality control, reliability, or performance requirements. The American National Standards Institute and its related program, the International Standards Organization, have key roles in the standardization of media for dissemination and communication. The physical qualities of the media, their packages, and their containers or carriers should be carefully delineated by national and international bodies. The lack of minimum standards for specific media storage, equipment necessary for its use, and evaluative criteria for selection are obstacles to the full utilization of nonprint media and are, therefore, of concern to professional librarians and audiovisual specialists alike.

The identification of specific needs that users, and potential users, of nonprint media have should be carefully researched first as a basis for further investigation and planning toward the bibliographic control of media. User needs, as they relate to the function of media, should be studied within the following contexts: education, research, historical developments, archives, institution, information, reference, and recreation.

User needs also should be studied in relation to the libraries, professional organizations, commercial interests, the general public, museums, foundations, schools, universities, governmental agencies, private collections, and religious institutions. The level and quantity of need and use of bibliographic tools by each of these groups will influence the fundamental form of citations, entries, facilities, and materials to be made available.

Recommendations

To establish a consistency of classification that will provide for translation grid computer programming for classification and meet the requirement of computer technology with the least cost to different computer systems, it is recommended that a basic classification scheme be utilized for all print and nonprint material. This seems particularly valid and urgent in view of the advantages of computer technology in handling vast quantities of information in a variety of formats.

There are already in existence a number of general classification schemes that cover the whole of knowledge as expressed in published works, and these have already been applied to many of the media, demonstrating that they can be used for this purpose. These schemes are detailed, can be revised when needed, and have the advantage of being applicable to print. It is recommended that the principle of classifying media by such a scheme be adopted and that the schemes to be used are, in order of preference, the Library of Congress subject classification scheme and then the Dewey Decimal scheme.

To be made as useful as possible within the recognized limitations inherent in both schemes, the Library of Congress (LC) subject classification scheme should be supported and enhanced by:

1. A subject index for ready explanation of the classification scheme. The index should be based on the author/title format employing selective listing for classification. A general index to the scheme will be needed and could be the basis of the subject indexes to be provided for particular users.

2. LC subject headings, extended with verbal statements as needed. The classification of the subject should be very specific, using words to extend the class mark as necessary.

3. A unique identifying number, whether the Standard Book Number or one constructed according to local rules, to specify the individual record within the class.

4. Computer utilization; employing the MARC II (latest version) format of organization of input bibliographic information and using its analysis of elements and system of tagging them. All information so far stipulated will fit into this format.

5. A revision of part 3, Non-Book Materials, of *Anglo-American Cataloging Rules.* Such a revision to show the principles of author-title. cataloging more clearly and to produce a simplified code for nonbook media would permit

more easily the cataloging of media in accordance with the principles of the code as set forth in parts 1 and 2. Standards for the physical forms of these media should be developed in conjunction with Association for Educational Communications and Technology.

To bring about these changes, it is further recommended that support for cataloging print and nonprint materials be secured by enlisting the use of the Library of Congress staff and facilities, that the services be paid for by a tax levy based on a prorated share of the cost of cataloging and assigning classification numbers identified above on a per unit cost basis to each piece of material—book, periodical, film, filmstrip, videotape, audiotape, and slide set.

As determined by cataloging competences outside the Library of Congress for the biblio-graphic organization of nonprint media, and in lieu of a tax levy for retrospective materials, it is recommended that each publisher or producer be requested to have their publications or productions cataloged and classified, as set forth for all current materials, by recognized competent catalogers. It is also recommended that purchasers of information products insist that their potential purchase be cataloged and classified as a condition of purchase.

The acceptance of specific schemes of classification according to subject area content is vital to the orderly and efficient development of a broad information-retrieval system necessary to the effective utilization of existing knowledge and ever expanding resources.

Classification schemes employed must be capable of incorporating all information, regardless of format.

A Plan for
Change: Diffusion and
Adoption Theory Applied

T. M. Williams

Recent findings in communication research, especially in the area of diffusion and adoption theory, seem relevant to the eventual acceptance of new systems and standards for circulation, distribution, and bibliographic control of nonprint media. It seems to me that a formal diffusion-adoption campaign will be in order once a program is properly developed. We have enjoyed some excellent preadoption publicity for our initial efforts as evidenced by the number of busy, important people who are here to observe, meet, and collaborate with us. Many others are interested or curious about the increasingly important role of nonprint-media activity in libraries and will wish to take part in an organized endeavor to develop bibliographic controls for these materials.

But, there are limits to how far we can and should go until the innovation or product is diffusible through the collective efforts of these individuals and groups. Appropriate publicity and interpersonal contact should be continued as the struggle is maintained to form and perfect the innovation. As the innovation begins to reach the point of diffusibility, appropriate and comprehensive diffusion-adoption design growing out of the work of Everett Rogers and other diffusion theorists may be adapted to our purpose and set forth for action.

A model for the concepts of diffusion and adoption of ideas was set forth by Everett Rogers.[1] It has been modified and extended for this institute group to illustrate the concept of diffusion-adoption in an actual problem-oriented program. Notations above the stairsteps designate stages in the diffusion-adoption process. Notations below each stage designation indicate communication techniques which might be uniquely appropriate in precipitating movement of the subjects to the next higher level. The diffusion-adoption campaign should be predicated upon careful preassessment of the state of the subjects—where on the scale the subjects now are—and the extent to which they seem to be open to change.

Constraints likely to impede information flow and other processes should be identified and appropriate countering strategies devised. Some campaigns will bypass or combine stages while some stages may have to be repeated with alternative strategies to get the subjects through them. Stages may occur simultaneously or independently, overlapping is often quite desirable.

Meanwhile, we should consider the process of perfecting a readily diffusible innovation, as suggested by the important but still emergent field of diffusion and adoption theory. Much is known today about how to carry out a diffusion-adoption campaign—how to in-

Assistant Professor of Communication, Brigham Young University, Provo, Utah.

[1]*Diffusion of Innovations* (New York: Free Pr., 1962).

72

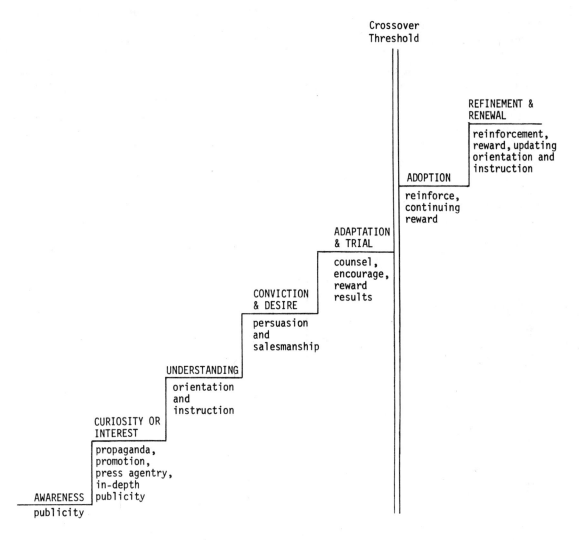

Fig. 1. Diffusion-adoption process

duce change in people and secure their adoption of new ideas, practices, and products which will work to their advantage and to the welfare of the communities in which they live. There are many factors—we should perhaps call them variables—which must ultimately be considered. However, for the present let us consider some basic factors that have been isolated by rather extensive research and experimentation during the last thirty years:

Relative advantage—degree to which the innovation is relatively superior to what it would replace. It matters little whether or not the innovation has advantages, as judged by experts in the field. What does matter is whether or not the individual perceives a relative advantage (a common weakness). Diffusion will take place more quickly and more universally if we can demonstrate a clear-cut relative advantage which suggests dedicated homework.

Compatibility—degree to which the innovation is consistent with existing values, past experiences, and practices currently in fa-

73

vor with potential adopters. An idea not compatible with prevalent values and norms of the system will not be adopted as easily as one that is compatible. Adopters need the feeling of security which comes with innovations not too far removed from what they are used to, such as birth control in pill form and LSD in sugar cubes.

Divisibility—degree to which the innovation may be tried out and proven on a limited or *pilot* basis prior to wholesale adoption. New methods which can be introduced on the installment plan will generally be adopted more quickly than those not divisible. In the widely heralded hybrid seed-corn adoption campaign, not one farmer adopted it without first trying it on a partial or trial basis.

Complexity—degree to which innovations are relatively difficult to explain and demonstrate. Innovations must be clearly comprehended and easily demonstrated; for example, the canasta craze in Brazil—slow diffusion through personal explanation; and the hoop craze in the United States—instant diffusion through demonstration on television.

Communicability—degree to which potential values and benefits of the innovation can be made attractively and compellingly visible to potential adopters.

These factors suggest that we begin now to look at our proposed new standardized system for bibliographic control of media in the light of what kind of fit will be required if it is to be adopted. We must take at the outset those actions which will help assure the desired results, a diffusible product. First, any grant proposals submitted should include the necessary budget for pilot projects and a method for field testing to perfect the product and increase the probability that it will be readily diffusible. Secondly, we must write into our grant proposals provisions for dissemination of the results of the pilot activity for a full-blown diffusion-adoption campaign.

Our purposes must be carefully examined so that we may delineate the task and evaluate our goals in light of the predispositions and concerns of the people to whom our messages

are to be directed. It is important that we know in advance what the attitudes and vested interests of persons in our target population are so that we can plan accordingly. Like successful salesmen we must devise ways of presenting our messages in terms of our prospects' thoughts and emotions.

The overriding factor is that there is no single rhetoric common to all the people we seek to convince. Therefore, we will need to design several messages, each adapted to the different categories of people with differing backgrounds and perceptions of the gravity of the problem and the action needed. What seems important and noteworthy to us may not be to them. Our logic may not be theirs; what we consider valid arguments and proof, they may consider irrelevant or lacking in validity. Unless we proceed with caution and finesse, anything we try to have instituted for nonprint-media control could be construed as an attack on the ego of the user. If, however, we approach the prospective user as a consultant, seeking his advice on applying the innovation to the movement in general, as a partner in devising ways of spreading the word to other prospective users, our level of success might be improved; for example, the University of Maryland project to obtain adoption by industry of NASA-developed innovations.

As we proceed, it will be desirable to develop strategies for inducing many changes within the target system. We should develop and select innovations which have clear-cut relative advantages—test, modify, and retest—under operational conditions until, it is hoped, clear-cut advantages emerge. The group should attempt wide-scale adoption only when we have advantages which can be forcefully demonstrated and compellingly communicated.

It is essential to establish an organization within the system to facilitate invention, tryout, and diffusion of innovations to bring about change and self-renewal in the system. It is also essential to operate on the premise that the whole organization is a system in need of continuing innovation. A formal procedure should be employed for informing those at the top, compellingly and promptly, of (1) needs for change at all levels, and (2) the actual consequences of innovations that are introduced. We may utilize personnel recruitment, selection, and training policies that encourage development of a staff oriented to innovative practices. A growing body of heuristic knowledge of both formal and informal communication can diffuse innovations.

Most of the problems to be faced in diffusing information about a product must be dealt with rhetorically. They are problems of persuasion geared to the realities that exist. There are certain rhetorical facts of life which we must arrive at searchingly and objectively. In formulating diffusion-adoption campaigns, a variety of orientational or persuasive techniques may be required to get the job done. The diffusion-adoption model illustrates what is typically involved and gives the communication techniques proven to be useful in helping people move through the stages of the process to the eventual adoption decision.

Speaking of decisions, the overriding aim of all that we do in a diffusion campaign is to precipitate some kind of decision about the innovation we ask people to consider. As a rule —because we have struggled with the innovation to a point where adoption of it would be to the best interest of our target population—we seek vigorously for wholesale adoption or group decision making. This goal may be rather precarious and should be undertaken with the realization that there exist alternative ways in which our target product might be embraced. The types of innovation decisions are:

Slow   *Optional*—made by an individual regardless of decisions of others in the target system.

Contingent—adopted only after approval by a majority of members in the adoption system; individuals not forced to conform to group decision.

Collective—adopted or rejected by consensus; all individuals agree to conform to the system's decision.

Authority—forced by those in a superordinate power position; individuals

Fast   told what it to be done.

In view of the foregoing, let us expect that,

Rate of Adoption

in spite of our best efforts, we will win some and lose some as we have in the past. But, as we fail, we must try again, seeking diligently to identify the cause for failure. We must analyze the reasons behind the indifference or resistance of those who fail to respond. We cannot assume that those we seek unsuccessfully to influence are hopelessly stupid or derelict. Some of the stupidity may be our own. In the vast plurality which typifies our time—with its fantastic array of options, alternatives, and viewpoints—we have no choice but to expect that some will view things differently and be willing to meet the resistance resulting therefrom with imaginative patience and persistence. Resistance to change is a natural and very important aspect of any stable society. But, the concept has been analyzed and broken into components of facilitating and impeding factors. Study of them can help one deal with resistance in constructive ways.

Change will be opposed if the nature and the implication of the change are not made clear to the people who will be affected by the change, or if different people perceive differing meanings relative to the change. Should those affected be caught in a crush between strong forces pushing them to make the change and strong forces militating against it, they will— to the degree that they as potential adopters are pressured without some say in the nature or direction of the change—resist change.

Resistance may be expected if the change is perceived as a reflection against personalities rather than an impersonal attack on the problems. If the proposed change ignores already established group norms and patterns of operation, it will face the unnecessary opposition of established groups. Resistance can be decreased to the degree that the change agent can help those affected by change to develop their own understandings of the need for change and demonstrates an explicit awareness of how they feel about the innovation and its implications for them. The facts which point to the need for change are best gathered by (or, at least, gathered with the knowledge and cooperation of) the persons most immediately affected by the change. This done, the change agent's job is to help those affected to see the implications of the data and how it argues for and against the proposed change.

To achieve this the agent must, of course, be an expert on people, and this requires knowledge of and consideration of a rather wide range of people differences and similarities—termed "variables" by behavioral scientists. Some of the important variables correlated with innovativeness in people have been identified. The diffusion theorists divide them into two basic categories:

Nonattitudinal

Age and proximity factors associated with it
Level of education and recency of schooling
Inherent personality factors
Cosmopoliteness (mobility)
Socioeconomic status and power position
Contact with change agencies
Interpersonal contact pattern and group loyalties
Dependence of opinion leaders

Attitudinal

Mental rigidity
Empathetic response capacity
Knowledgeability (desire to know)
Attitudes and disposition toward change (innovativeness)
Dominant value orientation
Achievement motivation
Career aspirations
Familial orientation
Interpersonal style
Conformity-deviancy disposition

As previously indicated, innovations should have clearly demonstrable advantages over existing practices, for marginal advantages are difficult to sell. Consequences of innovations are often difficult to measure, evaluate, and predict. Innovations in large systems, the kind we will be dealing with, encounter many structural barriers on the path toward full-scale adoption. A hierarchial system tends to perpetuate the status quo. Innovative decisions in educational systems are generally collective today rather than optional or enforced. The normal kind of collective choice takes time—perhaps more time than present-day conditions will permit. Assuming these conditions, one must ask, "What kind of timetable is needed to meet the need, given the state of our world?" and "What can be invented in the way of a change mechanism to speed things up?"

George S. Counts feels, "Today a great gulf stands between many of the stubborn realities of our industrial civilization and our customs, loyalties, understandings, and outlooks—between our closely integrated economy and our competitive spirit, between our shrunken world and our tradition of isolation, between our knowledge in almost every field and our ways of life. The task of bringing our minds and our practices into harmony with the physical conditions of the new age is a gigantic and urgent undertaking."[2]

We in the communications profession need to become more vigorous and accept a major part of the action to accomplish this task. Ours is a major aspect of the communication and instructional task. The elements of the diffusion process that undergird our efforts toward a new system for bibliographic control and widespread circulation of the nonprint information-bearing materials are to begin with an innovation, perfect idea, practice, or product which is perceived as new and communicated through certain channels such as convention speeches, television broadcasts, publications, and motion pictures to members of the target system (librarians, media specialists, teachers, administrators). They may adopt or reject the innovation over a period of time.

We must move forward with great vigor to perfect the great ideas and concepts generated by participants of this institute and implement the reform action they suggest. We must also articulate clearly and forcefully what is begun and not let this movement fall of its own weight because of our lack of initiative and professional resolve.

[2]"The Impact of Technological Change" in W. G. Bennes, *The Planning of Change* (New York: Holt, 1961).

Part 3

Access
Requirements
and Need
Projections

Studies concerning the future needs of media services have been undertaken by professional associations, the federal government, and private corporations in the United States and abroad. C. Walter Stone's survey for the American Library Association emphasized the rapidly expanding need for nonprint media and for talented professional personnel to facilitate its use.

Joseph Margolin analyzed the obstacles to the use of nonprint media by federal government personnel. Trevor Dupuy has conducted private surveys and personal interviews in various institutions of higher education in the United States and abroad. The analyses of them indicate a not-so-distant future society largely dependent upon enormous quantities of information in a variety of formats.

Future Media
Services and Media
Professions

C. Walter Stone

It is a privilege to be able to address the problems of bibliographic control of the newer media to a group which shares my feelings of concern. I am thinking chiefly of the lack of control of the newer media, the lack of indexes, guides, catalogs, and systems for finding out about their existence. Also, I welcome the opportunity to think with friends about the shape of the future and about what librarianship is going to become. What will be the definition of our job with respect to providing educational communication and information services in the future?

First, I want to share some philosophy with you because you ought to know something about the background of ideas relating to what I propose for the media field. I want to describe my perceptions of our profession and aspects of media service that we currently provide. Then I shall review the American Library Association *A-V Task Force Survey* project,[1] of which I was chairman over a two-year period. Although the recommendations which grew out of that report are addressed primarily to the American Library Association, they also are pertinent to other professional groups concerned. Finally, since I do not yet have all of the confidence I might have that all of our professional groups will immediately rush out to implement the task force's recommendations, I would like to give you a personal concept of what is required if we are to develop nationwide a satisfactory media information and availability program. It is the national approach I am most concerned about, rather than the ingredients that may be involved.

We may sometimes be led to assume, perhaps unconsciously, that the primary solutions to problems confronting us regarding what we should be doing in our profession today lie somewhere in the areas of the psychology or sociology of communication. Many of us believe now that if we learn to exploit to full advantage the laws of human communications behavior and to utilize the benefits of modern communications technology, then suddenly and miraculously we shall become effective. We as librarians or media service personnel will gain more status and public influence in and outside of our homes, communities and institutions, and so make the world a better place. Wouldn't that be lovely? I am sorry; I simply do not believe it.

The laws of individual and social communications behavior do not answer our questions concerning the assignment of human values, nor do they in and of themselves set either personal or vocational goals. Modern communications technology and media, including the bright, new, whirring reels of tape and

President, Joint Market Analysis Reports Company, Inc., Palo Alto, California

[1]Special summary prepared for the Audio-Visual Committee, American Library Assn. University of Pittsburgh Libraries, 1969; reprinted in *American Libraries* 1, no 1: 40–45 (Jan. 1970).

the blinking-light world of computers, can function just as effectively in serving one mission as another: to divide, separate, and terrorize, as well as to perform benevolent functions. While I agree that we must know who and what we are and use the tools available to perform our work, I submit that the chief problems of our profession are not those of communication as such. Rather, we have another, perhaps more difficult but certainly a more important, concern. We must order our work priorities in terms of commitments to meet basic needs.

I now believe the day has come when it is not enough for libraries or other media service agencies simply to provide access to materials or data, or to compilations, or to interpretations of data, which taken together add up to information. Instead, the library must be capable of assisting human beings to use information humanely to achieve human ends. To do this, librarians and others must understand themselves, what humanity is and requires, and what knowledge is all about. They must be capable of helping others to understand and make skillful use of communications processes, techniques, and media, many of which no longer require any reference to the world of print at all. My chief point, however, is a different one than this. Our task is not one chiefly of providing reservoirs of knowledge, nor guide to it, nor ease of access, both functional and psychological, although these are important. *Rather, our task is that of becoming direct partners in putting ideas and information to work.*

A corollary of this first point is that the day of the general library or information service center is over, finished, as is also that of the librarian or media generalist. That it is gone is documented repeatedly in our professional quest for new public-library goals, for more adequate and appropriate definitions of adult, youth, or children's library service; of our professional education; and of optimum institutional service roles. To become an effective partner in putting information to work, one must be able to identify and to become personally identified with a field of significant human concern, with its purpose, its accomplishments, and its failures. This means intensive work, study, specialization, and, perhaps most of all (to use a term from the space-age glossary), personal injection into all the orbits of that field in which we choose to work.

At least one recent study of library utilization and nonutilization suggests that the public library's greatest weakness, insofar as its efforts to encourage use are concerned, is not in resources or services but in the inadequacy of its publicity program. This is nonsense in my view. I believe that the greatest weakness of the public library, indeed of American library service generally (*library* now being used generically), is our failure to achieve basic relevance to the lives and work of those we serve. In our effort to be all things to all men and children, we have become impotent technicians who can do little for anyone.

Where then do we go from here? First, our missions must be redefined. Second, our institutions, whether they are libraries or information centers, must be restructured to help us accomplish the new missions selected. Third, our staffs, including all classes of library, communication, and information service personnel, must develop new competencies. Some of you are familiar with Sam Simon's "Simplistic Recipe for Cooking up Librarians," in which he talks about adult services. He says that a librarian or media service person should be someone who has the cultural background and the inquisitiveness of a Renaissance man; the heart, soul, and sensitivity of a Salvation Army volunteer; the practicality of a Medici banker; the public relations expertise of P. T. Barnum; and the missionary zeal and aggressiveness of an encyclopedia salesman.

I would be more specific and add a number of ingredients. There should be a basic knowledge of human communication processes. These are important: How does learning take place? How are attitudes formed? What are the causes of motivation? What roles can and do specific media play? How do you appraise communications effectiveness? How do you train patrons for self-guidance and growth in such areas? Also to be mastered are the knowledge and skills essential for effective utilization of the full range of modern communications technology. There would have to be the competencies of the subject specialist to function in one or more areas of vital human interest, constantly scanning its perimeters and parameters to identify limits and bring the focus of attention on that which is important.

Most important of all, I would require the learning, or indoctrination, requisite to formation by each individual of a set of reasonable human values which will yield commitments to this end and which will prepare individuals for sacrifice, if necessary, to perform their unique and socially essential function. It is almost axiomatic today that progress in every sector of life depends upon the successful performance of the library function. Those who manage the flow of ideas and information may be more important in society and to the development of society than any other vocational group.

Now to state our personnel qualifications in simpler and perhaps more practical terms: In the future a number of staff members must be attached to any library or information center or media center whose prime responsibility is to provide professional communications help to those who need it. In the public-library sector, for instance, for the small-business entrepreneur, these needs may be the development of a suitable on-the-job training program for new, perhaps marginally educated, employees. There is nothing new in the idea of providing service for program chairmen; it is just that we have done it so badly in many places. We, you, I, librarians, media specialists—whoever we are—we are not equipped, and we are not trained, and we are not prepared, and we are not organized, and we are not structured, and we are not yet committed to that kind of a goal for the institutions which we serve.

The nature and the range of human behavior in responding to communication are most complex. They cannot be understood easily. One requires major knowledge as well as many technical skills to analyze properly, interpret, and assess the process of communications. Yet such knowledge and skills are mandatory if the library job about which we are concerned—that is, making information, ideas, materials relevant and useful—is to be performed in something more than a perfunctory fashion by employing a Thanksgiving basket or a CARE package approach, the values of which, where

any exist, are more often than not quite accidental. We have been concerned with access and efficiency in providing access. To some extent, even as we approach the problem of awareness of the existence of media, we are concerned with access. Most of the systems which we have for the acquisition, storage, and distribution of educational information resources are archaic and clumsy mechanisms which need improvement in order that they make some kind of sense.

The systems we develop must be so designed as to make access relevant, so that a significant purpose, pluralistically derived in terms of values, may be accomplished. I do not think that our professions, our schools, or our institutions generally have yet come around to accepting ideas of this sort as a basis for defining our primary job. I think it is crucial that we do so.

I want to share something with you, because when I come to a general recommendation (and I am thinking about colleges and universities, and schools, and business, and industry, and the community), I am not thinking just of access, through whatever devices; I am also thinking of relevance.

During the years of 1967 to 1969, I was chairman of the American Library Association Audio-Visual Task Force. This was an ad hoc subcommittee of the Audio-Visual Committee of ALA, which was set up to do three things. The first was to develop a series of regional conversations, to try to find out what it was within or outside the American Library Association which made the association so unpalatable, so inhospitable, so inadequate as an organization to meet the requirements of librarians and others interested in providing audio-visual service. A second part of the task force effort was to distribute to the field a questionnaire which would discover those things which librarians, media specialists, and others considered must be done to improve the availability of information about media and their distribution and what the professional associations most concerned might do. The third part of the study was to ask a colleague, someone we could consult and to whom others would look with respect, to think personally about what our problems are in this area. We asked

James Brown of San Jose State College, not because he is identified with the audiovisual field, nor because he is the dean of graduate faculties there, but because he and a colleague had done some studies of ways in which media are being used in higher education on a national scale.

These are the priority needs as the conversations, as the letters I received, and as the individual interviews expressed them. The first is the need for the recruitment and improved training of people who will exhibit more favorable professional understanding and attitudes toward the job which has to be done in the provision of audiovisual services. We are not recruiting them; we are not training them; they are not there, apparently. A second priority is the need for compilation and publication of more complete and reliable information concerning items of equipment required to perfect the use of audiovisual materials in libraries. Some of the work of Library Technology Program is addressed to this today. Some of the work of the Educational Products Information Exchange is addressed to this. However, none of these endeavors is doing the job adequately at the moment. Third, there must be more concerted and productive efforts to promote the interests of librarians generally in adding to the roster of their responsibilities. Fourth, we need help with the development of special services which utilize audiovisual material and equipment in ways that may be of help to disadvantaged groups, to hospital patients, and in special education. There are groups for whom these may be the only media which can effectively reach across cultural barriers as they exist among minority groups in some sections of the country.

Those were the priority needs. What recommendations came out of the regional conversations, the letters, the responses to questionnaires? The first is that in our professional organizations we must pay more attention, continuing attention, to standards. We do have the new joint American Association of School Librarians and Department of Audiovisual Instruction standards for the schools. But, did their establishment do the job for the public, the college, the special, or other libraries? We need standards not only for media and media

forms and specifications but also for equipment, and, indeed, for the quality of services that are to be rendered. We must find ways to measure these.

The second recommendation is that we must find some way to accomplish the immense task required in listing, reviewing, and cataloging media. There are several hundred subject guides and lists organized by form of media or format—such as the National Information Center for Educational Media (NICEM) publications—and some very limited evaluation tools. We do not really approach any systematic cross-media evaluative guides for the range of material required today; we are not organized so that we can do an informational or instructional job that is really relevant. My colleagues are embarrassed, and I am embarrassed, and I hope you are, too. I hope our association is more embarrassed than anyone else. For ten years our professional groups have known about this chaos, but we have not apparently felt sufficiently ready to make an issue of it. The *Educational Media Index* was an attempt, but it really has not done the job.

Third, there is training. Through our professional associations we must attempt to identify the career ladders in our field. In terms of preservice, inservice, and retreading activities, we need major association support for those developments. We must put real teeth in the field of professional education. "Real teeth" means strengthening ALA accreditation activity and the activity of other accrediting agencies in order that training programs and professional education programs cannot proceed without giving adequate attention to these problems. We may need to provide some special scholarships.

We also need to provide an organizational home within ALA for media specialists. Nowhere do I hear that a new membership organization is the answer; there are too many membership organizations now. We require a focus of attention. An office could be established without diminishing the significance of existing divisional groups or committees. This office could serve as a clearinghouse; it could provide consultant services; it could help support legislative efforts; it could assure cooperation with, rather than duplication of, what other groups may undertake.

In 1967 there was an inventory of the various organizations, offices, and committees within the general framework of librarianship which were working in the audiovisual field or were providing guides, or lists, or training. We filed the report. You have probably never heard of it.

To the best of my knowledge, no one in our professional association, either members or staff, really knows the full range of activity in the field with which we are concerned here. Something will have to be done about it. We must find ways of promoting interest in and among librarians and the clientele served, and in the media services generally, so that these things will be supported. I submit to you, however, that our problem is not just that of promotion. If we really begin to provide staffs who know media well and free them to work in the various fields of work concerned to tap all the resources available and make these relevant, I submit to you that we will have all the promotion and publicity we need. But we are not doing that.

In 1958, I thought the United States Office of Education would one day set up centers of excellence which could demonstrate the difference which can be made with support of educational communications and information service activities and the difference which can be made by the provision of resources; but it did not. Rather than duplicating what is being done by foundations over this country, significant psychological and educational schools, colleges, universities, and private organizations, the regional laboratories, I think, should be dissemination centers; but they are not. They are competitive, research-oriented groups, for the most part narrowly dealing with difficult problems of learning. There is nothing wrong with research—we need it—but there is something wrong when we do not have demonstrations of everyday facilities and programs.

Today, the chief problems affecting the development and use of modern communications media, audiovisual media, and other forms of instructional or information technology differ from those of ten years ago chiefly in matters

of degree. American education and society still are plagued on all levels by the lack of qualified teachers and of other media or professional personnel trained to make optimum use of instructional and information media. Despite billions of dollars invested since 1956 in educational and instructional innovation on all levels, there is still among members of our profession too much lack of certainty regarding the optimum contributions which can be made to the processes of education through the use of newer communications media, including graphic and photographic materials, recordings, educational radio and television, programmed instruction, and computers.

Another debilitating problem is the continuing lack of a national information system capable of affording, in convenient format, listings and guides to resources currently available to assist instructional or information processes. Local, state, regional, or national reservoirs of media and equipment must be developed. Sufficient numbers of new demonstration and display centers must be created to which those interested may be referred to see at firsthand the benefits which can accrue from effective use of modern communications technology in a relevant way.

How can we find out where the materials are and who produces them? How can we get access to them? How can we distribute them? We are not talking here simply about needs for evaluation. We do need evaluation tools, of course; but that is not the problem, nor is it a problem only of more guides and indexes. We have to create a whole system which will afford a media information clearinghouse on a national basis. In partnership with commercial agencies which are prime producers and distributors, and without whose help we cannot do this, we must accomplish the creation of a national media information and distribution system. We do not have the money, the talent, or the wherewithal at local, state, or outlet levels to produce many of the types of materials we should have. We must find a way to support production functions cooperatively and new ways to store these new media, building into our systems a storage capacity for new products of many different kinds. These materials should be examined and sent out for previewing and for testing. Our film producers are tired of sending out preview prints which may be damaged or lost rather than purchased. They want some sensible kind of awareness and evaluation of their products. We should build into the demonstration and display agency the capacity to create an awareness of what exists, so that we can also provide counseling and training for effective use of what exists. There should be a research service function performed by our national media information system to develop efficiency of operations, to establish the effectiveness of media in various contexts, and to help design the service systems which ultimately will be used locally, regionally, and statewide for distribution. We can make use of modern computer and communications traffic systems, riding piggyback on these systems where they already exist for police, fire, water, highway, and other federal and state communications. We will be able to link the schools, the colleges, the educational institutions, the full range of library systems for information queries, information answers, and ultimate delivery of all or portions of what may be required to resolve a given media service problem.

All of the services we presently have today say very little about relevance. I am trying to share with you as honestly as I know how my concern about media evaluation and information, the chaos which arises in our field, the need for new tools, and ways of achieving production of these tools. This is not enough. Unless we build in a whole system, which on a nationwide basis serves the educational and instructional requirements of our society, which relates to the generation of new materials, the counseling and training that are involved, and the continuing research about the systems we create, and which constantly increases the effective use of our total resources; unless we tie all these together and use this highly vaunted technology which is available to us, then we are fools.

Comment: My general reaction is that I have heard this all before; we have all heard it *all* before. As I see it, evaluation is a very splendid notion, but I am particularly concerned that we are able to find the media after it has been evaluated.

Mr. Dupuy: I feel it is very important to know what is going on around the country; too little is known, and often that is found out by accident. Quite obviously, there is now no effective service to make available the materials that are potentially useful, and the suggestion of a national media information center, service, or clearinghouse is a very desirable one.

Comment: Dr. Stone's suggestion that an office should be set up within the American Library Association is long overdue. He is perfectly right. There is, of course, a possibility that money simply does not exist for implementing the recommendations Dr. Stone has made. However, when you look at some of the other programs ALA has been able to foster, then the excuse that ALA does not have the money is hardly palatable. Our efforts have been isolated and fragmented; we have been putting off the real demands and needs.

Comment: I personally feel inadequate when we talk in terms of relevance. I cannot dictate relevance to other people; it is an individual decision whether the information is relevant. I can only present the user with the information, and this is what I should be able to do more efficiently than I do now. We do not have the tools such a national media center would need. I can recommend materials to people, but I am not sure I can tell someone what is relevant to his situation.

Comment: The relevance statement may be the most important. You may have the most elaborate catalog system, the most elaborate dial-access system, and the best organized media center in the state, but no one will use it unless competent personnel are available to interpret it to the teacher who has placed his emphasis on learning rather than on the organization of media and resources.

Mr. Stone: This is the problem; now what do we do about it? How do we create the program, the system, and the activities that really make the media available? In most cases the problem is not in knowing the material exists, nor that it has been evaluated, or cataloged, or described. It is simply that we do not have the mechanisms that will get the material to the user when it is needed.

Individuals might very well raise questions of jurisdictional dispute. Who should provide what kind of resources to whom? Who has what salary? Who is supervisor? How do you resolve all of this? I think there is a very simple answer; I do not mean simple in execution, just simple in concept. It is to be found in the definition of the function to be served, whether it is a production, distribution, training, or demonstration function. When functions in terms of media service provision are discussed, jurisdictional lines which are divided by form of media begin to disappear, and there is a different orientation. Specifications and listing of the various jobs that have to be done in order to make available the full range of services must emerge. These are organized in a hundred different ways. There is not just one way for you to have an instructional materials center. There are a hundred ways in which those responsible for media service can cooperate and coordinate work. We should be discussing the functions that have to be served and worrying less about the administrative configuration. It is not really relevant, although it is a problem.

The question in all of our minds is the concept of relevance and our competence to provide counsel with regard to what is relevant to the solution of problems. Relevance, as I use it, is a goal towards which we work, not an absolute result in every case. No one says this job of ours is easy. The notion that somehow we can go through a master's degree in a year or two and receive the knowledge and skill essential for the management of the flow of ideas and information to society is unrealistic in our present educational system.

From our experience as teachers in various professional education agencies, we know that most of the basic curricula of library science can be taught and learned much faster than it is presently. If we invest the time, money, and effort to create the materials that are required, more time will be available for two important areas of specialization. One of them is in the area of the communications and learning process, and the other is specialization in an area of human problem concern. If I hire as a chemistry librarian an individual who does not know the language of chemistry,

who is not familiar with the range of research being done in chemistry, who cannot communicate with chemists about their needs, and who is not a specialist in the publications and information about that field, then all I have is a babysitter for books. If we can hire bench chemists with twenty years' experience behind them and teach them the necessary library and other media skills, they can be active partners in departments of chemistry in the area of identification and distribution of the literature, because they know what is relevant.

Coming back to the first response, because it stings a little bit—and I am grateful for the sting—I have heard it all before, too, and said some of it, but not at a time when there was a readiness to do something about it.

Question: Dr. Stone, you indicated that we have a considerable amount of research and development, that we do not have an adequate dissemination or utilization program. What kind of an agency would do this?

Mr. Stone: When I speak of sponsorship or support of research, I am speaking of case studies and operational studies of systems and services. This is a research rather than a report activity. We have a research office at the American Library Association which is doing some things in this area.

Question: Would the regional laboratory systems, though not specifically as they now operate, be likely to foster this research and its implementation?

Mr. Stone: Yes, but not in the way they are presently structured. We should use these laboratories as they were originally intended, but they have attracted to their staffs people who are bent towards research as an end in itself, and so they do not have effective dissemination programs or demonstrations. However, something like the regional laboratories could very well be expected to provide the services so desperately needed today.

Question: You said that we now have a lot of knowledge that is not being used and that perhaps we should begin using it in lieu of creating more. Does this situation have a direct relationship to the ERIC [Educational Resources Information Center] system?

Mr. Stone: Some of our distinguished specialists in the library and communication field, working with the research branch and bureaus as advisers, have said repeatedly that we need to find ways to put into practice what we already know. The emphasis in these advisory committees has been to place pressure on the Office of Education, the National Science Foundation, and other agencies to establish model demonstration and test activities.

Question: Since we have a lot of research in progress but very little dissemination or practical application of research, what would be your reaction to a moratorium? The efforts and support that would ordinarily go into research could then go into the dissemination process.

Mr. Stone: I find that to some extent emotionally appealing. However, the way to get more dissemination of research is not to freeze the development of ideas. Research ideas build upon those that have come before, taking them into account, and these may become far more important to the solution of problems than the ten or the hundred studies that may have preceded them. The support of dissemination at the expense of either a focused or a market-basket approach to research is not the answer. We must continue to support research in education and information science to the maximum extent that it is appropriate, while also building the dissemination and demonstration mechanisms.

Comment: The Health, Education and Welfare Office now being proposed with a general responsibility of evaluation and dissemination of research should have an impact similar to what you are suggesting. There would be a distribution of funds to achieve evaluation and dissemination rather than a total concentration of funds on research.

Comment: We must differentiate between evaluation of research and the evaluation of media. For instance, the Office of Education is embarking on a program of disseminating all of the media collected as a result of research projects. However, the evaluation of research has been taken on by ERIC. The difference between these two areas is creating a little pandemonium in the National Audiovisual Center. One has evaluations, decisions, and facts to collect and report galore. Could federal government agencies such as the National Audiovisual Center possibly assist if they were completely service oriented and not politically controlled?

Mr. Stone: I think the federal government's role should be focused, if possible, on strengthening the regional laboratories to become the sort of thing which they should have been in the first place, and which, indeed, many of them set out to be before they were distracted by local considerations. Secondly, working with and through states, federal government agencies can support the development of educational communication authorities, service agencies, studies, and commissions if society is to take advantage of modern communications technology. All over the United States there are commissions for television or for instructional broadcasting. It is now being recognized that these commissions should not limit themselves to television. Television is only one in the arsenal of tools needed to assist the instructional process. We need an *educational communications* commission. The creation of agencies of this sort at the state level with assistance from federal government should be encouraged.

The ALA office to which I have referred could have been funded long ago by the federal government as a pilot project. The government does not favor this kind of assistance for an association, but assuming there was a concerned acknowledgment among the professions, it could be given.

Question: What would you think of the idea of specialized collections of materials? For instance, we have a project now on narcotics because this is a national problem. We are collecting all materials produced in any media on narcotics. Where does this fit?

Mr. Stone: I think it fits in best as a contractual arrangement, where the support goes to that agency or institution best equipped for the job. Until we have a national communications authority, it is probably better done by that sort of arrangement than by setting it up within the federal agency itself or by creating another agency to do it.

Question: Do you think it is within reason that some of the existing agencies and organizations actually could disregard political implications and merge their efforts?

Mr. Stone: I think it is perfectly rational, logical, educationally sound, and impossible. The Educational Media Council was created for a similar purpose, with its membership being the executive secretaries and presidents of all the media-based organizations. They are to meet regularly to provide a clearinghouse, special projects agency, or forum, and they are to engage in the conduct of certain special programs which no one of the agencies or associations represented might undertake. That council still exists, although the executive secretary has never had from the constituent memberships of the various organizations involved the level of support that should have been forthcoming. EFLA is concerned about DAVI; DAVI is worried about ALA; ALA does not like the commercial influence of NAVA; NAVA is wondering about EIA; SMPTE wondered what it was doing there; and NSPI got disgusted with the lack of progress. All of the people involved are dedicated persons, devoted to the proposition that there shall be cooperation, coordination, and a sharing of effort. Although the idea deserves exploration, it would probably be unwise to propose any new organizational structure which blends the media professions.

Comment: In England we have the same setup that you have been describing here. The initials are different; the structure of the individual organizations may be different; we do not talk of federal agencies; we have our own terms, but the pattern is only too familiar. The media world in England is making an awful lot of fuss about media production, which amounts to approximately 10 percent of the books produced each year in Great Britain. What is the relative proportion in this country of the production of nonprint media and books?

Mr. Stone: There are statistics which reveal a similar ratio, with thousands of new books published for instruction and only a trickle of films and other media, but there is another factor that is tremendously important as we look at it, and that is what is happening in the learning process, the instruction, and the way we are using the materials. I acknowledge the fact that we have a primitive, unorganized trickle of good stuff coming out in the audio-visual field, by comparison with the world of print. Some of these materials are, however, having a tremendous exposure and considerable influence.

Question: Have you made the assumption throughout that these materials are educational tools?

Mr. Stone: And informational.

Comment: The informational, from what I have heard so far, has not popped up very much. You have all assumed automatically that these kinds of materials are handmaidens to the business of education. They are information and, like every other unit of information, can serve a great many purposes. At the moment they are being used mainly by the educational people, but if these things are here to stay, they will be used by many others, just as books are used by more than schoolteachers in the process of education.

How much of this is pure education, and how much are you just discussing in educational terms? You are talking quite narrowly if you really are thinking solely about this function, are you not?

Mr. Stone: You are reminding us most appropriately that we must take into account a broader range of materials and a broader range of usage to which we can put existing materials.

Comment: I made an analysis of the data bank at NICEM to see who was contributing to the information. I discovered that out of some 20,000 entries, we had almost 9,000 different contributors. Of all those 16mm titles, there were many contributors who claimed they distribute only one film, and there were only about twenty-eight firms with a large number of listings. Yet I would not think of disqualifying the small contributors.

Comment: It sounds as though your practice here is again rather like the practice in England, where, quite frankly, our media people are demanding machinery of very considerable sophistication to deal with a very primitive technology. It is not primitive in the technical sense, because they are making very pretty films, but they are demanding the kind of machinery that has been developed to deal with the whole enormous world of print to handle ten copies of nonprint media. You are asking for an extremely sophisticated machine for a relatively simple thing. Dr. Stone, in your address you suggested a very elaborate system. Is it possible that with all these splendid channels, you have the equivalent of Hoover Dam with a six-foot pool behind it, perhaps?

Mr. Stone: I do not know the amount of water behind the dam, but there is certainly a growing reservoir of resources. We are coming to the point very rapidly in this country, and in yours, where bits of information or ideas, visual or otherwise, urgently need to be distributed from central sources and reproduced on a one-at-a-time-publication basis.

The rather elaborate system to which I refer is not limited to audiovisual media at all but includes information in all forms. We need to be able to query the system to find out where the information is. I am really talking about a reservoir of information on which to draw, and while we have limited this discussion primarily to audiovisual media, they are only the present forms and formats of something much farther beyond. You are quite right that such an elaborate system for what we now have is not warranted, but the system that is going to serve the transfer, flow, and reproduction of knowledge in the future is essential and can be supported.

Analysis of Need for and Feasibility of the Distribution of Government-Supported Nonprint Materials

Joseph B. Margolin

The research project which is the subject of this paper has another year before completion. The Educational Policies group actually began working in the field of nonprint media about three years ago. Work done previously on computers and education made us aware of some of the problems with which we are presently concerned. Some of the reports presented at the institute have been very precise, and while I will not say that our study has been less than precise, we are precise about different things. We are trying to be exact about *why* things are done, before we begin to worry about *what* gets done. We are trying to build some behavioral objectives. When one of your institute members said earlier, "Clear first, consistent after," I considered filing that as our final project report.

Most of the people we encounter, and we have been across the country talking to many who use nonprint media, have no interest in who wrote something. Except for a few researchers particularly interested in authors, the vast majority seldom search for an item under its author. What we are trying to find out is just how do people use materials and how do

they search for the information? We have concluded that most of them would not care if authors were omitted, for they are interested only in the content or subject matter. We found this out not by sitting around and talking about it, but by researching the subject. To discover what is useful to one's critical user, one must survey and analyze actual users.

This report will serve at least two purposes:

1. To review the activities to date of the Educational Policies Project in performing the contract entitled *Analysis for the Need for and Feasibility of More Effective Distribution of Government-Supported Non-Written Material* (OEC-0-8-000716-4457-(016))
2. To present the current state of thinking of the staff with regard to the state of the dissemination of nonbook educational media and the method and design being applied to the research.

This research project is funded to study ways to improve the dissemination of government sponsored or produced nonprint materials in our educational system. The initial stages of our research effort included an intensive literature search including the use of the Defense Documentation Center, Office of Edu-

Director, Educational Policies Project, George Washington University, Washington

cation–Education Resources Information Center, National Library of Medicine, and Library of Congress sources as well as compilations from industry and a natural history study to determine the parameters and general characteristics of the field and to study a selected sample of organizations engaged in dissemination to sharpen our perceptions, tools, and methodology.

Exploration of the natural history of the process has produced some changes in our assumptions about the nature of the field. It has resulted in some alteration of design and the development of several new data-gathering and handling techniques. It has also pointed the way to several additional benefits that may be derived from the study. The natural history phase also assisted us in isolating the variables to be employed in the use of the case history, matrix, and other data-gathering techniques, producing changes in our initial assumptions.

In addition, the natural history study revealed the lack of clear definition and classification in the nonbook educational media area. We, therefore, developed a preliminary set of definitions for the purpose of staff communications. It made us keenly aware of the need for a good taxonomy to provide a basis for improved communication in the entire area. Because the staff does not include information scientists or librarians, we experienced great anxiety at this point in the research project.

Changes were taking place in the field affecting the direction of government and perhaps of educational activity. These include:

1. The organization of the General Services Administration-Archives central cataloging and sales outlet for audiovisual materials produced by government agencies.

2. The activities of other government agencies and voluntary educational groups directed toward change in the field of dissemination. Both the Departments of Commerce and Defense are currently producing and organizing materials in their own patterns while we still study and discuss the problems.

3. The activities and forthcoming report of the Commission on Instructional Technology.

The commission is incorporating our effort in its report. The commission was created as a result of United States congressional and chief executive office concern for the bibliographic control of nonprint media.

The Educational Policies group will remain flexible and sensitive to the changes produced by these activities and will attempt to use this experience in learning how to adapt an information system to continually changing circumstances.

The design of the study presents a multivariate approach designed to yield both macro and micro characteristics of the field of dissemination and to assure the validity of the data and the conclusions. The objectives remain the improved comprehension of the dissemination process and the development of alternative systems of dissemination and feedback to be applied as Office of Education policy makers determine.

The basic mission of this program is to improve the dissemination of nonbook educational material. In this service the Educational Policy group has accepted as the basic premise the need to define, outline, and comprehend the system commencing with:

1. Generation of these materials
2. Collection of them by the U.S. Office of Education or other agency or organization
3. Organization of materials collected for intellectual dissemination
4. Actual intellectual dissemination
5. Physical dissemination
6. Collection of information about the needs, demand for, effective use, and value of the materials.

Necessary steps to achieve the mission will include the development of criteria for an effective dissemination system for nonbook educational media. These criteria must be derived from a sound understanding of the characteristics of the dissemination systems, including their dynamics and effectiveness, and the needs and objectives of individuals and groups in education and areas related to it.

The Educational Policies group has been engaged in a massive effort to understand the nature of educational nonbook dissemination, both public and private, although with ultimate emphasis on the government and the Office of Education activities. We have been engaged in a very extensive and intensive study of the literature on the dissemination of educational materials and related products. We have studied the education market, its characteristics, and its natural history at all levels critical to dissemination. We have gathered information on past and current assessments of the need in the field[1] for materials and for educational services that may lead to the production of materials as well as the several approaches to dissemination, both public and private.

We have studied the methods employed to gather data about the several aspects of the dissemination process and have considered the accuracy and usefulness of much of this data collection. We are engaged in an effort to determine the system requirements for improved data gathering based upon the need for a continuing feedback of critical information relating to the dissemination process as well as to the generation of materials. We must also watch for changes in the field of education which will permit a continuous updating of the information.

The phases of the study thus far have included a natural history study which was designed to gain deeper insight into the characteristics of this field, and the conceptualization of the field in a manner that would permit us to handle the vast amount of material that pertains to the subject as well as to achieve the goals of the program. This conceptualization has permitted us to formalize and refine our methodology and to proceed to early stages of data collection.

We began on a theoretical basis which was derived from familiarity with the field of educational technology but which was lacking the intensive experience which would be required to formalize and test a methodology. On the basis of the natural history phase, we have been able to achieve more realistic formulations of operating systems and subsystems.

[1]Throughout this report the term *field* refers to the system for dissemination of nonbook educational materials in the schools.

The information we have been seeking will permit the construction of functioning systematic models which will yield understanding of the sources of materials, the need for materials, as well as the methods that have operated to bring supply and demand together or which fail to do so. Here we include the creative forces operating to produce materials, the economic and industrial process required to manufacture them, and the methods employed to index and catalog them, and as well as the advantages and limitations of the information and library subsystem which may alternatively facilitate or deter the dissemination of such materials.

We have explored the organization and characteristics of the user or demand systems —the direction, breadth, and force of the dissemination process in education which is determined by the educational needs, the economics and sociology of education, and the marketing process. The dissemination system ranges from the techniques for cataloging, which are so crucial in determining the ability of the user to reach for materials, to the expenditures by the disseminator at the several levels for contact with the individual user. The effectiveness of all that has gone before may be minimized or maximized by the nature, perception, responsiveness, and the effectiveness and vigor of the basic consumer group, the school system. Finally, we have examined the physical dissemination process itself.

There is much overlap in the levels described. A school system can be both a user and a disseminator, obtaining materials from government agencies or private vendors and disseminating them to its subdivisions and individual teachers. Thus we have a broad sweeping subject influenced by many factors outside the control of education. Many of these factors are outside of its awareness.

The first phase of our research supports graphically what we have anticipated. Education is both heterogeneous and pluralistic in nature with regard to needs, demography, levels of sophistication, economic variables, attitudes toward the use of nonbook materials, and attitudes toward the use of government materials. No less complex and vague is the state of definition of the field. There are many different kinds of audiovisual media and even more permutations and combinations of dissemination systems. The attempts at definition and arbitrary categorization have shed some light on the field, but, to our knowledge, an organized system of definition, classification, and conceptualization approaching a taxonomy has not been achieved. It would appear that such an effort would contribute to the solution of several problems of categorization and definition, to the development of effective storage and retrieval systems, and to research in dissemination. Some definitions have been attempted on an interim basis and for purposes of communication, but it is expected that a more organized system or taxonomy will emerge as a by-product of this research.

The field is characterized by the absence of valid, reliable, or meaningful information about the need for educational materials and their use, or even of criteria for the collection of such data. We have researched exhaustively the many sources of information about non-book products and materials and the nature of their market. These include available material; where the material can be obtained; estimates of past, present, and future markets; and some information on technical, training, and administrative issues. However, most of these efforts appear to be attempts to provide lists and crude estimates of demand rather than efforts to understand and improve the process of dissemination or even the process of the market. One article was found which attempted to comprehend some aspects of dissemination.[2]

It is also clear that no definition or conceptualization had been made by the information brokers, public or private, who either interpret need at crucial points in the dissemination system or even more positively control dissemination. Understanding the nature of these key positions, or gatekeepers, and how information may be gained from them or supplied to them emerges as a vital task for the study.

William Paisley, in describing the "knowledge linkers" or brokers, provides a useful analogy between the dissemination of scientific information and the dissemination of educational materials so clearly linked to scientific and professional activity. Despite the mechanization and commercialization of much product dissemination, Paisley feels one need only attend a professional meeting of educators to observe the "personal and pluralistic characteristics of the system.[3]

The close link between dissemination and the quality of research is further demonstrated by Paisley who suggests:

> Proof that they [product developers] have utilized the knowledge is the product they have to sell. Their agents, the marketers, seek to motivate groups of practitioners and to facilitate adoption of the product by them. In many cases, because of a close correspondence between knowledge elements and product attributes . . . adoption of the product implies acceptance of the knowledge that leads to its development.[4]

Thus, in several ways, it is not only the dissemination of educational materials, but also the eventual link between the dissemination of educational research information and educational practice information that must proceed side by side with the dissemination-of-materials process.

Another area that appeared more sharply was that of quality control, both technical and educational. This problem emerges from our inquiry at almost every level in the dissemination system, from government and industry and from educational administration and classroom teacher. While many aspects of the problem must be treated apart from this study, others may seriously affect the dissemination of government-generated materials.

The legal areas remain a source of ferment and development. New government procedures for granting limited copyright will have some

---

[2]"School Purchasing Decision Patterns," *School Product News* (Jan. 1, 1968). Published separately by Industrial Publishing Co.; 85p.

[3]Invited Address, Division E, American Educational Research Assn., Los Angeles, Feb. 6, 1969.
[4]Ibid., p.12.

impact on the dissemination process. The extent of such modifications of the basic public domain policy remain to be assessed in the context of the overall dissemination system. Its relationship to the system and subsequent effects will be studied.

There are quantum changes in government policy such as the development of the National Audiovisual Center and the small increments or modifications of procedure employed by the several government agencies in their legal, economic, and organization operation.

In our examination of the dissemination of nonbook educational materials, we were renewed in our awareness of the multiple effects of other systems on that of educational dissemination. Legal systems; political developments and new laws; changes in federal, state, and local fiscal and budgetary programs; and changes in tax laws and corporate finance are among the social processes to be considered. New technology provides new media as well as new channels for the transmission of information about older media. The social and the technological interact to further modify the environment into which research and development into the production and dissemination of new materials must take place. This continuing awareness of relevant changes in other systems is an essential aspect of this research and of an ongoing information system for the Office of Education.

The first phase of the study has made it clear that costly mail questionnaires do not provide the sole, nor a sufficient, vehicle for data collection. The nature of much of the data that are needed requires that it be holistic or macro in its nature, reflecting the operation of a system; come from secondary research, such as research into the structure of agencies or copyright law; and be personal. It further requires that the inquirer be able to follow new areas or trace leads introduced by the respondent. It may be necessary to pursue the same question in a different language attuned to the parlance of the respondent.

It has therefore been necessary to vary the methods of data collection by the staff to include direct-inquiry methods (i.e., focused interviews, depth interviews, case studies, and focused group interviews); key role players

(i.e., audiovisual specialists, teachers, catalog developers), critical incident studies and related techniques, seminars on key issues or subsystem problems, and questionnaires. We have also utilized indirect-inquiry methods such as matrix analysis, library research (e.g., studies of supply and demand), and content analysis. A number of issues have emerged as distinct entities, and it is anticipated that they will be developed in depth by individual consultants working closely with a staff member to maintain a relationship to the program.

We have traveled the country, interviewing senior executives in the Office of Education, those who fund research, those who handle information, those who do policy work and determine next year's budget; laboratory personnel of the research and development centers; regional office staffs; persons in state departments of education and in major city school systems; classroom teachers, secondary school students, and even elementary school-age youth. We wanted to know how those individuals access information about materials, and we were concerned in two ways. We are looking for models of organization of data that can be translated into a more effective system for the Office of Education and other governmental units. Perhaps a classroom teacher has set up a unique system for organizing materials so that her youngsters can get to them more quickly and more appropriately, or there might be a system as sophisticated as the Library of Congress. We are also looking for an appropriate interface with groups for whom we are working. What do states need? What do laboratories need? What do teachers need? What do children need?

The wide range of skills and experience required to provide data, perspective, alternative formulations, and conclusions about the dissemination process have required, as anticipated, that many consultants be employed. The initial phase of the study suggests that a number of areas of inquiry can be isolated briefly from the body of the research so that they can be developed more fully. These will be contracted for in the form of papers to be prepared by consultants who are highly competent in the subject area.

Unless the consultant has been working

closely with the staff, a member of the staff will collaborate with the consultant or will monitor the process to assure the relevance of approach and product and the compatibility of assumption, as well as to provide the consultant with necessary data or information from the project.

The areas currently envisioned for such treatment include:

1. Patent law and copyright law and regulation
2. Economics — nonbook media and the school budget
3. Marketing and marketing research practices
4. Indexing and cataloging for user needs
5. Personnel training (in-service and preservice) in application of nonbook media to education
6. Relationship of research to material development
7. Cost-benefit studies — How are they useful? What are proper measures of effect and benefit?
8. Methods for evaluation of dissemination of nonbook materials.

This particular use of consultants does not preclude continuing contact by the staff with other consultants.

We have coined three phrases that were found to be useful: intellectual dissemination, which is the transmission of the idea about something; physical dissemination, which is the material itself that might be delivered by truck, van, mail, television, or satellite; and motivational dissemination. We are still debating whether the latter is a subset of intellectual dissemination or whether it stands on its own. Motivation is essential, for if information arrives too late, is confusing, not appropriate, or not what was requested, the user's motivation is diminished. These are the three categories with which we are working, and then there is the vast area of use study. In our particular population, we can compile four pages of users of educational nonprint material and still fail to make clear that all nonprint media specialists fall into the system.

All of us know that information does not always travel through the traditional structure of the state department of education, large city or county departments, single school system, and on down through the several levels of administration. One of the most impedimental voices in the entire operation is in the state departments, and their very impedance has made for some difficulty. The audiovisual person in the state department of education is typically bypassed by everyone.

Feedback to the people who appropriate money, who make films, and who have something to do with the policy making does not take place. A congressman talks to an audiovisual specialist in his area or a teacher complains at a Parent-Teacher Association meeting. There is no systematic evaluation of what goes on at any level in this system, and it is not sent back to the people who are actually making the policy and shaping much of it.

Comment: It seems in terms of your model, or description, you are defining two kinds of things. One is the abstract or intellectual information and the other, intertwined with it, is the physical operation. But, how are they parallel?

Mr. Margolin: It is an informational, intellectual kind of problem that deals with gathering, organizing, disseminating, and using evaluation instruments. Parallel to that is a physical problem that relates to film, which is probably the biggest problem in the nonprint area.

Comment: In England, when we were thinking about the same problems and cleverly postulating what we thought was based on research, we identified the three areas in the problem of dissemination. At one point, we call it intellectual organization, organizing for dissemination. We then recognized the second, which was the flow of the object, maybe the physical object or an object in the shape of a printed document containing the results of data collection and organization. The third area we identified was that of dissemination within the receiving organization, which is not quite the same as that in your concept of use. We are now thinking more narrowly and have come to the conclusion that these separate problems and separate systems, which have to be divided in different ways but designed so that they work together. They are certainly related and have to be worked together for the design in one area, but for dissemination in another, it is obvious that the latter should be involved at the initial stage of system design.

Mr. Margolin: I agree with you and would reinforce the statement that the intertwining is to be a very critical aspect of the program. It is certainly true that the extent to which something does or does not get delivered has no effect on the attitude toward the information about it. You get a certain amount of intertwining and this is perhaps a simple illustration. To develop this with some degree of sophistication, I would break it down on the intellectual and physical levels and probably eventually on the nonprofit basis. There may be, however, a difference between educational use and other uses in this particular field.

During a recent professional conference I was wandering around the exhibits when someone approached me saying, "I would like to talk to you about insurance," and I replied, "An insurance salesman here?" He had interpreted the "Educational Policy Group" on my name tag to mean that I was selling insurance. How confusing labels are today. Our larger organization at George Washington University is called the Programs Studies of Science and Technology. It is an interdisciplinary group set up with cooperation between GWU and the National Aeronautics and Space Administration with most of the funds provided by NASA, which is the science component of the program of policy studies. The whole organization contains engineers, systems analysts, economists, sociologists, psychologists, and lawyers.

The Educational Policies Project has a wide range of interests, for example, in addition to this nonprint media availability study the group is concerned with replacement technology and its effect on man. It should be effective in the space program. The Educational Policy Group is primarily a psychology, sociology, behavioral science, and information science oriented group. The basic funds are from NASA, but this particular research project is funded from the U.S. Office of Educa-

tion. There are also funds from the National Science Foundation and the National Institute of Mental Health.

Four of the staff members are educators, one is an audiovisual specialist who was making films when we found her, one is a systems analyst, several are economists, and one is a sociologist. The educators range from elementary school to special education. They are from Minnesota, Louisiana, California, and two are New Yorkers, one of whom is from New York City. We take the talent where we find it regardless of regional origin. All but two of the people previously lived in Washington, D.C. Some specific projects, as mentioned earlier, are allocated to consultants.

The problem of geography is actually diminishing as a problem in this country because of the high mobility. Professional people seem to spend most of their time en route elsewhere. Our staff spends considerable periods of time in California, Washington, Chicago, Kansas, and West Texas.

Not only are we using questionnaires and interviews, but we are also trying to get several levels of interaction where possible. A television group in Hagerstown, Maryland, included a teacher, a librarian, an audiovisual chief, the producer of audiovisual material, and the budget director, all of whom sat around a table and interacted to the problems in Hagerstown in response to topics we would introduce. A few sparks were produced, several which led to major hostility that had been kept under control for years. People finally had to confront each other and talk about some of their differences, giving us a tape of this to analyze for its dynamics. We are utilizing means such as this to probe the dynamics, complications, and interrelationships between the various levels in these fields and in vested interests. Incidentally, one of the things we are doing with this wide range of data-gathering methods is to define and clarify some of them. Personnel in the Educational Resources Information Center (ERIC) Media Center are probably the best authorities on these techniques.

We hope to develop some models of methodology for other people to use in surveys. Frequently long lists of questions are sent out through the mail, and the solicitors sit on their hands waiting in vain for responses. A 10 percent return is fortunate, although one often finds it impossible to find meaning in the results, largely because the sample is self-selecting.

Our effort is directed towards the methods to find out what requirements are necessary to achieve a more satisfactory system. However, I work with a group of systems analysts who constantly emphasize to me that there is no isolated system and that you can ultimately reduce everything to one large system. The objective is to get a set of requirements for systems that we will offer. Once we have agreed on them it may become possible to build alternative systems which policy makers, decision makers, or government officials can mix or match as they choose. One further requirement is a basis for the continual feedback of critical information. It is very difficult to control any kind of research system.

Nevertheless, there still are creative forces in this field which will have an impact on education, on the kinds of things that happen in education, and we must understand, if not control, and be able to determine the impact of these forces. The economics of the industrial process of manufacturing operates in the field of education, too. Education administrators are resistant to the production of new material if old material will serve half as well. Many antiquated psychological tests, old films, and outdated books are being used today. Some of the tests will continue indefinitely if people are stupid enough to buy them. Some of the factors that are involved in industry will affect us, not the least of which is the capacity of the industry to spend money for advertising. This probably has a greater impact than the information dissemination methods we devise. Industry's methods are somewhat more aggressive than a card catalog or even a computer console. Even the more sophisticated computer requires that something be done in a specific location, whereas you may pick up a new product news release and items are dramatized for you wherever you are. A full-page ad gives the advertisers a weighted opinion.

Although the methods employed to index and catalog are important, they are not the sum of intellectual determination. I would venture that the growth of so many competing forces to inform people means that we as educators, audiovisual specialists, and librarians must become more aggressive in reaching the people whom we want to inform rather than asking them to come to us. This is particularly true of librarians.

Another dimension is needed to show how complicated is the concept of the nature of the information. There are things that teachers, superintendents, parents, and school boards want which may have nothing to do with conceptualizing the dissemination patterns of nonprint government-generated media. Much of what we are talking about is affected by the social structure of the school system, which is still somewhat of a feudal entity. The fact that the principal runs his principality may have something to do with the way we provide information to school systems to be used by someone working under, or dominated by, the principal.

The motivational area, briefly described before, is an essential element for the success or failure of the entire program, which is, in large measure, the attitude of the ultimate user. This has always been left to the audiovisual specialist, librarian, and teacher. However, with the continued growth of individualized programmed instruction and computer assisted instruction, the student himself becomes the ultimate consumer and has an increasingly greater decision-making role in the program. The extent to which the users are motivated by the access system will determine whether the media really has a beneficial impact on education. Sending the user to a card catalog and saying, "Go find it, and if you do not find it, you are stupid," may not be the way to get the media transmitted.

Mr. Tauber: I have looked at your data-gathering procedures. Could you tell me to what extent the studies actually go into the use of nonprint materials by those expected to use them? Are you making any studies on your own?

Mr. Margolin: We are asking the questions to get a typical answer to be sure the terminology is clear. We will have a sample but a somewhat more precise understanding when we complete the project. The questionnaire can be handled in many different ways, one being the effective method of gathering statistical data by mailing questionnaires anticipating a percentage of return. If you want to know how many of the schools with audiovisual equipment have overhead projectors, a questionnaire is probably an effective method to do this. However, in reference to motivational research, you know a questionnaire is a structured document and you cannot design a neutral questionnaire.

We found that the National Audiovisual Center has been advertising in a number of places and is increasingly being referred to as a source for distributing United States government films. We have characterized what NAC is at intervals of time during the period of our project through examination of their correspondence. We are also looking at the letters for specificity and generality of request.

Question: Have you been to any American Library Association offices or interviewed any librarians? Have you been to the nonprint units of the Library of Congress and interviewed any of those people?

Mr. Margolin: Some of their staff members are certainly scheduled to be visited. We have talked to a number of librarians and also the American Book Council. Incidentally, the Educational Media Selection Centers Program, administered by the National Book Committee, Incorporated, is doing a study parallel to ours using questionnaires only. The questionnaires they worked on for eighteen months are not being returned. The fear that this might happen perhaps persuaded us not to rely solely on questionnaires, and I am ever so grateful that we did not.

Because of your intellectual determination, the library-audiovisual professions have the gatekeepers in this whole system, the bibliographers. This is why I have been daring enough to say, Become more aggressive in addition to your preciseness and go out and see something, and I do not mean the displays in library windows either.

One assumption which is fairly well documented is that education is a terribly heterogeneous and pluralistic activity. Demographi-

cally, it is tremendously confusing, for generalizations cannot be made about geographic regions, the inner city, suburbs, or specific school districts. The level of sophistication of this field is uneven. The economic variables are becoming more confusing because of fluctuations in federal spending. At one time the central city was a very poor area. Then suddenly it became a favored area only to be reduced, at least in terms of education funding, to a very poor area again.

The range of teacher, principal, and even school system responses and attitudes toward media is tremendous. Some think an audiovisual specialist is usually a tall man who is able to carry large packages of film and put them up on shelves. Yet there are people who possess a high level of sophistication in science, advertising, administration, and nonprint media. The spread of backgrounds and research in this field is difficult to comprehend. Nevertheless, I hope you will all become involved in the activities for the Association for Educational Communications and Technology.

Arbitrary categorization is good, although we really do not have reliable, meaningful, or valid information about the needs for educational materials and how they are used. We know that there are differences between people in the way they function, particularly in how they perceive and organize things. How many of you have thoughtfully read about these differences and the cognitve process with the thought of applying it to the system you are establishing? I wonder how much research has already been done in psychology that could shed some light on how people at a given age level or in a given profession perceive their needs. Personality variables associated with different occupational groups are significant— engineers, physicians, and psychologists are all quite different. If you are serving one of these groups, you should know the differences even though they are subtle. It will equip you to know how the members perceive things and enable you to serve them better.

Mr. Tauber: However, from some of the idiosyncrasies of these groups come patterns of procedures that they do not realize are wasteful. I met with the Engineers Joint Council in relation to a particular American National Standards Institute [ANSI] assignment and helped to orient them.

Mr. Margolin: You are one man, and it is a question of trying to teach them all. I would rather, just for the sake of economy, see you program an intellectual access system that was oriented to them. Start from where they are and lead them into using the material so that Dr. Tauber does not have to visit every engineer in the country.

Mr. Tauber: I was not visiting every engineer. There were six editors of engineering journals who use bibliographical references and each one using a different system. I think we made the point that they should consider a standard system, which they would not admit earlier.

Mr. Margolin: What kind of a standard system?

Mr. Tauber: Whether we get it through our ANSI standards or whether the engineers develop one for themselves, all of them would agree to one uniform approach to documentation for their readers. Now there is a wide range of approaches.

Comment: There are about three separate points I would like to make here. One concerns practical economics, training librarians, and audiovisual specialists to be psychologists as well. The second point is related to this one. If I were running an engineering special library, I would be fascinated by the study you have just mentioned about engineers, but I would first need to know about it.

My third comment is on the business of research, testing, and evaluation. I am with you 100 percent, providing the context is clearly defined. Special librarians in special libraries in narrow fields run very peculiar libraries judged by average standards. Each peculiar library is a developing organism that specifically meets these variables you are talking about. They are not doing it on any scientific basis, but if you go into a special library serving a narrow public and suggest reorganizing the card catalog in a certain way, the special librarian will stand on his two hind feet and say, "I do my catalog this way because this is what users want."

Now this is empirical evidence. It might be interesting to contrast your research against this empirical evidence. When you said that we do not know or that we need to test or measure, there is this kind of evidence in the background. A dog cannot define a rabbit nor even statistically evaluate the possibility of its being in a particular wood, but he has a pretty good idea of where to go hunting rabbits.

Mr. Margolin: I quite agree and, of course, there is also this point that Dr. Tauber made: sometimes the specific field is a little less than efficient in its use.

Comment: Yes, and what is also needed is an interaction of the information person with the specific field.

Question: Are we not looking for something even more basic than you are indicating? You seem to be looking for points of divergence when in fact we are looking for common traits. Our emphasis should be on the commonalities of the engineer, psychologist, and librarian rather than divergences, which are probably learned.

Mr. Margolin: Some of the methods that we use suggest that there are divergences and that the system is not highly efficient; so our approach should be to find out why things are not working in order that we may associate the differences and seek solutions to this problem. It is very difficult because, conceptually and in terms of cognitive style, we have isolated academic subjects. For example, two professions that must use the same material, very largely, and yet are utterly different in the way their people think, are physics and engineering. To organize materials for these people, you find out how they are different and then devise as many ways as possible to get them all under one blanket.

Dr. Paisley has raised a question for the communications field with what he describes as the knowledge brokers or linkers. The general position would be that despite anything that has been done with mechanism, those beautiful computer programs and industrial systems, the character of communication in this field, the way in which decisions are made and information is carried from one person to another is still largely personal. To confound things, it is not only personal but also pluralistic in the sense that we have a Babel-like situation in which each of us tends to speak a slightly different language, not only in different countries, states, and associations, but also as individual people. If you listen to conversations, often you will realize that the words seem to fall short of both speakers, not quite reaching each other. Not only are we going to have to tie down precise meanings of words but also, in trying to be precise, we are going to have to clarify what needs to be done. Clarification is not simple, and it is seldom achieved by consensus alone because there are characteristics of drift that take place.

To get into some of the cognitive or psychological processes, we need some crossbreeding between the behavioral and information sciences for agreement among people on meanings that will serve their needs. They will then drift back and forth and mean what they need to mean within those disciplines rather than what is agreed among England, the United States, and Canada, or what is found in a compact of states, or among the people of the American Library Association.

We need to develop ways of sampling even after a consensus is reached to find out whether, five years after it is agreed upon, A still means A. To accomplish this we must know whether in California, in New York, and at the elementary, secondary, and graduate level in various libraries A still is being defined as A or whether a considerable amount of drift has occurred.

When you are presenting film material on, let us say, early childhood education, it looks like a plain straightforward film, and you can get descriptors that will characterize it. There needs to be an association between the material and the theoretical background upon which this material is based. I do not really know whose responsibility it is, but since you, the librarians, are in many respects the final path for the material before it reaches the user. It may very well be your responsibility to request that somebody down the line provide you with this kind of information. Eventually we are going to have to get a closer link between the language, educational research, and educational practice. When that is achieved, it will be possible to meet the requirement that I have just placed on you.

The job required is really twofold. One is getting people the information they need so that they know what is happening to the children they are trying to teach; what kind of theoretical material is influencing them. The other is that of bringing the science research information specialists together with the practitioners to gain some understanding of each other. There are those who would like to introduce the material that is available now by putting it into the ERIC problem. Considering the way ERIC is presently organized, this could lead to some painful encounters with computer programming.

The problem of quality control in this field would compound the situation. Teachers are upset about it for one set of reasons, the audiovisual specialists from another point of view, and parents from a third viewpoint. Despite the fact that a lot of production is shoddy, both technically and educationally, industry would like to do something about the problem.

The problem of standardization is very closely related to these concerns, too, as are the legal issues involved. It must be remembered that we operate rather close to the school of public law, which has a section on copyright law and a section on patents. The Office of Education has tried limited copyright, but the Department of Defense gives full copyright to the people who produce material with government help. Other government agencies operate still differently.

We are faced by these basic conflicts within the governmental structure; various units see themselves as *the* standard by which to improve the dissemination of material. Some feel that everything with a nickel of public money should be in the public domain, giving anyone free access to it. Others are reluctant, pointing out that the theory is acceptable but questioning whether or not private enterprise or individuals will put forth the capital or labor to produce, disseminate, or distribute something that is free. The present trend is toward a limited copyright in contrast to the public domain concept that was tried for years, apparently without success.

Government materials have been accumulated on shelves, due partially to our attitude that if they are free they have no value. The

National Audiovisual Center process is an example of a trend which should improve dissemination. The public system for government information dissemination is virtually nonexistent. What we hope to establish clearly is the variable that results in the failure to get things disseminated. The National Audiovisual Center is an element to be considered. Should it be the single agency that distributes nonprint media for the federal government? Can it be handled from one central source? Some feel it can handle certain kinds of nonprint materials but question its handling others, such as instructional resources.

Some United States governmental agencies cannot afford the services of the National Audiovisual Center, others refuse to use them, and still others have distribution systems vastly superior to that of the National Audiovisual Center. The Atomic Energy Commisson [AEC] system with regional, subregional, and area libraries is rather good. The NASA and AEC vans can get things around in a much more aggressive manner than any government system has ever done. These agencies are cooperating with the National Audiovisual Center. What will happen, I suspect, is the person controlling this particular area in the Bureau of the Budget will ultimately make a rather personal decision on the complex matter. When one looks at the broad scope of non-book-material dissemination, he must realize what multiple and complex effects are produced by other systems and be willing to take them into account.

Comment: Dr. Margolin, other than the one exception, the girl who has a film production background, you do not have an audiovisual specialist, librarian, or information scientist on your team. Was this deliberate or accidental?

Mr. Margolin: It was a question of circumstance, because we could not find a qualified person to join us at the right time for the right monetary figure.

Comment: You have been making points about the need for what technically we call deep indexing in England. We assume for the moment that you have evaluated and clearly stated all of the legal implications or educational implications and we librarians, while insisting on a very elaborate author-title structure within this, already have the subject content. This means that for one document we have our parameters clearly defined. There are a number of systems whereby this can be done, all of them are expensive. Are you doing any evaluating of the formal systems for distributing and disseminating information that now exist?

Mr. Margolin: Our economist concluded it will be a tremendously complex and expensive operation for us to evaluate. Therefore, I have no preliminary notion on this. We do know things are going to be expensive, but administrators continue to scream and write about communication problems and the information explosion. If money is advanced for fission research, we can produce the hydrogen bomb; or if funds are committed to a nuclear submarine, it can be built. It is a question of our determining whether we want to recommend this as one way of solving the information problem.

Question: Not only one way, but are you evaluating it in any way? I am not saying that you necessarily settle down, but it would be extremely useful to know, for example, if it costs more to index for the Universal Decimal Classification or the Library of Congress system. I suggest that what is not certain is the cost. Is this kind of thing done?

Mr. Margolin: I do not think that we will come up with data that specific. I do not know that we have the expertise to tackle something like this. We are spread a bit too thin anyway. But, is this not one of the kinds of research that library scientists should be doing?

Comment: No money.

Mr. Margolin: Another thing that may change our situation is the entry of industry into the information area. I suspect it will strive to find out what people need. It would be a combination of motivation research and good ethics to give people not what you can sell them, but what they need and you can sell them. This means that industry will have to start buying more and more methods for finding out what people need and then the ways of organizing it. The people, research,

100

and hardware essential to accomplish this will require changing many things, even the tax laws. Tax laws determine how much money is spent for research and development in industry and how much new equipment is purchased.

The new technology of computers, better film, new hardware for delivering images, and better sound is continuing to revolutionize the industry. Technical journals report cheaper and more rapid imprinting of images on film through the use of lasers.

With regard to the computer and advanced technology in general, the engineers have been the only ones who know the machine's capabilities. Educators are just beginning to realize that the engineers who build them will run them and dictate to the educator unless the latter gains an understanding of the logic and programming concepts essential to computer utilization. Computers are designed and built long before control programs and individual programs are constructed for educators. A chief engineer at International Business Machines [IBM] said, "If you will tell us what you need, we will build it; however, you keep taking our stock computers and complaining about what they will or will not do." He concluded, "If you do know what the field of education needs, tell us and we will build the necessary hardware."

Support for library and information science is decreasing, for these are industries, and government support of any industry is tenuous at best. However, there are, no doubt, problems in the library or information field with solutions of potential value to an organization like Borg-Warner, Raytheon, Science Research Associates, IBM, Encyclopaedia Britannica, or McGraw-Hill. An alert profession would start building projects that serve industries' needs and, at the same time, solve problems of the profession. Representatives of the national organization should then communicate the proposals to industry for mutual benefits.

Another aspect of the economic situation has to do with computers. If tax advantages encourage companies to write them off faster, we may have third-generation computers available sooner than expected, and at lower prices. It write-offs are stretched out, computers will

be more expensive. Should tax investment credit be wiped out, there will be cancellations in existing computer contracts with the companies that had planned on buying them and had even ordered them. IBM may even go back to bargain rates for colleges. These are developments outside the library science field.

Comment: Anyone who has ever been involved in an evaluation by a national organization would utilize the technique of faculty, library staff, student interviews: for example, National Council for Accreditation of Teacher Education and the North Central accreditation association.

Question: I would like to know what is the feasibility of more effective distribution for nonprint material. There has to be a need for it or at least a need for something to be done about it. When you talk to people at the grass roots level about government-sponsored material, they say, "I did not know there was any." In view of this I suppose it is possible to get a tremendous rate of growth. First, there is a need for something to be done about it and secondly, you can get a tremendous rate of growth if you start with zero. Since the Educational Resources Information Centers [ERIC] are research programs only and we are concerned with the distribution of materials, we must either get ERIC involved in this, changing their mission, or establish a parallel system.

Mr. Margolin: We now have regional offices of the Office of Education and other federal government units. There are also regional laboratories in education as well as research and development. Then, we also have state programs, state audiovisual offices and organizations, and library and information programs at the state levels. Do they work together or even know that each other exist? I am afraid that sometimes they do not.

The regional laboratories were set up with the assistance of the states, who then proceeded to ignore them until the blood was deep enough on the floor, whereupon they reclaimed them. Regional offices presumably are always supposed to relate to the state within which they exist. The only role state officials played was one of sabotaging everything that happened, for they were angry at being ignored. Unfortunately, they had no power with which to do anything constructive. I am not sure such a system of centers could function for the bibliographic control of non-print media because you have a variety of levels involved, you are dealing with an agency that is perhaps not universally efficient yet, and the varied problem of standardization of the evaluation will require a very precise operation.

The American system of funneling funds and everything else *down* leads to a lot of slippage. Direct federal subsidies to the working level have been infinitely more efficient than money passed through several levels, including the very inefficient user of tax funds, state government. A dissemination system would have difficulty operating with this crude method of assistance.

Question: How about professional groups, such as the bar association?

Mr. Margolin: While governmental centers look logical, we know that things are being accomplished under the support or supervision of associations. Foundations are playing a tremendous role in policy making in education.

Question: Do we have experience to guide us? The political breakdown tends to appear at all levels, whether in politics, status, or financial control.

Comment: I may go back to my professional group for guidance because my chances are better, more direct, and expedient. Assuming the program is long range, I should recognize that I am supported in part by state funds and should, therefore, lay some groundwork for these people.

Mr. Margolin: You are really making a good point, although there are certain political and financial facts of life that must be faced. If the federal-state tax-sharing plan is accepted, the likelihood is great that states will pressure for and get an envelope of monies labeled education.

The question then comes, how do you maintain a level of agreement, standardization, and cooperation across state lines. The balance of dollars, which is to some degree the balance of power, seems to be swinging from the influence of a wide range of professional groups

to industry, which tends to cross state lines, and foundations which are almost inevitably active at the national level. In these balance-of-power shifts, what is going to happen to efforts toward any kind of standardization?

Question: We are talking in terms of the power groups from your sketch. Is there any evidence that a better system can be had by simply improving the one we have, an improvement within the library system? Nothing to shout about, only a technical improvement, a better mousetrap. Is there any evidence, not necessarily in this field, but generally, that this can affect the distribution of nonprint media?

Mr. Margolin: It is a good question, Mr. Croghan, but would you direct it to the institute participants, for I would like them to tell me.

Mr. Brown: It is here that technology offers some disruption of the kind of flow chart you have presented. The national center becomes more and more central as our technology becomes more and more sophisticated. Our antiquated, eighteenth-century political system could not accept this technological level.

Question: Miss Macdonald, you have worked in England. Do you think, on the whole, that within the library profession the idea of cooperation between different levels is rather more widespread in England than here? You think it is. We have a regional grouping in Great Britain similar to the Educational Laboratory system in the United States. A number of very large regional groupings has begun to emerge. Does this help or hinder the situation? It simplifies things a little bit perhaps.

If you attempt worldwide standardization, achieving consensus becomes impossible, for everybody is weak, and it becomes terribly hard to get fifty or a hundred people or contending groups to agree. If you set up large power blocs like these state operations, you may reduce systems, but you also increase the power of the groups and their ability to resist change. Many groups could be in agreement, but then one could say, We do not like it and we represent twelve or thirteen states, a power bloc that might be large enough to do it alone.

Comment: Libraries are already organized

into regional groups with emerging networks of knowledge projecting the utilization of many kinds of electronic cooperation devices.

Comment: A typical breakdown occurs at the point of cooperative groups accepting a single standard.

Comment: Mr. Croghan, you have so much more tradition and yet seem to have more cooperation than we in the United States. It seems Dr. Brown is saying our problem is our tradition, our unwillingness to cooperate. However, if our tradition is placed in a historical perspective, including the English, we hardly have a tradition at all.

Comment: No, no, you have exactly as much tradition in libraries as we have. Your libraries started at about the same time ours did. In the English library profession, we are not as computerized as you are, but one thing is being thumped out right, left, and center; if you computerize, go for MARC II. This is already being done in Great Britain. Groups that have formats are deliberately modifying them or making positive assertions that they are going to MARC II; we are deliberately settling on this one. One other thing is partly the theory that we do in fact believe in cooperation. Also, the sheer brute economics of MARC, is going to force this on others.

Comment: I could say so many things about audiovisual people from state to state, but we do not really have regional groups working. Nevertheless, we have accepted two systems of classification of knowledge, the Dewey and Library of Congress classification system. This is a greater step toward standardization than any other national group of which I am aware has taken.

Comment: I was not setting my country Great Britain, up as any kind of paragon. I was using the comparative method of finding solutions to our common problems. Remember, Great Britain has only fifty million population and a very different history.

Comment: The degree of cooperation that is outlined here is slightly different from my notion of who cooperates more. In England I found, to my great joy, that they are not waiting until a national program is established to begin issuing library cards for a metropolitan area. Now, we have had one library card for the metropolitan area in Toronto only approximately one year. Is anything as basically simple as that so terribly difficult? I am thinking about Toronto, but I am wondering how prevalent this is in the United States. Surely this does not have to start at the top. But it is the type of cooperation I was pleased to see in Great Britain.

Comment: You are speaking of federal systems in contrast to the cooperation of states in a single country. We have the latter in this country and will continue to have it.

Comment: That is not what I am talking about. I am talking about Canadian borough councils. Why is it necessary to start any higher on this basic sort of thing? The Canadian borough councils agree the taxpayer in one municipality can use the library of another if the access is reciprocal. It does not exist in this country as far as I know and certainly not to the degree that is present in Canada and Great Britain.

Comment: In England we have as many charging systems as there are mice in a field of corn, but if you have a valid card in one borough, you can use it in another. They usually end, I might say, by writing it down on a little slip of paper and sticking it somewhere.

Comment: In addition to that, we in the United States have independent producers making cards themselves and giving them away. He is talking about the problems of implementation. After going through the sequence of procedures from Dr. Darling's Resources and Technical Services ad hoc committee on cataloging nonprint media, up to section level, to the appropriate division, the American Library Association itself, the American National Standards Institute, and International Standards Organization, we still face the problem of acceptance and implementation.

Comment: There are a great many areas of real cooperation that do not need that many levels of approval. Cooperation at all levels is the sort of thing I saw happening in England that I do not see in North America.

Mr. Margolin: Is information a public utility? Consider two different levels that can be related only subjectively. If this might legally be done in the United States, perhaps any federal support for a library system might very well require all library systems to open their program to any valid user. It is possible that a court case would decide this matter. On another level, you are faced with a critical question of communication of ideas, just as the communication of the human voice is a critical question. Despite the fact that there are some one hundred or more different telephone companies in the United States, they all use the same wave length and compatible equipment. Would it, therefore, be possible to say conceptually that the exchange of information is a public utility? A federal agency might be established similar to the Federal Communications Commission [FCC] or under the FCC to bring contending forces together and work out a system. However, such a bureaucratic structure does tend to slow the progress of more rapid movers in the field.

Comment: Do not muddle levels of information here. On the basic level, the primary level, what is contained in a document, represents capital invested. I would tend to doubt whether that should ever go into the public domain because if so, why the devil should anyone write another book?

In Great Britain we have accepted, I think without possibly even noticing it, the secondary level activity, the supply of information about information, as certainly in the public domain. We had a report that suggested setting up a national bibliographical center to be funded by the government to bring together the business of MEDLARS [Medical Literature Analysis and Retrieval System], the *British National Bibliography,* and a catalog of nonbook media. If it is bibliographical information that we are trying to set up, a major system to control the supply of this is intentionally free. Anyone can walk into a library and gain access to the data.

Comment: It raises the question of who really pays for the service that you have established, which is the difference between a federal system and those set up by cities, states, and other smaller units.

Comment: There is the question of capital involved. I would merely come straight to Dr. Margolin and say the question then has been answered in the United States. Information about information is a public utility.

Mr. Margolin: Except that it has incompatible elements to the system, which makes it unique and, therefore, an obstacle to public use.

Comment: But that is machinery and we are here to find a better machine. On the question of capital, I will say, the big public libraries in England, the Manchester Reference Library and others, are now beginning to raise a fairly considerable voice on the fact that 50 percent of our information is going to people outside our tax area. Although we do not want to take the crude line that nonresidents cannot come in, our supporters are beginning to say, We invested the capital and are, therefore, entitled to get some return on this.

Mr. Margolin: Information sciences have assumed the characteristics of a public utility, and they are important enough to be one although the elements are incompatible. Mr. Croghan dismissed this by saying that it is mechanical, but I would question that, and even say it is not mechanical. It is political, because of what we have been talking about here and the fact that with fifty states, there are possibly five or six power blocs if states go into compacts.

There are also foundations and professional groups with still different needs, and of course industry operates independently. There are political reasons that make it more than a mechanical thing and leave us two options: either allow the best force to win or decide it is like a telephone system and have the FCC or some comparable organization, maybe even the Library of Congress, standardize the system, consulting of course, as the FCC does, with the power groups that are involved.

My question is, simply, as the critical group in this trust, which would you favor? Would you favor a final, national decision, with some enforcement in regards to standardization, or would you like to operate independently, with the good rising above the poor, and not being restricted by the latter? The implications of either decision must be evaluated.

Comment: Your comments have, I think, particular significance, in the light of certain conversations we have had earlier in the week. We are arguing the virtues of a central government agency accomplishing what we are discussing vis-à-vis the virtues and vices of assigning this task to private industry. Now, you are suggesting that we can have the authority of the federal government with the more immediate and stable financing capability of private industry. The net result is that instead of the cost being borne by all taxpayers, it would be paid for by the users, but nevertheless subject to, in this case, a federal authority. I think it might be a reasonable answer, notwithstanding my personal feelings as a capitalist, being subjected to governmental control. As a realistic approach to getting the job done, this may be the answer.

Comment: We can get the United States Congress to legislate authority much more readily than we can get it to commit itself, over a long period of time, to the expenditure of funds.

Question: Are you forcing me to choose between your company, a much smaller endeavor, and Xerox, a large conglomerate?

Comment: That probably is not necessary. There are American Telephone and Telegraph [AT&T] and Midcontinent Telephone, with a variety of sizes in between. Rather than the telephone, I would favor the telegraph as an example, where it is not broken down geographically with the Telex, Teletypewriter Exchange Service, and a few others. You have a certain competitive element, and yet, the avariciousness associated with private enterprise is subject to the watchful scrutiny of the Federal Communications Commission.

Mr. Margolin: I believe a small company in the Middle West has just announced that it is going to set up microwave transmitters to substitute for American Telephone and Telegraph's long cables. They will be competitive, yet the FCC requires, no matter what they do in between, the signal to be of comparable quality and compatible with the receivers. When it reaches your telephone at home, the receiver, which is supplied by AT&T, will sound the same to you when you make the call.

Comment: Another advantage is that the various industrial participants will cooperate in the establishment of standards. Right now, the antitrust laws will not permit this. Once you inject the element of federal control, then cooperation is under federal sponsorship.

Comment: We are forgetting that information has to flow over these lines of communication. If we get a standard, for instance of an annotation, and it was in the public domain, no one would care then if it was copied or used verbatim right out of some publication. What happens now? Someone takes the annotation and feels they must rewrite it so no one will think they plagiarized it. This happens constantly.

Comment: I think you can draw a parallel to the airlines industry. There are no geographic barriers here. It is regulated and competitive, although certain elements are identical.

Comment: In the state of Washington, where a library network is being developed, institutions were developing two-way closed-circuit television so the instructors would have visual contact with groups of students around the state. It was found that the telephone and other communications companies could not carry the signals, which meant that the cooperative, the university or the state, had to establish its own statewide communications network. The state utilities commission made it known that this could be done and that an outside agent would be allowed to compete with the phone company for statewide communication. In other words, the commission was beginning to poke a few holes in the franchise that was granted to the telephone company. We have seen some great activity since, on the part of the telephone company, and find that it is willing to build and provide the equipment needed at competitive prices on a non-franchise basis with no strings attached.

Comment: The federal government should provide a certain degree of regulation, which would include the format of the information. An agency like the Federal Communications Commission would act somewhat as a referee or spokesman for the public interest, and individual companies would be working under the surveillance of the federal watchdog. Commercial investors would have to obtain their own financing, do their own marketing, and, most important, be able to cooperate without being accused of monopolistic practice, which would occur if the Xerox Corporation and IBM were to sit down today and discuss ways of coordinating their operation.

Mr. Margolin: Miss Carolyn Whitenack described the national system for library access which is, at present, a pencil, pen, and typewriter method of communication. Ultimately this entire system will be computerized. Because the computer now carries the largest part of telephone-line transmission, there is already activity in this area for the establishment of federal regulations and standards for the control of programs that operate interstate communication of computerized data.

If the system that Miss Whitenack described was computerized under the National Library of Medicine, or some other agency, so that she could communicate through a centralized computer system with libraries throughout the United States, we would then have standardization of computer programs as a wedge toward standardization. However, is the trade-off between standardization and the possible loss of creativity by allowing divergent approaches to cataloging worth it? Would there indeed be a loss of creativity under a federally regulated system?

Comment: If you look at this system as a utility, the two problems with monopoly are one. People can get together and reduce standards, reduce the quality, and they can get together and raise prices. However, if the quality and price are regulated, they would have to show great cause to raise prices or reduce quality. For example, telephone companies, even though private enterprises, cannot change prices or quality without a thorough investigation by the regulating agency. It seems to me this is the way to go, and it would not be stifling creativity. The stifling of creativity is not really the problem.

Question: Are not performance standards what we are really concerned about here? Performance standards need to be set, and then we should let the free-enterprise system work out how they can best be satisfied.

Comment: Except that free enterprise has to be a participant in the establishment of performance standards. Do not forget that when we talk of creativity, very often it is free enterprise that attracts the more creative people

due to its ability to pay more than nonprofit institutions.

Question: Part of our problem is that we do not have a salable product. We want information for its intellectual sake or for others, but how many of us would pay required fees? We have not been taught to pay, but rather to get it as a service. The problem of involving free enterprise is just who is going to pay.

Comment: I want to make two small points. Creativity in cataloging and classification is not one of the minor details of annotations, but the effort needed to create the intellectual structure that is then embodied in the record, classification schemes, or the computer structure. This is where real creativity comes in. Standards are no more than platforms that you build on. I do not think the standard holds anybody down; for example, the two-by-four-foot canvas has proved a considerable challenge to a very considerable number of artists.

Secondly, I would hate for anyone to think I was naïve enough to say it was just machinery, for, of course, it includes politics. Although our politics are of a somewhat different kind and may look English and mild and sort of pastoral from your angle, I can assure you, they are just as fierce and hard fought in our country as they are in yours. The detail may differ, but the spirit, the rancor, the venom, and the rest of it is just the same.

Mr. Margolin: This has been very useful to me, because I have seen the spectrum of problems you face. They go all the way from commas to problems of national import which relate to philosophies of government. Decisions cannot be made until very fundamental assumptions have been discussed. If, indeed, certain things are to be possible in a dissemination system, economic and political philosophy must be faced. To obtain standardization, one must be willing to trade it off with the loss of some elements of freedom and be willing to cooperate in governing the system that controls standardization. I have obtained from you some sense of the kinds of recommendations we can make and will tell you very succinctly that no single recommendation will be made to the government, but rather we will give a set of choices from which government may choose.

Academic
Media Services

Trevor N. Dupuy

We have now the question of organization and control of media, again in an academic context, and within all the information resources of a college. It is probably a good idea to make sure that we are in agreement on what is being organized and controlled, or at least on what might be eligible for such control.

There seem to be six categories of things that are eligible candidates to be considered, but that does not necessarily mean that I think all of these categories must be organized or administered by the librarian. Books, of course, are what is in the conventional library. Second, nonbook or nonprint media of several types should be considered. If you do not think of them as books, microforms would be included. Sound recordings and visual recordings are obviously nonbook media. Sound and/or visual representations of the creative or performing arts would come into this category, but I would exclude the responsibility of creating them. Similarly, the sound or visual recording of the output of communications media, radio and television, could be included, while excluding the creation or dissemination of this output. Compilations of data used in computer processing, such as tapes and punched cards, might also be considered. Third (and you may raise questions about

this, but bear with me for a moment at least) are media labs. Fourth, there are other instructional media devices and the services that go with them. The distinction which I make between these two is between the things that are essentially for learning purposes and the things that are used to facilitate learning or perhaps teaching. Fifth, we have processing facilities, and sixth, the bookstore. You may have some others in mind, and you may raise very serious questions about these.

In preparing that list, I went through the process of asking myself why I considered using these particular categories of things to find a relationship between the control of nonbook media and book media. This led me to formulate a philosophy which I wanted to use and which will influence the remainder of what I am about to say. I am talking about how to make the best possible use of a wide variety of things which contain information or intellectual output and which are useful to the learning process. We want to collect these things and organize them in such a way that all, not just some or most, are readily available and useful to those who need this information. Such people may need this information in learning or in teaching or for any other constructive purpose.

There are two different principal aspects to this philosophy. The first is the collection, just the physical collection, of things, information, or what we might otherwise call information-transfer resources. These come in a great vari-

Executive Director, Historical Evaluation and Research Organization, McLean, Virginia.

107

ety of information or intellectual content which could be useful to the clientele of the institution. The second aspect of this philosophy is the service which can be provided to the clientele to assure the acceptability of all of these things or resources which a user might wish to consult on any given subject, for which there is or may be information. For want of a better term, I have decided that the service I am speaking of I would call information resources service. The information resources service includes collecting and storing all available information-content resource items, from any and all media that are available. In other words, I am speaking of the total sum of information resources, whether in books or in any other form.

Organizing these in an integrated fashion for convenient use by the clientele would include, naturally, the inventory and catalog process, assisting the clientele to get out all information-content items that are on hand and actually available, and also assisting the clients to get at all possibly available information-content items that are not on hand. This does not include, in my opinion, tailoring course-content to resource-content items. This is the responsibility of either the student or the professor, depending upon what philosophy of education you have.

It does not include the preparation of new resource items, save possibly in the very specialized professional field of competence of the serving agents. It does not include the control of functional, administrative, procedural operations, or activities that are used by the serving agents or agencies, saving in those instances where it is the sole or major user. In other words, just because lighting is essential to the library, that does not mean that the librarian should be responsible for an electric-generating plant; however, I can see instances in which a library might want to run a book-binding plant. Now, there is a gray area between the things it should or should not do.

The person who is responsible for the organization of these resources might give assistance in the techniques of using and combining the media when the client needs it, even if the client is not always aware of the need. This might include assistance in techniques of

preparing new resource items in media other than print if there is no other source available for this kind of service. It might include maintenance and control of devices and facilities related to the exploration and use of the media, particularly where this contributes to the overall efficiency of the operation. This is why librarians are interested, for instance, even though they may fear the use of such things as copying machines or readers or viewers, even though the operation and maintenance of these things is obviously quite foreign to librarianship per se.

This may be a somewhat complex way of converting this philosophy into some kind of yardstick or standard, but it is the thought process I went through. I hope that in sharing the process with you, I have not lost you. Let us look down this list of six candidates, or items, and see how this philosophy applies.

Obviously the conventional book library fits, if only because that was the base from which I started, but I think one would find that it fits, in logic, anyhow. It seems to me self-evident also that if there were a comparable library of nonbook media items, this would be subject to the same kind of organizational control. It would include all of the things that I mentioned with one possible exception. These were microforms, sound recordings, visual recordings, sound or visual representation of the arts without the responsibility for creating these, and sound or visual recordings of the output of communications media, radio and television, again without the responsibility for creating or disseminating such communications output. I would doubt seriously, if, under normal circumstances, it should include compilations of data-processing tapes or cards. If the elaboration of my philosophy has any validity, the information resource service should include responsibility for the operational effectiveness of the media labs and for controlling and coordinating their use. It should also include responsibility for the coordination and control of all general-purpose devices, as opposed to special-purpose devices like science laboratory microscopes. It should also include the college bookstore. This list probably could be discussed at great length.

This is where I arrive by the thought process

which I described. Some of you, I am sure, will not agree, perhaps will not even agree with the process, and are likely not to agree with the results of the process. I do not think it is terribly important that you agree with me, so long as you are able to go through, in what appears to you to be a logical sequence of thought processes, and decide what should be included.

I would like to turn from the discussion of *what* should be controlled and organized to *how* it should be controlled and organized. There are three fundamental considerations in determining how the organization should be administered. First, the librarian is the person responsible for the print or book collection, which will be the largest element of the overall resources collection. He cannot and should not be a nonprint-media specialist in terms of technology and the employment of nonprint-media devices, even thought he may be responsible for the nonprint collection. I understand that in some places considerable emphasis is being given in library instruction to competence in nonbook-media technology. In my opinion a good librarian does not need to know a lot about the electronic processes or technology which produce that media.

Second, the media specialist is a person who is qualified in this technology and in the employment and maintenance of these devices. He should not be inhibited in the provision of services with these relatively new kinds of devices that are being adopted only cautiously by many teachers. He should not be deterred from being an evangelist, a missionary, or an enthusiast in propagating the use of these devices, simply because this is not the way librarians traditionally act.

Third, the media specialist must realize that any and all of his collections are properly part of the entire information resource potential of the college. For the most efficient use of the collections, they must be fully integrated with the larger resource collection. This is the most important thing that I have said, or will say. If you do not agree on this point, then we do have a real debate.

These fundamental considerations would suggest to some that there should be complete independence between the librarian and the media specialist, even though they closely coordinate their collections and the services related to these collections. My experience suggests, however, that complete coordination is impossible between two entirely independent people or agencies, even though they may report to a common superior and even though they may be people of very goodwill. Full coordination is possible only if one of the two is given both the responsibility and the authority to require coordination. My experiences and observations suggest to me that the coordinator, whether he is one of these two principals or a third supervisory authority, must be primarily resource service oriented, while the other should be effective for the benefit of clients needing to use the combined collection.

It is significant that a librarian, or someone oriented toward library thinking, is able to perform the coordination of the kind which I suggest. This has been attempted at several institutions I visited. In three of these the coordinator was primarily library oriented. Two of the media-oriented coordinators were less than fully successful because, in my opinion, they concentrated their interests, their efforts, and their attention on media and largely neglected the library and the librarian.

Both of the library-oriented coordinators, on the other hand, were quite successful, since they imposed their professional views on the media specialist only in terms of collection and office administration, while encouraging and supporting the media specialist with his noncollection service functions and missionary work. The third media-oriented coordinator also tended to leave the library operation alone, perhaps more than he should have, but before he did this, either intentionally or accidentally, he did a very important thing. He assured full library operational control over the combined library and media collection; thus the media collections became a major element within the library proper.

Organization charts never mean as much as the people who fill in the boxes that appear on the charts, but I do not agree that charts mean nothing and people everything. Good people can work effectively even if the organization is poor, but they work better and more productively if the organization is good. A good organization with mediocre people will probably work better than good people in a poorly designed organization. I could discuss this at great length on the basis of my military experience, but you might say that is not relevant.

This department should be fully coequal with other university or college departments. The coordinator might have the title of professor or dean of information resources service. Actually, the title of dean has been used in several places recently. The two major subordinates might have the title of professor of library services or professor of media services. This is not important.

There are some special problems, however, even under ideal circumstances. How does this information resources service cope with the use of media labs for audio-tutorial programs? It can work in a number of ways, but only if there are diplomacy and administrative skill and a certain amount of goodwill involved. The departments will almost always want to keep the labs under their control, if possible within their own departmental areas. They will also want to keep under their control all of the resources used in the audio-tutorial program. The extent to which the departmental demands are met or resisted quite simply depends on the use of the labs and the materials. If one department can efficiently and effectively use one or more of the labs on a full-time basis, then it probably should be assigned full responsibility for such labs. If, however, assigning labs to a department would mean that expensive equipment and space are allowed to sit idle for long periods of time, then the department should not have the responsibility; centralized control is best. The same is true of the resource items.

Question: Would you explain what you mean by media labs?

Mr. Dupuy: The best known, of course, is the language laboratory. There are also laboratories which are specifically designed for the media tutorial method, in which you have carrels with recorders, a small projector, and things of this sort.

Question: You say you are talking about the total situation, but you do not include communication, that is, radio and television. Where does that fit?

Mr. Dupuy: If your institution is large enough, it goes in some sort of a communications department. If not, it comes right back here to media services.

We have been talking peripherally about some esoteric ideas in educational philosophy, which I do not feel qualified to discuss, despite the strength of my feeling about them intuitively. I have tried to talk as an observer of these things, in terms such that everyone would know exactly what I was talking about. These are entities that exist. We can call them anything we want, but at the present time, *media* is being used essentially to distinguish certain kinds of information resource items from books. I have adapted myself to this in what I presented.

Comment: You are really defining the traditional concept most people have of librarians, of collecting, storing, and then retrieving information for the user's sake.

Mr. Dupuy: Right, but recognize the fact that with the media you have a new kind of technology involved, which means that you must have an additional service with a technical capability as well. The information resource coordinator could be at any level from immediately below the president to the dean's level, or even head of department.

Question: Will you discuss the concept of the active versus the responsive librarian?

Mr. Dupuy: I coined these expressions in one of my books, pointing out that an active librarian is one who is service oriented, whereas a responsive librarian is one who is collection oriented. I suggested that really both are thinking in terms of service *and* collection, but the active librarian is one who is trying to get out and persuade the faculty that this collection is available and show ways in which it can better be used. The responsive librarian may have the feeling that he should give the same kind of service that the active librarian does, but the faculty should come to him and ask.

Mr. Stone: I am a bit troubled by some of the discussion. The administrative configurations set before us are useful ways to describe what is and may help us, but I have a fear that they do not do the task, at least for the larger university, the larger college, indeed for education, very well.

I would propose a different approach, which is a different philosophy, not a better one, just different. We would go farther and get there faster, design better training programs, and design better organizational systems and structures in schools and colleges if we start, as others are suggesting, with the functions that have to be performed. We should start by defining the functions, in order to ensure that we produce and have available systems which will distribute and evaluate the results of training and otherwise make available the full range of communication resources. In order to do that, we must have units, agencies, and a whole cadre of different kinds of clerical, technical, and professional skills. Some of these relate to the generation of media. Some relate to the operation, switching systems, and distributive mechanisms, the indexing, cataloging, filing, and control of them. Others relate to teaching, to students, faculty, and others. Research is a vital ingredient.

There is an interlocking of these functions, from the background or base knowledge essential for their performance in the general area of the intellectual discipline of communications. It has been suggested that these functions are best conducted in a common managerial fashion, probably in common or connected facilities, and, at least at the top, probably under common administrative control. There are a hundred or a thousand different ways we can hook together the pieces that relate to production, distribution, research, counseling, and the catalog display. The use of communication technology is just one of these ways. The best way for us to worry about it at our own institutions is to think in terms of these functions and the conceptual interlock which relates them. The feasibility and cost factors relate them to each other.

The words we are using get very badly, seriously, detrimentally in the way of intelligent planning for the administrational services. The organization of knowledge resources can be managed far more effectively by a concern for subject than by a concern for form and character. I was not wanting to disagree with you, but I did want to present an alternative.

Part 4

State of
the Art

Authors in the United States, Canada, and Great Britain set forth a current state of the art in their countries with possible solutions to the bibliographic control of nonprint media. A review of the current situation in Canada by Janet Macdonald was followed by a challenge from Jean Riddle, also a Canadian, who called for international cooperation to solve those problems she was convinced can be satisfied only at the international level. Antony Croghan and his British colleague, Bernard Chibnall, analyzed the control of educational nonprint media in Great Britain and concluded that a coordinated program at the international level is essential to an orderly development of information exchange among nations.

Joseph Becker considered the feasibility of establishing a national control of nonprint media in the United States. Trevor Dupuy shared the results of his visits to academic libraries and audiovisual centers on university and college campuses in this country. Evaluating the results of two surveys for the same institutions done several years apart, Dupuy concluded that little progress was being made to enhance the effective utilization of nonprint media in institutions of higher education. He called for librarians, audiovisual specialists, and information scientists to cooperate for the benefit of the learner and our society.

Requirements for ease of access to information in many formats were put forth by institute participants directly involved in the development of bibliographic controls.

Bibliographic Control
of Nonprint Media in
the United States

Alma M. Tillin

In Tudor times a witch, Mother Shipton by name, is said to have prophesied, "Around the world thoughts shall fly in the twinkling of an eye." In the seventeenth century this vision was attributed to witchcraft. In the twentieth century the infallibility of this prophecy has been proven through modern technology and, in all probability, in dimensions far beyond those envisaged by Mother Shipton. Indeed, ample proof of this is the very fact that we are all gathered here to discuss the multitude of forms in which thoughts have been recorded and the many possible ways to make them accessible to everyone—in the twinkling of an eye. Perhaps, if Mother Shipton, in her all-seeing wisdom, had specified a method of keeping track of all these thoughts flying around the world, we would not now be faced with many of our current problems.

A historical review of efforts to establish bibliographic control of nonprint media in the United States reads like a contemporary novel of frustration. Several studies have been made, funded either by national associations or federal grants, each of which stressed the need for a system of bibliographic control and made recommendations that were not successfully implemented. It is disturbing to realize that each successive project duplicated work done in the previous projects.

Technical Services Librarian, Berkeley Unified School District, Berkeley, California

In 1955 the American Library Association, Special Committee on the Bibliographic Control of Audiovisual Materials, chaired by Eunice Keen, reported that every effort should be made to achieve standardization of the essential elements in cataloging audiovisual materials and that a standardized manual of procedure for the handling of these materials be prepared. In 1960 Margaret Rufsvold and Carolyn Guss stated that "a national descriptive bibliographic control system of the newer educational media is an urgent necessity." In 1968 an ad hoc committee of the American Library Association Resources and Technical Services Division, Cataloging and Classification Section, chaired by Richard Darling, was charged with the investigation of the feasibility of developing a national standard or standards for the organization of nonprint materials and the production of a manual that would guide libraries in the cataloging, classification, processing, and physical preparation for use of these materials. It would seem that we have come around again full circle.

In the absence of any standardized method or tools to assist them in organizing scattered and growing collections of nonprint media, those who felt responsible for the full potential utilization of these resources produced their own how-to-do-it books. From Michigan, New York, North Carolina, California, Arizona, and other states, manuals emanated, each worked on independently, each duplicating to a great extent the labor of the others.

These, together with handbooks prepared for local use by individual institutions, have had varying degrees of influence nationally. While they all recommend adaptation of the cataloging techniques used for books and are remarkably similar in their principal characteristics, they are different enough in many details to enhance confusion. Since none of these codes have had the official endorsement of the national library or audiovisual associations, they have been disregarded by many who prefer to do their own thing. Others, having chosen one of these manuals, have proceeded with caution and misgivings but yet are reluctant to support any national program that would change what they have started.

It was hoped that the 1967 *Anglo-American Cataloging Rules,* treating nonprint materials in part 3 would solve the problems of media catalogers by establishing rules for entry, format, and content as stable and acceptable as those for books. It soon became evident, however, that the rules permitted a variety of interpretations and contained many inconsistencies, making further revision essential.

Another ray of hope appeared in 1968 with the publication of *Standards for Cataloging, Coding and Scheduling Educational Media* by the Department of Audiovisual Instruction (DAVI). Here was an attempt to specify what elements should be incorporated in catalog descriptions, how they should be expressed and arranged on the catalog card or printed catalog, and how this information could be coded for computerized storage and retrieval. Although the DAVI code was a step forward toward the development of standards, it was admittedly a trial balloon. Further refinements must result from reaction and feedback from those working with instructional materials in the field.

One should not be misled into assuming that bibliographic assistance in the media field is entirely absent. Services and tools do exist, which range from the provision of commercially prepared catalog cards and kits to sophisticated computer information-retrieval systems. None of them, however, is comprehensive either in types of media or in coverage of current or prior productions. Without the guidance of accepted standards, each of these services has attempted bibliographic control in a different way, and it is rare to find in their various products the compatibility needed for intersystem communication.

The Library of Congress renders an invaluable service by providing printed cards and National Union Catalogs for films, filmstrips, and recordings. However, many items have not been cataloged, classification information is incomplete, and the receipt of cards is exceedingly slow. Sets of catalog cards, with or without labels for physical processing, are available from commercial cataloging firms—such as Bro-Dart, Specialized Service and Supply, and others—or directly from some producers who have had their materials cataloged by various agencies. Other facilities produce book catalogs of specific collections and will contract to provide access to their data banks. To ease the burden of selection, some associations and institutions, such as the Educational Media Council and the Educational Products Information Exchange, have issued availability information, usually treating each type of media separately.

There are encouraging and discouraging aspects in some recent developments. Now under consideration is the much needed revision of part 3 of the *Anglo-American Cataloging Rules,* based, to a great extent, on the proposals submitted by the Canadian committee. The latest edition of the Canadian cataloging manual, entitled *Non-Book Materials: The Organization of Integrated Collections,* demonstrates how these would work. The American Library Association Resources and Technical Services Division, Cataloging and Classification Section ad hoc audiovisual committee will study this *Manual* and report on whether or not it is acceptable as a standard cataloging guide. In our new book, *Developing Multi-Media Libraries,* Warren Hicks and I have attempted to pull together some of the scattered bits and pieces of media information and synthesize them into a practical and efficient procedure built on the intrinsic interrelationships between acquisition, selection, cataloging, physical processing, storage, and individualized use of nonprint material.

Commercial firms are continuing to expand

their services. The most recent catalog of Specialized Service and Supply lists more than 10,000 nonbook titles for which it will supply kits and spells out the modifications to the *Anglo-American Cataloging Rules* they have used. Bro-Dart has announced the availability of cataloging and processing of recordings according to the ANSCR scheme, the Alpha-Numeric System for Classification of Recordings. This system was designed specifically for browsing collections of recordings and has limited capability for integration with resources in other formats. The offering by some commercial firms of fully cataloged and processed multimedia curriculum programs is indicative of a current dangerous permissiveness on the part of all of us in the education profession. We seem to be willing to relinquish our responsibilities for the selection of media in exchange for any solution to the problems of bibliographic control.

There are several bibliographic tools that have recently appeared or are in the planning or production stage. Bowker has published the NICEM indexes to 16mm films, 8mm cartridge films, 35mm filmstrips, and overhead transparencies. Compiled from the data banks of the National Information Center for Educational Media, they are, as yet, the most comprehensive listing that we have of these materials. Since the data banks were built from the holdings of various collections, there is no assurance of complete coverage of all productions. Westinghouse Learning Corporation has scheduled the publication of *Learning Directory 1970,* described as "the comprehensive index to instructional material in all media." Indexing both print and nonprint materials together, it is expected to fill seven volumes with multimedia listings under a wide range of general and specific topics. The subject descriptors were determined by random selection of words out of context from titles and annotations in producers' catalogs, and all materials not specified as instructional are excluded. *The Catalog of U.S. Government Motion Pictures and Filmstrips for Sale by the National Audiovisual Center* is a welcome addition. Planning is now underway to disseminate similar information about other government audiovisual materials, both for sale and for rent.

On a more sophisticated level, some mechanized information-retrieval systems for media are in operation. At the National Medical Audiovisual Center in Atlanta, computer-generated compilations of film titles in several subject areas have been produced. Currently, tests are being run with an on-line hookup from the National Medical Audiovisual Center to the General Services computer facility some miles away. If these tests are successful, the data file could be available on-line countrywide. These activities are separate from the MEDLARS (Medical Literature Analysis and Research System) program at the National Library of Medicine and use different medical subject headings. However, planning for entering information on media into MEDLARS is in progress, and information on media for nurses training will soon be available.

A major breakthrough for bibliographic control on a national scale is the work of the Library of Congress on a MARC (Machine-Readable Cataloging) format for motion pictures, filmstrips, and other pictorial media intended for projection, such as slides, transparencies, videotapes, and electronic video recordings. It is hoped that impetus will be added to formulating national standards by the recently completed *Report of the Commission on Instructional Technology,* which recommends the establishment of a National Institute of Instructional Technology and the development of a system by which practicing educators in schools and colleges throughout the country would have ready access to the widest possible range of materials and resources for instruction in every medium and subject.

The work of this institute is an outstanding demonstration of what can be accomplished through cooperative effort. Those concerned with the organization and dissemination of knowledge—librarians, audiovisual specialists, information scientists, communications experts—reviewed the many problems related to bibliographic control and reached a common understanding of objectives. Working together as a united group, participants have urged national professional associations to assume responsibility and support the implementation of national standards. The institute has instigated action for the establishment in the American Library Association and the Association for Educational Communications and Technology of permanent entities for the coordination and development of nonprint-media activities. Its various committees have been working on the many aspects that are all part of bibliographic control: user needs, cataloging and classification, the MARC II format, terminology, statistics, nonprint-media standards, cooperation with producers, communication networks, and international relations. If we are ever to achieve national standards for the bibliographic control of nonprint media (the urgent need for them has been voiced through comments from individuals and resolutions from state professional associations), the projects and action started by this institute must be continued.

The picture I have sketched is a conglomeration of uncoordinated bits and pieces. It tells a story of duplication of effort, of continuous attempts to reinvent what has already been fabricated, of projects that have come to nought, of incompatibility resulting from insularity of interests. It shows only spotty recognition of the necessity of bibliographic control in every program of media services. Yet, in each of its separate parts, it demonstrates skills and techniques that are intrinsic in an art. It remains for us to combine our expertise to create a national, standard, media bibliographic-control format capable of producing bibliographic information on library catalog cards and in book format, capable of storing and retrieving bibliographic information on *all* media, and capable of easy assimilation into any network or system. It is our responsibility to do this, both as individuals and as professional associations. Only when we have produced this instrument can we truly say that bibliographic control of nonprint media in the United States has attained the state of an art.

Bibliographic Control of Nonprint Media in Canada

Janet E. Macdonald

The present lack of catalogs or even a "media in print" suggests that those traditionally responsible for buying and using nonprint media have never seen the need for such tools. To the librarian dedicated to the principle that you cannot use what you do not know exists, this situation is incomprehensible. In the hope that my bewilderment stemmed from ignorance, I contacted many people who I thought would or should be concerned about the problem. The results of this investigation, ranging from smug incomprehension through frustration to the reinvention of another solid gold-plated fifth wheel, will be familiar to you all.

Only two projects of any real significance emerged from these contacts. I will describe them as they were outlined to me and leave their evaluation to you. The following letter from Dr. Jean Lunn, Director of the Cataloguing Branch of the National Library in Ottawa, should amplify the situation there with regard to nonprint media:

> The coverage of films and filmstrips in *Canadiana* is not very complete at the moment. Within recent years the listings have been almost entirely National Film Board films. We are, however, about to renew our efforts to collect information from all Canadian producers and we are only awaiting delivery of a supply of form letters.

There is no legal requirement for producers to supply information so we must depend on their goodwill and perhaps the lure of a free advertisement in the form of a listing. The producers supply the summaries. These are short and factual, and I have no reason to suppose that they are not reliable—although I do not actually know.

> We intend to assign classification numbers and subject headings to films and filmstrips as soon as possible, even though the subject analysis will be based only on titles and summaries. We intend, also as soon as possible, to extend legal deposit requirements to educational kits and other AV material and to catalogue these items in *Canadiana*. We suffer, as who does not, from limitations of funds and staff. However, it seems fairly obvious that the whole production of *Canadiana* will be automated within the foreseeable future, and before that date we must do our utmost to give full treatment, especially subject, to everything listed in *Canadiana*.

The second project, *Film Canadiana*, published by the Canadian Film Institute, is described in the following letter from its editor, Andre LaRose:

> At the very beginning, we described *Film Canadiana* as Canada's national filmography. This definition implied the necessity for us to cope with all films and tele-

Chief Cataloger, Co-operative Book Centre of Canada, Ltd., Toronto

vision programmes available to Canadians, and this within a reasonable length of time. We decided, in the first issue which would be published in December 1969, to describe films and television programmes produced and released in Canada after January 1, 1969. Further issues would be published quarterly and would describe current releases. Productions released before January 1 would be gradually dealt with in future annual cumulative editions. To compile the documentation, two major tools are used—data reports filled in by Canadian distributors and producers whom we contact at regular intervals. The mailing list includes more than 800 companies, and we receive replies at a rate of 50 percent, a rate which will increase gradually as *Film Canadiana* becomes more and more known in the industry. To complement documentation sent by the above, the Institute's extensive records—more than 100,000 entries in periodicals, books, etc.—are used. Vol. I, no. 2 describes productions released in Canada during winter '70. More than 325 films and television programmes are described —of these, 118 are Canadian productions. We are studying possibilities of using modern retrieval methods in the compilation of the tremendous amount of material involved—current releases, releases after January 1, 1969, and a re-arrangement of documentation in order to publish the annual cumulative edition in this catalogue.

The main listing is by Universal Decimal Classification, an excellent choice for this type of listing, and the publication is indexed from every conceivable angle. I cannot resist observing that this comes closest to the ideal in bibliographic control I have ever seen, but its funding is uncertain, and it deals only with motion picture film and television.

In the meantime, our schools are acquiring filmstrips, transparencies, tapes, and multimedia kits. All the things which are not yet covered by either of the above. These materials are going into the school library, into an already existing information source, formally organized for maximum utilization.

A group of interested school library people in Toronto have explored a type of integration of the media which had hitherto not been seriously attempted. The result of this project is *Non-Book Materials: The Organization of Integrated Collections,* published by the Canadian Library Association. We found that the present arrangement for print could accommodate the media with no great difficulty. Because this can be done, there seems little point in elaborate and costly attempts to organize *a* slide collection or *a* record collection (the fifth wheels referred to earlier as gold-plated) in isolation from the much more comprehensive information source already available in the print field.

The state of the art in Canada is much the same as yours, as I see it. Everyone is doing his own thing. We must find something which will work for everyone, because all these fifth wheels are rolling us further and further from our objective.

Question: What about the multimedia packages?

Miss Macdonald: What is your problem with them?

Question: Under what media are you going to house it?

Miss Macdonald: This is a problem of terminology. What are you going to decide is in fact a kit? We have decided, for the purposes of getting something done—getting the things cataloged and on the shelf where people can find and use them—after a great deal of soul-searching and asking a great many questions of a great many people, that a kit is any two media, not three or more, just two or more. This means a filmstrip with a recorded sound accompaniment is a kit, not a sound filmstrip. There is no basic agreement on this point, which is the main problem. This is the terminology problem that we must solve. I think that Jean Riddle would like to amplify that.

Mrs. Riddle: When you have a filmstrip and recorded sound, you mean that you require that neither one can be used independently before you label it a kit.

Comment: It is a problem of definition. Do remember that in your own particular situation, it is possible for you to make the definitions. We have the problem here of the centralized ones. For your own working system, if you don't want to call a sound filmstrip a kit, you can say kits are everything that include two items, except for sound filmstrips which I am calling something different.

Comment: The idea is to develop the definitions and a system with some flexibility, knowing that the individual institution, depending on whether it is Harvard University with a hundred thousand slides or a small public library with twenty-five slides, must deviate at specific points to accommodate different needs. But, if the system was there, you could pull off what you want. It would be a service, and it would be within a general context of a system or a standard.

Miss Macdonald: I am glad you used the example of a sound filmstrip. This illustrates the basic problem. We speak of a filmstrip with an accompanying disc or tape as a sound filmstrip. Now, we are developing a filmstrip with the sound on the film, which is a real sound filmstrip. The others are filmstrips with accompanying sound. This distinction demonstrates the need for acceptable terminology that can be adapted to the new media. I am sure all of you have seen things at the exhibits here which you didn't know existed, particularly new combinations of individualized media. We must develop a system for media terminology standardization with this dimension of the problem in mind.

Question: What do you as a group, that has been slaving over this for so long, recommend to us when we try to select our descriptors? What do you think is going to be the national standard? Ultimately there is going to be a national standard, and every institution that wants to invest in something that is going to be stable will follow it.

Miss Macdonald: What do you mean by descriptors?

Comment: Well, the media descriptors, for instance.

Miss Macdonald: Are you talking about the names of physical objects rather than content descriptors?

Comment: Yes, we are looking for the system. You have made it clear there isn't one at the present time.

Comment: Can I have a commercial break here? I can afford to, you know, I'm English and I'm retiring to the Continent again. This is an enormous problem which must be solved. If you want a hand in solving it, get in the new divisions being formed in associations, because this is one of the things we want to do through professional groups. It also gives you a method by which you can tell us about this kind of thing. You know, put up or shut up, I think is the thing I'm saying. But the machinery to "put up" is a division structure in organizations. We need this so that you can tell us about it. You know how to talk to each other about the basic things, but I've sensed—I'll speak as an Englishman—that there is a feeling amongst the audiovisual people that you want to talk about this and you are not quite certain how or to whom. If you get a division in AECT [Association for Educational Communications and Technology], it will give you a method of doing this.

Question: Is there any pressure being brought on the commercial producers for cards or anything?

Miss Macdonald: I react to that question immediately because that is in fact what I do. I am a commercial cataloger. Our customers want cataloging for the audiovisual materials they buy. They have expressed this need to producers; the producers have done their best to find out how to provide the service, but the profession is unable to tell them. This is why there is such a multiplicity of methods of cataloging audiovisual material from commercial firms. Both Shirley [Mrs. Lewis, Canadian Book Wholesale Co.] and I were extremely reluctant to get into the field of audiovisual cataloging. Because we did, we were asked to contribute to a committee of school librarians, not so much as commercial catalogers, but as centralized catalogers. The problems are the same, whether you get us to do it or you do it for yourself on a centralized basis. In your own library, as Mr. Croghan said, you can call a kit what you like, but once you are cataloging it for more than your own library, you are in trouble. This is why Mrs. Lewis, Mrs. Riddle, and I got very interested in developing a method that we felt would not simply sell a product but would do something to improve library service. We hope what we have done will be useful to other people.

Comment: A meeting was called at the ALA conference in Kansas City in 1968 under the auspices of the Resources and Technical Services Division. Commercial interests were there to hear the results of a survey. Richard Darling chaired the meeting that was called to discuss this very problem. The commercial people said they have to do something to sell the product. They are waiting for the professions DAVI [Department of Audio-Visual Instruction], ALA, EFLA [Educational Film Library As-

sociation], MLA [Music Library Association], and others, to give them the guidelines for card and label production. If it is not forthcoming they cannot wait. They must get something out, for it seems they cannot sell their media without some way to organize it. The tragic situation is that each commercial company must go its own way, due to a lack of professional responsibility on our part. They know the added problems and risk of their investing even more in what they are doing, and perhaps being caught with an obsolete system. They are in a dilemma.

International Cooperation

Jean Riddle

I have assumed that the topic international cooperation means Canada's actual or intended role in the international cooperation in the bibliographic control of media. When one considers the vast lines of communication which must be established to have effective bibliographic control, one wonders if we are discussing an impossible ideal. Even prompt, reliable mail service within the boundaries of a metropolitan area sometimes is difficult to maintain.

Many people are concerned about the mail service because it affects their daily lives, but relatively few people in Canada are concerned about bibliographic control of media. This fact is hardly surprising. What is surprising is that so few librarians and media specialists are concerned with this problem. In preparation for this paper, I talked with librarians, audiovisual specialists, and producers. Their reactions ranged from incomprehension to disinterest. Except for a few librarians working directly with media cataloging, the most concerned person I have met all year is a teacher at Seneca College who lectures in astronomy. He was astounded and then enraged to find that he could not discover exactly what items are available in his field in the various media. I sincerely regret he does not hold a position that is politically valuable to those of us who wish to press for bibliographic control.

My personal observations on this general state of disinterest are that catalogers frequent-

ly work in isolation from the media world; that audiovisual specialists are unfamiliar with bibliographic procedures and are far more producer oriented than librarians are publisher oriented; and that the producers do not look, and are uninterested in looking, beyond their own catalogs into a larger bibliographic setup. In addition, the librarians who would benefit the most from standardized bibliographic control of media are the school librarians.

Generally, these audiovisual people are not well trained in cataloguing principles. Generally, catalogers do not handle media. I note this disinterest in order to emphasize the point that the only international cooperation towards the bibliographic control of media by Canadians is displayed by organizations already actively engaged in the bibliographic control of print materials.

There are two such Canadian organizations. First is the National Library of Canada. It differs from the Library of Congress in that it is not an open library serving a particular clientele but an archive preserving the Canadian heritage. Like LC it receives on deposit all books copyrighted in Canada. It publishes *Canadiana,* the national bibliography of Canada, which lists all books published in Canada, about Canada, or by Canadian authors. At present, trade books, pamphlets, federal and provincial government documents, microforms, films, and filmstrips are included in this list. In 1970 phonodiscs and phonotapes have been added. Many of these entries are fully cataloged and classified. The inclusion of other media is being considered in *Canadiana's* long-

Head, Library Technical Services, Borough of East York Board of Education, Toronto

range plans. At the present time educational kits are not deposited unless specifically requested. *Canadiana* issues proofsheets of its cataloging, which are sent to the Library of Congress as the Canadian contribution to the National Program for Acquisitions and Cataloging. The Library of Congress adapts the catalog entries for the *National Union Catalog*. And so in this way a major contribution is made to international bibliographic control. However, *Canadiana* does not list all types of media, nor does it attempt to search out all items produced in the media it does list. Like the Library of Congress, the National Library does not handle the media itself but catalogs from producers' sheets.

The second organization to concern itself with the bibliographic control of media is the Canadian Library Association. The *Anglo-American Cataloging Rules (AACR)* Revision Committee of the Technical Service Section of the CLA acted as consultant in the formulation of the *AACR*. This committee now contributes the Canadian point of view to the revision of these rules. Recently because of pressures brought to bear on it, this committee has interested itself in the revision of part 3 of *AACR*, which deals specifically with nonbook materials. This pressure was generated as a result of the research associated with the writing of *Non-Book Materials: The Organization of Integrated Collections.*

The committee which was associated with *Non-Book Materials* has been disbanded; it was only intended to be temporary, but this voice in bibliographic control has vanished. Still, all parties to the *AACR* revision have agreed that part 3 must be rewritten, and, of course, the Canadian Library Association will be an active participant.

State of the Art in
Great Britain

Antony Croghan

In Great Britain about three years ago our government took a look at the work that was being done in the audiovisual field within the educational system, which was by that time growing quite considerably. The government decided to formalize it by establishing the National Council for Educational Technology with the express purpose of proselytizing, or making certain that it grew in an organized fashion. As part of its effort, the government gave a special responsibility to the University of Sussex which caused the university and its Center for Media Studies to look around and attempt to collect the information within this area.

It became obvious that information was scattered, incomplete, and not very clear about the effectiveness of this newer media. The position was that many media catalogs were compiled in a haphazard fashion to conform to different patterns. The information within them was obviously of value, but not necessarily easy to find. It was not always clear whether they were comprehensive or what were the limits of these catalogs.

The one major catalog, the *British National Film Catalogue*, was organized by a book classification system, and had been working quite satisfactorily on this system for some years without any apparent difficulties. Also within this field were various information agencies, some with published catalogs. Their

job was disseminating information on these media, rather than organizing reference tools so that people could get at them. So the University of Sussex, in conjunction with the National Council for Educational Technology, set up a study for an integrated catalog of all nonbook media, a feasibility study for a catalog of multimedia. I was appointed as the research fellow with my brief being, quite simply, to find out if these media could be integrated within one catalog, and to look at the cataloging and classification of them.

It is remarkably interesting how our three countries—Canada, the United States, and Great Britain—starting off separately at about the same points in time, evidenced the same need almost simultaneously. We took the same definition of *nonbook* as did the Canadians. Any thing that was not a book, including machine-readable forms or -carried information that was not print on paper in words in a line, we looked at it. The basic conclusions that the study came to on the narrow question of an integrated catalog was that all nonbook media were sufficiently common with each other and with print media that they could legitimately be organized by the systems already developed for print media. It was possible to catalog these works and to classify them using the standard systems that already existed for organizing media. It was possible to put them into a computer format that already existed, the MARC II format.

This does not mean and nowhere in the study is the statement made that these systems are adequate of themselves as they stand

Lecturer, School of Librarianship, Northwestern Polytechnic, London

at the moment, to cover all of the problems of nonbook media. The schemes were developed for print, and for nonprint media they will need extending and amplifying. But it is only extension and amplification that is needed. Therefore, the basic devices are already being developed for organizing information-bearing media that happens to be print, and will also serve to organize the information-bearing media that happens to be nonprint.

It also became equally clear that the relatively narrow objective of setting up an integrated catalog for these media to record all of them was indeed a narrow one because it was passive. It would record them, but it made no attempt to advance their utilization. It sat there and needed to be used. Clearly, it should be part of a positive system of information flow, and this system should consist of essentially two parts: a recording of what was there and a method for getting this information, once recorded, into the hands of the people who need to use it, for direct use within the classroom and for other educational purposes.

The term *educational* is used here because the most positive use at the moment is in the educational field. But, do remember that all of us here are constantly being exposed to all of these media. And many of us here, I am certain, visit a favorite movie more than once, just as we reread a favorite book more than once. The generation growing up will expect to have media as readily accessible as we do print media today—in all contexts, not just as a teaching tool—because it will want to see its favorite movies all over again.

The final report of the study itself concluded that it was possible to produce a multimedia catalog. The means to organize it were there, although these means would need extending, and it should be part of a wider system. This report, in conjunction with this media institute that I have been attending, sparked the direction that the further work in his field is now taking in Great Britain. It is following two parallel paths, because there is already a study by the National Council for Educational Technology underway, of the system of information flow. The purposes of this study, it is assumed that we have access to the information. Then, given this, how does

it get into the hands of the people who need it? Should it go through libraries? Do educators prefer asking their colleagues? Do they like to use print tools? Could they pick up a phone and use a computer? These are the kinds of questions that are being asked about information flow. The second work being carried on in the study is, in fact, an extension and amplification of the tools we already have for organizing media.

Therefore, we are looking at the problem of classifying these media, but not from the direction of subject content, for we already know that subject classifications or systems of subject analysis will do this job. Information about audiovisuals remains the same whether on print, on audiotape, on videotape, or whatever. Anyone who is in doubt need only walk through an audiovisual exhibition where you will get information about audiovisual instruction thrown at you in each and every one of these forms. What does differ is the physical form. A videotape is not physically the same as a book. So work has been going on to try to describe and extend this particular area.

Work has also been going on in the attempt to define the special conditions of cataloging these media. A book may be cataloged under author or title. We may not decide which we want to catalog it under, but, at least in a book, we are fairly certain what constitutes an author and title. Even this degree of certainty does not exist in the nonbook field, although work is proceeding in an attempt to find a consensus on this particular matter. One of the ways in which this is being done has already been mentioned, the revision of the *Anglo-American Cataloging Rules.*

This is indeed a joint international code. The words *Anglo-American* are no flourish. This is a joint code among the British, Canadian, and American library associations. It is a geographical accident that the proposal for revision is formally situated in Great Britain for we are simply one partner in a joint project setting it up. This is one of the fields in which work has gone forward on the classification of the physical forms of nonprint media.

This is the direction in which the state of the art is now proceeding in Great Britain.

Question: It seems to be the consensus of your institute that the standard classification systems currently in existence are adequate to handle all media. I haven't personally worked with cataloging media, but the people on my staff who have, feel that there are real problems involved in the retrieval of individual slides, and I stress individual slides because I think they feel very strongly that individual slides need to be retrieved. Would you care to comment on this?

Mr. Croghan: For music I would say that you have got a fairly elaborate code in the chapter of *Anglo-American Cataloging Rules.* If you were to read that and follow it closely, you would come up with some pretty good cataloging for music.

Slides are a somewhat different problem. The basic problem with a slide is that it is a very small piece of information, a separate little bit of information and that you usually have a whole lot of them. When I said the systems that were already developed for book material, I wasn't limiting it solely to classification and I would agree with your people that classification will not handle slides. But the book system called "post-coordinate indexing," using subject descriptors, is one that is very useful for this. A slide usually does not require that many descriptors for it hasn't got enough information on it. Since you want to pull them out individually and no hierarchy is involved, I would certainly adopt a system for slide indexing that is, in fact, a post-coordinate system, using subject descriptors. However, you name your own poison when it comes to subject descriptors. If your slides are with a collection of medicine, for instance, you have MeSH (Medical Subject Headings) that MEDLARS has developed. In other fields, look for a specialized vocabulary and that would be the system I would use, not classification in this instance. But the point I would make to draw the moral, like the Red Queen, is that this is a print system originally which will work for a nonbook application. Not every print system will work for every nonbook media, but for every nonbook media there is an existing system that will work.

British Media-Control Research

Bernard Chibnall

British Organizations

Unless one understands the organizations, what they do, and something of the historical background, I do not think one can see why a particular event took place. There are three organizations in Britain concerned with the documentation of media: the British Film Institute, the National Committee for Audio Visual Aids in Education (NCAVAE) and its associated organization the Educational Foundation for Visual Aids (EFVA), and the National Council for Educational Technology. In addition, there are many small organizations often entirely voluntary or assisted only by one or two clerical staff.

The British Film Institute was established in 1933 to promote the use of films in all aspects of British society. One of its functions was to set up a National Film Archive, which it did in 1935. It is impossible to overestimate the importance of that archive for the whole concept of documentation and scholarly approach to media.

By way of introduction, it should be pointed out that because it was one of the first media (apart from books) to appear in quantity, film has been the media to which most attention has been given in considering the problems of documentation. This study has in the

Director, Media Service Unit; University of Sussex, Brighton

event been beneficial to all media, since film contains, in one form or another, most of the media which have subsequently developed— sound, still pictures, loops, and combinations of these.

Under the direction of its first and present curator, Ernest Lindgren, the archive from the beginning set a high academic standard for its work and soon considered the problem of cataloging film. The second edition of the *Rules for Cataloguing* had appeared by 1952.

In 1949, I was appointed, as a professional librarian, to set up a production, or "stockshot," library in the Shell Film Unit, which required different kinds of rules from an archive, and, as a result, a broadening body of expertise in film cataloging developed. In Paris, United Nations Educational, Scientific and Cultural Organization (UNESCO) had from its foundation been interested in preparing an international catalog of films, which raised cataloging problems of yet a different kind. To meet this need UNESCO, in collaboration with the National Film Archive and other interested organizations (and in consultation with the Library of Congress), published the preliminary edition of *Cataloguing Rules* in 1953 and the first edition in 1956.

So far the emphasis had been on arranging the material so that it could eventually be used by the serious student or scholar. Such persons were still rare, but in 1955, Sir Arthur Elton presented a paper to the annual conference of Aslib, "Film as a Source Material for History,"[1] which presented a detailed examination of the subject and emphasized its future importance. As an immediate result of this paper, the many film librarians in Britain decided to form a group within Aslib. At first it was primarily addressed to production libraries but subsequently included all film librarians. Within the last year, after a moribund period, this group has been reconstituted to concern itself with all media. This group, too, had cataloging problems and set out to produce a new set of cataloging rules, which were published by Aslib in 1963. These took account of the work of the archive, UNESCO, and other film libraries.

The growing interest in the organization of special film collections soon began to draw attention to the paucity of information about films which were available for distribution. The many film catalogs published by film distributors followed no standard pattern, and a vast number were needed to obtain a reasonably complete record of films available. As a result, pressure grew in Britain and in other countries where a similar situation prevailed for a comprehensive national catalog. UNESCO in 1960 set in hand an inquiry to see what national catalogs existed. At a meeting called in London to report to the UNESCO investigator, it was evident that much of the British information already existed, albeit in no one organization. A representative of the *British National Bibliography (BNB)* present at the meeting indicated that it would not be difficult to publish this in a form comparable to the *BNB* if the information could be coordinated.

As a result, steps were taken to establish an organization to do this, and the British National Film Catalogue Ltd. was set up in February 1963. The first bimonthly issue appeared in the same month. The terms of reference of the *Catalogue* were to list all films as they became available in Great Britain, and no attempt was made to document films already available before 1963. Thus by 1963 it was possible to claim that film was reasonably

well documented in the United Kingdom and that machinery existed to keep the documentation procedures up to date.

The next problem was to familiarize users with the information available. This has always been one of the major roles for the various voluntary groups within their own particular areas of interest, but there was clearly a severe limit on what such groups could achieve. The British government eventually recognized this and in 1963 set up a committee under the chairmanship of Professor (now Sir) Brynmor Jones to report on the use of audiovisual aids in higher education in science and technology. It is of interest to note that even as recently as 1963 audiovisual media were thought of only as aids, that it was felt that discussion could usefully be restricted to one section of education, and that it was only in science and technology that they merited consideration. The committee recognized that its terms of reference were unduly constraining and made broad recommendations when it reported in 1965 (Audio Visual Aids in Higher Scientific Education HMSO). They fell into two main categories: a national center, to be set up at a capital cost of £350,000 and a recurrent cost of £260,000, and local service units to be established at a capital cost of £7,000, and recurrent cost of £2,750.

The suggestions were not implemented in detail for several quite sound reasons:

1. There was a lack of finance.
2. The local service units did not exist, and it is not normal British practice to establish a central organization first. It would have therefore been an unusual British procedure to set up a national center before the local groups existed through which it could work.
3. It was clear that the national center would impinge on the work of EFVA and NCAVAE, and it was difficult to decide how to reconcile the interests of the established bodies with those of a quite new organization.

Accordingly, in 1967 the British government set up a National Council for Educational Technology (NCET) whose function was to be to correlate the activities of all the

---

[1] *Aslib Proceedings* 7:207–39 (Nov. 1955).

organizations in the field and, in particular, to advise the minister for education and science on the need for the national center (the negotiations on this topic are just now in hand in 1970). It is interesting, as a measure of developments in the field between 1963 and 1967, to note that audiovisual aids have now become educational technology, with the wider field of activity that phrase connotes, and that NCET is concerned with all education and training in any subject.

Research

With the establishment of NCET, it was possible to consider broad research into the problem of media information. The Office of Scientific and Technical Information (OSTI) set up several years earlier to consider print information, fortunately recognized the importance of organizing all sources of information, whatever their form. As a result, in 1968 I was awarded a research project in the University of Sussex to investigate the feasibility of publishing a multimedia catalog comparable to the now well-established *British National Film Catalogue*. The report, *A Feasibility Study of a Multi-Media Catalogue*, was published in July 1969. It is to be hoped that the publication of such a catalog will be related to the establishment of the National Bibliographic Service recommended by the Dainton Committee Report.[2] NCET was closely involved with the feasibility study and is itself experimenting with cataloging a small multimedia collection on physics.

Since the feasibility study was completed, the University of Sussex has placed particular emphasis on the importance of multimedia collections in the university library. The incorporation of such collections—as opposed to single media collections of slides, tapes, or films—raises many problems, and it is hoped to pursue these in a new research study in the near future.

NCET has also recognized that information stored is not useful in itself. It must be dis-

[2]Report of the National Libraries Committee HMSO 1969 no. 4028.

seminated, and it was soon evident that there was very little knowledge or understanding about how information at present flowed within the field of education. A study was therefore set up to investigate this, and a report is due later in 1970. It is already evident that this is likely to be a pilot study indicating further important fields of investigation.

Relationships between Librarians and Media Specialists and Teachers

It was evident from discussions in the United States that, at present, librarians and media specialists tend often to regard each others professions as having no common ground. However, as media collections grow, the media specialist realizes he needs help to organize them, and as the librarian acquires books with filmstrips, tapes, and gramophone records included, it is evident he has to become familiar with media. Reluctantly, therefore, the two professions are being forced together. It is the experience of some of us who have worked as librarians and in media that this reluctance is quite unnecessary; indeed, it may be positively harmful.

Consideration of media seem to bring to the librarian a much better understanding of what librarianship is all about. This is partly the benefit derived from transferring any activity from one media to another. For example, however lucidly we speak about a subject, it is always a great test of the speakers' understanding if he is required to transcribe his speech into a written text. Another reason may be that there is a tendency to treat the book as a complete unit; we underestimate its incompleteness and its selectivity.

Visual and sound records are obviously incomplete, for we have only what the camera or microphone recorded. Yet paradoxically they are much more difficult to describe completely. In searching through them, with perhaps new questions in our mind, we find so much information recorded which we had not previously noted. Media thus emphasize that information is always incomplete, either because it was not recorded or because we are not in a position to recognize what is recorded. Librarians handling media come to recognize this point as they catalog and classify them. They have continually to decide how significant is the omission of what was not recorded or what they have not noticed. They cannot avoid being selective and consequently must accept that something is left out of the record and of their interpretation of it. They develop their judgment in selection and gain confidence in accepting that something is omitted, and this gives the link to the librarianship of printed materials. In fact, selection and rejection or omission are basic to all library work, for the librarian has continually to decide what to acquire, how to store, and where to classify, and recognize that he is rejecting alternative procedures. If, therefore, media librarianship emphasizes the selection processes, it is reinforcing basic library procedures.

If we now turn to the media producer, he has to decide what to include in what media in what context.

Further, these two analyses can be linked by Lasswell's communication concept:

Who	Librarian	Producer
Says what	Acquires	Includes
In which channel	Stores	In which media
To whom	Classifies	In what context[3]

The teacher on the other hand decides what to say in what way in what context.

There is thus a clear correlation among the three professions, which is not surprising if we recognize that each is concerned with the process of communication. Each is involved with selection and exercises judgment in making it. By implication each has confidence in the process despite the fact that something has been omitted. The learner, too, must select from the information given him that which relates to his need and previous pattern of knowledge and must recognize that much that is offered him must be rejected. We thus see that the learner, teacher, librarian, and media producer have fundamental activities in common, activities which are the true concern of education to promote, those of exercising judgment and developing confidence in the handling of information.

[3]Harold Lasswell, "The Structure and Function of Communication in Society," in *Mass Communications,* ed. Wilbur Schramm (2d ed.; Urbana: Univ. of Illinois Pr., 1960), p.117.

A Feasibility Study
of a Multimedia Catalog

Antony Croghan

My project at Sussex for the National Council of Educational Technology was a feasibility study to see whether we could set up a national catalog for multimedia materials in educational technology.

The objectives of any catalog are:

1. To record the stock available
2. To do it in a way that allows accurate, fast retrieval of all relevant material
3. To provide the order that is the most helpful to the user
4. To provide all reasonable access points to this order
5. To provide for some purposes a substitute, the catalog entry for the actual item itself
6. To do all this in a way amenable to machine manipulation (really a subset of number 2).

The last is a purpose of a catalog that has only recently entered into catalog technology. It is a viable, purposeful one that should be in any catalog in the present day. For a national catalog I added two further objectives. One is the number present to provide a permanent inventory of the national intellectual output. This is one of the jobs of a national catalog as a permanent record. We still use Domesday books for some purposes in England, not very much, but we do use them. The second objective is to set bibliographical standards within the area being cataloged.

Lecturer, School of Librarianship, Northwestern Polytechnic, London

It may help to define terms. *National* is defined in two ways: by area, obviously Great Britain and Ireland, and by audience, and here is where I dropped the limitation of the term *educational*. All interested people in Great Britain, fifty million, might want to use media. This was my audience. If you have a very specialized audience, you may get an easy answer to your cataloging problems. With a very general audience you can fall back on general principles, for an audience of fifty million people does not have one clearly defined objective.

My definition of *multimedia* is a rather long and involved one: all media containing information that is not provided in the form of verbal information in a linear sequence conveyed to the medium of print on paper or any other direct reproduction of this, or nonbook media. It is a negative definition. It assumes that I am going to include everything that is not a book; I mean just that. I started off right from computer tapes down to the model that I use from domestic economy in our country, which has little folders showing herringbone or lazy daisy stitch. These are audiovisual teaching devices, and if they are produced and available for instruction, they should be included in a national catalog.

The method of investigation I used was twofold, only people and things. First of all, to survey I went around and talked to people mainly within the educational situation. Having been a librarian for a very long time, I assumed I knew how people approach libraries. I did go around to the various strata of our education system fairly selectively (I only had ten months for the whole project), relying for my basic selections of people to talk to on the knowledge of my project head, who had been in this field far longer than I had. Coupled with this and going on obviously at the same time was the comparative method for the technical problem. My approach to this was to take a standard that I knew, in this case the print-information solution, and use it as my yardstick against which to measure other things.

For users' needs I distinguished four main categories:

1. Subject information, with which author/titles are included. For my purposes, author/titles come under the generalized headings of subject information.

2. Evaluation of the materials. This was, I think, the most frequently expressed need.

3. Access to specific titles. They wanted to get to a particular film. This need is partly because, at the moment, our media catalogs in Great Britain are predicated on this particular method. This arrangement is what they were used to, and so this is what they said they wanted.

4. The learning need. This did not come up very often, but it was mentioned because of the situation I was in.

I started off on one or two basic assumptions because I was a librarian. The first one is that a good catalog is a good thing. At this point I was not worried that it was a good catalog or that nonprint media was a good thing. As a librarian, I appreciate a good tool and know what I can do with it. The second one, and this applies a little more precisely to the nonprint media, was that these materials were entitled to the utmost sophistication in cataloging that I knew was possible.

The first thing to construct was the actual record itself, the catalog record. A catalog normally describes an item by uniquely identifying it through the author, title, and description; by physically describing it; and by coding in some subject information. The author/title function in a catalog entry is the unique identification of a particular object. This meets, essentially, objective one: You record

that you have got this particular item in your library. The second part of a catalog entry is the description, and the basic function of this is both identification and amplification to meet objectives five and six, substitution and machine manipulation. These are all very general objectives and functions, quite closely interrelated, but I tend to narrow down subject information, which is actually subject description. This essentially meets objectives three and five, order and substitution. If you can learn from a record that the film is about physics and you want a film on chemistry, you have some useful information.

The *Anglo-American Cataloging Rules* does not specify, but it is inherent in the description of notes, that the basic function of any notes, in addition to amplifying the information you have already given, is to provide additional bibliographic data. They fall into two kinds: bibliographic, which essentially amplifies the statement on the catalog, and administrative, which enables one to administer either the record itself or the object; for example, a call number or the statement "This is not available for student loan." A tracing is an administrative note which deals with the administration of the record within a catalog.

The media, in fact, present some special characteristics when you look at them for cataloging. The first one is the problem of where you find the information to be included in the record, the authority for what goes into the record. In the print world, this has been predicated on the very sound principle that the basic authority is the object itself. Take the information from within the book. Because of the physical form of the book, the best authority is the title page itself.

There is a quite practical reason for making the authority inherent in the object rather than in an outside authority, such as a biographical dictionary. The object remains a constant. It is what you are looking for. It is what you will be looking for in a system in 2096 or 3096, and the information you are looking for is that contained within the object. No matter how systems vary, you are still looking for the same object. This is the only constant between systems, and much of the business of information retrieval or information finding is, in fact, searching for a known thing in an unknown system. I know a film exists, and I want to find it in a catalog. The authority of the object and the information that is basic to it are what any two systems will have in common. The user must know how to approach each system.

The problem with media is that this kind of authority does not exist at the moment. With some of the objects, it is not possible to tell where to start looking for the information, and it is not clear to a nonmedia person how much authority the information has. I take my example from film, which is one of the oldest, and certainly the major medium in terms of size. Authority is difficult to discern partly because film has been bedeviled by the trade union practice of everyone getting his name on it. The chap who sweeps the front steps at Paramount gets his name on the credit titles of a Paramount film, or so it seems. This really is a considerable problem if you are an unsophisticated cataloger tucked away with only the film itself to look at. You look at these; you know you want to put in names as handles, very potent retrieval handles, but which names? I think I saw the second production accountant listed in the credit titles of a recent film. He was some clerk who wrote up the bills, but he got his name on the credit titles. Unfortunately, one of our major film codes says that you transcribe the credits exactly. This practice results in an appalling situation.

The principle of proximity strikes me as being a very good one to apply to the information-bearing part of the record. The information nearest the content of the record will fit a title page of a book, or the frame on a filmstrip, or the credit titles on a film. And notice, it is independent of whether or not the credit title comes at the beginning or at the end of a film. It is the bit nearest to the record.

A second problem of cataloging is that media as a class is essentially one of collaborative work. It is very rare that a piece of media is totally the work of one man. The conjunction of the director and scriptwriter is felt in practically all of these media which one has to accept. In relation to print, the standard

I set up, these are what we call collaborative work. There is such a very, very, high proportion of them that I think the cataloging world is going to have to recognize our concept of diffuse authorship. We must assume that there are at least three names on each of these objects to be dealt with. They create a cataloging problem, and one that we would not accept in relation to books, where we tend to talk of a single author. What, in fact, is an author in these things? I am defining the author here as does the Anglo-American code definition, the person primarily responsible for the intellectual or artistic content of a work. Who is that in relation to a media? I am going to stick my neck out and say how I have defined the author for a film. It is a collaborative work, and there are essentially three authors: the director, the cameraman, and the scriptwriter. The director is the principal author, and the cameraman and scriptwriter are secondary authors. That is my definition, a print man's definition.

The one totally distinct area of media for my purposes is the area of physical description of the media, beyond the basic idea of the collation. There is nothing you can draw from the practice of print that will help with this particular problem. For my purposes I had to come up with collations for the media.

A fourth concern is the cataloging problem of dealing with media that are inconvenient to handle. You must plug in machines and insert software, while you need only pick up a book, a very convenient unit, and riffle through its leaves. You can get quite a lot from the book in thirty seconds. You cannot, offhand, riffle through a tape cassette. You have to set up the equipment. If one of the purposes of the catalog record is to provide a substitute for the object itself, this becomes far more important in cataloging media because you cannot get at the object any way quite so easily as you can the book. From the cataloger's point of view this is something we must recognize and accept.

These, I think, are the cataloging problems that are special to the media. There are other problems such as double authors, how many titles, and a choice between the director and the production company, which have essentially been solved in a print context in the Anglo-American code. Though we need actual editing of the code, from all I've heard here, the English version of the code was edited before it was printed and is, therefore, out somewhat before the American edition. Nevertheless, most of these problems have been solved by the code. It is now only a job of translation, not one of invention. Those who genuinely read the first part of the code and do not just dismiss its relevance will, in fact, get many of the solutions they need. The code is for all information-bearing documents, and in that sense a film and a book really do match each other.

On the matter of subject content, which we have been backing around, I will make a flat statement, and I am not open to argument on this one. There is no difference detectable by any of my antennae in the subject content surveyed in any of these media; the problems of cataloging are identical. If my words were being preserved on audiotape and if someone were also making a videotape or immortalizing me in 35mm cinemascope, prints could be made to produce a filmstrip, with or without monaural sound. Whether the final form is a kit, done up in brown, or engraved in Egyptian hieroglyphics on stone, the subject would still be the problems of cataloging nonbook media. The subject content would not vary because of the manner of presentation—media, multimedia, or book.

It is perfectly possible to use with media any of the tools that have derived for these purposes for books—with all their inherent faults, too, even as they are used for books. Applying it to multimedia does not suddenly cure the messiness of the Library of Congress subject headings.

The last special problem or major category we have to consider for the record is the physical form of the object. I have already said that this is an area where we need physical description and something a bit more basic, definitions. What indeed are multimedia? What are the objects? Because I must develop a classification of these, which is a necessity for the catalog and is also enjoined on it, I would say, by the final objective to set bibliographical standards. One of the objectives of this catalog is to develop this kind of taxonomy.

These considerations have given the bibliographical record a shape, one very much like the traditional catalog entry. I am coming up with what most United States librarians will nod their heads to in firm agreement. Rather than an invention of anything new, the result is a record very like a standard book catalog that contains the same kind of elements, some of them in fuller detail.

At this point I want to pull in another strand, which is objective six: to do all this in a way amenable to machine manipulation. One of the fundamentals of computer technology, any computer application, is to put in at the beginning anything you are going to want, anything at all, later from the machine. Going back to add to the store is very, very expensive. The day of the simplified catalog entry is gone forever. The format is not only that of a book, it is a very full record indeed.

Now, what in fact is the format of this record? I said it was a book format. Having these elements, I examined many computer formats, because a format on a card is a relatively simple thing to adjust. It is the computer format here that is the tricky one to decide. Since my method was a comparative one, I took the one I knew best, which was MARC II, examined that and then measured the others against it. Those used by the American Film Institute, the Museums Association, and many others were studied, but none were found to be as detailed as MARC. All contained the same elements; many had much the same kind of structure. The MARC format was the most clearly delineated, best structured, and the most coherent of any of them. Although MARC contained the elements of the other formats, many of them did not have elements included in the MARC format. So I settled at that point for the format based on MARC II, and again I must say based on British MARC II, because with the Library of Congress' permission we have done some development there as well.

With the elements and format of the records established, it is appropriate to consider the order in which these records should be put. Order is essentially an information-conveying device. You put things in order because it is meaningful; otherwise you might leave them in a heap on the floor. One very important order is that based on the learning principles inherent in the idea of educational technology. This is a viable and highly important order that will be needed in the future. I could not construct one in the short time available to me, nor could I find a sufficiently clear statement of one to enable me to produce a taxonomy of the order. Although there are many statements about this, it turned out that there are so many different ones I could not organize a taxonomy. First of all, there did not seem to be a sufficiently stable agreement, either in terminology or within the concepts hidden by the terminology, to enable me to construct a taxonomy. Secondly, I do not think that as of now in England enough people would want this order to make it viable for the catalog. But I would say that production of this other order is very much a future objective.

Related to this is what I have heard discussed here in the United States, but not so much in England, and that is the curriculum orders. All the curriculum orders that I have seen here, to my naïve English librarian's eyes, seem to be simply statements of subject arranged in varying degrees or varying groups or levels. Essentially, they seem to be no more than straightforward algebra, physics, chemistry, high school math, or what have you. If this is true, then curriculum order only becomes a problem of subject order, and we have been dealing with subjects for a very long time. I don't think *curriculum,* in the way I've heard it here, is a very special principle.

There are three standard ordering devices. The first one is the arranging of the records by author, and in relation to the media this one can be dismissed immediately. The author concept, as a concept, is so little developed in this area that it would be a meaningless catalog. This judgment is independent of the concept's merit, which will be dealt with later in this paper.

The second one is the title, and this was an expressed demand of the users. There is a technical point about the title as an arranging device, that is, essentially, an individualizing device. A title arrangement is an arrangement of single member classes, and although each title is designed uniquely to identify the object, it may not do so. Each author of a *Manual for the Cataloging on Nonbook Materials* thought he was labeling his own particular work quite uniquely. If one were producing an order of single member classes, this order would convey very little information. It allows very easy access to a specific item, but, except by accident of the alphabet (from the accident of generalized titles, perchance *Manual of the Cataloging of Nonbook Materials*), you get very little extra information from this kind of order. The construction of references then needed is an elaborate business and, in my view, not worth the candle.

The third method is to arrange the material by subject content. This order was a formally expressed wish, though not mentioned so often as the title, which was requested partially due to conditioning; if one has been accustomed to asking for these media by a particular method, then he tends to feel it is the only method. Subject information was a fairly widely expressed need of the educational user. It is certain that this is one of the primary needs of the ordinary user as expressed by libraries. My conclusion, quite firmly, was that this was going to be a subject catalog. Each of these decisions narrows down one's choice. One starts from fairly general objectives, and at each stage the elimination of things narrows them down. We must now address ourselves to the problem of subject order.

The subject of a document can be expressed primarily in two ways, either verbally (a statement using words) or encoded in some fashion. Both can be either structured or unstructured. Unstructured methods, whether verbal or coded, need a machine of some kind to deal with them. They will, therefore, be postponed until the discussion of computerization. It is assumed at this point in the catalog development that we are settling for a structured subject arrangement. This can be done verbally. The best example of structured verbal headings, and the one known most widely, is the Library of Congress subject headings. They unquestionably make up the largest collection of structured verbal headings in existence. It is also one of the worst subject heading lists we have. It is in its seventh edition, the first being started in 1896, and subject headings have been added since that date. Revisions have, in my view, been only slight revisions of specific terms and rearrangements, a fact which leaves us with a "layer cake" of subject headings, dating back some seventy years. We now have the biggest, if not the best, list, which is so difficult to use with consistency that I would never suggest that anyone making a serious catalog use it. Should one, in fact, want to use structured verbal headings, the energy needed to evolve a method for handling the Library of Congress list would be far better put into devising his own rules for constructing subject headings. They would be far more consistent than an attempt to tidy up someone else's.

It would be most valuable if the Library of Congress, which is putting the subject headings on tape, will use the capability of a machine to do this, in which case we would have a very good subject headings list. At the moment it cannot be done, although it is a perfectly viable system for structured verbal headings. A very good example is the *British Technology Index,* which has verbal subject headings arranged on a structured pattern, from which subject information can be retrieved quickly, providing you know the rules of the system. Unfortunately, the printed page is very messy. Part of the machinery is that there are references numbering far more than the average dictionary catalog in this country.

Catalogers get frightened when they put the fifth *see* or *see also* reference in front of a heading and begin to feel they should stop there, but often five or six *see also* references are needed. At times seven, eight, nine, or ten references may be required to assure retrieval of the information. Putting these in, in fact, produces a very complicated machinery, one so complicated that, frankly, for the average user it would not be worth it. So, I came back to the classified catalog. I was, generally throughout this project, trying to approach things with an unbiased attitude towards media. I tried not to make any assumptions at the outset. It was interesting to have a chance to measure these basic assumptions against something else, and so I genuinely worked through the idea of the subject catalog.

A subject classified catalog is based on a classification scheme, which brings to mind a point worth mentioning. The physical form of a printed book catalog minimizes one of the great disadvantages of a classification scheme, which is its notation. If you have an array of records in front of you, it helps to demonstrate the shape of the classification scheme. This, in turn, makes the notation more coherent and easy to understand. There are only three possible candidates for a general catalog to cover all subjects in Great Britain in 1969. The first is the Library of Congress Classification, and it was just dismissed straightaway for two reasons: it is not particularly well known or used in Great Britain, and for the purposes of machine manipulation, it is in my view, far less efficient than the other two candidates. These two reasons together were sufficient to discard it immediately.

The choice then, lay between the decimal classification of Melvil Dewey and the Universal Decimal Classification (UDC). There is a body of experimental evidence to show that any indexing system used to its full capacity has more or less the same relative efficiency. Both Dewey and UDC, considered solely as subject classification, work at about the same level. So the choice between these two then hinged on extraneous factors. The virture of UDC is that it is infinitely flexible, but this is not a virtue that is necessary in a printed catalog. A printed catalog's order has been chosen anyway, a fact which is advantageous in machine manipulation.

Dewey is much less specific and its order is more rigid, but against that, it has two advantages. It is the best-known classification in our country, not in technical terms, but when people talk of the numbers on the backs of the books, if you ask them for an example, they will invariably say a Dewey notation. The second advantage is that it is being used by our major national bibliographic agency, the *British National Bibliography.* These two were the basic arguments for choosing the Dewey Decimal Classification rather than the Universal Decimal Classification.

The major form of the catalogs is then a classified catalog, arranged by the decimal classification with a very full record. The subject entry is, I may say, totally specific. To accomplish this, we go as far as possible in Dewey, then extend the subject statement in Dewey with a verbal statement. The *British National Film Catalogue,* containing films only, is the type of classified catalog to which I have been referring. This particular one is actually arranged by the Universal Decimal with the verbal extension and a straightforward statement of the subject itself before the presentation of the record.

I will specify for my catalog an author arrangement within the subject, because if these media grow, as it appears they are going to over a period of years, who made the film is not going to become important. At the moment, you tend to take a film because, in England anyway, it is the only one on the subject, and you do not, to a certain extent, care who made it. Once you get to the stage that we have with books where you can choose among five histories of England, then you start asking who wrote which history. Having read a good history of England by a particular person, if you then want a history of France and find the same man has also written one, you can then take this as being valuable to your selection criteria. It is no more than a recognition of the author concept, and I want to sneak it in under the subject arrangement.

This way you provide an author index, *author* being the generalized person responsible, and you include with this a title index, because this is the need expressed most. People want to get at information by title. For this particular catalog I suggest that under the title we put a very brief entry sufficient to identify the work so that those who only want one particular film can get sufficient detail without having to go to a classified sequence. The user does not want, at that point, the information that a subject arrangement can give him, but rather he wishes to know about one particular film.

The subject index will also be of two kinds. One is the procedure called chain indexing, which simply repeats the order of the scheme. It is an economical way of producing a fairly deep index right down to the specific subject. Its limitation is that it shows only the relationship already built into the classification scheme,

actually a mirror image of these relationships. There is another technique of indexing called Selective Listing in Context (SLIC) which, in fact, permutes selective terms to show most of the possible relationships within these contexts. This is of course a much fuller index. A classified catalog with author and subject indexes with a considerable degree of detail creates a very full catalog.

The implementation of the catalog is a particularly significant aspect at the outset, for it is of little use to design a tool that will not work. A tool that is technically perfect but which no one is prepared to purchase, is hardly feasible. Even though it may be designed on the highest principles, it will not work because it is too expensive. The basic thing is to get the catalog implemented. To accomplish this, the concept of thrift or cost effectiveness must be applied. Cost effectiveness does not mean cutting costs, but rather getting value for what you spend—two very different ideas.

I began with the assumption that I was going to include everything that was nonbook, and up to now, no limitations of the media on these terms have been made; but at this point two kinds of media were firmly excluded. One was the whole field of recorded music as distinct from sound. There were two reasons for this. The first is theoretical, for to me music is a special cataloging problem requiring that it all be cataloged together in its various forms —sheet music and recorded sounds—as they belong, for indexing purposes, together. We have already in England a catalog of music. The second reason concerned implementation. Recorded music in fact, amounted to about 50 percent of the items to go into the catalog. By excluding one particular media, the size and therefore the physical cost and indexing cost were reduced. Through this, the cost of publishing the catalog was reduced sufficiently to make publication possible. If recordings could have been gotten in cheaply, they would have been put in, but it was going to cost a great deal to include this one media.

The second minor exclusion may be grouped as microforms. In my view, the record of a microform of a book belongs with the appropriate entry in a catalog listing of books; it is simply another form of reproduction. The record of that microform will be identical to the book record except for the collation and statement "microform" or whatever. At this point they are excluded from the nonbook catalog.

Implementation of the catalog was always intended right from the first as being in two forms. One was a printed form and the other a machine-readable form, the latter eventually to generate the printed form. There are a relatively small number of these multimedia items, perhaps only three thousand a year published in Great Britain: 10 percent of the number of book titles published in Great Britain each year. It is a small amount in terms of organization. So, it was intended that the cataloging be done on the scale appropriate to machine-readable records; that is to say, very full indeed. For the printed version, which was to appear during the first five years, a subset will be used. It involved an element of redundancy in terms of cataloging effort and in rental space because I wrote in that these full records had to be kept. When the cost of the input machine system is amortized over five years, cost effectiveness and thrift, but not cost saving, result. Immediate costs could have been reduced quickly by simply reducing the level of indexing, but, in fact, I did not.

It looks very much as though the machine capabilities are going to come much earlier than I thought, which will be a real bonus. The MARC format was accepted not only because it was the best format, but because I am thrifty and I realized that the MARC personnel are going to catalog all books published in Great Britain and the United Kingdom. People are going to be using MARC and developing programs and techniques and working with them. I want to be able to come along in five years' time and borrow them or take the spin-off from all this effort. MARC is a sort of basic tool for the purpose of cataloging. The technological spin-off from the surface of cataloging was an additional reason for using MARC. The media field will not be able to generate programs, for it is not big enough to afford them, but it is big enough to use them if someone else will pay for their development.

Cataloging will initially be from paper; that is, information about the media rather than the media themselves. It would cost too much to buy three thousand items a year just to catalog them and then throw them away. If you are performing a bibliographical service not attached to any particular institution, this is what you do, which means that it was not going to be feasible for my project. In fact, events again overtook me during the year, and the idea of a national collection of media material is now in the wind. A national center would, of course, acquire the material, thus enabling the cataloging to be made, most of the time, from the object itself. However, the initial assumption was, I am afraid, that we would catalog it from paper. Three separate recommendations are in order: one, that we start a separate national discography (though I do leave out this particular media), and that work should start immediately on cataloging our gramophone records. Two, that the catalog should not be considered to have reached its final form until its fifth year of publication. I was not designing a complete system for the first issue but an initial catalog that was going to grow over five years. My final recommendation is that, before these five years are up, considerations should be given to incorporating the multimedia catalog with the book catalog and the discography as well.

This presentation began as a study for a multimedia catalog and ends with an outline for a possible media catalog, because it seems to me far more useful in these terms. We as learners and users need our information and learning tools in all of the various media.

Question: I put the initial article on the right side of the title, but there are many people in this country who still feel that the article is sacred and must remain on the left side of the title. Would you comment on this?

Mr. Croghan: Until you brought my attention to it, I had not even noticed and frankly do not care. I have no strong view, but I would certainly disregard the article in any filing system.

Question: Would this placement be confusing on a general basis?

Mr. Croghan: No, for the patron is not looking at the whole of this system, but rather for only one particular citation. He only wants one of these media from those displayed on the page. He looks at the printed arrangement, which helps isolate the item. Now if he really *does* want everything on a subject without winnowing, it can only be guaranteed by the use of this kind of machinery. He might not like the machinery, but he will accept it. Today a library catalog is not the concern of a layman. You cannot design a very highly sophisticated system to deal with the extremely complex knowledge we have now, with the layman or the junior high school boy in mind. But, in point of fact, a junior high school boy can compete. We are much less nervous about notation in Great Britain. In England long Dewey numbers are a nuisance, not a problem; that really is the attitude. We would rather have short numbers, but we do not worry about it.

Question: What is the decision-making body concerned with your feasibility study?

Mr. Croghan: It was a joint project of the Office of Scientific and Technical Information and the National Council for Educational Technology. My project head is officially on committees of both.

Question: Can we go back to this point of user needs and level of sophistication?

Mr. Croghan: I was designing this catalog for the bullied, persecuted British reader who can hardly sneak into our public libraries without being terrified by the likes of me. We have him where he will accept anything we give him. For Americans it is genuinely different; they are much less frightened of the librarians. Nevertheless, I did get a very fine integrated multimedia catalog from the independent

schools in San Diego and had quite a long correspondence with them about the catalog. It is a very fine example indeed of a catalog arranged by *Dewey.*

American classifications are relatively simple, you know. Some of their creators actually refuse to give up the decimal point. Because I had the impression that Americans do not like classified catalogs, I asked the librarians if the users have had much difficulty in using classified catalogs or not. I got back a flat statement from the San Diego school system that they had no difficulty is using it' and appreciated the virtue of a classified directory.

Comment: I think it is a matter of orientation, because there is much concern now that the LC list will become classified. If it ever does, you know there will be a lot of changes in the whole user orientation to information.

Mr. Croghan: I should perhaps break it to you good and early that the *British National Bibliography* is coming up with a very elaborate classification that will do an enormous number of things, far more than UDC will do. If you want three-figure *Dewey,* you have to accept three-figure *Dewey* order with all the limitations. If you want a sophisticated, flexible, highly manipulative device for information retrieval, which is the least we can demand in 1969, one of the penalties you must pay, and cannot escape, is a concentrated notation. You make it as simple as possible, but you cannot make it a simple effort. Luckily, the computer can cope with any kind of complicated notation, provided you can define what the complications are.

Feasibility
of Establishing
Bibliographic Control
of Media

Joseph Becker

In the library profession we have used the word *standards* before. We have public library standards, for instance, but they have been more concerned with quality objectives of the profession than with the rigid rules and regulations which must support the problems of bibliographic control. When we think of standards, we have to adjust our thinking a little from the kind of standards we have been accustomed to talking about. As far as bibliographic-control standards are concerned, historically within the library profession we have accepted common practices for the handling of bibliographic data. These have been formalized to the extent that within the American Library Association there have been intensive sessions over a number of years to establish, for example, the American Library Association cataloging rules. These went through several revisions, and, most of us know, produced a volume about two inches thick. It represents a consensus of views within the profession on the way in which printed materials are to be treated bibliographically.

There have been other informal, or less formal, types of common practices established, the existing teletypewriter networks among various libraries, for instance. When a group of

President, Becker and Hayes, Inc., Bethesda, Maryland (library automation consultants)

libraries becomes involved in a teletypewriter network, representatives generally meet to establish a method of operation. They establish, for instance, the times of the day in which the network will operate; the way in which information will be communicated back and forth over the devices so that there would be some commonality in terms of appearance on the printed page and some commonality with respect to the kinds of bibliographic information which will accompany an interlibrary loan request. In some places, they actually display the bibliographic elements of information in the format of the American Library Association interlibrary loan form, in order to encourage commonality of understanding.

Formal machinery is available in this country for establishing standards and even bibliographic-control standards. This machinery is a bit fragmented, but it has some kind of homogeneity to it. There is the National Bureau of Standards, for example, whose job it is to do just this sort of thing. The National Bureau of Standards generally acts after the fact rather than before. Historically, the National Bureau of Standards has waited until some segment of our national society has done something, which, in turn, has been proved through practice. At this point, all parties meet and they establish the standard. Rarely is the standard established in advance, as you might expect. The second organization is the American National Standards Institute, which has a number of subdivisions concerned with various kinds of standards for many segments of our national life. Most of them have nothing to do with libraries, but there is one group within the American National Standards Institute, which does concern itself with libraries, the Z39 Committee. Jerrold Orne of North Carolina, as the chairman, invites librarians to work with him in this area of bibliographic standards. We do have liaison with both the American National Standards Institute, which is the principal standards institute in the United States, and the National Bureau of Standards for developing and establishing formal standards if we so desire. There is also the International Standards Organization, which is an international body. It meets periodically to discuss the same issues. For example, the International Standards Organization group has been very much concerned recently with problems of copyright, and it has also discussed questions of bibliographic control. Henriette Avram, who was largely responsible for the MARC II project at the Library of Congress, delivered an address last year to the International Standards Organization. She has had discussions with them about the possibility of their accepting Machine Readable Cataloging (MARC) as a standard.

If we speak of bibliographic control of the media and how we go about developing standards for it, maybe the thing to do is to look at the way in which MARC was developed, because basically I view it as a standard. This experience took a little more than two years from beginning to end in terms of total cycle time. I think it represents a good case study of the way in which you might proceed. There are a number of elements to MARC's history. There was a developmental stage; there was an interface stage; there was a synthesis stage: an approval stage; and there was an implementation stage. In the development stage the Council on Library Resources gave seed money to the Library of Congress, which led to a first attempt at a bibliographic standard.

Mrs. Avram is not a librarian, although I think after two or three years, she may have become one whether she realizes it or not. She is basically a computer programmer who has had considerable experience in the computer field and in the handling of nonnumerical records. She learned something about cataloging through her discussions at the Library of Congress. Then she designed the MARC I format, which was a first step in laying out on a magnetic tape all the bibliographic elements of information that she and her colleagues at Library of Congress could perceive would ever be wanted. This meant organizing the various elements of data and, from her viewpoint, laying them out in such a way that it would facilitate computer processing for both processing purposes and collection purposes.

Officials of the Library of Congress invited various libraries to participate in a pilot group. They intended to make available the MARC I tapes, not in any periodic manner, that is not week after week, but once in a while. These tapes, with some small associated programs, were to be made available to the pilot group of libraries who were to work with them any way they wanted, experimentally, provided that the sum and substance of their review would be shared with other experimenters at some time. This worked very well. Sixteen libraries requested to participate in MARC I, far more than Library of Congress anticipated. They were mostly university libraries, but they also included one public library among them, one state library system, and possibly one school system as well. Various types of libraries, then, had an opportunity to work with the tapes and review their experience with them. That type of pragmatic approach to the MARC tapes led to questions and discussions and a more general understanding about the potential of the tapes.

At the end of the MARC I phase, there was not only a written record of this experience but a much clearer understanding of just how to go about shaping MARC II, in terms of its format, for a practical working library situation. We saw the establishment of a strawman, to be knocked down and changed somewhat by the libraries that were actually working in different settings with bibliographic data. All this activity led to the MARC report as well as to a change in the content of the MARC record itself. Those discussions were not easy ones to conduct, but they did result in a much wider consensus and agreement with respect to the elements of data that should be included on the tape. This activity not only led to changes in the identification of new elements, or changes in the way they were being tested, but also to a new concept developed by Mrs. Avram of the most efficient way for the computer to treat and process the data, based on what she understood would be their size, length, and the number of characters. Some libraries needed to suppress some of the information, and some others needed to add new information. That initial experimental period was valuable. It was valuable to the libraries, because they understood more clearly the kinds of processing that would be involved in MARC. It was valuable to the profession, because it caused the group to decide on the basic elements of information which should be included in MARC. It was valuable to the Library of Congress, because through it Mrs. Avram was able to perceive a much more efficient approach to the treatment of the record as far as the computer was concerned and an awareness of the ways in which this particular record would have to interface with other things. I have just now concluded the discussion of the development part of this cycle.

The interface, after the development of this record, divided finally into three basic parts. One was computer processing, or how the elements of information are put on the tape in order to facilitate processing by computer. Mrs. Avram capitalized on developments within the computer field itself within the last ten years. For example, at the head of the MARC record, there is a leader which is essentially a label to facilitate the processing of the MARC tape by any computer installation. There is a standard way in which to examine the beginning of any file in order to understand what is on that file itself, in terms not only of the kinds of data which are on it but also of the sequence in which they are stored. There is also a built-in system for locating specific information. There is a numerical record at the beginning of the tape designating at what point on the tape a particular tag is located, and what number of characters follow that particular tag. In this way, there is an index to the whole layout of the tape itself. From the processing viewpoint,

it simplifies the way in which the tape is searched and the way in which users will print the various elements of information which are on the tape. There is an important relationship to computer processing, and that structure, that sequence, that layout is at the moment very efficient in terms of processing in a third-generation computer. It was not just a casual arrangement, but a very important interface problem that Mrs. Avram faced.

The second interface area that she recognized had to do with communications. The American National Standards Institute and the National Bureau of Standards have agreed to something called the ASCII, the American Standard Code for Information Interchange. This code was designed long before librarians became interested in mechanized bibliographic control. It was designed by communications people and computer people at the time that the second-generation machines were becoming passé, and they were planning the third-generation machines. They wanted to make the interface between communications and computers as smooth as possible. Manufacturers, who had been organizing their bits for the different characters of their particular system in different ways, agreed that they would adopt an American code for the exchange of information between computers and communications.

Communications manufacturers built their equipment in such a way that they could anticipate that an *A* would always be an *A*, a *B* would always be a *B*, and a slash mark would always contain a certain number of bits and be arranged in a certain way. They agreed on the way in which information was to be mechanically transferred from a computer to a communications device and back again. Mrs. Avram was aware of this, and in the development of MARC, she made sure the MARC data was laid out so that, without any complications or additional processing, the data could leave a computer, enter a communications system, and return again. The communications interface, and particularly with the ASCII, was another secondary area to which she had to pay considerable attention.

The third area had to do with electronic printing. In bibliographic control you cannot ignore the requirements for printing, whether it is for a book catalog or a selected bibliography or anything else. You must think in terms of the kinds of diacritical marks required or the types of symbols needed. The library profession did not understand what character set constituted our particular domain or printing interest in the drive in electronic photocomposition machines. Many sessions were held at the Library of Congress trying to iron out exactly how far to go. Do you include all the letters of the Greek alphabet, for example? The character set prescribed in the ASCII did not take into account Greek characters, but we know for our printing purposes that we *do* have to take into account Greek characters. Mrs. Avram had to anticipate the requirements for printing with electronic devices and build her character set accordingly, to be nearly universal, to satisfy as many needs as possible.

These are the three areas of interface. One is computer processing, the layout of the record. One is communications, to be sure that the contents of that record can be transmitted and received easily over communications lines. The third is to make absolutely certain that we have taken into account as much as we can in terms of the needs of printing. Maybe you can think of others; I cannot, not even in terms of bibliographic standards for the new media.

I mentioned the development, the interface of the three parts, and then the synthesis of the results. The latter was accomplished through a series of meetings at the Library of Congress, and they led to the MARC II record itself. The fourth stage is approval. How do you go about getting approval for a bibliographic standard? First, we felt that before proceeding to the Z39 Committee of the American National Standards Institute there was some work to do within the profession. The Information Science and Automation Division, the Reference Services Division, and the Resources and Technical Services Division, all divisions of the American Library Association, were given an opportunity to react. The three divisions formed an interdivisional committee which eventually endorsed the MARC II record and format. The format was also submitted to COSATI, the Committee on Scientific and

Technical Information, in Washington, which led to an agreement among the federal agencies that considered using it. The Library of Congress, the National Library of Medicine, and the National Agricultural Library agreed that they will indeed use the MARC format for materials which they process. This agreement was an important step in itself, since usage often dictates standards. Richard Kalb, of the *British National Bibliography,* spent six weeks with the Library of Congress, working in the direction of putting the *British National Bibliography* (BNB) in MARC II format. I understand the British are accepting the format almost as is with very slight modifications.

Comment: They have added some slight extension that gives it a more related format within the same process. The basic format only calls for classification numbers, but the *BNB* format is deliberately going to press and cards are already being printed from the MARC tapes.

Mr. Becker: The National Central Library of Florence has been publishing, through its national bibliography, monthly lists of the books published by Italian publishers for the last eight years. They have done a complete conversion of the monthly lists for the last eight years by keypunch, one of the largest conversion jobs that I have ever seen anywhere in my experience. It amounts to several millions of characters and something like 600,000 different titles, which were later placed on tape. Fause produced a 30-volume cumulative set of these 960 monthly publications, so that now Italian bibliographers can actually go to one source for all the titles of a given author or given subject. Diego Montavia, who is head of the national bibliography, is also thinking in terms of MARC. Just as the Library of Congress gets two copies of everything that is copyrighted, so the national bibliography of Florence is on the list for all publishers. All Italian imprints are sent to Dr. Montavia, and he catalogs them. If he were to catalog them according to a MARC worksheet, he would be able to produce, as Britain is going to produce, tapes for the Italian national bibliography that would be equivalent to the MARC tapes for American imprints and the British tapes for

British imprints. The tremendous opportunity that this presents eventually for an exchange of tapes should be obvious. We would be getting the best-quality processing of national bibliographies in each country available to the others. If these interfaces for communications and printing are taken into account, then the exchange does not necessarily have to be through the mail. It can lead to the printing of cumulative bibliographies in whatever type font and style we choose to have. This rosy relationship I described in Britain and Italy does not apply to France, and I do not think it applies to Germany, although West Germany has been making overtures recently to the Library of Congress about this.

In speaking about standards, common practices and protocols, mentioning the historical development of MARC and the various ways in which it developed, including the process of informal approval by professional endorsement, national library acceptance, and international usage, my purpose has been to encourage you to think in terms of using either the MARC approach or the format itself for the media. While I am not so familiar with the requirements of the media as you are, I do know that the format is not designed exclusively for monographs. It can be applied to serials or to maps; it can be applied to various forms of information. Why not apply it to the media?

Comment: The computer interface, the communications interface, and the electronic printing interface have already been taken care of for us. Now we need seed money, some development effort, some experimentation, and we should draw some conclusions on how to proceed.

Comment: Sometimes a steering group is needed. If you proceed on the premise that the MARC II format is applicable to nonprint media, and I can assure you from a mechanical viewpoint it is, then a steering group decides from a substantive or subjective viewpoint what the tag layout will be. It seems to me that you can follow the process of development which has been described. Perhaps a dozen places in the country might test it for a while to see what "bugs" develop. From that experi-

ence, we may be able to reach agreement on how it should be accomplished.

Comment: It would appear to me that to get an organization which already has a large data bank to change to the MARC format, there will have to be some kind of an incentive.

Comment: There is no claim in the MARC format that you should change immediately. The point about standardizing is that when you reach the point of change for your old system needs, there is something which you can consider when you need to change. I would not expect any working system to change over to the MARC format if it has a workable format of its own, except at the point where its own system provokes the need for change. The central core of the MARC format is that MARC is designed with a flexible format so that you don't have to say, "MARC format," but you say, "I want this kind of catalog." There are some libraries now that have their materials in a format other than MARC, but in a machine-readable form, and have written programs. They can convert or transpose the data which were in another format into the MARC format. This is simple, mechanically; although it may be difficult professionally when you are using a different authority file. Strictly from a machine conversion viewpoint, it is possible to go from one to another in most cases.

Comment: The Educational Media Index was conceived originally as a noncopyrighted item, to be open and available to everyone. The idea was a good one then, and still is. However, a great mistake was made in letting the *Index* go to a private publisher rather than ultimately requiring the government to print it. Publishers bid for the right to publish, and there were several bids, but no one was willing to publish without the copyright. That is where the real problem came. The only way we will ever really attack the problem is to have a government agency perform the service. Where do you go when you cannot get support from the federal government? You go to private business. This is the way these things go. I do not think we can really continue that kind of arrangement. We have to have the same thing for media that we have for books.

Modern College Libraries

Trevor N. Dupuy

It has been twelve to eighteen months since I completed the *Study to Develop a Research Program for the Design Development of Modern College Libraries.* In preparation for this paper, I thought I should inquire about what had been happening since then in the academic library world. In particular, I wanted to contact some of those institutions which could give me considerable insight into the new developments, either because they had progressed so rapidly in the past or had progressed so little in the past. I felt I could get some useful reactions and that I could observe trends in what they had to say about these developments in the past year and a half. I prepared a questionnaire (Appendix, p.151), which I sent to thirty-eight people, twenty-four of whom responded. Of these twenty-four, nineteen responded directly to the questions; five of the responders supplied useful data which did not match the questionnaire.

These responses contribute to whatever is new in my thoughts on current trends in college programs and multimedia programs beyond what you can find in the slightly outdated material in my two books.[1] The material in these books, however, is not as outdated as I would have hoped, and the movement has not been as great as I had hoped.

I did get some other helpful reactions. For instance, I had a visit from Robert Taylor, director of the Hampshire College Library. Here is a man who is truly exploring the frontiers of academic librarianship as I, an outsider, observe it. He and his people are producing papers and holding meetings, with some substantial funding, to help him produce a first-rate library. You may wish to explore what he is doing in trying to make his library a local information center, in which books and all of the other things are as integrated as their differing formats will permit. He has a concept of the extended and experimenting college library which I think that most of you will find quite interesting.

Robert Hayes, director of the Institute of Library Research at the University of California at Los Angeles, in quite a different way, is also exploring the frontiers of modern academic librarianship.

I would now like to comment on the various responses that I got to my questionnaire. First, however, I should speak about the problems of interpreting these responses. This questionnaire went to places where there had either been considerable forward-looking activty when I was doing my research a year ago or to places that I felt were quite backward. I interpret each of the responses quite differently. Sometimes a *no* or a *no change*

Executive Director, Historical Evaluation and Research Organization, McLean, Virginia

[1]*Ferment in College Libraries: The Impact of Information Technology* (Washington, D.C.: Communications Service Corp., 1968) and *Modern Libraries for Modern Colleges* (Washington, D.C.: Communications Service Corp., 1968)

means that the considerable activity that was going on a year ago is still going on. For instance, most of my responses from Oral Roberts University were *no* or *no change,* but this does not mean that nothing is being done at Oral Roberts University. I think that the number of yeses and noes gives a false impression.

First, in the response to automation in college libraries, the relationship of two to fifteen, I am afraid, is one which does not need to be interpreted. The use of computers continues to move slowly, disappointingly slowly, in light of the state of the art of computer science. In light of the unquestioned potential of the use of computers for administrative purposes and for important information control purposes in the future, I think that this warrants an investigation. Why does the situation as I discussed it in my report still seem to be continuing?

In the use of microforms the situation is considerably better. The potentialities of microform are still far from being fully explored or exploited, but a number of them have been discovered and are being pursued vigorously. In my preparation of this questionnaire, I did not think to raise questions about ultramicroforms, but I think that they, too, can be of increasing use to all academic libraries, particularly new libraries. By this I mean libraries of new colleges which have to build up their collections quite quickly.

The question on the use of other nonprint media is one that was obviously rather poorly phrased. It was too general, too vague, and the response certainly required some interpretation. The noes included all of those institutions which were making considerable use of all kinds of media and also included those libraries and institutions where media are controlled completely outside of the library. In the light of the institutions from which the yeses did come, I interpret the response as reflecting a substantially growing awareness of and interest in the potentiality of nonprint media in the learning process at schools which had been slower in the past than some of the more advanced institutions.

The dial-access response of one yes and fifteen noes was to me surprisingly negative and suggests even more emphatically the need

for research. The completely negative response on programmed learning was even more surprising, however. Perhaps my sample was too small, or perhaps I did not phrase this quite correctly.

On reprography the response is not as negative as it appears. The use of reprography was almost as widespread as it could possibly be when I first made my survey. I have included it here adjacent to a query on networks mostly to see if it stimulated any comments about linking reprography with networks; however, I suspect that there cannot be too much progress in this area until the question of application of the copyright law to current reprography practices is clarified. Networks can be either very, very simple and rudimentary or they can be quite complex, but I was thinking of a more sophisticated electronic network of the kind that EDUCOM (Interuniversity Communications Council) is holding out as the potentiality of the future, a highly sophisticated electronic network. There probably can not be as much progress in the area as one would hope until the application of copyright laws is clarified.

Networks. Here the balance of twelve noes to three yeses is a valid reflection of what has seemed to me to be a somewhat dismal lack of progress in cooperation. There are more sophisticated ways of answering this, which really are, at least theoretically, available. The three yeses represented a very rudimentary kind of progress such as the facilitation of interlibrary loan procedures. I still see the kind of networks which EDUCOM has been talking about as being beyond the beginning of the next century.

One of the more promising network experiments which was going on when I was doing my survey, the New England network, has apparently failed to operate as planned. Unfortunately, I did not get a reply from the man who I think could have answered this for me. I suspect the reason I did not was because this project of which he was so confident had not gone well. Because of the somewhat ambiguous response I received from one person connected with the Pittsburgh library center, I had gotten the impression that the Pittsburgh network activity had not gone as well as had been hoped. Walter Stone has reassured me, however, that it is moving in the direction of true cooperation among the numerous libraries in Pittsburgh and the immediate vicinity. Perhaps my negative interpretation is too negative. Responses on educational television indicate that here, too, the progress is very slow.

The question on the mechanization of administration probably should not have been included, for it is doubtful that the subject warrants it. In the area of selective dissemination of information, progress seems to be inadequate, but again the query was perhaps inadequate. I have been thinking in terms of capabilities of modern information storage and retrieval. Again, I have to suggest that the query was not properly worded. The other information systems activities in mind were thought of very specifically in terms of information storage and retrieval, and I had hoped that a general query would elicit more response; obviously I was wrong.

On the use of electronic carrels, the fifteen to one negative response is, you will note, identical to that on the dial-access systems, and I think that the comments to be made are also identical. Several of the responders noted that the use of audio-tutorial techniques did not seem to them to be a library responsibility, and this belief unquestionably had some influence on the twelve to four response. However, I do interpret the results more positively than this numerical relationship, in part for the same reason that I took a favorable view on the thirteen to four response on the question of media in general. There is a clear trend in the direction of the use of audio-tutorial techniques. I personally think this is a good thing despite the remarks of those who felt this was outside the field of library interests. I firmly believe this is of significance to librarians.

I have in one way or another reflected the comments that I got in reply to question 2 in what I just said on the queries under question 1. Now, questions 3, 4, and 5 are closely related; all have to do with the issue of the relationship of the library to media services and the coordination of library services and media services, either voluntarily or through administrative control. In general, I would say that the results of these questions, at least, were encouraging. There is a trend toward greater voluntary collaboration, while the various administrations are also apparently beginning to recognize the need for coordination and control from the standpoint of efficiency and cost effectiveness. On question 6, concerned with faculty attitudes and practices, the results are at least mildly encouraging. Bearing in mind again that some of the responders come from institutions which have been active in exploring new approaches, these responses suggest that there is a definitely increasing use of both library and media services by faculty and students. Faculty members are increasingly recognizing their responsibility to encourage students to research and explore for themselves. Similarly, there seems to be real interest among faculty members in experimenting with new teaching techniques. The library college movement does not seem to have made much progress, a phenomenon to me somewhat surprising in the light of the intensive effort of the library college advocates to drum up enthusiasm. I suspect that most of the potential membership find the concept somewhat unreal and see other more practical ways to attack the problems which the library college movement is intended to solve. I find it very difficult to reconcile the responses to the query 6g on educational use of computers with the responses to questions 1a and 1e.

For the most part, the responders to question 7 saw little or no significance in the pattern of responses to question 6. Four, however, did see some significance, and I think I got some of the more valuable results of my questionnaire from those four responses. Patricia Knapp, of the Department of Library Science at Wayne State University College of Education, said about questions 6 and 7 together:

For a number of obvious reasons, college and university faculty members, I believe, are much more inclined to pay attention to teaching methods than they were eighteen months ago. Recognizing a problem, they are more open to the possibility of innovative methods. I don't think they see the use of the library as innovative, so I don't think their attitudes or practices with respect to it have changed. Newer teaching methods may stimulate more use of the library, and if the media are packaged for individual student access they may stimulate student use of the media. But whatever innovations there are with respect to methods which call for independent exploration and inquiries seem to me to be little related either to a different or more extensive use of library resources or to use of media.

In other words, she does not think that attitudes have changed, and, interestingly, Bob Jordan, of Federal City College, agrees at least in part. He also does not think there have been any significant changes in attitude, but with a greater availability of things, there is more use of those things. The "yes" comments were received from two people very much involved in dial-access pioneering, from Oral Roberts and the University of South Florida. They indirectly tend to confirm what both Knapp and Jordan wrote, while they completely and independently corroborate each other's views. They say that the availability of dial-access equipment stimulates greater use by professors in course presentation and greater involvement by both faculty and students in a variety of uses of dial access. Both also commented that as the faculty gets involved, the fears of technology tend to disappear. I want to pass on one comment which Robert Taylor made to me, and which, I should add, agrees with my own independently reached conclusion. Whatever is done in the way of bibliographic control of the media, the present bibliographic control of books is probably too rigid to be applied to all of the media, but there must be some compatibility between them if they are going to be equally useful information resources.

To sum up my earlier observations, then, and indicate how I see current trends in college libraries and multimedia programs, I would say generally that technology and events are moving much faster than our institutions and their facilities are responding. There has been some progress in moving towards the kind of coordinated control of all means of information systems and information-transfer systems, the kind of control which is essential if our minds and capabilities are to catch up with the machinery and techniques they have developed. I would say not enough progress has been made at the moment. I am not very optimistic about the near future, of academic librarianship and its relationship to the media, and I am afraid that the situation is probably going to get worse before it gets better. Perhaps there will be increasing awareness of the potentialities which the technology offers if we can only get it under control.

Mr. Stone: I agree fully with Colonel Dupuy that the technology available is moving much faster than the institutions' readiness to absorb it and make effective use of that technology. The slowness of academe to respond to communication resources is evident in the recent experience I had with the Association of Research Libraries [ARL]. This organization has a very effective lobby in Washington doing great work. But when we put before them the notion that ARL as an organization ought to look at the problem of administering and planning for effective organization and utilization of communication information resources, the board's response was that it was not ready to consider this kind of problem at the present time.

I believe that we should strive for efficiency in terms of the educational process. It was suggested that requirements for cost effectiveness are going to be forced through administrative channels. The media professional groups are not going to have very much to say in this unless they are out in front, ready with suggestions for the dollars that are forthcoming. College presidents, junior college presidents in particular, and school superintendents from large cities are going to insist these things be put together efficiently and now. The slowness of response is going to be overcome by the force of administrative imposition, and the sad part of this is that we are probably not ready to give the kind of guidance which is needed to produce appropriate systems.

With regard to questions that related essentially to the use of computers and the development of programmed learning devices and techniques, in my opinion, we had a gross overestimation in the early days of the immediate promise represented in what was a diagnostic technique for determining the nature of the learning process. We also had a considerable underestimation of the task required to produce even a significant segment of material in any form which can depart from and relate to changes in behavior. As yet, we cannot even state our instructional objectives in behavioral terms and, therefore, are not ready to go beyond this point.

Mr. Dupuy, you said the networking promise that was in the Networks for Knowledge Bill, the EDUCOM idea, and a variety of others was not moving us forward very rapidly. I also understood you to say we have gone very slowly on this and that you thought there would be a considerable length of time before we advanced toward the more elaborate kinds of information-transfer systems contemplated on a state, regional, and national basis. However, state after state has an educational television commission evolving into an educational media commission. In some states—for example, in California—library networks and systems are being tied in with the state agencies. They are all tied together in one way or another with the governmental communications systems, police, fire, traffic and water safety, and federal or state business transactions. The possibility that education could ride piggyback on some of these systems and services which provide electronic transfer of information of data is going forward in the development of a number of these commissions. These state commission efforts are moving from television to a broader media base and are being applied to other communication problems—state, federal, and regional—so that we might accelerate the entire network movement and have some expectation that it will be a realization far before the twenty-first century.

Mr. Dupuy: Dr. Stone has raised one completely new thought which had not crossed my mind. That is the fact that these individual state activities are, in effect, becoming the genesis of a network in each state, and thus each can become a state or regional center which can eventually be linked together. Because of the cost of education, state governments are going to demand efficiency and this in turn will be demanded by the federal government.

Appendix: Questionnaire

**Follow-up on
"Study to Develop a Research Program
for the Design Development of
Modern College Libraries"**

Name: Institution:

1. Have there been any significant changes in the activities of your installation (library, media center, learning center, or college in general) since your interview with T. N. Dupuy? Please indicate as follows:

	Yes	No
a. Use of computers	2	15
b. Use of microform	7	9
c. Use of other nonprint media	4	13
d. Application of Dial Access System	1	15
e. Use of programmed learning	0	15
f. Use of reprography	2	14
g. Network participation	3	12
h. Educational Television	2	13
i. Mechanization of administration (other than computers)	1	15
j. Selective dissemination of information	1	15
k. Other information systems activities	0	14
l. Use of electronic carrels	1	15
m. Use of audio-tutorial techniques	4	12

2. If your answer to any of the above is *yes*, please expand your remarks below, if necessary for clarity.

3. Has there been any trend *toward* greater collaboration, or coordination of efforts, between library and media staffs:
Yes 8   No 10
Remarks:

4. Has there been any trend *away* from former collaboration or coordination of efforts, between library and media staffs?
Yes 2   No 17
Remarks:

5. Has there been any effort by college or university administration to centralize control or coordination of library and media functions?
Yes 8   No 10
Remarks:

6. How would you rate faculty attitudes and practices today (as compared to 18 months ago) in the following respects:

	Greater	Less	No Change
a. Use of library	10	1	7
b. Use of media	11	0	5
c. Encourage student use of library	8	0	9
d. Encourage student use of media	8	0	6
e. Experimentation in new teaching techniques	9	0	7
f. Knowledge of interest in Library College Movement	2	0	15
g. Interest in educational use of computers	7	0	9

7. Do you attach any particular significance to the pattern of your responses to question 6, or to any single response? If so, please elaborate below, or on an additional sheet of paper.
Yes 4   No 7

Part 5

Centers for Organization and Dissemination

Information research and service centers at the national level in several countries offer some evidence of progress toward the bibliographic control of both print and nonprint media. Recent projects begun at the Library of Congress, National Library of Medicine, National Medical Audiovisual Center, National Audiovisual Center, National Information Center for Educational Media, and the ERIC Media Center lend significant weight to developments in the United States. Parallel efforts are found in Canada and Great Britain. These centers are active in both the organization and dissemination of information.

Those individuals most directly responsible for nonprint media in the national centers pro-

vided progress reports on their programs and discussed the contributions their centers are making and can make in the future toward a national system for maximum availability of media in all formats.

In contrast to the existing centers that are dedicated to research and service on a national level, Richard L. Darling described a local public school service which has enlarged its outreach beyond the county to include other school districts within a single state. The two approaches, one beginning at the national level and the other at the local level, both substantiate the need for standardized terminology, organizational procedures, and bibliographic data.

The Library of Congress and Nonprint Media

Katharine Clugston

The problems faced by the Library of Congress are very different from those faced by school libraries. The Library of Congress is large; it is *the* library of *the* Congress, which means that we bow to the whims of Congress.

We have an unusual and unique collection of film material. More than 40,000 titles of motion pictures are in our collection, more than 90 million feet of film. The collection is very old, dating back to 1894, when Fred Ott sneezed. Fred Ott was the mustachioed gentleman who dipped snuff and sneezed in front of one of Edison's cameras. A record of that sneeze was registered for copyright in 1894, and thus became the first motion picture to be deposited in the Library of Congress. At that time the copyright law did not provide for the registration of motion pictures. Edison, in registering that film, had to print it frame by frame on photographic paper and register it as a series of photographs. As a result, we have a roll of still photographs showing Fred Ott as he dipped his snuff and sneezed soulfully.

Another characteristic of our collection, which makes it different from most of yours, is that it is largely uncataloged, and the films are not available for distribution. Of course, the latter applies to our books too. The types and sizes of films that we have vary from the paper print which is the record of Fred Ott's sneeze, the tiny paper roll which would fit into a one-inch can, to the enormous reels of cinerama film which stand several feet high and take up twenty feet of shelf space each. Because of this great variance in the size of the materials themselves, you can see why we have to have fixed locations. We cannot afford to shelve our films according to any kind of a classification system at all, nor can we shelve them alphabetically. We put them in place mostly according to their size and leave them there more or less permanently.

In our collection there are a great many foreign films as well as films produced by our own producers. There are captured war films, Russian, German, and Japanese films, which were confiscated during the wars and turned over to us by the alien property custodian. Comparatively few of the films in the Library of Congress are classroom films, since the Library of Congress does not specialize in the collection of classroom materials, either in book form or in motion-picture form.

The basic collection of films in the Library of Congress dates back to 1942. The early films which were produced in this country were not covered by the Copyright Act. Nevertheless it was because of the inadequacy of the Copyright Act that we have a substantial record of the films produced before 1912. Approximately 3,000 films were registered for copyright as photographs between 1894 and 1912. In 1942, when the library was cleaning out its cellar, it found some large cartons containing rolls of pictures printed on photographic paper. It turned out that those rolls were the reproductions of the work of the

Head, Audiovisual Section, Descriptive Cataloging Division, Processing Department, Library of Congress, Washington.

early producers of motion pictures, a magnificent collection of the earliest films produced in this country and registered for copyright. We call them our paper print collection.

In 1912 the copyright law was amended to cover motion pictures. Because of the problems associated with nitrate film, the library's collection is woefully deficient from 1912 until the advent of acetate film. As soon as provison was made for the inclusion of motion pictures in the Copyright Act, an arrangement was made with the producers to send their copyright deposit films back to them, because the Library of Congress at that time had no particular interest in films and had very limited facilities for storing nitrate film. The Washington Fire Department ordered the Copyright Office to dispose of the films within twenty-four hours. Consequently, they were examined for copyright, returned to the producer, and lost to the Library of Congress. Now the American Film Institute is trying to find prints or negatives for these old films and bring them back into a national collection which is being housed at the library.

When the paper prints were discovered, the library for the first time began to think that there might be something in films that would be of use to Congress and to research scholars. By that time industry and the military forces were interested in films for training purposes. Therefore it was decided that something should be done to add films to the collection of the library. We received a grant from the Rockefeller Foundation to provide for the selection of films to be added to the library's collection. We contracted with the Museum of Modern Art to make that selection for us, since the library at that time had no one who was particularly interested in film material. That project was a failure. Either the films could not be located, or no one wanted to give them to the library. Furthermore, the library had no appropriations with which to buy them. Interest in films had been aroused, however. The next year President Roosevelt issued a directive to the National Archivist and the Librarian of Congress to draw up plans for a national motion-picture repository. That seemed a step in the right direction, but Congress failed to appropriate any money for the

drawing up of these plans, even though we were directed to do so. That plan failed also, and we still do not have a building for motion pictures.

However, in 1945, we did get an appropriation from Congress to establish a motion-picture project at the library. This project was to be concerned with the selection, service, and storage of motion-picture film, and the staff was to be responsible for building up the collection and studying ways to bring it under control. The project was a failure. Just as the project was getting well started, Congress failed to renew the appropriation of funds for it, and we were back where we started.

Help came in 1946 when the Copyright Cataloging Division underwent a great upheaval. The newly appointed Register of Copyrights, Sam Warner, was interested in increasing the bibliographic value of the copyright catalogs and making them of greater use to scholars as well as to publishers and lawyers concerned with legal aspects of those catalogs. He thought that there was considerable research value in the catalog, particularly in the film catalog. Instead of entering motion pictures in the weekly catalogs under the claimant, whom no one knew, they were entered under title and described in some detail. Before this project was disbanded, the staff of the motion-picture project sent a questionnaire to public libraries, film libraries, theater libraries, and any other libraries that had a collection of films. The questionnaire asked for a statement of opinion on various aspects of film cataloging, but the project was dissolved before the questionnaires were analyzed.

The Copyright Office pulled them out of the files in 1946, and we used those questionnaires and any other information we could find as a basis for drawing up rules for cataloging motion pictures. There was not a great deal of interest in those days in cataloging films, and the Copyright Office had absolutely no preconceived notions about how films should be cataloged. It was not bound by any code of rules, but it wanted to make the cards and the catalogs as useful as possible. The 1946 copyright film catalog was published as an annual and after that was issued semiannually. I did cause some interest in film circles and library circles. Requests began to come in for our printed cards for film materials.

We were not, at that time, adding any films to the collections of the library. We had appropriations from Congress sufficient only to take care of the films on hand. Since we did not lend films or do any reference work on films, we had no current films of our own to print cards for, but we did have information about new films which were being registered for copyright. The library was not very eager to go into the printed card business at this time.

At an international film conference in 1951, sponsored by Eastman House and the Film Council of America, representatives from Canada and England were present, as well as UNESCO representatives. The latest revision of the rules from the Copyright Office was discussed and approved for use. The library was urged to publish those rules and to begin printed cards based on them. The film companies that were represented at the Rochester conference agreed to send into the library information about their films on data sheets so that it would speed up the cataloging of the films themselves.

Two top men in the library, Al Walter, head of the Card Division, and Richard Angell, head of the Cataloging Division, went on a tour of the country to find out what the consensus of opinion was regarding printed cards for motion pictures. On several trips they were gone virtually six months. They traveled all over this country and Canada, holding meetings and seminars at various places along the route to determine what people wanted and how people could cooperate to get what they wanted. The medical film libraries were very much interested, and so were the government agencies. Arrangements were made with both of them to send data to the library. The current copyrighted films continued to be cataloged in the Copyright Office, but new films that were *not* copyrighted, as well as films produced prior to 1947, were cataloged from data supplied by producers and other participants in the film-card program. The printing of cards began in November 1951. Since that time Library of Congress cards have been printed for 72,000 motion pictures and film-strips. Of these, 3,600 were theatrical films for which cards were printed prior to 1958, when the printing of cards for copyrighted theatricals was discontinued.

In 1953, two years after the first conference at Rochester, a UNESCO conference on cataloging was held in Washington, in which the Library of Congress *Rules* formed the basis of the discussion. As a result of that conference, minor changes were made to bring the library *Rules* in accord with the international standards that were agreed upon. The *Rules*, of course, have been changed from time to time. You cannot expect rules to remain static. There is a new revision in the mill now to extend the coverage to sets of slides and to sets of transparencies. These changes have been approved by the American Library Association, and it is anticipated that a new booklet incorporating these changes will be issued in the future. Actually, we expected that we would begin cataloging and printing cards for sets of slides and sets of transparencies on the first of July, but Congress again did not treat us as kindly as we had expected, and we are still waiting for our appropriations to be approved. In the meantime, we have had to cut out the cataloging of some of our own film collection, because we feel that our first obligation is to the people who send data sheets to us to provide cards for films.

The library is now printing cards for other nonbook materials besides motion pictures and filmstrips. We have cataloging rules for phonorecords, which include both the discs and the tapes. We have sheet music as well as discs and tapes and books about music. We have all types of artwork, including three-dimensional works. We do not print cards for them, but we do maintain cards for our own collection. Those for some of the signed prints, have, in addition to the description of the work, an inset in the upper righthand corner of the card in which there is a small reproduction of the work itself. Users of the reference collection find the inset very useful. We have had printed cards for some time for maps and atlases and for globes, but we do not print cards for the works in our manuscript collection.

In all of these materials, whether we print

cards for them or not, we still must observe the rules which are observed for the cataloging of book material, because the cards are interfiled with the cards for books in our own catalog. We cite bibliographic data on cards in much the same way for all types of material. Furthermore, we use the same subject headings for all types of materials because the cards are interfiled in the same catalog. We do not expect other people always to like our subjects or to use our subjects indiscriminately. We expect users of the cards to adapt them to meet their own personal needs. As a concession to children's libraries, we have adopted certain changes in the subject headings for children's literature. You probably have read about those. We have also added bracketed subjects in addition to the regular printed subjects in some areas so that anyone who wants to can eliminate the formal subject headings and use those for special materials.

There are a number of very valuable tools that we have at the Library of Congress in addition to the *Anglo-American Cataloging Rules* which have been agreed upon by the American, Canadian, and English Library Associations. I think the biggest bargain of all is the seventh edition of the Library of Congress subject headings. That is a 1432-page book, rather large, and it sells for a mere $15. I think that it is the biggest bargain in the market. We use the seventeenth edition of *Dewey* for the film cards and for certain book cards too. The eighteenth edition is on its way. An abridged edition has been published which is usable for smaller collections. Then there is the MARC format, which some of you have seen. The MARC format is available for books and for maps, and the one for serials is just out, as a working document only. The MARC format for motion pictures is in preparation.

Library of Congress printed cards are available from the Card Division. They can be bought singly or in sets. The cheapest way to buy them is in what we call wholesale lots. Arrangement for such purchases should be made with the Chief of the Card Division, Library of Congress. Each set of cards contains from four to ten cards, depending on the number of subjects and added entries. *The National Union Catalog* issues as one of its parts

Motion Pictures and Filmstrips. That catalog is published quarterly and cumulated annually and quinquennially. The quinquennial volume for 1963 to 1967 is published and available for purchase from Edwards Brothers. The cumulations have to be ordered directly from Edwards Brothers for $45.

Comment: You certainly see the difference in what is available from the Government Printing Office and what is available from a commercial company.

Question: Mrs. Clugston, what relationship does the Library of Congress have with the American Film Institute in Washington?

Mrs. Clugston: The American Film Institute has an office in the Library of Congress, and it is trying to bring into the Library of Congress the films that were issued during the gap in our acquisitions policy. You see, from 1912 until the advent of acetate film, which was in the late forties, we were not able to add to our collection any motion pictures because we had almost no facilities for storing nitrate film. The institute is trying to get prints of those early materials and to get reproductions on safety stock that we can add to our collection.

The institute is also interested in the research value of theatrical materials, and it is providing a great many points of access to them. The institute wants a key to the performers, as well as to the credits, which we do not take care of in our ordinary cataloging.

Question: I make the assumption that when you are describing subject information, there is no difference between books and any other media from the subject content, so I certainly accept the general principle that you can use your book of subject headings. You have said that subject classification was done on the basis of a description on an annotation provided by the descriptive cataloger. Could you elaborate a little more on how an actual subject heading gets into a book?

Mrs. Clugston: There is a difference between the way it gets on the card for books and the way it gets on cards for films. When the books are processed, they come in to the preliminary cataloger, who makes a rough card in many copies. That card goes to the descriptive cataloger, who adds the commas, changes the capitalization, and makes the other necessary changes to make the card a good bibliographic record. Then the card and the book go together to the subject cataloger, who adds the subjects that seem to be necessary, using the book as a guide, and adds the class number. It goes then to the shelf lister, who "cutters" it to see that the book gets in the correct place on the shelf.

The film materials come first to the cataloger, who has the data sheet and other bits of material such as a teacher's guide. If it is a feature picture, there will very likely be a complete cutting continuity. This may be accompanied by reviews, synopses, press boards; any number of other pieces of literature may accompany the films, but the data sheet is the main thing. The data sheet has on it the producer's summary. Those of you who have read producers' summaries know that the adjectives are not omitted. The cataloger, using the producer's summary as well as the descriptive material, writes a factual synopsis of the content of the film, theoretically beginning with a topic sentence followed by a sentence or two giving more specific details. We try to limit the summary to five or six lines so that it will all go on one card. Sometimes it will not. After revision, the completed card only is forwarded to the subject cataloger, who reads the summary, the title, and the series, and assigns to that card the subjects which he thinks are appropriate. There is no classification number assigned by the subject cataloger. The descriptive cataloger assigns the Dewey number.

Question: The general system seems to me a complicated flow, into which you have built an element of feedback and control of the system because they go to different people. Is this a deliberate design within a system, or did it, like Topsy, just grow?

Mrs. Clugston: It was deliberately done.

Question: How is the current staff able to keep up with the cataloging?

Mrs. Clugston: If you had asked me a few months ago, I would have been able to give you a better answer than I can now. It takes quite a while at the present time for things to go through the mill. We have catagories which have been set up at the library, 1 through

7, I believe. Film cards at the present are in category 4, which means the materials in categories 1, 2, and 3 are processed before the staff is supposed to take on category 4. Since the cataloging of audiovisual materials is done only in the audiovisual section, category 4 is our first priority. If there are wholesale card orders, then they go into category 2, and they go through rather quickly. Under the best circumstances, it now takes a month for the card to go through. Under the worst of circumstances, it could take a year. That is when the card has to have a new subject, which calls for conferences.

We have been very much interested in the reactions to our subject headings. When our film-card program was initiated in 1952, people did not want Library of Congress subject headings on Library of Congress cards for films. They thought they were altogether too complicated and too specific. However, we were geared to give the Library of Congress subject headings and no other, and that was all we could do. Therefore we settled for Library of Congress subject headings when we started the program. Gradually the complaints have lessened, until now we get almost no complaints about subject headings being too specific. This is because other collections are growing and they feel the need of entering a film about lions and pigs under both *lions* and *pigs* instead of under *animals.*

Question: It seems to me that one of our problems is centered around this concept of a national library. I wonder if you would care to comment on whether you think the Library of Congress should become such a thing and perhaps better serve the entire country, or should another organization be established, allowing the Library of Congress to go back to what it is supposed to be?

Mrs. Clugston: You put me on the spot. The Library of Congress is considered by many people as a national library, and it functions as such. It devotes most of its energies to serving Congress and the research needs of the country. We do a lot of research and provide a lot of materials for research for a lot of people all over the country through our bibliographies, our union catalogs, our *Union List of Serials,* and things of that sort by making the body of information which we have on hand available for research. It is truly a national library, in spite of the fact that Congress does not call it that.

Comment: If you really want improvement in the cataloging and classification of audiovisual media at the Library of Congress, then do what the book librarians do, and that is, become a lobbying group. See that Katharine Clugston's division has the money it needs to do the job we want at the source. That's my speech for the two weeks, and I am going to push it, as Mr. Croghan says, for the whole time I am here.

Comment: Well, the answer is to elect the Librarian. I would like to make one comment on Carolyn Whitenack's aspiration. I am a little less sanguine than she that lobbying will persuade Congress to give this matter the priority that all of us feel that it should. This is where the commercial firms can make a substantial contribution. Now the Library of Congress, because it is nonprofit, can publish a book for $15 whereas the commercial publisher may charge twice this amount, but commercial publishers can take the initiative.

They can make an independent judgment to invest money, which means that all of us pay a little more but that the job can get done. Unless there is some way found to persuade Congress, then we will have to look to the commercial firms to provide the financial initiative. The commercial firms, in turn, must look to the Library of Congress and the professional organizations for providing the structure and the content of the work to be done. This will be a more practical and more obtainable answer than waiting for Congress.

Comment: The commercial people are picking us up to use for their profit. I see no objection to our saying, "Okay, you take a profit but take a profit by doing the things that we want." We can use them as pilot projects. To this eloquent plea on the behalf of the virtues of capital, I can only say that this enlightened capitalism does not get people to use safety in an industry that has really come on big. The automobile industry is a very good example of a heavily funded industry producing the item that people want, but is it being built up to the standards really needed?

Cataloging Audiovisual Materials at the Library of Congress

C. Sumner Spalding

I would like to review the Library of Congress activity in cataloging audiovisual materials and speculate on the outlook for the future. In the past we have felt that we were not doing a really adequate job of coverage in the field of motion pictures and filmstrips. This cataloging is really a general bibliographic service, since the library itself does not collect extensively in this field. Therefore, we reconsidered whether we ought to reduce the program to cover only what we collect or to expand the service to a reasonable degree of comprehensiveness. We have now decided to adopt the latter course and expand the cataloging of United States productions of motion pictures and filmstrips as fully as possible, and, in order to implement this decision, we have requested additional personnel in the 1971 budget. This will enable us to cover not only commercial productions but also United States government films in a way we have not been able to do in recent years.

At the end of the fiscal year 1968 we had a very serious reduction in force at the Library, and a number of positions in the cataloging area had to be dropped. This had a severe effect on our audiovisual program in fiscal 1969. So far in fiscal year 1970 we have been able to do much better, but it will take authorization of more positions to bring us up

Assistant Director, Cataloging and Processing Department, Library of Congress, Washington

to the level that should be our goal. Another serious problem we have to contend with is our severe shortage of space for this activity. In 1971, if the Congress is willing to recognize the validity of the program I have outlined, we do hope to do a much better job in the field of motion pictures and filmstrips.

At the same time we reconsidered our role in the audiovisual field, we concluded that we would not be able to function effectively in the field of the newer media developed primarily for young students and for the classroom situation. We do not collect these materials, and because we do not collect them, we are not familiar with them and, therefore, do not have the expertise required for their effective organization. Some audiovisual media are of broad interest to general libraries as well as to school media centers, and in this area we do have the competence. Here we can try to serve the whole library community, but for audiovisual materials of special interest to a particular type of library, I think it is not going to be possible for you to look to the Library of Congress for coverage.

I hope that we can work this out together. Our main concern in this area is the cataloging rules, because we are so involved in the *Anglo-American Cataloging Rules*. Participation in the development of the code is still an obligation of the Library of Congress, and one in which I have a particular interest as the editor of the original publication.

Question: How can we break the budget dilemma?

Mr. Spalding: I think nothing can be done for fiscal year 1970. The regular appropriation for the Library of Congress has already been passed, and the appropriation for the Health, Education and Welfare Department, from which the library receives funds for cataloging materials for the research library community, is still in limbo after Mr. Nixon's veto.

Question: We seem to have two problems. One is the cataloging in the Library of Congress with or without the media collection, and the other is that of standardization. The latter is important, but it does not matter which body does it.

Mr. Spalding: The library is working very closely with all interested parties. When the Descriptive Cataloging Committee meets, Mr. Croghan, Mrs. Riddle, and I will be present to give our respective views of what needs to be done in this area. We will see how much progress can be made at the meeting here. I do not think we are going to solve all of the problems, but we should make a little progress and go back home with the determination to do more.

Question: Is there a possibility of getting other organizations involved? Why shouldn't the cataloging of tape be performed by another group? Would you consider seeing this established at subpoints?

Mr. Spalding: This would be somewhat similar to the procedures of large state universities which catalog the documents of their states and send the bibliographical data to LC for processing and distribution. This is what we call cooperative cataloging. The Library of Congress' experience with this sort of arrangement reveals that it is not a very satisfactory way to accomplish the job. We have come around to a preference for what we call centralized cataloging. With cooperative cataloging we found that the administrative problems often tend to offset any theoretical benefits. Many questions of details arise; all of the

headings must be compatible; some of the descriptions may be nonstandard. We have to write the cooperating libraries to find out if they will accept changes. Often we would not have received the material when the cataloging copy came in, or, contrariwise, we would have the material but the copy would be missing. We had to maintain records just to keep track of the location of the material or the copy. Under centralized cataloging, particularly under the Shared Cataloging Program, with the strong support of the Higher Education Act, we were able to increase the level of production considerably, and we think that this is the kind of situation with which we are best able to work.

Question: Since you have referred to the desperate space problem several times, can we as a body, representing all those working for bibliographic control of nonbook media, aid in your getting the Madison Building or another building erected? We need your assistance now, but there is an exceptionally impressive group of people here representing many national groups that would also be affected by such a program. Would the Library of Congress be receptive to this type of support?

William Welsh (director of the Processing Department): We have been asked this question a number of times. In 1965 we cataloged just over 100,000 titles. This year, with the support we received from the Association of Research Libraries in the passage of Title II-C of the Higher Education Act, we hope to double our efforts, cataloging over 200,000 items. In order to do this we had to recruit and train the staff, which took quite a bit of time. We have already run out of space. We are trying to do some things well, rather than a number of things superficially, and our goal of full coverage of motion pictures and filmstrips as a segment of the audiovisual field is a reflection of that policy. Whether we can succeed with the difficulties we have had in getting budget and space is debatable.

Bibliographic Control
and the National
Library of Medicine

Malcolm S. Ferguson

The library of the Surgeon General's Office, United States Army, under the direction of Dr. John Shaw Billings, initiated the first comprehensive index of medical journal literature in 1879. This publication, *Index Medicus,* was replaced from 1927 to 1956 by the *Quarterly Cumulative Index Medicus,* a publication of the American Medical Association. In 1956 the library was transferred to the Public Health Service, U.S. Department of Health Education and Welfare, and renamed the National Library of Medicine. The *Index Medicus* reappeared as a library publication in 1960 and was produced by a partially mechanized system using papertape typewriters, tabulating cards, and an Instamatic camera.

Even this more modern system of publication could not meet demands for quick retrieval of citations from the rapidly expanding health sciences literature. To provide better control of this literature, the National Library of Medicine (NLM) developed specifications for a computer-oriented information storage and retrieval system called MEDLARS (Medical Literature Analysis and Retrieval System). In January 1964 the system became operational in the library's new building in Bethesda, Maryland. MEDLARS joins the intellectual talents of trained literature analysts and the processing capabilities of a high-speed electronic compu-

ter. The literature analysts, using terms from Medical Subject Headings (MeSH) and the thesaurus of MEDLARS, index biomedical journal articles and assign the MeSH descriptors which characterize the content of the articles. The data are entered into the computer and transferred to magnetic tapes for storage and rapid retrieval. Publication of these citations is accomplished through an electronic phototypesetter driven by the computer.

The principal objective of MEDLARS is to provide references to the literature for individuals engaged in clinical practice, biomedical research, medical and allied education, and related health science activities. This is accomplished through:

1. Preparation of citations for publication in the monthly *Index Medicus* (citations to periodical literature) and the monthly *Current Catalog* (citations to publications cataloged by NLM).
2. Preparation of eighteen recurring bibliographies on specialized subjects of wide interest
3. Preparation of retrospective, one-time bibliographies (demand searchers). The objective is achieved by rapid search through the file of citations to journal articles in response to specific requests. Since 1964 more than one million citations have been entered into the computer file.

The bibliographic services provided by NLM

Audiovisual Specialist, Special Projects Office, National Library of Medicine, Bethesda, Maryland

through MEDLARS are widely used in the United States and to an increasing extent in other countries, through the establishment of MEDLARS Search Centers in libraries and information centers. Magnetic tapes containing citations are periodically distributed to these centers, where they are processed by computer to provide demand searches. Through this decentralization of searching, the requestor receives desired bibliographic information much quicker than if all searching were done at NLM in Bethesda.

The bibliographic control in the United States of audiovisual materials such as motion pictures, videotapes, slides, filmstrips, audiotapes, and other nonbook media in the health sciences is diffuse and chaotic. There is no one source to which one can go to obtain information about the titles, subject content, and availability of these media. There are several hundred small catalogs or lists of media, mostly motion pictures, and only a few of them are comprehensive, and almost none are multimedia in scope. There is the large catalog of *Medical and Surgical Motion Pictures of the American Medical Association* (4,800 titles), the equally large *Film Reference Guide for Medicine and Allied Sciences,* the annual *Catalog of the National Medical Audiovisual Center* (more than 1,000 titles), and the *Film Catalog of the American Dental Association.* Pharmaceutical companies issue catalogs of their own films. A catalog of more than 1,000 8mm motion pictures in the health sciences has recently been published. Recently, a multimedia catalog of more than 500 training units for nurses was compiled. There are also several lists or small catalogs of audiotapes on various specialties in the health sciences. Reference to available videotapes can be found in the catalogs of the Network for Continuing Medical Education, the Association of Medical TV Broadcasters, and the Medical Television Network (California). It is estimated that there are some 2,500 distributors and sales sources for biomedical nonprint media. Many of them have catalogs, primarily of film.

The National Library of Medicine had only minimal concern with the bibliographic control of nonprint media prior to 1967. That year the audiovisual facility of the Public Health Service in Atlanta, Georgia, was transferred to NLM from the National Communicable Disease Center and redesignated the National Medical Audiovisual Center (NMAC). NMAC had its origin in 1942, when a small unit to produce audiovisual training aids for malaria control was created within the organization in Atlanta known as Malaria Control in War Areas (MCWA). MCWA was reorganized as the Communicable Disease Center in 1947. By 1967 the audiovisual unit, now NMAC, had a large staff and was equipped with complete and modern audiovisual facilities, including a television production capability. Another and very important function of the center was its distribution of motion pictures, filmstrips, and slide sets to health-related organizations from its large film library.

Concurrent with the development over the years of the audiovisual productions and film distribution activities, the center and its predecessors have produced catalogs of the holdings in the distribution library in Atlanta. In cooperation with the medical departments of the military services, the Veterans Administration and the Armed Forces Institute of Pathology, NMAC has for several years produced annually the *Film Reference Guide for Medicine and Allied Sciences.* The content of this catalog is made up of films produced and distributed by the federal medical organizations, together with a number of nongovernment motion pictures that have been found useful in educational and training programs.

A listing of health science films, known as the *International Index of Medical Film Data,* has been accumulated over the years at NMAC. This noncritically developed file now contains more than 25,000 titles of motion pictures. It is interesting to note here that this file was started after World War II in Washington, D.C., at the National Library of Medicine, when it was known as the Armed Forces Medical Library. This original collection of a few thousand film titles was transferred to Atlanta in 1961. The *International Index* has been used extensively at NMAC to provide requesters with information regarding motion pictures on specific subjects. It has also been used to prepare specialized film lists that have been published and distributed widely on such subjects as dentistry, neurological diseases, cancer, space medicine, mental health, drug abuse, and the history of medicine.

The searching involved in answering requests for film information, and in preparing the lists of motion pictures, was done manually until recently. The preparation of the catalogs and film lists was only partially mechanized through the use of typewriters, data cards, and a specialized camera. In 1969 the information in the *International Index of Medical Film Data* was transferred to magnetic tape for the computer in Atlanta. Hundreds of demand searches and specialized filmographies (film lists) have been processed by computer for NMAC.

The subject headings developed at NMAC and used to characterize for the computer the film data input for its *International Index* and cataloging purposes are not compatible with the medical subject headings used at NLM for MEDLARS. Recently, the decision has been made that NMAC will convert information in the *Index* to the NLM MEDLARS format using MeSH, and initial steps for this conversion are now underway. It is proposed that citations to motion pictures, filmstrips, videotapes, and other nonprint media will be published in a catalog similar to the NLM *Current Catalog* rather than in *Index Medicus*. The latter would require the indexing of the content of the various media. Attention will be paid to evaluative information on media to be cited in the *Current Catalog*. Titles to be included will be those known to be of professional quality, current in content, and readily available on loan or on a purchase basis.

The subject matter of the nonprint media to be included in the NLM *Current Catalog* is similar to that of the literature cited in the various MEDLARS publications. No problems will be encountered with the present MEDLARS format in producing media catalogs by subject area. It is not possible to produce catalogs of media by intended audience and purpose by this format. However, this will be feasible after MEDLARS II, the successor to the first MEDLARS format, becomes operational in 1971. Additional details regarding media such at 16mm, 8mm, color, and sound will be searchable items with MEDLARS II.

With citations to literature soon to be supplemented by references to audiovisual materials in the MEDLARS file, the health sciences field in this country is approaching the time when a researcher, clinician, teacher, or other interested individual will have rapid access to a wider spectrum of information sources than can serve his particular needs. It is to be hoped that there will be worldwide cooperation in the development of compatible, linking, automated information systems for nonprint media so that there will be few impediments to the international flow of data regarding them.

The system of regional medical libraries, with MEDLARS tapes, computer terminals and data banks—such as the State University of New York at Buffalo Medical Library—is growing in number, information available, and the variety of materials retained for service. The Lister Hill National Center for Biomedical Communication is planning for a network in cooperation with various existing programs that will link libraries, institutions of higher education, hospitals, research centers, and even physicians' offices through the utilization of computers, television facilities, and satellite communications.

Although the bibliographic control of medical nonprint media is yet to be realized, there is a growing recognition of the potential for visualization of medical sciences information. Its integral role in centralized resource collections and regional library networks is becoming increasingly important.

National Medical Audiovisual Center

Margaret Brooks ·

What is now the National Medical Audiovisual Center was founded in Atlanta in 1942, as a part of the Malaria Control in War Areas program. It came into existence during World War II when emergency training efforts proved that visual teaching media were efficient tools for instructing military and civilian personnel in new, sometimes highly specialized jobs. With the formation of the Communicable Disease Center in 1947, the audiovisual program became a branch of the center and was later designated the Public Health Service audiovisual facility. When it became a part of the National Library of Medicine in 1967, it was renamed the National Medical Audiovisual Center, and with the library, in 1968 became a component of the National Institutes of Health. Director of the center and associate director of the National Library of Medicine for audiovisual and telecommunications is Assistant Surgeon General James Lieberman.

The purpose of the center is to:

Operate the central facility in the Public Health Service for the development, production, distribution, evaluation, and utilization of motion pictures, videotapes, and other audiovisual forms

Coordinate a comprehensive audiovisual program for the service to assure maximum responsiveness and economy of funds and manpower

Provide consultation and assistance in the development of specialized audiovisual activities

Encourage the production, dissemination, and utilization of medical films and other audiovisuals in the schools of health professions and elsewhere

Operate a national clearinghouse and archival program

Act as a national/international film and videotape center for the distribution and exchange of biomedical audiovisuals.

These functions are carried out by the production branch, the acquisition, distribution and reference branch, and the educational systems and development branch.

The International Index of Medical Film Data, one of the world's largest collections of abstracts on medically related audiovisuals, forms the nucleus of our reference program. The name is not entirely self-explanatory. It is an index in that items are listed, briefly described, and their location pinpointed; it is international in scope. However, *medical* is not a completely accurate term, nor is film. Since it was originally conceived that the center would serve the entire Public Health Service, the scope of the index included not only medicine but also such aspects of public health as accident prevention, safe driving, civil defense, and water safety. Having established a reputation for reference service in these areas, we have continued to add data which is oriented to broad health-related programs. In addition to motion pictures, the *Index* includes

Chief, Reference and Archival Section, Media Resources Branch, National Medical Audiovisual Center, Atlanta

filmstrips, audio- and videotapes, and slide sets.

We have developed a standardized format for cataloging *Index* entries. It is a combination of several existing formats, no one of which we felt suitable for the needs of the many users of our reference service. We selected parts of the American Library Association rules, and we utilized parts of the Library of Congress rules and National Education Association suggestions.

A seven-digit title number is assigned to each citation. This number is a numeric representation of the title and serves as a file location number. Following the title line is a producer/sponsor line, which also includes country and year of production, or an asterisk if the date is unknown. The physical description line varies with the media being described. When an audiovisual is in a language other than English, a notation of this is made before the series line. A brief content synopsis fellows the series line and then restrictions, such as "professional use only," are shown as required. No evaluative words or phrases, either commendatory or condemnatory, are included in the summary. Sale and rental sources are listed in code, and, of course, any filmography we prepare is accompanied by a key to these code numbers.

Subject cataloging for the *Index* is based entirely on our own classification scheme, which was designed to meet our own needs in handling the requests of our rather diverse user groups. We are a public service organization, dealing with both professionals and non-professionals, and must be more specific in certain subject areas than medical reference services dealing primarily with professionals.

Our classification scheme is similar to the Medical Subject Headings (MeSH) system. Our scheme has a hierarchy of 65 subjects, descending from general to specific. In all, there are approximately 1,800 subject categories, with each specific subject represented by eight numbers. The first three represent the general subject area; the second three represent the subdivision; and the final two, the specific subject. There is ample room for expansion within the scheme.

Input for the *Index* is both orderly and chaotic. It is orderly in that we annually request from all sale and rental sources an updating of their additions and deletions. It is orderly in that five government agencies systematically provide us with current information on their holdings. It is orderly in that we scan the professional and industrial media journals for lists of new productions. On the other hand, our input is chaotic in that we are constantly inundated with individual new-title flyers from myriad sources, with catalogs from new producers or film libraries, and with actual films sent us by mistake.

For each title added, a computer input document is compiled and processed. From this data two file cards are created, a master copy similar to a shelflist and a subject index copy. With this accumulated data we perform, basically, three reference services.

We select and organize titles to be included in catalogs published by the National Medical Audiovisual Center (NMAC). We compile listings of audiovisuals on specific subjects as requested by individuals, and we answer requests for information on specific titles. The published catalogs are of two types, both recurrent and specialized. Our own NMAC catalog is an annual listing of the audiovisuals that we distribute. We also publish annually the *Film Reference Guide for Medicine and Allied Sciences,* known affectionately as the FRG. This is a combined listing of audiovisuals available from member agencies of the Federal Advisory Council on Medical Training Aids. This group encompasses, in addition to the National Library of Medicine, the Departments of the Air Force, Army, and Navy, the Armed Forces Institute of Pathology, and the Veterans Administration.

We have now computerized the *International Index of Medical Film Data* containing approximately 27,000 audiovisuals in the health-medical field. Approximately 200 new titles are added to the *Index* each month. Using this data, we prepare special listings upon request. In the first half of this fiscal year, we furnished 1,595 selected listings in response to 326 individual requests. When the number of individual requests in a specific area reflects a widespread concern with the subject, we produce a specialized catalog. We have recently prepared selected listings to cover organ transplants, mental health, dentistry, and addictions.

In response to requests, we supply information concerning the source of specific film titles. These may be requests for single titles or lists numbering 100 or more titles. In the last six months we have responded to more than 3,000 such requests from Amsterdam, Chile, Tel Aviv, the Congo, Sweden, and all the English-speaking world.

We are presently negotiating with a number of medical schools and professional health organizations to begin a program of cooperative cataloging. We are convinced that this is one of the most practical approaches to the problem of information communication. These cooperative programs will put the information where it is needed, into the hands of the health practitioner, student, and patient.

National Audiovisual Center

Glenn D. McMurry

The unique ability of the motion-picture camera to record events for historical purposes was recognized by a provision in the act establishing the United States National Archives in June 1934. In a 1939 issue of *American Archivist*, Dorothy Arbaugh also notes that the act authorized, in addition to motion pictures from governmental agencies, the acceptance from nongovernmental sources of motion pictures illustrative of American history.[1] A system for the care of these materials was established earlier. When a film arrived at the National Archives, a reviewer indicated the subject matter of the reel, compiled what was known about its sources and history, recorded its title, completed credit information, prepared a synopsis of the action, and recorded details of the scenic content and sound sequence. An alphabetical card catalog was begun to index the films and the inspection reports by titles, subjects, important persons, and source. According to Arbaugh, "the cataloguers engaged in this work, planning for the use of these pictures far into the future, are adapting library bibliographical methods to the special characteristics of motion-picture film." Six suggestions were made by Arbaugh in 1939 for the future development of the archives film collection, of which two dealt with "a library of motion-picture films created that would be comparable to the library for government publications maintained in the office of the Superintendent of Documents" and "a central library to serve the nation much as the Library of Congress serves it in the field of books and printed literature."[2]

For many years the federal government, through its many agencies, has been involved in the production of media: slides, motion pictures, filmstrips, recordings, and other audio or visual records of communication. Each agency that was producing materials soon discovered a system had to be established to circulate copies of the material, the by-product of their production. As with any new venture, government or otherwise, such a procedure did not exist, so it "grew like Topsy," with all of the ensuing problems.

The military services established effective internal distribution services and offered limited free loan service to the public. A few major nonmilitary agencies organized cooperative federal-state free loan distribution systems. As for the others, there was no particular overall plan.

As long as only a few copies of the materials existed, the secretary in the office handled the physical job of storing the prints and sending them to the users. When many requests had to be filled and large numbers of film titles had to be handled, the procedure became intolerable.

The predecessor of the present U.S. Office of Education produced between 1941 and

Chief, Distribution Branch, National Audiovisual Center, Washington

[1]"Motion Pictures and the Future Historian," *American Archivist* 2:106–14 (Apr. 1939).

[2]Ibid.

1946 a series of more than five hundred motion pictures and filmstrips designed to train World War II workers. Distribution of the films was accomplished on a "sales only" basis through a commercial seller selected on the open-bid system. Many other federal agencies offered their firms for sale through the same seller over a period of twenty-seven years. Some agencies offered their media prints for sale directly and enlisted the services of private laboratories to prepare and ship new copies of media to the purchaser.

The bidding process developed competition and, consequently, lower bids with little profit for the commercial seller adversely affected service to the United States government and its public. This contract letting to one group after another, with all its problems, attracted the attention of the Federal Interagency Media Committee and a special audiovisual study group was appointed by the Archivist of the United States. It became evident, as a result of investigation and study, that a central clearinghouse for information, sales, and distribution services was urgently needed to handle government nonprint media. The National Audiovisual Center was authorized on October 30, 1968, and established in July 1969 to meet this need. It was to be a division of the National Archives and Records Service, General Services Administration, to serve the federal government, industry, educational institutions, and the general public as a central information, sales, and distribution point for most government motion pictures, filmstrips, audiotapes, videotapes, and other audiovisual materials.

The center serves as a central information clearinghouse of government-produced media. All federal agencies are required to furnish information to the center on the materials they produce. Detailed information is gathered on all relevant materials produced by or for the federal agencies and made available on request. The center's distribution program includes sales, loans, and rentals to both government agencies and the public. The response to these services by the general public has been most gratifying. More than 80 percent of the correspondence comes from schools and colleges throughout the United States, Canada, and abroad. The center also offers to government agencies limited technical assistance related to media production, processing, and distribution. The center provides a uniform, efficient, and economical loan service of audiovisual materials, primarily 16mm motion pictures, deposited in the center by various government agencies. A sizable catalog of films for sale is available upon request from the center. Soon to be published is a supplement to the catalog which will include the first titles available for rent.

The inventory consists of thousands of titles produced over a span of thirty years, including many World War II training films, as well as later productions. New titles are being added weekly, among which are selected titles produced for and by the United States Information Agency for use abroad. Currently, a large number of prints of drug abuse films sponsored by the National Institute of Mental Health are being circulated to the general public.

More and more agencies consult with the center's staff regarding their needs for service. The center fills an important gap between the government and the general public. Its growth has been faster than expected, and its future looks promising, as more films are released by the agencies for sale, free loan, and/or rental through the center. The Department of Agriculture, with a large film library, and the Department of the Interior are not listed in the center's catalogs as yet. However, central organization, promotion, sales, and correspondence with the public is proving to be effective and efficient, as indicated in the recent "Survey of User Initiated Written Requests for Federal Audiovisual Materials."[3]

[3]Preliminary draft of a research report prepared by Jenny K. Johnson for the Educational Policy Group, George Washington University, Washington, D.C., June 1970.

The ERIC
Media Center

William J. Paisley

I am trained as a social psychologist with a specialty in communications, my academic business is teaching graduate students in communications research, and my role as an information specialist is to manage the Educational Resources Information Center (ERIC) Clearinghouse on Educational Media and Technology. This paper is limited to the problems perceived from behavioral studies that have been conducted on the uses of information systems and the problems that information systems present to their users in indexing systems, in transactions with files, and with the personnel who run such systems. The reason that we have been conducting such studies and that many other investigators have been interested in the utilization problem is that the level of utilization of most information systems is scandalously low, especially when you depend on mission-oriented funding sources such as the United States Office of Education.

Although many people have had some involvement with ERIC, the system is changing so fast that a constant up-dating is essential for one to remain current on the center's research programs and services. Those who have not been looking in on ERIC for some time might be surprised to know that ERIC now seems to be successful in spite of itself. There are many reasons why an information system like this would not even be initiated. A bal-

anced review of how this print system has been initiated and of the roles that it cannot play should demonstrate the necessary complementary relationship between systems for organizing print and nonprint resources.

It is always gratifying to realize that the ERIC system, which encompasses all of education from reading instruction to library science and the administration of junior colleges, had its origin in the National Defense Education Act (NDEA) Title VII. The media research title of NDEA in 1958, written into the United States Office of Education (USOE) operating code for the first time, provided a dissemination responsibility. Title VII of the act created a watershed of research findings on educational media, while Title VII-A required the USOE to look for instruments for the proper dissemination of these findings. It is an extremely mission-oriented title which said, in effect, that the research evidence collected under Title VII-A could not be allowed to languish in the USOE's own library, which had been the case with much, if not most, of the office's previous research. Unfortunately, no mechanism for dissemination had been devised. A narrow interpretation of Title VII-A would have led to some small information systems specifically for the rapid reporting of media research results. But some people in the USOE at that time, such as Tom Clemens and Andy Mona, thought this could be the nucleus of an educational information system that would bring together research under the Cooperative Research Act and subsequent research legislation that might be passed.

Director, ERIC Clearinghouse on Educational Media and Technology, Palo Alto, California

171

Title VII-A authorized funds to do feasibility studies for the ERIC system in 1959. However, ERIC was not administratively functional until the end of 1965. It represents an interesting experiment in federally supported information systems. Most federal systems are located in only one geographical location; for example, the Defense Documentation Center is located in Cameron, Virginia, and the Clearinghouse for Federal Scientific and Technical Information is located in Alexandria, Virginia. A much larger and earlier counterpart of educational information is the National Library of Medicine. These are centralized information systems.

After years of experience in setting up centralized information systems, information specialists began to realize that certain things are sacrificed when an information system is set up in one location. Under these circumstances subject experts must be highly mobile and ready to leave any moment for Washington, either temporarily or permanently. There will be less subject expertise for the benefit of the information system than would be available to run the information system from the many places where the subject specialists prefer to live. It was decided to try decentralization for ERIC, in spite of the problems of coordination which would inevitably arise among academicians running independent information centers, often a prescription for chaos.

In 1966 ERIC began publishing an abstract journal entitled *Research in Education*. The first issue contained 40 research résumés, with monthly supplements containing 900 additional résumés covering all fields of education. The total document flow each year is approximately 10,000 research reports.

In the structure of ERIC, a network of information systems in education is emerging that is similar to the Air Transport Network. The many autonomous elements of the latter, often in competition with each other, are nonetheless able to coalesce into a network. That is not true in our case, because authorities tell us what is required. Each individual in each component of our information network realizes the other person is doing something that really cannot be combined with his own operation. A contrast may be drawn between the organization of print material and that of nonprint material.

Media projects that come into our clearinghouse consist of a document plus a filmstrip and an audiotape, or another type of media, and we usually get as far as the document. We then must consider the filmstrip, tape, or other media. The different requirements for processing print and nonprint materials illustrate my theme, that an information network for education would have to represent the coalescence of operations that are perhaps logically combined but are likely to continue separately.

According to its established guidelines, ERIC is organized primarily to serve elementary and secondary education in this country, while, by contrast, an organization like EDUCOM (Interuniversity Communications Council), I believe, has no responsibility for elementary and secondary education. It might, therefore, be of use to know a little bit about ERIC's structure simply because it is one of the components that should eventually combine with other components into what, we hope, would be called the complete educational information system.

ERIC has gone through three stages up to the present, and at least as many additional stages have been blocked out in long-range planning. The first stage of the ERIC system was the creation of a computer processing facility so that the staff could meet a monthly deadline for publishing an abstract journal, while accepting input in various forms of bibliographical accuracy from a centralized clearinghouse extending from New York City to San Francisco. The ERIC staff was fortunate to find one company with existing computer software appropriate for the applications. The ERIC indexes were produced with the computer programs North American Rockwell Corporation has developed for its own nationwide internal information-management system. Some of the big corporations are just about as big as government agencies, so it was easy to transfer the software from one to the other.

The second phase of the ERIC system was to reach a certain level of bibliographic precision so that our publication did not always look like a poor cousin to *Psychological Ab-*

stracts or the *Education Index*. This second phase was much more difficult than the first. Nevertheless, by the middle of 1968, we had managed to achieve a minimum level of library professionalism, so that wherever in the system a résumé originated, it would contain a certain predictability about the format of the field's content. These are the two mechanical phases of the ERIC system.

We are now in the third phase, that of information analysis. In education, where the document load is not of uniform quality, it is very important to supply the products of information analysis to school personnel. It is especially helpful to those unaccustomed to the obscurity that educational research specialists inevitably include in their reports. It takes skilled reviewers and synthesizers to go through these reports and show that certain exemplary programs are being validated and well documented.

Each clearinghouse has taken on the responsibility for producing these products and is, in effect, its own publishing company. This arrangement gives us the necessary insight to see targets of opportunity: for example, a paper on film resources for ethnic studies that was obtained from San Francisco State College when it was setting up its Black Studies Program. Other special projects undertaken include a paper on evaluating educational research products and another on the kinds of royalty payments that are appropriate for instructors, especially in higher education. Some instructors create videotapes that are used over and again, which causes a royalty problem that many professors do not realize can be resolved to their benefit.

Our publications are cheaply produced so multiple copies may be made for distribution to school systems. Results of information analysis by the media clearinghouse that have been considered important enough to publish are:

Media and the Disadvantaged: A Review of the Literature

Learning from Television: What the Research Says

A Basic Reference Shelf on Individualized Instruction

A Basic Reference Shelf on Audio-Visual Instruction

A Basic Reference Shelf on Computer Assisted Instruction

A Basic Reference Shelf on Programmed Instruction

A Basic Shelf on the Uses of New Media for Teacher Training

A Reference Shelf on Facilities for Educational Media

A Review of Educational Applications of the Computer Including Those in Instruction, Administration, and Guidance

A Reference Shelf on Instructional Media Research

A Basic Reference Shelf on Learning Theories.

We wanted to emphasize the point that education is first of all a social and psychological process and that even a media center should not begin accepting hardware without recognizing preeminently the psychological problems in learning. Therefore, the three phases that the ERIC system has passed through thus far are the establishment of a computerized publication facility, the coordination of a decentralized network, and the production of information analysis products to assist school personnel in utilizing a vast array of unevaluated literature. The two major types of publications available from ERIC are the abstract journal *Research in Education* and the *Current Index to Journals in Education*. The system also makes available the documents themselves. Microfiche was selected as a format for dissemination of documents, not because it is anyone's favorite medium, but rather because the alternative hard copy would have been prohibitively expensive. The cost of deploying a large number of hard-copy collections around the country would have rendered the entire system economically unviable. The ERIC collection now includes more than 20,000 documents, the size of a small library, which in microfiche format is easily contained on one wall of an office.

As the optical characteristics of microfiche readers improve, and as companies produce low cost microfiche reader-printers which give hard copy from the individual frames of microfiche, the medium will gain acceptance by the public. Microfiche is not, as yet, a trouble-free medium. We are running into some prejudices when people simply refuse to consider using the microfiche collection. However, the slow process of diffusing an innovation is being accomplished and I feel we have passed the critical point in that those other than the experimentalists have now decided to acquire microfiche.

The ERIC system has gone on-line, which means that from a number of places in the country it is potentially possible to connect one of your computer terminals with one or more of ERIC's computers. One can, thereby, complete the bibliographic part of a search in real time, even though the documents themselves are not held in a computer file. No one has yet solved the problem of storing large quantities of unprocessed data in a computer console. It is clear that the console can be cost effective, for experiments have been made showing that a manual search will cost more than a search at the console, even when computer and long-distance telephone costs are included. For this reason, all ERIC clearing houses will automate their document-processing operations.

We still have some very tedious manual processing such as that done by anyone who is trying to organize nonprint materials. These are the processes of checking for duplication and precedence and reviewing the history of index terms usage. These can be incredibly tedious when manual tools are used. You want to see exactly how many times a descriptor like *curriculum guide* has been used and in connection with which specific documents. Such a review is necessary to preserve the integrity of the indexing system. When this is done on-line, it is very convenient to review any number of past documents that have been posted to any term.

We are automating our in-house processes for two reasons: first, it saves money in spite of on-line computer costs which are quite high, and second, it produces an unexpected but very agreeable boost in staff morale. We have observed that those engaged in an indexing and abstracting operation become somewhat strained after a while. Children at the Computer-Assisted Instruction (CAI) console may

not be learning much more than they would learn in the classroom, in some cases less, but the benefit in student morale and their willingness to repeat lessons more than offsets this parity of achievement.

It is absolutely necessary that the document delivery system catch up with the bibliographic-access system. In a traditional library it takes roughly the same amount of time to use the card catalog as it does to get something from the shelves. One spends fifteen minutes at the card catalog and an equal amount of time awaiting the delivery of the material. There is a kind of parity in search time and access time. As we move toward on-line bibliographic access, we find that a very complicated coordinate search of a large file can be completed in a few minutes, even one ordinarily requiring several days of searching in a large collection like the Library of Congress. The trade-off in time is great indeed.

Computer coordination of terms yields a powerful time reduction in the search program, but access to the documents themselves in modern information systems is somewhat slower than it is in traditional libraries. There is a paradox in this as shown when the user has completed his fast search of the file, he has very limited options for putting his hands on the document. He may be close to one of the ERIC respositories or to a university library that would have an original copy of the document. If, however, neither of these conditions prevail, which is quite likely in school districts, he spends five minutes filling out an order form to secure microfiche or hard copy from the ERIC Document Reproduction Service and awaits the arrival of the document in two or three weeks. An absolutely essential future phase in the development of the ERIC program is a document delivery system that is equivalent to the technological sophistication of the bibliographic search system. There are many ways in which this can be done with existing technology, such as using the Ampex video-file system for the entire ERIC document collection. Every page of every document could be held on a couple of standard two-inch videotape reels. The entire ERIC system could be held on perhaps half a dozen Electronic Videotape Recording (EVR) cartridges. It is not at all unreasonable to think about the combination of slow-scan television, which could use standard television facilities and either one of these electronic files. It is possible to hold the video file in one central location and to advance the tape playback mechanism to the appropriate document, using a digital code. This is actually a very simple and efficient system whereby slow scan television then transmits the images of those papers to the user.

The cathode ray tube used for the search itself would also be appropriate for displaying an electronic image of the document. Thus we have two future phases in mind which are in agreement with the thinking of those in other large information systems. One is that you must guarantee rapid document delivery, and two, files are increasingly being organized by thesauri that require coordinate searching which in turn necessitates an on-line computer to derive from the indexing effort, the coordinating power of thesauri. Unlike the Dewey Decimal Classification (DDC) or the Library of Congress Classification, most of the indexing systems being used by federally supported information services are designed for coordinate searching.

Therefore, if one is using DDC, a single number is posted to a document, and he then uses an in-the-hand inspection to decide whether that document has the other attributes desired. One might be looking for documents at the intersection of bibliography, media, and the DDC. There is the possibility of a bibliography of media, but it seems that one would have to use the DDC access, either through media or through bibliographic procedures. Then, by an inspection of a table of contents, one could decide if the document satisfies a requirement through its call number.

In coordinate searching, many terms are posted to any one document, while a manual information tool like an index does not allow the creation of coordinate possibilities. When a manual index is used, even though the thesaurus itself has been designed for coordinate searching, the user must still use one entry point or the other. Following a search under bibliographic procedures, one must then find

some other way of deciding if the same document treats media.

If the search was initiated under media, one would have to look for other evidence of bibliographic procedural content. There are ways of achieving coordinate search power with manual tools such as cards, which can be flipped simultaneously to coordinate a term on one card with another term on another card, the Termitrex system, for example. However, all are extremely tedious to maintain. The unique power of the computer is its capacity for searching, a task of infinite complexity without a system of logic.

Some confusion arises about the bibliographic status of the media themselves, due partially to the organizational title, ERIC Clearinghouse on Educational Media and Technology. This title is ambiguous, leading many people to think the clearinghouse is responsible for organizing media such as tapes and films. Some people have sent us material on this assumption, only to find that media is our substantive problem and not our vehicle. We organize only print materials and only those print materials that deal with media and technology. The ERIC system is print bound now and will undoubtedly be print bound in the future. In view of the information network we envision, it will not be necessary for us to encompass nonprint media, for it will already be organized by other people who may also assume the responsibility for the dissemination of nonprint products.

ERIC began as the Educational Information Center and quickly changed its role to the Educational Resources Information Center in acknowledgment of the fact that many of the documents of some benefit to education are not research documents. Researchers who come to visit the clearinghouse are surprised to see how few research documents we have in our collection.

Education, I believe, is being moved forward by philosophical essays, descriptions of exemplary programs, and detailed explanations of how education proceeds, not by the value of research alone. Therefore, we maintain materials ranging from printed speeches and arguments to formal research reports. Access is supplied to these documents through the ERIC Document Reproduction Service in Bethesda, Maryland. The system also maintains twenty regional facilities, nineteen clearinghouses and a central facility in Washington, D.C., each with the entire ERIC depository collection. These collections are located within three hundred miles of any point in the country. Since each of the clearinghouses is located at a center where there was previous work in that specialty, we are also able to supply scholarly and practical support to patrons. There are many places in the country where important media research has been taking place. Research scholars are attracted to Stanford University because it has an extensive data file. Some stay for several weeks at a time, especially those on post-doctoral and sabbatical leaves.

A blueprint for the educational information network is contained in the Elementary and Secondary Education Act (ESEA) of 1965. It provided for a number of experimental quasi-governmental institutions enabling the establishment of research and development centers around the country, such as the Stanford Center for Research and Development of Teaching and the Wisconsin Center for Research and Development of Cognate Skills.

The ESEA also allowed the creation of a network of regional laboratories, such as the Center for Urban Education in New York City; the Far West Regional Educational Laboratory in Berkeley; the Southwest Regional Educational Laboratories, of which there are three; and the Northwest Regional Educational Laboratory in Portland. Regional laboratories, unlike the research and development centers, are located wherever the Office of Education considered there was a sufficient mass of research expertise to keep a certain area moving forward. The centers have no local responsibilities, a fact which is annoying to those with zeal for getting information out to people. On the other hand, the regional laboratories are quite different and do have a local mission.

The ESEA also established supplementary education centers under Title III that are exclusively local in purpose and service. The supplementary resource centers are attached to school districts and are funded on the basis

of proposals to remedy some educational problems in the district. Title III or Project to Advance Creativity in Education (PACE) Center treats local problems such as minority-group education, rural schools, and the problems of isolation. The ERIC system itself was also provided by ESEA funds. It seems obvious that the beginnings of an education information network are present.

Research and development centers are responsible for producing the research information that ERIC disseminates. Much of the research is also disseminated from districts and universities not affiliated with the centers. ERIC is responsible for processing the information somewhat remote from the perspective of the ultimate user. Regional laboratories and Title III centers are sufficiently local that they develop close ties with local educational administrations and serve as excellent dissemination points for the information system.

The regional laboratory is probably in a better position from which to disseminate information about exemplary programs. The research and development centers have experimental classrooms and multimedia installations. Title III centers are the ideal one-step local information dissemination points to serve the entire system. These centers are viewed around the country as points of convergence of many independent systems.

A distinction should be made among information centers, media centers, and resource centers. A media center is a place where films, tapes, and various nonprint materials are made available. An information center answers queries and makes available print materials. The resource center, which is catching the imagination of many people, is a combination of the best elements from information and media centers. The purpose of local instructional resource centers should be to serve as document and media dissemination points. Progress in education is hindered if either of these services is unavailable to the local educational practitioner. There are too many systems in the country where money is available for hardware but unavailable for the supplementary documentation which reports how the hardware is to be used.

The instructional resources center would

first supply the documents needed to learn about multimedia instruction or individualized instruction and then supply materials that are needed to implement the programs described. Network centers are then needed to bring together, at the point of local convergence, services from each of the information systems. After dealing with educational documents for our ERIC media center, I believe it would be inadvisable to bring nonprint materials under the same bibliographical system, where a 150-page report may be indexed with up to fifteen descriptors using an alien thesaurus.

At the beginning of this year, we began to process all media information, print and nonprint, in technology journals for a new publication called *Current Index to Journals in Education*. The space problem has begun all over again with the journal index, and now there is less and less space for people to occupy in the ERIC center. The ERIC clearinghouse for media deals primarily with unpublished literature in print format. Our collection is not housed on shelves but rather in vertical files. We now add one four-drawer file each quarter, or sixteen file drawers each year.

One way in which to bring this array of bibliographic data under control is through the computer. Central to our research facility is the small data cell of an IBM 360 model 40 which could hold in its file perhaps the entire card catalog of the University of Oklahoma and the municipal tax rolls of a fairsized city. Both could be placed on a single cylinder, which demonstrates its enormous storage capacity. In fact, one of the cylinders or cells, now accommodates the ERIC file very comfortably. Our on-line information retriever is not available all day long, for it is too expensive a device to keep idle until someone wants to use it. The same computer, therefore, must serve many other functions at different times. Once a day, for a two-hour period, we mount the data cell that contains the ERIC file. However, our primary device for producing bibliographies, which is one of our major outlets of these searches, is simply a line printer.

We not only do a number of searches for our own document-processing operation but also accept letters and personal queries from media specialists. If they are unable to sit at the console themselves, which we encourage them to do whenever possible, we conduct the on-line search for them. The bibliographic results of the search are then printed out on the line printer and turned over to them. A great deal of money is spent on this kind of user service, and it is very inefficient from the Washington cost-benefit accounting point of view. This may be true when you consider a one and a half hour struggle trying to satisfy the query contained in a letter from a North Dakota school district, but we feel differently about such an information system and continue to fight the cost effectiveness battle with Washington accountants. We have the entire ERIC file in addition to our local file which is updated by the computer contractor, North American Rockwell Corporation, so that at any given moment a relatively current file can be searched. This is the facility of "interquery," and the computer reports are located elsewhere.

Stanford University has an information system referred to as the Stanford Public Information Retrieval System, which was developed originally as a physics information system by Edwin Parker. It became the core of the Stanford Library Automation Project under a contract from the Office of Education and later became a general purpose public facility. We ran our ERIC tapes into it, and if we wanted, we could use both consoles simultaneously. However, we found that when there was a choice, we preferred to use the cathode tube, for we are able to page through the abstracts much faster and complete the search more quickly.

The system we are using is called the dialog system, which is explained in our user's manual for this particular system. The dialog system was developed by the Lockheed Aircraft Corporation under a contract to the National Aeronautics and Space Administration (NASA). We felt a little apologetic about asking Lockheed to take over our 20,000-item ERIC file, but we found that NASA's performance records were good. The company was able to handle 500,000 items without any noticeable lag in searching. As the computer goes through the data cell, looking for all bibliographic entries to satisfy any given request, the person at the console is not really aware that half a million NASA documents are being searched. The response is too fast for one to believe the computer is searching half a million documents.

Our complete ERIC citation, down to the bottom of the descriptive fields, may be shown on a cathode ray tube (CRT) display. In a complete ERIC citation you will find in the upper left corner the ERIC document number, title, author, and institutional source. Also shown is the price of the ERIC document reproduction service. The same information could be printed out on the auxiliary printer if a copy was needed for preservation. However, these printers, being modified electric typewriters, move at Selectric typewriter speeds, and so they are used only when is absolutely necessary.

Because it is a human-engineered system, we find that a person without any previous exposure to any kind of computing or bibliographic retrieval beyond the card catalog can use this system of coordinate searching. Our clearinghouse staff members in charge of indoctrinating people into the system find about fifteen minutes is sufficient. We also use the system ourselves each day to do cumulative searching operations and locate documents.

Expansion is one of the unique powers of a computer information system allowing a computer file to become, in reality, several files in one. A search goes into the linear files of all citations posted in a section number order that is known as the master file, but for searching efficiency each of the fields of the master file that ought to be searched is broken out and turned into an inverted file. That is, all index terms are broken out of the master file and become files of their own.

The master file in a conventional system is the shelflist. A card catalog is created by breaking out of the shelflist each of the indexing terms and author's name and title. Although they are usually mixed together in the card catalog, it is equally possible to have one card catalog for subject terms and another for authors' names. These inverted files are kept logically separated in the computer and are expansions of the inverted files of indexing terms. With this feature one is able to look at nearby descriptors. After the computer displays the expansion of the inverted file, it is ready for the next command. The computer will also show the thesaurus with its hierarchical structure. The hierarchical display is most important because it brings together terms which are logically related but alphabetically different. The thesaurus indicates that the terms the searcher is looking at have a hierarchical relationship.

As an illustration of what happens when you create a thesaurus on a priori principles —that is, when you have a kind of systematics that guides you in creating the thesaurus, and then only later are documents ever posted to any of the terms—you may have 900 documents posted to *instructional materials*, one document posted to *educational materials*, and no documents for any of the other terms. Even though the file is now larger than 20,000 items, there are many terms in the thesaurus that have never been used and a large number of terms that have been used only once. The problem of any a priori indexing scheme of any kind is that you can argue over the merits of a term for hours and then, with a split vote, insert it into the thesaurus, where two years may elapse without it being used. There are, however, equally difficult problems in creating a post hoc indexing system in which terms are entered only after someone wants to use them.

Question: What kinds of lexicographic skills are available to the ERIC media center?

Mr. Paisley: The ERIC system has its chief lexicographer James Eller, who, before he came to the Office of Education, was one of the prime movers in creating the Department of Defense thesaurus, which is much larger and more complicated than that of the ERIC system. He is a first-rate lexicographer, a man of strong opinion, as all lexicographers seem to be. Local clearinghouses do not have lexicographers but index specialists. The latter need not be etymological experts, but the professional lexicographer needs these highly specialized skills.

Question: You used a nice, intellectual

phrase earlier, "we gambled on microfiche." How did you gamble on it, and why did you not proceed with microcards at the time?

Mr. Paisley: We gambled on microfiche because there is now, more or less, a coordinated federal attitude toward information processing which is organized by the Committee on Scientific and Technical Information. Within the executive office of the president there is the Office of Science and Technology. Its Committee on Scientific and Technical Information set up a standard for microform, 105mm microfiche. By the time we had to make the decision, the Department of Defense, NASA, National Science Foundation, and others had already made the commitment to 105mm microfiche. It is more than just a size standard, it is a frame standard, sixty to seventy-two frames depending on whether you have a readable reader or not, and an eighteen to twenty magnification ratio.

It is a gamble, not in terms of technology, because that was already adopted by other federal agencies, but rather in terms of whether educators would use microform at all. User studies show that microform is resisted by people, for they like to carry recorded information with them.

Question: Why did they not use microcard, an opaque card?

Mr. Paisley: It is not used as much in the particular circle in which we would be circulating reports. The decision for a 105mm standard was a bit of a compromise between government offices because while the Department of Defense had been using a three-by-five-inch card, NASA had been using a five-by-eight-inch card, and they compromised on the 105-mm size. I am sure there are two or three systems in every shop that has a microfilm archives. Only the future will vindicate this decision to introduce still another standard at this time.

Question: Can you amplify your statement that you would keep a system for the organization of nonprint material separate?

Mr. Paisley: I think the theory of descriptive cataloging and of indexing data indicates that the heterogeneity of the items that can be put in the same file is the result of the number of fields they can share versus the number of fields that have to be set aside for one component of the file and not used at all by another component. If you are working through an arrangement of print material, you have a difficult enough problem bringing journal articles, unpublished reports, theses, and books into the same file, especially in the descriptive cataloging stage but also to some extent in the indexing. You have fields that are usable for only one of those components. The journal article citation field is wasted space for all the other report media.

Comment: You made the point about the collection of tapes for the purpose of organizing information content. Although it is understandable that actual physical objects must be dealt with in different ways, when you realize the many things we do within a system, the physical handling of objects is a relatively small part. Are not the objects only physical carriers of information?

Mr. Paisley: That is not an issue at all. The attribute of the object would have to be posted somewhere. The attributes are sufficiently similar so that you can post them in similar fields, and then one descriptive cataloging and index system can be expanded to serve the purpose. But even though the physical property of the objects is not an issue, there are attributes for the nonprint media that have to be put into some field that are completely unknown. Terms used in descriptive cataloging and indexing—such as length of feet in the film, size of the film, and black and white or color—are specific attributes. Do you not think they are necessarily particular physical attributes and, therefore, should be posted in different fields?

Comment: All you are saying is that you do not search on the collation at the moment. In libraries a number of librarians are quite happy to retrieve books on the basis of their being printed on vellum, which is a purely physical attribute. This is, in fact, machine searchable in MARC, and I would say you would not use it very often. You use it more in media, I would grant.

Mr. Paisley: There is a difference between computerized indexing systems and the number of attributes that can be tolerated in a system.

Comment: Yes, and I have been talking it over with the computerized systems people, but the computerized system designs are all basically principles established for the manual system, particularly the human-oriented system. What if it were being machine oriented so effectively that you only press a button at the beginning? For MARC those parameters are in sight. The MARC II format is an example of a significant development in this direction.

Mr. Paisley: Yes, as soon as the computer file gets MARC, we will try to cut back drastically on the number of attributes that are posted. The number of attributes acceptable to MARC II is manyfold larger than the number we would consider. Perhaps in the future no one is going to mount MARC II as an on-line retrieval facility.

Comment: I am sorry to hear you say that, for MARC II will probably be in use in Great Britain in an experimental form within ten years.

Mr. Paisley: How large a retrieval file do you think you could maintain in the MARC II format?

Comment: The MARC II format is a manipulable one, and this brings one back to the point that a straightforward, sequential, and chronologically designed MARC format may be restructured or reformatted for differing purposes. By saying this, I am really defining the very first step as not changing the format of the record but using that format in a differing order. For machine retrieval, I for one, would simply put a Dewey decimal on it.

Comment: There is little doubt in any technician's mind that the statements Mr. Croghan has made are true. But your statement, Dr. Paisley, that you tend to reduce the number of items to sort on as the pile grows larger is of particular concern to me. I hope you will refrain from that, because the larger the file gets, the more valuable those small items become.

Mr. Paisley: A distinction should be made between the number of dimensions of classification versus the sublety of any given dimension. One of the dimensions by itself is the indexing system, while another dimension all by itself is object dimension. A file of educational reports can be handled completely in about four dimensions, and one of them is necessarily a subtle dimension, the indexing dimension, which should be broken up no matter how large the file grows.

The distinction I am making between a computerized descriptive cataloging file and an additional library file is based on the procedure at the Stanford Library, which integrates ordering, acquisitions, and accessioning attributes together with descriptive attributes. By the time the list is completed, there are some 140 different things that you can say about a document from its ordering information to the final shelf location. To maintain the record of 140 attributes for each entry in the computer file would require random access storage much larger than we have now in the large file. We are talking in terms of six to ten attributes. Six attributes means six dimensions of classification, of which only one is the subject index. I would not reduce the number of terms in the index to create a more compact computer record, that is not the issue.

Question: Why do I need a computer to locate the document?

Mr. Paisley: You would not, for you have the manual indexes.

Question: Why would I need an on-line computer to coordinate the searchable material?

Mr. Paisley: To complete a power search in the same sense, you should have an on-line computer to give you the full power of the card catalog. This is the new technology.

Question: You are giving the patron without computer facilities everything that he would have if you had no computer system at all, and providing additional service for those who do have a computer?

Mr. Paisley: Yes, the on-line movement does not require computers at your location. It requires only that you are willing to pay IBM the monthly rent for a terminal, which is not expensive, and the long-distance line charges for the actual on-line time you use of the centralized computers. This sounds formidable, but it is really very simple.

I do not think that there are subtleties in nonbook classification that are of a different order of complexity from book classification. The difficulty of the past has resulted from attempting to transfer nonbook classification indexing systems that were developed for books. This is really just an exercise of the mind that comes under the general heading of taxonomy. Taxonimizing goes on in all fields.

Comment: Dr. Paisley, you raise the point of post-coordinate methods that do not use classification in any way at all. You can transfer classification, using it for the purpose for which it was intended, in the way that it was intended, which was not post-coordinate, over to the nonbook media. And, I would aver flatly that most of the systems already developed for the information content of print media can be transferred, in the appropriate situation, over to the control of nonbook media, and you can use post-coordinate methods.

The subject of a work remains the same, whatever its physical form. You have discussed ERIC at some length. Your presentation could be print on paper, videotape, audiotape, or a filmstrip for the content would remain exactly the same. Regardless of the format, the subject remains that of ERIC at Stanford.

The system that has been developed from subject indexing can, in fact, cope with any particular indexing system. The problem is transferring it into an appropriate form. If you are saying that you tried to use book subject classification for nonbook media in your computer system, the problem was not the nonbook media, it was the fact that you were using the wrong tool for your system.

Mr. Paisley: The ERIC thesaurus would be completely inappropriate for cataloging nonbook material.

Question: Why should it be?

Mr. Paisley: It covered the wrong subject content. If we had films to go along with educational research projects, it would be, but films are not on educational research projects. They are on the substance of the instruction, and the thesaurus is not developed for that.

Comment: I know of at least one film that is going to deal with educational research within this group, and I would be very much surprised if there was not, educational media under the broad heading "educational research." It will be in the form of films. You yourself told us to think in terms of informa-

tion and not educational research. Once you start talking about educational information, there is a considerable range of educational information on film, and I do not mean merely media used for education, but the principles of education on film, which is entirely appropriate to your ERIC center and its data bank.

Mr. Paisley: An indexing system has to be sufficiently precise at its lowest level of specificity for the distinctions that exist among the objects to be indexed to persevere. The ERIC thesaurus will have a term like *biology* that will be its lowest level of specificity because the subsequent content of the report to be processed will require further specificity. You can have ten instructional films on biology, and there will be multiple distinctions among those films that the thesaurus can not represent.

Question: Are you saying that your thesaurus is rather an inefficient tool?

Mr. Paisley: No, not for the purpose that it was intended to serve.

Comment: On the whole, a rather inefficient tool, judged purely as a thesaurus and in view of my professional interest, which is this particular area.

Question: What would you recommend for the organization of nonprint media if you do feel both can not be combined in your system?

Comment: I suggest we examine the Ohio State University communications system, which is the result of a research project.

Mr. Paisley: That is a very special example. I wish I could design an indexing system to represent that product.

Comment: They could both be handled by the same indexing system.

Mr. Paisley: Indeed they could, because they were produced in parallel. I am concerned about how you take the catalogs of Encyclopaedia Britannica and Coronet films and an ad hoc file of videotapes and a file of single-concept loops and audiotapes and somehow put them in the same system.

Comment: You do not take the entire output of Encyclopaedia Britannica, but you break it up into subject fields, and those that pertain to adult education go to the ERIC Clearinghouse on Adult Education, and those that pertain to media technology go to the

ERIC Center for Media Technology. You do not try to put all media into the media technology program, for it should be placed according to subject fields.

Mr. Paisley: Let me make a point that may clarify what would happen if you did that with a card catalog. ERIC is not in a position to process textbooks. You could have ten textbooks for social studies on the secondary school level, but the thesaurus could not make distinctions among those textbooks that would be useful.

The substantative content as well as instructional strategy and environmental considerations, such as student achievement and motivation, are all facets of the thesaurus. When you are trying to classify a textbook, all the distinctions that might be important in classifying a textbook are virtually absent from the thesaurus. Now the Britannica film, which is very much like a textbook, is very strong in substantive content, but it does not utilize at all the depth of the thesaurus on environmental considerations of facilities.

Question: Could you make the same statement for ten textbooks on educational media? It would not be appropriate for them either?

Mr. Paisley: We process a few textbooks, those sent as announcements, such as the revised edition of James Brown's textbook. The indexing for a textbook is really very meager—audiovisual instruction, teaching methods. This kind of self-evident indexing does not have to be there at all.

Comment: My point is that you do not have to take the entire Britannica output. You are limiting yourself in the world of print. As you just said, you are only dealing with certain areas that relate to research in very specific fields of study, and you do not even include textbooks of these areas. Equally as well, you could take the world of film and omit those films that do not apply. But I assure you there are films that do apply, a good number of them.

Comment: Dr. Paisley, you did start off with a general statement that you can not transfer indexing systems for print material to nonbook. What you are now qualifying hastily, I believe, is that your particular system and your particular parameters, on the whole, do

not match audiovisual parameters. That is an entirely acceptable statement. You define your system to meet the parameters which you have laid down, and no one can properly quarrel with that. But your initial statement is open to very considerable question; in fact, it is not true.

Mr. Paisley: Well, I have a fair familiarity with indexing systems set up for print material, and there is one limiting case in which they could be applied well to nonprint material. That would be the limiting case in which the producer of the nonprint material had been so unimaginative as to simply create in a nonprint format the equivalent of print substance.

Comment: I have taken the performing arts, a very specific area of film that is perhaps the most devoid of subject content, and have developed a classification for this that works quite well, even if I must say so myself. I am sorry but your statement is not true.

Question: Could you say why you could not apply a system for one to the other? Could you be more specific from your background as an index specialist?

Mr. Paisley: The distinction, I think, is that nonprint materials are capable of more dimensional aspects than print materials. Only the most limited and unimaginative use on nonprint material gives the kind of identity in which the film is only the equivalent of the content of print media.

Question: Could you give an example of this?

Mr. Paisley: The film version of a history book could be indexed to the indexing system utilized for the history book itself. However, I do not agree that an imaginative nonprint production is going to be indexed according to that same system. I can index anything in any system, but the first question is, is it retrievable in that system; second, are the users satisfied with the results in that system; and third, are there dimensions of content to which we are completely oblivious and with which we think we are doing a good job but are not?

Question: I would like to ask, if there is difficulty in handling the creative elements of film, how would you construct a system for this purpose?

Mr. Paisley: I would set up a different indexing system, but it would still have the same hierarchical structure, or lack of hierarchical structure. The dimensions of a print indexing system are quite different. A good indexing system is a meshing of multiple dimensions of perceivable differences in content, and the dimensions of perceivable differences in print media are different from the perceivable differences of nonprint material.

Comment: There is a vast array of material which will be inaccessible unless we find a way to index it, and I believe that is why we are here.

Mr. Paisley: There is one further distinc-tion I would like to make. It would not strain even the inappropriately used ERIC system to classify instructional film, as has been proven with the teaching of anatomy. We could do that easily because we have the descriptors for it, but consider the problem of screening the product. It is much more difficult than the problem of screening print material. You would really want to make the indexing so specific that by the time you get to a screening stage, you are pretty confident that what you are screening is what you really want. There are several dimensions of perceivable differences that the ERIC thesaurus could not capture.

National Information Center for Educational Media

Glenn D. McMurry

The library at the University of Southern California has no motion-picture films. All university film materials, other than some specialized collections, are located in the Division of Cinema, Film Distribution Section. This Cinema Division is the oldest and largest of its kind in the world. Many students have passed through its doors since its creation back in the 1930s. Since its opening, students have made many films that have potential use by schools and colleges throughout the country as well as by the University of Southern California (USC).

In 1950 a film library was begun and its use has been promoted throughout the United States. Realizing that the greatest number of potential users of film were schools and colleges and the problem was communication with the classroom teacher, an extensive catalog listing of the USC collection was prepared. By the time the hand-typed catalog was finished, the project had exceeded its budget and the material was out-of-date. This was troubling, especially when funds were difficult to obtain and no visible results could be seen from the catalog to support even the initiation of a supplement.

An application of a keypunch machine was then investigated to ascertain if it could be utilized in preparing listings, or camera-ready copy for a catalog. At this time, the late 1950s, not much had been done to support or question the theory. With the help of another department that had acquired some unit-card equipment, film distribution personnel were able to prepare some materials on punch cards and prepare listings. The resulting printout was not considered top graphic quality, but it was readable and was certainly a breakthrough in film catalog composition and production.

The initial work in automated cataloging at the University of Southern California consisted of establishing certain formats for printing. It was soon discovered that a line length had to be established in order to get proper reduction in printing. A report form was devised in order that a smooth procedure could be established for transferring data from written material to machine-readable cards. The original work was done entirely by unit card, with no computers involved. This became a barrier, however, when it was discovered that a "memory" was needed to retain certain bibliographical facts to be printed at random throughout the printout. The Graduate School of Business at the University had a computer of the IBM 1401 series, with 8,000 core positions and 2 tape drives. Thanks to company engineers, the writing of Autocoder was quickly learned, and a magnetic tape record was constructed that would include critical data pertaining to film.

From this early and rather crude beginning,

Former Director of NICEM; now Chief, Distribution Branch, National Audiovisual Center, Washington

procedures for inputting data began to take shape. Forms were developed for translating data from typewritten form to machine-readable cards, and for processing and editing. Because of the realization that these problems were universal, consideration was given to sharing ideas about automated cataloging with other audiovisual coordinators in Southern California. Interest grew until it was suggested that a grant be sought from the U.S. Office of Education. This was done with the help of the Audio Visual Education Association of Southern California, and a project grant of approximately $114,000 was awarded. Its purpose was to ascertain whether a central computer with a data bank of information about media could prepare unique catalogs for selected schools in Southern California more economically than each school could prepare its own.

The project, now known as the Southern California Automated Cataloging Project, covered a two-year period, 1964 through 1966. Accomplishments of the project included the establishment of guidelines for computerized cataloging, later used by both the state of California and the Department of Audiovisual Instruction; more than 350 individual catalogs for schools and colleges throughout the United States; and a massive data bank, the contents of which were first published by McGraw-Hill Book Company and subsequently by the Bowker Company. The data bank at the University of Southern California includes information not only on film, but data on filmstrips, overhead transparencies, slides, and a number of other media compatible with the requirements of the individual schools requiring catalogs.

The project would never have succeeded without the help of the Department of Cinema, the Graduate School of Business, and International Business Machines (IBM). The freedom to search out new ways of doing things was an accepted fact at the university. Thus approval was given to proceed with minimum restraint. The IBM 1403 printer proved to be a technical wonder, for it required a minimum of maintenance as a printing medium, and, coupled with the 1401 computer, made a perfect match for the project.

Another important outcome was the development of the "call card." Based upon user needs instead of data-processing convenience, this card was used to trigger the computer to print complete data about a particular title and merge specific organizational information for that title in a printout. An order number, for instance, could mean only one thing, a specific school's order number. Too, specific grade-level indications and color codes would be assigned to films that another group could not accept. Information that could be standardized, such as title and bibliographical data, was utilized in all catalogs.

Subject headings remained a problem throughout the project because most of the organizations needed their own subject headings. This was not by design or by tradition for the question "Would they use the service if forced to utilize general headings set up by the project?" was answered in the negative. Therefore, each catalog had its own subject section designed by its user. The patterns are now changing, however.

Soon after the project ended in 1966, McGraw-Hill Book Company published the *Index to 16mm Educational Films* (1967) and the *Index to 35mm Educational Filmstrips* (1968). Both were circulated widely throughout the country. Done in computer printout, both books represented the holdings at USC of those groups contributing to the project between 1960 and 1967. The subject section and indexes were added as requested by the publisher. The books *did not* represent a comprehensive listing of materials, but rather the university's holdings as of the publishing date.

Among the contributors to the project were the producers and distributors of materials, evidence of the spirit of cooperation that existed from the beginning of the project. Developed with the cooperation of the Library of Congress was a report form, which led to uniform reporting both to the center and to the Library of Congress.

The center at the University of Southern California is now known as the National Information Center for Educational Media (NICEM). Its services are available to schools, colleges, and other interested groups for the preparation of customized catalogs utilizing the data bank, the most comprehensive in the world. Information from the data bank is now being used extensively throughout the United States as many data centers utilize all or portions of the automated cataloging system to set up their own information systems.

The future promises a complete computerized network utilizing the standards and information gained from the automated cataloging project. Complex computers are able to process and transmit information at extremely high rates of speed and at a decreasing price. Instant information, as well as upper- and lowercase conversion, is becoming practical. Consistent cataloging, using the guidelines set up by the project, will guarantee a consistent output that is usable. The saying "garbage in, garbage out" is a truism that must be reckoned with in the information field. The human being can never shirk his responsiblity in maintaining a data bank if integrity is the goal.

The two earlier NICEM publications published by McGraw-Hill, *Index to 16mm Educational Films* and *Index to 35mm Educational Filmstrips,* were revised in 1969 and 1970 respectively and published by Bowker. Additional publications of the center's nonprint-media resources are the *Index to 8mm Motion Cartridges* and the *Index to Overhead Transparencies,* both published by Bowker in 1969. The National Information Center for Educational Media makes possible these special media catalogs obtained electronically from its data bank containing over 70,000 titles of nonprint material stored on computer tape.

Instructional Materials Services for Montgomery County Public Schools

Richard L. Darling

I discovered a problem when I was librarian at the University High School in Ann Arbor, Michigan, and was attempting to catalog a collection of records. I did not begin to know there was a solution until almost twenty years later, when I was with the Livonia, Michigan, Public Schools. There Ted Samore and I drew up a plan for cataloging the film library and presented it annually to our board of education, only to have the request deleted each year. That plan did not get very far, although in our processing center, we did catalog and classify recordings. We did something else that I realize is in total disrepute; we established a color coding system. I am not apologizing for it; we did it.

The next and most serious experience I had with audiovisual materials and their problems was when I went to the Montgomery County, Maryland, Public Schools. This county is a unified school district with about 127,000 pupils. It is one of the twenty largest school districts in the country, with 180 schools, so that when we set out to do something, it was for a very large school system indeed. When we started processing nonprint materials, we were by no means just beginning to put them into our school system. In fact, the preface

to the library handbook in 1938 said that the school library was the repository for filmstrips, slides, and all other educational media. It was not really until much later, however, that something systematic was done.

The Montgomery County School System unified the audiovisual and school library programs in 1961, as the result of a survey done by James Brown from San Jose State College. In a report called *Instructional Materials Services for Montgomery County Schools* he recommended to the superintendent that the division of instructional materials be created by combining the offices of the supervisor of audiovisual services and the supervisor of library services. He also recommended that centralized cataloging and processing be established. Among the functions for that office, he recommended "catalog all instructional materials for county and individual school card catalogs," and "process all instructional materials, books, films and all, to ready them for distribution and use in the schools or in the county center." The processing center began as soon as it was practicable to implement this survey.

The obvious first step in setting up the processing center was to start where there was a fund of knowledge and experience; therefore, it began with printed materials. It was not until the 1962–63 school year that we first began work with nonprint materials in

Director, Department of Educational Media and Technology, Montgomery County Public Schools, Rockville, Maryland

the processing center, using again that unfavored approach of colorbands, a color coding system. That year, the processing center produced approximately one million printed cards, sorted them, and distributed them to the schools for interfiling in school library card catalogs. This first effort, which was only for the county central inventory, included films, filmstrips, slides, transparencies, maps, globes, art prints, sculpture, models, and kits. In the second year 998 more items of nonprint material were added, completing the same process for those. After a two-year effort we had cataloged, on cards, the entire collection of the Central Instructional Materials Department and had deposited and interfiled this complete catalog in each of some 150 card catalogs throughout the system.

It was not until the following year that the processing center began to provide service on nonprint materials for school collections. In that year we added filmstrip cataloging as a service to the schools, and from that point on, we cataloged every filmstrip that went into the school libraries. We accomplished this by purchasing Library of Congress cards for 6,300 filmstrips and by using the Library of Congress cataloging exclusively. For the other materials we had used our own.

In the 1965–66 school year we added all other types of nonprint materials to our processing center service for the schools, provided that they were published under Title II of the Elementary and Secondary Education Act. Our state plan for Title II was set up in such a way that we had no alternative but to consider the materials we purchased as school library resources. Those not familiar with Title II may not understand the significance of this reference. Title II provides funds for the purchase of school library resources, textbooks, and other instructional materials. When you begin to read the fine print, you discover that school library resources and other instructional materials are exactly the same thing except that one is in an organized collection. The state plan required that ours be organized, so organize it we did.

In 1966–67 alone we processed 37,461 items of nonprint instructional material. Ob-

viously, in order to do this, we had to establish some kind of bibliographic control. We had to determine what our procedures would be and what our cataloging policies would be. We had a little experience with bibliographic control through the issuing of our approved lists of materials for school purchase, one for elementary schools, the other for secondary schools. The amount of bibliographic information included is limited indeed, and for a number of reasons. One was our lack of experience and another the even greater lack of experience of the people in our computer department who worked with us on this. The lists are basically subject lists arranged alphabetically by title within subject, with several indexes. After a code number the entries have information, where it is appropriate, on learning groups and reading levels; give full title, format, the medium, publisher, and an arbitrary item number; and indicate color or black and white and if it is other than an individual item cost. These lists were based on evaluations done by committees made up of teachers, supervisors, librarians, and other members of the professional staff of the school system.

In 1965 we issued only the elementary list, and in each subsequent year we have done a new edition, four of them through the 1969 edition, which will be the final edition of this monumental work, although there will be other kinds of lists. At the end of each year, before the volumes were printed, the computer interfiled all of the added titles and deleted those that had gone out of print or had been removed from the list for other reasons, and the volumes were printed by offset from computer printouts.

The cards that we designed that first year were very poor indeed. They were done for the central inventory during the first year in a primitive attempt to catalog a wide range of audiovisual materials. The format has been revised since, and currently we are hewing closely to more standard cataloging practice.

Question: The answer to this may be obvious to librarians, but is there a standardized code of color?

Mr. Darling: No, there are as many color codes as there are places using them. I do not defend the use of color. Our current plans are to go to computer-produced catalogs soon. Since our computer is incapable of producing color, we will be abandoning it of necessity. The computer is one reason it is much too late for the adoption of a color code nationally, even if it were desirable. So many library systems and audiovisual centers are utilizing computer production of catalogs that the whole issue of color coding is basically a dead one anyhow. This one had some psychological advantages when it was adopted a number of years ago which are no longer valid. At one time the color indicated that certain things were not in the individual school but were located in the county center.

For our central collection, which is a closed collection in which people cannot come to browse, a fixed location number is assigned, which was found as useful as any other type of number. We encouraged classification in the schools, and our processing center today includes a Dewey classification number on every set of cards. We use Sears subject headings both for the central collection and the schools and have continued to include a descriptive note or a contents note on every card. Our practice has been to include such subject headings as would be useful. Original descriptions are written if one is not found from another source. They are simply to give people some information about what they are going to find. When the title is fairly specific, the summary may not add much information at all. It is questionable whether annotations are necessary for any media other than motion-picture film unless the title may not be explanatory.

Comment: I would disagree violently with you that summaries are of no value. Basically, you need annotations for additional information; it is irrelevant what the form of the material is. If the title of the film is perfectly descriptive, and you do not want to give additional information about sequence and division, then you do not. However, if you have a film called *Wheels,* and it is an explanation of a relativity theory, then you must add that or the title is misleading.

Mr. Darling: In a school, particularly when you give children access to all of your ma-

terials, the titles are not going to be of much significance to the children. Rather, the subjects are of primary importance. The same thing is true for teachers if they are trying to use materials to support the instructional program. Perhaps when they order films just before Christmas, subject headings do not make a difference in the ordering but, throughout most of the year, teachers are looking for films that are related directly to the curriculum.

Comment: There was an experiment done with another medium, book material, called Operation Top Soil. It was based on the idea that the most-used catalog cards get grubbiest. The majority of them were subject headings rather than title or author.

Comment: I think the most authoritative annotations that I have come across are those prepared by the Indiana University Audiovisual Center. The center has designed the annotation so that the first sentence contains the essence of the description and then additional sentences may elaborate. If you want it concise for economical reasons, as is very often necessary, then you can use just that first statement. If you can afford a more elaborate description, then you build on that first essential statement.

Comment: Our purpose is to state in one sentence what the film contains, then to go on and elaborate in more detail. As far as economics are concerned, it does cost more, but the feeling on that is that a teacher in the classroom probably does not have, or take, the time to preview the film before using it, as all good utilization rules recommend. This detailed description gives the teacher more information about the film's contents. Perhaps, in fact, we are supporting that type of action.

Mr. Darling: How about the date? We do indicate dates now, whenever we have them, but this is one of the curses of most of the audiovisual media, that the producers quite deliberately do not give dates on the materials. Every time we have an item without a date now, we write a letter to the producer. I do not know if it is doing any good, but we think that ultimately he may get tired of our letters and start putting dates on them.

Comment: Might this problem be alleviated somewhat by a kind of circumvention? Everything gets a date, and if you do not know what it is, you estimate. If you give the item in hand a current date, at least ten years later you could have dated it that much.

Mr. Darling: One of the things we added to our county center recently was a lunar globe. The date would have been very important on this item even if we had to supply one, because this globe was made before the far side of the moon had been photographed and was blank on one side to show that nothing was known of it.

Comment: The Anglo-American code has rules for supplying dates. These do not fit all circumstances, of course, but they are a guideline if you must supply a date.

Question: Is it possible with computer cataloging to have a color-banded card? Many of us see the advantage of a banded card, but this possibly requires a certain piece of equipment.

Mr. Darling: Color codes can be used easily if you want to. You can have your stock preprinted with the color band on it. One of the published manuals states you must put the color strips on by hand. That just is not so. There are machine methods for achieving this purpose.

I want to stress that many of these decisions were made before I went to Montgomery County Public Schools. However, when you have a million or two cards in the catalog, you do not send out a notice that you are going to erase all those color bands, nor do you invest in another two million cards to replace them. As someone has pointed out, once you have done it, whatever it is, you are likely to be stuck with it. When you are providing catalogs for 180 schools, which is what we have this year, the job of redoing any part of it would be fantastically expensive. We now write out as part of the call number, the full name, *transparency,* or whatever it is. If you do not use something on the card for identification, then banding would be necessary. As long as you have something on the card, either in the call number or in the description that tells what the media is, that would tend to signal the user that he has to have a machine, if indeed he does. Obviously, you do not need a machine to look at an art print or maps or globes or charts.

Comment: One other advantage to banded cards in a dictionary catalog is that frequently they are interfiled, and presently we might have 3,000 nonprint items and 15,000 printed items, and it does call attention to those particular types of items, which may be located in different places.

Mr. Darling: The Montgomery County Department of Educational Media and Technology is made up of five divisions: the Division of Instructional Media, the Division of Instructional Technology, Processing Services, Publication Services, and TV Services. The total staff of this department, including the director, is 114 people. Instructional media is responsible for all of the software in the system, for the consultant and advisory services with the schools, for personnel recruitment in the media program, and for working on design of the media centers with the technology division. Technology is responsible for all the hardware. Its staff writes the specifications for all of our audiovisual equipment; they do design work; they inspect work on closed circuit TV systems and the school dial-access systems. Processing division duties should be obvious. Publications is the division that is responsible for all of the publishing and printing for the school system. It is made up of a staff of editors, artists, and typesetters. They do not set manual type; they work with IBM magnetic tape composing systems. The artists do the layout and illustration. Printing and binding is also a part of this division; we have six presses at the moment. The television division is responsible for production of television for broadcast and ultimately, when the system is constructed, will have the responsibility for a four-channel 2500 megahertz distribution system.

Question: Do you not have a production center on the district level?

Mr. Darling: The Graphic Arts Department does design; it has an elaborate setup. Also in technology there is a production section, although no original art is done there. The section in instructional technology duplicates slides, transparencies, and microfilm. I simply forgot to mention that.

Question: Does your Graphic Arts Department work between those two?

Mr. Darling: The reproduction section is manned by clerks who can snap cameras on a copying machine or a microfilm camera, or run things through from pre-prepared masters, which may be done in graphic arts or may be commercially produced. Ordinarily we do not prepare things for the schools unless we are going to do them in large quantities for a lot of schools. Every school has its own production facility as part of its learning center.

I report to the Assistant Superintendent for Instructional and Pupil Service, who is one of five assistant superintendents. The other four are the Assistant Superintendent for Administration, who runs the schools; the Assistant Superintendent for Business and Financial Services; the Assistant Superintendent for Personnel; and the Assistant Superintendent for Educational Information Analysis, the person who is in charge of all computer operations. The directors of the Department for Supervision and Curriculum Development, the Department of Pupil Services, the Department of Pupil and Program Appraisal, and my department make up the Division of Instruction.

Question: Could you tell me who are the people on the building level that run the instructional media center, or whatever you call it, and what kind of persons they are? Is there one person, one professional person, three paraprofessionals, or what?

Mr. Darling: That depends on the size of the school. There are generally from one to three professionals. We have the largest staffs in the high schools of about 2,000 enrollment—six people, including three professional librarians, who work under a state certification system, and three supporting services persons, who as professional media center personnel are required to have eighteen hours of library science. We hire librarians and retread them or, occasionally, get a person with an audiovisual degree and retread him or her with the eighteen hours.

The Media Division runs an enormous in-service education program; in fact, we have one specialist in this division whose sole duties relate to in-service education in media. We conduct workshops for professional staff, both teachers and media specialists, and also for our supporting people. When we design the media centers or rennovate old ones, we plan a production center into each of them. The production centers have the facilities for making transparencies, mounting pictures, and laminating.

Question: What facilities and services do you have in your central instructional media center and where do you take care of evaluation and reviewing?

Mr. Darling: The Instructional Media Division is made up of four sections. One is the Media Center Services Section, which does the consultant work with the schools and with in-service education. The Educational Materials Laboratory, our system-wide professional library for the staff, is a media library which is open every Monday through Thursday, from 8:30 in the morning until 9:00 at night and on Saturday from 9:00 in the morning until 3:00 in the afternoon. The third section of Instructional Media is the Central Film Library. The fourth area is the Review and Evaluation Section, which is responsible for such things as our lists of recommended materials. The Review Section coordinates the work of about sixty committees that evaluate materials. It also coordinates a tremendous number of additional evaluations done in individual schools. The job of this section is to bring in the materials from vendors or publishers, get it to the people or committees who will review it, take the evaluations that result, and issue lists of recommended materials which are then distributed to the schools. The staff have been doing four basic lists, but, in addition to that, they do special subject lists such as elementary science. They have just issued a supplement to one published last year, *Negroes in American Life,* which is a bibliography of materials for elementary school. Shortly, they are going to do a similar one for secondary schools, and, increasingly, they are working on special subject areas in issuing their lists in bibliographies. While we have about 114 people in the department, if we count the people in schools, then the total exceeds 400.

Question: How many schools does the division serve all together?

Mr. Darling: There are 180 schools in our own system, but the processing center serves 300 other schools. It serves all the private schools in the state of Maryland where there are Title II materials. We purchase, catalog, process, and lend the materials to these non-public schools under contract with the state Department of Education. Actually, we process for 480 schools, but not the complete collections for private schools.

Question: Could you explain to me what are your reasons for reorganizing the computer evaluation process?

Mr. Darling: Formerly the committees did everything, but it has become too big and too complex. We could not get done; that is the reason. Also, in response to all the outcry, strikes, and the other demands for decentralization, this seemed the appropriate time to decentralize much of the evaluation process. Under the new process we have the evaluation done at the school level for all materials except textbooks and 16mm motion picture film. We still will continue to manage all the logistics related to acquiring the materials and getting them to the schools. Another element in changing our evaluation system is that I have been convinced for a long time that there are people doing reviews for *Booklist* and *Library Journal* and other reviewing media who are just as smart as our own personnel. We will begin accepting reviews in professional journals, which we have not done for years. It took me six years to convince some of our staff that everything need not be read, viewed or listened to in our own school system.

Question: Do you have any cost figures available on your processing?

Mr. Darling: I knew you were going to ask that, but I do not recall precisely what they are. We have had to figure our cost because of a state contract which is based on actual expenses; we do not make a profit. Our cost for processing is a little lower for books than for nonprint media, about sixty-five to seventy-five cents per item. This includes procurement costs, as well as cataloging and processing, and is therefore not directly comparable to the price of commercial processing. Incidentally, we occasionally buy preprocessed materials. If a single senior or junior high school is opening, we may buy the collection from a commercial processing firm.

Question: Do you maintain a district stan-dard on all of your cataloging? Do all your high schools have the same cataloging and classification specifications?

Mr. Darling: We do not do custom cataloging for anyone. Some of the private schools complained, but none of the parochial schools did. Several exclusive private schools in the suburbs wanted us to do custom cataloging of the material they were being loaned. The state department pointed out to them that these *were* loans and that ours was, in fact, the state's cataloging. We have had a standard within the county and the schools ever since the processing center was begun in 1961. Prior to that I suspect it was chaos. However, we did not do extensive recataloging. Perhaps some of the schools did, but they were encouraged not to. We felt that in a very few years the materials they had organized would be worn out or replaced. Replacement titles would come through the processing center, and usually, unless the school had directed otherwise, they would receive a new set of cards.

Not all of the cataloging and processing of material is done at the center. I wish that it were, but it really is not. About the time that Title II began, the board of education doubled our local book budget. But when they doubled the book budget, I could not convince them that they ought to put some extra people in the processing center. For about two and a half years we were running eight to ten months behind. We did have plans to add a media each year, starting with filmstrips in the 1964–65 school year. It took us until last year to catch up. We now process materials in four to six weeks and plan to add other media. We have processed all books and filmstrips purchased with Title II funds. This is far from the full range of media. The other nonprint items purchased by the schools have had to be done in each individual school. This is terribly wasteful, but we could not do otherwise, when our processing center was in danger of collapsing because of this immense increase in the work load. This past year, the staff cataloged for the schools, our own, and the Title II private schools, about 330,000 items. There is not another processing center connected with a school system or library system that has the volume we have done. This is what Tauber and Hines say in the survey report they made of our system.

The schools do all of their own selection. They work from lists of recommended materials, but they go beyond that and make the selections. The relationship of our processing center to the schools is no different from that of a jobber, a wholesaler relationship, except that we manage the funds. They send us the order forms, and we order from a jobber or publisher. When they get the materials, they are ready for use.

Question: Have you thought of going to computers for this?

Mr. Darling: Have I *thought* about it? I have been thinking about it for a long time and have gone back through all the annual reports for the department from its creation as the Division of Instructional Materials in 1961. Beginning with the organizational report submitted to the school board when the division had been set up for about two months, and in every annual report since, this has been one of the recommendations. For a variety of reasons we have delayed. We now have an analyst assigned to begin designing systems. I am not sure yet what kind, but we hope that in two or three years something will be ready.

Part 6

Systems
and
Standards

Schemes, plans, and programs have been developed for the logical organization of media. These have been simple, complicated, related to library classification, arbitrary, logical, full of loopholes and problems, very particularly local, widely applicable, incomplete, or overwhelmingly detailed. Individual librarians or media administrators in local situations have developed their own systems. Professional committees and groups have discussed and adopted schemes. Some have been published.

Adequate media utilization is not possible due, in large part, to the lack of proper organization for its bibliographic control. Presentations by some specialists brought together to consider this obstruction to the use of non-print media are included here as an introduction to the broad concepts of systems and standards for the control of media. The speakers and their colleagues agreed that information scientists, media specialists, and librarians must find appropriate ways to organize these rapidly expanding formats of technology to make possible their effective use by society.

Specific codes conceived in different countries were discussed and analyzed in relationship to possible international standards. Per-

sonnel responsible for the Machine-Readable Cataloging format (MARC format) program at the Library of Congress responded to requests and with the assistance of institute participants developed a MARC format for projected images. Various steps in this program were described by those directly involved. Speaking before the 1970 DAVI convention, Louis Brown stressed his work with the MARC project, expressing the expectation that it will "solve our major problem, bibliographic control." Brown feels that it will give educators and students control over educational resources essential in our "ever increasing student population, students whose differences are beginning to be recognized."

Mr. Leni relates previous activities of the International Film and Television Council and its European subgroup and explains his involvement in a report on a meeting held before the media institute in Norman, Oklahoma. He reviews deliberations held between subsequent institute sessions and gives a final report of his council's European subgroups at the last institute session held in Detroit, some nine months after the institute's initial session in Oklahoma.

The Anglo-American
Cataloging Rules

C. Sumner Spalding

All of us here realize a growing sense of urgency in the area of audiovisual or media librarianship. I know that practitioners in this wide field are anxious to find solutions to the problems of bibliographic control. Pearce Grove conceived the idea of bringing together representatives from many different organizations in order that the problems may be properly surveyed with a view to try to regularize, standardize, and advance those aspects which have to do with bibliographic control of the various media.

I am scheduled to speak on the *Anglo-American Cataloging Rules*, which were published in 1967 as the official rules of the American Library Association, the Library Association (Great Britain), the Canadian Library Association, and the Library of Congress. All of these bodies actively participated in their development. These *rules* really constitute a multimedia approach. They are rules for cataloging various kinds of materials or media so that a library collecting these materials will be able to make compatible entries for the various types of media in the same catalog.

I am now using the term *media* to include books as well as nonbook materials. Within the term *books* are various subcategories like pamphlets, multilith documents, publications which appear serially and in parts, periodicals and other continuing publications, facsimile

reprints and microform copies of any of these publications, and, finally, original manuscripts. The rules for nonbook media include those for maps, music, phonorecords, motion pictures, filmstrips, pictures and other types of two-dimensional representations.

The code of rules is divided into three major parts. The first deals with entry and headings. By this we mean the determination of the actual words under which one presents the description of what is being cataloged. Normally these are the names of the authors, secondary authors, editors, corporate bodies or governmental agencies which may have sponsored the publication, and the title. They also cover the titles of series in which the publication is issued. These entries provide the approaches that are needed to locate the particular publication.

We make a distinction between the main entry under which the publication is to be entered and the added entries. In a multiple-entry catalog, whether it is in book, card, or machine format, you may use many entries. However, if all the entries thought to be necessary are used, the main entry is of little consequence. The selection of the main entry does matter if you are going to make a single-entry listing, because you will then have to decide how the publications are going to be listed, whether under the title, the personal *Anglo-American Cataloging Rules'* author, corporate author, or editor. A great many listings, as you know, are single-entry listings.

Although this distinction may be a theoretical matter for multiple-entry catalogs, it is a

Assistant Director, Cataloging and Processing Department, Library of Congress, Washington

practical matter of significant import to the single-entry catalog. It is also important for the specific citation to all types of publications, for without a standard mode of citing bibliographic entries, you have no guidelines for searching. Therefore, we are necessarily involved in the question of establishing the main entry. The *Rules* deal first with the selection of the main entry, and second with what other entries should be utilized for any given publication. These rules for headings deal with the ways you represent the names of personal or corporate authors, authors whose names are Chinese, authors whose names are Arabic, or even authors with Italian names who live in England and publish in French.

The second part of the *Anglo-American Cataloging Rules* deals with description. As were the rules for entry in the first part, the rules for description have been organized primarily for book material. Part 3 deals with the special problems of nonbook material, but the rules for entry, headings, and description for books also apply in the cataloging of nonbook materials. Often there is no reason for special treatment because the material is nonbook. This third part deals only with the special characteristics of such nonbook materials as maps, manuscripts, music, phonorecords, filmstrips, and pictures.

The cataloging rules were designed primarily for the needs of research libraries, although public or popular libraries were kept in mind. When work was first begun on the *Rules*, it was thought that in some cases, or even in many cases, the needs of public libraries would be considerably different from those of university libraries and that possibly there should be two sets of rules, one for research libraries and another for public libraries. We proceeded with this in mind, but as we developed the rules, we found that there were very few of these cases, and such conflicts were resolved by including alternative rules. In addition, the rules were set forth with the clear understanding that a popular library might not wish to include as much cataloging detail as an academic research institution.

As we consider the problems of audiovisual media, there is the possibility that the same kind of conflict may occur. It is conceivable that there may be some conflict among the cataloging needs of the school, public, or academic library. There might be valid variations in the terminology of audiovisual materials for school purposes and for university or adult purposes. In the case of phonorecords, some conflict of interest may arise between a music library, which is essentially a research library, and a general educational institution using the same type of material. There may be differing needs for an art library and a school library using art materials.

Ideally, we should try to find a way to use standard descriptions and terminology that would work for any of these conflict situations. While we certainly should have this as a goal, it is conceivable that we may find it unworkable in some instances. It should then be possible to provide alternative rules, as we did in the case of differing needs of research and public libraries for print materials.

What are the problems to be faced as we start to record nonprint media? The *Rules* do not provide instructions for description of many of the newer media which have been produced in great numbers by commercial firms serving the interests of our educational community. While we have dealt with phonorecords, filmstrips, and motion pictures in the *Anglo-American Rules*, we must provide for slide sets, transparencies, realia, kits, and other types of nonprint media.

Questions have been raised concerning the structure of the *Rules* and whether their basic organization is sound. Once the necessary rules are developed to cover nonprint media, it may be that another structure would be more suitable. There are certain inconsistencies between the rules for one media and another which are presently being reexamined.

The established methodology for making changes in the *Rules* is for the Descriptive Cataloging Committee, a unit of the American Library Association, to approve or disapprove for ALA. However, these are the rules of the Library Association, the Canadian Library Association, the American Library Association, and the Library of Congress. All four of the cooperating bodies will be represented at a meeting (January 1970) with the ALA Descriptive Cataloging Committee, with

Antony Croghan, a participant in this institute, acting as a representative for the Cataloging Rules Subcommittee of the Library Association. Although full representation is not possible at this time, nevertheless, we are going to address ourselves to the problems of nonprint media.

Although ideally certain logical steps should be accomplished in sequence, this achievement will probably be impossible. We are currently working on some of the more advanced steps, while the very first step is yet to be completed. However, the job will not be finished until all phases have been completed.

The first step, in my view, is the identification of media under consideration. Rules for describing media are not possible unless one can state exactly the kind of media for which the rule is intended. One of the requirements for the identification of media is standard terminology. There must be a way to assign a term or phrase to each discrete medium that merits special rules for description. The Technical Services Committee of the Canadian School Library Association has been working on this problem and is preparing a list of these terms. However, one group cannot do the job by itself, for there are too many individuals and organizations concerned with the problem who must achieve agreement. Although it is a slow process, this identification and terminology characterization of the media must be developed.

A possible problem is the determination of what is a medium and what is a form of a medium. In the book field, is a paperback book different from a hardback book or a multilith publication? We have not treated them as though they are different, although they could be described somewhat differently. On the other hand, if we reproduce a publication on microfilm and must use a machine in order to get the message, even though the content is the same, we will have a rather special sort of material that would warrant special rules. These would not be special rules for entry or headings, but rather, special rules for description. In other cases like this, the same content may appear in different media. For example, we may have the original painting of the Rafael Madonna, a photographic slide of that original, and a study print of the same.

After we have sorted out the media and reached agreement on the proper terms for them, we must decide whether any special rules for entry are necessary. Motion pictures and filmstrips are presently exceptions to the general rules of entry for other media, in that the main entry is arbitrarily the title. Obviously, other entries are required, but the main entry is the title. There are filmstrips of books by a specific author in which the entire text is in audio form, with the illustrations filmed for projection. What then should be done with this filmstrip that has all of the content characteristics of a book? Should an exception be made for a movie by Charles Chaplin in which he conceived the whole story, wrote the scenario, played the principal part, and composed the music?

Although these situations arise occasionally, in most cases there will not be any grave problem in the determination of main entries. Should we decide to adopt the general rules and enter films under the person or the corporate body primarily responsible for the intellectual or artistic content, with entry under title when there is no primary responsibility? Many film catalogers have thought that most films would come out with entry under title. But would they? *Coney Island Holiday* is a short subject by Warner Brothers. There are credits for a director, writer, narrator, composer, photographer, and film editor; certainly the personal responsibility is diffuse. What about corporate responsibility? Isn't Warner Brothers totally responsible for creating the entire intellectual and artistic content of the film as a product of its corporate activity? Will the application of the general cataloging rules for the main entry really be more satisfactory than the present arbitrary rule for entry under title?

What aspects of a medium must be described? What is it that we really need to know when we look at a description in a catalog? Certainly information about the content of the materials is needed because it will influence the decision on the selection of particular items. Information about the physical characteristics of the materials is needed if certain equipment is necessary to use it. These are things of consequence to the user, but other things will be important to the library which houses and services the media.

Once rules for entry and rules for description are developed for all media, they must be properly integrated into the pattern with other cataloging rules to achieve a satisfactory multimedia code.

Finally, a machine-readable cataloging format for information exchange and retrieval must be developed. Work has been done toward this development by the Library of Congress. Henriette Avram and her staff have prepared a preliminary draft format in the MARC structure. In its first draft this format is based on the MARC format for books and the cataloging rules previously developed for motion pictures and filmstrips. It is hospitable to other types of audiovisual media, but de-

tails for the other media will have to be integrated a step at a time. The forthcoming Descriptive Cataloging Committee meeting will concern itself primarily with chapter 12 of the *Anglo-American Cataloging Rules,* dealing with motion pictures and filmstrips. These *Rules* were originally developed between 1946 and 1951 by the Library of Congress in cooperation with the Office of Education, the National Archives, the American Library Association, the Educational Film Library Association, and the National Audio-Visual Association. They were thought at the time to be hospitable to all audiovisual works for projection, but it is entirely possible that another chapter is needed for other special educational media. We intend to continue searching for solutions to the problems of cataloging nonprint media.

Canadian Cataloging Code Revision

Jean Riddle

It is often said that educational institutions are organized for the convenience of their administration and that the students stand in the way of a smooth operation of the educational system. While this is unquestionably an exaggeration, there is more than a germ of truth in this statement. A danger exists in all institutions that they will be so organized that the needs and aspirations of professionals will be placed before those of their constituents. Libraries and librarians are no exception in this regard. It seems that sometimes libraries are organized for the use of librarians, and catalogers catalog for the approbation of other catalogers.

Librarians and media specialists must keep in mind constantly the obvious fact that they exist to serve the public, who either directly or indirectly pays the bill. Library users are largely uninformed about cataloging rules. Even those who have had to take library orientation courses during their school years have retained little more than a general concept of cataloging principles. This is not surprising, for cataloging rules, like legal documents, tend to be highly technical and obviously not easily comprehensible to the layman. Therefore, the library must either have sufficient staff to help the patron interpret the catalog and find the materials or, preferably, must construct a catalog which can be used with little instruction.

My experience as a librarian—and I have been connected with university, public, school, and college libraries—leads me to believe that there are generally three types of library users. First, there are those who are looking for material on a given subject. The second group wishes to obtain the work of a particular author, composer, or artist and is concerned with what editions or representations are available. The third group wants a book, sound recording, or art reproduction without having a specific item or subject in mind. These are the browsers.

A catalog should be constructed so as to serve the needs of these users. Separate catalogs for each medium will not, I suggest, accomplish this purpose. Those who are looking for material on a specific subject cannot be expected to pursue it through several catalogs and various library departments. An integrated multimedia catalog will provide a complete alphabetical listing of the library's collection, regardless of format and medium.

For those who seek editions or representations of a work, the integrated multimedia catalog has obvious advantages. The information they seek will be found in one place in one catalog, rather than in two or more catalogs. Even the browser will derive certain advantages from a multimedia catalog, because coincidental with the use of integrated cataloging methods, materials on the same subject will likely be stored in one location.

By now you are all aware that I am an advocate of the integrated multimedia catalog. I believe a well-indexed, well-cataloged, well-filed multimedia catalog gives the best service

Head, Library Technical Services, Borough of East York Board of Education, Toronto

to the public. Because it must, of necessity, be larger than catalogs that index only one medium, it is more difficult for the library to administer. This internal library staff problem should not be used as an excuse for library service that is anything less than first class.

I suggest that the type of medium or format is not of primary concern to most library users. If a selection of materials on a given subject is available, the user then considers the medium. Can the material be used at home or at work? Is special equipment required? It is necessary to use the library's equipment, or can the content of material be obtained with the equipment generally available in the home? The catalog cards should answer these questions quickly. It is necessary, therefore, to indicate the medium in a clearly established position on the card.

In order to achieve the above objectives, we believe that part 3 of *Anglo-American Cataloging Rules* should be revised. Three revisions are basic to the construction of the multimedia catalog. Other revisions proposed in the Canadian code revision briefs are refinements of cataloging and not fundamental to the structure of the multimedia catalog.

We believe that the first major revision should be that the rules of entry in part 1 be applied to all materials, both book and nonbook. The general principle which states "entry should be under title for works whose authorship is diffuse, indeterminate or unknown" should be extended to make this rule pertinent to nonbook materials. Under the current rules a work reproduced in diverse media may not be entered in the same manner. This means than two items containing the same subject matter may be widely separated in the catalog, for example, a set of art prints of Renoir's paintings will be entered under the artist. The same prints photographed and made into a slide set will be entered under the title of the slide set. If the library patron approached these through impressionism in art, he would not find these two similar items standing together in the catalog. It may very well be that one of these items will be lost to him if he is not knowledgeable about the structure of the catalog.

Many audiovisual producers are hiring well-known authorities to edit, write, put together, or, in other words, undertake the authorship function for nonbook materials in the field of their specialty. Edward Radlauer has written many books about motorcycles which are widely read by teenage boys. He is cited as the author of many nonbook materials on motorcycles including a multimedia kit. It seems reasonable that all materials by him should stand together in the subject listing.

The second major revision that we propose is the establishment of a list of media designations which can be adopted by librarians and media specialists. Terminology in the nonbook field is complicated by the interchangeable use of trade names and generic terms. Media designations should be generic terms, defined for cataloging purposes only in such a way that the cataloger knows which media designation to select for the particular item he wishes to describe.

We sent out a list of media designations to 200 specialists in North America and Great Britain; approximately 100 people sent back answers. We found that by far the most difficult part of the book which we are about to bring out was deciding on the media designations list. We are not at all satisfied with this list. It is going to require a great deal more research.

The list of media designations should also establish clearly the placement of the media designation on the catalog card. The multimedia catalog could be used much more efficiently if the media designation is always found in the same position on the card. Whether it is placed after the title, in the collation, in notes, or some other place is a secondary consideration.

The third revision which we in Canada feel should be incorporated into the *Anglo-American Cataloging Rules* results from the diversity of titles found on nonbook materials. We have suggested an order of precedence for establishing the correct title. The exact wording of this rule is yet to be decided.

The three authors of *Non-Book Materials: The Organization of Integrated Collections* have discussed the *Anglo-American Cataloging Rules* revision for almost a year. We have written briefs, attended meetings, and expressed our opinions on many occasions. Our book is based on the *Anglo-American Cataloging Rules* and incorporates the revisions which we have proposed. We have field tested these ideas, and we think that they produce a service-oriented multimedia catalog. We are not completely happy with the book, for some areas of it need more research. However, it is a preliminary edition, and we hope that in

about eighteen months either the Canadian Library Association by itself or the Canadian Library Association, the American Library Association, and the Association for Educational Communications and Technology together will bring out a much more definitive work. We hope that in the months to come you will tell us where we have succeeded and where we have failed.

Catalog Code Revision
from the English
Point of View

Antony Croghan

When it became known to me that I was going to follow Sumner Spalding, editor of the *Anglo-American Cataloging Rules (AACR)*, suddenly I had a very, very vivid realization of how the sorcerer's apprentice must have felt. To you, Mr. Spalding, a full apology, for I am talking now to members of the Bibliographic Control Institute. I shall shortly be talking to you officially, as a part of the *Anglo-American Cataloging Rules* Revision Committee.

This code is an Anglo-American code of cataloging rules. We in Great Britain look on this code with a slightly different philosophy, I think, than the Library of Congress certainly does. We view the 1967 code as a fairly complete one and want to see how this particular code, which has got a different shape and a different structure from the earlier codes of 1908 and 1949, works out. So the English committee has not originated very much revision of the code thus far. Quite deliberately, we have been holding back to see how the latest code, with its present structure, works.

The committee, of which I am not formally a member, though I am well aware of what it is doing, has limited itself to considering amendments brought forward by the Library of Congress, American Library Association, or Canadian Library Association, and whether

it should adopt them or not. This procedure raises one technical point of some importance, and that is that the English side, and indeed the American side, have the right unilaterally to adopt the revisions of its own if it so wishes. These do not then become a part of the Anglo-American code, but remain a British or American rule. One of the things that the English side did on the edition that it published was to make some revisions of part 3 even before it was published. The chapters on maps and music differ between the American and English editions of the code. The Revision Committee also took the decision that it was not prepared to accept further piecemeal amendments of part 3 for nonbook material. It felt that if this was to be amended at all, it should be amended as a complete thing. This decision was taken very shortly after the publication of the code. It antedates our thinking as an institute quite a long time.

We want to cooperate on this, the business of revision. The English committee is publishing a bulletin which shows the revisions that are being done and publicizes them as much as possible. It is against this background that I bring up now, and I say the sorcerer's apprentice is brought even more vividly to mind, the proposals that are being made for the revision of part 3 nonbook materials, in Great Britain, by me actually.

The aims of the project, as I put them forward, are to revise the rules in part 3 and ensure that rules for these kinds of material are

Lecturer, School of Librarianship, Northwestern Polytechnic, London in accordance with the principles laid down in parts 1 and 2, either directly, or where the nature of the materials demands a departure from these principles, by demonstrating why it is necessary. This is to be done in such a way as to produce a self-contained code for the cataloging of nonprint materials. It will not be as detailed as parts 1 and 2 of *AACR* for books, but it will rely explicitly on these two parts for any further extension that may be needed of the information in part 3. So the intention of this is quite clearly to integrate part 3 even more tightly with parts 1 and 2.

The basic work that I saw as needing to be done fell into three parts. The first was that of comparison within the code itself of part 3 with parts 1 and 2 to see where the differences occur; also, comparisons with the special codes for these materials that do exist. I did some work on this comparison well before this and finished it in June of this year. This was *A Feasibility Study of a Multi-Media Catalogue,* containing a recommendation that the code to be adopted for this is *AACR,* and I quote myself, "because it is unquestionably the best code that has been produced so far for the cataloging of these materials."

The second part of the work to be done was direct consultation with other bodies interested in this problem, both in this country and Great Britain. The third part is the consolidation of the solutions arrived at through these processes and the drafting of the new code to bring out the specific relations with parts 1 and 2.

So, the intention is to tidy up part 3, and I would not put it, in essence, any higher than that. I do not envision a structural alteration of part 3. To deal with the problems that have been enumerated many times, we must identify the media, check then what should be the rules for entry and the rules for description, and produce a pattern that would be used relating to these rules in the first part.

I will only say that I am mildly optimistic about this project actually succeeding. If it does succeed, it will be an English committee which goes ahead to revise part 3. We proceed, through, with the hope that we can, in fact, get agreement from all four parties on this, and that this will, indeed, be an Anglo-American revision. The time limit I have allowed calls for the job to be done within twelve months, so with any luck, there will be a revision of part 3 quite soon.

Since I am so far steeped in nonbook bibliographical organization, I might as well wade in even farther. The first object put forward by many is the need to identify the media and produce a standard terminology. I am also preparing a small publication intended to identify the statement of the media, the physical form of nonbook media. I think I have identified about sixty-five separately described media, for which I am publishing a small separate classification, a classification of the media according to their nature and a thesaurus of the verbal description of these that have cropped up. Like the Canadian code, it is a preliminary edition, and I will be grateful for suggested amendments.

Normally one always feels that the third man down working on the same subject, is going to be saying exactly the same thing everyone else has said. And indeed, I think we all three—Jean Riddle, Sumner Spalding, and Antony Croghan—have said the same thing, with different emphasis, and this, I think, is probably the most reassuring thing about the whole business, that though we start from different points of view and though we put different emphasis on it (an educational librarian, a pure cataloger, and a teacher of cataloging and classification), we end up talking about and recognizing the same problem. All we have left is to resolve our separate solutions to these problems, a task which is, I hope, a rather minor thing.

MARC Format
for Nonprint Media

Henriette D. Avram

Nonprint material is becoming an increasingly popular media for education today. Consequently, the need to exercise better control over this material in libraries and other institutions is apparent. The Library of Congress (LC), recognizing this need, has developed, with experts in the field of motion pictures and filmstrips, a format for this material as one of the series of Machine-Readable Cataloging (MARC) formats. I appreciate the opportunity to describe what is meant when we use the word *format* and to suggest how this particular concept might relate to materials other than printed monographs and serials.

I did recognize very early, about 1966, that it was not possible, within a reasonable time period, to design a format for all materials. What was needed was a format structure that would be hospitable to the bibliographic description of all forms of material, and the actual content to be recorded in the format and the explicit identification of the content would then be determined for each particular form of material as required.

The result of these early efforts was a communication format, a medium for the interchange of information between institutions, rather than a processing format for a particular institution. The design of the format structure took into account different types of computers as well as the need to manipulate information for a variety of uses in different institutions.

The communications format is divided into three basic elements: a basic structure which is the same for the description of all material, content designators to identify uniquely the content of the data for a particular form of material, and the content itself.

The basic structure of the format consists of three major parts: the leader, the record directory, and the variable fields. The leader is much like a title page of a book, and one of its functions is to identify the record. Since we are not certain how machine files will be organized, the information in the leader is used to identify uniquely the kinds of records in machine-readable form. We may, for example, wish to distribute from the Library of Congress machine-readable records for printed books and film material. Individual users may wish to keep both kinds of records in the same file or to maintain these records in separate files. The information in the leader enables a particular installation to exclude or include records, depending on its file organization or collection.

The record directory is comparable to the table of contents in a book and specifies what fields are in the record, the length of these fields and the location of the fields in the machine record. Since bibliographic information is variable, it never consists of a set number of characters in machine-readable form. There are several ways of retrieving data from variable length fields, and we have adopted a directory technique (or a map technique). There are record directory entries for all variable fields in the machine record, and if a

Director, MARC Development Office, Library of Congress, Washington

search is made for all subject headings or a particular subject heading, the record directory entries are examined for the appropriate tags. If these tags are not in the record directory entries, the remainder of the record is not searched, and the next record is searched for the tags. This technique allows more efficient manipulation of records and also more efficient updating procedures.

The format also includes what we have termed, at the Library of Congress, as variable fixed fields. For example, the Library of Congress catalog card number is used for our control number or identification number. We know exactly how long the number is in length of characters. In machine terminology this type of field is called a "fixed" field. However, when the structure of the format was designed, it was recognized that one could not dictate the length of every control number used in every institution. One convention of the format requires that all institutions use the same tag (001) for the control number. The inclusion of tag 001 is the directory and the placing of the control number after the last entry in the directory allow this field to be fixed within an organization but variable across organizations.

A machine cannot recognize the meaning of information unless it has been explicitly identified. The format has three different kinds of content designators: tags, indicators, and subfield codes. Tags consist of three numeric characters which identify fields of information, such as a physical description field, a title field, or a subject field. Within the physical description field, there are several data elements such as length, width, and sound. The identification of data elements within a field is achieved by the use of subfield codes. Indicators are used to tell us more about a particular field of information. For example, the tag will specify the kind of subject heading: a personal name, a corporate name, a uniform title heading, a topical heading, or a geographic heading. Then for a personal name subject heading, the indicator will show the kind of personal name: a single surname, a forename, multiple forename, or family name.

The third element of the communications format is the content or data itself. The content designators in the MARC formats may be

different according to the form of the material, although the format structure will be the same. For example, the map format has a scale note but the monograph format does not. The tag used to identify the scale note will be a unique one, and it will never be repeated in any of the formats unless the meaning of the data is identical.

The first LC document describing both the structure of the format and the content designators and content for monographs was published in January 1968. The concept of a legend is described. The legend is made up of two categories of data, the type of record and the bibliographic level. It is the legend that indicates to the processor the type of material described in this particular record. The legend serves two primary functions. The first allows an institution, such as the Library of Congress, the possiblity of including in its distribution service, records for more than one form of material. The user, by testing the legend codes, has the option of including or excluding the record from his data base. The second purpose is to notify the computer system that a particular record is to be processed that may have unique content designators. The legend provides the flexibility for the implementation of modular computer programs; that is, using a subroutine that is common to data elements across all forms of material (e.g., title) and tailor-made subroutines called into execution for exception data fields (e.g., scale for maps).

The legend contains two codes for type of record and bibliographic level which allow this flexibility in processing. The type-of-record code indicates the type of library material being processed, from printed books to computer media. These types have been designated according to the different kinds of library materials described in the *Anglo-American Cataloging Rules*. The bibliographic-level code designates whether the item being cataloged is an analytic, a monograph, a serial, or a collection. These terms are defined as follows: an analytic is a work not published separately but as a part of a larger bibliographic entity and includes such items as a chapter of a book, a journal article, or a single volume of a multivolume set; a monograph is a publication that is nonserial because it is complete at the time of publication or is to be issued in a known number of parts; a serial is a publication issued in successive parts bearing numerical or chronological designations and intended to be continued indefinitely; a collection consists of a group of manuscripts, pamphlets, et cetera, which are gathered together and cataloged as a single unit. Twelve types of materials have been identified by codes and together with the four codes of bibliographic level, these positions of the leader provide the capability of using the MARC format to describe a variety of material.

The Library of Congress, in the design of its format for motion pictures and filmstrips, has had the very active cooperation of many interested organizations. LC staff members met with representatives from this institute, as well as representatives from the Department of Audiovisual Instruction (DAVI), the American Library Association (ALA), and the Motion Picture Section of the Library of Congress. We are anxious for you to comment on what we have done, although we know that our proposed format is lacking in some details. Our intent is to define the format for motion pictures and filmstrips before we investigate the format requirements for slides or other audiovisual material.

Question: There is a need to provide for changes that occur in media fields that probably will not happen in any of the other areas. A company may produce an item and give it to another organization to distribute, and, to complicate matters further, that distributor may sell, assign, deposit, or exchange the item with another organization at a later date. This is a data element that one needs to identify; that is, the distributor as apart from the producer. I look at the distributor in most instances as the producer. Should it be needed, both of these categories can be identified. Once you update anything in the machine-readable form, you are going to update a distributor who was the producer to another distributor. We need both categories. Therefore, are you going to consider this, and if so, what kind of distinction will be required between producer and distributor, and does it change when the distributor changes?

Mrs. Avram: This is one of the reasons that we are here presenting the MARC format proposal for motion pictures and filmstrips. We are asking for comments and guidelines, proceeding in the way we did for the format for books; that is, considering the requirements that are necessary for the majority of users. The MARC record can be updated. At the Library of Congress we have what is supplied by the original producer of film. This information is the basis for our cataloging and is what will be recorded in the MARC record. It is the initial record. If, sometime later, someone else is distributing the film, the Library of Congress will not know this. We have input for the first time and have no basis to update the record because a distributor has changed. However, if an institution was using the magnetic tapes, that institution could provide the updating required if it is aware of changes. We have studied a number of the fields trying to arrive at some best method of encoding a particular condition. One of the most difficult is that field dealing with the intellectual level.

Question: One of these difficult fields is the dimension field. Is it possible to make multiple use of this? And if we are going to consider every single dimension, then it seems we still have a lot of codes.

Mrs. Avram: We are considering handling this by encoding as many dimensions as required. This has been done by using a technique of six possible characters to describe a dimension such as color, width, et cetera, and any number of sets of these six possible characters can be used to describe each dimension.

Question: There are three different fields describing sound, and I wonder if you could tell us the reason for three rather than putting them in one field?

Mrs. Avram: Again, this was the first attempt at the definition of content of the record. We are aware that modifications may be forthcoming. The codes for sound were considered not mutually exclusive, and it appeared to be more efficient to code them separately.

Comment: I think that there was one other point on which we would very definitely agree. It is extremely interesting that nonbook material should fit into the MARC format so easily. We have made these comments about the elements we have discussed, but basically we felt that what we were trying to do was to improve an already very, very good instrument. We were doing a little bit of detail work. I have always felt that MARC was a very fine instrument on the communication side.

Mrs. Avram: What Mr. Croghan just said in terms of the same format being used for monographs, serials, and maps for nonbook material is what I described as the basic structure of the record with the addition of the legend to allow for this flexibility.

The MARC Project and MARC Records for Film Material

Lenore S. Maruyama

MARC (Machine-Readable Cataloging) has taken its place as an additional method of recording and disseminating cataloging information that has been created by the Library of Congress. In the past libraries have obtained cataloging data from the Library of Congress by purchasing printed cards and printed book catalogs. The introduction of the machine-readable record has allowed users greater flexibility in specifying products for their institutions. MARC records can be used as the basis for a retrieval system, for production of book catalogs or printed cards, or for production of secondary products such as spine labels or book pockets and book cards.

In terms of actual expenditure by a user, the cost of the MARC tapes is probably the smallest unit of cost. For the current subscription year beginning in April 1970, a subscription for the MARC Distribution Service is $800 per annum, and it is estimated that more than 60,000 records for English-language monographs will be distributed during this year. Before the MARC tapes can be utilized, the following requirements must be met: (1) access to a computer and peripheral equipment must be available; (2) computer programs must be written to process the MARC records and to produce the desired products; and (3)

qualified personnel must be available to do the systems analysis, write the programs, and provide a liaison between the library staff and the computer specialists.

Data on MARC records have been supplied by the Processing Department of the Library of Congress as part of its cataloging operations. Although the actual machine record is not created until after the catalog record has been completed, the cataloging information itself remains the responsibility of the various cataloging divisions.

Background of the MARC Project

In order to understand fully the implications of machine-readable catalog records, it is necessary to give some of the historical aspects of the MARC project. Recognizing the need for the creation of machine-readable data bases, the Council on Library Resources sponsored a study in 1964 to investigate this problem.[1] Three conferences on machine-readable catalog copy were held during 1965 and 1966 to discuss: (1) the results of the above study; (2) a proposed format for machine-readable records; and (3) implementation of a MARC pilot project. The MARC I format was designed in the Library of Congress, and in November 1966 the library began distribut-

---

Library Information Systems Specialist, MARC Development Office, Library of Congress, Washington

[1] Lawrence F. Buckland, *The Recording of Library of Congress Bibliographical Data in Machine Form* (Washington, D.C.: Council on Library Resources, 1965), 54p.

ing weekly tapes to sixteen libraries. These libraries were selected on the basis of: (1) type of library; (2) geographic location; (3) availability of funds, personnel, and equipment to utilize tapes; (4) proposed use of MARC data; and (5) willingness to evaluate the use of the data for a final report.

By the end of the pilot project in June 1968, approximately 50,000 records had been distributed to the participating libraries. The final report on this project was issued in 1968.[2] For institutions expecting to introduce automated techniques into their libraries, this report is an extremely valuable document because it pinpoints all the problems encountered by the participants and the Library of Congress. Long before the end of the pilot project, work was begun on evaluation of the format used and the development of a new one. The Library of Congress began using the MARC II format with the implementation of the MARC Distribution Service in March 1969.

Structure of the MARC II Format

One of the most important criteria in the design of the new format was that it should have enough flexibility to serve as the standardized communications format for a wide variety of bibliographic data. Since it was not possible to analyze and categorize completely the data elements for material other than printed book material during the development stages of the MARC II format, it was felt that the format should be structured in such a way that it would be hospitable to all types of bibliographic information. In other words, the structure of all machine records would be identical, but for any given type of material —such as books, maps, music, motion pictures —the components of the format may have specific meanings and unique characteristics. In the work to date at the Library of Congress, the detailed analysis, development of definitions, and tags have been restricted to those data elements found in the bibliographic descriptions of monographic and serial book ma-

terials, maps, manuscripts, and film material. Other kinds of materials such as music, sound recordings, or pictorial material will be analyzed at a later date.

Another goal was to develop a format which could be used in a wide variety of computers to manipulate machine-readable bibliographic data. The analysis took into consideration both character and word machines and the use of different programming languages. Since it was difficult to design a record for optimal use for all library functions, the designers of the MARC II format tried to take into account many library activities and a variety of users. Because of their computer configuration or proposed uses of MARC data, individual users of the MARC tapes may find it necessary to develop their own processing format, but there should be only one communications format in which to transmit data to and from other installations.

The basic premise of a machine record is that all data must be explicitly identified. In contrast, data on catalog records or printed cards are identified implicitly; that is, there is no means by which to identify the collation statement or the imprint statement automatically other than the order in relation to other items, the indention on the printed card, et cetera. A format is the means by which data can be recorded and organized so that the parts can de identified explicitly.

A machine record has the following hierarchical arrangement. The data element is the lowest unit of information and consists of such items as a Dewey Decimal Classification number or place of publication. A field is a logical grouping of data elements, such as an imprint statement, consisting of place of publication, publisher, and date of publication (each is a data element) and corresponds roughly to the separate items on a catalog card such as the main entry, title, and imprint statement. A field can be of two types, fixed or variable. A fixed-field element is fixed in length, such as a three-character alphabetic code for language of the text; a variable-field element is variable in length, such as a title which can range from one character to fifty characters. A record is a collection of all the fields treated as a unit.

[2]Henriette D. Avram, *The MARC Pilot Project: Final Report on a Project Sponsored by the Council on Library Resources, Inc.* (Washington, D.C.: Library of Congress, 1968).

The MARC II format has a structure much as a book has a structure consisting of a title page, table of contents, and the text. The structure of the MARC II format consists of the leader, record directory, and variable fields. The leader serves a function similar to the title page of a book; it indicates the kind of record and the kind of material being cataloged. This information is found in a portion of the leader called the legend, which in turn is divided into two parts. The type-of-record portion consists of a number of codes to show whether the work is printed book material, sound recordings, film material, maps, or manuscripts. The bibliographic-level portion indicates whether the work is a monograph, serial, collection, or analytic. These codes in the legend enable a user to store records for different kinds of materials in one data base or to store them separately. The entire leader is fixed in length at twenty-four characters.

The next part of a machine record is the record directory, which is similar to the table of contents in a book, in that it shows what variable fields are in the record. There is a record directory entry for each variable field, and each record directory entry is twelve characters long and consists of the tag, the length of the field, and the location in the machine record of that field.

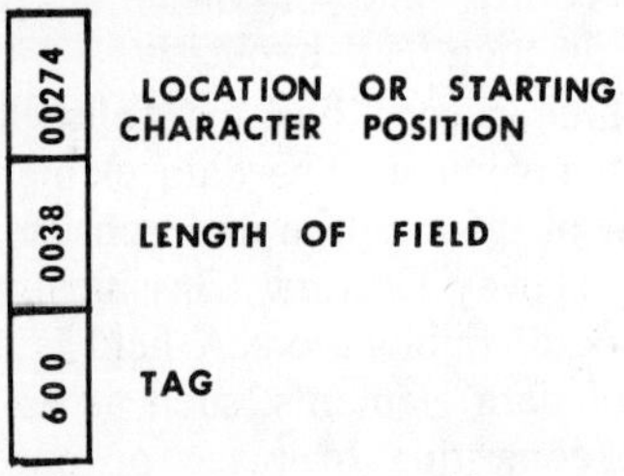

Fig. 1. Record directory entry

The tag consists of three numeric characters which identify fields of data. Tags in the MARC II format are assigned by function according to traditional cataloging usage so that main entries begin with 1, subject headings with 6, et cetera. In figure 1, the tag 600 is for a subject that is a personal name. The tags also show the kind of name used in the field, and the same pattern is used when-

ever names appear in the record. A personal name main entry is tag 100, a subject heading that is a personal name is 600, a personal name added entry is tag 700, and so on.

The remaining part of the machine record structure is the variable-field portion, which consists of most of the cataloging data found on a printed card. At the beginning of a variable field are two characters called indicators, which supply additional information about the data in the field. In figure 2 the first indicator

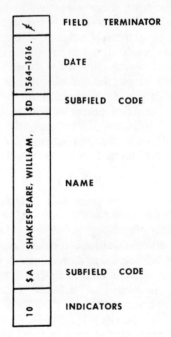

Fig. 2. Subject heading in the machine record

shows the type of personal name, with the code 1 designating a single surname. The second indicator shows the source of the subject heading, and the code 0 designates an LC subject heading, as opposed to a National Library of Medicine subject heading. Each variable field also has subfield codes which identify the separate data elements within the field. In the example there are two subfield codes for the name portion and the person's birth and death dates. At the end of each variable field is a special character called a field terminator to show the end of the field.

The MARC II format structure, consisting of a leader, record directory, and variable fields, is an implementation of the American National Standards Institute *Format for Bibliographic Information Interchange of Magnetic Tape*. It has been adopted as a standard by the Committee on Scientific and Technical Information of the Federal Council for Science and Technology and by the International Nuclear Information System. The format structure and the communications format for printed books have been adopted as standards by the American Library Association, the Special Library Association, the Association of Research Libraries, and the three national libraries. The communications format for printed books is also being used by the British National Bibliography for a UK/MARC project.

MARC Format for Film Material

The draft document, "Motion Pictures, Filmstrips, and Pictorial Media Intended for Projection: A MARC Format," is the latest in a series of MARC communications formats. In each of the MARC formats developed at the Library of Congress an effort has been made to have the identifying elements or content designators (tags, indicators, and subfield codes) alike when describing the same kinds of information. For example, a title field would appear in each format and would be identified by the same tag, 245. If a data element is unique to any particular format, a different tag which is not found in any of the other formats will be used.

The MARC format for film material describes two basic kinds of information: data that are generally found on LC printed cards and data that are needed to describe and control films in archival collections. Although only the first category of data would be distributed on a regular basis in machine-readable form, an attempt was made to include as much information of interest to film archivists as possible so that they would have the guidelines needed for standard representation of data about film material. The rules for entry and description follow the proposed revision to chapter 12 on motion pictures, filmstrips, and similar audiovisual works in the *Anglo-American Cataloging Rules*.

The Library of Congress plans to use the machine-readable records for film material to produce the printed book catalog for motion pictures and filmstrips, to produce printed cards, and possibly to expand the MARC Distribution Service to cover film material. The success of the MARC pilot project and the MARC Distribution Service has already demonstrated the feasibility of distributing machine-readable records. The Library of Congress is primarily interested in using MARC records for film material as test data in the production of its book catalogs. The publication of the format for film material will be the first step in achieving all of these goals, and the valuable assistance of the Office of Education Institute on Systems and Standards for the Bibliographic Control of Nonprint Media is gratefully acknowledged in this endeavor.

A Proposed International System for Bibliographic Control

Jules Leni

A preliminary proposal was developed following a meeting to explore possible avenues for funding a research and development project for an international system of bibliographic control of nonprint media. In Washington, September 1969, Pearce Grove, Malcolm Ferguson, Glenn McMurry, Robert Snider, and the author, meeting as a steering committee, discussed several organizations as possible vehicles for the project but postponed any final decision regarding an organizational home for it. This initial proposal was to be submitted for possible funding as an independent outgrowth of the United States Office of Education (USOE) Institute on Systems and Standards for the Bibliographic Control of Nonprint Media.

Background

In the last ten years a number of efforts have been made to achieve some degree of standardization in the bibliographic control of nonprint media. They generally have consisted of individual publications, committee studies, or assemblies of librarians and media experts and have been relatively ineffective except in areas of restricted applicability. The most recent attempt in this direction is the Institute on Systems and Standards for the Bibliographic Control of Media. This institute brought together for three weeks of intense and frank discussion a cross-section of academic authorities, commercial experts, and practicing media librarians. The proposal that follows reflects several conclusions reached during the three-week deliberation of the institute:

1. The urgency of the problem demands an efficient procedure for evolving workable solutions.
2. The complexity of the problem points to the need for a systems approach for developing compatible alternative methods of information management.
3. The growing use of media on a worldwide scale should be taken into account.

Plan of Action

The proposal envisions a research and development project, with the emphasis on development of a workable information management system that will be flexible enough to accommodate differing user requirements and will gain acceptance on the strength of its merits. The implementation of the proposed project will be carried out by a paid staff under the supervision of an advisory board. The board will consist of leading representatives of the academic community, professional organizations, governmental agencies, and commercial media information specialists. Seven participants of the USOE institute have already agreed to serve as an executive committee of the board.

Vice President, Comprehensive Service Corp., New York City (a company offering diversified services for motion picture film)

The project will be divided into two distinct phases. The first phase would consist of the following steps:

1. As a starting point a survey of published and unpublished literature and other related government- and foundation-funded projects in related fields should be made to ascertain whether any parallel efforts are already being made in this direction. This effort will achieve a degree of coordination that does not exist at present and will avoid unnecessary overlapping.

2. Procedures will be developed and implemented for surveying media users in various functional and organizational categories in order to compile some statistical data that can be translated into performance standards.

3. Investigation will be made of the impact on bibliographic control of developing changes in the patterns of media utilization.

4. The information gathered thus far should be synthesized into detailed statements of current practices, performance standards, and constraint on the development of systems for the organization of data, classification of content identifiers, and dissemination of information.

Publication of this information will lay the groundwork for the second phase of this project: namely, the design of an operating system that will be broad enough to fulfill the diverse spectrum of requirements and will be specific enough to be workable. The techno-logical factor that will permit such apparently contradictory criteria to be met is the twofold use of a computer. One is the ability of the computer to digest vast amounts of information in distinct but compatible formats, and the other is the use of the computer as a tool for system design. Taking advantage of this capability, a computer-based model will be constructed to simulate the transition from current practices which are uncoordinated and incompatible to updated methods of organizing and disseminating bibliographic data that will permit easy access by all media users.

There is another intangible benefit to be realized from taking a computer-oriented approach towards the solution of an extremely complex information-handling problem; that is, the discipline that computer systems impose, the precision and thoroughness in the statement of a problem. It is hoped that this project will avoid the pitfall of many other studies in wandering far afield and becoming lost in an avalanche of words. It can be expected that well before completion of the first phase of the project, the scope and direction of a second, or design phase, will become clear.

It is estimated that the first phase will take approximately two years and will require a total funding of $150,000. Even if the project goes no farther than to coordinate efforts previously made in this area and to produce concise statements of performance standards and constraints, it will do much to clear up the confusion that now exists in this area.

Proposed
Standard for
Bibliographic References

Maurice F. Tauber

One would not think it would take four years to prepare this document [Appendix, page 250], but it has. As a matter of fact, there was a previous committee that worked on it for three years and gave it up as an impossible assignment. Thus, this is a seven-year-old project of a subcommittee of the Z39 Committee of the United States of American Standards Institute, formerly the American Standards Associations, and now renamed the American National Standards Institute (ANSI).

The Standards Institute is primarily interested in hardware or other measurable items. The PH5 Committee of ANSI deals with photographic equipment, and librarians are represented on this particular committee. The Z39 Committee was developed solely for the purpose of identifying library standards. The subcommittees of Z39 are as follows: .2, machine-input records; .3, periodical title abbreviations; .4, bibliographic references; .5, transliterations; .6, abstracts; .7, library statistics; .8, proof directions; and .9, terminology. Other subcommittees are concerned with indexing, trade catalogs and directories, standard book numbering, book publishing statistics, book publishing advertising, standard serial coding, and, finally, title leaves of a book. Many of these particular subcommittees are working with very tangible goals, such as title leaves of books and standard serial coding. Our assignment was to set up bibliographic references that will be standardized for all fields of effort, including engineering, music, and literature, as well as publishing and other crafts. Professional workers in the biomedical and physical sciences, who have their own ideas about bibliographic citations, were prominent among our consultants.

Jerrold Orne, the Z39 Committee chairman, says that this subcommittee has had more correspondence than any other subcommittee. There is nothing so difficult as directing a writer to cite in a particular way, which has been our basic obstacle. The preliminary draft included with this paper indicates we have had correspondence with publishers, individuals in learned societies, editors, librarians, and people in library-related activities. We have also had a Columbia University committee—Nathalie C. Batts, Theodore C. Hines, Oliver L. Lilley, Ellis Mount, and myself—because I wanted to be able to assemble them within a short time for meetings.

This is the fifth draft of this document, and I believe its essence is simplicity. I hope we can go through the document item by item, in order to understand the terms of the assignment, and to get some idea of your reaction to this particular document. I understand that you are trying to alter the rules in the AA code [Anglo-American Cataloging Rules] for nonbook materials. They are problems in

Chairman, ANSI Z39.4 subcommittee; Professor, School of Library Service, Columbia University, New York City

themselves. There are very few libraries that are able to follow rules for nonbook materials. I know this because I have worked with audiovisual organizations, including Richard Darling's school library operation in Maryland, where he set up his own rules. His code of practice in the handling of audiovisual materials represents the application of experience to his problem.

We have in this document been more or less influenced by the development of comparable documents in other countries. The American National Standards Institute is related to the International Standards Organization (ISO). Therefore, in the development of this document we have used the British Standard, the Indian Standard, the United Nations manual, the Library of Congress work toward standardization of bibliographic references, and other documents of this type. In the mail this week I received the Swedish standard for bibliographic references. The bibliography subcommittee membership has been asked to tell ISO what we in the United States think of this standard. The committee will review it and comment on it for ISO. Our proposed U.S. standard, which we are about to examine, was just distributed to the subcommittee members last week. I was given permission by Dr. Orne to reproduce it for this United States Office of Education (USOE) media institute.

With these preliminary remarks, I would like to go through the document, referring to each section of the proposal by reference.[1] In the table of contents you will see that we have identified Purpose, and indicated Definition and Function, Forms of Reference, General Guidelines, Elements and Their Order, Detailed Recommendations, and Miscellany, which deals with abbreviations, transliterations, and such matters as punctuation and typography. Virtually every type of material was given to us as being susceptible for inclusion in this document. We have not, however, tried to include every publication or audiovisual item in existence. The Library of Congress and the *Anglo-American Cataloging*

[1]Numbers in the text refer to the sections and paragraphs of the Proposed Standard, the appendix to this paper, pages 250–55.

Rules really do not attempt to do this either. We have limited ourselves to books, serials, periodicals, articles, and nonbook materials such as manuscripts, maps, film, music, and patents.

Definition and Function, section 2, of a bibliographic reference is a statement containing information which describes a published or unpublished work that functions to enable the user to identify and obtain the precise item. This is the basic point of the committee's orientation. What does it mean to a user to have or not to have certain elements in a bibliographic citation, or a bibliographic reference as we would call it? In Forms of Reference we have tried to include the examples directly with the items being discussed. We had these as a separate appendix and were advised by those who criticized the most recent draft that they were undesirable. This change is what held up the issuance of this revision for at least eight weeks. Many of the new examples were provided in the document we are discussing.

Consider in the section Forms of Reference paragraph 3.1, An Entry in a Bibliographic List. . . . We have four examples which look like traditional library citations. One of the real criticisms that we have had from the engineers was that we tend to be too library oriented, which is all right if you think of it as a guide for an engineering publication. Some engineers think that they have invented the wheel and that they know how to cite while no one else does. I met with the Joint Engineers Council in connection with its particular publications, which differ widely. The council has recently tried to get its editors to use the same sort of citing for its particular publications. This urging comes from a central source, which means that this organization is moving closer to what we are trying to accomplish.

Paragraphs 3.2, A Note Appended to a Text . . ., and 3.3, A Statement Partly or Wholly Contained in the Body of the Text, crystallize our thinking so that materials can be identified in bibliographic citations. If you can think of something else that cannot be subsumed under one of these headings, we would like to know it. The effort is for simplicity and distillation.

General Guidelines, section 4, is a reference to the bibliography. I think this is probably a full bibliography on bibliographic citations. The bibliography in this report was done by three people and the committee examined every one of these items. It is an important part of this document. We have delineated, so far as we know, everything in these documents that could be standardized. Similarly, in regard to elements and their order, as depicted by items in the bibliography, the only thing you can say about order in relation to different disciplines is that there is some disorder.

So we had, as I indicated in standard development, taken a point of view, and we have adhered to it in this particular listing. As you see, we are alert to overdoing, and hence, despite the fact that we have more than six elements, we have suggested that there might be a minimum of six elements. If we stopped at that, we would still be within the framework of standards for separately published works: the author, title, edition number, place of publication, publisher, and the year. This procedure is beginning to sound like what is done in libraries, and there should not be anything wrong with it, because it has been fairly successful for separately published works. It is not necessary to spend too much time with book materials, as many of you are quite familiar with them. However, it is probably important that they be quickly reviewed.

The quotation of a passage from a book, or other separately issued publication, has been handled in so many different ways by different libraries that we thought it necessary at least to indicate what we consider to be a reasonable solution to that particular item. It is given in the example for 5.1.1. For 5.1.2, Contribution to a Book or Other Separately Issued Publication, you have an example in Malinowski's work. These are the areas where there has been general resolution.

However, 5.1.3, Technical and Other Specialized Reports, is the start of a real controversy, for reports are handled in at least fifteen or twenty different ways. On the basis of our examination of the variety of steps taken in handling technical reports, we have agreed on these particular items: a corporate source, title, dates, personal authors, pagination, and the document numbers of various kinds. Those who know what technical reports are realize that they are identified by numbers that meet government requirements as well as provide security identification, which has had influence on the character of the elements in the citation. For security classification there are two examples of this type of report; one is relatively simple, but the other gets more complex.

Question: Dr. Tauber, may I ask a fairly general question arising out of these? Have you mitigated your terminology for this as a general standard? Can you translate, "5.1.3," as corporate author and title with the date as part of the title? In the first example, January 1966 is the date that the study was set up and is, therefore, part of the title. In this one, personal authors become added authors in the normal sense that they are reporting. It would then seem logical to put in date of publication of the study, or is that exactly the same as the date at the top? This is an American experience for me: security classification, document numbers, and series titles. You could use all of these items in what I would call a standard library terminology. Did you mitigate this deliberately on the grounds that the people who look at this would wonder what the devil you were talking about?

Mr. Tauber: That is partly true. The technical report is a complex item, and it has given much trouble to those libraries that are depositories for this type of publication. If you worry about the bibliographic control of other multimedia materials, technical reports represent as complex a group as any of them. To say an engineer will find a document if he really wants to is not the point any more than saying someone will find a microfilm if he really wants to.

I do not want to get too involved with technical report literature, because it is really peripheral to your particular interest. It has been regarded as literature of interest only to the people who are working in the field, and more than that, there is a feeling that technical report literature is a secondary type of publication and that any findings of significance from technical reports will get into other open literature. It is not true at all, which we found through the study that Oliver L. Lilley and

I did for the Office of Education. It is also not true of audiovisual research, but less so than for the technical report literature.

Question: Will you tell this group about your USOE study?

Mr. Tauber: The Office of Education asked Lilley and me to undertake a study with a very complex title, *Feasibility Study for the Establishment of a Center for the Dissemination of Findings in Research in Educational Media.* How many of you have ever seen that report? Just two. This is a good example of the Office of Education giving an assignment and then not making the results of it easily available.

Question: Was ERIC [Educational Resources Information Center] an outgrowth of this?

Mr. Tauber: ERIC is definitely related to it.

Comment: Then it really did not stay under the bushel but did finally come out.

Mr. Tauber: In itself it is a very difficult document to find. This particular document had three parts to it. The first was an examination of a sampling of studies in audiovisual research and research studies in audiovisual applications. We found that this was an area in which there was very little dissemination of research in indexes, abstracts, and educational publications of various kinds. We set up a classification system which, I think, was not used. It was a faceted classification that Dr. Lilley worked on primarily. The third part of the document was a list of subject headings in the field of audiovisual materials. The Office of Education asked us to continue it, but for some reason or other, personal reasons I think, we did not take it, and it went to Case Western Reserve, where Jesse Shera, Allen Kent, Alan Rees, and several others issued a series of documents, that preceded the development of ERIC centers. There was a relevance between this particular study and the development of ERIC centers.

Question: What was the time gap?

Mr. Tauber: Six or seven years. The State University of Pennsylvania in University Park at that time had a number of individuals who were using audiovisual materials extensively in classroom teaching and in research, and they thought that the Office of Education

should turn the centers over to private or state institutions rather than have the program developed in Washington. If they had, the centers probably would have been put into operation faster. The Office of Education retained supervision of the program because it was federally funded. However, they have distributed ERIC centers throughout the country. The study was reprinted twice, once at Columbia University, and we are still getting requests for it, at least a dozen a year. It must be xeroxed or filmed because it is just too long to retype.

In 5.1.4, Abstracts and Reviews, we tried, as you have noticed, to coordinate any particular item with a previous item in order to be consistent. This does not represent, in any way, a difficult type of citation.

In 5.1.5, we get into another very difficult area of bibliographic citation, Conferences, Congresses, Symposia. It is difficult to locate publications of this type in the Columbia University card catalog. The examples presented to us in correspondence have resulted in the simplicity of this paragraph.

Question: Would you consider the addition of an added author, or the director as an added entry, for we often remember the name of the director and not the complex name of a particular institute? Your workshop is a good example, for it is known by your name. Unfortunately, I couldn't find it in a hundred years in the Purdue University catalog, as there is no entry for the institute director.

Mr. Tauber: This is a very good suggestion, and we probably ought to change the examples to include that. The amazing thing about this particular remark by Miss Whitenack is that I directed a conference at Columbia University in 1952 entitled The Subject Analysis of Library Materials, and at Atlantic City seventeen years later, there was another conference with the same title. The 1952 conference was cosponsored by the Catalog Division of the American Library Association, which has subsequently undergone a title change. The 1952 workshop report was cataloged by the Library of Congress under the entry "Institute on the Subject Analysis of Library Materials," but has not, to my knowledge, been cited by anyone by this entry except me. It has not been cited with the word *institute* preceding the title. Although we have come up with this example, maybe we are wrong. Mortimer Taube, who was in the Library of Congress Technical Division, suggested three rules of cataloging, and the basic one is that, if a personal name appears on the title page, make sure the name occurs somewhere in the entry and as the main entry, if you can select it with clarity.

These are complex rules in terms of book cataloging. I have tried to use the *Anglo-American Cataloging Rules* as a teaching instrument in the library school, only to find out how difficult it is for the layman (the student is a layman for a while) to understand how conflicting rules are in many cases.

The Periodicals or Other Serial Publications paragraph, 5.2, is useful to anyone in the library field. I understand some of you are not. The rules are representative of a wide range of citations by people from different fields, including the short ones in medical journals and other scientific publications. Reference to Proceedings of a Conference, Congress or Symposium, 5.2.2, is worth calling to your attention, for again, there is a very large body of literature which falls under this particular rule of procedure.

The next rule, 5.3, is basic not only in terms of the ordinary periodical article, but also in the terms of multimedia, particularly since many articles are being put on microfilm, microcard, and other kinds of photographic reproductions. Hence, there is a problem of identifying them. One of the complaints I have found in many institutions is that some catalogers always regard micromaterials as of secondary importance, and if they have arrears, they will likely include microforms, despite the fact that many of them are important titles for the library.

One of the major goals of this conference is to bring these situations under control. Some of them can be done in a national pool of some sort, but a lot has to be done on the local level, in your own library or center, if you are going to make your program the service agency it should be. The items under 5.3 are

likely to receive heavy criticism from the individuals to which this is being sent.

Actually, there are many manuals in the bibliography [p.255] which suggest how one might cite. The University of Oklahoma has different rules for citing articles in dissertations from those used at Columbia University. We have the University of Chicago's manual as well as others. Although we have tried to standardize usage at Columbia, there remain different schools in the university that require different bibliographic citation formats. Apparently the important thing is to be consistent.

The items in 5.3.1 should be useful in any bibliographic citation for an article. We have worked and reworked until we are now back to the form originally suggested. We would be grateful for comments on this, because it has been one of the areas criticized most by those who have had this particular document.

Comment: I notice that you have given up underlining titles throughout the bibliography.

Mr. Tauber: That's right. We think if it's going to be a printed document, they will probably be italicized. We decided that we would not underline on the basis of observations from people who have looked at these references. I do not think it is essential.

Comment: How would the user know what to italicize?

Mr. Tauber: Well, it's pretty obvious, isn't it?

Comment: Not to a typist, for example. To a bibliographer it would be, and maybe a typesetter, but not to others.

Mr. Tauber: Well, it was dropped on the basis of the criticism of the field.

Question: Are you saying titles *should* be italicized if printed?

Mr. Tauber: Yes, although it does not have to be. Sometimes it is set off in darker or bold type.

Question: Should not this be a part of the standard?

Mr. Tauber: No, because we were told that it is too variable, and we are trying to eliminate variables. Printing represents a variable, and under the section Miscellany you will see that we have some general statements about punctuation, typography, abbreviations, and relevant matters. We have even tried to standardize general statements of that sort, so that within the framework of the general standard you can do what you like to make your format most attractive. There is no restriction on format except that it be logical.

I am not so sure that this document I am reviewing with you is as clear as possible in terms of the actual format or presentation. When it's printed, however, it will be, because it will follow something similar to the Swedish standard, which has different forms of type. It will also follow the American National Standards Institute form of presentation, as it has a particular form. The August 1969 issue of *American Documentation* has a standard printed in it.

Question: I assume that the issue number in the second example [under 5.3.1] will appear in parentheses. It might be clearer if, in your order for the issue number, the citation read, "Issue number in parentheses."

Question: Isn't this the general thing? I don't know about the American publishers, but English publishers are very touchy on what they call their house style. They will accept a degree of control over what information is going into the book, but the minute you start trying to dictate the physical form of the book, even relatively unessential things like parentheses and underlining, they will throw out the baby with the bath water. Instead of saying, We won't use the particular typographical conventions but will use the information, they will probably conclude these typographical conventions laid down here are useless; therefore, the whole document is useless. The fact that you can demonstrate that this is a logical absurdity has nothing to do with it.

Mr. Tauber: This particular element was put in, really, at the dominant request of the critics. I think from the user's point of view it makes a lot of sense to search for a particular issue. I know it helps me if I am looking for a thing to know the issue number.

Question: Do we often differentiate between items by using arabic numerals?

Mr. Tauber: We have generally used arabic figures throughout. This is a very important thing in terms of preferences. However, you will find that a journal would not think of altering its use of roman numbers if that has been its practice.

Comment: When we begin to utilize this information in computers, one of the questions asked is, Does it need to be fielded, meaning isolated, to the point where you can get at it in a very simple fashion on the computer? When you generalize so in these statements, it gives us no clue, really, to what is important. Computer personnel who want to help you need to know what is important. Every time you field something, it means you can sort on it, sort in a hierarchy and get information.

Comment: There are two stages, and Dr. Tauber has done the first. First, you have to identify the elements that can be fielded. What you are saying then, Mr. McMurry, is that Dr. Tauber has not said what are the important ones. But this is within an individual system. Providing he has, as he's done here, recognized the elements in a bibliographical citation, these can be fielded. What you then say is, you have got to ask the user in a particular computer center which of these varied elements are important to him so that you can field or pull out typography if you want computer typesetting or something like that. They are two distinct things. The second one, what is important, Dr. Tauber has not attempted to do nor, I would say, can he.

Mr. Tauber: Well, that's not completely true. I think what we have tried to do really is to extract some elements from the many that could be given. We will see these possibilities in the audiovisual field. For example, what do you put on an entry for a motion picture? Here, I believe, is what Antony Croghan has referred to as basic elements. If you take a look at those examples and drop off the issue number, month, or any other items there, you will have an incomplete citation. The procedure that we have followed has been parsimonious, particularly in the possibility of computer application, to make it as simple as possible for the computer people.

Theodore C. Hines, our computer faculty member at Columbia University, has identified the different approaches to computerization of book catalogs. He and Jessica Harris probably did one of the first book catalogs, that of the Farmingdale Schools on Long Island, New York, which was an extensive catalog for the elementary schools. (You may wonder why should they need a book catalog, but they have about forty schools in Farmingdale.) Book catalogs are being issued in rapidly increasing numbers.

One of the things in the citations that we were interested in was the application for computerization. In a sense, what we have done here is to look at computerization as a possible goal and to indicate pretty clearly that you can go only so far without giving incomplete information. This is true, you know, of some book catalogs. Some of them give incomplete information. The compilers want to put everything on one or two lines. Sometimes you cannot do so without giving up service. At the Pennsylvania State University, for example, a computer staff member was trying to computerize acquisitions, cataloging, and other activities. One of the things that happened in the computerization of serials was that titles were shortened or abbreviated to the extent that often they could not be identified. I think this is not helpful to the user and is a disservice to the library staff. They will have to rework things that should have been obvious from the first presentation.

Question: In the general rules that you have written, have you indicated that the title is that given in the book and that you do not abbreviate the title of the book?

Mr. Tauber: You will see when we get to the Miscellany.

Question: Dr. Tauber, in the last example under 5.3.1, is this a typographical error, or did you intend to invert *American Chemical Society. Journal?*

Mr. Tauber: It is a corporate inversion.

Question: Does the society publish a lot of different materials?

Mr. Tauber: Yes, it has a whole series of publications, and I think the period indicates this very clearly. It really is not the American Chemical Society Journal, but the Journal of the American Chemical Society. This follows our rule of using the best of those practices represented in the field of bibliography. We have tried to select the best bibliographical efforts that have been made in the past to use

them when they seem applicable. There has been no objecion from the chemists on this.

Question: Does this mean that this is the *Journal of the American Chemical Society* and you are suggesting it be cited in this way? Will other titles beginning with "Journal of" be cited in the same way?

Mr. Tauber: If it is the only journal of a particular association, I would say no. But the American Chemical Society publishes many items, and this particular way of citing one of its journals is the simplest and most practical one we have developed. Generally, in libraries the journal or bulletin of a society is placed under the organization if it is a part of the title.

Question: If the American Chemical Society is to be an exception, could this exception be explained?

Mr. Tauber: It may not be an exception, but rather the generalization that we have made for this type of entry. I am glad it was brought up. We have tried to stay away from exceptions which could wreck the document if there were too many. It is like filing rules; there is only one filing rule and that is file alphabetically. Then there are scores of exceptions because of the complexity of filing. We have tried to eliminate, as far as possible, the exceptions. If this represents an exception, a corporate entry, then we have to establish the fact that it is an exception and follow the rule of corporate entry.

Question: Dr. Tauber, is this the way *Chemical Abstracts* lists it? Did you utilize major abstracting and indexing tools?

Mr. Tauber: I will check that, Mr. Grove. Any point of this sort is useful to the committee. This is a very delicate instrument we are tampering with, and a period makes a significant difference. So, if anything at all occurs to you, please do not consider it irrelavant or naïve in any way. You would be surprised how much deliberation has gone into each of the examples and each of the phrasings, to make sure that we do not lose anyone, or tell people how to do things which are against their habits or judgment of what is best as their publication policies.

Question: Well, that really encourages me to ask something that is really near the beginning under Forms of Reference. Did you give any consideration to placing the date of the publication in a much earlier position in the entry? For instance, some people are placing it right after the author, because of the increased emphasis on currency and the speed at which things are becoming out-of-date.

Dr. Tauber: The order has been, more or less, consistent with the order of most of the journals or other publications that are cited. The Queensborough Public Library in New York City had been putting the date after the title for the last forty years, but it changed this practice when it began using Library of Congress cards more extensively. Until a few years ago, it put the date right after the title for the very purpose that you cited. People want the date as quickly as possible. In general, if you drop publisher or place of publication, you always retain the date. Even a small library has the date. Let our committee work with that, but I think this has been settled, whether it is the right or wrong decision.

Question: Wouldn't that lead to a lot of confusion, though, for it might be the date when a convention occurred. You might have four or five dates in the citation.

Comment: That is why I asked. You are right; it does cause confusion. The problem is not restricted to a scientific list to indicate what is the most recent knowledge, but rather it is becoming a more widespread concern to all disciplines for the reasons given above.

Mr. Tauber: Well, I made a note of it, but I think this is something on which we have probably followed the great majority of counsel.

In item 5.3.2, Newspapers, you may have some questions about newspapers.

Question: I have one that deals specifically with news reports and possibly those which come with other media. Do you list the news service that might be responsible for the editorial opinion in the news story such as the AP [Associated Press] or UPI [United Press International]?

Mr. Tauber: No. I could give you a list of maybe 500 similar items that have come up in relation to a wide range of concerns.

Comment: A news story on a given activity in the Far East from UPI could be a significant factor, but that is evaluation of the content.

Comment: I don't think so. The source of the information is an important bibliographic aspect of the citation. If we get two stories in the same paper, which is quite possible in our larger papers, the stories from different sources could even be listed under the same title.

Mr. Tauber: I suspect that on the basic principle of assisting the user, you could make a case for this. However, we have tried not to get ourselves involved with special elements of this sort and did eliminate that particular element. Notice, however, that if the article is signed and in a newspaper, the authorship has been retained. This specifically identifies the source for people who are knowledgeable about newspaper writers. I doubt if we could include the particular item on source of a news story, although your concern is certainly valid. Does anyone want to support the view that the source ought to be identified for a newspaper citation?

Question: If you have no specific author, what would you use in the author position?

Mr. Tauber: He wanted to insert the writer as a note, not in the author position. You would use the title, probably, with a note.

Question: Would it not be a corporate author if you didn't have an individual?

Comment: United Press International is responsible for it. I can see where that could start complicating things.

Comment: May I say that it seems to me, the whole of this discussion is an exemplification of one of the basic problems we have, and this relates to the disorganized state of the basic material. Librarians are organizing basically what they are getting, but there is a limit to the amount of order you can put on something amorphous. If, in fact, you try to cover everything, you over elaborate. We must strike a balance between extreme sophistication that only bibliographers can cope with and something too simple for the needs of library patrons.

Are we going back to the problem of "Can we control the stuff right from the source?" I must say, my answer is a despairing no. I will settle for the lesser problem of trying to control what we get, occasionally trying to dam or divert the stream. You obviously want to tackle the full problem, when you keep on fondly saying, "We must tell the producers to do thus and so." I wish you all the luck in the world, but I haven't seen anything like it since Stanley set out for the Congo.

Question: How do you handle a column? There are two kinds of authors in a newspaper. One has a by-line, which just means that this person wrote the story, supposedly objectively. The other has a column, in which he is giving his opinions. In your deliberations did you feel that it was not necessary to separate these?

Mr. Tauber: Again, this is a detail the user ought to find out for himself after he locates the item. Otherwise the burden of evaluating is put on the person making the citation. We have tried to keep the form simple, and I think because of its simplicity, we might get this standard approved. If a person going through a document of this sort finds five or six or a dozen little items of that sort, he is prone to throw the whole thing out. You should see the nasty letters we have received. After an item was inserted, someone tells us to take it out and then another demands it be reinserted.

There is one other point made in 5.3.2, which I think is worth calling attention to. Why do we have Boston after *Christian Science Monitor* in the Stanford example, and not New York after *Wall Street Journal* in the preceding example? I think perhaps Boston is not necessary, although there is a Pacific Coast edition of the newspaper. We are very much interested in not only adequate presentation but also the avoidance of excessive presentation.

Question: May I ask whether in fact any rules are given for determining editions? In England most of our major papers are published in three different editions, in different places, with different contents. There is not an awful lot of difference, but the *Northern Daily Mail* is different from the *Southern Daily Mail.*

Mr. Tauber: The edition is definitely important, then, in identifying paging and the location of the item. We have not overlooked this point in general, and we do suggest the edi-

tion of the newspaper be included if it is given.

The item 5.4, is also about as tough as they come: Laws; Legal References. The various library associations and learned societies have been given the opportunity of looking at the revised draft. Sometimes we receive letters that represent the views of twenty people or even more. Literally hundreds of people have commented on this draft. In view of all this, the legal reference is one of the toughest. Even in the *Anglo-American Cataloging Rules* we had a great deal of conflict with the American Association of Law Libraries. We made concessions, but at times the concessions resulted in confusion. So here you have two examples which are quite similar to the old cataloging rules. The one on legislative council and law statutes, which is a form heading, is very much disliked by even non-law librarians.

Comment: There is a wording here that has created considerable ambiguity in my mind: "Laws should be listed by the country, state, or other jurisdiction to which they refer." Now, in my own country, which is Great Britain, the Parliament could make a law referring to the county of Lancashire. Lancashire would not be the author or originator, but the law refers quite specifically to Lancashire. Your wording there would suggest that this law would be entered under Lancashire. Do you mean this?

Comment: That would not happen in America, for our Congress could not make a law that referred only to Kentucky. It makes laws for the United States in general; Kentucky makes laws for its own state needs. The same is true for all states.

Mr. Tauber: I would imagine that if this particular document were distributed in Great Britain, it would get a very rough reception. However, it is a United States standard.

Comment: Well, if there is no ambiguity in the United States, I will withdraw the point.

Mr. Tauber: I think the wording can be improved. The next section, beginning with 5.5, deals with nonbook materials. I have gone through this first part to indicate that there is a very direct relationship between these basic rules and the handling of nonbook materials. The nonbook materials, your major interest, just do not hang in the air by themselves.

Just as Dr. Hines is the computer person at Columbia University, D. Marie Grieco is the person there who has been most concerned with and most involved with nonbook materials. She teaches a course in them and has raised questions about the *Anglo-American Cataloging Rules* for nonbook materials. Miss Grieco reviewed this document, recommending changes, some of which were made. We have had many others in the special field of nonbook materials take a look at these rules. We have tried to get a distillation of observations concerning the relevant bibliographical items for this document.

This is a very fragile part of the document. We are venturing here, so help us. The general rule for nonbook materials is to record, as fully as possible, the existing elements as recommended in paragraph 5.1, the description of separately published works. The rule is to supply the title in English and, if necessary, enclose it in parentheses. The proposed standard for section 5.5, Nonbook Materials, also requires adding "information characteristic of the form." Now, reverting to 5.1, note that we have not tried to lift any type of common elements but have indicated that these paricular types of materials have their own common elements. Actually, we did have common elements for these in an earlier draft but removed them after they created such dissension among those who read the earlier drafts.

Question: Did you have any communication with the DAVI [Department of Audiovisual Instruction] committee, of which William Quinly is chairman? Did you work with this committee in arriving at your proposed standard for nonprint media?

Mr. Tauber: Yes, I believe it has been given the documents for criticism.

Question: Have you seen the committee document?

Mr. Tauber: No.

Question: On the example of the two maps, the size of one is given in inches and the other in centimeters. Is there a reason for this, and which do you prefer?

Mr. Tauber: I gave this document to Luther Evans at Columbia University, who is working on various projects for the Library. Luther Evans was responsible for the simplifica-

tion of descriptive cataloging at the Library of Congress, and I was in on those conferences many years ago. He had a copy of the proposed standard last Thursday and gave it back to me on Monday, saying, "Except for some flyspecks on this document, it is excellent." Well, I believe this is one of the flyspecks. I don't know why they are different. I prefer inches.

Some years ago when I was at the University of Chicago as head of the Catalog Department, we used to exchange cards with the University of Illinois. I noticed after a little while that the University of Illinois only had size on the cards when they represented very large or very small books. All the cards that represented books in between had no size. When I wrote to ask why, they replied that most of the books were about the same size. I instituted this policy at the University of Chicago and also at Columbia University. We tend to think of books as needing a size to facilitate their storage, location, and use, and I personally do not see a reason for using centimeters. Now why it occurs that way, I am not sure, but I think it came from Melvil Dewey, who was interested in the metric system.

For our examples concerning maps we took one example with centimeters and one with inches. Is there any question about the item for maps? The geographers do not use this form, which follows the *Anglo-American Cataloging Rules* rather than the rules of the geographers, who use the place as the major heading.

Question: I am curious about why you include the size of the envelope in which it comes. Is this really of some importance that I am not aware of, not being a librarian or a geographer?

Mr. Tauber: Yes, for locating. It could be a very small map in a big envelope, or it might be a very large map, which you fold and put in a small envelope. If you did not give the envelope size, you may be looking for something several times larger or smaller than the actual map.

Question: I realize that the *Anglo-American Cataloging Rules* will indicate that "Horton, Robert C." would be the proper entry, but would one be looking for certain geological formations in Nevada under the entry Horton?

Comment: This is a basic question in map cataloging. It is not actually related to the cataloging, but to your initial decision about your system. A fundamental aspect of map cataloging is whether one enters a map under its originator or under the subject content of the map. You can decide one or the other. But please, let's not start that one here and now, for it is a debate that has raged for at least thirty-seven years and can go on forever. All we can do is settle on the one or the other and show what the alternatives are.

Mr. Tauber: We have already been attacked by the geographers on this.

Question: But you would have added entries, wouldn't you?

Mr. Tauber: That is one of the most wonderful things about cataloging, added entries. You can't make a mistake if you are consistent.

Comment: Unless you forget to add them.

Question: In other words, you are saying that these are rather rough guidelines because, in essence, when you actually organize something on your own, you will probably do what you want to anyway?

Mr. Tauber: I hope that I did not give you that impression by my remarks. We used to have an editor of publications at the Columbia University Graduate School of Library Service who made the syllabi and reading lists consistent, but when she left, we never replaced her. In the years following her departure, each faculty member went off on his own, and of the group of teachers there, I will guess there are not two of them that follow exactly the same rules within a particular document. The students have caught this very quickly. If we can make this particular document useful in just one library school, or all library schools, it may be influential to others. If it is used by journals, a large group of journals, we will think we have been successful. We cannot convince everyone to make identical bibliographic citations, and there are certain eccentric writers dreaming up ways we haven't even thought about yet.

Comment: If you genuinely mean that, you are abdicating your responsibility. If you are writing *American* standards, then you are, in fact, producing only an in-house document. However, the theory behind a standard is that everyone, the eccentric ones as well, pause and think, "I am doing it this way; ought I for the general good of the intellectual community adopt the style of the American standard?" You know they sit there talking like this, these eccentric writers. Certainly, this is our next hope, human nature being what it is.

Basically, this is a teaching instrument, and I am now going to make a splendid generalization that, please, let's argue about very, very much later. A teacher has to teach the ideal as far as possible, though being human, we know that this ideal is rarely attained. These standards are laying down what everyone should do, and that is your aim, sir, if you are writing standards.

Mr. Tauber: I am glad you are here.

Comment: The reason I raise the question is that if it is a standard we are supposed to abide by, I need to know so that when I get back to my office, and start using these rules that specify tapes be measured in millimeters, I want an authority to cite when the staff says, "You're nit-picking, McMurry."

Question: Are we questioning whether to quote the size at all, or are we quarreling about the specifics for the size?

Comment: It is a detail which you are being invited to comment on. Your mind is still open, isn't it, Dr. Tauber? The whole of this session is predicated on the presupposition that we can educate Dr. Tauber.

Mr. Tauber: That was my opening sentence.

Comment: The Western world is going to the metric system, while the United States is one of the few countries dragging its feet.

Comment: That may be true, but I would dare say there is not a single one of us using a half-inch or a one inch or a two inch tape that could convert it to millimeters.

Comment: But the point is, shouldn't we? We use inches because the producers use inches, not because we want to work out standards as professional people. The cataloger has a ruler with the scale right on his desk; therefore, it's no problem for him.

Comment: I think there is another point.

We talk about satisfying user needs, a thread all through this conference, but, the user knows tape only in inches, regardless of whether he uses millimeters for film.

Question: Dr. Tauber, would the standard we are discussing be strictly a U.S. standard?

Mr. Tauber: Well, I said that each country prepares its own standard. I referred to the Swedish one, and said we used the British one, the Indian one, and several others. If this proposal is revised and accepted as an American standard, it will be distributed to foreign countries through the International Standards Organization. It will send our standard around, as it did the Swedish standard, to countries belonging to the ISO. The appropriate standards committees in these countries will comment on the American standard and compare it with the British, Indian, Swedish, and the standards of other countries and perhaps recommend that one of the standards be made international. International standards are very difficult to establish.

Question: Could I ask whether we have already accepted millimeter as a standard and whether by a particular time we will convert from inches to centimeters?

Mr. Tauber: This is certainly relevant. I mentioned at the outset that this particular subcommittee is only a small part of ANSI. The PH5 Committee has probably already established the millimeter as the standard.

Question: A procedural question. How are you going to handle the serial form in nonprint material such as motion pictures, audiotapes, phonodiscs, or EVR [Electronic Videotape Recording] cartridges? We have heard from Joe Becker that an engineering serial publication is going to be produced in the form of electronic videotape recording. We already have serials in the form of filmstrips and slide sets and serials on tape cartridges and audiotapes in medical libraries.

Mr. Tauber: I would think that the rule for serials in print format would be the primary rule. You would identify the fact that it appears in a special form.

Comment: Could we ask Gerald Brong to review the AA code, which has a very good and elaborate distinction between series and serials in the context of print, to see how far that would meet his problems in film? This would be a very useful thing for you to do from the librarian's point of view.

Question: The engineering journal Becker mentioned is going to come out in 1971 with volume 1, number 1. Is it not a serial?

Comment: Yes, as librarians, we would say it is a serial. Would you look at our solutions embodied in the code and see whether they seem to meet what you, as a film man, need?

Comment: It would seem to me that we are going to have to consider form for everything.

Mr. Tauber: This is why I said there is no separation between the first and second parts for the kinds of rules that we would develop. If a particular type of publication is in a serial form, the rule for serial publication is the dominant rule, and the form is identified. If we have basic rules in the first part that are applicable in the second part, we can refer back to 5.1 or whatever section is applicable and use it for the particular publication.

Question: How many of you audiovisual specialists would prefer to see the proposed standard developed in this way?

Comment: Many of us feel this must be done.

Comment: No, the point is that the basic principles are there. Now, instead of just listing these without thinking, our audiovisual friends need to take the proposed standard and translate it. For instance, it now says to list the title and director, obviously using director here as a translation of the author.

Comment: We should use title, form, and producer just as it is in the draft.

Comment: Is there an indication of format, such as reel to reel or loop film? What type of sound does the media have? These should be indicated. I do not know who in AECT [Association for Educational Communications and Technology] had a crack at this, but I know the Cataloging Committee did not. For historical purposes you might use terms like *sepia,* but not for recent productions.

Question: Since you have used both inches and millimeters for maps, why not use both for nonprint materials?

Mr. Tauber: What you said earlier, Miss

Whitenack, is probably involved here. I don't believe ANSI has a committee dealing with maps, but it does have one dealing with motion pictures and film. If that committee knows nothing about bibliography or bibliographic entry, then it ought to pass that over to Z39. Whenever one committee faces difficulty of this sort, it passes it to another committee for consideration.

Comment: Well, if your subcommittee did not get the DAVI media standards, then I am really concerned.

Mr. Tauber: I have already made a note of that.

Question: Dr. Tauber, in item 5.5.5, the examples of audiorecords includes two phonodiscs but no audiotape. Are you attempting to present a comprehensive listing of the various media forms with examples?

Comment: In book media, you have a place, publisher, and date. You should have a place, producer, and date for nonprint media.

Comment: But, since you do not say "published by," I would suggest dropping out "released by."

Mr. Tauber: No, I am sorry, films may be made by one and released by another. The actual producer may be somewhat like the printer. We have made a decison in the library world that the printer is irrelevant. Does it serve some purpose for nonprint media?

Comment: Yes. Many people will purchase a film if they know the producer and have confidence in his work.

Comment: In the example under 5.5.2, why do you put the distributor and the producer at the end, when normally they would come up before the release and all other information? The citation format should follow place, publisher, and date, and I think the director and the producer are out of bibliographic unity.

Mr. Tauber: We have been led to believe that it is much more helpful to have all the information concerning the film first, and the producer and the editor at the end. They stand out that way, instead of being meshed in with a lot of other details about the motion picture that are not monographic print materials.

Question: I am raising these questions for consideration of your subcommittee. One other idea that we have considered is the problem of finding a date on some of nonprint media. If you do not find a date, would you use *n.d.* to indicate no date?

Mr. Tauber: I think one of the general assumptions for this standard is that you supply the information that something is lacking. If you use *n.d.* with brackets, you know the information in lacking.

Comment: If we have a television program that was not originally a film, it could not be synonymous with a commercial motion picture, where Columbia Pictures is the organization and the producer is a particular person. Actually, WGBH is the organization that produced this program; therefore, the producer is not the producer in the same sense that he is in a Hollywood movie. The television producer does not usually do the same things and, in fact, the directors of television stations are so mobile that it could be one today and another the next. The quality is not necessarily dependent on a particular man, but on the organization backing that man. Therefore, the producer, in this sense, is not that important.

Comment: Mr. Koskey, so that the librarians here know that, would you write it down? To us, the word in both instances is *producer*. The media are both visual; therefore, only the media person, one as steeped in it as you are, would know the distinction. It is not a distinction that we could make from the information we normally get. This is what we want you to tell us.

Question: Don't you have to take what is given in the credits on the film? If they say producer and give you a man's name, I do not see that you have a choice in the matter.

Comment: We could be interested in the producer, but I do not think anyone in the film business cares about the film editor.

Comment: Mr. Clarke is quite right when he says that what the producer puts in the credits should be used for the citation. Like a collaborator for a book, if the name appears, you use it in the citation. You see, if the producer considers the name important enough to put it in the credits, the bibliographer should use it.

Comment: For any information other than

this, you may be assuming that the organization is a prime force in the production.

Question: Could *title page* be changed to *title credits?*

Comment: No.

Question: But how, then, can we equate them?

Comment: Read the DAVI media standard which specifies what a producer is, what a distributor is, and what production credit stands for. It is very specific.

Comment: It tells you how to place these elements in your entry, but it does not tell you how to make the decision about whether a film is actually produced by so-and-so, or how you could find out if the film was produced as described in the DAVI code.

Comment: And second, the DAVI code requires production credits. Have you looked at some of the production credits that appear at the beginning of a film? They include the bootblack who polishes the director's shoes. Do you seriously want, as a part of your computer tape, the equivalent of a producer's bootblack?

Comment: I feel there is an inconsistency here. Since I was a film editor for many years, let me make the point that the word *editor* was just thrown in here. Ordinarily, in a film the producer and the director would be the two main people. If the editor is mentioned, it is because he has won an Academy Award for editing or something of that nature. The film editor is not the same as the editor of a written work.

Mr. Tauber: You would not include this?

Comment: The first person responsible for a film is the director. The producer would be significant if it was a particularly outstanding individual or organization. The editor would be listed only if it was a particularly significant editing feat, or if he had won an unusual award.

Mr. Tauber: I think we need to review these examples because of your comments.

Comment: That is straight out of the DAVI code, which defines the producer as the organization or individual responsible for determining both the content and form of the material or for executing the wishes of the sponsor.

Question: That is a very nice definition, but when I am confronted by a film with credits on it, and that film lists the producer, how am I to decide whether it is a true statement?

Comment: In relation to film, the name of the producer is a very potent retrieval device, because, on the whole, most producers do produce their own films. Gene Koskey has told me that the producer, in a differing but very similar context—such as television—is *not* that important. This is the first time I have really had this difference between two media spelled out. Within one media we have to assume if they say producer, they mean producer. The fact that everyone in the place knows that he is a stinking drunk and that the film was actually made by the clapper boy is irrelevant.

Comment: You do not try to find out whether an author really wrote a book or whether some graduate student wrote it.

Comment: Among the things you must remember in cataloging nonbook media is that you cannot equate the title page of a book with the credits of a film, because they are different. If you are to catalog effectively you must be acquainted with the media you are going to catalog.

Comment: This is why we are here.

Comment: Apparently my verbal communication is not very good. I am not asking for a title page but for the equivalent integrity given to a title page. Does this make sense at all? It must be there somewhere.

Comment: In our experience at Indiana University, the person or organization responsible for the content is what we attempt to list as the producer. Sometimes the only real clue we have is the copyright information—if the media under consideration has been copyrighted. When there is no copyright, we lean on past experience. We must get producers to do the same thing that publishers have done for many years, which, of course, only solves the problem from this date forward.

Question: In looking over the listing of nonbook material in your proposed standard, I have not been able to see where you have treated transparencies, study prints, or art prints. There is also the problem of kits, all the various possible combinations, and how they should be listed. For example, should we follow the definition of sound filmstrips or define kits as any combination of two or more media?

Comment: In books we publish kits of assembled print media. They are called journals, and we have set out rules for them. The answer to your question is that we set up a series of rules for kits, considered as a whole, and you can then do analytics if you wish. What you need, in fact, is a series of rules for the total entity, a kit.

Comment: Still, there must be some examples of kits, or some statement of how a kit should be done in the accepted standards for nonprint media.

Question: Did I understand you, Mr. Croghan, to say you would handle the nonprint elements in a kit the same way you would handle elements in a journal?

Comment: For the purposes of a catalog record, yes. I can take a journal and simply classify it as the *Journal of Engineering History,* or I can make analytics for the separate journal articles by the authors, or I can make separate subject entries for the graphs. These are differing methods. So, for the multimedia history-teaching kit which will contain pamphlets, a tape giving the Gettysburg speech, a film, and a filmstrip, I have two levels. I can catalog it as a kit, all together, or I may catalog only some of the separate parts.

Comment: What you have just said needs to be in this proposed document.

Comment: I would think so. Kits actually are one of the things that have not really been recognized in most of the documents I have seen. I do not see that they pose any enormous problem, but they have to be recognized as a separate media kit.

Mr. Tauber: What you are asking for, primarily, in my observation, are more examples, rather than specific rules.

Comment: I think you ought to include examples of every type.

Comment: Yes, the rules are fine. There's nothing wrong with the rules, but not enough examples are included to clarify how the rules are to be applied.

Mr. Tauber: Dr. Hines and I did a study at Rockville, Maryland, last year. We were asked to take a look at centralized processing there for the Department of Instructional Materials, and there was a publication issued. One of the things which struck us about the Rockville activity was that they did include globes, slides, games, transparencies, kits, art prints, and so forth. We have had this document a year and a half now, and I have come to the conclusion that these are so special, for us to get involved with them for a standard would only bring more critics into the arena.

Comment (many voices): No, no, no, no.

Mr. Tauber: Let me ask you two questions. First, do you think we ought to have a stipulated statement about each one of these forms of materials? Second, could we get away from doing this sort of thing by just having a list of examples?

Comment: You will never know whether the examples will work until you do it for each type, so that's why you have to go through the process. Once you do it, you can see whether you have a general principle. Then you can use examples.

Comment: Maybe it would be helpful if you got together with some of the media people and took the broader categories of media, giving examples under each.

Comment: A lot of these may seem like new media, but in fact you can categorize them as old media with an infinitesimal difference. Now the infinitesimal difference is the one that is always stressed when the products are being sold, because this is their selling point. If they brought out a sepia-colored transparency base, they would call it something like sepia-trans, and the manufacturers would thump this solely, since the sepia gives an added sepia phonic dimension to the overhead transparency or what not. A naïve person would tend to think of this as a totally new thing when, in fact, it is basically a transparency with a very little difference. Ninety percent of the basic rules that are already worked out will apply, and all you need is the extra rule for the difference. This is possible, however, only if you recognize the likenesses.

Mr. Tauber: Well, it looks like we may have not only a sixth draft of these standards, but perhaps a seventh, too.

Comment: There is an added problem here that has never been reconciled, which is the definition of terms, and perhaps your committee could be helpful in this. We need to resolve the apparent confusion about sound filmstrips and kits. If a sound filmstrip is a kit, *sound filmstrips* should be dropped and *kit* used.

Comment: No, if you say a sound filmstrip is a kit, then you look at the general rule that we have evolved for kits and ask how it applies to this special example of a kit. Now this gives you a two-way situation enabling you to check on your initial decision that this new media falls into the category of a kit. Then, if the rule seems to solve a lot of your problems (no rule will ever solve every problem on a totally new thing), then you are probably in the right area. If it does not seem to match at all, then you have made a wrong initial decision about what the new thing is.

Comment: One thing we probably should give recognition to is the DAVI code.

Mr. Tauber: When did that come out? I have never seen it before.

Comment: We have made a gross mistake in the past by not getting these guidelines to our chief bibliographers.

Comment: This was a publication put out by DAVI largely for bibliographers and catalogers, but they were not involved in the development of it.

Comment (several): That's right.

Comment: Wait, wait; Katharine Clugston from the Library of Congress met with us the very first day on that one.

Comment: Once and for all, I am sick and tired of hearing people refer to this as the Bible. It is not. It simply was a guideline developed to wake up the American Library Association's Resources and Technical Services Division to do something to make *Anglo-American Cataloging Rules* a better tool. That was the sole purpose of the DAVI effort originally.

Comment: We have certainly gotten your point and will accept within this group that it is not a bible. However, what can we do about the 200 million minus 45 that see the word *standards* on the publication? You see, this is the dilemma. The term *standards* has become very ambiguous in our society. In general, it means goals for which to strive. When you say *standards* in relation to the standards that Dr. Tauber is talking about, it is a genuine and complex goal. For example, the *Standards for School Media Programs* are actually guidelines.

Comment: Mr. Croghan has a good point, for the title does indicate it is *the* standard rather than a preliminary statement.

Comment: We know this was not your choice, Miss Whitenack, but the document exists with the word on it, and this is our dilemma.

Comment: It was quite to the point, though, for when DAVI issued this code, it was for one purpose, and that was to get reactions which it has not gotten from librarians and catalogers in the field.

Comment: It disturbs me professionally to think of the contacts that have apparently existed between Dr. Tauber and Dr. Darling, and know that the DAVI code was not referred to the ANSI standards subcommittee. This lack of communications among the experts is a detriment to any kind of meaningful bibliographic control of nonprint media.

Comment: Dr. Tauber, you represent a group that is coming up with standards, an influential group. You are dealing with an area called media and, therefore, have the responsibility of contacting professional groups in this field.

Mr. Tauber: We did. We established contact with everyone in the country who we thought was interested.

Comment (many): Not me, not everyone.

Comment: Dr. Tauber did say, too, there is a PH5 standards group in motion pictures that should have contacted this Z39 subcommittee, but has not.

Comment: In the media field we need the help of our bibliographers. Heaven only knows how badly we need them; however, we must see that these people get our guidelines.

Comment: You are getting now to one of the central purposes of the institute. It has come out over and over, an audiovisual person stressing the importance of having a bibliographer involved. And too, you librarians are now asking for statements from the audio-visual specialists.

Question: How many people in the library world know what Z39 is? Very few people, I would judge, and as a result, we are reinventing the wheel out in Podunk in an attempt to compile bibliographic guides that are much less successful than this standard being proposed by ANSI's Z39 subcommittee.

Comment: When we started the Canadian Library Association project, realizing Canadians cannot deviate too far from the Americans because it is too expensive for us, I wrote all over the United States to get the views of American librarians. I wrote countless letters to people whose names had been given to me, asking for advice and assistance on the Canadian code, and the only person who replied in the entire United States was Mr. Quinly. Other than that the responses received said, "I have passed your letter to Mrs. Jane Brown, who will reply shortly," but she never did.

Comment: I agree with Mr. Clarke that we in the media profession have never assumed our responsibilities for the organization of nonprint media. Nevertheless, when I began working on standards in the state of Washington for a bibliographic control network, a part of the state library network, our committee wrote to Richard L. Darling as chairman of the ALA RTSD [Resources and Technical Services Division] ad hoc committee concerned with the organization of nonprint media.

Comment: May I make an aside, too? I took Sumner Spalding's proposed revision of the AA code regarding audiovisual materials to Dr. Darling's ALA committee meeting in June 1969, only to find the committee had never heard of it.

Comment: I have had an exchange of several letters with ALA, only to learn that there was apparently no activity in this area.

Comment: Let me say that ALA and the Library of Congress are certainly not synonymous. They can be working almost completely without knowledge of each other's activities. However, it is unbelievable how little interest there is in DAVI. There are now three committees in this organization concerned with the control of nonprint media, and, of those

three committees, only one is functioning, and that is Mr. Quinly's.

Comment: Maybe one constructive thing we could come up with in this particular institute is a communications procedure.

Comment: One of our problems is our personnel in both professional organizations. Although there is sporadic communication at some levels, no formal structure exists for the meaningful interchange of ideas and cooperative endeavors. Robert C. Snider has been our DAVI contact for Z39.

Mr. Tauber: We will see that DAVI is kept informed.

Question: Dr. Tauber, instead of having them kept informed, couldn't they be *involved?* Really, this is the difference.

Mr. Tauber: All right, involved. I do not know how that document escaped us, because Nathalie Batts is probably as alert to the developments in this area of our responsibility as anyone in this country. As one of our committee members, she really has been responsible for the bibliography of this particular document. How this slipped through, I do not know.

Comment: You do have people at Columbia like Philip Lang who could be added to your group to help do this very part. I can appreciate all the work that has gone into this, for those who have worked in bibliographic control know how many hours you have donated to developing this tool. This is free labor, and don't think that we are not appreciative.

Mr. Tauber: No, I think this is absolutely tremendous. I expected considerable criticism and questioning because of the nature of the project.

Comment: I would like to return to a point Harlow Clarke brought up earlier concerning a communications procedure which was not taken up and followed through. I suggest a flow chart be developed with the committees and persons of every professional organization we are aware of that would have authority in these areas. We should establish a chart of contact personnel, or a flow chart of some dimension, so that you would know who to contact.

Mr. Tauber: You know, in certain ways this

is quite amusing to me. Here I am being put on the spot for failing to be associated with DAVI. Do you know, only in the last few days I have become aware that the abstracting subcommittee of Z39 should have been constantly informed by me. I have not been doing it. They are working without the bibliography subcommittee's thinking in terms of responsibility for citing abstracts. Just before I left, I sent them fourteen copies of this document in order to get that committee involved. I think the DAVI code discussed here is very, very important, especially when it is called standards. Do not minimize this, for anytime you put *standards* on something, people think of it is something more than mere guidelines.

Question: Concerning the controversy about centimeters and inches on a map and other things, would it be useful in your development of these standards to include the dimensions as given on the document? If it is given in inches, it is recorded in inches; if it is given in centimeters, it is recorded in centimeters, with the other designation in parenthesis, so that you have both.

Mr. Tauber: It's worth considering.

Question: But why do you need both? Isn't that the point of a standard? One of the objects is to simplify so that you are not giving two pieces or two versions of the same information. On the whole, I would have thought it simpler only to give one and make up our minds which one.

Question: In cataloging we have a provision for adding extraneous material to titles by putting things in brackets. The precedent is set, so why not apply it to the various things like inches and centimeters, adding in brackets that which is not originally part of the produced material, but which is helpful in defining what that material is?

Comment: We certainly have this provision as a safety valve. It is also, however, part of our cataloging philosophy that you should use it as sparingly as possible.

Mr. Tauber: In the area of maps, rather than following the approach of most cartographers and geographers, who, as was indicated by Mr. Croghan, place the most importance on the place or subject and do not care

in most cases who the cartographer is, we have followed what you would call the more standardized approach.

On motion pictures, filmstrips, and videotapes, I have become aware of your thoughts, and I think that these can be clarified on the basis of your comments.

In respect to 5.5.3, Music, it seems rather skimpy for the subject, even if only in terms of examples. A comment was made in connection with cataloging particular types of materials that you need people who know the field. This is absolutely true in the case of music. As a former head cataloger, I always looked for a musican first and then sent him to take a catalog course, if he did not have such a background, rather than looking for a cataloger and trying to train him how to prepare music cataloging. Basically, the items in this draft are those which we regarded as important in the cataloging of music.

Question: I am puzzled. The proposed standard uses the term *form: music.* Would you explain what that means?

Mr. Tauber: If the item itself is not identifiable as music, you have to describe it as music. That is a note.

Comment: In other words, that particular element will always read *music.* I suggest that *form,* to a musican, means the type of form that the piece of music uses as the basic structure of the music itself. This might be a useful element to include here, for instance, with form meaning symphony or sonata allegro.

Question: Not quite, but if you had a composition called *Zeeclus for Two Compounds and Tensionometers,* then you might want to identify that as music, electronic music. That is probably why that term is included. However, in the example that is given, it says *Music around the Clock for Soprano and Two Tenor Recorders.* Why report the term *music* when the intention is already described in the title?

Comment: It could mean sheet music rather than a phonodisc or phonotape.

Comment: In a book entitled *Elizabethan Lute Music,* the wording on the title page is such that it is very hard indeed to distinguish, until you get down to the collation, that it is not sheet music.

Question: Was that the agreed definition, that music means printed notes?

Question: Music seems so general. Why wouldn't it say *score*?

Comment: It could mean both score and sheet music.

Mr. Tauber: It means any type of music.

Question: What does the AA code recommend?

Mr. Tauber: It is more specific, using the term *score.* Do you think the term *music* is too general? I am listening.

Comment: Music is really a subject description.

Question: Does *score* mean anything to anyone who is not a musician?

Comment: It sounds like baseball to me.

Mr. Tauber: Do not forget what the standards are for. We tend to forget general bibliography or a footnote. Standard bibliography distinguishes the fact that it is music, which is not necessarily clear from the title.

Comment: Music includes aural as well as visual in terms of defining the word. I do not think it is clear whether you are saying aural or visual.

Question: Dr. Tauber, doesn't the Music Library Association have a classification scheme with definitions?

Mr. Tauber: Yes, I would like to know if there are general reactions to the fact that this is not more specific than *music.* I do not think that this particular title requires anything, but, supposing there were titles that should have been idenified more specifically, would you then prefer another term such as *score?*

Comment: There are at least two ways to view that. First, perhaps *Music* as the title of section 5.5.3 is too general. You might entitle it *Musical Scores.* That would get you out of that hassle. Now, the AA code gives a notation, *The City in the Sea,* which is the title, and then "poem for orchestra, chorus of mixed voices and baritone solo." This is what you have suggested. Your proposal states "instrument(s) or group for which written." The problem is in the punctuation, because I do not know if *Music around the Clock for Soprano or Tenor Recorder* is the title, or if the title is *Music around the Clock,* and "for soprano or tenor recorder," is the next element

which indicates the instruments or groups for which it was written.

Comment: My guess is that this is the title. You really do not know if it is a story about music around the clock.

Mr. Tauber: It is a book, a piece of music.

Question: Is 5.5 nonbook materials? You have switched and included print material in the same section with motion pictures. Music is a different media, and you call this particular section, 5.5, Nonbook Materials. Since your example is a book, or printed words, are we back to book materials?

Mr. Tauber: If you are thinking of codex, I think of codex as a book. Music is usually printed in pamphlet or book form. When we are talking about music, in the context of nonbook, we are probably thinking of it in comparison to the typical monograph, serial, or pamphlet, as compared to something which has content other than music print. I think this is the reason why the Library of Congress includes music in its nonbook materials, and also why it is done generally. This is what may be described as an in-between type of media, not clearly print or nonprint.

Question: Can it be made more specific?

Mr. Tauber: I would add a note such as symphony, sonata, or whatever it is.

Comment (many): No, no. More specific categories such as *score* are needed.

Comment: The point being made here is that this ought to be in your conventional title anyway.

Mr. Tauber: If we were cataloging according to the Library of Congress *Rules,* which we are not doing here, this would be right.

Question: Are you throwing out the whole concept of a conventional title? You do not make any provision here, except you say *title.* In present music bibliographic form a conventional title is one of the more important aspects.

Mr. Tauber: Actually in a citation?

Comment: In grouping things together, for location, yes.

Mr. Tauber: I do not want to lose track of our particular proposed standard. We are not cataloging music the way it is necessarily done at the Library of Congress.

Comment: For standard bibliographic control, not only in the music field but also in the legal field and in the English literature field with Shakespeare, we should utilize conventional title identification, so that we can group these items together in one location.

Comment: In the organization of musical recordings you cannot just say it is a performance on a record. It is a performance of specific music and/or sound, if you want to so describe it.

Comment: You are not cataloging each individual piece on a record for which there is a performance, but a recording, and more specifically, a recording is of a performance, not the individual pieces.

Comment: When I catalog an anthology of English poetry, I do not attempt to enter separate entries for Tennyson, Auden, or all the 177 poets. That is the problem of a composite work, and there are principles behind it. Pick the one you need, but let us not start rearguing principles again on this one.

Comment: I do not think we are. I think what Mr. McFarland is saying, going back to musical scores, is that the entry is under composer, but it is not consistent. It is consistent under title. Maybe you need to make that a subdivision.

Mr. Tauber: I understood this point completely.

Question: Getting out of the musical frame of reference for a minute, what are you going to do when you have lectures on audiotape? It seems you must put them under lecturer, because the title would have less meaning to the user.

Comment: Of course, this is a work by a named author. A lot of these problems have been solved in principle. Look for the principle and see whether or not it does apply.

Comment: The principle has not been solved on this one. I have been working on this for two years, and there is no solution.

Mr. Tauber: I have the point, and I certainly will put this before my committee.

Question: Setting all existing rules aside, *AACR* [*Anglo-American Cataloging Rules*] or whatever, view with me a physical collection of materials such as a record by Brubeck entitled *Jazz Improvisations* and a record of Tchaikovsky, *Symphony No. 1,* performed by Eugene Ormandy. I contend that no greater contribution is made by Brubeck than by Ormandy, and if we are entering the *Jazz Improvisations* under Brubeck, who is the performer, giving the record his own style, why are we not entering Tchaikovsky's *Symphony No. 1* under Ormandy, who is also creating a work, giving it his own style, with his own interpretation of the work? Ormandy is a conductor and Brubeck a performer.

Question: Rather than having *title* under the list of elements, would it be more appropriate to have author first and then in parentheses, the composer or performer, whichever seems to have the greater importance?

Comment: George Abbott's previous question is a very valid one. A hundred years from now we may have another very famous conductor, who will do another Tchaikovsky, but we will not have another jazz performance duplicating Brubeck.

Comment: We will not have another performance of Tchaikovsky that will be an exact duplicate of Ormandy's.

Comment: There will be many different performances of Tchaikovsky all together in your catalog by conductor. But, Dave Brubeck is not only the performer of jazz, he is the author. That is the difference.

Comment: I contend that his improvisations are no more important than Ormandy's interpretation of Tchaikovsky's score. They are equally important, for they both have their own style.

Comment: If there is someone who originated what Brubeck is doing, then it would be entered under that name first, and then Brubeck as the performer or conductor. You are right in your thinking, but you would have to know who did the original.

Comment: It need not be put under the original. I think that, for *Ellington at Newport,* the title is sufficient. I do not think the performer, unless we decide he deserves prominence, is important enough to be cited first. Taped lectures and spoken records are different problems.

Comment: As a user, if I am really hip on Tchaikovsky, I would like to have ten different performances, but what I really want are

Tchaikovsky recordings and not necessarily a particular performance.

Comment: However, you might very well want a specific interpretation.

Comment: Mr. Abbott, it is not as simple as saying you can choose one or the other. The cataloging of books presents similar dilemmas.

Mr. Tauber: Let's not go back to cataloging but stay with bibliographic citations. You worry me with some of this discussion, because I think you are going back to cataloging with your concerns for added entries, cross references, and subject headings.

Comment: But you really cannot separate them, in the final analysis.

Mr. Tauber: But these are bibliographic citations which may be cited perhaps once in the footnote of a document.

Comment: In determining an author for a book, it is not just an A or B situation. That is the reason the *Anglo-American Cataloging Rules* was written, to tell you the C, D, E, F, G, H, and I. You cannot use the term *either/or* for audiorecord either. I am suggesting that we consider what is extremely relevant in the field which encompasses library users and that we consider the performer in his bona fide position. Just the same as Shakespeare writing one of his plays the Bee Gees or the Beatles would be "authoring" their records. They are just as much an author as Shakespeare. I am suggesting that we consider this as an added facet, because performance is one of those things which is essential to the audiorecord of any type.

Question: How do we handle a recording with jazz improvisations that has twelve different pieces by twelve composers?

Comment: May I make a point as a musician, a listener, and as a teacher in this area of music? For the vast majority of works on records, virtually no one would be selecting recordings by conductor, primarily because there is not that much difference. Ormandy and Toscanini may be exceptions, but we are considering a basic standard for bibliographic entry. The conductor is not that important when we look at the entire collection.

Question: Was any consideration given to suggesting where this title information was to come from for a disc? It is all very well to say that this is *Ellington at Newport,* but those three words will have been juxtaposed at least twice on that recording. Now, which version of those three words are you going to use as the title for the citation? This is one of the major problems in phonograph records.

Mr. Tauber: You do not think *Ellington at Newport* was on the disc?

Question: I would like to know which is the official title, the one on the front of the sleeve, the back of the sleeve, the spine of the sleeve, or the disc itself? They can be very different renditions of the same phrase.

Mr. Tauber: I do not know what is given in the catalog of Columbia Records, but the chances are, the citation you would use is what is listed there.

Question: Mr. Abbott, do you feel that the title of the lecture is more important than the performer?

Comment: I am not saying that the performer is unimportant, but I wish to point out the inconsistency involved. I see arguments for entering it under performer and equally valid points for placing it under title.

Comment: Consistency does not mean doing everything in the same way. It can mean consistent variation, and this is what we have. If you are really worried, there is no inconsistency in what we have been saying, because we arrive at our choice for the items that should go under the title, performer, author, composer, or, if you like, under the color of the record sleeve. We can arrive at these consistently. It is important that we identify the variables that require consistency. Let's not have the illusion that consistency means doing everything one way, for you cannot do everything one way. It is totally impossible, but you *can* be consistent in the different ways you do things.

Question: When you make master files and put them in the computer, you want to be able to dump that file in the most economical fashion and not have to make expensive sorts. Are you referring to the entry that goes into the master file, so that if I have only one opportunity to dump the file into some order, it is this one entry, the important entry, that I will have?

Comment: This is why the problem of getting at the right author is a genuine one, and why it is worth arguing about; which is the approach that will give you the most economic order in the first place? Inherent in your system, inherent in any author catalog that puts in a subject approach, is the assumption that we must, having decided the most economical way, also provide a machinery to get at it by other approaches.

Question: I can do that, but I want to know, how is the first file, the main entry listing, supposed to look?

Mr. Tauber: Our basic problem is one of sufficient identification to get the particular item that the user wants into his hands. You cannot worry about cross references, added entries, and other kinds of devices for a catalog system. This is strictly a bibliographic control system.

Question: Then what we are trying to do here is to produce the single dump requested by Glenn McMurry, in which you give as much information as possible. Is that what you are after?

Mr. Tauber: Right. And, if "Ellington at Newport" is enough, you do not need an entry for Brubeck or anyone else.

Question: When you say "disc or tape speed, diameter of tape reel or disc, recording channels, monaural or stereo," are you recommending that only these things be included, and not such things as standards for notation?

Mr. Tauber: The *Anglo-American Cataloging Rules,* and the DAVI publication both go into great detail. My suggestion is that we set this within the framework of acceptable guides. You can include other items if you wish. We did not want to undergo the torture of enumerating the variety of information that you can use in identifying media.

Question: Have we agreed to change the entry for spoken recordings? It seems ridiculous to have a title entry for a lecture.

Comment: There is no essential difference between the two. If for *performance* you were to substitute *Tchaikovsky Conducting His Own Works,* you have the same thing as a lecturer reading his own notes. There is no fundamental difference, and the principles that solve one will solve the other.

Mr. Tauber: Lectures are located under 5.7., Oral Communications, in the proposed standards, which now seem to me, to be out of place. I do not know the extent to which you people are concerned about this, except that again, within the framework of special collections, you are likely to have this type of material. I think the examples indicate pretty clearly what we are trying to do with Unpublished Materials in 5.6.

Comment: There can be tape recordings on different widths of audiotape, one-quarter inch, one-half inch, and one-inch tape. A master eight-track recording will very likely appear on a one-inch audiotape. Therefore, you might want to have some kind of designation for the width of the tape.

You might also consider combining the two paragraphs 5.5.5., Audiorecords, and 5.7, Oral Communications, for the medium seems to be the same.

Mr. Tauber: But the complications of the entry for Audiorecords follow those of music rather than the kinds of things that you have under Oral Communications.

Comment: When you say *audiorecord,* the term is too broad, if you are confining that to just music. A lecture on a tape is to me an audiorecord, just as a piece of music is an audiorecord.

Comment: We have not touched on archival records. Today even small libraries are establishing archive collections. However, there are no citations or references in the proposed standard.

Comment: But, unpublished material would be in an archive, which is essentially a collection of unpublished material. The published works included are usually treated as other published materials.

Comment: There is a difference between manuscripts and archives. Although I do not think we need to go into this in detail, there are archival groups, and references are made to them, not to the individual item.

Mr. Tauber: That is a proper observation. The distinction between individual manuscripts with which we have been concerned here and groups of manuscripts, or archive collections, is an important one. There are certain manuscript collections which are only identified by a general heading, such as the comprehensive manuscript catalog issued by the Library of Congress.

Question: What do you consider unpublished in the case of an audiotape?

Mr. Tauber: One that is unique, and there is only one.

Question: Therefore, is anything that has more than one copy a published document?

Mr. Tauber: With today's copying facilities, I do not know if that is true. But, usually when it has not been printed in a journal, book, or some other method of publication, it is thought of as being unpublished.

Question: Do not copyright lawyers have a definition of *unpublished?* I thought it was set down very clearly.

Mr. Tauber: No. I did a report in 1962 on Australian libraries. There were six manuscript copies of the report, but the National Library of Australia reproduced it in 100 photographed copies for general and Australian libraries. Ten copies of the report may be located in the United States. I consider it published, although it was never printed.

Question: Would these citations we are discussing here ever be incorporated into a union catalog?

Mr. Tauber: They could be in a union catalog. As a matter of fact, it is very unusual, but this is the kind of thing that G. K. Hall of Boston is doing, photographing card files and making book catalogs of them. Hall published the Columbia University School of Library Service card catalog in book form. In 1956 I did a study of the shelflist section of the Library of Congress, which is an unreleased report by the Library of Congress. I gave a copy to the library school but said not to send a copy of the catalog card to the Union Catalog. Nevertheless, it is in the G. K. Hall printed catalog of the library school. Consequently, some people want xeroxed copies of this study of the Library of Congress shelflist system, which is one of the few studies of its kind. I would call this an unpublished manuscript, despite the fact that a lot of people know about it.

Comment: Well, if we are talking about this citation's possibly being used in a union cata-

log, there is a statement in the AA code that says a brief note may be given for the topic or topics of a letter and that such a note is especially important for entries intended to be included in a union catalog. I still feel that some subject analysis, not a cataloging approach, is important and, therefore, that a small note about the topic of the letter would be advisable.

Mr. Tauber: Well, I will put a note here with a question mark.

Question: Would you make a statement about what constitutes unpublished material in the audio and video categories?

Mr. Tauber: It would be a unique item.

Comment: I can cite a case in which something has been published and only one item exists, a master tape. If you were to say quite firmly, "I will supply copies at such and such a price to anyone who cares to ask," then, even though there is only one unique copy, the statement that you will supply copies constitutes a publication. Until someone pays his five dollars, you have a published item that exists in one copy only. Uniqueness is not a criteria for publication.

Question: Then would our interpretation be that anything which is recorded in audio or video form would be considered published?

Comment: Yes, if it is made available in multiple copies to a stated audience, defined either by price or by a statement on the actual object itself. There must be a definition of the audience, and I would exclude multiple copies produced for administrative purposes only within an organization or a system. This will eliminate in-house reports that are never intended to go outside the walls of International Business Machines (IBM), while still retaining the manual on how to store an IBM tape that IBM produces and offers free to all librarians who write in. The latter is published, but an internal document, a research report on storage problems on IBM tape, which is only meant for scientists within the company, remains essentially unpublished.

Mr. Tauber: Let me ask you, if fifteen libraries own microfilm copies of President Buchanan's papers, would it be considered published?

Comment: That is published, in my definition. They exist in multiple copies for a selected audience, who have probably paid in some way for them.

Question: May I ask a question here, and this is a matter of fact that I am not quite certain about. In this country is copyright dependent upon publication? In Great Britain, copyright is inherent in the document.

Mr. Tauber: No, you can have copyright on one copy.

Comment: It is absolutely inherent in Great Britain. If you produce it, you have got the copyright.

Mr. Tauber: Another thing completely unexpected is the question of what is a manuscript. I would hesitate to say the distinctions that we have made here for the use of the word *unpublished* would hold true in all cases. For example, Theses and Dissertations, 5.6.2, are involved in this question. The usual practice nowadays is to deposit a dissertation at University Microfilms, Ann Arbor, and copies are sold from there. The dissertation is cited in *Dissertation Abstracts,* and you can get a copy of it very quickly. This is really the depositing of a unique copy, with copies being made from it.

Comment: Since we are considering the total field of media, there should be some kind of note in your standard explaining how audio and video materials fit into the descriptions.

Mr. Tauber: Definitely, for theses and dissertations and microforms represent extensive collections in many libraries.

Comment: Speaking of microforms, it seems that these must be a terrific problem for bibliographers, and you have not mentioned them.

Mr. Tauber: Microforms represent a particular treatment of the material that is already in there. You must, however, indicate that it is a microfilm, microfiche, or microcard.

Question: If we are being this exact in terminology, isn't the term *bibliographic controls* a misnomer, for *biblio* means, in my terminology, *book.*

Comment: The term *biblio* derives from book, but you can always extend the meaning of a term.

Mr. Tauber: I think that is what we have

done here, which may not be right, but I think it can probably be adequately explained in the foreword. *Bibliographic* is the word we have been using, and the question is whether we are proper in using it that way. In terms of authorship, in terms of title, in terms of the other elements, *bibliographic* is used generically.

Perhaps 5.6.3 should have been Unpublished Official Reports and Papers, as I reread it on the basis of the question that was raised. That gives it a little different character than that designed for unpublished manuscripts.

I think 5.6.4, Letters, does not appear to contain anything that should disturb you. It is a relatively simple type of document in which you can easily identify the individuals involved.

In 5.6.5, Privately Printed Works, the idea was to give the type of entry that you would develop for a privately printed work. I do not think it is too different from the regularly printed work, except for the note.

Question: This creates a question in my mind about what is privately printed and what is published. For instance, some of us saw a document which was commercially printed; Dr. Snider's bibliography of his own book collection. This is not circulated that I know of, unless he gave a copy to friends. However, it is printed, and there are multiple copies. Does this fall under 5.6.5, or would it fall under published works?

Mr. Tauber: I think if he did it himself, it would be privately printed by the author. This note unsually appears on the title page, by the way.

Question: Even though it is commercially printed?

Mr. Tauber: Yes, it would not have the name of the printer necessarily.

Question: I keep wondering, what is the difference between this standard you are recommending and a style manual such as *Turabian?* Are they much the same thing?

Mr. Tauber: I think so; there is a good deal of relationship between the two, except we are trying to use a form that is acceptable to more individuals. The phrase "Privately printed by the author" is a very important note in terms of trying to locate a copy.

Mr. Koskey asked how 5.7, Oral Communications differs from aural materials? Actually, this has not been identified in any situation as being aural; oral communications, but not aural.

Question: How are these recorded?

Mr. Tauber: Probably transcriptions rather than disc or tape.

Question: Since we used *microform* earlier, why wouldn't it be consistent here to also indicate the form, if it is an audiotape or a transcription?

Mr. Tauber: Well, I would say that both 5.7.1, Lectures, and 5.7.2, Interviews, Conversations, Discussions, if they were on tape or on discs, would fall under the notes that you use for this type of material.

Question: Could this also be a manuscript a secretary has typed?

Mr. Tauber: Yes, it could be.

Question: Would this category also include the type of presentation that Mr. Clarke referred to earlier, let's say, a recording of Maurice Evans reading Shakespeare? This is obviously not music, and yet it is a performance, and you could not consider it, bibliographically speaking, an oral communication. Would it really belong under audiorecords?

Mr. Tauber: I think, in the section dealing with audiorecords, we have to make a distinction between musical audiorecords and nonmusical audiorecords. That became quite clear after Mr. Koskey raised the question.

Question: What about the private tape of the private performance of an unpublished composition by a well-known, recognized composer? The criteria that you have grouped under here, and I rather agree, are for unpublished items. I assume, since you put it under unpublished, that you meant oral recorded, because, if you have an oral communication that is written down, it is either manuscript and still unpublished, or print and probably published.

Mr. Tauber: Probably unpublished. There is an oral history project at Columbia University with which some of you may be familiar. People come in and talk, and then the recordings are reduced to manuscript, whereupon the tapes are destroyed.

Comment: What a pity.

Mr. Tauber: A lot of people agree with you. However, the oral history project staff is doing this because of the cost, care, and control of the materials and because of the desire on the part of some people who participated and do not want their tapes preserved. That is part of the arrangement, that after a certain number of years the tapes will be destroyed.

Question: Are they considered unpublished?

Mr. Tauber: I would call them unpublished.

Comment: If in fact, as you are saying, the audiovisual media are only intermediate steps to getting print on paper, then for heaven's sakes, let's stop. And this is a librarian talking. The whole virtue of tape is that you can get a man's voice, which is a part of him, as distinct from just print on paper.

Mr. Tauber: This is being done every day, you know, using the tape recorder to obtain a speech and then erasing the tape when it has been transcribed.

Comment: I am appalled by the fact that you are taking oral communication and transferring it to the medieval form of print. In view of the expanding oral history movement, I am utterly appalled.

Mr. Tauber: I had nothing to do with it. As a matter of fact, I found out about it accidentally about two months ago.

Comment: We have to consider the purpose of a record. Suppose that someone records an interview. Under the context of this outline, it is oral communication. As soon as it becomes published and is sold to schools, it becomes an audiorecord and, therefore, is no longer an oral communication. This element of purpose or dissemination is going to affect the classification of the material.

Mr. Tauber: There are three more items which represent again the special problems and appear in bibliographical citation. Paragraph 5.8, Works in Preparation or Being Printed, should be very commonly used. Sometimes the books never appear but become bibliographic ghosts. Probably, *in preparation* should mean that the work is pretty far along and may even be in the hands of the printer.

Rules given under 5.9, Reference Embodied in the Text, do not, I believe, present any special difficulties.

The two remaining sections of the document are 6., Detailed Recommendations, and 7., Miscellany. In the first section, 6., we have tried to identify and clarify what we mean by certain terms, such as author, title, edition, date of publication, series statement, collation, pagination, and illustration. Under the detailed recommendations of item 6., the first item, 6.1, concerns the Author. Following the general statement, the personal author citation, 6.1.1, is given. The author is a person, persons, a corporate body, or bodies responsible for intellectual content of a work. The recommendations apply to whole works and parts of works: for example, an article in a journal or an encyclopedia, or a section of a composite work.

Question: May I suggest the AA code be added for this type of description? Is it intellectual, or aesthetic, or emotional in content? The code uses a definition that brings in works of art, as well as facts. The term *intellectual* seems to me a little narrow, although I think the AA code stretches it a bit. Right at the very front, attention is called to the creation of the intellectual or the artistic content of a work. Since we have accepted that aspect, we may be concerned with tapes or things like that.

Mr. Tauber: I think it is very desirable, Mr. Croghan. The paragraph on personal author recommends you list the names of each author when there are one to three authors of a particular work. When there are more than three authors, give the name of the first followed by "and others." This follows the *Anglo-American Cataloging Rules.* However, I do not know whether this particular rule is desirable from the point of view of some private works in multimedia.

Comment: The answer is yes, simply on the grounds that we accept the fact that multimedia integrate with books. I think there is a feeling here that we should do this. Therefore, we will stick with the AA code. I would like to ask the American librarians assembled here, does anyone know where the "rule of three" comes from? I have heard various suggestions going back to the theological concept of the Trinity. So, although the answer is stick to the rule of three because it is consistent with the AA code, we should look at why the AA code fusses about the rule of three.

Mr. Tauber: And particularly in view of the theory someone has suggested, that the fourth author may be the one who did it.

Comment: Ah, this is a muddle here, isn't it? The fourth author, solely on his position on the title page, is relegated to oblivion. But, if you really decided that he is the fellow who did it, he is the principal author and should appear first in your record.

Mr. Tauber: The rule says that if you have four, you forget the fourth person.

Comment: The basic principle of the AA code says that you put it under the principal author once you have determined him. If there are then four or more, you can ignore this, but you go first to the principal author and enter it under his name. It is only if you have four authors with no principal author that it becomes a composite work with a diffuse authorship. So that if you have a title page that states A, B, and C under the general direction of X, in very large letters, were responsible for the manuscript, then this is typographical evidence that it is really X who did the work and he is giving credit to his three assistants. I think this is the accepted interpretation of the code. Typographical evidence enables you to determine the principal author. Then only if you cannot determine a principal author does the idea of diffuseness and four authors become a factor.

Comment: But if you said, "under the direction of this," is that evidence enough of what is actually being conveyed about who is really responsible for the intellectual content of the item?

Comment: Can I stop a catalogers' argument at this point? I will have a lovely argument with you later, Mrs. Britton, on what constitutes typographical or other evidence for determining the principal author. Meanwhile, if you can determine the principal author, that is the principle that I would go by.

Mr. Tauber: Do you need five or six authors cited for certain areas of the audiovisual field? I want to be sure that I am clear on this particular point because, as has been suggested, the selection of three is arbitrary.

Question: Are there certain other aspects about the use of the form of names given in the publication which suggests that you forget about real names and use pseudonyms?

Mr. Tauber: Yes, except that the *Anglo-American Cataloging Rules* now permissively indicates that you can use pseudonyms. Actually, many public and some other libraries have been using pseudonyms for many years. We have a specific item on pseudonyms. The third item under 6.1.1 gives the generally accepted practice. These rules are definitely following the *Anglo-American Cataloging Rules*. This is also true in respect to the Corporate Author, 6.1.2. If no personal author is associated with the work, it should then be listed under the corporate author. When there is lacking any identifiable author, list it under title.

Question: This would suggest that when you have identified both the corporate author and a personal author—and this is a very common practice in publications—the personal author is effectively a subordinate author. That is to say, the corporation is primarily responsible for the content of the work, and Joe Doaks, an executive of the corporation, has written the report and got his name on it. Do you follow me?

Mr. Tauber: Yes.

Comment: Making Joe Doaks the secondary author would, nonetheless, suggest that you enter it under "Doaks, Joseph," because of your proposed standard. If no personal author is associated with the work, it is, of course, listed under a corporate author. But if you have both a personal and a corporate author, this direction would still require you to place it under the personal author.

Mr. Tauber: Do you object to this, Mr. Croghan?

Comment: Yes, I object quite strongly. The principle is to put it under the principal author, and if the principal author happens to be a corporate name, it should be put under that. If you have a secondary author who is a person and you go by function, he is a secondary author and deserves an added entry or none at all. But we should stick to the basic principle of the main author, corporate or personal, for authorship is the criterion here, not the kind of authorship.

Mr. Tauber: The effort here is to identify

the publication with the personal author if there is one, regardless of the appearance of a corporate body on the title page. In terms of this particular document, a "Proposed USA Standard Bibliographic References," we are not interested in added entries, but only in basic bibliographical references.

Comment: In doing this you would be going against your definition of author, personal or corporate, for the corporation in the example is responsible for the intellectual content of the publication. You would be going down to a subordinate person for the primary, indeed the only, entry.

Comment: The function of the bibliographical reference is to take the user to another tool, the whole point of having a reference. The reader is almost certain to begin his search at the library catalog. So if you are at variance with what the libraries are doing, then you know you are going to have a two-step process. If you put under personal authors the works that libraries are going to place under corporate authors, the user will probably find it because, in a large catalog, there will be an added entry on it, but he will then have to complete an otherwise unnecessary second step. It is surely better to allow for the libaries that do not put in added entries or rely on a single-entry automated printout and stick to the centralized standard.

Mr. Tauber: This is one of the most delicate parts of this document, and the reason that it appears this way is because we have had pressure from the various fields who do not like what librarians do. They want the personal author, if his name is on the page, regardless of the corporate entry involved, as the citation directs. If someone edits a work issued by a corporation, they will want that person's name as the editor. I would like to have your further comments on this, as it is very important. We do not follow the AA code in this. Government publications are also involved in this procedure.

Question: Is this because it might best be known, and is currently owned, by the person, or would it be like an IBM or Library of Congress report?

Mr. Tauber: This is one of the late Mortimer

Taube's three rules—his first, in fact. If there is a person's name on a title page, cite it under that name.

Comment: Yes, and Mortimer Taube is wrong.

Mr. Tauber: He was chief of the Science and Technology Division of LC and considered this procedure the most effective way of retrieving a document.

Comment: If God issued the Ten Commandments under a personal name when it was a corporate doctrine, God would be wrong. Although we all know now that something is the work of Joe Doaks, within fifty years' time people are going to look at it as an IBM report or an Office of Education report. We are like Ozymandias, king of kings. Antony Croghan, who does the research report for OSTI [Office of Scientific and Technical Information], we all know now in our own small circles. However, fifty years from now it will be a government document on the cataloging of nonbook media, and users will start from the fact that it is an education document, because government departments and institutions have a lot longer life than individuals.

Comment: You are being very British. We in America put the individual before the corporation.

Comment: Then America is wrong. I would remind you, Miss Whitenack, that America, as expressed in its cataloging rules for the Anglo-American joint code, does not put it under the personal heading.

Comment: I think we need to be reminded again of what Dr. Tauber said about the user being very important. The user would not go to the corporate entry.

Comment: The user fifty years from now will go to the corporate entry.

Mr. Margolin: If a research scholar is doing research on how policies developed in the United States Office of Education or IBM and has accumulated a group of documents under a single corporate entry, he is not going to have much to work with to understand which contending forces were shaping the policy. It seems to me we could help the eventual user by giving him names.

Comment: The eventual user, if he is going to try and reconstruct the internal policy of IBM from catalog records and not go back to the original document, which will have many more names attached to it than will ever appear in any library catalog, no matter how deeply it is indexed, is lacking in research methodology. If he is really doing research on this basis, then I am honestly not very much impressed by this user. He should go to the original document.

Question: Isn't the purpose of this draft to serve as a citation source for documents that will last for hundreds of years? Assuming that I have the personal name of an author and that a copy of his paper is deposited in the local public library, surely some cataloger would have been good enough to provide an added entry under either the corporate or the editor entry.

Comment: One might consider that a personal name today may be longer lasting than the corporate name, which is ever changing and thus may not supply the continuity throughout a number of years as envisioned by Mr. Croghan. Corporations are constantly merging and changing their names today.

Looking at this question from the user's standpoint, I use books once in a while and I do not find documents that I need that are published by the USOE. I will never find anything if I have to look under USOE and its multiple subheadings. What I remember is who directed the project, did the research, or wrote the report.

Question: Fifty years from now, will people still remember that?

Comment: We are using the names now of earlier works that could be buried under corporate titles that are forgotten or are too cumbersome to utilize for bibliographical citations.

Mr. Tauber: I think this is so basic that if we do not accomplish another thing. I want your thinking on this matter, for agreed upon bibliographic citations are equally as important to nonprint as to print media.

Comment: Dr. Tauber, in teaching basic cataloging, I almost invariably give my students a *World Almanac* to play with. In your recommendation, would that be cataloged under the author or under the name that appears on the title page?

Mr. Tauber: That is a serial which is a different kind of publication. We are considering only an individual publication or report of some kind sponsored by an institution or a governmental agency that has the personal name on the title page. Nonlibrarians have suggested that the individual name be given the first note citation if you are citing it bibliographically. The proponents of this author citation agree that it is helpful to call attention in the body of the description to the fact that it was prepared under the sponsorship of an organization. The pressure for this came from industry, science, and technology.

Comment: As a professional librarian I agree with your proposal for bibliographic citation. I do not agree with it for cataloging, but that is a different end. As to bibliographic citations, the individual who is making the citation often has no library background and cannot determine the correct corporate entry or whatever, and so encourage him to put it under personal entry.

Mr. Tauber: It is a very technical and professional job to establish correct entries. These last few days, before I came here, I was looking for a report by an author on the feasibility studies for processing centers in Pennsylvania. Do you know there is no entry in the catalog under the author, but we finally found it under Pennsylvania after much searching.

Comment: Let me give you a very recent example of the problem. Yesterday, I telephoned the Columbia University Graduate School of Library Service library to get the feasibility study by Dr. Tauber that he has just discussed. The librarians could not find it in the catalog. They looked under his name and every other conceivable entry but could not find it because the title was not exact and the study was entered under the corporate body, the U.S. Office of Education. The point is, if it had been entered under his name, we would have gotten it. This example is actually more illustrative of cataloging deficiencies than the bibliographic citation, but it does indicate our reliance on specific references that may not be held elsewhere.

Mr. Tauber: All the bibliographical citations I have seen of that item have been under my name.

Comment: They are not in your library school library.

Comment: As you are sharing user reaction and justifying the reason for the person's name to be used, I am reminded of similar experiences at the Purdue University Library. I went in to find Jim Finn's reports on the technology project, and I could not find them in a hundred years by looking in the catalog. Finally, I went to the shelves and hunted around, and because I am a librarian, I found the material needed. However, anyone other than a desperate graduate student would have given up. I think we ought to consider our user.

Comment: The bulk of use, I think, will come so close upon the production of the work itself that the fifty-year concept, although important, should not be the overriding factor.

Comment: If you use a name as the citation, and the library that is following the AA code has not made an added entry of that name, you have given a blind reference, not in the cataloging sense, but because it cannot be found. If you give the name of the committee in the citation and the user brings it to the library, which is what we are arguing about, the item should be located quite easily.

Mr. Tauber: I want you to remember that this proposed standard, if acceptable, is going to go to many publishers, editors, and others who are not really concerned about the *Anglo-American Cataloging Rules*. I can assure you, on the basis of the letters that I have received, that if we demand the use of the corporate body instead of the personal name when personal names appear on the title page, this draft will probably not be approved.

Comment: I for one now accept this argument, and I will stop arguing directly to that point, Dr. Tauber. You have considered all our reasons, and I am perfectly certain that you are well aware of the argument of corporate bodies; but, in view of your limited context and of the argument for the other one, which is so overriding that you are going to settle for it, I will now accept the decision and merely say that as librarians we are going to have to adjust to this problem. Although I feel it is an unnecessary problem, I will now merely say that we recognize it and that the American standards have done this so that bibliographical references in the future are going to be oriented towards the personal author.

I am now going to steer away slightly from the purposes of your document and ask this group to consider one thing. Libraries have been in the business of organizing books for quite a long time, and they quite admittedly invented the idea of the corporate author and worked out its considerable and complex ramification. Do you honestly think that librarians would go to the trouble of defining this, the elaboration and all the rest of it, unless they genuinely thought that it was needed as a tool? We need this concept. Our complex system of bibliography will not work without it. As a matter of practice, it was developed about seventy years ago in this country by Charles A. Cutter. There has been a whole range of libraries in Europe that refused the concept of the corporate author, the Germanic and Scandinavian libraries, and they have gotten their catalogs into a much worse mess than ours. I cannot find my way around the German catalog. While I cannot speak for the rest of my colleagues, I can find my way around any moderately good English or American catalog. The degree of difficulty will depend upon the degree of skill put into the catalog, but I can find my way around it. However, I cannot find my way around even a good German catalog. Any of you who have used the British Museum catalog, which is predicated on personal author entry and a dislike for corporate entry, have undoubtedly had difficulty.

Mr. Tauber: I am going to interrupt you, if you do not mind, for I do not believe what you have just said is in relationship to the purpose of this document. You are talking about catalogs again. David Nevin cleared this up for me when he said that he would not accept this for a catalog department, but he would for bibliographic references. This is the point that I have tried to make, and it is a very important point. The fact that they could not find my name in the Columbia library school catalog has nothing to do with this document. It simply reflects inadequate cataloging.

It is a controversial issue, but we have had to go out on a limb and attempt to establish a standard for a very diverse audience. It is being done under pressure from users. This decision has a very direct relationship to the bibliographical reference for audiovisual materials or multimedia, because of the complexity of individuals intertwined with organizations and producing companies.

Comment: What would happen if it is found that in certain cases a citation under the National Film Board of Canada would be more relevant to the fact than the name of the person who wrote' it or produced it?

Mr. Tauber: Within the citation of a particular item coming from the film board, there would be either as publisher or issuing agency, the inclusion of the National Film Board, wouldn't there? Somewhere in the citation there would be this sort of lead.

Question: Think in terms of the master file with everything alike on computer tape, in sequential title order. If you decide that this entry should be from the standpoint of the author, I am still going to have to put the title in the title position and other entries in their positions. We must have a consistent file so all materials will fall under their titles only as you dump the file. If you want to get it by author, why of course, you sort the file by author. To accomplish this, you must be consistent in the initial form and get everything by title, or author, or by publisher, or what have you.

Comment: I think this is a computer problem.

Comment: I am thinking of the master file, the master citation that we have been discussing.

Comment: It is a computer problem and can be solved quite easily between the two.

Mr. Tauber: Let's go on to Title, 6.2, which is not as bad as corporate authors, but very controversial too. The title should be an exact transcription of as much of the title of the work as is necessary for identification, followed by transliteration if needed. This was also a concession to industry, which did not want long titles. People who write and people who cite do this without your having to tell them to do it. They shorten at times by using three dots, stop at the semicolons, use subtitles, and things of that nature. Long titles may be shortened, but initial words may not be omitted nor the entry title changed. Subtitles or other clarifying elements should be included if needed for precise identification, such as music or fiction. For works in foreign languages you give the original title, followed by a translation in parenthesis if needed. Periodicals, including journals and newspapers, having distinctive titles should be listed under title, whether or not the name of the editor is given.

Question: For a recording, where do I find this title?

Mr. Tauber: Do you feel the label on a recording is more important than the label on an album?

Comment: It is certainly going to last longer than the sleeve will, but the label is not necessarily more accurate. Accuracy at this point is not crucial. What really matters is being able to recognize and identify which of the choices open to you have been used by someone else. Janet Macdonald feels the title to use is the one that is the nearest to the material, which enables me, when I get exactly the same choices, to know which choice she has made and if I want to correspond with her, I can use the same choice. This is an abstract thing. By laying down this principle, I can work out relatively easily which one she has chosen. But notice, the principle is not based on accuracy of cataloging or anything; but, in this case, the principle is based on physical proximity. Nonetheless, it is a principle on which you can work.

Comment: We tried to stick to the principle that the things that cannot be separated from the material itself, that cannot be torn off easily, are the best sources of data. When our authority reference is easily opened, torn, or lost, new considerations are involved.

Question: Should we utilize the title on the nonprint media itself? If so, which list of credits is closest to the exact data that others will recognize?

Mr. Tauber: A person who uses bibliographical references either has the thing in his hand that he is citing from or a reference that someone used. Very seldom will he sit down and try to manufacture a title.

Comment: You may have a record, tape, slide, or film in your hand which has three titles on it. On a disc recording it may be on the slip cover, the jacket, the box, or the record.

Mr. Tauber: Well, I have not heard of the *proximity* approach to cataloging before, but it does sound logical to me.

Comment: We have proposed to the ALA RTSD ad hoc AV cataloging committee that it consider our problems.

Comment: The DAVI rules say the official title is that which appears on the material itself.

Comment: I would agree with you except that there are three versions of that title on the material itself. Now, which one do you want to use?

Mr. Tauber: Why not use the first one?

Comment: The code indicates subtitles frequently become names which are further explanatory information under the main title. The subtitle should be included in the catalog entry. Again, the correct subtitle should be entered, insofar as possible, as it appears on the material, including the producer's punctuation, which separates the main title from the subtitle. If the producer has not indicated punctuation for this work, the main title should be separated from the subtitle by the use of a dash. In no case, even though the producer has done it, should parentheses be used for this purpose, since parentheses are to be used for other functions.

Mr. Tauber: On the basis of that particular statement, do you favor the item in this particular document that says long titles may be shortened?

Comment (several): Yes, yes.

Question: Concerning the omission of initial words, we on the cataloging level run into problems with such titles as *Bennett Cerf's Book of Jokes,* which is placed under *Bennett* rather than *Book.*

Question: Isn't there a National Institute of Health grant for the Association of Research Libraries to establish an authority for journal titles?

Mr. Tauber: There is an effort to establish such an authority, but right now, as Mrs. Britton is indicating, there are difficulties, regardless of the authority; for example, *Ulrich* and the *Union List of Serials.*

Comment: This problem is being worked on, with a preliminary report having been submitted to the Library of Congress, the National Agricultural Library, National Library of Medicine, and the Joint Union List of Serials Committees at the 1969 ALA Conference held in Atlantic City.

Mr. Tauber: Coden has been an effort to try and standardize abbreviations of journal titles. It is one of the Z39 Committee projects.

In regard to the questions of edition, place of publication, and publisher, we have tried in the proposed standard to follow standard cataloging procedures rather than deviate in any of these situations. It has been indicated rather specifically, however, that the publisher should be given in full or in a distinctive shortened form. If neither the publisher nor the distributor is given in the work, the printer's name may be listed. The place of publication follows the general *Anglo-American Cataloging Rules.*

Question: To come back to computer applications, don't you think it is best not to use title page, copyright, or date of printing because this terminology is book oriented? Will the audiovisual specialists present give us a similar set of terminology for the nonbook media? We will use them, but we need to be told very specifically what they are. In relation to a book, title page, copyright date, and date of printing are three specifics, very specific indeed, so we have an order of priorities. Now what are the equivalent specifics on a film? Is there, in fact, a processing date on a film copy that is equivalent to a date of printing? Is the date of printing effectively a processing date?

Comment: In nonprint media we have discovered that if you produce something, that may mean that you took a camera and shot something as of, say, 1917, before World War I. You saved the footage, and today you have made a film that utilizes that footage. This does not mean that it was produced in 1969. However, a print of it was released in 1969, and as of this date it is alive and usable.

Question: Can I stop you there on this point, because that is content, and I am not worried about that. I have in my hand two physical objects, one a book and the other a film. For the purposes of finding dates on them, I have three specifics in this book. I can look on the title page. If the book was published 200 years ago, that approach will still work. I can look for the copyright date within this object, or I can look for the date of printing.

Now, where would I look on the reel of film in my hand for the three equivalent dates for this physical object?

Comment: To begin with, most titles are generally on packages, whereas film comes in a can. By the term *title* we refer to a sequence of the film itself on which the title is imprinted.

There is rarely a copyright date on the film, but it will have a release date which may or may not have anything to do with the printing. The film may be released the year in which the copyright is taken or several years later. Therefore, the release date is really more of a publication date than a copyright date. We have no real specific terms equivalent to those on the book title page, but I would say simply that when the title is on the film, it is accepted.

Comment: I think it would be helpful if you added a printing or release date.

Mr. Tauber: The paragraph 6.7, Series Statement, looks untroublesome, but I do not know. You have a lot of series in multimedia materials, don't you?

Question: Columbia Records calls all it records Columbia Masterworks, and LC uses that as a series title. However, it is not a series title but a commercial title applied to a whole realm of products.

Mr. Tauber: Do you think that we ought to say something about that here? Is Columbia Records the only one that does it?

Comment: No, but it is also a book publisher's sin. Penguin book number 83 is an exact equivalent of it.

Mr. Tauber: Could you think of an adjective that we might put in before series?

Comment: Publisher's series, the same as we do for books.

Comment: No, he is requesting a positive statement for a type of series that is needed, an adjective that is related.

Comment: I think that we are talking about two different things. You can have a series that is very tightly one thing and very tightly related to the other, or you can have a very loosely related series like this example of Masterworks. One has nothing whatsoever to do with the other and can stand absolutely alone, whereas the type of series cannot stand absolutely alone.

Question: How about the term *interrelated*?

Question: Are series usually related to a specific subject?

Comment: There is a filmstrip series entitled Close-Up Photography which uses different filmstrips for different parts of the topic. Although you can use one without the other, to get the whole idea of close-up photography, you need all of them. Now, contrast that with the Masterworks of Columbia Records, where one has nothing whatsoever to do with the other except that they are all classical selections as opposed to popular ones.

Comment: Could we use the term *interrelated item,* meaning produced under the direction and sponsorship of one organization, for the same audience, and for the same general purpose? If so, we must keep several problems in mind. Producers are notoriously negligent in their responsibilities when they produce these things; for example, they may say nothing about a particular film being part of a series.

Mr. Tauber: Let's look at collation, for it is a very serious problem. I was asked by Miss Whitenack to include the fact that we might have under collation not only an item relating to books, but also one relating to nonprint materials. It occurred to me that audiovisual rules and examples might be given under each one of these items in section 6. Does this seem desirable? You agree. Is there any discussion on 6.8?

Question: Would it be possible to add a number of explanatory items in parentheses such as *painted, volumes, frames,* and *footage*?

Mr. Tauber: I was going to make a separate entry for that, but you people combined it.

Comment: No, in the preliminary statement.

Comment: Are you going to take the whole series of items and rewrite them in term of media?

Mr. Tauber: No, I have made a note of

this suggestion. We will work at it from either way it seems possible.

Comment: In the interest of integration, rather than segregation, this might be better, as two entries would indicate two different kinds of things.

Mr. Tauber: This is why I have given additional examples as a possible first choice. The suggestion that we add audiovisual examples under each section is good. In 6.8.1 the same thing occurs in connection with nonbook materials.

Comment: Illustrations, I think, are entirely a book rule, except that you really cannot talk of putting illustrations in the collation of a filmstrip, for a filmstrip *is* illustrations.

Mr. Tauber: This is not either or.

Question: Would it be possible for the media catalog to go farther into illustration technique? I mean the way you would use it yourself.

Mr. Tauber: We have already done it. I thought you were phrasing it for me.

Comment: No, you cannot describe everything in collation.

Mr. Tauber: The three items under Miscellany refer to overall problems of abbreviation, transliteration, and typography, and we have talked just briefly about transliteration. I do not believe that abbreviations ought to cause any difficulty. In these general rules we follow standards of specified abbreviations, to be used sparingly. I do not know how the computer would absorb abbreviations.

Comment: It all depends on what it is. If you are trying to use the computer to file for you and you abbreviate, you are in trouble. For the film title *I, Leonardo da Vinci,* if you want the computer to file this in with other titles and you drop off the *I* just because you want to call it Leonardo da Vinci, you have a problem.

Comment: It will file just the way the letters occur in your abbreviation. If you have them all that way, you are fine. For instance, if you are going to abbreviate *United States,* you have to decide whether it is going to be *U.S.* or *US.* You have to make decisions, or you have to tell the computer to do it. When you deviate from the rules, you raise costs. It is our problem at this point of designing a structure, and the economic advantages must be considered in each situation.

Mr. Tauber: Is there a degree lower than sparingly?

Comment: I do not think the abbreviations are the question, but I do think that the rules of what and how the computer sorts should be a part of the standardization, so that if the user decides to put a period under the *U.S.* he will realize that the period is going to come at a certain sequence.

Comment: You are talking about computer coding and not bibliographic citation.

Comment: It is actually computer filing. These are two distinct things, and they have not touched the basic problem. What do the letters *CLA* mean to you, Dr. Tauber? What does that abbreviation mean to you?

Mr. Tauber: California Library Association.

Comment: No, the Canadian Library Association. You must be clear first, and consistent afterwards.

Comment: The standard is supposed to provide consistency, and I think that abbreviation rules are put in not because the computer has anything to do with them, but as a matter of consistency.

Mr. Tauber: We could spend an hour on transliteration, but I do not want to. It is a very complex thing, and the Library of Congress, as you know, uses its own transliteration system, which is different from other transliteration systems.

Question: I can hardly recognize standard sources. Can you recommend a guide for this purpose?

Mr. Tauber: Osterman, I believe, is a standard source, and a lot of journals use *Osterman.* It is a problem to have the editors in the United States to agree on a transliteration sys-

tem. I got a deeper insight into this when I was chairman of the Z39 subcommittee for Cyrillic translation. Dr. Orne is making progress on this subcommittee.

The last item, 7.3, is Punctuation and Typography. They should be such as to make the reference readily intelligible. Uniformity and consistency are the criteria.

Question: Is there a reason for placing this information, which I think is so needed, at the end rather than the beginning of your proposed standard? It might be more helpful to place all the general information at the beginning.

Mr. Tauber: We will consider it. Does anyone else feel as she does?

Comment (many): Very good.

Comment: I prefer a different order than your order of items.

Mr. Tauber: I have found that the order needs reevaluating. I am going to stop now. Thank you again for going through the draft, because it is very important, and there are many very serious and controversial problems involved. I cannot tell you how grateful I am that you made us take another good look at this document, particularly the last section concerning nonbook materials. To have pursued it to this extent is the epitome of persistence and a compliment to each of you. There is national interest in this project and apparently a genuine need for the standard for bibliographic citations we are proposing.

The proposed Standard for Bibliographic References was not approved by the Z39 member organizations when it was submitted to a vote in the spring of 1970. It is anticipated that a reorganized subcommittee will make use of the previous subcommittee and of the constructive criticism and comment they have received.

Appendix: Proposed USA Standard Bibliographic References

1. PURPOSE

This standard is a guide in formulating bibliographic references to books, serials, periodicals, articles, and nonbook materials such as manuscripts, films, maps, music and patents.

2. DEFINITION AND FUNCTION

A bibliographic reference is a statement containing information which describes a published or unpublished work. It functions to enable the user to identify and to obtain the precise item.

3. FORMS OF REFERENCE

References can take many forms, all of which contain certain elements. A bibliographic reference may be:

3.1 An Entry in a Bibliographic list or Catalog of Whole Works or Parts of Works.

Examples:

Riker, James. Revised history of Harlem and early annals. N.Y., New Harlem Publishing Co., 1904.

Roosevelt, Theodore. New York. N.Y. and London, Longmans Green & Co., 1891.

Schuyler, George W. Colonial New York. N.Y., Charles Scribner's Sons, 1885. 2 v.

Ulmann, Albert. A landmark history of New York, N.Y., D. Appleton-Century Co., 1939.

3.2 A Note Appended to a Text, Wherever Located, e.g., Footnote, End of Chapter Note.

Examples:

(15) Description taken from Ulmann, Albert, A landmark history of New York, N.Y., D. Appleton-Century Co., 1939. p. 82.

3.3 A statement Partly or Wholly Contained in the Body of the Text.

Example:

Upper Seventh Avenue was planned as a wide and stately boulevard with a central mall. Plans for the area above 110th Street are mentioned briefly in Riker, James. Revised history of Harlem and early annals. N.Y., New Harlem Publishing Co., 1904. p. 100ff.

4. GENERAL GUIDELINES

Entries should be complete enough to identify an item exactly. Standard sources should be used for specific details or citations. (See list of sources in Appendix.)

Prepared by the Z39.4 Subcommittee—Nathalie C. Batts, Theodore C. Hines, Oliver L. Lilley, Ellis Mount, and Maurice F. Tauber, Chairman—for submission to the American National Standards Institute, Z39 Library Work and Documentation, August 1969.

5. ELEMENTS AND THEIR ORDER

References should include the following elements, taken from the material cited. The minimum should be the first six elements: Author . . . Year of Publication.

5.1 Separately Published Works.
Author.
Title, with translation or Romanization if needed.
Edition number.
Place of publication.
Publisher.
Year of Publication. If copyright date differs, use both.
Page, or inclusive paging, or volume number if multi-volume work.
Series statement if one appears in the work.
Notes of other important identifying information, including microforms or paperbacks.

Examples:

Oliver, Roland and Fage, J. D. A short history of Africa. Baltimore, Penguin Books, 1962. 280 p. (Penguin African Library.)

Strahler, Arthur N. Physical geography. 2nd ed. N.Y., John Wiley & Sons, 1960. vii, 534 p.

Toussaint, Augusta. History of the Indian Ocean. Chicago, University of Chicago Press, 1966. x, 292 p. Translated by June Guicharnaud.

United States. Internal Revenue Service. Statistics Division. Statistics of income, 1963: corporation income tax returns, with accounting periods ended July 1963–June 1964. Washington, Government Printing Office, 1968. 429 p. (Publication No. 16(3–68).)

5.1.1 Quotation or Passage from a Book or other Separately Issued Publication.
The basic elements (see 5.1) if applicable, plus: include specific paging of portion referred to; also, the volume number, if part of a set.

Example:

"Stimulus-response theory." IN Hall, Calvin S. and Lindzey, Gardner. Theories of personality. N.Y., John Wiley & Sons, 1957. pp. 420–466.

5.1.2 Contribution to a Book or other Separately Issued Publication.
Author(s) of contribution.
Title of contribution.
The word IN, followed by reference to the work containing the contribution (see 5.1 for details).
Inclusive paking of contribution.

Examples:

Malinowski, Bronislaw. "Traders of the Trobriands." IN Coon, Carleton S. A reader in general anthropology. N.Y., Henry Halt and Co., 1958. pp. 293–321.

Gabel, Creighton. "Prehistoric Populations of Africa." IN Butler, J., ed. Boston University Papers on Africa. Boston, Boston Univ. Press, 1966. v. 2, p. 1–37.

5.1.3 Technical and Other Specialized Reports.
Corporate source.
Title.
Date(s)
Personal author(s).
Pagination.
Document numbers, e.g., contract number, project number, grant number, report number and accession number.
Security classification if applicable.

Examples:

Mexican-American Study Project. Mexican immigration to the United States: the record and its implications. Jan. 1966. By Leo Grebler. Division of Research, Graduate School of Business Administration, University of California at Los Angeles. Advance report 2. 1 v.

System Development Corporation. A system study of abstracting and indexing in the United States. Falls Church, Va. Dec. 16, 1966. ix, 228 p. Technical Memorandum TM-WD-394. (Contract NSF-C-464.)

5.1.4 Abstracts and Reviews.
The basic elements (see 5.1) if applicable, plus:
Indicate that it is an abstract or review.
Give author, title and source of publication as stated in abstract or review.

Examples:

Carlquist, Sherwin. Island life: a natural history of the islands of the world. Garden City, N.Y., Natural History Press, 1965. Review in The Geographical Review, 56:612–613, 1966.

Burton, Thomas L. "A day in the country: a survey of leisure activity at Box Hill in Surrey." Chartered Surveyor, 98:378–380, 1966. Abstract by Alan Gillies in Geographical Abstracts D, Social Geography, 1967/4, p. 228.

5.1.5 Conferences, Congresses, Symposia.
The basic elements (see 5.1) if applicable, plus:
List under specific name of the Conference, Congress or Symposium.
Number of the meeting, if numbered.
Place at which held.
Date.
Title.
Publisher, if other than sponsor.

Examples:

Man's role in changing the face of the earth. International symposium sponsored by the Wenner-Gren Foundation for Anthropological Research. Princeton, N.J. June 1952. Chicago, University of Chicago Press, 1956. xxxviii, 1193 p.

Yale Conference on the teaching of English. 12th, New Haven, 1966. Report. New Haven, Yale Univ., Office of Teacher Training, 1966. 85 p.

5.2 Periodicals or Other Serial Publications.

5.2.1 Reference to Entire Volume(s).
Title, with translation or Romanization if needed.
Place of publication.
Sponsoring body or publisher if not included in the title.
Number(s) and date(s) of volume(s).
Mention summaries or abstracts in other languages.

Examples:

"Dimensions of cultural change in the Middle East." Special issue. Human Organization, 24:1–104, Spring 1965.

Geographical Review. N.Y., American Geographical Society. v. 26–35, 1936–1945.

5.2.2 Reference to Proceedings of a Conference, Congress or Symposium.
Give citation as in 5.1.5
The word IN followed by reference to journal containing the proceedings (see 5.2.1 for details).
Inclusive paging of proceedings.

Examples:

"Charismatic leadership in Asia: a symposium." IN Asian Survey, 7:341–88, June 1967.

The World Conference on Church and Society, Geneva, Switzerland, July 12–26, 1966. Report by Archibald A. Evans. IN International Labor Review, 96:24–42, July 1967.

5.3 Articles.

5.3.1 In Periodicals other than Newspapers.
Author of article.
Title of article.
Title of periodical, with place of publication if needed for identification. (See 6.2 Title.)
Volume number, in Arabic figures.
Issue number.
Specific page(s) of article.
Date of issue, in Arabic figures.

Examples:

Bengur, A. R. "Financial aspects of Libya's oil economy." Finance and Development, 4:56–64, March 1967.

Francis, Karl E. "Outpost agriculture: the case of Alaska." Geographical Review, 57(3): 496–505, Oct. 1967.

Jones, Harry R. and Brown, Alfred K. "Theory of the hydrogen bond." American Chemical

Society. Journal. 45(3):345–422, Mar. 15, 1964.

"Tanzanian girl students win illiteracy prize." School and Society, 96:84–6, February 3, 1968.

5.3.2 In Newspapers.
Author, if given.
Title or heading.
Title of newspaper, and place of publication if not given in the title.
Date of newspaper.
Edition of newspaper, if given.
Section of newspaper, e.g., pictorial magazine; number or letter of section.
Page(s) of article.
Column of newspaper, if identifiable.

Examples:

"Job training programs for poor get more help from unions." Wall Street Journal, October 1, 1968. p. 1, colm. 5.

Stanford, Neal. "Another shot at the sun." Christian Science Monitor, Boston. Jan. 25, 1968. Eastern ed. 2nd ed. p. 9.

5.4 Laws; Legal References.
Laws should be listed by the county, state, or other jurisdiction to which they refer. Legal references comprise a specialized body of materials which should be listed as recommended in the standard guides to the field, e.g., Price, Miles O. and Bitner, Harry. Effective legal research. Englewood Cliffs, N.J., Prentice-Hall, Inc., 1953. 633 p.

Examples:

Kansas. Legislative Council. 1967 Report and recommendations, submitted to the 1968 legislature. December 15, 1967. Topeka, Kansas, 1967. 198 p.

Vermont. Laws, statutes, etc. Acts and resolves passed by the General Assembly at the forty-ninth biennial session, 1967 [Jan. 4–Apr. 15, 1967] and the special session January 5–March 12, 1966. Montpelier, Vt., Vermont State library, 1967. 920 p.

5.5 Non-book Materials.
Record as fully as possible the existing elements as in the description of separately published works (see 5.1). Indicate form of the material. If necessary, supply title in English, and enclose it in parentheses. Add information characteristic of the form, e.g.:

5.5.1 Maps.
Follow title with description of form, e.g., map, atlas. Include the number of maps, their size(s) and form, e.g., topographic, serial. Give scale(s) of the maps.

Examples:

Horton, Robert C. Barite occurrences in Nevada. Map, 89x84 cm. fold. in envelope 29x23 cm. 1: 1,000,000. Data compiled by Rob-

ert C. Horton, Cartography by Ronald V. Wilson. Reno, Nevada, Bureau of Mines, 1962.

Vietnam, Cambodia, Laos, and Thailand. Map, 30x37½ in. 1: 1,900,800. Washington, National Geographic Society, 1967.

5.5.2 Motion Pictures, Filmstrips and Videotapes.
Follow title with designation of form, e.g., motion picture, filmstrip, videotape. Give facts relating to production, release, date, and director of film or tape, if possible. Include length, running time or number of frames; sound or silent; color, sepia, or black and white; width of film or tape in millimeters.

Examples:

LSD: Lettvin vs. Leary. Motion Picture 51 min. Sound. Black & white. 16mm. National Education Television. Made by MGBH-TV. Released by Indiana University, Audio Visual Center, 1968. (NET Journal) Producer, Austin Hoyt; editor, Boyd Estus.

Small farm. Motion picture. Sterling Educational, 1967. 11 min., sound, color. 16mm.

South Pacific by Rodgers and Hammerstein. Filmstrip. Black & white, with color sequences. 35mm. Educational Audio Visual, 1967. (Music appreciation series.)

5.5.3 Music.
Composer.
Title.
Form: Music.
Instrument(s) or group for which written.
Date, if given.
Opus and number.

Example:

Newman, Harold. Music around the clock for soprano or tenor recorder. Music. N.Y., Hargail Music Press, 1965. 36 p.

5.5.4 Patents and Patent Applications.
Issuing country designation, usually abbreviated according to standard forms.
Indicate that it is a patent or patent application.
Patent number; indicate if a special type of patent, e.g., plant patent.
International classification symbol.
National office classification symbol.
Patent title.
Patentee(s).
Assignee.
Publication date.
Application or priority date. When a patent includes both an application date and a priority date, i.e., date of application in a country other than the country of issue, only the priority date should be given.

Examples:

U. S. Patent 3,222,455 (Cl. 188-79.4) Adjustable ratchet for speedometer. Brown, James L. and Rollins, Harold R. (to Eagle Mechanism Co.) Nov. 3, 1965. Appl. Oct. 2, 1962.

British Patent 1,322,134 (Intl. Cl. B 24d) (Cl. B 3 DIG2). Constant tension adjustment screw. Allen, Alfred (to Bedwin Spring Works, Ltd.) Apr. 14, 1967; German appl. Mar. 3, 1966.

5.5.5 Audiorecords.
Title.
Statement or form, e.g., phonodisc, audio tape.
Performing artist(s), group, soloist (if any) and conductor when applicable.
Trade name of the publisher and album and record numbers.
Disc or tape speed, diameter of tape reel or disc, recording channels, monaural or stereo.

Examples:

Ellington at Newport. Phonodisc. N.Y., Columbia Records, 1956. CL 934. 33⅓ rpm.

Tschaikovsky, Peter I. Symphony no. 4 in F minor, opus 36. Phonodisc. Constantin Silvestri conducting the Philharmonica Orchestra. Angel Records. 35565. 33⅓ rpm.

5.6 Unpublished Materials.
Record as fully as possible the existing elements as in the description for separately published works (see 5.1). State that material is unpublished. Add information characteristic of the form, e.g.:

5.6.1 Manuscripts.
The basic elements (see 5.1) if applicable, plus:
Indicate that it is a manuscript.
Include note of special features, e.g., illustrations.
If part of a larger collection, add the word IN followed by a citation to that collection.

Examples:

Flad, Harvey K. Agricultural terracing: a study of the spatial distribution on an anthropogeomorphologic example in tropical Affrica. Manuscript. 1968.

Whiteman, Walt. Crossing Brooklyn Ferry. Poem. Brooklyn, December 1855. Autograph manuscript, signed. 3 p.

5.6.2 Theses and Dissertations.
The basic elements (see 5.1) if applicable, plus: indicate that it is a thesis and the degree for which it was submitted. Include the name of the school by which it was accepted.

Examples:

Keiderling, Wallace E. The Japanese immigration in Paraguay. Master's thesis, University of Florida. Feb. 1962, vi, 139 p.

McConnell, Ruth Ethel. Iterative imagery in the fiction of Joseph Conrad. Ph.D. thesis, Univ. of California. Berkeley, Calif., 1967. iv, 401 1.

5.6.3 Unpublished Reports and Papers.
The basic elements (see 5.1) if applicable, plus: indicate that the material is unpublished and give present location of copy.

Example:

Purvis, Malcolm J. The food economy of Malaysia and Brunei. Unpublished report, submitted to the National Planning Association by the Department of Agricultural Economics, New York State College of Agriculture, Cornell University. May 1965.

5.6.4 Letters.
Author.
Indicate to whom the letter was written and the date.
If necessary, supply date and enclose it in parentheses.

Examples:

Gordon, Charles. Letter to Augusta Gordon, Sept. 2, 1877.

Smith, John Howes. Letter from John Howes Smith to Grace Hart Crane, December 10, 1911. Autograph letter, signed. 1 p.

5.6.5 Privately Printed Works.
The basic elements (see 5.1) if applicable, plus: indicate that it is privately printed, for whom, by whom, place and date.

Example:

Oehser, Paul H. Fifty poems. Privately printed by the author. Washington, 1956. 60 p.

5.7 Oral Communications.
Give information characteristic of the form:

5.7.1 Lectures.
Author.
Title.
Place lecture was presented.
Date.
Sponsoring body.
Series, if applicable.
If unpublished, identify with note.

Example:

Lowenthal, David. The American scene. The American Academy of Arts and Letters, New York. Lecture, Feb. 10, 1968. Sponsored by the American Geographical Society in the 1968 series of public sittings.

5.7.2 Interviews, Conversations, Discussions.
Names of participants.
Subject(s)
Date.
Place, if pertinent.

253

Examples:

Conversation by Georgia O'Keeffe, John V. Lindsay and Bertrand Russell on trends in women's fashions. Mar. 10, 1968. Paris.

A major tells how firmness stopped riots: interview with Jersey City's mayor Thomas J. Whalen. U.S. News & World report, 63:40–2, Aug. 14, 1967.

5.8 Works in Preparation or Being Printed.
The basic elements (see 5.1) if applicable, plus: appropriate statement of status, e.g., In preparation; In press.

Example:

Everyman, John. Peace in the world. N.Y., United Nations. In preparation.

5.9 Reference Embodied in the Text.
Describe elements as fully as possible:

5.9.1 Citing an Entire Work.
Indicate author and title. Include place of publication, publisher, date of publication, total number of pages and series note.

Example:

The Library has a copy of William H. Fitchett's The unrealized logic of religion; a study in credibilities. N.Y., Eaton & Mains, 1905. 275 p. (The 35th Fernley lecture).

5.9.2 Citing Part of a Work.
Indicate author and title. Include place of publication, publisher, date of publication and series note (if applicable). List inclusive pages of part cited.

Example:

The story concerning the invention of the word "quiz" is related by Frank T. Porter in his Gleanings and reminiscences. Dublin, Hodges, Foster, 1875. pp. 31–35.

6. DETAILED RECOMMENDATIONS

6.1 Author.
An author is the person(s) or corporate body (bodies) responsible for the intellectual content of a work. The recommendations below apply to whole works and also parts of works, e.g., an article in a journal or an encyclopedia, a section of a composite book.

6.1.1 Personal Author.
When there are one to three authors, list the names of each.
When there are more than three authors, give the name of the first followed by "and others"; if none is listed as mainly responsible for the work give the title followed by the names of the authors, or by the name of the first author given with "and others."
Use the form of name(s) given in the publication.
List the author's surname followed by forename, or initials, and other identifying

elements, if needed; editors or compilers, or translators, should be listed in the same way followed by the abbreviation ed. or comp., as appropriate.
For pseudonymous works use the form of name which appears in the work, followed by (pseud.).

Examples:

The French Renaissance and its heritage: essays presented to Alan M. Boase by colleagues, pupils and friends. London, Methuen, 1968. 206 p.

Kostelanetz, Richard, comp. Beyond left and right; radical thought for our times. New York, Morrow, 1968. 436 p.

Polanyi, K., C. M. Arensberg, and H. W. Pearson, eds. Trade and market in the early empires, Glencoe, Ill., The Free Press, 1957.

6.1.2 Corporate Author.
If no personal author its associated with the work list it under corporate author when there is one. Lacking any identifiable author enter under title (see 6.2).
A corporate author is a society, institution, government department or other organization which authorizes or issues a work.
Serial publications of a corporate body, other than periodicals having distinctive titles (see 6.2) should be listed under the name of the corporate body.
Use the form of corporate name given in the publication.

Examples:

Operations and Policy Research, Inc., Washington, D.C. Institute for the comparative study of Political Systems. Venezuela election factbook, December 1, 1968. Washington, 1969. 50 p.

United States. Bureau of the Census. Statistical abstract of the United States, 1967. Washington, Government Printing Office, July 1967. xii + 1050 p. bibl. tables. charts, maps. (88 an. ed.)

6.2 Title.
The title should be an exact transcription of as much of the title of the work as is necessary for identification, followed by transliteration if needed. It should be given as it appears in the publication. Long titles may be shortened, but initial words should not be omitted nor the sense of the title changed. Subtitles or other clarifying elements should be included if needed for precise identification. For works in foreign languages give the original title, followed by a translation in parentheses, if needed. Periodicals, including journals and newspapers, having distinctive titles should be listed under title, whether or not the name of the editor is given. Further identifying

elements may be added if needed, e.g., Gazette (Plainfield, Vt.).

Examples:

The Economist . . . v. 1- Sept. 2, 1843, London, C. Reynell, printer, 1843–19 .

Frazer, James George. The golden bough, a study in magic and religion. 3rd ed. London, Macmillan, 1935. 12 v.

Frazer, James George. The new golden bough; a new abridgement of the classic work. N.Y., New American Library 1964, 1959. 832 p.

Rama, C. M. Sociologia del Uruguay (Sociology of Uruguay). Buenos Aires, Eudeba, 1965. 111 p.

6.3 Edition.
Use the words given in the text, abbreviated in accordance with standard abbreviations.

6.4 Place of Publication.
Use the form of name which appears in the book. When several places are listed use United States location if given; otherwise use the first place listed.

6.5 Publisher.
Publisher's name should be given in full or in a distinctive shortened form. If neither publisher nor distributor is given in the work, the printer's name may be listed.

Example:

Cockcroft, James D. Intellectual precursors of the Mexican Revolution, 1900–1913. Austin, Published for the Institute of Latin American Studies by the Univ. of Texas Press, 1968. x, 329 p. group port., map.

6.6 Date of Publication.
Give the date which reflects the actual publication of the work. When title page or copyright date is not listed, use date of printing, if given. If a reprint, give original date as well as reprint date.

Examples:

Horowitz, Israel Albert. How to win in the middle game of chess. N.Y., Cornerstone Library 1961, 1955. 190 p.

Spencer, Herbert. The principles of sociology. N.Y., Appleton, 1880–96. 3 v. in 5.

6.7 Series Statement.
When the work is part of a series, show the series name and the number of the work in the series, if given.

Example:

Crozier, Ralph Charles. Traditional medicine in modern China (Harvard Univ. East Asian Research Center. Harvard East Asian Series, 34). Cambridge, Mass., Harvard Univ. Press, 1968.

6.8 Collation.
List the number of pages or volumes, and note important illustrations, maps, etc. in the work.

Example:

Nahai, Lotfollah. India's iron and steel industry. Washington, Dept. of the Interior, Bureau of Mines, 1961. ii, 40 p., illus., fold. map, diagrs.

6.8.1 Pagination.
Numbering should correspond to that used in the work. If paging is complex, or includes many series, it may be listed as: 1 v.

Example:

Four fugitive slave narratives. With introductions by Rodin W. Winks and others. Reading, Mass., Addison-Wesley Publ. Co., 1969. iv. (various paging).

6.8.2 Illustrations, etc.
When illustrations, bibliographies, etc. contribute to the value of the work, indicate them by the appropriate word or abbreviation.

7. MISCELLANY

7.1 Abbreviations.
Abbreviations should be used sparingly and should be taken from recognized standard sources, e.g., United States of America Standards Institute. Sectional Committee on Standardization of Library Work, Documentation, and Related Publishing Practices, Z39. American standard for periodical title abbreviations. N.Y., 163. 19 p. (Z39.5-1963) (Revision currently—1969—in process.) Unusual or specialized abbreviations should be followed by their full or complete form if known or their sources should be given, whenever possible.

7.2 Transliteration.
Transliteration of Cyrillic and other non-Roman alphabets should follow the rules used in recognized standard sources.

7.3 Punctuation and Typography.
Punctuation and typography should be such as to make the reference readily intelligible. Whatever method is adopted, the presentation should be uniform and consistent in any given work or list.

LIST OF SOURCES

This list represents some of the tools used by various groups in their particular fields. The forms set forth in these tools do not always agree with our recommendations, as indicated previously. They are included as an indication of materials we have used and as sources of additional help for the specialist.

1. American Chemical Society. Chemical Abstracts Service. Directions for abstractors. Revised 1967. Columbus, Ohio, Ohio State University, 1967.

2. American Institute of Biological Sciences. Style manual for biological journals. Washington, 1966. 2d ed. 11 leaves.

3. American Institute of Physics. Publication Board. Style manual for guidance in the preparation of papers for journals published by the American Institute of Physics. 2d ed., rev. N.Y., 1967. 42 p.

4. American Psychological Association. Publication manual. 1957 rev. Washington, 1957. 70 p.

5. American Society for Testing and Materials. Coden for periodical titles. DS23A. Philadelphia, 1966. 1102 p.

6. Anglo-American cataloging rules. Prepared by the American Library Association, the Library of Congress, the Library Association and the Canadian Library Association. North American text. Chicago, American Library Association, 1967. 400 p.

7. Appel, Livia. Bibliographical citation in the social sciences and the humanities; a handbook of style for authors, editors and students. 3d ed. Madison, University of Wisconsin Press, c. 1949. 32 p.

8. Applied Mechanics Reviews. Manual for preparing of bibliographical headings (citations) in the AMR Editorial Office. San Antonio, Texas, 1967. 46 p. (AMR Report No. 46).

9. British Standards Institution. British standard for bibliographical references, B.S.1629:1950. Incorporating amendment issued May 1951. London, 1950. 18 p. (Revision currently—1969—in process.)

10. Chicago. University. Press. A manual of style, for authors, editors and copywriters. 12th ed., rev. Chicago, University of Chicago Press, 1969. 546 p.

11. Cross, Louise Montgomery. Preparation of medical literature. Philadelphia, Lippincott, 1959. 451 p.

12. Engineers Joint Council. Recommended practice for style of references in engineering publications. N.Y., 1966. 2 leaves.

13. Gatner, Elliott S. M. and Cordasco, Francesco. Research and report writing. N.Y., Barnes & Noble, 1956. 142 p. (College outline series, 78)

14. Harvard Law Review Association. A uniform system of citation; form of citation and abbreviations. 9th ed. Cambridge, Mass., 1955. 92 p.

15. Hendricks, King and Stoddart, L. A. Technical writing. Logan, Utah State Agricultural College, 1948. 117 p.

16. Higgins, Marion V. Bibliography; a beginner's guide to the making, evaluation and use of bibliographies. N.Y., H. W. Wilson Co., 1941. 42 p.

17. Hubbell, George S. Writing documented papers. 3rd ed. N.Y., Barnes & Noble, 1951. 164 p. (College outline series, 37)

18. Hurt, Peyton. Bibliography and footnotes; a style manual for students and writers. Revised and enlarged by Mary L. Hunt Richmond. Berkeley, Univ. of California Press, 1968. 163 p.

19. Indian Standards Institution. Indian standard; recommendations for bibliographical reference. New Delhi, 1963. 11 p. (IS:2381-1963)

20. International Organization for Standardization. Bibliographical references: essential and supplementary elements. Revised text, Mar. 1967. Geneva, 1967. 16 p. (Draft ISO recommendation No. 722, revised text)

21. Iowa State University of Science and Technology, Ames. Graduate College. Manual on thesis writing. 3d ed. Ames, 1951. 78 p.

22. Joughin, George L. Basic reference forms; a guide to established practice in bibliography, quotations, footnotes, and thesis format. N.Y., Crofts, 1941. 94 p.

23. Kent, Sherman. Writing history. 2d ed. N.Y., Crifts, 1967. 143 p.

24. Lester, John. A guide to the preparation of research papers. Rev. ed. Haverford, Pa., Haverford College, 1949. 26 p.

25. Leube, Sigrid and Chamberlin, Waldo. How to cite United Nations documents (in) footnotes (and) bibliographies. N.Y., New York University, 1952. 17 p. (New York University Conference on United Nations Documents, May 19, 1952. Paper No. 2) Mimeographed.

26. McGraw-Hill Publishing Co., Inc. Typographical stylebook; prepared as a standard of usage and practice for the McGraw-Hill publications. N.Y., 1949. 127 p.

27. Modern Language Association of America. The MLA style sheet, compiled by William Riley Parker. Rev. ed. N.Y., 1959. 30 p.

28. Moor, Carol C. and Chamberlin, Waldo. How to use United Nations documents. N.Y., New York University Press, 1952. 26 p. (New York University Libraries. Occasional papers, no. 1)

29. Nixon, Emily C. and Chamberlin, Waldo. How to catalog United Nations documents. N.Y., New York University, 1952? 47 leaves. (New New York University, 1952. 47 leaves. (New Documents, May 19, 1952. Paper No. 3) Mimeographed.

30. Price, Miles O. and Bitner, Harry. Effective legal research. Student ed. rev. Boston, Little, Brown. 1962. 496 p.

31. Schellenberg, Theodore R. The management of archives. N.Y., Columbia Univ. Press, 1965. xvi, 383 p. (Columbia University studies in library service, No. 14)

32. Sharp, Eleanor. Stylebook of The Encyclopedia Americana. Chicago, Americana Corp., 1946. 259 p.

33. Special Libraries Association. Science-Technology Division. Technical libraries: their organization and management. Edited by Lucille Jackson. N.Y., 1951. 202 p.

34. Stanford University. Press. Publisher briefs author; a manual for Stanford authors. Stanford, Calif., 1951. 31 p.

35. Trelease, Sam F. How to write scientific and technical papers. Baltimore, Williams & Wilkins, 1958. 185 p.

36. Turabian, Kate L. A manual for writers of term papers, theses, and dissertations. 3d ed., rev.

Chicago, University of Chicago Press, 1967. 164 p.

37. United Nations. Dag Hammarskjold Library. Bibliographical style manual. N.Y., United Nations, 1963. 62 p.

38. U.S. National Library of Medicine. Library manual: R-R-6. Washington, 1952. 4 p.

39. U.S. National Agricultural Library. Bibliographic style; a manual for use in the Division of Bibliography of the Library. Prepared under the direction of Margaret S. Bryant, Chief, Division of Bibliography. Washington, U.S. Govt. Print. Off., 1951. 30 p. (U.S. Dept. of Agriculture. Bibliographical bulletin, No. 16)

40. U.S. Federal Council for Science and Technology. Committee on Scientific and Technical Information. Standard for descriptive cataloging of government scientific and technical reports. Revision no. 1, Oct. 1966. Washington, Distributed by Clearinghouse for Federal Scientific and Technical Information, 1966. 50 p. (AD641092) (PB-173314)

41. U.S. Geological Survey. Suggestions to authors of reports of the United States Geological Survey, with directions to typists, by George McLane Wood. 5th ed. Washington, U.S. Govt. Print. Off., 1958. 255 p.

42. U.S. Library of Congress. General Reference and Bibliography Division. Bibliographical procedures and style; a manual for bibliographers in the Library of Congress. Washington, Library of Congress, 1954. (Reprinted 1966 with a list of abbreviations) 133 p.

43. United States of America Standards Institute. Sectional Committee on Standardization in the Field of Library Work, Documentation and Related Publishing Practices, Z39. American standard for periodical title abbreviations. N.Y., United States of America Standards Institute, 1969. 14 p. (Z39.5-1969)

44. Wiley, John and Sons, Inc. Author's guide for preparing manuscript and handling proof. N.Y., 1950. 80 p.

45. Williams, Cecil B. and Stevenson, Allan H. A research manual for college studies and papers. Rev. ed. N.Y., Harper, 1951. 194 p.

46. Wistar Institute of Anatomy and Biology, Philadelphia. Style brief; a guide for authors in preparing manuscripts and drawings for the most effective and economical method of publishing biological research. Prepared by the cooperative efforts of the editors of journals published in the Wistar Institute and the staff of the Wistar Institute Press. Philadelphia, Wistar Institute Press, 1934. 169 p.

American National Standards Institute Z39 Committee

Jerrold Orne

I am pleased to talk with you and also pleased that you are willing to let me come, for I had begun to get the general impression that you never would let me come near you because of what I have done and have not done. I think perhaps my acquaintance with Maurice Tauber goes farther back than does that of anyone here, except possibly Sumner Spalding. I went to school with Maurice Tauber in 1940, and we have been close friends since. I love him as much as any of you, but at the same time, in my function as chairman of Z39, I have had to do some things, like it or not, that may seem to belie this affection.

These things grow out of a system about which David Nevin said, very properly, we need to know a great deal more. No one is to be blamed for not knowing it, because the systematics of standards production is very complex, very difficult, and little known except to those who give full time to it. I have been in this work now about eight years, four of those years as chairman of the Z39 Standards Committee. Sumner Spalding was in it even before me. There was a time, some eight years ago, when as chairman of a Z39 subcommittee Spalding threw up his hands and said you can have the whole business right back. It was at that point that I came into it. Sumner's assignment passed to me, and I unwittingly took

Chairman ANSI Z39 Committee; Librarian, University of North Carolina, Chapel Hill

it. So when I speak with some vehemence, it is with very good reason. My purposes in being here are to give you counsel, to warn you of the difficulties, and to let you know that I am fully aware of your concerns.

One member of your group wrote to me rather heatedly, reproaching me severely; I was not surprised. It happens all the time because of the things I have to do to keep our standards work on the track. The bibliographic standard has been in progress for six years. One of the worst chores I have is to get anybody to bring work to a conclusion, and this is what you are going to inherit if you get into the standards business. It is a tiresome bore, a taxing battle, costly, hard work with very little thanks for it and with hardly anyone willing to listen to you. You will do it because you are as vulnerable as I am, and you will do it well; but it will take time, money, determination, and a lot more than any of you have thought of up to now. The Anglo-American code was started in 1908, but long before that there were extended efforts that resulted in this first code. There are those who say that 1908 code is still the best ever done.

I will tell you, as briefly as I can, what it takes to do a job in the American National Standards Institute (ANSI), as it is now called. You will find it is, in many ways, just another big organization like the American Library Association (ALA) or the Association for Educational Communications and Technology (AECT) and that you have to plow your way through. Personalities and personal problems must be considered if you are going to fight through a standard proposal. ANSI officials are constantly revising their methodology, and you must keep up with the changes. The initial stage is only the beginning, although it takes a lot of time and effort. Some of the decisions I have made that affected you so strongly were not really mine but those imposed upon me by the ANSI system.

You must first find a sponsor and propose a standards committee to ANSI. The review of your proposal will determine whether what you have proposed to do conflicts with other standards committees. You will note, if you have seen the ANSI catalog, that there are several hundred standards committees, each with subdivisions. Finding a unique area where you will not infringe on the responsibilities of other committees is difficult indeed. After a committee is established with a sponsor, money, and people, it may begin to produce standards. Then, as these standards are started through the system of review, you may find that you have failed to maintain liaison with someone or to coordinate your work with someone or that you are crossing into someone else's area and you are in trouble.

One place where you will invariably get in trouble is with codes which you will need to plan for machine application. There is a standards committee called X3. It has X3.2, .3, .4, and .5 and heaven knows how many subcommittees. All codes with machine-manipulation capability cross the scope of X4, business machines. We did. The ALA Library Technology Program, an organization concerned with library equipment, produced a typewriter keyboard and, in all innocence, proposed that Z39 process it as the keyboard for libraries. Yes, you guessed it, there is a keyboard committee. The committee asked what we were doing with keyboards, for they were its concern. Not knowing what to do with the proposal, I gave it back to the Library Technology Program director, Forrest Carhart. There are such disappointments all the way down the line, and you are going to experience them.

The Z39 Committee and its many subcommittees are concerned with libraries and doc-

umentation, and with publishing practices related to them. These concerns also border on someone else's business. Initially, ALA was the sponsor of Z39 and supported it to about the same degree as it did PH5, Photocopying, $300 for postage and stationery. The Z39 Committee now enjoys support to the extent of $40,000 a year through grants from the Council on Library Resources and the National Science Foundation. This funding was obtained by presenting a program and doing something with it, and it continues only because we do accomplish things.

There are today some 38 subcommittees of Z39. I heard mentioned today that there are 29 to 65 different types of audiovisual media. You can look forward to 65 if not 165 subcommittees of your standards committee. Now all you have to do is go out and get the money to enable subcommittees to meet and work on standards. The two remaining chores are to get the people to work on these standards and to find some tough geezer who will stand up there and say, "Give it to me." Every three months I require a report from all subcommittee chairmen. That is the only way I get any action. If they do not give me a report, if they do not move, I either close out the chairman or the subcommittee. Now that makes me a ruddy S.O.B., but it also makes Z39 produce.

When I first learned of Maurice Tauber's discussion with you, which resulted in the preceding chapter entitled "Proposed Standard for Bibliographic References," I said, "That is great, that is just what I need, more delay." If we do not get them out, our financial support will vanish. We have to produce standards. Now I am not the kind of a genius who actually produces them; others do that, and I stand behind them with a prod.

I love Maurice Tauber, but, by God, he seems to have a tough time finishing something. Now he is in the hospital, and I have got that standard. I got it from a lady in his office who gave me the final copy. He agreed to it, but it took a couple of telephone calls and some pressure to get him to let go. This was the only way I could do it. I take all the responsibility for it, and so if you want to harpoon me, go right ahead. I told Maurice, "We cannot wait any longer." This is a specific problem, and from what I have heard here, you have still got a large piece of it left. The standard could not wait for nonprint media.

This is the whole story! The basic work accomplished by your institute with Maurice Tauber should be continued with the expectation of its becoming a supplement or equal component of the standard for print media. It will obviously require more attention, but is a genuine need that must be met. National and international standardization of the bibliographic components for nonprint media has become increasingly clear to me and will, I am sure, in the near future be recognized by many professional groups. Therefore, I urge you to continue your fine work in this area.

While I was at the Air University for six years, one-third of my entire library organization was audiovisual. The unit was directed by John Mitchell and had an annual budget of one-half million dollars. It had an art section, a photographic laboratory, a film library, and other things with which you are concerned. I knew a great deal about it and still have an affection for it. With this kind of knowledge I was eager to talk to you and explain the process whereby library standards are brought into existence. Thank you for letting me do it.

Question: Could you tell us more about the American National Standards Institute, the director to whom you are responsible, and its form of government?

Mr. Orne: ANSI is not a government organization. In this we differ from many other countries, where their standards institutes or standards associations are usually a government agency. Our institute is not an agency of the national government by deliberate intent, because we live in a democracy and believe the standards association should not be regulatory. All American National Standards are voluntary standards. There is no compulsion on anyone to use the standards published by ANSI.

Here it might help to distinguish between the products of the American National Standards Institute and those standards developed and published within the federal government. The United States National Bureau of Standards (NBS) has recently announced computer code standards; these are mandatory only for federal agencies. Nevertheless, the federal government utilizes nearly 70 percent of all computer products, which gives its standards a strong influence. Even so, the fact remains that federal standards are not binding on the private sector of our economy.

I report to our sponsor, the Council of National Library Associations, attending its meetings biannually to report on our activities. By regulation I also make an annual report to the American National Standards Institute, on our activities as well as to the International Standards Organization concerning activities that have a bearing on its work.

For a proposal to become a standard, the subcommittee first develops it, and then the Z39 membership passes on it, with every member having one vote. There are something like forty-six member organizations of Z39, such as American Library Association, American Society for Testing Materials, and the Library of Congress. If the proposed standard is approved by the membership and seen by everyone concerned, it should be approved and become truly a representative standard. The remaining steps are not concerned with content, but rather with procedural matters relating to transmission and various stages of approval with ANSI.

The American National Standards Institute designates one member of its staff who monitors a number of standards committees and steers recommendations through the ANSI procedure to the main body, which is a standards board. The standards board is made up of some ten people from various fields whose main function is to determine that the standard has been reviewed by all concerned and that it is within the scope of the submitting standards committee.

The board decides whether the standard affects or overlaps another committee. That is where you often get kicked, for the standards board passes on proposals submitted by a large number of standards committees. There are about ten or twelve standards boards, each of which encompasses a wide but related range. Should the proposed standard be passed, it is then announced to the public. If all steps are successfully completed, it is passed, published by ANSI, and offered for sale. There are other problems such as announcement, distribution, and bringing about its use.

Question: Who supports ANSI financially?

Mr. Orne: ANSI gets its support from its member organizations, who are primarily industrial organizations. Their interest initially lay in commercial products which have a very large dollar volume. The financial support for libraries and audiovisual media has come from the Council on Library Resources and the National Science Foundation.

Question: Is there any provision within ANSI for subcommittees to work together on something? For instance, take the example you gave with the keyboard. It would be conceivable that the keyboard group does not know enough about the specific content to develop it properly and that perhaps your committee did not know enough about keyboards. Is there any provision for coordination?

Mr. Orne: Yes, there is indeed. By agreement you may have a delegate from one committee assigned to the other. We have a person who represents ALA on X3, computing machinery, and also represents Z39 on X3.4, the committee that held up the MARC II standard for a year. That standard went in complete and approved and ready to go to the standards board, but it was suspended because someone said the code subcommittee of X3 had not been consulted. Subcommittees X3.5 and X3.2 were also involved, and a series of meetings and telephone discussions were required to resolve the matter. By bringing together Henriette Avram, David Weisbrod, and two people from X3, the problem was resolved. This solution goes on to the annual meeting of X3 with an agreement that it should clear the MARC II format for publication. It has been a year since we turned it in.

Question: Who chose the name Z39?

Mr. Orne: The alphabet and numbers are used because of the need for an almost unlimited expansion. The letter *Z* is designated miscellaneous, and the *39* represents the 39th committee of standards established under *Z*.

Question: It must be exasperating to have to consult all those committees. Do you find that if you do not, it is even worse because the things you fail to learn from other committees make your work invalid?

Mr. Orne: You simply must. For if you do not, somebody kicks you in the head before you get your standard accepted. The ANSI standards process assures a very thorough screening, which is as it should be. When a proposed standard is approved, it is a valid standard and is used. There are an infinite number of standards which are not national standards but are called standards. ALA publishes standards, as do other professional groups and an industry itself, but a national standard should be one that will be adopted nationally.

Question: Could you help us think through the development of a bibliographic standard for media and consider whether or not we should first develop the cataloging principles? We are now looking at part 3 of the Anglo-American code in depth. Would it be better to revise this code and then create the bibliographic standard from the code, or can these be done at the same time?

Dr. Orne: From what I have heard here, you are on the right track. You should begin with the basic elements and define what you are talking about. I would recommend that you review the list of data elements in the early manual devised for the MARC program. The Z39 Committee funded and produced this collection of data elements, which was the first step in establishing the MARC format as a standard. These data elements for machine input of bibliographic data were published as a small booklet, which has had two printings and is being used by those who are establishing a machine system for handling library data.

You are on the right track with the identification of your subject. Each type of material must be isolated and standards proposed which say what it is, how you handle it, how you identify it, what you call it, and everything else relating to it. You will end up with a whole series of standards, one for each type of material. This is what really scared the devil out of me, when it began to appear that our bibliographic references would wait on all of this.

Question: There has been a good deal of

discussion here in terms of relating the media that is nonprint to print material. Can we not employ much of the standards work already completed for print material for nonprint formats?

Mr. Orne: Yes, any work in these areas is ultimately related. The experience already gained with some of the products is certainly relevant and should be used.

Question: If we have sixty-five different versions of the containers for bibliographical elements, should we be writing standards for the containers or for the elements themselves? Your standard does not refer particularly to paperbacks or pamphlets as such, except very incidentally. In fact, when you come down to nonbook media, I think you will find, as did the catalogers, that there are not that many basic forms. There is a fair amount of proliferation in any one basic form; such as different physical forms of videotapes which are important because of machine and storage requirements. A videotape is a videotape is a videotape, whether is it half an inch wide or an inch wide.

Sumner Spalding: This is what I was referring to when I was trying to distinguish between media and form. It is not easy, but it is the first step. We have to know how many different media we have, because it may require different steps, but the forms of the various media are simply details.

Question: It may seem a stupid question, but how long does a media have to be a media to be a media?

Mr. Orne: This is one of the definitions that you will have to establish. This is the tough part, where you start and stop, but I understand that the distinction is being made, and it is a proper one. When you attempt an agreement on a standard, you have a far more difficult situation than we have with standard library problems because you will have the manufacturers and other commercial interests with which to contend. The computer X3 sub-

committee personnel will become quite concerned with your proposed standards, for there are very important economic considerations which apply to the area of standards for nonprint material.

Comment: We are receiving more and more combination multimedia kits from producers, which leads to the thought that we may be dealing with elements rather than a single container. We should really try to think of common things rather than 65, or 85, or 105 separate media.

Mr. Orne: That is why you had better get into this standards business before you are snowed under. It is happening to us in the print field. Right now Encyclopaedia Britannica is proposing a miniature library over which there is quite a hassle.

Question: Did the Z39.4 Bibliographic References Committee dabble in the citations for media earlier and then, for matters of expedience, drop them?

Mr. Orne: I would guess that this section 5.5 was included because someone happened to mention it during one of the first five drafts, but it was not explored farther because we were not aware of the magnitude of the problem. If nonprint media had been considered from the start, some five or six years ago, it would be better covered, but it would still not be complete, for you have yet to complete the basic steps in this complex project. If the current proposal is approved and published, a year later you might double its size.

Comment: Your mention of the numbers twenty-nine or sixty-five different media brings to mind something that Frances Neel Cheney said recently when she made a reference to her life-long love affair with government documents. I think that we could liken this to our love of media and say that we have had a mad running love affair with multimedia resources for many years, but as the numbers proliferate, they become more and more difficult to embrace.

International Film and Television Council European Subgroup Conference

Jules Leni

The International Film and Television Council (IFTC), a nongovernmental organization created by UNESCO, sponsored a two-day meeting in Paris in February 1968, to consider the possibilities of international cooperation and standardization in the development of computerized techniques for the cataloging of films and television programs. The American delegation to the meeting included Glenn Mc-Murry, Carolyn Guss, Carolyn Whitenack, and me. At that meeting it was decided to establish a working party of experts belonging to the IFTC member organizations to explore this subject in detail, and Anna Hyer, then executive secretary, appointed me to represent the Department of Audiovisual Instruction (DAVI) on this working party at its first meeting in Rome, October 1968.

Since the working party proved to be too unwieldy as an investigating and idea-formulating body, a standing working group was formed among representatives at the Rome meeting. For purposes of close coordination it was divided into European and North American subgroups. The DAVI and the American Film Institute (AFI), the other American film-related organization participating in the IFTC, were asked to organize the North American subgroup. From our discussions in Rome,

however, it was apparent that the aspirations and the approach of the two organizations were so different that, for the time being, we decided to pursue the subject independently.

In the meantime, there was the media institute session in Oklahoma, which represented a real step toward organizing standards and establishing some form of communication. We saw there the benefit of maintaining an international outlook in our effort through the presence of English and Canadian representatives at the institute. At one of the institute meetings it was decided to make an effort to broaden international participation. With an International Relations Committee, of which I am chairman, the gap created by the nonparticipation of AFI and DAVI was about to be filled. This committee met several times in Washington, between August and December, to make plans for bringing European representatives to attend the institute meeting being held in conjunction with the DAVI convention in April.

The European subgroup met in February 1969, to organize with representation from England, France, Italy, and Belgium. The members were assigned tasks to be reported on and discussed at the next meeting the following December 1969. The chairman of the European subgroup of IFTC invited me to attend the December meeting in London, and members of my committee and DAVI gave me

Vice-President, Comprehensive Service Corp., New York City

strong encouragement to attend. I attended the three-day conference on the application of electronic methods to the cataloging of film and television programs. I had anticipated the nine-member European subgroup to be an ideal size for informal discussion. However, the meeting was opened to representatives of all interested organizations, and there were more than fifty persons in attendance, including delegates from Germany and Sweden. The meeting was conducted under provisions of protocol, as most United Nations-sponsored meetings are. The presidium of the meeting consisted of the president of IFTC, John Madison, retired British government official; the chairman of the work party, Dr. Robert LaFranc, who is director of Audio-Visual Services of the French National Commission of Education, Science, and Culture; and the chairman of the subgroup, Jacques d'Olier, director of documentation of the French National Center for Scientific Research.

Educational and bibliographic professions were definitely in the minority at this meeting. Most of those present represented only the archival interest in cataloging films and the concern of the European state-operated television organizations for retrieval of information on television programs, including news broadcasts. Reports were given by subgroup members assigned to compile a list of experts in the field and propose a program for the exchange of information; compile a minimum content list for catalog records; review the practices of staff training and techniques for cataloging audiovisual materials; survey the existing approaches to classification; and study the problems of cataloging educational films. Obviously they had not learned that American organizations have already invented the wheel. With the exception of the presentation of a proposed minimum content list, no significant progress was reported on any of these assignments. Since I had gone there hoping to hear of activities comparable to what had transpired in Oklahoma, I was very disappointed.

The paper on the minimum content list was quite interesting and provoked considerable discussion. While it was written from the viewpoint of a film archivist, it reflected an approach which is entirely viable and perhaps essential if some degree of interdisciplinary compatibility is going to be achieved among organizations with interests in cataloging. Another interesting point was raised that should be considered, particularly in view of the development of Electronic Videotape Recording (EVR), and that is the question of sequential analysis, which occupied a considerable part of the discussion time at the meeting.

When called upon to deliver a report on the nonexistent North American subgroup, I took advantage of the opportunity to speak out at some length, and with considerable enthusiasm, of what had happened in Oklahoma. Sorry that I had not taken a copy of the institute song, which crystalizes the essence of our activities, I substituted my own verbal description which was well received and enthusiastically commented upon.

The IFTC as an organization is very strong on ceremony and very weak in leadership and organization. In the absence of national government or UNESCO support or the availability of such volunteer effort as has really enriched the activities of this institute, the IFTC will accomplish nothing more than international communication among interested parties on the subject which would, frankly, not otherwise occur. Extending the scope of our communication is a task which the IFTC is willing to do, and I feel that this modest achievement, in itself, justifies continuing support by DAVI and the institute. The European audiovisual community definitely looks to American leadership in the application of technology to education.

The final result of the meeting was to plan a conference, under the sponsorship of the IFTC, concurrent with the DAVI national convention and the institute meeting in Detroit. Therefore, I am going to propose to Howard Hitchens, current executive secretary, DAVI, that in view of the 1970 national convention emphasis on international education, a concurrent meeting of the IFTC working party would be an event of considerable interest. Our committee has drawn up a list of experts whose presence would be of great help to our whole effort.

My participation in this IFTC program has been personally rewarding. We represent one narrow point of view, people concerned with film as a media of communication, but IFTC embraces those people who are concerned with films because they love films. This is quite a different viewpoint, and when we meet together in April, it should be a broadening experience for representatives of both points of view.

Part 7

Activity in the Professions

All professional associations directly concerned with the organization of nonprint media were represented by participants in the media institute. They shared their points of view, expertise, and concerns. Officials in several organizations were also invited as speaker-participants for a two-day period. Richard Ducote, chairman of the American Library Association Coordinating Audiovisual Committee, discussed the activity of committees in that organization (there are some twenty-five) and Robert Snider, associate director of the National Education Association's Department of Audiovisual Instruction (DAVI), related the historical accomplishments and current interests of his association. (The latter organization's name was changed to the Association for Educational Communications Technology during the last session of the institute which was held in conjunction with the organization's annual convention in Detroit.)

Presidents of the two national associations, speaking before the institute's session in Chicago, gave their perspectives of the problem and delineated their organization's responsibility for bibliographic controls. Their positions were heard and commented upon by Mortimer Adler.

Paul Ward, executive secretary of the American Historical Association, asked to address the institute and share his professional association's venture into the field of nonprint-media production for curriculum use in academic institutions. Recognizing the reluctance of librarians to embrace media in formats other than those of traditional print, the American Historical Association's executive secretary urged librarians to apply their bibliographic expertise and accept materials in film format to be organized and made available to college students in multimedia kits.

Academic Librarianship and Newer Media

C. Walter Stone

I have a habit, as some of you know, of looking at my horoscope each day at breakfast. Today, it read, "Go to the top if you have a gripe. Don't take it to the underlings who can't do anything!" Despite restlessness in some media groups regarding the librarians who now are taking over the media field, I believe I *have* gone to the top. Insofar as I can tell, this institute has recruited individuals to attend as well as address it who are working directly for sound development of media services.

I would like to begin my remarks by referring to recommendations advanced during last evening's presentation [speeches by Becker, Adler, Gerletti and Dix]. I do have much respect for all who addressed us and for what they had to say; indeed, three are personal friends. But I do retain some unsatisfied feelings, because the essence of the profession and the professional organization emphasis which these gentlemen described relates in content to the provision of communication and information services and systems. This is perhaps a fine theoretical way to say that we are all part of one family. To my way of thinking, the difficulties which are now of primary concern to media service professions are not those of theory but of practical, professional politics, logistics, administration, and management.

Take the matter of personnel, for instance. The recruitment of qualified individuals for training in the media service areas highlighted last evening is still conducted as if each field was complete and separate in itself. The integrated approach which is recommended and which is supposed to be emerging does not, in fact, exist.

Second, administrative arrangements on a campus, in a community, and within the typical school system are still archaic.

Third, goals generally posited in this area are frequently misguided or simply follow the turn of events. Support levels are insufficient and inefficient, fiscally and otherwise. We don't have the dollars. Nor do we have as yet the information necessary to provide the kinds of media service wanted and needed.

The library of the future may be more concerned, far more concerned, with providing or obtaining access to information about media than with provision for local acquisition of media in specific forms and quantities. As for bibliographic control, we are not even close to being on top of what exists, where it is, and what educational and informational values and relevance it possesses. We do not yet agree on how to describe instructional media in too many cases. Nor are we agreed on whether the prime responsibility here should be assigned to the public or private sector, to individual institutions or professional associations, or to consortium-like arrangements. Divisive and debilitating competition which is

President, Joint Market Analysis Reports Company, Inc., Palo Alto, California characteristic of our present operations must be eliminated.

My chief responsibility here is to discuss the role of academic librarianship in media organization. I found that at least two interpretations of my topic were inappropriate. The title assigned does not refer to campus library responsibilities nor to academic library contributions to the organization of media as these might be represented in bibliographies or printed catalogs. Rather, I have been invited to consider the academic library interests in what the American Library Association can and should do through its existing committee structure, subdivisions, and offices. I have, therefore, been thinking about each of these in relationship specifically to the ALA *A-V Task Force Survey*.[1] I have also been trying to identify a few major issues which honestly do divide thinking about related questions.

For instance, should there be a new and separate division in ALA which would work primarily in areas of concern to this institute group? I do not think so. First, such a division might well rob responsibility from other units within the profession which should be concerned. Second, and perhaps more important, a new division could well prove offensive politically to colleagues whose prime allegiance is to other media organizations rather than to ALA.

What about a new ALA headquarters office? Could we support it? How might it be staffed, and what functions should be considered primary? Answers to these questions have been given before, but let me repeat them. I do think an office should be set up within ALA to serve the whole association as a clearinghouse, liaison agent, research sponsor, reservoir of ideas, reporting agency, and special projects manager. Such an office could, for instance, encourage audiovisual library research, experimentation, and demonstration programs, as well as perform various types of service operations such as providing information on logistics, administrative arrangements, and costs.

The office could also work on a continuing basis for increased and improved publication of relevant materials, manuals, and reviewing media. It could assist in development of both technical and service staffs. It could assist in or speed the development of regional specialized reservoirs of media from which all of us might draw. I would also hope that the new office might assist recruitment and training as well as accreditation of professional education of media service personnel. I would hope it might take steps necessary to encourage more universities to serve as "yardstick" producers of materials and to assume responsibility for provision of demonstration services, for instance, in the development of oral history collections. Working with other offices within the association, such as the Library Technology Program (LTP), the office would seek development of the new kinds of equipment required; for instance, a hand *fiche* reader and other devices required for effective media use.

What kind of organization might be needed? I do not think it has to be large, but I would certainly suggest that two, three, or four professional people, working in and out of Chicago, would be needed to perform the functions I identified, as well as to inform their colleagues at headquarters.

How might we support the new office? Initially, I would suppose a government grant or a contract might be sought to demonstrate its utility. Here the problem, despite a drying-up of federal funds, is not so much the dollar shortage as it is one of priorities. If ALA really wants such an office, it can be created and it can be maintained.

Now another question that has been raised concerns the role of the ACRL [Association of College and Research Libraries] Audiovisual Committee, and indeed of the ALA Audiovisual Committee as such. What can and should these committees do to support academic librarianship? Here are some answers to these questions. I think the subcommittee [the ACRL committee] can serve as advisers with respect to the new headquarters office and, until that headquarters office exists, as proponents and advocates and pound-on-the-

[1]Special summary prepared for the Audiovisual Committee, American Library Assn. University of Pittsburgh Libraries, 1969; reprinted in *American Libraries* 1, no.1: 40–44 (Jan. 1970).

table, lapel-grabbing pushers, lobbyists, or whatever may be necessary, to get the office launched. Second, I think the personnel of these committees can take on special problems such as program meetings and institutes, discussion of standards, identification of needs for legislation, an inventory of new service programs across the country, and editions of special publications relating the new thought we need in academic librarianship, which thought is required to ensure proper recognition of the need for redefining library functions in the media field.

You have heard me say before that the library is not a place; it is a function, or a set of functions, or a cluster of functions which may be described in this way: distribution (production and reproduction of recorded knowledge); research, having to do with the effectiveness of services provided and of the media themselves; demonstration and display services, counseling and training activities; and the effective harnessing of modern computer technology to make knowledge truly accessible. These are the library functions. They cannot be performed by a single profession. They must be performed by a cluster of professional, technical, subprofessional, and clerical groups. A whole cadre of personnel will be recruited to support this kind of activity. The future requires a professional background which is far wider than most of us are prepared to accept. It must be far more penetrating in depth of approach than frequently will be economically feasible for us to support. This is where we are headed, and I think it would be effrontery on the part of library or audiovisual education specialists or information science schools to presume that they are doing adequately the job of professional education for provision of the kinds of communication and information services with which you are concerned.

Comment: The American Library Association must provide some formal structure so that it relates to the rest of the world in the area of nonprint media. Unless it has some structure, I do not see how it can relate with either the commercial world, or with other associations, or with any individuals who are concerned about media. I think that we know it is impossible to carry on this work in an organized way with committee structure alone. The proposed office is the minimum requirement in order to implement the programs we have identified as essential. I am intrigued about this problem of structure, which seems to me a "chicken and egg" situation.

There is also the question of training, but what the appropriate training agency would be, I am not sure. Shouldn't we develop a closer relationship with some appropriate body now in order to provide the necessary training programs? The library schools are apparently not doing the job.

Mr. Stone: There is a review of some of the activity in library education currently underway, under the direction of Irving Lieberman of the University of Washington School of Librarianship, similar to the study done ten years ago. Some schools are developing cooperative programs which cross traditional professional school lines. They are providing some access to the range of special knowledge requirements. Hope seems to lie in the interdisciplinary approach. We are dealing with a cluster of functions, which includes the functions of production, research, and demonstration. It includes communication technology and computer technology, as well as a variety of skills, knowledge, and integrated abilities. The key is staffing the program for maintenance of the *library function* with the competencies required, but these competencies come from a variety of disciplines which must be properly focused for resolution of the instructional research problems of institutions.

Effective library information distribution can be accomplished only by the most capable personnel. To achieve this efficiency, we should look increasingly to junior colleges and lower-division levels for the recruitment and preparation of a variety of specialized clerical and technical personnel needed to staff the various units within our communication information service complex.

We must also look to a wide variety of first professional level schools in the various media and subject fields, where there is a concern to provide the necessary background in areas such as finance, cost effectiveness, space, facilities, and utilization. I would begin with the functions to be performed, the kind of programs required, and the competencies needed for effectiveness. For these competencies I would look to our junior colleges and lower divisions to provide techniques, technicians, and technologists. I would also look to a variety of professional schools in business, engi-neering, library, audiovisual, radio-television, and computer science to provide some of the individuals needed to work within the framework of communications information services. They should be brought together in an integrated manner at the specialist level, probably in an interdisciplinary program.

The Booklist Nonprint Reviewing Program

Paul Brawley

With the growing acceptance by libraries of the multimedia approach to learning and with the ever increasing volume of new audiovisual materials, librarians expressed a need for reviewing and selection tools for nonprint media comparable to those for books. As a step in this direction the American Library Association Editorial Committee, at its 1967 Midwinter meeting in New Orleans, established an advisory and planning subcommittee to prepare long-range plans for reviewing nonprint materials in *The Booklist*, ALA's book review periodical, and to determine steps for implementing these plans.

The report submitted by the advisory and planning subcommittee identified the needs for reviewing nonprint materials. The committee ascertained the amount of nonprint materials produced each year to determine the size of the undertaking and the feasibility of reviewing these materials in *The Booklist*. It established the priorities of media to be reviewed, the scope and method of the operation, and the steps for implementation of all recommendations. Early in its deliberations the committee realized that reviewing would have to be undertaken in stages. Considerable study and lengthy discussion of the reviewing needs —which included research into library activities reflecting interest in nonprint materials, ex-

amination of retrospective and current sources of nonprint reviews, and tabulation of the needs as experienced by committee members and their colleagues—resulted in a tentative list of reviewing priorities. This list was submitted to representative segments of the profession, including state and large city school library supervisors, heads of audiovisual departments in large public libraries, and college and university librarians interested in nonprint materials, to ascertain the extent of agreement or disagreement with the committee's priorities.

In its final report the committee recommended the following order of priorities: filmstrips, 8mm film loops, transparencies, nonmusical recordings, and 16mm films. It also recommended that after the reviewing of the five top-priority media was established, *The Booklist* should plan to publish periodically reviews of other media such as slide sets, study prints, globes, maps, and multimedia kits. These reviews would be in the form of bibliographic essays compiled by subject specialists in the field and would be similar to *The Booklist's* compilations of recommended foreign-language books.

Reviews of filmstrips and 8mm film loops have appeared in each issue of *The Booklist* since September 1, 1969. After a reconsideration of priorities in the fall of 1969, it was decided to add reviews of 16mm films and nonmusical recordings on discs, tapes, and tape cassettes, starting with the September 1, 1970 issue. Since 1956 quarterly reviews of

Editor, Nonprint Material Reviews, *The Booklist,* American Library Association, Chicago

16mm films have been compiled and edited by a group of dedicated public library film librarians, serving as a subcommittee of the American Library Association Audiovisual Committee. This committee was dissolved after compilation of the July 1, 1970, issue.

The program includes newly released materials in all subject areas and for all age levels, preschool through adult, which are available for purchase or long-term lease from United States producers and distributors. Foreign-language teaching materials will be excluded, as will those of a religious or sectarian nature, highly technical materials intended for a professional audience, items of limited local interest, free loan materials which cannot be secured on a permanent basis, musical recordings, programmed instruction, and audio-tutorial materials.

Producers and distributors submit newly released materials to *The Booklist* nonprint reviews office for examination by the reviewing staff, and those within the scope of the program are assigned and mailed to two different consultant groups skilled in the evaluation of audiovisual media. These consultants are selected from top-ranking elementary and secondary school districts, public libraries, junior colleges, universities, and graduate schools of library science nationwide. *The Booklist* nonprint editorial office has identified and enlisted the consultative services of nearly 200 of these groups.

A variety of evaluators—such as librarians, teachers, media specialists, and students—examine the materials according to the criteria and evaluation form developed by *The Booklist* nonprint editorial staff and its advisory subcommittee. The selection criteria fall into the following categories: authenticity, content, technical quality, and utilization. Completed evaluation forms, reflecting consensus of the consultant group, are returned to *The Booklist* nonprint reviews office, where a reviewer screens or auditions the material. On the basis of the consultants' evaluations and his own examination, the reviewer writes the annotation summarizing content, pointing out specific audiences, age level, and limitations of use, and, where appropriate, making comparison with other audiovisual materials on the same subject.

Consistent with the existing editorial policies and practices for listing books, only reviews of items recommended for purchase will be published. In addition to publishing reviews, *The Booklist* provides feedback to producers and distributors for all materials submitted for review by relaying the evaluations of the consultant groups to them. Criticism contained in the evaluations should have a positive effect on the kinds and quality of materials produced in the future.

Previous Nonprint-Media Activity in the American Library Association

Evelyn G. Clement

We have spoken unhappily about the frequent reinvention of the wheel. There is an often repeated phrase from George Santayana that "He who cannot remember the past is condemned to repeat it." But how can we remember the past if we were not there when major events, or even minor developments, occurred and if no one considered it important enough to record the event in permanent form, preserving the information and providing access to it?

Do you think, as I did not long ago, that ALA's concern with nonprint media in libraries is rather recent? In 1906, Melvil Dewey conceded that if a picture provided the information required by the user, it had every right to a place on the library's shelves, right along with the book. Perhaps if Dewey had given nonprint media the energy and attention he gave to simplified spelling, we would not need to give it so much of our own energy and attention. We might, however, have to spell *catalog* with a *ue*!

During the period before and just after World War I, libraries were circulating and

Institute Assistant Director; Doctoral Candidate, Graduate Library School, Indiana University, Bloomington

housing music rolls, lantern slides, photographs, cylinder recordings, and stereographs. Many articles appeared in the professional journals discussing ways of housing, distributing, and even organizing these materials. Some discussion touching on these special materials occurred in the sessions of the Art Reference Round Table before 1924, when the ALA Council approved the establishment of the Committee on Relations between Libraries and Moving Pictures.

At the Seattle conference in 1925, under the chairmanship of Clarence E. Sherman, the committee made three recommendations. Two of these directly concerned public libraries, recommending that they be urged to establish and maintain film libraries. The third recommendation was, "In view of the amount of detail involved in the task of developing and sustaining a consecutive program of cooperation between public libraries and the moving picture producers, the services of an executive clerk, working at the headquarters of the American Library Association or at the office of the Motion Picture Producers and Distributors of America, Incorporated, should be secured. It is believed that in the event that the ALA is unable to finance this proposal, the necessary funds can be obtained elsewhere."

In 1928 the committee decided to enlarge

its scope and to include in its charge "the study of library activities as they relate not only to moving pictures, but to lantern slides, stereopticon reproductions, microscopic equipment, educational exhibits, and museum material," and to designate it as the Committee on Visual Methods. The title recommendation is ironic in view of the development of commercially feasible audio recording on photographic film that same year.

The primary emphasis of the Visual Methods Committee for the next few years was on cooperation among commercial film producers and distributors, the local theaters, and libraries. Bookmarks, booklists, lantern slides, and other publicity devices were widely used in the theaters to call attention to libraries, and a plan for early previewing of Hollywood films by librarians in Los Angeles and New York was consummated.

Halsey Wilson was an active member of the committee during the 1930s and made his great contribution through the publication of the *Educational Film Guide.*

Interest was so great in the meetings of the Visual Methods Committee, that in 1929 a Visual Methods Round Table was established. Librarians, educators, and members of the motion-picture industry were all involved in assisting the committee in its work of extending the use of visual aids in the library.

At a joint meeting of the Visual Methods Committee with the Adult Education Round Table, Adult Education Board, and the Library Radio Broadcasting Committee in 1940, attention was focused on audiovisual media for education of concern to libraries. The name of the committee itself was changed in 1941 to the Audio-Visual Committee. A Joint Committee on Educational Films and Libraries was formed with the responsibility of planning and directing a study of the responsibilities which libraries have or may have in the handling and use of educational films. Gerald D. McDonald of the New York Public Library was principal investigator for the committee, conducting a survey under a grant from the Rockefeller Foundation. The American Film Center, Association of School Film Libraries, the Motion Picture Project of the American Council on Education, and ALA cooperated on the com-

mittee. The resulting publication was the topic of discussion for several years to follow (at least when World War II was not immediately the center of conversation.)

In 1945, Mary Rothrock as chairman reported that "no other committee objective is as important as the need for funds to make possible an immediate film advisory service and field service from ALA Headquarters." Mrs. Aubrey Lee Graham, chairman in 1947, reported that "a grant of $27,000 was received from the Carnegie Corporation for a two-year program to provide for film advisory service." A professional film adviser, Patricia Blair, was hired to begin her duties at ALA headquarters in June 1947. Hoyt Galvin began preparation of a film manual for public libraries, and the Film Council of America was organized.

A request was made to the ALA Executive Board that the Audio-Visual Committee be made a board, "because the concept of the library has changed to include all the media of our times," and because the need for continuity and the multiplicity of demands in this field make it impossible for a committee to do the job that should be done. This recommendation was approved by Council at Atlantic City in June 1948. The board was organized in 1949 with Mary Rothrock as chairman, and a number of committees under this board were instituted. One of these was a Uniform Statistics and Records Committee.

A restatement of the purposes of the Audio-Visual Board in 1952 was "To study and to promote the use of all media and all materials of an audio-visual nature as they are related to public, school, college, and other libraries, and to further the establishment of national or regional clearing houses. To cooperate with other committees and agencies having similar functions."

By this time, in 1952, the Carnegie grant had run out and was not renewed. Patricia Blair had become Mrs. Cory, and though she was not working for ALA in an official position, she still assisted as a member of the board. Irving Lieberman conducted a Pre-Conference Audio-Visual Workshop at the 1953 annual conference. A recommendation (a familiar one by now) came from this workshop that an office of film specialist be established at ALA headquarters, to be subsidized jointly by the several divisions interested in audiovisual materials. Chairman Quincy Mumford passed along the recommendation to the ALA Executive Board. But in 1954 the board authorized Grace Stevenson to redraft the proposal for an office for a film specialist at headquarters. The Fund for Adult Education had not been able to make a grant for this purpose.

Lee Cochran, then president of DAVI, was present at one meeting of the board to discuss closer cooperation between DAVI and the ALA/AV board. A joint committee of the two organizations was appointed. At the Philadelphia conference in 1955, the Audio-Visual Board met with members of the Descriptive Cataloging Committee to discuss a proposed joint Audio-Visual Board and Descriptive Cataloging Committee on Bibliographic Control of Audio-Visual Materials. However, during this meeting it was decided that this task was properly a function of the Descriptive Cataloging Committee, which would establish such a committee unilaterally.

The Audio-Visual Board once again became the Audio-Visual Committee. This was not a demotion, but rather a result of the ALA reorganization in the late 1950s. This then brings our review of the association's nonprint media activity up to the point where Eunice Keen began her description of her involvement in the Descriptive Cataloging Committee on Bibliographic Control of Audio-Visual Materials and the publication of her manual in 1956.

We were talking with C. Walter Stone earlier concerning his recommendation for an audiovisual office in ALA, particularly one which would be truly interdivisional, a clearinghouse type of office. While his recommendation is certainly not a new notion in the association, it is a much broader and more fundamental proposal that he is making. It will be interesting to see in what way this recommendation can be influenced or, perhaps, implemented through our dialogue here. Perhaps the movement for change within the association, the recommendations of the *A-V Task Force Survey,*[1] and the meeting of this institute, all converging in this time and place, are propitious.

[1]Special summary prepared for the Audiovisual Committee, American Library Assn. University of Pittsburgh Libraries, 1969; reprinted in *American Libraries* 1, no.1: 40–44 (Jan. 1970).

American Library Association Audiovisual Committee

Richard L. Ducote

It is somewhat frightening, but always interesting, to look at yourself in historical perspective. The analysis Evelyn Clement has just given of the American Library Association's long involvement in nonprint media indicates to me that we do not necessarily have a revolution at hand. If anything, we are at a stage of development in our evolutionary process when a greater acceptance of nonprint media can be expected.

The *A-V Task Force Survey* was authorized by the American Library Association in the summer of 1967 and actually begun in September of that year with a commission to study the needs for a membership unit within ALA for nonprint media, accompanied by the office staff necessary for an advisory coordinating service to libraries. The survey came about because of the increasing number of groups and individual librarians interested in nonprint media within the library profession as a whole and because of concern that ALA had not been adequately providing information assistance needed regarding audiovisual services. We must, however, keep in mind that the field has been changing rapidly and that the need for more rapid changes in our attitude and for the assumption of professional responsiblity is obvious.

The recruitment and training of personnel who will exhibit more favorable professional attitudes toward the development of audiovisual services by libraries, and the regular gathering, compilation, and publication of more complete and reliable information about audiovisual materials and equipment required for more effective acquisition and utilization of audiovisual materials in libraries were identified by the survey as high priorities. More productive efforts to promote the interest of librarians in audiovisual services and to explain the importance of such services were stressed, as well as the development of special services which utilize audiovisual materials and equipment, including those established for hospital patients, disadvantaged groups and special education programs.

In Walter Stone's report on the survey, he identified inadequacies in the area of personnel. I would stress this inadequacy, not only in numbers or in kind, but also in our ability to recruit personnel and to attract them into the multimedia field. I should mention too our own inadequacy as administrators in the library audiovisual program in being able to identify the new kinds of people we require as we go about the marriage of libraries and audiovisual services. In the area of administration our methods are archaic. With technology bombarding us from all sides, we are evolving some exciting new concepts and ideas, but we are attempting to superimpose these on old administrative structures that barely, perhaps

Chairman, Audiovisual Committee; Director of Instructional Resources, College of DuPage, Glen Ellyn, Illinois

never, functioned well in the past. Our expectation of order from this chaos is simply beyond reason.

Dr. Stone said our goals have been discarded, but if I read between the lines correctly, perhaps we really have never determined our goals. We may be engaged in systems for education without having our goals and objectives clearly delineated. We are also suffering from inadequate funding, which affects all areas of our professional service.

As chairman of the American Library Association Audiovisual Committee, I propose a four-point program in order to begin implementing the Task Force Survey recommendations. From the data tabulated, these recommendations represent a good consensus of opinion regarding some of the problems involved. Before we make any recommendations, the ALA Audiovisual Committee will study the survey report in detail and interpret it for present relationships to present audiovisual activities, not only to ALA but to its subsidiaries as well. One of the primary tasks is to define the role of the library within media services and the role of the media within library services.

What functions are we trying to provide with media in libraries? What are we trying to do? At Du Page we think we have solved our institution's problem by outlining a program of what we want to do. I have heard you referring to intershelving and any number of things that we have had to learn by ourselves during the last three years. Our *Instructional Resources Center Handbook* indicates an integrative approach to media and libraries. We do not separate them, for we think they belong together and, of course, we have organized them together. We have approached this organization from the functional standpoint in in which we have a materials production division, materials utilization and distribution division, and a materials acquisition and preparation division.

We still have audiovisual specialists who refuse to accept the book as a viable carrier of information, thinking it went into an eclipse around 1900. There are also librarians who are still reluctant to embrace newer formats for information. However, the majority of librarians do not feel that they invented media, nor are they trying to put it under their wing. Technological developments in recent years and their application to education have permeated all areas of society.

I am particularly concerned that we avoid duplication of things which are already being done quite adequately. In the community college field most of us are new and are initiating new programs, and we must be able to identify a program and say this is what we want to do, then relate people and services and materials to it.

Finally, the area in which you have been most interested through your participation in this institute is the area of bibliographic control. Dr. Stone has recognized this as a critical factor. The wonderful things which this institute has been contributing to the field should help us to make progress. These are the kinds of problems we can share regardless of our area of educational interest or expertise. Librarians, and perhaps all educational communications specialists, will at some future point look back upon Dr. Stone's efforts with great appreciation.

American Historical Association Nonprint-Media Concerns

Paul Ward

I come here out of a need for cooperation, and I will try to put my case as clearly as possible. It is a rather complicated project in which we are engaged. Key representatives from my association have just met and agreed to embark on a multimedia program for educational enrichment, utilizing thirty-minute cartridges for the production of special audiovisual collections from motion-picture films. Carefully developed book lists will be combined with the cartridges to form media kits for individual study at the college level.

For example, a booklet has been prepared with appropriate selections of material for a medieval history course and tried out in a University of Chicago class. We are anxious to see how effective this combination of film and print will be for homework papers or a week's assignment in standard college and university courses. This combination could catch the imaginative spirit of youngsters and stimulate their independent reading and understanding of historical concepts. Scholarship is dependent upon the creative application of imagination, and it, in turn, can guide and discipline the mind.

The booklets we have developed contain both source and secondary readings for use in the standard academic teaching fashion. A very heavy usage of these materials is expected,

and I think you, as librarians, may have a central concern, for it is hoped the film cartridge can be handed out conveniently, like any book, from the reserve desks and viewed with hardware in much the same fashion as the *New York Times* microfilm is consulted. A large number of these cartridges are envisioned, and several are nearly ready now.

The American Historical Association favors more effective use of audiovisual materials and will be persuading college and university faculty to use them in their instruction programs. Although it is difficult to alter the pattern of general-purpose film viewing in large groups, the use of film cartridges in individual studies, at the convenience of the student and researcher, seems more appropriate to the learning of history. A further complication is the necessity of studying film along with print material. They are of equal importance and, therefore, need to be coordinated for their most effective use. There are a number of intellectual problems upon which I will not dwell, but let me assure you that historians are facing up to these.

The American Historial Association committee that launched this program includes a past chairman of the history department at the University of Chicago, W. H. McNeill. You perhaps know of him as the author of the book *Rise of the West*. There are subcommittees, including many scholars, who have done a great deal of work with films. They announced the project, received applications, and have

Executive Secretary, American Historical Association, Washington

carried out the program like any normal, high-level research program. The response was good. The technical film work is being done on quality control of the film itself, and it is now obvious that I have found the right group to work with in the development of proper coding for bibliographic control.

We decided that if we were going to change expectations, we must develop a more effective catalyst and that would, of necessity, involve the use of the film medium. Rather than attempt film production work, the historians decided to take clips from both educational and entertainment films, domestic and foreign, and combine the best elements of each for use in higher education. This project was conceived out of a genuine concern for the lack of an appreciation and understanding of history by the college student of today.

I am here to talk to you because we need the cooperation of librarians if we are going to make this something of a revolution in the use of film. We historians want, above all, to see the multimedia kit designed and constructed for maximum convenience and availability to the potential learner in the university, high school, and adult and continuing education programs. As executive secretary of the American Historical Association, I am assisting the work of several committees that seek to establish new patterns for the learning of history. We have the film material free from the owners and hope to open up a nonprofit, scholarly oriented integration of print and nonprint media. The success of this undertaking may rest, in large part, with the willingness of librarians to accept multimedia materials. Therefore, I come before you, asking that you accept nonprint media as equally important to that of print and that you join us in this endeavor.

Media Cults
and Mythology

Robert C. Snider

The Department of Audiovisual Instruction (DAVI) was founded as a department of the National Education Association (NEA) in 1923, when two national organizations united at the San Francisco convention to found the NEA's Department of Visual Education. This relatively small group, whose major concern in 1923 was the stereoscope and the lantern slide, met annually in connection with the American Association of School Administrators.

Until 1946 the main item on the agenda was often, "Should we try to continue this organization for one more year?" Edgar Dale, Charlie Hoban, Walt Wittich, Ole Larson, and some of the old guard were the leaders then. They did continue for another year, and another. Some of the more progressive members thought that they ought to change the name. In 1947 radio was well established, and they wanted to add *audio* to *visual*. They also had had phonograph records for some time, and that had started quite a discussion in the group. Many of them said, "Let's not expand into a department of *audio*visual education." "After all, we haven't solved the problem of visual education, so let's not take on the problems of audio education, too." But the liberals prevailed, and it became audiovisual.

The same kind of liberal-conservative pull has happened during my relatively brief tenure on the staff. In 1960 we published a 740-

page book, *Teaching Machines and Programmed Learning* by Art Lumsdaine and Bob Glaser, which took about all the financial resources that DAVI had. When we were working on it in 1959, no commercial publisher in the world would have touched the manuscript. Since then there have been a good many commercial publishers who have touched manuscripts somewhat inferior in quality to ours, and our book is still selling at about fifty copies a month. A professional association *should* publish a book like this, one which is premature for the commercial industry.

However, when we brought that book out in 1960, a number of our members were saying exactly the same thing they were saying in 1947, "Teaching machines and programmed learning are neither audio nor video, and we have not solved the problems of audiovisual instruction yet, so for heaven's sake, let's not take on programmed instruction, operant conditioning, and heaven knows what else goes with it!" We are now hoping to publish a book that will probably be called *Remote Accessibility* or *Remote Access to Learning and Individual Instruction*. This should present the whole concept of remote accessibility of instructional materials in much the same way as we presented the concept of programmed instruction a decade ago. This will be another very important book published by our association.

DAVI is one of some twenty national organizations that are concerned with media in some way, and is probably the most catholic in its concern. Its central concern has always

Assistant Director, Division of Educational Technology, National Education Association, Washington

been the improvement of instruction, rather than a primary concern with any particular medium. Within the past several months, some very important changes have taken place in DAVI, which now has about 10,000 members.

The National Education Association has thirty-five departments, representing special interest groups in education and having varying degrees of autonomy. In a major reorganization it was decided that all departments must elect one of three kinds of relationship with NEA. Most departments have taken the route that DAVI's board of directors elected to take and become, in the summer of 1969, national affiliates of NEA. Four departments decided to remain as departments under the new structure, totally dependent on the NEA. National affiliates recommend their members join NEA but do not demand that they do so. From NEA we get such benefits as negotiable room rent, telephone rent, and duplicating services. DAVI is not quite as close to its parent NEA as it has been, but it is still quite close. Personally, I think it is quite important for DAVI to maintain a close relationship with the organized teaching profession.

We are voting this fall on a new constitution for DAVI. This constitution provides for a very flexible affiliation with divisions that is not unlike the American Library Association and its divisions. This will make it possible for many of the groups that have been meeting with DAVI at our conventions to become affiliated as divisions. After a four-year debate over a more appropriate name, DAVI members voted in 1970 to call their organization the Association for Educational Communications and Technology (AECT).

Anna L. Hyer, who had been the executive secretary of DAVI for a number of years, decided she would remain with NEA as director of the Division of Educational Technology. I resigned as associate executive secretary of DAVI to continue full-time as assistant executive director of the NEA's Division of Educational Technology. After a careful search by the board, Howard Hitchens was named executive director of AECT, and Richard Nibeck was named deputy director.

For a group that is concerned with nonbook media, AECT has done a great deal of pub-

lishing. We have about forty-five titles in print at any given time. For seventeen years we have published a quarterly journal, the *AV Communication Review,* with readers in eighty-four countries outside North America. Our monthly magazine, *Audiovisual Instruction,* had a picture recently showing a man with a copy of *AV Communications* on Antarctica, where the navy base down there apparently gets it.

Another important activity of AECT is our annual convention. In Portland, Oregon, last April, we had more than 8,000 people present, with a trade show of more than 500 exhibits.

The NEA Division of Educational Technology was a prime mover fifteen years ago in persuading the Federal Communications Commission to reserve, in the public interest for education use, certain television channels. We are now at work filing briefs, doing the same for cable television, which is active in many communities. We want a certain percentage of each cable reserved for educational use. We are doing the same thing in terms of communication satellites.

The Division of Educational Technology was founded in 1945 as the Division of Audio-Visual Instructional Service. It has two functions, basically: to serve the staff and members of NEA and to improve American education through the more effective use of educational technology.

When the board of directors changed the name of our division from Audio-Visual to Educational Technology three years ago, we were in the process of issuing a very popular eight-page annotated bibliography on the use of the computer to schedule high school classes. Now that is neither audio nor visual, but, I submit, it is educational technology.

For the last three years we have been active and effective in helping the United States Congress revise the copyright law which was signed by Theodore Roosevelt. This law has probably outlived its usefulness, since everyone here who copies something on a Xerox machine is probably violating the copyright law. The NEA is one of the large effective lobbies in Washington, lobbying in what we consider to be the public interest.

I should also mention the Educational Media Council (EMC), which is made up of national organizations that are concerned in one way or the other with educational media. The Educational Media Council is an important group composed of representatives from both commercial and professional organizations. The commercial groups include the electronics industry, the audiovisual dealers, and book publishers as members of the council. The professional organizations include AECT, the Educational Film Library Association, the American Library Association, the National Society for Programmed Instruction, the Society of Motion Picture and Television Engineers, the University Film Producers, the Audio-Visual Division of the University Extension Association, and the National Association of Educational Broadcasters (NAEB).

Historically speaking, whenever a new communications machine has been invented, a national association has sprung up almost worshipfully around this machine. The National Society for Programmed Instruction is an example. The NAEB used to be educational radio, then educational television, and now educational broadcasting. The Association for Educational Data Systems (AEDS), which is about eight years old now, is made up of computer people in education. The Educational Film Library Association (EFLA) has obviously limited its interest to films and filmstrips. In all of these organizations, and others, there is a parochial concern for a small sector of the media pie rather than the larger pantry of technology. However, all of these groups tend to broaden their interests as time passes, and several have already proposed changing their names to something concerning educational technology, with a strong feeling that they were really not limited to television or to programmed instruction.

However, the controlling interests in these groups often wish to remain parochial in terms of their particular interest in a media. At the second annual meeting of AEDS, I met a man who had just been hired by one of the largest school districts in the country as the director of data processing. This man was formerly in the insurance business, but he was attending an AEDS meeting because he happened to have a job where he was processing educa-

tional data. NAEB is controlled by station managers who tend to come from commercial stations. They are professional station managers, who are good and really know their business, but they happen to be televising educational messages. The technology is where you find this parochialism. National associations spring up around these specific inventions. Their primary, basic concern is with a particular media, and the educational application of the media is all too often a secondary concern.

There are a number of superintendents who have said, "You were libraries, but now you are going to be educational media centers." Unfortunately, this is usually nothing but a semantic exercise, with very little change accomplished. We have the same problem in AECT. We have a lot of audiovisual people who want to leave things the way they have always been. They do not want to become involved in new developments.

At the annual convention in Milwaukee three years ago, our theme was *The Media Specialist: Object or Agent of Change*. Some audiovisual people and some librarians are really making an effort to become media specialists. But are these media specialists going to be objects of change or agents of change? First, we must know where we are and where we are going, so that we can better judge what to do and how to do it. Then we can begin to take action in this kind of environment.

I think the library media question is academic; it is of no consequence, really, in terms of what is going on in the schools. The relationship between librarians and media people today is not unlike two other groups who were caught in 1900 in another order of change. The blacksmith and the livery stable owner knew about the internal combustion engine and the horseless carriage, although many of them did not believe in them. They were unable to anticipate what was to come and how it would change their vocations, but today there are no livery stables or blacksmiths. We have all kinds of people, in special capacities, serving the vast complex needs of our transportation industry today, the needs that were filled so simply by these two men just seventy years ago. In far less than seventy years, there are going to be no librarians or media people, but a great many people tending to the information processes, which will be much more complex.

I am convinced that nothing will stop instructional technology. With any technology comes specialization, and you have to watch the specialization or you will become sterile. Technology is not a panacea, but it is an established fact. We have to learn to make the most of it, to adapt it as best we can to maximize humanization. There is a need for a closer relationship between blacksmith and livery stable operators—excuse me, I mean librarians and media specialists. To get down to a very practical suggestion, there have been during the last several years several useful starts in the area of control or retrieval. I hesitate to use the word *catalog* for somebody always jumps on me. In March of 1968, DAVI published *Standards for Cataloging, Coding, and Scheduling Educational Media* as a tentative statement. The hope was expressed in the introduction of the book that specialists would look at it, react to it, and suggest changes in it. You might give serious thought to recommending revisions to our document. Update or revise the AECT statement and others in the area of management of media—cataloging, storage, and retrieval of materials. I urge that you give thought to something as practical and as important as these changes because you and the people you represent are the best-qualified people in the world to accomplish such revisions.

Question: In speaking of increased specialization, I must comment that you can certainly produce faster when you have specialization, but you may actually realize no benefit if you cannot find the specialist. A few weeks ago I was trying to locate a person knowledgeable about ultramicrofiche. I telephoned some fifteen people, only to learn that none of them happened to know about ultramicrofiche, nor could they tell me who did. Long after the deadline, someone telephoned me and said, "I know a lot about ultramicrofiche." By then it was too late. What are we going to do about the problem of locating the specialists?

Mr. Snider: It's what we learned yesterday and this morning that is earning us our keep. This is an age of constant, continual learning in any profession, and the more the profession gets involved with technology, the more this is true.

Question: Does AECT expect to provide answers to problems, or is it the function of this particular organization to ask the questions?

Mr. Diamond: It depends on the stage of evolution of the particular group with which you are involved. Basically, the degrees of sophistication in different areas are at entirely different points along the spectrum. Questions are asked at meetings, then you will see people work with the problem, then come to the next meeting with specific things they have tried, things that worked and things that did not work.

Dr. Snider commented on the lack of coordination between the two groups, librarians and media specialists. I was in a conference recently which was composed of the chief librarians and audiovisual persons from each of our states. The lack of communication among those present made it obvious that they had lost sight that they were there because they were part of an educational *system*. Each was concerned is his parochial way about his own function, structure, and organization within the system.

We cannot have effective individualization of instruction without the coordination which makes resources available to students and teachers. To accomplish this we must identify the needs, design the functions to meet these needs, then design the structure and train the people appropriate to the task. There is a need for the generalist in this world of specialists. We need a new type of person, the catalyst for change, who can work with teachers, students, and administrators to evolve the concepts and identify the specialists available at the appropriate time. Quite often we bring the specialists in too soon. For instance, television was ruined as an educational tool for perhaps twenty years. We need the person who has a broader scope, who knows what is happening, and who can say at the proper time and place, "These are the resources; these are the people; this is the procedure."

Comment: You talk as though librarians are *all* librarians in academic institutions, formally involved in teaching institutions. The librarian is the generalist for whom you are looking. Now, you all know the academician's cry, "Not my field, not my specialty, outside my area of specialty." No librarian ever makes this cry, because he takes a classification scheme, Dewey, LC, or you name it, and operates from the whole of knowledge. The librarian specialist is indeed a generalist.

Mr. Diamond: There is a key element missing here, and although the librarians may disagree, I feel librarians have not been catalysts and salesmen of change. The traditional librarian expects people to come to him asking for help. Today, with things in the process of change, someone must ask certain questions long before you start on the specifics. It must be a person other than the curriculum specialist, for he is within a rigid frame of reference. This person must be a learning specialist who says, "Before you proceed further, what are our objectives and specific goals?" This is the systems approach. Then at a certain time, it is asked, "What are the resources we have available? What are the alternatives we can use to solve this problem?" The traditional library function comes in at this point. The generalist I am talking about is the one who is involved at the earlier stages of instructional change. This has not been the traditional role of the librarian.

Comment: Your semantics are muddled, If you are asking for a new person who is to be the learning generalist, how could this possibly have been the role of the traditional librarian? I'm not really arguing this. We really need this person, and it might be that it will evolve from the librarian. You are speaking of librarians in a much narrower context than I would accept. A librarian, to me, is someone who can work in the educational field, or in something completely different. The librarian who is working for Metal Box Company is just as much a librarian as someone working in Purdue University.

Mr. Diamond: I used both the traditional role of the librarian and the traditional role of the media person. Ideally, these roles should be much broader than they are traditionally pictured.

Comment: Audiovisual people may have a very myopic point of view, but perhaps a comfortable one, that librarians just stack and carry books. As a coordinator of a combined media program, I have found that librarians are much more prone to meet the kind of changes you are talking about than are media people.

Mr. Diamond: Both sides are tremendously frustrated. I think this whole clash between the two fields has been a major calamity. Our common problems are not being identified. I never had an experience like this before, for I have a librarian who talks to me, and I talk to him. We're combining out efforts every day, and this has a major effect on what we can do.

Comment: Are we going to limit our considerations primarily to formal education, to the instructional, rather than to education in the broad sense? What about the librarian at the chemical firm? The law office has a librarian. Many of their problems are similar, certainly. They all need to obtain information, although from a slightly different standpoint. We need to convey information in the most palatable, most readily acceptable, most readily available form. We must think of the patron who walks into our public library, our college library, our school library, and wants information about a subject.

Comment: I am convinced that we are all in the information business, but there are people who say it is information but not instruction. There is no common term, but there really are no differences among the school library, public library, industrial library, law library, and any other. People come to the collections for some kind of knowledge that they did not have before, whether it is in the hands of the people who operate it or in storage units. I think part of our problem is that we compartmentalize our vocabulary, as well as compartmentalize our specialty.

Comment: I have been watching the adrenalin rise and drop, and people agreeing and disagreeing with these various ideas, and a thought has come to mind. When we discuss persons or positions and functions, we are using specific instances, and, therefore, when we are discussing librarians and audiovisual people, we are referring back to a stereotyped concept. All of us from varied backgrounds were brought together to apply our expertise to the problems of bibliographic control of media. Not that one is going to get more out of the session than another, but that the group of people assembled here might come up with a common and useful tool for a multitude of purposes.

Comment: I am not really concerned that an audiovisual person become bibliographical, for I am confident that the librarian can in fact organize the whole range of media into a retrieval system that I can use. I do not really think that audiovisual people should concern themselves with becoming good librarians in the sense of contributing knowledge about how to organize media, for librarians are fully competent to do this. What I am concerned about is that as an instructional technologist or media strategist, I do not want to take on the responsibility of organization and retrieval.

Comment: Along with many other librarians, I have been thrust into a new role, with new objectives for which I have no training.

Comment: Do you mean as a librarian your new role is to become a designer of instructional systems or to increase your holding of information?

Comment: I have been forced into coping with physical objects, which have not been a great portion of my training. Unfortunately, I think a great many librarians have not gone past the stage of being compulsive organizers; they feel that is their role. We have now been forced into the role of controlling different-sized physical objects. This is why I am here. I do not feel that I am equipped to deal with them, but I do need help from the people who have invented these physical objects to define them for me.

Comment: If one group had the answers, it would not be asking for help from the other, but moving out ahead and offering answers to our problems. The fact that we are here is proof that we are desperate and in need of total cooperation of all our resources.

Nonprint Media
and the
Audiovisual Profession

Robert Gerletti

The Department of Audiovisual Instruction, now the Association for Educational Communications and Technology (AECT), has had an interest in this problem which you have been discussing since about 1923, when we joined the National Education Association. In Los Angeles County we started a visual-aid program in 1916. During the last ten years, the notion of merging nonprint and print materials has really become a problem. One of our districts has discovered it has 57,000 pieces of nonprint material, and it is trying to merge those with a 250,000-volume book library. It poses rather an interesting problem and, I think, helps crystallize the idea for us.

AECT has just over 10,000 members. The 30 or 35 different types of members include librarians, interestingly enough, about 200 or 300 of them. With such a large and diverse group of people, the needs are tremendous and we are trying to meet their needs in the association. If we do not meet them, we are going to cease to exist as an organization. We hear many voices; we hear them constantly telling us what we ought to be doing. Pluralism is easy to talk about, much easier than it is to live with. Last year we designed a new constitution which establishes divisions within

AECT. We have had geographical representation with affiliated organizations in most of the states, but now we are making provision for interest groups, such as for television or data processing, within the division structure. We hope that this framework will prove a fruitful one for us.

What is the essence of AECT? There are really two, I think, and I will try to make them clear. The first essence of AECT is the use of specific media in instruction. This is a point of view which has been prevalent in our field for some time. This idea has a research tradition in its own right, but it is part of a larger idea, the idea of the technology or instruction, or instructional technology. Many audiovisual people define their field of interest by referring to the special communication devices, such as films, filmstrips, television, and radio. In this process the teacher is considered to be the center of the universe of instruction. This is what Jim Finn called the "Ptolemaic concept." Materials and equipment under this concept are generally appliquéd onto the instructional program. That is one essence or point of view of AECT. The second essence is the instructional technology concept, which is primarily oriented toward psychological principles and empirical data based on a total teaching-learning process. One definition you have seen in print, or course, is the "systematic application of organized knowledge to the solution of practical problems facing the teacher and the learners in the learning process." At the cen-

President, Association for Educational Communications and Technology; Director, Divisional Educational Media, Office of Los Angeles County Superintendent of Schools, Los Angeles

ter of this universe is the student and the learning process.

If you subscribe to the first point of view, the problem of bibliographic control will be no different than it has been. It will not change. We will locate materials and documents as we have before, not information. We will have lists, card catalogs, and computer-generated book catalogs. We will have warehouses full of materials waiting to be used. Review, professional assessments, needs assessments, priority selections, purchasing, cataloging, filing, circulating, repairing, and discarding will continue. You are probably aware of some of the recent projects, such as the Educational Media Council, Educational Products Information Exchange, National Information Center for Educational Media, National Book Committee, and the Los Angeles City Schools project to study bibliographic control systems and to develop national evaluation and/or assessment programs.

If you subscribe to the second essence of AECT, you have a development which may be in its infancy in terms of what ought to be, but is really much older in concept than the first. With this idea the business of teaching and learning becomes much more complex from the point of view of arranging for learning. Among other things that bother us in AECT about this second notion is that you have to start to plan far in advance for instruction. Planning for the specific use of materials is much more detailed and requires much more time from start to finish, as the process is much more exacting. Large amounts of money, time, and expertise will be required initially for planning, experimentation, and revision, with allowance made for trial and error. Specification of task performance requires the allocation of resources to solve that specific task. Material and equipment generally are tailor-made. The ideas must be tested, revised, and then produced. More expertise is needed. Long-range planning will require additional checks to make certain that strategies develop systematically along a previously determined course. The logistics are frightening to us at times.

What, briefly, are some of the implications of these two points of view? We are going to live with both points of view for some time. I was talking with a Los Angeles City Schools representative who said he could not see that they can change over to a complete information system within the next five years. They are going to have to phase out and do it on a pilot project basis, school by school. School districts will be moving on many fronts in connection with this information system concept. If we accept this, then we will have the kind of bibliographic control that now exists, and we will continue to need that kind of control. At the same time, our institutions will be making severe demands on our information systems such as individually prescribed instruction and computer-assisted instruction.

Recently, when I was visiting one of the schools in Pasadena, I watched a professor go through an ERIC (Educational Resources Information Center) file, looking for a document which he knew existed but he did not know where it was. It took him about two hours to go through the indexes and the several monthly supplements, and he did not find what he was looking for. Somehow the indexes were lacking something needed for him to recall what he wanted. That is one of the problems with which we are faced.

This suggests to us that some kind of systems analysis should be applied. I heard today that printed matter has to be converted into machine-readable form. Systems may provide new intellectual concepts of information organization that are better than those we use now. Systems may show us how to reorganize the information constantly in order to maintain an active, usable source. You do not just put information in storage and permanently leave it there. Systems may be of help to us if we do not let our so-called professionalism get in our way. The information stored must be communicated and displayed rapidly in a form suitable for use, and in the future this may mean using perhaps unconventional systems. I would hope that we would take a good look at all kinds of systems.

The performance of descriptive terms and access points must be determined within a total system. That is a key point so far as we are concerned. Our efficiency of recall and our precision is not as high as we would like.

Perhaps some of the reasons are that we need better classification, we need better quality control, and we need the publication of a standard reference vocabulary. We have to "out-organize" the human lack of precision. A user apparently selects a different set of materials on any given day; a user in Chicago selects differently than he would if he were in Seattle; the sequence in which information is read apparently affects the use of the material or the information. Each user's assessment of materials differs from his colleague's. We have an unstable, dynamic, and very subjective problem where there is a need for evaluative criteria which meet the user's needs.

It bothers me somewhat that we often have two or more parallel systems operating at the same time, so that we fractionate our efforts. We should bring some of this into focus to work for consistently financed programs that we do not duplicate efforts. I am concerned that we are talking about systems not related to a total learning process. We ought to have some models for experimentation which will help us to provide needed data. We cannot accept automation blindly without evaluative techniques which will judge and control the quality of a new system. I would hope that we would do that.

We in AECT are watching and supporting developments all around the United States. We are concerned with the vast support systems necessary, the copyright law, equal access to information by learners, and the variation in current instructional patterns. We are more than willing to work with all interested groups to bring about solutions to these problems.

There is a thought from *Alice in Wonderland* which may be appropriate for closing. " 'The question is,' said Alice, 'whether you can make words mean so many different things.' 'The question is,' said Humpty-Dumpty, 'which is to be master, that's all.' "

Nonprint Media
and the
Library Profession

William Dix

The traditional function of the library is to collect, organize, and transmit the documentary record of men and society. This record by no means consists entirely of books and manuscripts. We as librarians have indeed recognized that a part of this record is the responsibility of others. But by far the greater part of the record is the primary responsibility of the library. I include in this part most of the nonprint media and, as a part of this responsibility, the transmission of these records of human communication. The library is not a dormant warehouse but an active instrument of communication.

We have not accomplished all of this. One of the earlier forms of communication, for example, is art, but from cave painting to dadaism, libraries, by and large, have not dealt, I think, with certain kinds of paintings and sculpture in the original form. We have set up museums to deal with them. I think perhaps this was a mistake for they could have all been considered and retained together simply as other forms of communication.

To me, the essence of the library, then, is this record of communication, the assembling of it for use. Our responsibility is not just to store records of the past but to use them and make them available to others who need them. This flow of activity is the business of the

library. Obviously then, my definition includes all forms of media so long as there is a record. Librarians have not been concerned, for example, with communication by telephone, because this does not normally leave a record. We feel we must have something to preserve and pass on to others.

The American Library Association's archival records indicate it has been interested in the purpose and concerns of this institute. The American Library Association (ALA) headquarters staff has supplied me with a few facts, some which were unfamiliar to me. In 1940 the ALA Audiovisual Committee was founded and merged with the earlier ALA Visual Methods Committee. In 1947, ALA received a film library grant from the Carnegie Corporation to assist the program by expanding library film services and to develop the concept of film circuits. At the association's 1967 annual conference the Audiovisual Committee heard reports from some fifteen units of ALA concerning audiovisual related activities, which represented only a few of the audiovisual groups in the association.

The American Association of School Librarians–Department of Audiovisual Instruction joint committee, with the cooperation of the ALA Children's Services Division, listed producers of television network shows and the production of bibliographic materials and tools by several ALA units. The Information Science and Automation Division, an ALA division of which Mr. Becker has been presi-

President, American Library Association; Librarian, Princeton University, Princeton, New Jersey

dent, is also interested in the listing of audio-visual materials by computer and the development of bibliographic control, your particular concern here with these materials. The Reference Services Division has for many years sponsored noonday film showings at meetings by a subcommittee of the ALA Audiovisual Committee.

The association's publications in this field are quite numerous. As far back as 1947, ALA published papers presented at the University of Chicago library institute on Youth Communication in Libraries. The publication *Films for Public Libraries* was compiled by the ALA Audiovisual Board in 1955, with a supplement appearing two years later. The following year Pat Blair Cory and Violet J. Myer prepared for publication by the association a survey of public library film cooperatives made by the ALA Office of Adult Education. A basic review journal, *The Booklist,* began publishing film reviews in 1956; *Films for Libraries* was compiled by a subcommittee of the association's Audiovisual Committee and published in 1962.

In 1969 the American Association of School Librarians and the Department of Audiovisual Instruction cooperated with ALA in the writing of standards for school media programs covering both printed and nonprint materials.

Only last year a new section of *The Booklist,* the nonprint-material review section, was begun. Walter Stone's report of the *A-V Task Force Survey* was printed in the first issue of a new serial publication, replacing the *ALA Bulletin* and entitled *American Libraries.*

The American Library Association has, I think, demonstrated an interest in nonprint media for a good many years, and it seems to me quite within the scope of my definition and, I think, most people's concept of a library. The specific subject of this institute, bibliographic control, is, of course, a primary concern, a logical and historical concern, of professional librarians. We specialize in the art of cataloging things, making lists, and bringing things under bibliographic control. Librarians are trained to organize materials for repeated use by others.

I do not think we are prepared to view part of the technology as something outside our area of interest. However, should this happen we would still, I think, become involved in the organization of this material, the dissemination of knowledge about it, and the interface between the user and the institution. We are particularly concerned with the organization, promotion, effective and efficient use, and preservation of all media for the communication of information beneficial to human society.

A Philosopher's Response

Mortimer J. Adler

I am delighted to be here, but am not sure I am properly here. Of the three addresses that I listened to, I understood one and did not understand the other two. This is simply a reflection on my own ignorance as a philosopher. Philosophers are persons who have ideas but know very little else. I heard the words and most of their meanings but did not understand them exactly, which indicates how specialized these things have become. I understood the comments about books, libraries, and information in general and cataloging and handling things, but obviously, most of technology and the techniques involved are way beyond me.

To indicate my confusion even further, let me tell you why I thought I might have some relevance to this program. I have been engaged for the last year and a half, still actively engaged, in a project that I would say has some relevance to your concern as librarians and persons involved in the systematic handling, cataloging, and ordering of materials. As I listened to what was said, I can not tell whether the thing I am talking about is nonprint material or audiovisual material, as you will see in a moment. I think the items are print and visual, but not in the ordinary sense. Perhaps just by exhibiting my difficulties, I will be able to provoke you to explain some things to one another, if not to me.

I am engaged in the project of producing

Director, Institute for Philosophical Research, Chicago

on microfiche, at a reduction ratio of about a thousand pages on a small card, of a 20,000-volume Library of American Civilization. While I am interested in the technology, I am only vaguely acquainted with it. I am concerned with the editing of this library, the compiling of it as a resource and research library, and with the cataloging and indexing of it. I would like to know, before the discussion goes on, whether a microfiche card, which contains a book or a microbook, is print material? Yes, good. Then obviously I am not concerned at all about nonprint material. I am just an old-fashioned bookman with a new fall publishing list.

It seems to me that Dr. Dix's account of the history of these matters should be projected one step farther from oral communications to written communications, to manuscripts, to printing with movable type. By the way, each of these new developments makes communication more efficient and the transfer of information more efficient. We have now come to another major stage of publication, the production of reading matter on microform or microfiche, to be read from an optical instrument rather than from the printed page itself. The advantage of this might be likened to the same kind of advantage that primitive movable type had over ordinary manuscript production.

As you think now of new libraries being created, not only in the United States, but all over the world, and as access to learning is spread across the globe, there will be many books, rare books, books in small quantities, books out of print that will now be available. This library, for example, will consist of 20,000 volumes, some 6 million pages on microfiche cards that will provide schools and colleges, not only in this country but also abroad, with materials they could not get otherwise because they simply are not available. The production of this library collection indicates what I thought was the relevance of this undertaking to your interest.

We have conceived the library not as just a collection of books, but as something that will be both cataloged and indexed. One of the problems of retrieval, as other speakers have indicated, is finding the optimal ways of determining the kind of information and material that different persons with all sorts of interests will want to pull out of a collection of material. Clearly, the normal orthodox card catalog system, which has been used for some years now to make the book content of the library accessible to readers, researchers, and students of all kinds, is an extraordinarily flexible instrument. However, in my judgment it is not refined enough for this 20,000-volume Library of the American Civilization. Therefore, we did provide, in addition to the ordinary catalog cards for every item, a kind of topical index which will make the contents of that library, unit by unit, book by book, available under a topical analysis of that whole field of learning in American civilization. There will be something like 500 to 1,000 topics. Topic by topic, there will be *Biblio-Guides* for the library as well as ordinary library cards. This, I thought was relevant, but I gather that it is not really because it is so orthodox. It really is not far out at all but rather a library made available in a new media, cataloged and indexed, I think, in a special sense.

It seems to me that if it can be done with these materials, the problems raised by Mr. Becker and Dr. Gerletti are solvable too. No one's material has intellectual content or informational content of any kind that cannot be properly indexed. So far as I know, these are conventional intellectual tools for retrieving from a vast collection the things that an individual wants to find and for ordering them and classifying them in such a way that they

are accessible, using the human hand or machine retrieval of some kind.

American Civilization is the first of twenty libraries that we are planning to produce, so this is only the beginning of a long undertaking. A colleague of mine in this undertaking, Charles Van Doren, will also be speaking with you. We have one more word and that is technology, in all of its forms. This meeting would not occur if it were not for the pressures upon the educational profession and upon the library profession of new technological equipment of one kind or another. Technology creates problems for us that are not new but intellectual problems that remain very much the same.

The librarian of the ancient library of Alexandria, full of papyri, had the problem under those very primitive conditions of handling material in some systematic way to make it usable by persons who had access to this library. The intellectual problem he faced is no different, really. Our problem is no different from the intellectual problem he faced, though we face it under much more complicated conditions, with machinery and instrumentalities vastly more powerful. Still, the human mind remains exactly the same kind of instrument. Definition, cataloging, inventorying, classifying, thinking of categories under which things are to be placed is the same old intellectual process it always was. It is useful to remember that when we are overwhelmed by all the technological advances that surround us, that they are no better, finally, than the human mind. The utility of their value to us cannot be any greater than our own intellectual resources.

Question: Dr. Gerletti,[1] are the two points of view you described as the essence of DAVI compatible or diametrically opposed one to the other, and if they do come together, what kind of offspring are they going to have?

Mr. Gerletti: My own personal opinion is that the first point of view is a subsystem of the larger point of view of instructional tech-

[1]This paper and the two preceding were presented as part of a panel discussion. During the open discussion that followed, questions could have been addressed to any of the members of the panel.

nology. Apparently, it is the system to which we have evolved. Apparently, we must go through it in order to arrive at the other, because the other is far too complex to spring all of a sudden. I think that we are going to go concurrently along with both, and I do not know if or when the first will ever phase out, because that affects my library considerably. I do not think it will ever phase out completely, but there will be new uses or new combinations into which these things go. Instructional technology requires such a vast amount of energy in terms of money and time that we can only hope to evolve to it, utilizing examples whenever they arise throughout the United States and elsewhere in the world.

Question: Dr. Adler, please describe the preparation of the microfiche catalog and index.

Mr. Adler: There were three stages in this process. The first was the job of selecting the titles that constitute the 20,000-volume Library of American Civilization. Imagine a library started from scratch, having no books at all, and you wanted to supply it with 20,000 volumes with a fairly representative sampling of the research and source materials in the field of American civilization. This collection is neither very large nor very small; it is about medium size. The first job is selecting the 20,000 volumes from 200,000 to 300,000 items.

Second, when the titles have been chosen, there is the job of cataloging the collection. Third, after they are put on microfiche cards, the volumes will be indexed not from the books but from the microfiche cards. There will be 20,000 microfiche cards in envelopes on the face of which the library card will be printed. We think that these library cards in the envelopes will be made machine readable so that you will not even have to go through them but can place them in a sorting machine and get any book that you want by number. Now, the indexing is the most elaborate part of this process, largely on the part of the persons who will have to read all of these 20,000 volumes in order to index them in more detail than is normally involved in the cataloging process.

Question: Is this similar to *Syntopicon*?

Mr. Adler: It is, in the sense that we are going to apply the same techniques that we used to do a rather small job, the topical indexing of almost 400 books. However, this new project is going to involve an initial collection of 20,000 books.

Question: The indexing is by topic?

Mr. Adler: Yes, this is a model of topical indexing.

Question: If you have just collected these and have not started cataloging or devising the general index, when do you suppose it will be available?

Mr. Adler: Early in 1971. This is one of the things, as far as I know, that cannot be done by machines. You need people to do this, for indexing remains an intellectual process. We think that with a large enough staff it can be done, and the library on microfiche cards will be cataloged and made available in 1971. Indexing will be done a year later, in 1972.

Question: If these 20,000 volumes were already published, would you use the cataloging information that is already available from the Library of Congress?

Mr. Adler: The Library of Congress card will serve us for the most part.

Question: What are going to be your criteria for indexing in general?

Mr. Adler: I am afraid that my answer is going to be so simple that we could not strike relevance on this matter. We have in mind somewhere between 500 and 700 topics that we think do a good job of indexing the whole area of American civilization, the topics of interest that represent most approaches to the contents of this material. When the index staff reads materials in the library, it will book by book, item by item, place it under the topics of which the whole book, or that portion of the book, is relevant. It is what we did over a number of years in constructing topics under the Great Books. The process has to be checked and rechecked, although it was not very difficult to establish this process. It is different from word indexes. We are not indexing words; it is the notion of a topic, that is, a place, a common place, an area of discussion.

Question: In view of what you have heard

this evening and what you already know about this technology, whether in the library or elsewhere, what is the future of libraries?

Mr. Adler: New institutions—and I don't include Harvard, Princeton, California, Yale, Oxford, or the British Museum—are growing up all around us. Both the impossibility of collecting the books needed and the expense of housing the collections will make many libraries in the future of necessity turn to microforms such as microfiche. This is particularly true in the developing countries where whole libraries may be created with printed resources on microfilm and microfiche. The status of older libraries that have extraordinary collections in printed formats will not change, however.

Question: Dr. Dix, what do you perceive will be the impact of technology on libraries in the next three decades?

Mr. Dix: I agree with Mr. Adler that we are going to have more tiny little pictures of books than we now have, proportionately, in our collections, for a variety of reasons. The controlling factor in all these things is, to a large extent, an economic factor. As I understand it, the duplication of copies of ultra-microfiche is rather high. The cast suggests then a special edition approved to publication, such as you are doing, Mr. Adler. The problem then becomes one of how many individuals and organizations need and can buy a ready-made library of 20,000 volumes. This, I think, would not be of much use to us at Princeton University, where I hope we have most of these texts already.

I see here a technology hunting for the right kind of application within economic constraints. The same thing is true in computer technology, omitting the internal, clerical operations. We are going to provide many services for user needs that simply could never before be satisfied, assuming we can afford it. Actually, we are going to have to afford it, because our users are going to demand it. For example, the whole 1970 census, I understand, will be available in machine-readable form. I have seen various estimates, and the cost of this thing is certainly going to be more than $100,000.

At Princeton University we have one of the best centers of demography in the country. Our demographers, studying population, are going to want to use this material, although I am not at all sure we can afford $100,000 every ten years for the cost of the tapes, much less the necessary servicing and searching that will be a continuing expense. A service center concept for this type of data must be developed. A group of research institutions could support one center. In that way we can afford to give our demographers access to the raw data on these tapes. Let us take the position that we must have support for it. A growing tension between the economics of newer media and the demand for its utilization appears obvious. The limitation placed on new kinds of research emerging in a number of fields is largely economic.

Question: One of the major interests of academic libraries in the past has been the development of manuscript collections, original work. How do you view the documents of new discoveries, for example, our landing on the moon, where the originals are available only in videotape format? How do you see their relationship to our past concept of manuscript collections?

Mr. Dix: I think it is the same thing. In my definition, the library is first of all a collection of the records of communication. Now the record of that first man stepping down out of the capsule onto the moon may be on videotape, but it is recorded. This is a document, and libraries deal in documents. We must alter our programs to include these new formats whereby historical events are preserved for future generations. Fifty years ago the Art Department at Princeton University began to develop an extraordinarily good collection of slides on art history used in teaching. It is well cataloged and well used but does not happen to be part of the library, and it seems to me, the location does not matter, for it is an arbitrary, administrative kind of decision.

Thirty years ago the Princeton University Library had a collection of musical recordings because no one else on the campus did. When our music department was established, this was obviously something it could handle better than the library. Therefore, our library does not now have a collection of musical recordings. In a different kind of institution it might be administratively feasible to pull all of these things together in the library, but this seems to be an arbitrary administrative kind of regulation. The significant matter is that these records be preserved and made available for those who need them.

Question: Are we trying to fit this tremendous new technology into an old framework?

Mr. Dix: We certainly know already how to do a great many useful things. The fact that we can not afford to do them is part of the basic problem. Viewing this concern against the ever expanding need, university research libraries are facing a real crisis. I do not think we can afford to continue for more than another twenty or thirty years the way we are going. We have known for twenty or thirty years that university libraries double in size every twelve to sixteen years. We have got to share our resources in some way, and the new technology gives us the means to accomplish this.

We have not as yet anything like an economically feasible way of sending large masses of materials from one institution to another. The United States Postal Service and the United States Parcel Service are still about the best methods we have. Perhaps facsimile transmission by a satellite will become more feasible. This too involves an order of magnitude, but it may still be cheaper than doubling the size of the Harvard University Library every twenty years.

Mr. Gerletti: Maybe there is an unconventional system that we may have to search for. If we have strength enough to arrange our prejudices, we may find it. We have the knowledge, and I think we have the ability. With people like this group, I think we may find an answer to these perplexing problems.

Question: Librarians have this expertise we spoke of, this bibliographic background. In view of the enormous development in the field of nonprint material, Dr. Dix, is it conceivable that, with the new structure in the American Library Association (ALA), we might expect recognition of this field?

Mr. Dix: I really cannot answer that. As you know, we in ALA are undergoing this year a serious soul-searching about what we are and what an organization of this kind is about. This is not peculiar to ALA, for it is common to every professional society that I know in the country right now. It would be difficult to predict what is going to come out of our own self-examination. One of the problems in ALA is rather obvious: one in every seven of our 40,000 members is involved in the activities of the association. He is on a committee or holds some kind of an office. This is beginning to break down under its own weight. Somehow we must find a way to streamline this thing and at the same time respond to the demand for democratic participation.

We must find a way to make this organization respond to the needs of the sort you are stating here. We must find a home in the organization for a group of people with similar interests who have an idea of what they want to accomplish. Like the Information Science and Automation Division that we established just three years ago, perhaps this is another field that is different, which ought to be recognized as a division or a similar unit within the association. In another year we will know a little better how this whole thing is going to shape up and will see how we can best mold an organization to carry on the interests of the profession.

Part 8

Commercial Endeavors

Those who manufacture and sell materials experience resistance to the acquisition of products that are not adequately listed, evaluated, cataloged, and classified at a central source, stored, or retrieved. Therefore, commercial producers and distributors have made numerous attempts to assist with the organization of nonprint media. They have developed and utilized various methods and services which have only led to further confusion and incompatibility.

Evelyn Clement, former media librarian at Oral Roberts University and associate director of the institute, summarized commercial cataloging of nonprint media by four companies in the United States and Canada which were represented at the institute. The contributions of each have been overshadowed by the necessity to devise unique and therefore incompatible schemes and procedures for the organization of the materials sold or distributed.

David Nevin reviewed the care given television media but found virtually no concern for the retrieval of this material beyond its original exposure. Charles Van Doren described the development of an elaborate system for the production, storage, retrieval, and use of highly reduced microfiche, while Ronald Randall explained the rationale behind his company's decision to produce a simplified though comprehensive directory of integrated print and nonprint learning resources for all age levels.

Alma Tillin discussed the problem of adequate containers for various nonprint media and offered specific solutions that would enable librarians to integrate all media on traditional library shelves.

Commercial Cataloging of Nonbook Media

Evelyn G. Clement

Alanar Processing Services

When the Contra Costa County library began to do centralized cataloging and processing for its own system in the early 1950s, Bertha Hellum suggested that someone ought to provide this service on a commercial scale. Officials of Bro-Dart Industries agreed with the idea, but they concluded that in order to do the job properly, the firm which began such a service should already be in the book distribution business. Although Bro-Dart was definitely not in the book distribution business then, it firmly believed this commercial processing idea made good sense and tried to convince a number of major book distributors to try it out. Unable to convince any other firms that they should begin to offer cataloged and processed books to their customers, Bro-Dart decided to try it itself. The first library that ever used a commercial cataloging service was in Winachee, Washington, in 1957.

Since that small beginning, Bro-Dart has cataloged and processed more than ten million books. It now operates three plants in the United States and two in Canada. Libraries may request anything from single, standardized processing to fully customized service, but they do pay for the difference. This cataloging service within Bro-Dart Industries was established as Alanar Processing Services, Incorporated.

Institute Assistant Director; Doctoral Candidate. Graduate Library School, Indiana University, Bloomington

Bro-Dart was probably the first firm to offer cataloging of nonprint materials, although it did not act as jobber for the media as it did for books. It began producing cataloging kits in conjunction with the publication of the *Elementary School Library Collection,* issuing cards for the audiovisual titles selected for the Gaver list. It also began to supply catalog kits for producers of media. Unfortunately, Bro-Dart elected to follow the guidelines of the DAVI *Standards,* including the media designations recommended in that document. Since librarians had by no means agreed to accept the recommendations of this document as standard practice, many were reluctant to purchase Bro-Dart's card sets.

Bro-Dart began as a manufacturer of library supplies and has expanded from the supplying of cards, pockets, and labels to the distribution of adhesives and sprays, to the manufacture of library furniture. Through its book distribution business it has also become heavily involved in computer technology. Since Bro-Dart opened this Pandora's box, other firms have begun to supply cataloged and processed books, cards sets and labels, and, in some cases, fully processed media as well. Most of the firms follow the abridged Dewey classification, Sears subject headings, and for entry and descriptive cataloging, they follow the *Anglo-American Cataloging Rules.* Many of the processors modify these general authorities in actual practice, based on the expressed needs of their customers or the past experience of their catalogers.

Professional Library Service

In addition to cataloging and processing books and media, Professional Library Service (PLS) is producing computer-generated book catalogs. It also processes cataloging kits which commercial producers will distribute with their materials. The cataloging rules used by PLS are modified from the *Anglo-American Cataloging Rules,* with guidance from the DAVI code and interpretation by the chief cataloger, Elizabeth Pasternak. PLS has a collection of about 5,000 audiovisual titles in its data bank, along with more than 100,000 book titles.

Canadian Book Wholesale

Although Canadian Book Wholesale sells books to many libraries in Canada, it catalogs only for schools. This cataloging and processing is very standardized, operating in exactly the same manner as any centralized processing service in a school system, although the company offers a more general jobbing and cataloging service to Canadian libraries.

In cataloging, Canadian Book Wholesale offers only the ninth abridged *Dewey Decimal Classification* and only Sears subject headings, with the addition of the Canadian Library Association *List of Canadian Subject Headings* where appropriate. Where Sears is totally lacking a subject heading, the cataloger may add a Library of Congress heading, but this is done sparingly.

The processing is complete, and no variations are offered to the customer. The pocket is one size only and is applied at the back of the book; spine labels are placed one inch from the bottom; circulation cards are white. If the customer wants any variations in these, he will have to find another firm. According to Shirley Lewis, head of the Cataloging Department, the principal purpose of this extreme rigidity is speed. The company has found that this is the only way that it can provide fast, efficient service without a reduction in the quality of the cataloging or an increase in costs. Canadian Book Wholesale markets kits as prepackaged units for 10,000 titles and publishes a checklist from which they may be ordered. This list will continue to expand annually.

Last year for the first time a selection guide entitled *Audiovisual: A Selection of Audiovisual Materials for the Elementary School Library* was published. Since the firm is currently considering entrance into the audiovisual software field, this selection guide is a first step. If this is successful, it will publish a revised edition and make catalog kits available for each item selected.

Canadian Book Wholesale Company, Limited, is a subsidiary of the Ancorp National Services. The parent company, of course, is watching the progress with great interest, since it is not, at the moment, deeply involved in cataloging and processing in the United States. Canadian Book Wholesale only does one thing, but then does it well. The firm has quadrupled its business in the three years since starting the cataloging service, Ancorp may assume that the service is successful.

Cooperative Book Centre

The Cooperative Book Centre was started about twelve years ago by a group of Canadian publishers' agents, publishers, and the Canadian Library Association to try and bring some meaning out of the chaos which is Canadian publishing. It was established to provide Canadian libraries with one source for all their acquisition needs. This is a nonprofit organization whose charter states that it must not make a profit. It cannot sell to individuals, nor to anyone who is going to resell the books. This in effect narrows the field to schools and libraries; it does not deal with bookstores. The cooperative was organized so that libraries could send all their orders, for whatever publisher, in whatever part of the world, to one place where orders would be dispatched to the right place, then filled, and sent back to the Centre, which then delivers them to the requesting library. The cataloging department developed because the cooperative was dealing with schools and libraries only. The Centre now offers four different styles of cataloging: seventeenth edition of *Dewey* with Library of Congress subject headings; seventeenth *Dewey* with Sears subject headings; ninth abridged *Dewey* with Sears subject headings; and ninth abridged *Dewey* with Library of Congress subject headings. These present problems, of course, but the Centre is dealing with all types of libraries. It, like Canadian Book Wholesale, has one style of processing. However, according to Janet Macdonald, head cataloger, "We are foolish enough to say that if you want the pocket in the front, or if you want some other variation in the processing, we will provide this for a price." Many librarians decide that pink book cards are not nearly as vital to them as the twenty-five cents.

When the Centre began, materials were processed the way any library asked to have it done. At one point, there were no less than thirty-six different colors and combinations of colors on the book cards. In terms of speed, or of providing any kind of service at all, the service came to a standstill. The books were cataloged, but the processing was up to the roof and beyond. In fact, all processing ceased for one whole summer. Catalog cards were supplied, but the cooperative did no processing. After a survey of its records about what present customers required, a standard method of processing was developed which is now being supplied.

Bibliographic Control
of Television Media

David G. Nevin

More properly this paper might be entitled "Access to Commercial Television Documentaries and Prime Time Specials," since it is limited to one rather small but significant aspect of that very broad topic. In September 1969, I received a letter from NBC Educational Enterprises, Inc., announcing that it had or was going to establish an NBC National Educational Film Library. It was introduced as follows:

> Teachers have long been clamoring for quicker classroom access to important television documentaries, prime time specials and other pertinent network programming. Now with a unique plan for film distribution developed by NBC . . . various outstanding programs of the NBC Television Network will be available to the educational community almost immediately after broadcast—in some instances, the day after broadcast!

The letter went on to list twelve university film libraries where copies of NBC productions would be deposited. If a copy was wanted, it could be either purchased directly from NBC Educational Enterprises or rented from a nearby university film library.

Having had to search for hours through many distributors' catalogs to discover who had the 16mm film rights to which part of which television series (and whether it was

listed by series or individual program title), I thought the idea was a particularly good one. It would be especially helpful if productions from every network were as easy to locate. Since they are ostensibly in business to provide services to educators and others interested in both the television industry and television programming, I decided to make the following proposal to the Television Information Office and wrote to Roy Danish, TIO's director:

> Enclosed is a copy of a letter from an organization funded, I assume, by one of your sponsor television networks, NBC. Although I would hope that the Television Information Office was already aware of NBC Educational Enterprises and the *NBC National Educational Film Library,* I am forwarding the copy with the particular recommendation that ALL the networks, through the Television Information Office, consider the inestimable value of this or a similar solution to a perennial problem facing educators at all levels.

> It has always been bothersome at best to keep track of who is distributing which network kinescopes, for which series, for whom, et cetera; especially when distribution rights have the rather nasty habit of changing hands. The *Library* described by NBC is a very useful attempt by one network to keep much of what is most valuable in commercial television from being *lost* upon completion of the initial telecast or an occasional rerun. In sponsoring

Director, Audio-Visual Department, Washington University Libraries, St. Louis

Teachers' Guides to Television, TIO has performed a valuable service to the classroom instructor in making him or her aware of some of the very significant programming by the various networks. But unless the program can be worked into the curriculum or course plan at the particular time of broadcast, its value is considerably diminished. Correspondence with TIO and/or the various networks has usually been able to turn up a distributor who owns the 16mm rights and is more than happy to sell a print which can be used at a more convenient time. Unfortunately, this is not only a time-consuming task for which the average classroom teacher has not sufficient time, but, even assuming receipt of information in time for use in the particular course when needed, all too often the individual school does not have sufficient funds in the budget for other than rental. The result, in all too many cases, is frustration and ill will.

Not that I am recommending NBC's particular approach, in spite of its many excellent features, but they have at least recognized the problem and provided a solution. As an equally valid response and to prevent possible resistance by other networks due to the "NIH (not invented here) syndrome," I would like to propose a solution entirely within presently existing organizational structures.

My recommendation, then, is that either TIO, directly, or *Teachers' Guides . . .,* as a logical extension of their present services, provide educators with a listing of both purchase and rental sources for network productions, past, present, and future. To be most useful, such a compilation should indicate network sponsorship, individual program titles, and series titles. When 16mm rights changed hands, it would be a relatively small matter to indicate such changes. (Individual distributors would more than appreciate a single, comprehensive source for some of the wares and, indeed, might even be willing to share in footing the bill.)

I am forwarding copies of this letter to several people who have been instrumen-tal in providing similar services for feature and 8mm films in the hope that they may be able to reinforce my arguments concerning the urgent need for positive and more rapid "access to important television documentaries, prime time specials, and other pertinent network programming." In addition, of course, they represent a source for considerably more expertise and practical advice concerning such a service that I, as an "ivory tower librarian" feel capable of providing.

The proposal is far from being the final solution to the bibliographic control of media. It does, however, represent, I feel, a practical and down-to-earth solution in one increasingly important area for resources in instruction and education . . . an area which is presently lacking any semblance of control and which is both sufficiently large and suitably specialized to warrant having its own bibliographic tool. Such control would provide an additional source of good will for the networks, additional income for both networks and 16mm distributors through (hopefully) increased sales, and make TIO and/or *Teachers' Guides* . . . services of even more value. I sincerely hope that both you and your sponsoring TV networks will give it serious consideration.

Those whom I mentioned as having been forwarded copies of the letter were Joan Clark, chairman, Film Library Information Council; James Limbacher and Esmé Dick, president and executive director, respectively, Educational Film Library Association (EFLA); Pearce Grove, director of this institute; and Jules Leni, vice-president, Comprehensive Service Corporation, a participant in the institute. All responded favorably to the proposal, although one or two expressed doubts about whether the networks would buy it.

The proposal was simply that the Television Information Office should develop or oversee the development of a listing of television prime time specials and documentaries. It needs no particular form, no annotations except when a title might be nondescriptive, no specific cataloging code. It would be a simple list program and series title, giving sources for purchase or rental. Catherine Heinz, the librarian of the Television Information Office, in Mr. Danish's behalf replied that this idea had, indeed, been one of their "pet projects for some years." I was sufficiently encouraged by this reaction to spend three days in New York City, working primarily out of the EFLA offices, in contact with TIO, Jules Leni, and a number of the individual networks.

Apparently the Television Information Office has insufficient staff to tackle such a project and is not sufficiently independent in funding to be able to hire additional staff without additional support from its parent organization,

the National Association of Broadcasters, which is, if course, made up of and supported by the individual networks. Despite many letters and conversations with network people, I received one letter (from CBS) which clearly indicated that the sender was unable to recognize the problem even when it was presented directly.

What I had hoped would be a progress report is, I am afraid, merely a recounting of an incident which momentarily ruffled the status quo. I had hoped to be able to report with at least some encouragement, but any action toward a bibliography of television specials is still in the future.

The Bibliographic Demands of Microbook Service

Charles Van Doren

Collections of microfiche on broad subject areas are to be produced and issued with published indexes and guides by the Encyclopaedia Britannica Incorporated. Each library in the Microbook series will be a definitive collection, carefully selected by leading scholars in the field. More than forty distinguished college and university faculty members, preeminent in American studies, have participated in selecting the material for the first library, the Library of American Civilization. Their combined judgments led to a collection of some 19,000 titles in Americana of which few of the largest university libraries have more than 50 to 60 percent. To film the selections, it was necessary to supplement the resources of three major college and university libraries with material from the Library of Congress and other research libraries.

Microbook Format

The Microbook System reduces each page photographically from fifty-five to ninety times, depending on the page size. The publishers term this "bookrange reduction." This range of reduction has never before been used in micropublishing. It permits the reproduction of up to 1,000 page images on a single *fiche*, which suffices for most books.

Few *fiche* contain 1,000 pages. The princi-

ple of unitization—putting only one title on a fiche, except for special material—makes it possible for the librarian to shelve, retrieve, and circulate each title as he would a book. The three-by-five-inch size of the Microbook *fiche*—as contrasted with the usual four-by-six-inch size—matches the size of standard library catalog card drawers, making it easy to file and convenient to handle.

In the Microbook filming operation, each page is filmed separately rather than two at a time, which is the conventional method. This eliminates border distortion of the image and protects the source document from damage during filming.

Readers

Two new readers, a desk reader and a lap reader, each with unique characteristics, make up a critical component in the Microbook System. Of special interest is the four and one-half pound lap or portable reader, to be manufactured by Technicolor, which is described as "the key which will free microfilm for circulation." This lightweight unit, selling for $165, can be used at home or in the office. The reader makes it practical to circulate *fiche* as books so that the use of microform material is no longer restricted to the confines of the library microform room. The lap reader can be used comfortably and can be conveniently carried. The desk reader, being manufactured by the DuKane Corporation and selling for $450, has an eight and one-half inch by twelve

Associate Director, Institute for Philosophical Research, Chicago

inch screen, permitting most material to be enlarged to greater than original size.

The two readers will be followed by a reader-printer that will make hard-copy printouts of any Microbook page. Specifications are complete, and the units will be available in the near future.

As a consultant to Library Resources Incorporated (LRI), I have been charged with planning retrieval devices for the series of libraries that the company will bring out starting in 1971. The plans for the first such collection, the 19,000-volume Library of American Civilization, are now final, and other libraries will contain similar retrieval devices.

Basically, there are two devices, cataloging and indexing. The Library of American Civilization (LAC) will carry with it three separate catalogs. The first of these is an author catalog, arranged alphabetically by author. Each entry contains all of the information, corrected and up-to-date, on the Library of Congress card for the title, including bibliographical information and subject tracings. In the author catalog (fig. 1) the LAC number is of course also included for each entry.

The second catalog (fig. 2) is arranged alphabetically by title. For each entry, the title, the place and date of publication, and the author's name (with his dates) are included, but there is no other information from the original Library of Congress card. The LAC number appears too, of course.

The third catalog (fig. 3) is a subject list, arranged alphabetically by subject and, under each subject, alphabetically by author. Each title is listed under every subject traced on the main entry card, so that many titles are listed more than once. Information includes author's name, title of work, place, and date of publication, as well as the LAC number.

These catalogs accompany the library in both book and *fiche* form, five sets of book catalogs and ten sets of the same catalogs on *fiche*. An optional item may be ordered by the purchaser: a card catalog consisting of more than 40,000 cards which, by computer format, provide one printed *main entry* and added entry card for each title as well as separately printed cards for all title and subject references. This resource enables the purchasing library

to file the cards without additional processing.

I am particularly intrigued by what I believe is an ingenious additional cataloging device. Each separate *fiche* (fig. 4) in LAC is contained in a special envelope (fig. 5) which shows prominently the short title of the contents and its LAC number. The side of this envelope also contains the cataloging information contained in the author catalog. In effect, as the user flips through a drawer of Microbooks, he has the impression that he is going through a drawer of catalog cards—but in fact, at the same time, he is going through a drawer of books.

So much for the cataloging, which LRI feels, and I agree, has been done on an unprecedented scale. Each library will also carry with it a set of what are called *BiblioGuides*. I have been particularly active in the creation of these, and would, therefore, like to describe them in some detail.

Our feeling was that ordinary subject cataloging is done on a very wide sweep, as it were, but that although useful to librarians, it is not too useful to students and scholars. We, therefore, undertook to provide much finer topical indexing for the books and other materials in LAC, indexing that we hoped would be of use to researchers of any degree of expertise. We first drew up a list of something more than 500 topics, or rubrics as we call them, that we felt a priori would be discussed in our library of approximately 19,000 volumes. We then subjected this list of rubrics to an extensive test, reading and indexing a portion of the actual materials to be included in the library. This, of course, produced many modifications in the original list, but we eventually produced a list that we were satisfied with and that we thought would hold up. We have been using it now for some ten months, and I am pleased to report that it does hold up and that almost everything that our staff of indexers comes up with fits somewhere in the list of rubrics and, of course, often under several or many rubrics.

This indexing, as I say, is relatively fine. Whole books are indexed, but perspicuous parts are also cited when they treat of matters that are different from the subject of the book as a whole. Let me explain "perspicuous parts."

LAC 10092

Davidson, Jay Brownlee, 1880–1957.
Farm machinery and farm motors, by J. Brownlee Davidson [and] Leon Wilson Chase. New York, Orange Judd company, 1908.

vi, 513 p. incl. front., illus., diagrs.
"Literature which has been consulted in the preparation of 'Farm machinery and farm motors' ": p. [503] 504.
I. Agricultural machinery. I. Chase, Leon Wilson, joint author.

LAC 10150

Dunbar, Charles Franklin, 1830–1900.
Economic essays by Charles Franklin Dunbar. Ed. by O. M. W. Sprague with an introduction [biographical sketch] by F. W. Taussig. New York, The Macmillan company; London, Macmillan & co., ltd., 1904.

xvii, 372 p.

LAC 10100

Ellis, Ellen Deborah, 1878–
An introduction to the history of sugar as a commodity. Philadelphia, The John C. Winston co., 1905.

2, 117 p.
Thesis (PH. D.)–Bryn Mawr, 1905.
Life.
Also published as vol. IV of the "Bryn Mawr college monographs. Monograph series".
Bibliography: p. 113–117.
I. Sugar–History. 2. Sugar trade.

LAC 10030

Evans, David Morier, 1819–1874.
The history of the commercial crisis, 1857–58, and the stock exchange panic of 1859. London, Groombridge and sons, 1859.

3, [v]–viii, 212, ccxlvii p.
I. Depressions–1857.

LAC 10104

Fessenden, Thomas Green, 1771–1837.
The American kitchen gardener; containing practical directions for the culture of vegetables. Also, garden fruits, strawberry, raspberry, gooseberry, currants, melons, &c., &c. Rev. from the 35th ed., and adapted to the use of families, by a practical gardener. New York, C. M. Saxton, 1852.

viii, [11]–120 p.
I. Vegetable gardening–U. S.

LAC 10031

Fite, Emerson David, 1874–1953.
Social and industrial conditions in the North during the civil war. New York, The Macmillan company, 1910.

vii, 318 p.
I. U. S.–Economic conditions–To 1865. 2. U. S.–History–Civil war–Finance, commerce, confiscations, etc. I. Title.

LAC 10005

Fink, Henry, 1831–1912.
Regulation of railway rates on interstate freight traffic. 2d ed. New York, The Evening post job printing office, 1905.

v, 236 p.
I. Railroads–U. S.–Rates. 2. Railroads and state–U. S.

LAC 10033

Flint, Henry Martyn, 1829–1868.
The railroads of the United States; their history and statistics: comprising the progress and present condition of the various lines with their earnings and expenses... To which are added a synopsis of the railroad laws of the United States, and an article on the comparative merits of iron and steel rails. Philadelphia, John E. Potter and company, 1868.

5–452 p.
I. Railroads–U. S.

LAC 10039

Gunton, George, 1845–1919.
Trusts and the public. [Popular ed.] New York, D. Appleton and company, 1899.

v, 245 p.

LAC 10216

Hayes, John Lord, 1812–1887.
The Angora goat; its origin, culture, and products. Containing the most recent observations of eminent breeders. With an appendix on the Alpaca and its congeners; or, The wool-bearing animals of the cordilleras of the Andes. New York, Orange Judd company, 1882.

viii, 178 p. col. front.
I. Angora goat.

LAC 10114

Hunt, Thomas Forsyth, 1862–1927.
The cereals in America. New York, Orange Judd company; [etc., etc.] 1904.

4, 421 p. incl. front., illus., diagrs.
"Collateral reading" at end of some of the chapters.
I. Grain.

LAC 10115

Hunt, Thomas Forsyth, 1862–1927.
Lectures on the history of agriculture and rural economics. Columbus, Sheppard & company, printers, 1899.

xiv, 15–154 p. charts.
I. Agriculture–History. 2. Agriculture–Economic aspects. I. Title.

LAC 10087

Johnson, Samuel William, 1830–1909.
Essays on peat, muck, and commercial manures. Hartford, Brown & Gross, 1859.

4, ii [7] 58, ii, [61] 178 p.
I. Fertilizers and manures–Analysis. 2. Peat. 3. Humus. I. Title.

LAC 10082

James, George Wharton, 1858–1923.
Reclaiming the arid West; the story of the United States reclamation service. New York, Dodd, Mead and company, 1917.

3, v–xxii, 411 p. front. (port.) plates.
I. U. S. Bureau of reclamation. 2. Reclamation of land–The West. 3. Irrigation–The West. 4. Arid regions. I. Title.

Fig. 1. Page from Library of American Civilization author catalog. This and other pages from LAC are samples only and do not represent the pages as they actually appear.

LAC 10099

American farms; their condition and future. 2d. ed.
New York,& London, G. P. Putnam's sons, 1890.
Elliott, James Rupert.

LAC 10104

The American kitchen gardener; containing practical directions for the culture of vegetables. Also, garden fruits, strawberry, raspberry, gooseberry, currants, melons, &c., &c. Rev. from the 35th ed., and adapted to the use of families, by a practical gardener. New York, C. M. Saxton, 1852.
Fessenden, Thomas Green, 1771—1837.

LAC 10216

The Angora goat; its origin, culture, and products. Containing the most recent observations of eminent breeders. With an appendix on the Alpaca and its congeners; or, The wool-bearing animals of the cordilleras of the Andes. New York, Orange Judd company, 1882.
Hayes, John Lord, 1812—1887.

LAC 10056

Beet-root sugar and cultivation of the beet. Boston, Lee and Shepard, 1867.
Grant, E. B.

LAC 10095

The book of wheat; an economic history and practical manual of the wheat industry. New York, Orange Judd company, 1912 [c1908]
Dondlinger, Peter Tracy, 1877–

LAC 10114

The cereals in America. New York, Orange Judd company; [etc., etc.]1904.
Hunt, Thomas Forsyth, 1862-1927.

LAC 10105

The complete farmer and rural economist; containing a compendious epitome of the most important branches of agriculture and rural economy. 10th ed. rev. New York, C. M. Saxton, Agricultural book publisher, 1852.
Fessenden, Thomas Green, 1771–1837.

LAC 10150

Economic essays by Charles Franklin Dunbar. Ed. by O. M. W. Sprague with an introduction [biographical sketch] by F. W. Taussig, New York, The Macmillan company; London, Macmillan & co., ltd., 1904.
Dunbar, Charles Franklin, 1830–1900.

LAC 10087

Essays on peat, muck, and commercial manures. Hartford, Brown & Gross, 1859.
Johnson, Samuel William, 1830–1909.

LAC 10092

Farm machinery and farm motors, by J. Brownlee Davidson [and] Leon Wilson Chase. New York, Orange Judd company, 1908.

LAC 10112

The history of agriculture in Dane county, Wisconsin. Madison, Wis., 1905.
Hibbard, Benjamin Horace, 1870–

LAC 10030

The history of the commercial crisis, 1857-58, and the stock exchange panic of 1859. London, Groombridge and sons, 1859.
Evans, David Morier, 1819–1874.

LAC 10201

Inland waterways, their relation to transportation. Philadelphia, American academy of political and social science, 1893.
Johnson, Emory Richard, 1864–

LAC 10100

An introduction to the history of sugar as a commodity. Philadelphia, The John C. Winston co., 1905.
Ellis, Ellen Deborah, 1878–

LAC 10109

The Jersey, Alderney, and Guernsey cow; their history, nature and management. Showing how to choose a good cow; how to feed, to manage, to milk, and to breed to the most profit. Ed. from the writings of Edward P. P. Fowler and others. 10th ed. Philadelphia, Porter and Coats [c1872].
Hazard, Willis Pope, 1825–1913.

LAC 10115

Lectures on the history of agriculture and rural economics. Columbus, Sheppard & company, printers, 1899.
Hunt, Thomas Forsyth, 1862-1927.

LAC 10025

Monopolies and trusts, New York, The Macmillan company; London, Macmillan & co., ltd., 1912, [c1900].
Ely, Richard Theodore, 1854–1943.

LAC 10026

Problems of to-day; a discussion of protective tariffs, taxation, and monopolies. New ed., rev. and greatly enl. New York, T. Y. Crowell & company [c1888].
Ely, Richard Theodore, 1854–1943.

LAC 10033

The railroads of the United States; their history and statistics: comprising the progress and present condition of the various lines with their earnings and expenses... To which are added a synopsis of the railroad laws of the United States, and an article on the comparative merits of iron and steel rails. Philadelphia, John E. Potter and company, 1868.
Flint, Henry Martyn, 1829–1868.

LAC 10082

Reclaiming the arid West; the story of the United States reclamation service. New York, Dodd, Mead and company, 1917.
James, George Wharton, 1858–1923.

LAC 10005

Regulation of railway rates on interstate freight traffic. 2d ed. New York, The Evening post job printing office, 1905.
Fink, Henry, 1831–1912.

Fig. 2. Page from Library of American Civilization title catalog

AGRICULTURE

LAC 10092

Davidson, Jay Brownlee, 1880–1957.
Farm machinery and farm motors, by J. Brownlee Davidson [and] Leon Wilson Chase. New York, Orange Judd company, 1908.

LAC 10095

Dondlinger, Peter Tracy, 1877–
The book of wheat; an economic history and practical manual of the wheat industry. New York, Orange Judd company, 1912, [c1908].

LAC 10099

Elliott, James Rupert.
American farms; their condition and future. 2d ed. New York, & London, G. P. Putnam's sons, 1890.

LAC 10100

Ellis, Ellen Deborah, 1878–
An introduction to the history of sugar as a commodity. Philadelphia, The John C. Winston co., 1905.

LAC 10103

Farrington, Edward Holyoke, 1860–1934.
Testing milk and its products. A manual for dairy students, creamery and cheese factory operators and dairy farmers, by E. H. Farrington and F. W. Woll. 6th rev. enl. ed. Madison, Wis., Mendota book company, 1900, [c1899]

LAC 10104

Fessenden, Thomas Green, 1771–1837.
The American kitchen gardener; containing practical directions for the culture of vegetables. Also, garden fruits, strawberry, raspberry, gooseberry, currants, melons, &c., &c. Rev. from the 35th ed., and adapted to the use of families, by a practical gardener. New York, C. M. Saxton, 1852.

LAC 10105

Fessenden, Thomas Green, 1771–1837.
The complete farmer and rural economist; containing a compendious epitome of the most important branches of agriculture and rural economy. 10th ed. rev. New York, C. M. Saxton, Agricultural book publisher, 1852.

LAC 10056

Grant, E B.
Beet-root sugar and cultivation of the beet. Boston, Lee and Shepard, 1867.

LAC 10039

Gunton, George, 1845–1919.
Trusts and the public. [Popular ed.] New York, D. Appleton and company, 1899.

LAC 10216

Hayes, John Lord, 1812–1887.
The Angora goat; its origin, culture, and products. Containing the most recent observations of eminent breeders. With an appendix on the Alpaca and its congeners; or, The wool-bearing animals of the cordilleras of the Andes. New York, Orange Judd company, 1882.

LAC 10109

Hazard, Willis Pope, 1825–1913.
The Jersey, Alderney, and Guernsey cow: their history, nature and management. Showing how to choose a good cow; how to feed, to manage, to milk, and to breed to the most profit. Ed., from the writings of Edward P. P. Fowler and others. 10th ed. Philadelphia, Porter and Coates [c1872]

LAC 10111

Herrick, Myron Timothy, 1854–1929.
Rural credits, land and cooperative. by Myron T. Herrick and R. Ingalls. New York and London, D. Appleton and company, 1914.

LAC 10112

Hibbard, Benjamin Horace, 1870–
The history of agriculture in Dane county, Wisconsin. Madison, Wis., 1905.

LAC 10114

Hunt, Thomas Forsyth, 1862–1927.
The cereals in America. New York, Orange Judd company; [etc., etc.] 1904.

LAC 10115

Hunt, Thomas Forsyth, 1862–1927.
Lectures on the history of agriculture and rural economics. Columbus, Sheppard & company, printers, 1899.

LAC 10087

Johnson, Samuel William, 1830–1909.
Essays on peat, muck, and commercial mannures. Hartford, Brown & Gross, 1859.

ECONOMICS

LAC 10150

Dunbar, Charles Franklin, 1830–1900.
Economic essays by Charles Franklin Dunbar. Ed. by O. M. W. Sprague with an introduction [biographical sketch] by F. W. Taussig. New York, The Macmillan company; London, Macmillan & co., ltd., 1904.

LAC 10025

Ely, Richard Theodore, 1854–1943.
Monopolies and trusts. New York, The Macmillan company; London, Macmillan & co., ltd., 1912, [c1900]

LAC 10026

Ely, Richard Theodore, 1854–1943.
Problems of to-day; a discussion of protective tariffs, taxation, and monopolies. New ed., rev. and greatly enl. New York, T. Y. Crowell & company [c1888]

LAC 10028

Emery, Henry Crosby, 1872–1924.
Speculation on the stock and produce exchange of the United States. New York, 1896.

LAC 10030

Evans, David Morier, 1819–1874.
The history of the commercial crisis, 1857–58, and the stock exchange panic of 1859. London, Groombridge and sons, 1859.

LAC 10031

Fite, Emerson David, 1874–1953.
Social and industrial conditions in the North during the civil war. New York, The Macmillan company, 1910.

Fig. 3. Page from Library of American Civilization subject catalog

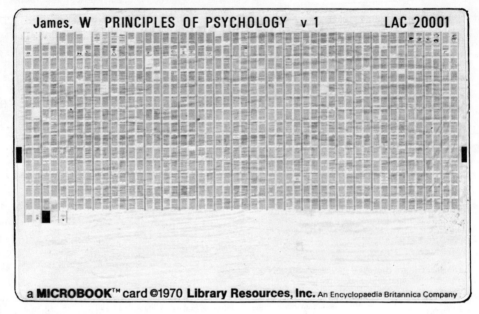

Fig. 4. A Microbook card

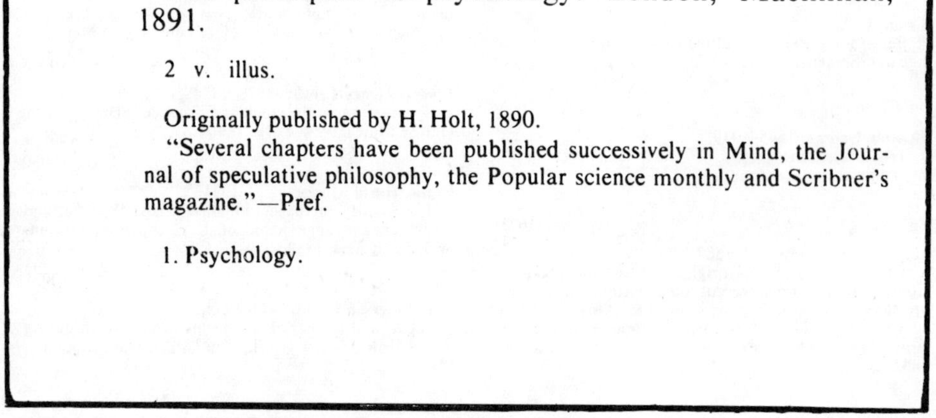

James, W.   PRINCIPLES OF PSYCHOLOGY v.1   LAC 20001

LAC 20001

James, William, 1842-1910.
    The principles of psychology. London, Macmillan,
1891.

    2 v. illus.

    Originally published by H. Holt, 1890.
    "Several chapters have been published successively in Mind, the Jour-
nal of speculative philosophy, the Popular science monthly and Scribner's
magazine."—Pref.

    1. Psychology.

Fig. 5. A Microbook envelope

(18.1. General histories and studies of American business, commerce and industry: bibliographies)

18.1.1.
General economic theory: the theory and practice of free enterprise; the role of the business corporation

Under this heading whole works appear first, followed by parts of works. In each case the listing is alphabetical by author. A list of periodical articles, organized according to and listed alphabetically by their source, follows the citation of works.

The materials under this heading deal generally with the theory and practice of American business. Included are books and other materials on basic economic theory, including economic organization, prices, money, and consumer concerns; discussions of free enterprise both as an ideal and as a matter of business practice, including discussions of monopoly; treatments of the role of the business corporation, its problems and practices; and discussions of the role of capital and wealth in the economic process. Also included here are materials about the general role of the businessman in American life.

More particular treatments of these and other economic matters are cited under other headings in this chapter. Colonial commerce is covered in 18.2., 18.3. and 18.4. and their subheadings list readings about various branches of commerce, industry, and manufacturing. Money and banking are covered in 18.5.; taxation in 18.9.; foreign trade in 18.10. But the most general discussions of these subjects are also cited here.

The student who is interested in the history of American business in the broadest sense of the term should also refer to the appropriate headings in Ch. 4: POLITICS AND GOVERNMENT, Ch. 5: MILITARY HISTORY, and Ch. 6: FOREIGN POLICY for additional relevant readings in LAC.

References

Andrews, E.B. WEALTH AND MORAL LAW	LAC 10347
Atkinson, E. THE DISTRIBUTION OF PRODUCTS	LAC 10703
Benner, S. BENNER'S PROPHECIES OF FUTURE UPS	LAC 10164
Bouroff, B.A. THE IMPENDING CRISES	LAC 10462
Bowen, F. PRINCIPLES OF POLITICAL ECONOMY	LAC 10427
Carey, H.C. PRINCIPLES OF POLITICAL ECONOMY	LAC 20116 -17
Carey, H.C. PRINCIPLES OF SOCIAL SCIENCE	LAC 20118 -19
Carey, H.C. THE PAST, PRESENT, AND THE FUTURE	LAC 10499
Carey, H.C. THE UNITY OF LAW	LAC 10500
Clark, J.B. THE DISTRIBUTION OF WEALTH	LAC 10502
Clark, J.B. THE PHILOSOPHY OF WEALTH	LAC 10503
Cook, W.W. THE CORPORATION PROBLEM	LAC 10189
Cooper, P. IDEAS FOR A SCIENCE OF GOOD GOVERNMENT	LAC 10737
Davis, J.P CORPORATIONS: STUDY OF ORIGIN 2V.	LAC 20021
Dew, T. R. LECTURES ON THE RESTRICTIVE SYSTEM	LAC 13106
Dunbar, C.F. ECONOMIC ESSAYS	LAC 10150
Ely, R.T. MONOPOLIES AND TRUSTS	LAC 10025
Ely, R.T. PROBLEMS OF TODAY; A DISCUSSION	LAC 10026
Fisher, I. WHY IS THE DOLLAR SHRINKING?	LAC 10006
Ghent, W.J. OUR BENEVOLENT FEUDALISM	LAC 10434

Gunton, G. TRUSTS AND THE PUBLIC	LAC 10039
Howt, H. M. PROTECTION VERSUS FREE TRADE	LAC 10401
Kellogg, E. A NEW MONETARY SYSTEM	LAC 10751
King, W.I. WEALTH AND INCOME OF PEOPLE OF THE U.S.	LAC 10170
Mun, T. ENGLAND'S TREASURE BY FOREIGN TRADE	LAC 10154
Patten, S.N. ECONOMIC BASIS OF PROTECTION	LAC 10541
Patten, S.N. THE NEW BASIS OF CIVILIZATION	LAC 10542
Patten, S.N. PREMISES OF POLITICAL ECONOMY	LAC 10543
Perry, A.L. ELEMENTS OF POLITICAL ECONOMY	LAC 10546
Perry, A.L. PRINCIPLES OF POLITICAL ECONOMY	LAC 10449
Phillips, W.A. MANUAL OF POLITICAL ECONOMY	LAC 10451
Seager, H.R. INTRODUCTION TO ECONOMICS	LAC 10442
Seligman, E.R.A. ECONOMIC INTERPRETATION OF HISTORY	LAC 10443
Baker, E. L. CREEDS OF GREAT BUSINESS MEN In [Business: Corporations and Career Guides]	LAC 40048
Sinclair, U.B. INDUSTRIAL REPUBLIC; A STUDY	LAC 10483
Small, A.W. CAMERALISTS, PIONEERS OF GERMAN	LAC 10353
Veblen, T. THEORY OF BUSINESS ENTERPRISE	LAC 10562
Walker, F.A. LAND AND ITS RENT	LAC 10763
Walker, F.A. MONEY IN ITS RELATIONS TO TRADE	LAC 10309
Walker, F.A. MONEY	LAC 10308
Walker, A. SCIENCE OF WEALTH: A MANUAL	LAC 10564
Walling, W.E. SOCIALISM AS IT IS: A SURVEY	LAC 10566
Watkins, G.P. THE GROWTH OF LARGE FORTUNES	LAC 10310
Wells, D.A. RECENT ECONOMIC CHANGES	LAC 10311
Wood, H. NATURAL LAW IN THE BUSINESS WORLD	LAC 10571
Baker, C.W. MONOPOLIES AND THE PEOPLE	LAC 10009
Carnegie, A. THE GOSPEL OF WEALTH	LAC 10395
Haven, J. MORAL PHILOSOPHY	LAC 10521

Baker, C.W. MONOPOLIES AND THE PEOPLE chs. 10-13, 15	LAC 10009
Brooks, J. G. SOCIAL UNREST: STUDIES IN LABOR chs. 7-13	LAC 11263
Carnegie, A. THE GOSPEL OF WEALTH pp. 1-46	LAC 10395
Kellog, E. CURRENCY; THE EVIL AND THE REMEDY In [Currency Question] pp. 3-6, 10-19	LAC 40001
Haven, J. MORAL PHILOSOPHY pt. 2, ch. 3	LAC 10521
Van Rise, C.R. CONCENTRATION AND CONTROL ch. 1	LAC 10215
Walker, F.A. DISCUSSIONS IN ECON AND STATS v. 1, v. 2, pp. 29-45, 405-413	LAC 20132
Wells, D.A. PRACTICAL ECONOMICS; A COLLECTION pp. 235-259	LAC 10355

Periodicals

ANDOVER REVIEW
15 (LAC 30523) Tucker 613
ATLANTIC MONTHLY
45 (LAC 30045) Atchinson, E. 742
CATHOLIC WORLD
45 (LAC 30455) O'Keefe, C.M. 635; 47 (LAC 30457) Cain, J.A. 545
FORUM
6 (LAC 30611) Atkinson, E. 19, 350, 474; 9 (LAC 30614) Abbott, L. 658; 12 (LAC 30617) Walker, A. F. 505
HARPERS MONTHLY
70 (LAC 30171) Ely, R.T. 452; 74 (LAC 30175-76) Ely, R.T. 970; 75 (LAC 30177) Ely, R.T. 71, 259; 105 (LAC 30213) Ely, R.T. 38
NORTH AMERICAN REVIEW
72 (LAC 30138-19) 396; 121 (LAC 30352) Newcomb, S. 241; 137 (LAC 30365) Walker, F. 147, Newton, R.H. 327; Senslow, V.B. 372, George, H. 584; 153 (LAC 30380) Thurber, F. 79; 180 (LAC 30407) Hollander, J.H. 249

Fig. 6. Sample of rubric indexing

I mean chapters, parts, even beginning and ending page numbers when there are no other divisions, and, in the case of periodicals, articles, even if they are no more than a few pages in length.

Figure 6 is a preliminary sample of the indexing under one rubric. This first rubric in chapter 18 of the *BiblioGuide,* which is entitled "Business and industry: taxation," is a relatively general one. As such it is to be contrasted with other rubrics in this chapter; for example, 18.3.1.1, "Railroad financing: railroad stock manipulation and speculation," or 18.9.2, "Internal revenues: taxes on interstate commerce; income taxes."

In figure 6, the number and title of the rubric appear at the beginning of the page. They are followed by a short headnote that helps to define the topic and also indicates the range and character of the material that is cited under it. The headnote also indicates some cross references. Following the headnote appear the references, which in this case are divided into three groups: books, parts of books, and articles in periodicals. An LAC number is included in each case. The citations under this rubric in figure 6 are by no means all of the ones that will be cited under it in the final *BiblioGuide.* Many more citations will appear, providing an extensive resource for any student or scholar interested in tracing this subject through the 6,500,000 pages of LAC.

The Learning Directory

Ronald K. Randall

The educational library of the future will increasingly be faced with the problem of the proliferation of teaching materials and the use of a greater variety of media than in the past. Already the teacher may find a large number of purely educational materials in media other than textbook form. Despite the fact that modern teaching practice emphasizes coordinated use of many different media, the educator has no presently available tool for finding those things that exist in all media to meet his specific needs.

The usual approach to this problem today is to collect bookshelves full of catalogs offered by the major publishers and audiovisual materials producers. However, the collection of catalogs becomes increasingly difficult to use as it approaches comprehensiveness. Another approach has been the collection of materials indexes published by several sources. Problems encountered here include the lack of currency and the need to use a different index for each different media, each with its unique subject-matter breakdown. There are, furthermore, no indexes to such interesting media as games, charts, or discovery learning kits.

Westinghouse Learning Corporation is investing several million dollars in a project called Project PLAN to create an individualized instruction curriculum for grades one to twelve in all major subjects. The curriculum is being defined not in such broad terms as *arithmetic* or *earth science*, but rather by thousands of detailed learning objectives. After each instructional objective is formulated, we select, from all the instructional materials in all media available on the market, those which can most effectively be used to help students master that objective.

We are realistically facing the problem of discovering what is available that can help students learn about detailed subjects. We are searching for all different kinds of media that might be used individually or in combination; we are trying to find materials from as many different publishers and producers as possible; and we are also trying to select from everything that we find those items judged as having the greatest interest-generating potential for the students.

This is a difficult job. As a first step we are preparing a printed *Learning Directory*. This will not be a publication which makes decisions on selection of instructional materials for the educator. Rather it will enable him to discover easily and rapidly what his options are, so that he may spend proportionately more of his time in careful evaluation and selection. The *Learning Directory 1970–1971* will give its user a capability to select a detailed instructional topic and with a rapid look under that subject, to find every instructional item that deals with that specific topic at his desired audience level, whether it is a book, movie, filmstrip, specimen, or computer-assisted instructional program. He will also find on that page certain descriptive data about each item designed to help him choose those warranting further investigation and evaluation.

You can imagine that this is a vast undertaking. We are attempting to produce a com-

Manager, Learning Systems and Media, Westinghouse Learning Corp., New York City

prehensive *Learning Directory* which is not too broad. It will cover just those items considered intrinsically instructional. We are trying to index just those forms of knowledge designed for pedagogical purposes. Obviously we are running into some problems of gray area. We try to include textbooks and related printed matter, but not trade books or reference books; educational games, but not games serving more an entertainment function; materials presenting instruction on a detailed topic, but not materials with only a diffuse or indirect pedagogical intent. We recognize that many items excluded by our criteria will, in fact, be needed or useful in teaching applications, but since almost every book ever written or almost any sample of natural or manufactured product could potentially be used in instruction, and since an index to absolutely everything would be so bulky as to be self-defeating, we have attempted to limit ourselves as I have described.

The form to be taken by the *Learning Directory* is modeled after the telephone book. We will attempt to produce a comprehensive index once a year and then update the *Directory* on an annual basis, completely revising the prior edition. While I may have emphasized comprehensiveness of coverage as a major goal in developing the *Learning Directory,* ease of use is a prime objective in the design of the publication itself. I know this group is particularly interested in how we will be able to bring together information on hundreds of thousands of different items and still make it easy for the person using the *Learning Directory* to find exactly what he wants. We are doing this by use of an interesting indexing scheme which we might label "redundant, judgmental, keyword-out-of-context indexing."

Our indexing effort begins with a review of the title and a complete description of each instructional item as prepared by its publisher or producer. We then select, using human indexers rather than a blind computer program, those specific topics that best characterize the subject matter taught by each item. The topics selected are as specific as possible and may include synonyms or other words developed by the indexer, as well as keywords selected from the publisher's title and description. These topics become the index terms under which the listing will appear.

We are not aiming for a hierarchical indexing scheme, in which there might be some ambiguity about the classification of a particular item. Our feeling is that hierarchical classifications become increasingly difficult to use as they become detailed, whereas classification schemes with fewer categories provide decreasing assistance in a search as the total number of items indexed approaches the 200,000 we anticipate. We plan to avoid the use of cross-references by assigning more than one topic to each item. Rather than relying on such directions as *see* and *see also,* the user of the *Learning Directory,* we hope, will find what he wants where he first looks, as well as where he might have been directed by such a comment. Such physical redundancy of listing under several topics, in combination with the large number of items indexed, will maximize the likelihood that a user will find a variety of materials under the particular topic he chooses to look up.

We are providing identification of what is available and facilitating the quest for further information or samples, but we are not attempting to evaluate or describe in detail the contents or efficacy of each item. We do not think the Westinghouse Learning Corporation, or anyone else, can tell educators which materials they should use in their own programs. They must decide for themselves. Our plan is to help people identify what can be used to meet their needs without prejudicing their selections.

By using computer systems to maintain our files, we have considerable flexibility in updating and adjusting our publication format to meet varying requirements. We will offer many different kinds of services to the academic world, the instructional materials industry, educational researchers, and others to help each group meet its specific informational needs about available instructional materials.

Question: Why did you elect not to cross-reference? It would appear that you must have perfect indexers, who know all the user needs, in order to eliminate structured subject headings in favor of an unlimited range of topics.

Mr. Randall: The use of multiple, redundant index terms for each item, producing a listing for the item under each of those terms, takes the place of cross-references. Additionally, the *Learning Directory* is designed to serve the person who knows the specific topic for which he is seeking instructional materials, not the person who must rely on someone else's subject matter outline to discover what he should be teaching.

Question: If you are applying only the criterion of being "intrinsically instructional" to the inclusion of an item, would you miss a great number of items of value to the specific user who has a broader orientation in his search for information from which to teach?

Mr. Randall: I am sure we will miss many items which many people would have wanted included. Trying to include too much would defeat the usefulness of the *Learning Directory* as much as setting too narrow a limitation on materials indexed. Many of the items we will be omitting are easily found in other listings. Reactions to the first edition of the *Learning Directory* will guide us in our inclusion/exclusion procedures for succeeding editions.

Question: We really need something to help focus our attention on the best instructional materials. From your description it appears that the *Learning Directory* will just present everything offered without discrimination as regards educational quality.

Mr. Randall: We are simply doing one thing and trying to do that well: to eliminate the problem of searching and identifying potentially useful materials. This is something we can do of unquestioned value. People can make their own decisions about which of the items found are the most useful or the best.

Question: Do you have a list of your media classifications?

Mr. Randall: Yes, they were taken with minor alterations from the DAVI [Department of Audiovisual Instruction] *Standards for Cataloging, Coding, and Scheduling Educational Media.* The media classifications we are using include: audio cartridge, tape cassette, or reel; book; card; chart; CAI [Computer-Assisted Instruction] program; equipment; filmstrip; game; globe; kinescope; kit; map; microform; microcard; microfiche; microfilm; model; movie 8mm loop (or reel); movie super-8mm loop (or reel); movie 16mm reel; movie 35mm reel; multimedia; periodical; phonodisc of unspecified rpm, or with 16, 33, 45, or 78 rpm specified; printed matter; programmed instruction in book or special media; slides; slide, microscope; sound filmstrip; specimen; study print; transparency; videotape of unspecified width or in one-quarter, one-half, one, or two-inch width; workbook; and others.

Multimedia Containers

Alma M. Tillin

In the spring of 1968 the Resources and Technical Services Division Planning Committee called for new project ideas to be considered at the forthcoming American Library Association annual conference. In response to this invitation I submitted a proposal that expressed my concern about the storage of nonprint media. This was done in the hope that a practical answer could be found to solve many of the exasperating storage problems described to me by librarians working with multimedia resources. The proposal read as follows:

> *Problem.* The storage of audiovisual materials of various sizes and shapes in integrated media libraries: to design, produce, and test packaging for nonbook materials, made to accepted standard minimum specifications, which would accomplish maximum physical integration of all media resources (book and audiovisual) in all types of libraries.
>
> *Proposed Solution.* Develop a family of standard modular enclosures of dimensions approximating those of books which could be stored with books on standard library shelving. These enclosures to be fitted with various internal removable spacers or inserts designed to accommodate the majority of standard sizes and shapes of the most commonly used audiovisual resources such as filmstrips, films, teaching guides, disc and tape recordings, slides, and transparencies. Containers and inserts to be

fabricated from a durable and attractive material (such as plastic) inexpensive enough to be practical for all libraries.

This proposal was not accepted for further development. However, I was contacted by several people who were interested in integrated shelving and were trying to work out their own ideas. Two ways of attacking the problem seemed to predominate in these designs. One was to modify the shelving to conform to the requirements of the material; the other was to consider the container as part of the material itself, so that the box and all that it contained was removed from the shelf and circulated as a unit.

Since both of these approaches are different from mine, I continued to develop my idea as time permitted. My husband, who is an engineer, is collaborating in this effort. Together we designed a system to accomplish maximum integration of all media resources, book and audiovisual. The name of this system is MIMS, Modular Integrated Media Shelver system. The basic part of the MIMS system is the container which is shelved on standard library shelving together with books. When materials are circulated, they are removed from the box, which usually remains on the shelf, since it may contain other items that are not needed at that particular time. Upon return they are reshelved in the container in their proper call number position. This multimedia container is based on the concept that the physical integration of the many different types of materials brings together knowledge on any subject, even though it is carried in various formats.

Technical Services Librarian, Berkeley Unified School District, Berkeley, California

To guide us in the design, we set up certain criteria. The container must be as flexible as possible. It must have a set of standard specifications to permit complete interchange of modular dividers. It should accommodate the maximum number of various media. Finally, it needs to be inexpensive enough to be practical for use in quantity in all libraries.

Storage is a very real problem in the bibliographic control of nonprint media and is often a determining factor in decisions about what classification system is used and the extent of cataloging that should be used. There will, of course, always be oversize items, such as framed art prints and wall maps mounted on spring rollers, which will require special storage facilities, but MIMS can accommodate the majority of audiovisual materials: films, filmstrips, disc recordings, cassettes, all sizes of audiotape reels, slides, transparencies, folded charts and maps, and study guides.

The box is equipped on the inside perimeter with a series of small notches, or teeth, on which the various interior shelves can slide and rest. The two standard sizes will be 10½ and 12½ inches in height, to take care of 10- and 12-inch records. Inserts can be arranged in any combination dictated by the materials in the collection. Vertical dividers are used for the storage of disc recordings, and there is a filmstrip module. A typical MIMS assembly successfully keeps all materials on any one subject together. For example, let us consider nature study or ecology, with the Dewey classification number of 574. The box stands on the shelf together with books labeled 574 and contains records, transparencies, guides, flash cards, cassettes, slides, super-8mm films, and filmstrips, all classified 574. In addition to keeping like subject matter together, MIMS also permits a one-location storage of items with accompanying material. It obviates the necessity of searching in three different places for the various components of a sound filmstrip—in the filmstrip cabinet for the filmstrip, in the record bin for the recording, and in the vertical file for the study guide. Finally, books and MIMS containers stand together on standard library shelving.

One of the most important features of the multimedia shelver is its flexibility. According to the fluctuations of the materials collections, boxes may be added or removed to other locations to take care of expansion, and inserts may be rearranged in various combinations to store different types of materials. A container of this kind should give great impetus to the use of nonprint media. I have found that one of the greatest deterrents to librarians' acceptance of media is their concern about proper storage and care of the materials and patron access to them. They do not have funds to buy several special cabinets designed for filmstrips, or records, or 16mm films, and do not, therefore, want to embark on building up a collection of these resources.

Both time and work are yet needed to perfect the design of the container, determine its fabricating material, and field test it. It is important that it be developed in cooperation with producers, for they could package their offerings in the same standard container, which could then be used on the library shelf, modified as needed by rearrangement of modular inserts. Pearce Grove has suggested that MIMS might be a feasible subject for a grant-supported research project. I hope that someone among you will want to join me in following through on this idea.

Question: One of the most important considerations to be pondered in storage is the uniqueness of each kind of media itself. Let me illustrate this for you. In addition to providing shelves, racks, and other physical apparatus for storage, it is essential to maintain the quality of film by controlling the humidity and temperature. These will differ from one media to another. What I would question is the basic assumption that these can be integrated in terms of the material itself.

Mrs. Tillin: There may be two different points of view here. I would see your viewpoint as that of a large collection supervisor whose needs are not being met in this approach to storage and retrieval of nonprint media. Of course, I always try to promote the use of these materials, especially by the individual, and would want their circulation to be as continuous as possible. It seems to me that the maintenance of these materials is an inherent problem regardless of storage devices, which seem to have little effect on their preservation.

Comment: This is a case where large collections and those developed for archival purposes have different requirements. However, it is better if those in constant use for educational purposes are stored with other learning materials. Ease of access and stimulation of use demand that they be integrated wherever it is feasible to do so.

Comment: These containers could be used for a variety of different purposes in a media center, library, archive, or large university collection. In a closed or open space you could still utilize this concept in storing a variety of materials that are proliferating at a tremendous rate.

Part 9

Systems for Bibliographic Control

Specific schemes for the systematic control of nonprint media are presented by their authors and criticized in view of the contribution each makes to standards in design and function.

Eunice Keen made the first impact on a broad scale with her manual for the cataloging of audiovisual aids. In reviewing that development she also related it to an active role in the American Library Association and public school libraries.

Alma Tillin provided background information and her rationale for the decisions made in a manual by her and Warren Hicks to organize nonprint media in California. It was subsequently revised and published under the title *Developing Multi-Media Libraries*. Jean Riddle gave a similar presentation for her Canadian Library Association manual.

Wendell Simons and Robert Diamond explained their separate work, with grant support, to devise systems for the organization of 35mm and two-by-two-inch slides. The strengths and weaknesses of both were brought out through participants' comments and dialogue between the designers of the two systems.

Roger McFarland shared the process whereby he constructed a logical, sequential, and expandable system of phonorecord classification. Its limitation to a single format of media was questioned and analyzed by designer and participants.

Revisions of many schemes including the Anglo-American Cataloging Rules and continued work toward a MARC format for all nonprint media indicate a trend toward standardization, simplicity, and the integration of formats in bibliographic-control design.

The Design of
Control Systems

Jules Leni

I am not a librarian or a media man, but a systems engineer, trained in the techniques of problem solving. My interest in the cataloging of audiovisual material is an outcome of management studies I have conducted on the operation of educational film libraries. The clearly defined goals of these studies were to increase quantitatively and qualitatively the utilization of 16mm films by teachers and students. Therefore, I look at bibliographic control as a means to this goal, and not as an end in itself.

Much of the discussion I have heard revolves around the library center, or in educational usage the learning resources center, which might be called a library with an infusion of nonprint materials. The system for handling information in this environment differs from the requirements of a circulating film library in one fundamental way. In a learning resources center the material user must come to the source of information, where he also has access to the materials themselves. This is not true for a 16mm film library, which is inaccessible to the user, and thus a motivational element must be injected into the dissemination of information.

While my topic is within the specific context of 16mm educational film libraries, much of my concern will have general application. It is particularly important that we emphasize the consideration of the users' motivation and the accessibility of the materials as factors in the design of bibliographic control systems.

In its narrowest aspect bibliographic control is the specification and organization of descriptive data about the physical entity and its content. In such a context the utilization of the material is irrelevant; that is, the cataloger need not be acquainted with how the material is to be used in order to perform his function. This approach certainly simplifies the bibliographic process; furthermore, it has worked successfully in the cataloging of print material for years.

Information scientists must look at bibliographic control as a problem in communications as well as organization. As a discipline it must deal with the transfer process, as well as the structure of information. Therefore, the term *information system* rather than *bibliographic control* is preferred, to emphasize the inclusion of the latter as a component of the former. The latter by itself is like a radio transmitter without a receiver.

Figure 1 depicts an exercise in system analysis rather than a proposed plan of action. It is a procedure followed more easily by individuals who are not involved in the practice of the particular program being analyzed, since it is unfair, if not impossible, to expect adherents of existing systems to discard them during the hypothetical discussions that may lead to the formulation of ideal solutions. The evolution of practical answers will be illustrated by application of the procedure to the problems of classifying and disseminating information

Vice-President, Comprehensive Services Corp., New York City

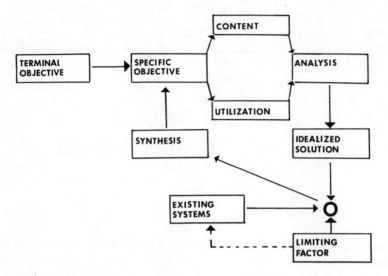

Fig. 1. Flow chart of information system parameters

pertaining to 16mm films for use in schools and universities:

Terminal objective—to improve utilization

Specific objective—to disseminate information in an easy-to-use form for the selection of films

Utilization parameters—to make accessible films used in fulfillment of instructional objectives or lesson plans information

Content parameters — physical description; content description, including annotations, subject headings and classification, and key-concept analysis

Ideal solutions and synthesis (dissemination)—user-scheduled electronic transmission of film, electronic inquiry (direct or time-delayed) access and response, electronic inquiry and mail response, library card file, printed book form catalog, and microfiche

Limiting factors (dissemination)—restricted availability of hardware, copyright restrictions, cost of communications equipment, too slow, not sufficiently accessible, economic feasibility related to number of entries and copies, and relative unavailability or inaccessibility of hardware

Ideal solutions and synthesis (classification)—exact correlation to curricular design (grade, subject, unit, lesson plan), correlation to in-structional objectives (purpose of use), and broad, in-depth curriculum classification

Limiting factors (classification)—cost of implementation and terminology not yet developed.

We have used curriculum-oriented classification quite effectively in catalog preparation. The computer retrieval system makes allowance for differences in curricular structure and terminology. For example, *sex education,* which appears under *personal development* under *guidance,* might be classified under *health and safety, personal health,* if this is the curricular emphasis given to it. The category *communications* is a newer term for what is more commonly called *language arts.*

Significantly, we have been asking teachers using these catalogs for their recommendations on improving the clarity of the classification. We are working currently on a major revision which, among other improvements, will divide the general category *science* into four, or possibly five, areas so that teachers' choices will be limited to a maximum of seven films for a given subtopic. Larger libraries will require a more detailed classification.

It may be helpful to say a few words about the use of a computer in the cataloging process. Computers have developed such a mystique among laymen that many regard them as a panacea. Let me offer a little perspective and clarification.

A computer can perform three functions: it can count, it can sort or select between two units of information, and it can store. Historically, the computer has been used and developed principally for accounting and scientific purposes, where the machine's capacity for nearly instantaneous calculation eliminates hours and sometimes days of arduous manual effort. The early efforts in the development of mechanical aids for sorting and indexing information involved the use of punched cards. Again, the transfer of these mechanical means to electronic means has vastly increased the volume of information that can be handled with minimum mechanical effort and time.

There is one fly in the ointment, however. Here let me clarify some terminology with multiple meanings. In computer jargon the word *program* refers to a sequence of steps which the computer circuitry must perform in order to execute a certain requirement. In some instances those sequences may be quite simple; in others they may be quite complex. A complete set of interrelated programs is called a system.

A system for the tabulation and sorting of numerical data, such as personnel and attendance data, is quite different from the technique required for indexing of catalog information. The latter function is considerably more complex. A particularly difficult application of the computer is to operate an automated phototype-composition machine. Therefore, while many of us may have computer equipment at our disposal, the likelihood is that the principal intended use of the computer installation is to process numerical or accounting data, and that the system in use is not compatible for catalog data handling.

A computer system need not be inflexible if the ability to handle data modifications is designed into the system. One of the utilization parameters for Comprehensive Services' systems is the ability to customize utilization data. Another parameter is the requirement that the catalog be easy to read; hence the system contains a typesetting program which produces camera-ready copy in a variety of type styles and faces. That data bank itself consists of two sets of files: one is the master file containing nearly 20,000 16mm films; the other is a set of separate magnetic tape records for each catalog. These records are

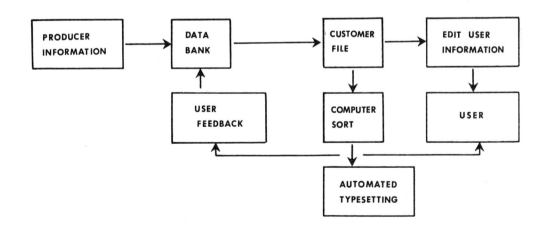

Fig. 2. Flow chart of information-handling system

merged back into the master file after each catalog is completed.

Master File	Customer File
Title and edition	Master data
Producer/distributor	Call number
Release date	Rental (if applicable)
Type	Type
Running time	Number of prints
Descripton	Number of requests
Grade level	Number of bookings
Subject heading codes	
Dewey Decimal numbers	

Figure 2 describes the structure of our information handling system, the automated typesetting process. The content analysis may be designed for general use, although I maintain that the classification must be capable of translation into a structure tailored to the users' needs. The experience factor must represent a constant feedback to the process of content analysis. While in practice we may have to run as fast as we can to keep up with the constant influx of new materials, we should at least have the capability of updating the information we have already.

Any system developed must have the capability of functioning in some future communications network and yet be applicable to the present card files, which, I believe, will continue on the present highly individualized basis.

Nonprint-Media Organization in the American Library Association

Richard L. Darling

The Resources and Technical Services Division's (RTSD) Cataloging and Classification Section (CCS) approved the establishment of an ad hoc Audiovisual Media in Libraries Committee to investigate and recommend to its parent unit the feasibility of developing a national standard or standards which would guide libraries in the organization of nonbook materials. This includes the cataloging, classification, processing, and physical preparation of these materials for shelving and use.

It is recognized that very little attention has been given by the American Library Association to the wide variety of extremely complex problems involved in organizing nonbook materials. Notable exceptions to a paucity of materials are descriptive cataloging and entry guidelines in the audiovisual section of the *Anglo-American Cataloging Rules.*

The committee called an open meeting for the association's Kansas City convention in 1969 to identify areas of concern to the library profession, commercial agencies who wish to serve libraries, and publishers of nonbook materials. Areas agreed upon as obstacles to progress included: the uncertainty of actual needs by media publishers, an obvious lack of standardization in cataloging and classification, variation in coding of materials, questionable circulation procedures, lack of adequately prepared notations on catalog cards, and an uncertainty of the data processing on media utilization in libraries. It was concluded that an early identification of a nationally acceptable cataloging and classification manual is urgently needed.

In response to the interest evidenced at the Kansas City meeting, committee members began collecting and analyzing manuals currently in use: manuals and guides from local libraries and school systems, state departments of education, state associations, private publishers, the National Education Association's (NEA) Department of Audiovisual Instruction (DAVI), and the Canadian School Library Association. Four were selected for close scrutiny because of their wide usage and influence on the treatment of audiovisual materials in the United States.

The Michigan manual[1] is basically a local school system guide, reflecting local practice, while the California manual[2] was prepared at

Director, Department of Educational Media and Technology, Montgomery County Public Schools, Rockville, Maryland; and Chairman, ALA Resources and Technical Services Division, Cataloging and Classification Section, Committee on Audiovisual Media in Libraries

[1]Judith Loveys Westhuis and Julia M. DeYoung, *Cataloging Manual for Nonbook Materials in Learning Centers and School Libraries* (Ann Arbor: Michigan Assn. of School Librarians, 1966).

[2]Warren B. Hicks and Alma M. Tillin, with Mildred M. Brackett, *The Organization of Non-Book Materials in School Libraries* (Sacramento: California State Dept. of Education, 1967).

the request of the Bureau of Audiovisual and School Library Education for the entire state. In 1968 two committees of NEA-DAVI issued their separate products in a single volume entitled *Standards for Cataloging, Coding, and Scheduling Educational Media*.[3] Rather than providing sections for individual media, this national association publication describes general rules for descriptive cataloging of audiovisual media and treats subject headings and classifications. The second part of the volume gives several codes for computerized cataloging, including a code for media.

The Canadian School Library Association's Technical Services Committee presented a preliminary manual to its parent organization in 1968.[4] Subsequent editions have gained considerable favor in the United States and, to some extent, in Great Britain. The Canadian Library Association has since published it in a preliminary edition as its national standard.[5]

The elements common to all four manuals outweigh the differences and emphasize support of the *Anglo-American Cataloging Rules* (*AACR*). Due probably to its appearance before the *AACR* was published, the Michigan manual departs most radically from this generally accepted standard.

Both the California and DAVI guides use title consistently for main entry, departing from the Anglo-American policy of using author, artist, or composer as main entry when appropriate. The California guide adopts titles, giving authors, artists, and composers added entries. The DAVI does not discuss author, artist, or composer as possible main entries or added entries. The Canadian manual follows *AACR*, using author, artist, or composer as main entry when appropriate and using title main entry otherwise.

Another difference among the guides is outside the scope of the *Anglo-American Cataloging Rules*. Two devices are recommended for identification of each medium as part of the call number. The Michigan manual recommends both an alphabetical and a color code for each medium. California discusses and lists both but recommends an alphabetical code. The Canadian manual urges the adoption of an alphabetical code and itself adopts the code proposed in part 2 of the DAVI publication. A few commercial cataloging firms and many libraries use the full name of the medium as part of the call number. While the manuals of both California and Canada give different reasons for not adopting color coding, it is significant that only the Michigan manual, published earliest, recommends its use. There appears to be a decisive trend away from color coding, perhaps augmented by the fact that many libraries look to the use of computers for catalog production in the near future. For computer-produced catalogs the DAVI media code offers the best solution to the need for standardization, although it contains ambiguities which require clarification.

All but the Canadian manual recommend that cataloging for audiovisual media include information on the maturity range or level of the material. Although this information may be needed more for central libraries serving other libraries than for those directly serving individuals, a good case can be made for its value to all audiovisual media collections. The DAVI designation of levels is more comprehensive than the others and can be used as a standard for maturity range. Only the DAVI guide gives a list of items for physical description or collation of nonbook materials. While it omits some useful information, with augmentations from the *AACR* it can supply a valuable addition to a national standard.

All of the guides recommend the use of Dewey Decimal or Library of Congress classification schemes or the Educational Film Library Association (EFLA) film numbers and standard lists of published subject headings, such as those developed by Sears and the Library of Congress. Not one recommends the use of accession number, though the California and Canadian manuals discuss its advantages and disadvantages.

On the basis of their examination of these

---

[3]Washington, D.C.: DAVI, 1968

[4]*The Organization of Non-Book Materials in Libraries* (rev. ed. with amendments; Ottawa: Canadian School Library Assn. 1969).

[5]Jean Riddle, Shirley Lewis, and Janet Macdonald, *Non-Book Materials: The Organization of Integrated Collections* (Ottawa: Canadian Library Assn., 1970).

guides, the committee members recommended to RTSD that a national standard for cataloging issued by the American Library Association include the following elements, based on the most common practice in widely used guides for organization of nonbook materials:

1. Use of *Anglo-American Cataloging Rules* for the main entry of all media
2. Adoption of the DAVI media code as a standard for both traditional and computer-based cataloging. Color coding should not be used.
3. Use of the DAVI designation of maturity range in cataloging nonbook materials
4. Development of a manual for national and international use with a specific treatment of each media, with sample cards, as in the California and Canadian manuals
5. Inclusion in the national manual of recommendations for physical handling of audiovisual media, such as the recommendations in the California manual
6. Inclusion in the manual of recommendations relating to methods of circulation for audiovisual media
7. Inclusion in the national manual of recommendations for classification of audiovisual media and guidance for handling the special classification problems they present.

An outline for a code or manual was drafted by the committee with the anticipation that it be issued in an inexpensive preliminary edition to suggest a national standard or standards for the organization (cataloging, classification, and physical processing) of nonbook materials in libraries and other media centers.

It was the committee's thinking that an editor and advisory board should be selected with representation from the appropriate divisions of ALA. The committee also recognized that although the manual will have a greater impact on the elementary, secondary, and junior college level of media center service, the advisory board should also include representation from all types of libraries and appropriate divisions of the American Library Association. The preliminary outline for the publication of an official code or manual for media organization delineates the variety and complexity of the committee's responsibility.

Code or Manual of Organization of Media in Libraries and Media Centers

I. Preface describing the efforts and giving acknowledgments
II. Introduction covering:
   A. Rationale
      1. Definition of media center, generically for all types or type by type. Focus should be on a comprehensive view rather than to the booking center, as in the case of DAVI's code, et cetera, or other special programs.
   B. History of efforts to set guidelines
      1. LC involvement
      2. DAVI efforts
      3. Various state manuals
      4. Impact of workshops and institutes
      5. Related programs such as NICEM [National Information Center for Educational Media]
   C. Purpose and plan of the manual; its use by types of libraries
   D. The future: plans to update and re-evaluate as the field develops with new media, methods, and technology; the impact of MARC and automation
III. Acquisitions
   Not specific procedures as much as an attempt to identify the primitive state of the art along with some of the pressing problems, questions, and philosophies.
   An attempt to relate particularly the problems of acquisitions to the approaches to cataloging and processing.
IV. Cataloging
   A. General
      Discussion as preface to B, C, D, and E, and section V below. Comment on cataloging standards and standard options.
   B. Descriptive cataloging
      Essentially an endorsement of the *Anglo-American Cataloging Rules.*
      Suggested alternatives such as omission of certain cataloging details, the inclusion of level and other user information.

C. Entry choice and formation

Essentially an endorsement of the *Anglo-American Cataloging Rules.*

Suggested alternatives such as adding certain entries for in-depth analysis, or the omission of certain entries as nonessential to a type of library program.

D. Subject cataloging

Endorsement of a standard list of subject headings and supplements as subject indexing authority.

Where additional headings are required or a different philosophy of application is in order, perhaps an alternative list and accompanying statement of policy could be worked out with LC's Subject Cataloging Division—as has been done for its Juvenile Cataloging Program (Bulletin no.86, January 1969 of the LC Cataloging Service).

V. Classification or call number systems

A. Classification

Endorsement of *Dewey* in its latest unabridged or abridged editions for those libraries which intend to integrate nonbook materials with book collection classified by *Dewey.*

Endorsement of a standard list of classification systems for those libraries desiring to integrate nonbook materials with book collection classified.

Identify other classification systems which are being kept up-to-date and which may be used for application in special collections of nonprint media, e.g., Universal Decimal Classification and ANSCR [Alpha-Numeric System for Classification of Recordings] (for browsing disc and tape collections).

B. Call number systems

Endorse the DAVI symbol codes to represent various media concisely in call numbers on both catalog cards and in machine-readable cataloging records.

Recognize that specialized programs may find traditional book-oriented schemes difficult or impractical to use, especially in the case of the film booking center, the automated media center, et cetera.

Refer to the systems suggested by DAVI, for example, supplying commentary to guide the user of the manual in his evaluation of their short- and long-term advantages and disadvantages.

C. Summary

Endorsement of the AASL [American Association of School Librarians] and ALA Standards which encourage multimedia programs and, thus, imply a uniform approach to the organization of all media and its retrieval.

While the committee may not endorse the idea of intershelving or interfiling various types of media, certainly it should seriously consider endorsing a common scheme of organization wherever practical.

VI. Data processing applications to the acquisitions, cataloging, and organizing media for use

A reaffirmation of MARC as the standard for communicating machine-readable cataloging information for nonbook materials.

Encouragement of libraries to consider in their policy formulation and systems planning the advantages which standardization in technical services can mean in the age of data processing as opposed to the cost and disadvantages of being nonstandard in such an age.

VII. Catalog card format, coding, et cetera

Endorsement of the MARC II formats.

Suggest alternatives such as omission of unwanted detail, the addition of user information such as level of interest. The omission or addition of data while maintaining a standard format assures the widest possible acceptance of standard cataloging and uniform systems for using that cataloging.

Discourage the use of color or black band coding of catalog cards. Offset printing and book catalog and other data processing display methods make such coding impractical.

As suggested in section V B, the name or a standard letter symbol for the media can be included in the call number, in addition to being recorded in the descriptive cataloging information.

VIII. Physical preparation of media for use

Description of some of the concepts of use, the limitations of storage, the problems of publisher packaging, the difficulties created because of lack of standardization, and the new problems caused by changing media and emerging forms.

A discussion by type of media of processing methods, assuming focus on generalities rather than exceptions and discussing concepts rather than the specifics of implementation in unusual cases.

An identification of the need for concern for library and media center storage and display problems on the part of the publishers.

A discussion of the need for standardization where possible on the part of publishers of media so that equipment and furniture manufacturers will be encouraged to develop more flexible and appropriate storage facilities and equipment.

IX. Card catalog, book catalog, or other media collection indexes

Encourage the interfiling of entries for book and nonbook materials in one catalog.

X. Circulation of media

Identification of generally accepted methods of circulating media by type of library or media center. Recommendation for the housing and care of materials and of equipment.

XI. Maintenance

Conceptual discussion of maintenance, repair, reassembly, and related problems in housing a media collection.

Referral may be made here to manuals or specific equipment which can be evaluated by each center or library.

Generic descriptions only are utilized, for the purpose in this section is maintenance of the overall system.

XII. Annotated bibliography and mediagraphy

Arrange by the general areas listed above.

Comprehensive treatment of submanuals such as the DAVI code.

XIII. Appendix of illustrations

Catalog cards

Classification systems

Book catalog indexes

XIV. General index

The RTSD CCS ad hoc committee, established to investigate and make recommendations concerning the feasibility of a national standard or standards for the organization of nonbook materials, has done so. However, it further recommends that ALA create a permanent committee to serve as advisory liaison with the Library of Congress (LC) similar to the Children's Literature Committee that has endorsed LC's new juvenile cataloging program as the national standard for school and children's libraries. While this committee could not set policy, it would have a significant advisory capacity as a liaison between fields of library and information service and the Library of Congress.

The recommendations of the committee were submitted to the Bibliographic Control of Media Institute for consideration by participants and staff. Their reactions included the following points of emphasis:

1. Deletion of the Michigan code as a potential national code
2. Support of the Library of Congress in two areas: proper funding for the cataloging of media, and establishing standards for the bibliographic control of media
3. Support of the Audiovisual Media in Libraries Committee (ad hoc) recommendations
4. Utilization of standard lists of subject headings for subject descriptors
5. A standard code for all media, print and nonprint

6. Cataloging data on cards which would encourage interfiling of entries for the various media

7. Development of generic terms for media technology and materials as a potential aid for the identification and naming of future media not yet created

8. Encouragement of cataloging firms, by conferral and dialogue, to apply their *efficiency* techniques to bibliographic problems of media control

9. The time lag in the implementation of the committee's recommendations, as well as the possible channels for implementation

10. Establishment of a federal agency to combine efforts and to add emphasis to the bibliographic control of media in the United States. Professional associations such as DAVI (now AECT) and ALA should provide the leadership in the pursuit of this goal.

Cataloging
and Classification of
Audiovisual Materials

Eunice Keen

In the summer of 1949, while attending the University of Chicago Graduate Library School, I proposed a project concerning the processing of audiovisual materials. I had previously been a cataloger in the Duke University and University of Florida libraries, where we had no audiovisual materials. Starting work in a high school library, I found that we had films, filmstrips, phonorecords, slides, and a few other items. Because neither I nor anyone else with whom I came in contact knew what to do with these materials, I decided, while at the University of Chicago, to get together some information that would help me, and perhaps others, in the future. I called it "A Manual for Use in the Cataloging and Classification of Audiovisual Materials for a High School Library." Under the guidance of Dr. Jesse H. Shera, dean of the library school, I made a lengthy bibliography and began to assemble different ideas and schemes according to types of materials, such as films, filmstrips, and records. By the close of the summer session, I had organized enough material to have it mimeographed for my own use and for others. Buoyed by the quick disappearance of all copies, I decided to go a little deeper and revise the manual. In 1954, I went to Western Reserve University to continue work under the guidance of Dean Shera. That sum-

mer I pulled together something that was not perfect by any means and did not include everything, but it did include the most important items of immediate concern to school libraries. In the Preface, Dean Shera wrote:

> The period following the close of the Second World War has brought with it an unprecedented use, on the part of all educational agencies, of audio-visual materials. This increase is due in part to greatly improved techniques of reproduction of films, filmstrips, microfilm, sound recordings, and the like. In the wake of these new techniques has come an increasing realization of the opportunities that these media offer for dramatizing the content of the instructional program and in extending the resources of the libraries serving the educational system.
>
> This growing popularity of audio-visual aids has brought with it a substantial body of professional literature on the organization and care of such material, but most of this has been directed toward the needs of the larger libraries, especially those serving higher education and advanced study. The *curatorship* of such aids at the elementary and high school levels has received but scant attention, and it is this hiatus that this (Miss Keen's) manual is designed to fill.

The introduction written at the time gives the purpose of this undertaking.

Former librarian, Lakeland High School, Lakeland, Florida; now retired

This manual has been prepared for the use of school librarians with the purpose of filling a definite need in their libraries in the processing of audio-visual materials. The object is to provide as complete a manual as possible, with explanations and sample catalog cards for the cataloging and classification of the materials which will be found in the average high school library. This manual is a complete revision of a preliminary edition begun in 1949 and published in mimeographed form for limited distribution during the same year. The response to this preliminary edition has encouraged the author to believe that it met a real need and that a more extensive treatment is desirable.

So far as I have been able to ascertain, there has been very little written from the standpoint of a high school library on cataloging and classification of audiovisual materials. There is no standard code for cataloging the materials for any library. Each library which has made a system, made it to fit its own individual needs as much as possible, and it is the ideas from these various schemes, together with a few original additions and modifications, that I have prepared this manual.

It seems that such material should have a common code just as there is for books, which could be modified slightly to fit the individual needs of each library, but until recently no one has attempted such an undertaking. The Library of Congress has in its *Rules for Descriptive Cataloging,* a section on maps and microfilm, also a preliminary pamphlet of *Rules for Descriptive Cataloging for Motion Pictures and Filmstrips,* as well as one for phonorecords, and it is now printing catalog cards based on these rules. These cards, like those for books, are available to libraries.

In 1949, when this manual was begun, I had no guidelines, but I did write to Lucille Morsch at the Library of Congress, who was most helpful. Then, in 1954 she sent me pamphlets which were a great help, a tangible point from which to proceed. One was LC's preliminary edition (1952) of *Rules for Descriptive Cata-*

loging in the Library of Congress: Motion Pictures and Filmstrips.

To continue with the introduction to the manual:

A number of schemes now in use employ symbols and/or colored catalog cards to differentiate the types of materials. Some use a symbol with the accession number as a call number; others use either a part or the whole Dewey Decimal Classification code for one particular type of material, as does W. S. Vincent for the phonograph record collection in a high school library and as does the American Geographical Society for their map collection. Each has made some modifications beginning with the 000's through the 900's. The Cleveland Museum of Art uses the combination of figures from 100 through 300 for their architecture, painting, and sculpture slides. All are excellent schemes for a library for the one type of material only. These would be somewhat confusing in a high school library where other types of materials would be classified in those same numbers, even though they were not shelved together, but the catalog cards would be filed in the card catalog with books and other materials.

You can see how confusing this situation would be, to find a slide on architecture classified somewhere between 100 and 300 in the catalog with books in the library that are classified according to Dewey in that 300 classification.

The Chicago Public Library and the University of Chicago Library have their own individual schemes for these materials, as does the Western Reserve University of Cleveland.

In some libraries the catalog cards are filed in the union catalog, just as cards for books, while other libraries have either a separate card file for them or no catalog. In most instances there is a separate shelf-list file, due to the nature of the call number, while others have no shelflist file, since the materials are not classified but are arranged by accession numbers or alphabetically by title. The Music Library Association has made an excellent code for cataloging music and phonograph records, which may be modified to meet individual needs. Other aids which may be used to advantage are the *American Library Association Cataloging Rules, Sears List of Subject Headings, The Educational Film Guide, The Filmstrip Guide,* as well as the *Dewey Decimal Classification* scheme.

The Educational Film Guide and *The Filmstrip Guide* have been discontinued, but they are still useful in many respects.

The sections of this manual are given in alphabetical order as listed in the table of contents. Each section has information on the cataloging and classification of one type of material, such as films, followed by the information which should appear on the catalog card in the order set forth by the Library of Congress *Rules,* together with sample catalog cards showing the different forms as used.

The section on filmstrips follows the same pattern as that on films, and the other types are similarly treated, but with the variations due to the type of material. If the filmstrip is accompanied by a record, a notation should be made on the card to that effect, together with the call number for the record, which should be same class number with its own symbol, since it would be filed with a filmstrip.

In the past there were many 3¼-by-4-inch slides; now the 2-by-2-inch miniature slides are in common use. There are sample cards for both sizes, single slides, and sets. Also shown is the form of entry for each size of individual slides and sets. There are many different types of entry for the main catalog card for maps, area, subject, and title. I did not include sample cards for atlases, globes, and relief models, as I did not have access to these particular types at the time, but I did give the necessary information for each. Microfilm is not as commonly used in high school as other types of materials, but for those who may need it, information is included, together with sample catalog cards based on the Library of Congress rules for microfilm.

Phonograph records are to me the most difficult to catalog. There are the single record and multirecord album, including speech and music records and the record accompanying a filmstrip. A single record may have a dozen selections on its two sides. Each part must be treated as a separate entry and tied to the main entry card for the record. The set or album should be treated in a similar manner, as shown on the sample catalog cards.

Stereographs are a bit old-fashioned, but there are still many libraries with large collections. A description is given of them, with sample catalog cards. Part of the information is on the front, at the top or bottom, or both, and some is found on the back of cards. Information for stereographs is meager and is mainly the same as for slides; thus they should be treated similarly.

A selective bibliography on the cataloging and classification of audiovisual materials is located in the back of the manual. The articles selected are largely related to the subjects dealt with in this manual, divided into a general section, followed by types of materials included.

Question: Miss Keen, do you really think of microfilm and microform as being, in our sense (cataloging and classification for our problems here), a media? As you know, there is the hard-cover edition, the paperback edition, and then there is the bit that happens to be on microfilm.

Miss Keen: It is based mainly on the original, and there should be a note on the card that it is a microfilm. Otherwise it would be confusing to the reader. The cataloging would be a little different because you would state the number of reels just as you would for films, whether it was positive or negative, the length, and the number of frames. The collation is different from what it would be for books. The information for *Later American Plays,* by Robert Roden, is given just as it would come from the book at the beginning of the microfilm. You have to tie it together in order to know its original source.

Question: In the years that this has been used, have you had feedback about this particular way of doing things? If you were to write a revised edition, are there any changes you would make in the information that you would include or not include?

Miss Keen: Yes, there is one thing I would

add, a section including relief models, globes, and atlases. That is the only criticism I have ever had concerning the information in it, and that was from only one person, a Canadian librarian. I probably would not make any revisions in the cataloging.

I have a record of every copy of the manual that has been sold, who bought it, and in what location. Among the foreign countries are Brazil; Canada with fourteen copies; two to England; and one each to Africa, Cuba, France, Finland, Italy, and Japan. The Japanese who ordered one said it was the only thing he had found that would serve his purpose, and he wanted to know if I would give permission for it to be translated into Japanese language. Copies have also been ordered from Norway, Saudi Arabia, Thailand, Alaska, and Hawaii. A number were ordered through jobbers that I know went to foreign countries. They do not tell where they are being sent, although you know from the jobber that they are for foreign distribution. Montana State University has purchased more than sixty copies, but East Tennessee State University is tops with about two hundred copies.

The manual was copyrighted when it was published, and the copyright statement placed on the back of the title page, just as it is for any other book. Two copies were submitted as required when it was released from the publisher. Later I was distressed to receive a letter from the Library of Congress requesting another copy or two. I thought the copyright was being questioned. I sent the copies as requested and wrote that the book was copyrighted and gave the data of the copyright. I received a nice letter explaining that the writer was not investigating the copyright at all; he wanted the copies for use in the Processing Department. I was quite relieved.

Question: Why do we have to call a 2-inch-by-2-inch slide a lantern slide?

Miss Keen: The 3¼-by-4 inch slides at that time were called lantern slides, and the small ones were called miniature or Kodachrome slides; so I just grouped them together. Now, for the most part, the 2-by-2-inch slide is more popular, and if I were to revise the manual, I would possibly call them all slides and give

the two sizes. If a call number was assigned, a symbol would have to be used to differentiate between the two sizes, since they would not be filed together because of the size. Many librarians told me they had large quantities of the 3¼-by-4-inch slides which they referred to as lantern slides.

Comment: But even in 1955 we were using the 2-inch-by-2-inch slides.

Miss Keen: I know, but I just grouped them together because they are treated similarly, and I used the symbols to differentiate between the two sizes. If you will note the information on page 10 and the sample catalog cards and slides given on page 11, I think that will help you better understand. The Division of Visual Education in the Cleveland Public Schools, where I spent quite a bit of time, had thousands and thousands of lantern slides. These slides—that is, the 3¼-by-4-inch lantern slides—were housed in the huge building. The Cleveland Museum of Art library had thousands of miniature slides—that is, the 2-by-2 inch—so that I got information from those two places on the types of slides.

Question: What about the *Anglo-American Cataloging Rules?* Have you in any way been influenced by the publication of that code? Or do you feel that you have pretty much settled on your program and would not want to make any changes?

Miss Keen: At the time I wrote the manual there was no *Anglo-American Cataloging Rules* published.

Mr. Grove: Miss Keen is retired and enjoying the fishing in Florida. We brought her out of retirement to give you a historical perspective, both on the manual and her activity in the American Library Association. Miss Keen, would you proceed with the latter?

Miss Keen: This manual came out in the summer of 1955, during the American Library Association conference in Philadelphia. I had twenty-five copies sent directly to me there from the publisher. Dr. Shera, my adviser, was the first person to receive a copy. Others around at the time, seeing them, wanted copies.

During a meeting of the Division of Cataloging and Classification (DCC) at this conference, the bibliographic control of audiovisual materials was discussed. When they reached the stage of appointing a chairman to head the committee, my name came up frequently, and finally they settled on me as the chairman of the Special Committee on the Bibliographic Control of Audiovisual Materials. The chairman of the DCC at that time wrote to ask if I would consider such a task. After much thought and consideration and correspondence, I accepted the challenge.

The committee was composed of Raynard C. Swank of Stanford University Library; Shirley Ellis from the Chicago Public Library Visual Materials Center; Helen Stevens from the Library of Congress; and Frances Hamman, cataloger from the University of Michigan. Our assignment was to survey the needs and existing practices and to make recommendations for further action in the cataloging and classification of these materials. In carrying out the first part of the assignment, the committee decided that the best method of obtaining the needed information was through a questionnaire.

First, it would be limited to motion-picture films, filmstrips, and phonorecords. Second, it would be sent only to those libraries that had had audiovisual collections for some time and, hence, had had an opportunity to consider and work out problems of cataloging and classification. Third, it would investigate what cataloging and classification procedure was employed and why it was used. The questionnaire would include a request for sample catalog cards and local manuals of procedure. In formulating the questionnaire the committee decided to use the Library of Congress descriptive rules for films and for phonorecords as a basis for the terminology, because they were known and were the most accessible standards. A tentative draft of the questionnaire, drawn up prior to the Miami Beach conference in 1956, was sent to members of the DCC executive board, the Audiovisual Board and the Audiovisual Round Table for criticism and suggestions. Their many useful and valuable comments were discussed by the committee at the 1956 ALA Conference at Miami Beach. In the fall of 1956, a final draft of the questionnaire was approved by all committee mem-

bers and mailed to the libraries on a list prepared by Shirley Ellis.

Questionnaires were sent to 300 libraries with phonorecord collections, 100 to each of three types of libraries: public, college, and school libraries. The questionnaires were sent to 203 film libraries; 46 to public libraries; 66 to college and university libraries; and 91 to school libraries. Libraries were selected in accordance with the committee's decision to send the questionnaire to relatively large, established institutions which had had the most experience with film and phonorecords. Public libraries with film collections listed in the American Library Association, *Public Library Film Statistics, 1955* indicating the date of establishment as 1951 or before and having a collection of at least 300 titles were selected. College and university library film collections were selected from the 100 largest institutions as indicated by the Office of Education, *Education Directory, 1951–52; Part 3, Higher Education* as having film libraries established on or before 1951, and Seerley Reid's *Directory of 2002 16mm Film Libraries* and a survey of the general catalogs of these schools for 1951–52.

School libraries were chosen from those listed in Reid's directory as having at least 376 film titles. Since a selected list of the largest and longest established music libraries was not available, the size of the cities and colleges and universities was the most practicable criterion for compiling the list for phonorecord collections. Accordingly, the public libraries and the school libraries of the 100 largest cities in the United States and the 100 largest universities and colleges were selected.

The questionnaire was divided into films, motion pictures and filmstrips, and phonorecords, and the four types as they are listed in the LC rules for cataloging phonorecords (preliminary edition): phonodisc, phonocylinder, phonofilm, and phonoroll.

The question "Does your library have collections of the following materials?" revealed that ninety-seven libraries had motion picture films; seventy-seven indicated they had filmstrips. In response to the question about where cataloging is done, we had a variety of responses for films and phonorecords. Twenty-eight said it was done in the cataloging department, and ten in other places, among which were the film department, audiovisual department, personnel and circulating service, administrative office, business section, community relations sections, general reference, a separate catalog department, the materials center in the library, and the state library. In some they were cataloged by a secretary, and sometimes not at all.

We divided the United States into five areas and gave each committee member a list of the institutions from which he was a receive questionnaires. When all were returned, each member compiled a list of what he had and sent it to me, along with the completed questionnaires. I made a complete compilation and sent a copy back to each committee member for further development.

Our final analysis of the reports received from the questionnaires was given at the meeting of the Cataloging and Classification Section (CCS) and the Audiovisual Round Table meeting of the 1957 ALA convention in Kansas City. When we had finished our final part of it, I asked Frances Hamman, a member of the committee, to write it up for publication for the Fall 1957 issue of *Library Resources and Technical Services* (LRTS).

About the time we completed this work, Esther Piercy, editor of *Library Resources and Technical Services,* asked me to chair another committee to work up a bibliography that would be helpful in cataloging and classifying and working with these materials. Reluctantly, I agreed and started the list. Each person on the committee sent bibliographic entries to me, and I in turn made a compilation which I sent to Miss Piercy for publication in the same issue of *LRTS* in which the report of our committee appeared.

I had not listed my "Manual for Use in the Cataloging and Classification of Audio-Visual Materials for a High School Library" in the bibliography, and so Miss Piercy requested that it be listed, along with Margaret Rufsvold's *Audiovisual School Library Service,* which had a few pages on the subject. At this time my manual was the first and only one that had gathered the information together for the different types of audiovisual materials; so on

that basis I became involved in the Special Committee for Bibliographic Control of Audio-Visual Materials for the ALA Division of Cataloging and Classification.

At the Kansas City convention Maude Louise Moseley, new chairman of CCS, asked me to consider writing a standardized manual of procedure for handling audiovisual materials. This was recommended by the committee, provided we could determine that no other was being prepared elsewhere. I was instructed to write to the National Education Association Department of Audiovisual Instruction (DAVI), Music Library Association (MLA), American Association of School Libraries (AASL), and any other organization I could to determine whether any of them were contemplating such or had one in progress.

Anna L. Hyer, associate executive secretary of DAVI, reported that no committee was undertaking a similar project at that time and expressed much interest in the one that I had been asked to undertake. Myrtle Hoverson, of AASL, also stated there was nothing being planned of which she was aware. Virginia Cunningham said the MLA was planning to issue a pamphlet on how to organize a music library, but she was doubtful that it would provide the information we wanted.

John F. Harvey, chairman of the Association of College and Research Libraries Audiovisual Committee, asked if I would be interested in another project. His committee wished to compile a directory of audiovisual resources available to researchers in the United States, and he wanted to know if any members of the special committee would be interested. My committee members agreed that we could not undertake such a project at that time. I suggested several persons who I thought would be interested in the task, one being William Quinly, a member of this institute staff.

I also had a letter from Bella E. Shachtman, chairman of the ALA CCS Committee on Cataloging Policy and Research, concerning a follow-up on a recommendation that her committee study the approach of users to audiovisual material. She asked for some information concerning it, but since our committee did not go into that subject, we could offer no information. She thought that if the executive board of CCS appointed a person or persons to prepare a standardized manual of procedure for use in the cataloging and processing of audiovisual materials, the study of the user approach should be done as a basic step to, and in cooperation with, individuals working on a manual.

I kept Miss Moseley and the executive board informed of all the follow-up, but no final decision was reached, that I know of, before Miss Moseley died. I did not begin work on the manual that she had asked about, for I had not completed all the contacts she asked be made before beginning on the work. For three years I was kept busy on the committee work and follow-up, but I felt quite relieved when it was over, even though I enjoyed it all.

The California Manual

Alma M. Tillin

In between our long and short discussions here, I have been carrying on some private conversations with myself, and I think that many of you have also been conversing in a similar manner. In this personal dialogue I keep trying to find the answers to two questions. The first is, "What can be my positive contribution to this effort?" And the second is, "What specific new information am I getting which will be of value in solving the problems that appear so great to those with whom I work?"

At this point in our proceedings it is evidently impossible to formulate a definite answer to the second question. Presumably, however, I can make a contribution because I am the coauthor of what is now referred to as the *California Manual*. The actual title of this work is *The Organization of Nonbook Materials in School Libraries*. My associate in writing this book was Warren B. Hicks, director of library services at Chabot College in Hayward, California. It was published by the Bureau of Audiovisual and School Library Education of the California State Department of Education in 1967 and subsequently used as a basic text in a series of workshops held throughout the state.

Because of the differences in training and spheres of operation among the institute participants, we have such varying interpretations of terminology that to attempt to assess certain specific elements in the manual which I had hoped to emphasize would be out of order at this time. My approach here, therefore, is directed from a learning point of view rather than from a descriptive one. I am going to use the *California Manual* as an example, pulling from it, and from my own experiences with it, some ideas that may be of value to us.

Why did we write the *California Manual*? For the same reason, scaled to smaller proportion, that we are here today. Throughout the state, school librarians were faced with the challenge of providing and interpreting knowledge no longer restricted to one media. They had neither the research resources that would inform and thereby assist them in devising a method to meet this challenge nor the time that would be needed to conduct any extensive search. They wanted immediate answers because they were pressured by an immediate demand. Although the manual was prepared to satisfy the need expressed by this group and is oriented to school libraries, basically the method it proposes is flexible enough to be adapted to any type of library.

What was our procedure and how did we arrive at our decisions? We used the logic of systems analysis, with each of the various components of the basic system included, not because it was traditionally there before but because it was essential in producing the desired outcome. Additional input would be variable in accordance with the pecularities of the specific situation and would be a matter for decision at the local level. If we were to create a usable instrument, we must identify and clearly delineate the limits within which we were working. If we did not proceed from the known, utilizing skills and tools already in existence, our effort would fall into a nonproductive vacuum. Our job was *not* to provide

Technical Services Librarian, Berkeley Unified School District, Berkeley, California

yet another book on the technique of cataloging, nor to devise an entirely new system which would require an additional complete training course. Our task was to show how to create, through the evolutionary process, a revised method adequate for organizing knowledge in whatever form it is carried.

In the introductory section of the manual we included the reasoning that determined our approach and an explanation of the project boundaries that we set. All decisions were based on a fundamental principle that the organization of knowledge by subject, whether it is carried in print or audiovisual form, reinforces the learning and extension of experience and skills already acquired by students and teachers. The use of standard library cataloging practices as a base is natural because they employ this same approach. Their purpose in producing a catalog is to enable the user to determine easily, and locate rapidly, all types of resources which might be useful for improving the teaching and learning process. Basically, the system should be sufficiently simple and flexible to permit adaptation for varying local conditions, expansion of the materials collection, and possibly future automation.

We discussed some of the factors to be considered in designing the system so that it is relevant to the situation in which it will perform. We examined here matters such as the union catalog, circulation policies, storage, integration of the collection, student use of equipment, accession number and Dewey Decimal Classification systems, and color coding. We alert the librarian to conditions that could create problems, and we emphasize the importance of thinking through the entire procedure and of visualizing the probable result.

The manual shows the cataloging and physical processing rules and procedures essential to the system and how they are applied for twenty-two different types of material. Elements considered essential and common to all types of material are designated, and those which can be modified because of local demand are identified.

There were certain elements which we considered essential and common to the various types of media, such as title, series, and subject headings. Those of you who are familiar with cataloging will note one major variation from a rule established for print material, in that we have adopted the title main entry for all types of materials. We did this for two main reasons. From our experience we found that material is most often requested by title and that the user is often confused by main entries that, according to the cataloger's interpretation, encompass a variety of personal and corporate names and titles. In addition, those working out in the field who would be responsible for this cataloging did not have the time to determine what main entry, among the various possibilities described in the *Anglo-American Cataloging Rules,* should take priority. Since this is a how-to-do-it manual, the illustrations also show the standard form and the specifics of spacing that should be used.

There are examples of classification by both the Dewey decimal and the accession number system. Throughout the book, on the sample catalog cards for all the different kinds of media, we showed the application of both systems because there were too many varying conditions to permit the absolute negation of one or the other. We felt that this was a decision that must be made at the local level. The symbols we adopted for identification of the media were taken from the University of Southern California Automated Cataloging Project. In each instance in the examples, we pointed out optional items, which can be used according to the needs of the user in the particular locale.

The illustrations showing the cataloging of a recording of spoken material demonstrate how title instead of author main entry is used. If a library wishes to keep materials by one author or one artist together, it can easily be done by making a possessive out of the person's name, but it still remains a title main entry. For instance, such an entry would read, "Shakespeare's Richard III."

The manual has been field tested for two years. It served as a basic text in a series of successful workshops. Those who participated seemed to understand what was going on and soon lost their fear of tackling the problems of nonprint-media organization.

From my experience in developing the *Cali-*

fornia Manual, I submit my conclusions about a national manual in the form of the following recommendations:

1. That we use the subject approach to knowledge in designing a national system for the bibliographical control of nonprint media.
2. That we use what has already been established in the organization of print materials as a starting point, that we pull from it those basic elements which we judge to be essential, and that we employ our combined knowledge, skills, and creativity to determine those additional components which are necessary for nonprint media and computerization. Much of this work has already been done in the DAVI *Standards for Cataloging, Coding, and Scheduling Educational Media,* and I strongly feel that we should try to complete the work that was started here.
3. That we use the Library of Congress list of subject headings as the primary source of descriptors or identifiers and work on its revision to make it more pertinent to nonprint media.
4. That the classification scheme permit compatibility to existing collections, computerized or not, and adaptation to all grade levels.

5. That we work closely with producers of nonprint materials, providing them with information and guidance which will assist them in supplying products in combinations, formats, and packaging to reduce both the time and the cost of our organizational procedures.

Question: What does your fourth point mean?

Comment: It means that the major system ought to be a large reservoir from which you can drain off, according to your needs. The reservoir must be so designed that if your need is for sufficient water to run a hydroelectric station or to turn on the tap to get a glass of water, you have got built in a system that will give you the water for both. A system that will run only a hydroelectric station or serve only a domestic supply is not going to be of very much use. We are in the situation where we already have people with taps and we already have hydroelectric systems. We do not want to design separate systems because that is going to use an awful lot of water—and water, in the sense of indexing skills and knowledge about this media, is getting pretty scarce.

Mrs. Tillin: Thank you, Mr. Croghan, you have translated my thoughts beautifully.

The Canadian Library Association's Manual for the Organization of Nonprint Media

Jean Riddle

The work on *Non-Book Materials: The Organization of Integrated Collections* was started more than two years ago in response to the obvious need for some standardized system of cataloging media. Originally it was the intention to set standards for metropolitan Toronto and its environs, an area which is thickly populated and has for the most part well-developed school libraries with growing budgets. However, as research on this project proceeded, it became increasingly evident that it was highly impractical to develop principles only for the school library cataloging world. Indeed, the approach which is now being taken is toward generic cataloging for all resource centers. Our goal is an integrated, multimedia catalog which can be used easily by young people in the primary grades and researchers at the university level, and which is economical to produce.

As the work on this manual progressed, it was tested in various school systems and by one commercial cataloging firm, Canadian Book Wholesale. The inclusion of commercial catalogers on this project is very important. They bring considerations of economic feasibility to discussions of ideal systems of media

control. Librarians in each province of Canada discussed the content of the manual, and sometimes loud disagreements ensued. We have received comment even from the Yukon and from many American librarians. The work is still in progress. We never seem to be finished because new problems present themselves constantly. This coming autumn *Non-Book Materials: The Organization of Integrated Collections* will be published by the Canadian Library Association. This will be the preliminary edition of a definitive work to be published a year later. In this preliminary edition we will give directions and explore possibilities. We hope that in the year that elapses between the publication of the preliminary edition and the definitive work, Canadian librarians will use the preliminary edition to test its ideas in practical situations. We also hope that librarians will write to the Canadian Library Association, to tell us how well or how poorly the manual solves the problem of multimedia cataloging. We welcome, indeed we would be overjoyed to receive, the help of American librarians.

Before discussing *Non-Book Materials* itself, I would like to state its frame of reference. We defined several problems. The first is, how do you organize nonbook materials within the framework that already exists for

Head, Library Technical Services, Borough of East York Board of Education, Toronto

our present large print collections in Canadian school libraries? In Canada, generally, books and other media are housed in a resource center, which is usually one room, but possibly, in more sophisticated school systems, a complex of rooms. With ever growing budgets for all types of media and equipment, the contents of the shelves of Canadian school libraries are beginning to approximate the joint standards advocated by the American Library Association (ALA), Canadian Library Association (CLA), and the Department of Audiovisual Instruction (DAVI). The second problem of organization is the unfortunate fact that the staff available to manage the resource center has not kept pace with its growing media budget, thus leaving almost all the resource centers understaffed.

Therefore, while our parameters extended to the Canadian school student whose grade level ranged from kindergarten to grade twelve or thirteen, we had to recognize that the retrieval system would be used mostly by the student who would receive very little, if any, staff help. Consequently, Canadian school libraries need a catalog which will allow students to retrieve easily their particular requirements. By this we do not mean a simplistic scheme such as those developed and discarded for juvenile book catalogs, but rather a unified approach to cataloging all media with rules that can be applied universally and that can be taught to, and understood by, the young. I wish to emphasize that we gave very little consideration to the implications of computerized cataloging, nor are we likely to do so during the useful length of this edition of the manual. However, to the best of our knowledge, our principles are compatible with computer use.

Non-Book Materials has three ingredients: the *Anglo-American Cataloging Rules,* the DAVI code, and common sense. Because our objective is an integrated multimedia catalog, and because the books on our shelves have been adequately cataloged by long-standing rules, we have tried to apply the rules governing book cataloging to other media as far as is consistent with good sense. We find parts of the *Anglo-American Cataloging Rules* inconsistent in their approach to nonbook cataloging. We have submitted to the American Library Association, Resources and Technical Services Division, Cataloging and Classification Section, Descriptive Cataloging Committee a request for a revision of part 3 of the *Anglo-American Cataloging Rules.*

Until this spring we were using the DAVI media code, together with a Dewey number and appropriate call letters, as the total call number. The DAVI media code, however, was never designed for the card catalog. It was chosen because it seemed the most comprehensive media code approved by a large American organization. We thought that it would be universally adopted. Because the call number must locate, and the DAVI media code does not do this in a sufficient number of cases, we have now decided to discard this media code and any other media code as an integral part of the call number, such as FS 599 MAM. *FS* stands for both filmstrip and filmslip, according to the DAVI manual. The Dewey number of mammals is 599, and we have assumed a filmstrip or filmslip titled *Mammals of the World.* A child who is using the catalog sees that call number and will go immediately to the place where the little round canisters are stored. If this particular item happens to be a filmslip, which is long and can be in a rigid jacket, he will not find it among the canisters. We have found time and time again, when cataloging a medium which is produced in varying sizes and shapes, that the materials are not located easily when the media code is appended to the call number. Quite frequently only the collation tells the student where the item might be housed and this, of course, is not a function of the collation. Location should be a function of the call number. So we have reluctantly discarded a media code. We have not solved the problem of location, and much more work must be done in this area.

We believe that the goal of integrating the informational content of all media can best be met in the following ways. First, nonbook cataloging should be built on the long-standing rules for book cataloging; therefore, the *Anglo-American Cataloging Rules* should be the basis of all cataloging rules. We have satisfied ourselves that the cataloging principles embodied in part 1 and part 2 of the *Anglo-American Cataloging Rules,* together with the classification schemes and subject analysis systems already in use in our libraries, will do an adequate retrieval job. As I mentioned before, we have asked for revisions in part 3 which we feel will bring it in line with the theory in parts 1 and 2.

Second, an accepted list of terms is essential to standardized cataloging. We should begin to build this list with the large number of bibliographic citations already in current use: for example, terms from the *Anglo-American Cataloging Rules*. The audiovisual people can make a great contribution by providing a list of standard terms for the newer media. They can help us answer some cataloging questions. Do we need to distinguish between a chart and a study print? Is it nec-

essary to have different media designations to indicate anything other than physical form? If there is a fine line between media, what is it? There are many areas here that need discussion. We feel that we should accept the terminology in the *Anglo-American Cataloging Rules* and develop names other than trade names for the newer media.

Third, we have rejected color coding because it militates against the integration of media.

I have briefly mentioned some of the points by which we developed the philosophical base for this cataloging system. The details can be worked out when the large principles have been settled.

A Retrieval System for for 35mm Slides Utilized in Art and Humanities Instruction

Robert M. Diamond

Traditionally, the organization of slides has been handled by people who look at slides as the creation of painters. However, historians have become interested and they view slides from a different perspective. They may be interested in the subject, a ruler of a country who was painted two hundred years after his death. In another discipline the armament of the period might be of the greatest interest. So we found that the traditional cataloging and shelving system just did not allow adequate retrieval for a variety of disciplines. To remedy this situation, we proposed a research project to begin at an elementary level with the disciplines of literature, history, and art and to evolve a logic for a search and retrieval system for 35mm slides. We picked a relatively small area that would serve as our prototype, European history of the seventeenth century, but it could have been any period of time and place.

We are now in the first phase of the project, the objectives of which are threefold: first, to evolve a logic and rationale for a retrieval system that would permit the different disciplines to utilize a single 35mm slide collection; second, to develop a prototype list of identifiers that would meet the requirements of the different subject fields (for the purpose

of this project, an identifier is defined as one of a series of terms that can be used to describe a given slide for retrieval purposes); and third, to test the general practicability and logic of the system by assigning these identifiers to a random selection of approximately 150 slides.

It is anticipated that later projects will expand and field test the practicality of the approach reported here. The system developed in this project is designed for search and retrieval and should *not* be confused with a shelving or cataloging system. Therefore, while some of the terms used are identical and while both systems are designed to assist the user, the basic approach of this project and that of the shelving system being developed by Simons and Tansey[1] differ considerably. A shelving system, while usually designed to assist a person in searching for materials, is primarily an organization system for item cataloging. It may range from the Library of Congress and Dewey Decimal systems to the general approach used in the yellow pages of a phone book. A search and retrieval system, on the other hand, is designed to permit the user to locate, with a minimum of time and effort, any item in a collection that meets his specific

Director, Instructional Resources Center, State University College, Fredonia, New York

[1]Wendell W. Simons and Luraine C. Tansey, *A Universal Slide Classification System with Automatic Indexing* (Santa Cruz: University of California, 1969), 183p.

needs. For example, while a single slide will have one shelving or cataloging number, it may have as many as thirty or more retrieval numbers, each indicating a specific element of its content. The Simons and Tansey report does not solve some of the unique problems in slide retrieval. For maximum utilization of materials, a combination of the two systems may be appropriate, each serving a specific need.

As noted earlier, the system developed in this project is designed primarily to permit individuals from different disciplines to locate, rapidly and as specifically as possible, all items in a slide collection that fill their specific needs.

Need

The last decade has seen a major increase in the use of instructional media. By 1962, 96 percent of all elementary and secondary schools reported owning slide-filmstrip projectors, with nearly 100 percent having at least one picture projector.[2] This growth has not been limited to the public schools. Most institutions of higher learning now have instructional support units developed primarily to assist faculty in the selection and use of audiovisual techniques and materials. In a concerted effort to handle large numbers of students, many colleges and universities have embarked on major building programs. High priority in the majority of these cases is given to the construction of large lecture halls for hundreds of students, providing, for the first time, teaching spaces designed to utilize effectively all media for quality instruction: film, slides, filmstrips, transparencies, and television.

Of all the available teaching aids one of the most flexible and most easily used is the slide projector. It is, therefore, somewhat surprising to find that, when compared with other equipment in a national survey, this projector was next to last in both incidence and frequency of use in the public schools.[3] Even in those subject areas where two-by-two-inch slides are ideally suited for instruction, they are not be-

ing fully utilized. In this survey fewer than one out of every five fine arts and social science teachers reported using slides.[4]

A key reason for this limited use has been the problem of accessibility. The number and scope of items in a slide collection create a major problem of cataloging. How can a large collection of slides of diverse utility be cataloged so as to permit retrieval of individual items with precision? Conventional cataloging systems are usually organized under a limited number of identifiers, thus restricting utilization by teachers from various disciplines. History teachers, for example, find it difficult to locate specific slides when filed in a collection developed by an art department; and a specialist in literature might wish to use a completely different series of categories from those of a historian. Therefore, while the slide might be the same, the titles under which it is filed will differ substantially, depending on the specific interests and needs of the individuals or departments doing the filing.

In the last few years there has been developed a search and retrieval logic that has been applied successfully to document cataloging in a variety of fields. The most comprehensive of these projects has been the development of the Office of Education's Educational Resources Information Centers. Under this project a number of specialized information clearinghouses have been established, and each, following an established guideline, has developed a set of identifying terms for use in its particular field.[5] With this process it has become possible for an item to be cross-filed under a comprehensive list of identifiers, thus permitting easy and quick retrieval by anyone using the system.

In summary, this project was designed to explore the practicability of applying this same basic search and retrieval logic to a collection of 35mm slides used by individuals from various subject areas. It provides an approach that would permit users from various disciplines to locate slides that meet their unique needs with a minimum of time and effort.

[2]Eleanor P. Godfrey, *Audiovisual Programs in the Public Schools,* (Washington, D.C.: Bureau of Social Science Research, Inc., 1964), p.12.
[3]Ibid., p.44.

[4]Ibid., p.26.
[5]*ERIC—Guidelines for the Development of a Thesaurus of Educational Terms* (Washington, D.C.: U.S. Office of Education, 1966).

Procedure

Since the main emphasis of the project was to develop a set of guidelines for a search and retrieval system using the collection of 35mm slides, it was decided to limit the actual list of identifiers, as much as possible, to a single representative period. This system would then form the framework and logic for the development of a more comprehensive and complete set of identifiers. Seventeenth-century Europe (Hapsburg Empire, England, France, Germany, and Italy) was selected arbitrarily to serve this purpose. When certain lists were unduly restricted by this specific time period (artists, authors, etc.) it was removed from the general list to permit the development of a comprehensive system.

The following developmental procedure was followed:

1. Subject specialists from the fields of European history, art history, and seventeenth-century literature developed preliminary lists of identifiers for their individual disciplines.

2. The three lists of identifiers were field tested on a random sample of slides and then combined into a single system.

3. The list of identifiers and a description of the proposed retrieval logic were then sent to the advisory committee for its critical evaluation.

4. At a joint conference the subject specialists and advisory committee reviewed the identifier list and agreed on an overall strategy.

5. The individual items and general organization of the identifier list were then revised according to conference recommendations.

6. The final identifier list was, as the final step to this project, applied to a random sample of slides to evaluate the general feasibility of the proposed plan for an identifier assignment.

The problems faced by this group were unique and required a retrieval logic that, while it is being used by research libraries, has not yet been applied to nonbook materials. It was, for example, apparent from the beginning that each of the three disciplines would often use entirely different terms and logic to search for an identical slide. As the project progressed, this difference proved to be far more extensive than originally anticipated. For example, while the art specialist might be interested in the artist, technique, and media, the historian would focus on date of the subject, the activities being shown, and the historical relationship of the content. At the same time, the literature specialist would use the same slide to depict the social climate that existed during the developmental period of an author or to illustrate a particular sequence in a given novel.

A second major problem was the establishment of appropriate dates. While the art field required the date of production, other areas were more concerned with the date of the subject. For example, a slide produced in the twentieth century depicting a battle during the Civil War would, for retrieval purposes, need to be filed under different dates to meet the needs of the various disciplines. The same type of variation exists in identifying the location, with the art instructor usually interested in place of producion, while the historian and literature specialist prefer to identify the location of the area being shown.

It became apparent that if the system was to be developed, it had to have the following capabilities:

1. It had to be workable with various shelving systems that now exist.

2. It had to be compatible with either a computer-based or manual retrieval system and thus be usable in major as well as minor slide collections.

3. It had to be open-ended, permitting individual collections with specialized interests to add new identifier terms easily.

4. It had to provide the capability for the various disciplines to use the same collection of materials without major limitations.

5. It had to be easy to use with a retrieval logic that could be readily explained to the new user.

6. Once instituted, the system had to offer a minimum of operational problems.

How the System Works

To facilitate use, the identifiers themselves have been divided into six major areas selected to follow a logical search sequence. These categories are as follows:

1. What is it—applied art, architecture, drawing, painting, or sculpture
2. Who made it (artist)
3. When
   a. Date of production
   b. Date of subject
4. Where
   a. Where produced
   b. Location of subject
5. Subject (content and/or function, i.e., battle sites, general category of content, type of building, geographical, authors, type of portrait, and type of weapons shown)
6. Collection (where now located)

While the identifiers selected for use on this pilot project are broad in scope and comprehensive, they are by no means complete. As noted earlier, emphasis was placed on developing a logic that would work rather than on developing a specific, comprehensive list of content identifiers. A more comprehensive list of content identifiers will be found in the Simons and Tansey report.

For retrieval purposes each identifier is given a number. While these numbers are arbitrary, they must be assigned and used for simple retrieval. For example:

28. Drawing	31. Pastel
29. Charcoal	32. Sanguine
30. Pencil	33. Silver-point

To handle the critical problem of dates—date of execution and date of the subject—a simple but extremely efficient system has been evolved. Each is handled separately but in an identical manner. Identification by individual years becomes possible with the use of three terms:

1. *B.C.* or *A.D.*
2. Century (1–20)
3. Year (0–99)

Thus, the year *1857* would be shown by combining *A.D.* with *19th century* and the year *57*.

If an individual library wished to permit broader searching by ten-year intervals, it could be done by simply adding to the system identifier terms and numbers for 0–9, 10–19, 20–29, et cetera. When a painting was produced over several years, the midyear has been arbitrarily used for the date of production.

Adding Identifiers

One advantage of the proposed system is that additional identifier terms can be easily added by an individual library or on a national level. For example, in an earlier draft of the identifier list used in this project, the type of media used in painting and sculpture was omitted. The new terms were added, placed in the system in their proper position, and assigned the next available identifier numbers. Painting now appears as follows:

35. Painting
   36. Ceiling (dome)
   37. Miniature
   38. Mural (wall)
   39. Portable
   Media
      668. Oil
      669. Tempera
      670. Watercolor
      671. Other

By this process specialized collections can add detailed identifiers to meet their unique needs, and new terms, as they become accepted, can also be included. It should be noted, however, that experiences with other retrieval systems have indicated that the fewer the number of terms in a system, the easier it is for most individuals to use.

Placing a Slide in the System

Upon acquisition each slide is assigned the maximum number of identifier terms that describe its characteristics. For example, a hypothetical oil portrait of the French king Francis II (1559–60) produced in 1665 by the Spanish artist Alonso Caro might be assigned the following terms (For the purpose of this example, the king is dressed in his regalia and some of the regal jewelry is clearly pictured.):

3. Clothing	376. 59
7. Jewelry	422. Europe and Medi-
35. Painting	terranean Basin
668. Oil	(production
147. Alonso Caro	location)
174. A.D.	430. Iberian Peninsula
191. 17th century	455. Europe and Medi-
260. 65	terranean Basin
296. A.D.	(subject location)
312. 16th century	460. Gaul/France
	499. Figure
	500. Kings and execu-
	tives
	586. Portrait
	587. Single
	516. British Museum,
	London

In the above example the identifiers *174* (A.D.), *191* (17th century), and *260* (65) combine to give the date of production, 1665. The next three identifiers—*296* (A.D.), *312* (16th century), and *376* (59)—convey the date of the subject, 1559. If Francis II had played a key role in a piece of poetry (560) written in sonnet form (563) by Lesage (547), these additional terms would have been added.

To assure proper assignment of identifiers, it is proposed that a specialist from each of the fields of art, history, and literature be involved in the assignment process for each slide in the collection.

Slide Retrieval

The logic of locating slides in a collection is relatively simple with this technique. An art historian wishing to find all aerial views of cathedral domes built in France during the seventeenth century would simply combine *18* (aerial view), *19* (domes), 174 (A.D.), *191* (*17th century*), *427* (*Gaul/France*), and *491* (*churches and temples*). A historian seeking illustrations of transportation used in the cities during the same period would use the date of the subject identifiers A.D., (296), *17th century* (313), plus *cities, towns, and villages* (494), and *transportation* (597). A specialist in literature would combine the name of the author and the term *portrait* (586) to locate any slides of the individual in question. The major advantage of this system is that it per-

mits the user to utilize any combination of terms he requires to locate all the slides in the collection that meet his specific needs.

This approach is designed to work with either a computer-based or manual retrieval system. In a computerized system the user would simply type in his list of identifiers, *18-19-174-191-427-491* (for our art historian seeking aerial views of 17th-century cathedral domes), and the computer would print out a list of all slides in the collection that meet his requirements. The printout could simply be a shelving number and title or could include additional descriptive information. Several members of the advisory committee felt that having available to the user the complete list of identifiers under which a slide is cataloged would provide an additional instructional function proving particularly valuable to those using the collection for research purposes.

While less sophisticated, the alternative manual, or optical retrieval, system does permit almost every slide library to install an operational retrieval system within the range of most budgets. The total cost of equipment for most systems of this type is less than $2,000. In an optical system a series of identifier cards is combined to indicate those slides in the system which meet the user's requirements. There are two major limitations of the manual retrieval system. First, since each identifier card can accommodate a maximum of 10,000 items, larger collections require subdivision. Second, since only numbers can be used for individual slide identification, the system requires either that the slides be numbered by acquisition or that a system be available to translate the numbers used in the optical retrieval system to the shelving system used in the collection.

Conclusions

1. Slide collections should be broad in concept and not be limited to a single subject area, since the slides tend to have application in more than one discipline.
2. The application of retrieval logic in a multidisciplinary collection of slides serving art, literature, and history is possible and practical.
3. Differences between disciplines regarding terms used in slide content identification

were far greater than previously believed, with less duplication than first anticipated.

4. These differences, although very real, will not inhibit the implementation of a retrieval system, even though the development sequence of identifier terms must be modified to ensure inclusion of terms designed to meet the need of each discipline.

5. A slide collection will have maximum utilization only when it is designed to permit the user to locate items using the terminology he is familiar with.

6. The search and retrieval system and logic developed in this project will facilitate maximum collection utilization by:

    a. Permitting a user to locate, with a minimum of time and effort, those slides in a collection that meet his individual needs.

    b. Permitting individuals from different subject fields to utilize the terminology of their own disciplines.

    In addition, the system is easy to use, compatible with any shelving or cataloging system, and designed for use with either a computerized or manual retrieval system.

7. Further refinement of the identifier lists is desired and will entail many hours of expert opinion, extensive cross-referencing, professional validation, and extensive data searching.

Recommendations

The 35mm slide is a major instructional resource serving teachers, students, and researchers. Cataloging and retrieving problems have, however, seriously limited utilization, with most collections designed to serve only a small portion of the potential users. The following recommendations are made to facilitate maximum utilization of these collections with a minimum of duplicated effort:

1. A national interdisciplinary system of slide labeling and shelving be established for use by both libraries and commercial publishers.

2. A national list of content identifiers be established along the guidelines and logic developed in this project, and all the disciplines using slide collections be involved in the developing of this list.

3. To facilitate utilization, separate identifier lists be developed for those collections that lend themselves to separation (Far Eastern, primitive, etc.).

4. Before national adoption, the filing, search, and retrieval systems be field tested in representative collections serving different populations.

5. After establishment of an accepted list of identifiers, a series of cooperative projects be supported to assign identifiers to individual slides and collections and to produce guides that would include shelving numbers and specific identifier assignments.

Question: Did you spend an inordinate amount of time on this project?

Mr. Diamond: No, it went very fast after we compiled the identifier terms. Although the number of people you can have look at each slide is limitless, we decided upon two in each discipline. They proceeded quickly once they knew the identifiers in the system. Work really progressed much faster than I had originally anticipated. It saved time and worked more smoothly to begin with the artists, who then passed their identifier list on to the historians, who in turn gave everything to the literature specialists. This progression was particularly important, for many categories overlap with each other.

Question: What is the size of your slide collection?

Mr. Diamond: The project has not been used on the State College at Fredonia's slide collection. It was a pilot study. The purpose of the project was to evolve a logic that would be applicable to all collections. We just ran 150 slides through the project to see what would happen, and we were pleased with the outcome.

Question: If a standard list was made up, it would not take a group of people to look at every slide, would it?

Mr. Diamond: No, although you would want the different disciplines involved. The discipline representatives only have to look at the slides once.

Question: Would this effort be cut down with some kind of agreed-upon list?

Mr. Diamond: No, we have an agreed-upon

list. The problem is that when literature people, for example, examine a slide, they may come up with identifiers based on the relationship of the characters in it. Art and history people often would not know what they were talking about. We need someone in each discipline who now knows its terms and can apply them to slide analysis.

Question: Is this not more the exception than the rule? Could it be done later if someone looking through your collection says, "There is a new identifier for you"?

Comment: The most expensive way of inputting into the system is piecemeal after you have done the identifying.

Comment: That is to be expected, but if it arises later, put it in.

Mr. Diamond: No. I mean, look at it at the time, because putting it in later means retrieving all the data you have, all the records you have already made to add one extra piece of information. It is even more expensive to have the computer search through a highly structured file within the computer memory or storage to alter an item already held in the system. There is no cheap way of adding information after the initial entry. We ran into this problem in our media library. We finally agreed to concentrate on current items and forego the computerization of earlier materials.

Comment: And what was the cost of your slide project?

Mr. Diamond: The entire Office of Education project cost less than $8,000. We got a lot for the money by using a graduate student under the direction of a faculty member as the discipline representative. It took the literature people the least time to view these 150 slides, a little longer for history, and somewhat longer for art. Art had more representatives than history and literature, but the amount of time spent in this area was surprisingly short.

Question: For the enlightenment of others, would you just assume that you are the user coming in to locate something and run through the actual process?

Mr. Diamond: First, you become familiar with the identifier system's logic. We have a circular file with entry strips in it that a person would come in and run very rapidly through

to see what the categories are. We are just setting up our entire slide system.

Question: You say "entire slide system." How many slides do you have?

Mr. Diamond: I have broken our collections down into potential 10,000-item elements because I may want to use the manual retrieval system, and I have done this arbitrarily and made many errors.

First, the patron must identify the correct broad category, or identifier, each with its own card. He would then go and pull out the cards. To identify those with the particular combination he wishes, he puts them on the light box and the light will come through the holes of those cards that bear the identifiers he has selected. This is the manual approach, which is quite inexpensive.

With the computer facility you punch in the numbers, and a previously written program instructs the machinery to search its system. To demonstrate the process, assume an interest in oil painting, an oil painting on a ceiling to be fancy; you might pull out *668* or another. For the computer system I would put the data into the computer for a printout of what I wanted.

Question: How do you have your slides physically housed?

Mr. Diamond: I have not gotten into this element of the system.

Comment: It is relatively unimportant. You can house them in boxes.

Mr. Diamond: Our slide collection has been put into three-ring binders with the plastic sheets to make it available for browsing.

Question: I still want it clear how you locate your 10,000 slides. Do you expect to generate, in addition to your identifier cards, 10,000 additional cards?

Mr. Diamond: No, a slide is shelved in the optical retrieval system by acquisition numbers within the established categories. The next slide is given the next sequential number. When the cards are put together, a light will show through a grid which refers to the shelving number.

Question: Could there be two slides at that number?

Mr. Diamond: Each one of these identifier cards is good for 10,000 items.

Question: Were you not insisting on a unified catalog for the search of all nonprint media?

Mr. Diamond: No, we type a single card for each search. We also type an author card and a title card. But the search card contains a list of all the identifiers that have been given to a particular item in the collection. The artists like this very much, because a student can take a slide to study it along with the search card to see all the different identifiers that have been given to that particular slide. It becomes an instructional process to teach something about the slide.

Comment: Now one of the things you asked for was an agreed-upon list of descriptors, covering a wide range of subjects, to be regularly updated by consensus of the people using the material. It already exists. That is exactly what the Universal Decimal Classification (UDC) is, a classified list of subject terms which has a machinery and, in fact, an interational machinery for bringing together and updating the thing. It is in enormous detail, but, with indexes, you can get at it. This is a list of descriptors and not applied UDC notation.

Question: Have you integrated any of this material into a centralized catalog?

Mr. Diamond: We are looking at the slide element only. My own feeling is that I would like anything on any nonbook materials in the card catalog.

Question: How would you put this in the card catalog?

Mr. Diamond: You would use whatever traditional card cataloging system you have, for you probably could not have this large a number of identifiers in the basic card file system. That is why we have evolved this alternative approach to slide management.

Comment: In fact, the physical forms are incompatible, but it is only the physical forms. If you have your data within a computer, you can, using the same system or a similar one, take books and feed the information from them directly into that store in the computer; there the two physical forms can meet. The computer can print out any information you design the program to give.

Question: Do you find that most of your use is from the faculty?

Mr. Diamond: Our collection is designed primarily for student and faculty use, but members of the faculty are our major users.

Question: About the question of authority, I assume that you are naming faculty members as your resource people.

Mr. Diamond: We brought in nationally known authorities in each discipline.

Question: Well now, are these authorities so recognized that if disputed elsewhere, you could defend the choices made?

Mr. Diamond: I do not know a recognized authority who would not be disputed somewhere. I suggested top people in the field be brought together to evolve something to which the field would agree. Our identifier list has holes in it and needs modification. Although this change is important, our purpose on this project was not to analyze an identifier list but to bring into existence a system with a logic that works, and I think that we have done this.

Question: Did you determine the overall cost of processing each slide and a per item cost?

Mr. Diamond: No, I think that a national project should include this with perhaps other analysis, too. It was relatively inexpensive the way we were doing it, but I cannot vouch for the accuracy or actual cost. One publisher has remarked that if we come out with an identifier list on the slide, he will publish a document for each slide with its identifier list.

Comment: The cost of indexing is a combinaton of two factors. One is the skill of the indexer. If you are going to hire national art experts to identify them, their salaries are going to come pretty high, and the second factor is the time that they spend on it. If the indexer is a national art expert, he will spend less time on indexing than somebody straight out of library school, who would have to go to an authority or authority file. Against that, the chap out of library school will receive much less money. Actually, someone who has been indexing slides for six months, even if he began with very little information, will, through the constant use of a deep indexing process and the use of tools that are provided, become something of an expert on indexing art slides. If you insist on an authority, the cost is going to be pretty high. If, in fact, you settle on indexing skills, you can purchase them more cheaply. I am talking now in English terms, for in Great Britain you lose out on the formal authority approach. You cannot say professors X and Y agreed on this, and it is, therefore, the proper identifier for professor Z and his students to use.

Comment: Most of the basic data that you need is already available for you on the slide. You do not need a level of sophistication for this problem.

Mr. Diamond: There are certain things that have limited characteristics and applications, such as the transparency project with which we are also dealing. It is a specialized retrieval system. I find that when you get into larger elements, such as motion pictures, you need a broader characterization. Slides are much easier to handle.

Comment: Could I disagree slightly with that? This is the depth of indexing and has nothing to do with characterization unless you mean to use both terms in the same sense. So it takes you five minutes to index a slide in depth. To index a film to the same standard is going to take you two, three, or four hours, but once you have indexed to that standard, you have the indexing materials, and this kind of machinery will cover it quite easily. You can certainly coordinate it.

Comment: You are fully turned around here. A motion picture is going to take two or three hours, for you must look at the picture, study it, and get it properly indexed before you put the data into a system. This is not feasible when it comes to the type of work the audiovisual specialists are doing. We are charged with the responsibility of getting a list out as quickly as we can of all of the material that we have in hand.

Comment: The implication here is that we are spending too little time and money to come up with a real quality project.

Comment: I was only making a quite technical point. The two systems were quite compatible, but to make them acceptable, we are going to have cost effectiveness.

Comment: We talk about all these grand plans of doing things, but are we going to be able to implement them?

Comment: Not unless we are willing to pay for the in-depth indexing.

Mr. Diamond: The one purpose our committee now has is to try and coordinate a group of nationally interested people to move in this direction on a major project. We have too much activity going on with little or no coordination. A Title III project in California was mentioned to me by your institute director. I did not know about the Simons project in California until about halfway through my project. Only through a well-coordinated and supported national group can this complex task be properly carried out.

Comment: A United States Office of Education representative telephoned just recently concerning a research proposal for the evaluation of materials in community colleges. It seems that four or five persons had submitted a project, and he wanted it evaluated. I immediately picked up the telephone and in one call got what was needed. In California during the last ten years, a group has viewed and evaluated 17,000 films and come up with a catalog on more than 7,000. This example demonstrates the need for a formal organization to coordinate the wealth of literature and research available so we will not be reinventing these things again and again. That one telephone call stopped a federal effort to once again evaluate community college films.

Question: Do you see any basic difference between what you call identifiers for slides and subject headings on regular catalog cards?

Comment: The identifiers are single concepts with no relationship built into them. You say "king, 15th century, 65." A subject heading is almost invariably, unless it is entirely simple, not a relationship, but coordinated. It is *Kings, England*. Now that is two concepts. Here it will be split into *Kings* and *England*.

Comment: Take a very elementary example, *The Book of the States*, which is a commonly known book found in every junior-senior high library. It lists the birds, the flags, the flowers, and some twenty other subject headings that are listed on the card. Is there any basic difference between this and a listing of your slide identifiers?

Mr. Diamond: The difference is in the way they are used within the retrieval logic. There may be 100 percent agreement, additional terms may be used, or some of the terms not used. The difference is in how the user goes about locating it. Does he utilize the random or specific approach to information? The second step is to use them at random in any combination for identifiers.

Comment: What I think did not come out here that had been mentioned earlier was that in this type of identifier list there is no hierarchy.

Mr. Diamond: No. If you say that, you are thinking of numbering systems, because this becomes a numbering system. This means then that under each one of these subject heading lists, you must have a complete numbering system. With the thought of helping the user, we have picked up six major categories. We have come up with a system so you can scan and locate the identifier terms you want to use. Two terms came in later, and they logically belonged in the system so we just added them. It makes no difference what the identifier term numbers are.

Comment: The fact that you are doing it manually means that you do not even need a number on it.

Mr. Diamond: Yes, but the number is to help you locate the card in the deck.

Comment: The system is a good one, and would certainly work on the lion's share of things, but the major pitfall with this kind of system is that as your terms grow, you get the problems of terminology control. It is fine if you have a short list of terms so that you can spot the word *kings,* but if someone tends to think in terms of monarchs, they look for *monarchs.* If it is not there and they do not think of *kings,* the material is just as effectively lost; so you must build in some method of control of synonyms.

Mr. Diamond: Well, I can cheat on this one, for the project was designed for the seventeenth century, when there were no presidents. Seriously, it is one of the fallacies, and I have a retrieval list of these terms. Decisions are made every minute when you are working on terms—dropping some, adding others, or inserting synonyms. I hope that an agreement will evolve from this meeting to go into a national project and take, perhaps, initially, the collection of slides on America, because it is limited in years, depth, and scope. Iden-

tifier terms would be set up, the slides would be put in the system, and the program would be installed in public libraries, colleges, and public schools to see what happens when people try to use the system to locate material in the 35mm slide format. This is a type of field testing that would demonstrate the value of the retrieval system.

We did a similar program in psychology on terminology with cartoons and were field testing it when it became apparent that one of our study groups was quite upset. Without realizing it we had built in a branch that put the group out of the activity, and it never got back into the main program. If we had not field tested it, we would certainly have been shot down.

Still, we have to start somewhere, and so I favor taking something definable that people will endorse and experiment for results. If it works, you have data with which to approach the next aspect of the problem. When one programs for the first time, he makes many assumptions about students that are completely invalid. When that error is recognized, he can make more realistic assessments the next time. After a while, he becomes more efficient in what he is doing.

Question: You said that you got very effective utilization by your faculty members, but did you give them personal instructions on how to use the system?

Mr. Diamond: We are getting a very high utilization on a shelving system we have evolved that is pretty specific. It helps people from all disciplines locate items in it.

Question: You have designed a system that is appropriate for use within your framework, but I wonder, as does Helen Britton, could this be field tested in a public library without giving personal instruction on utilization?

Mr. Diamond: For our retrieval system in research, one must acquaint himself with a single sheet of operational instructions and he is ready to begin. We have not given the faculty an orientation program on this.

Comment: Our biggest problem with its use in a public library would be the loss of a descriptor card, with data from possibly 240 slides punched into it. Patrons might not return it, misfile it, or step on it, and if so, we would be in considerable difficulty. A backup system might be required under these circumstances.

Comment: What is the limit of field testing? We have done more than three hundred catalogs based on certain systems. What percentage of these customers must you please to claim success? Some people who have done four or five catalogs and field tested them get the response that they have a great system. What do you consider accurate field testing?

Mr. Diamond: When we were working on behavioral objectives in program instruction, we felt that we had been successful when we reached the behavioral objectives we were after. My behavioral objectives in this system are that people coming in can locate what they are after in a reasonable amount of time and get what is there. Unless they can do this, we have no workable system. In some cases we can field test in a very small population and assume we are successful if we have no problems at all. In others we must keep revising. Rapidly changing terminology creates a problem we are going to have continually which will require modifications on a regular basis.

Question: In view of what you have done and what we are thinking about here—a national group getting together and making decisions on how to do this, that, and the other —do you see this project as having made a real contribution, and helping with the national decision that we have to make?

Comment: That is not fair. The speakers are, in fact, presenting the evidence. We really cannot ask them to give the verdict as well.

Mr. Diamond: I am not sure in my own mind what bibliographic control of media means. What I would like to see happen, very honestly, is that a group from this institute would become interested enough to get involved and start coordinating a national effort to solve this problem. I am also looking for someone to take over as chairman of my Department of Audiovisual Instruction (now Association for Educational Communications and Technology) committee next year. The participants here are sufficiently varied in their backgrounds and experiences that from this group may come a nucleus of people to start coordinating a national program.

Question: I think what we are asking you is that, from your experiments with your committee and the project, do you feel that there is some common denominator that we can use for a national basis?

Mr. Diamond: I would like to see a systemized approach to the application of the logic utilized in our project on a quality basis with a careful assessment of the results.

Question: In your opinion, is the common denominator the logic, the systems approach, that you have used in designing the program?

Mr. Diamond: The common denominator is the search and retrieval logic of random access of identifiers for the retrieval of materials. Perhaps 35mm slides are easiest to work with, and so I suggest that work start with them.

Question: Will this logic apply to any non-book media?

Mr. Diamond: The logic will. The identifiers will have to be different. For example, you do not get into the date problem as extensively, that is, the date of production versus the date of content. I may be wrong on this.

Question: Are you considering only commercially available slides?

Mr. Diamond: Yes.

Question: What do you see happening in the case of locally produced slides?

Mr. Diamond: They would be given a number "plugged" into the system.

Question: Let us say they were a collection of locally produced slides that were found to be very good and worthy of more than local distribution. Now, would this entail, because of limited local expertise, some of these identifiers having to be reworked?

Mr. Diamond: For local production you are going to have specific local identifiers that will only be in your own system. You would do as you do in any system; you would say this is a national system of identifiers but with our own local option.

Question: What happens in the future when other kinds of identifiers, that perhaps we have not even thought of, come into existence?

Mr. Diamond: Two things could happen. We might decide it is new, and we should search for every detail available on it and decide how it fits into our scheme. Or, we could say we are not bothering about it but will put a date after it so the person looking at it knows that his term came into use in this system beyond this date. Before that date, he would have to use older terms or just go through and have someone read them individually.

Question: Could you speculate on how we might set up a system for a specific media?

Mr. Diamond: Bring together experts in different disciplines and get them to divulge the terms they use in their search for data.

Question: Could you use existing subject authorities for this?

Mr. Diamond: I am sure you could if they were available.

Comment: There is in existence a classification of the performing arts which, in fact, would exclude terms peculiar to the motion picture industry and deliberately exclusive subject terms. If you get a film about metal forging, this particular classification will deal with the film aspect of it and then tell you its instructions. If you then want to use more technical language about the metal, look in the Universal Decimal Classification and use the word for steel, because you can not possibly write in all the subject terms for films.

Mr. Diamond: This is a specialized retrieval system on the film itself. Now we raise the question, are we after the instructional content or the process of filming? I believe we are saying you have to modify it and develop a logical retrieval system for nonbook materials.

Question: Would this mean that a library with five kinds of media would have five sets?

Mr. Diamond: No, one for everything. A single identifier for all media and books.

Comment: Specialized descriptors would only apply to one media.

Mr. Diamond: There could be a subject field—for example, a graduate program in instructional television—where documents may require an additional thirty or forty terms for specialized television research at the local level.

Question: Would you give a personal opinion about how many descriptors you could include and still utilize your system? Where would you define the limits of your system?

Mr. Diamond: I cannot answer your question, because I would make broader sub-categories with subcategories for them. You "branch" the user immediately from the broad categories if he can agree to the terms he wishes to use.

Comment: There has been some considerable testing of retrieval systems done, but it was a field experiment. I cannot remember the exact figure, but it showed that there was a break-off point that would retrieve up to about 80 percent with a relatively small number of items, perhaps twenty. After that, the return drops rapidly. As you go from twenty to fifty, the retrieval rate goes from 80 percent to 88 percent. A relatively small number of terms retrieves a relatively high percentage of the material. If you really want 100 percent retrieval, you have to do a great deal of indexing, for there is a break-off point which has been constructed.

Question: This would, I imagine, vary from field to field?

Comment: No, although that would seem to be the situation, there has been quite a lot of testing done, and the "relevance recall" does seem to hold validity for the different subject fields. It varies in proportion to the amount of indexing. You could use this retrieval rate to decide the extent of indexing, once you have designed the system and worked out the parameters.

Mr. Diamond: We were amazed at the number of identifier terms that we put in a system that were never used by the people. We got too sophisticated.

Question: But you do have an upper limit when you are using a matrix system, do you not?

Mr. Diamond: No, it is an optical system, and the only limit is in the number of items and the number of collections, not in the number of identifiers.

Comment: Or the other way around, you can limit your vocabulary to ten thousand but, if necessary, have half a million separate cards. You use a card for the item and punch in the identifier.

Mr. Diamond: Either way. The other way is faster because it is a single card filing system. There is no limit. Again, we had 750 and it works fine, but we are dropping down to 150 identifiers.

Comment: I have been doing this with as many media as I have books, and I find no great difference in identifiers from one media to another.

Comment: The media are conveying information. The information could be tape recorded, it could be written on paper, it could be recorded on a phonodisc, or it might be on videotape. These are different media, but the content would be exactly the same.

Mr. Diamond: I, as a classroom teacher, do not care who the author is and quite often do not even care who the producer is. A teacher may or may not be interested in a particular media or in whether it is a filmstrip or a film. Teachers are rarely interested in producers.

Question: Can we generalize things, though? All we are saying is that if you ignore a possible indexing factor, it will not be available when you want it.

Comment: Of the eight thousand items we have collected, we cannot assume that some are going to be needed and some are not. We would be very happy to insert them all if it were economically possible. Actually, I think we are going over some items with a camel's hair brush.

Comment: No, no, you are missing this one. Until we can say what techniques are available, I agree with you on it, but there is already in existence the Machine-Readable Cataloging (MARC) format which allows you to specify in considerable detail all the elements that will go into an entry. If people do not know about MARC, they ought to be told, first of all.

Mr. Diamond: We have been trying to get a workable system that will be accepted. The minute we hire people to help us do this job, we are criticized because they are not graduates of Harvard or have not graduated from a particular library school. I hope we can find the kind of people and qualities of teaching you will accept.

Mr. Snider: As a sort of hobby, I am working on a book, a history of one of the finest photographic achievements of this century: Farm Security Administration's photographic projects, which involved some of the great photographers of this century. The painter Ben Shahn worked as a photographer with Walker Evans and Arthur Rothstein, who is now photographic editor of *Look,* and a whole group of fine people who, in 1935 to 1941, amassed one of the great photographic records of our time, of the depression. There was recently, in Washington and California, a photographic exhibit called "Just before the War," the history of urban America as seen by the photographers of the Farm Security Administration. The exhibit was drawn from a great photographic file of 250,000 negatives that are extremely well organized and are an important source of history in our nation. They are in the Library of Congress.

Last week I spent all day at the University of Wisconsin with Paul Vanderbilt of the Wisconsin State Historical Society who organized this file of photographs. You can find from the file who took the negative, when it was taken, where it was taken, how it was taken, and what comments the photographer made when he took these particular pictures. This file is enormously interesting from the point of view of a growing number of historians. It is a primary source of information and, I feel, a very important subject area. I would recommend that in terms of photographic files Paul Vanderbilt is a very important resource, a person you might get involved at some point in some of these discussions.

Question: How is the file organized?

Mr. Snider: I am not sure how the pictures are organized; by subjects, I believe. There is also a file, by photographers, with proof sheets and information on the pictures. You can refer from this to the larger photograph in the master file, or the reverse. When the photographers shot these pictures, they had to turn in what they call captions; where, when, who, what, et cetera, which helps make it a very useful source of picture material.

A man came to my office from Pathé News about five years ago and said, "You know, we have been shooting newsreels since 1895 and have hundreds of millions of feet of historical film in vaults in Connecticut; *Theodore Roosevelt and the Panama Canal Construction,* for example. Can something be done with all of this to help the schools?" I assured him that there were all kinds of things we could do: organize it, get some kind of cataloging, and establish a system of retrieval. Just think of this, hundreds of millions of feet.

Another example of insufficient bibliographic organization is the museums. The extension division of the National Gallery during the Works Progress Administration days had groups of artists who were trained in making exact reproductions, the grain of wood and so forth, and they went into historically significant homes during this period, drawing furntiure and other items in the homes. For instance, there is a magnificent collection of drawings of early Shaker furniture which is stacked almost literally on the floor. The director says, "I do not know what to do with it. I have not got it filed, it is all original artwork, and the drawings are almost priceless now." Grubbing through it is a man who is writing a book about it. Here again is a great collection of Americana that few know exists and no one knows quite what to do with it, which is unfortunate. This is all original artwork which should be properly organized, listed, and made available in bibliographic data to a wide audience.

Question: Does anyone know how far visual recognition by computer is coming along, because it is a way in which this information could be stored. If we can get to the stage where film can be fed into the computer, where it is scanned and stored, we are on the way to solving this kind of problem. I know that trials have been made.

Question: The visual recognition of exactly what?

Comment: Of the image on film so that it can be stored in a digital form. Then, to initiate a search, you feed in a picture of what you want—a piece of Shaker furniture, for example—instructing the machine to scan for that particular pattern.

Development of a Universal Classification System for Two-by-Two-Inch Slide Collections

Wendell Simons

Very little has been published on the classification of slides, a fact which you probably realize if you have ever tried to find help in the literature. A slide classification project has been under development at the University of California, Santa Cruz, for a period of at least five years. A year and a half of the work was funded by grants from the Council on Library Resources. Our system is unique, or at least unusual, in several respects: first, because it has been developed within the context of a general library, and there are not many general libraries that have undertaken slide collections; second, because its goal was to create a universal collection—that is, one covering all subject fields; and third, because of automatic indexing capability built into the classification concepts.

The most primitive method of slide organization, to my mind, is that which is practiced by vacationers, arranging their slides in travelogue sequence, recalling the details in the same order in which they were first encountered. For a vacationer showing his slides in his living room, this is perfectly adequate. Another approach, classroom oriented, is equally primitive in placing the slides in an order that follows the text of a course or a lecture. This is not uncommon, and it works beautifully for one course, but the limitations are obvious. Another stage of organization, in the context of art, is an alphabetical arrangement by artist's name. A good many slide collections are arranged this way. However, a collection that has any significant amount of historical material is bound to have as much anonymous art as it does art by known artists. The whole body of material outside of art can in no way be accommodated in a scheme based on the name of an artist. The best-developed slide libraries have generally been those in the field of art, and the artist's most common approach to organization is organization by art form. The most widely followed slide classification in the country is that of the Fogg Museum at Harvard University. Its classification has been mimeographed and widely distributed around the country.

Division by art form serves the rather narrow interest of the artist who is media oriented. A painter may think of all art in terms of painting, a sculptor in terms of sculpture. But in organizing a collection this way, material is scattered in the files so that material relating to any period of history, or any country, is fragmented, and the person who is searching on an historical or cultural front is not well served. Some libraries have attempted

Assistant Director of Libraries, University of California, Santa Cruz to use existing book classification schemes, such as Dewey or Library of Congress, but I think most of these attempts either are abandoned or the modification necessary is so extensive that the advantage of using something ready-made is completely lost.

We tried to take a completely fresh approach and devise something that would suit our purposes and that would be useful to a good many other people. During the formative period of the University of California, Santa Cruz campus (prior to 1965), the whole question of where and how slides for the campus should be collected and serviced was carefully considered. There was ample opportunity to consider the question without the pressure of immediate demand. We were well aware that in most academic institutions slide collections are housed in teaching departments. It is a rare campus that has a central, all-encompassing slide collection made avaliable to everyone in all disciplines. Typically, faculty members have private collections that they keep in their desk drawers, and these, of course, are unknown and unavailable to anyone else. Even if departmental or private collections are made available to other people, they may not be organized or indexed in such a way that they will be useful to an outsider, a person whose interest is different. And so we decided that this was not the kind of tradition we wished to follow.

The need at Santa Cruz was for a collection that would support a highly interdisciplinary approach to teaching. This is one of the features of the campus. Most of art history, for instance, is not taught as a discrete course but rather is integrated and synthesized into larger concepts such as world civilization, culture and society, cosmos and the arts, and the third world. Art is integrated in most cases with the history, culture, philosophy, religion, and science of the civilization under study. This interdisciplinary approach in teaching strongly suggested a central location and administration of the slide collection as opposed to departmental fragmentation. The university library, with its strong resources in cataloging and data processing, took on the responsibility for collecting and organizing slides.

Before the actual work of organizing a collection was begun, we laid down four basic requirements as goals for a system:

1. The collection should be universal; that is, encompassing all subject matter of all academic disciplines.
2. The arrangement of the collection should reflect a broad historical, cultural approach to teaching.
3. The filing arrangement of the collection should encourage and facilitate browsing; that is, the visual inspection and comparison of slides in the file.
4. In addition to being filed for easy browsing, the collection should be fully cataloged or indexed, preferably by automated means.

I think that Robert Diamond and I may agree on these points except for the question of classification, or what I call arrangement for browsing. This is where our two approaches differ very sharply. I will spend a good deal of time on the need for browsing, not to sound defensive, but simply to make clear the reasons why we made this a major requirement.

To the best of our knowledge or ability to discover, no existing slide classification scheme fulfilled all four requirements, particularly those of universality and indexability. Thus it was decided to embark on the creation of a new scheme and, with a grant from the Council on Library Resources, we undertook some intensive development. We have a collection of 50,000 slides which by now is serving a fully operational campus. The collection has served as the testing ground for ideas that developed, and 30,000 to 40,000 of the slides are fully cataloged in this scheme, keypunched and computer listed.

The system was consciously conceived and designed for a general academic setting. In doing this we have assumed that a completely general and universal collection of slides will be heavily weighted in the arts, just as you would expect a universal collection of recordings to be heavily weighted in music, or a general collection of books to be heavily weighted in literature. In our system, we have devoted more time, effort, and space to the development of art than we have to some of the other areas. I think it is justifiable, because it does reflect what a truly general pictorial collection will have in it. The approach is definitely one of universality, expecting that the collection will incorporate every conceivable subject. Perhaps the existence of a tool such as this will serve to encourage librarians to consolidate scattered slide collections and build for interdisciplinary use. The obvious target is the academic library or academic materials center.

In seeking a tool for classification, we considered trying to use the Dewey Decimal or the Library of Congress systems, but it soon became apparent to us that pictorial information simply cannot be ordered in the same fashion as verbal information can be. Consider philosophy, which is a major segment of any book classification. Try to imagine a picture of philosophy, an illustration of philosophy. I think about all you will come up with is a picture of a philosopher. In my mind, that is not a philosophical function, but rather a biographical function. Biography is history. Consider religion. Religion is rich in pictorial tradition but is this not really art? Art is the means of making visible the essence of religion, but religion itself is not a visual phenomenon. Those aspects of religion that are not art, again, I think, are going to become biographical or historical. Consider what can actually be pictured?

Most of the commonly accepted hierarchies used in book classification simply have no meaning in trying to classify slides or pictures. After struggling with this philosophical problem for a long time, we finally settled on three basic divisions of knowledge that are capable of pictorial representation and thus are a suitable base for a slide classification system: history, art, and science. *History,* in this context, means the pictorial representations of people, of the events in the history of mankind, the natural, social, and economic environments. History is an umbrella term that covers everything but art and science. It covers such things as agriculture, business, government, education, sociology, religion— all the commonly thought-of subject fields except art and science. *Art* is used to cover the arts, artifacts, and artificial environments of

mankind. *Science* is used to portray natural elements and principles that exist without context of time and place and the representation of scientific research.

It was only after we had worked all this out and decided on this three-part system that something was discovered in research that I found comforting. Francis Bacon, in his *Chart of Human Learning,* had divided all human knowledge into three groups, which he called history, poesy, and philosophy. His definitions are: history, the memories of things observed; poesy, the flights of imaginations; and philosophy, the analysis and classification of impressions. In 1870, W. T. Harris renamed these three groups history, art, and science, and then Melvil Dewey took Harris' three-part classification and made it into ten parts.

History and art have in common a context of time and place, and art can easily be viewed as a part of history. In this scheme, slides in both history and art are arranged first by historical period, then by country. Each slide is primarily grouped by the time period it represents in history and the part of the world it comes from. In a collection so arranged, every aspect of life in any particular era or culture is readily brought together; cultures are easily compared, and human history is laid out in a logical flow from past to present.

Science requires a different treatment all together, because the principles of pure science know no age or national origin. The law of gravity cannot be assigned to a period in history or to any country, but the discovery of it can be assigned to an historical context. The science portion of our classification has been arranged in a subject order very much like a traditional book classification. Is it better to class the discovery of the principles with the principles, or to place scientific research and discovery in its historical context? We have tried to construct our tables to allow the user either option.

A similar problem arises in dealing with the product of research. The product, in my mind, becomes a part of the social or economic environment of the time and place. We are now in the midst of tremendous research in space. This is scientific research and would logically fit into the classification of pure science. When the time comes that you can buy a ticket on Trans World Airlines to go to the moon, space becomes a facet of transportation, a part of the economic and social environment of the day and age. That kind of space travel I would class in history, not in science.

Classification relegates an item to one fixed location in a file where it bears some logical relationship to the things around it. Once a thing has been put in one place, you have lost all the other places where it might have been put with equal logic. Cataloging is the next step, the process by which you go back and recapture all the places that you might have put the thing in the first place. The two processes are what make up traditional library organization: classification and cataloging.

An artist, particularly, needs to see what he is going to use; he would rarely be satisfied with a verbal description of slides in the files. Slides are a visual tool. Their whole impact is visual, and the person using them, I believe, normally has to have visual contact with the thing to know that is what he wants or to know if it suits his needs.

Question: How do you browse through a drawer of slides? Do you put them in a projector or take them out and look at them?

Mr. Simons: Actually, the initial browsing is of the labels on the tops of the slides. It is just like flipping through cards in a card catalog. When you come to a slide of interest, you can pull it out and take a look. If you have a handful you are interested in, then you can take them to a light table which is adjacent to the file.

Comment: The best or most desirable thing would be some setup, where these are arranged in little trays or perhaps put in a machine of some kind.

Mr. Simons: This is a matter of storage space. It gets expensive to spread these out. We are filing as compactly as we can.

Mr. Diamond: You can make contact sheets and print black and white copies to put in the hands of the department to achieve local browsing. If you start from scratch, it is not too big a job, and it is not that expensive to make contact sheets.

Mr. Simons: Right, but there is the factor

of size. We are thinking of collections of hundreds of thousands of slides, and that is a lot of material to duplicate.

As an illustration of the advantages of browsing, we have a group of slides of Chartres Cathedral in France. There are at least 100 slides of this building in our collection. How would you select the one you wanted? The easiest way is simply by observation. There is a variety of views from a variety of distances, night views as well as day, from a variety of angles in a variety of colors. One has a greenish cast; another is more pink. A critical artist would want to pick out the one he thinks best represents the cathedral as it is.

The file is arranged in such an order that you move in a logical progression through the building. We move toward the front, we move up to a door, to the statuary that flanks the doors; pick out a single figure, the head, and right down to the fingernails, if you care to. Next we find the rose window, from the outside and then from the inside, and a general view of the interior. I feel that this kind of browsing is the way that people wanting to use material on Chartres Cathedral search in order to find what they need. They simply will not be able to tell from a written or verbal description, nor perhaps even be able to specify what they are looking for.

There is another important reason for browsing, and that is serendipity, finding things that you did not know were there, or never would have thought of or asked for. In this drawer of slides we saw Chartres, a fourteenth-century French cathedral, illustrating the high Gothic period of France. Adjacent to it, there is Cologne Cathedral, which is high Gothic in Germany, and Milan, which is high Gothic in Italy, built in the same century. The Winchester Cathedral is fourteenth-century English. These provide a comparison, a graphic and visual comparison, of what was happening all around Europe at one particular time. The architecture is quite different and yet very similar when compared to areas outside western Europe. Does anyone have any notion what was going on in Norway in the fourteenth century? The Suborstine Church in Norway is an example of fourteenth-century architecture which is completely unlike the others. There is a mosque in Persia of about the same period. The heart of the medieval period in Europe corresponded roughly with the height of the late Mayan in southern Mexico. This is the kind of thing you discover by browsing. This was very important to us as we developed this system. The visual medium simply requires visual searching.

I believe that a majority of slide collections are classified to some degree, but almost none are cataloged. The approach that Dr. Diamond described he would not call cataloging, but in the context of my definitions, I would call it cataloging without classification. Cataloging is commonly understood in terms of books. Catalog cards describe a book in verbal terms. They can easily convey the content, the usefulness, the pertinence of a book because the book itself is verbal. A catalog card or verbal representation cannot describe music: that is, it cannot describe the *sound* of music by using words. In the same sense, we believe that a verbal description does not describe pictorial material adequately to serve a person whose whole interest is visual and pictorial. With only a general understanding of a classification system, a user can go to the files and have direct access to much in which he is interested.

Classification is the grouping of like things together and the separating of things that are not alike. It becomes a matter of very careful definition of terms. Each classification schedule drawn up should be a list of words or terms that are mutually exclusive. Any cataloger or classifier who uses a system marks it up as he goes, redefining terms or making specific definitions that fit his own specific needs or the needs of his own specific collection.

Having developed and defined a group of terms, it is then necessary to decide in what order to list the terms. There are three basic choices; we could have listed terms in alphabetical order, in chronological order, or in an associational order. Our primary schedules in history and art are both arranged in chronological order, from prehistoric down to the twenty-first century. Science is different. Here we are not concerned with historical development, but with pure science, science that has

no context of time or place. There, the division has to be subject oriented much as the book classifications with which we are familiar. Science is an alphabetical list.

Most classification schemes depend heavily on associational ordering. In our scheme we have minimized associational order in favor of chronological or alphabetical. In associational ordering you tend to create a list, putting in an order that makes sense to you because of some association. It might be chronological, or alphabetical, or left to right, or local context, or you could associate in terms of population or economic importance, as the rationale becomes more and more subjective. This subjectivity is a weakness in most classifications.

For example, both Dewey and Library of Congress classification schemes start their lists of European countries with Great Britain. One reason might be the left-to-right approach, or perhaps it is because Great Britain is most closely related to the United States in terms of history and culture. From Great Britain both systems move across the map in different patterns. The logic of this kind of file depends on subjective associations as they are understood or imagined by the person who created the file. The average person browsing through a file like that is lost. He does not know whether to move forward or backward from Sweden in order to find Portugal. For this reason we have chosen to minimize this kind of organization. We have used chronological order where it makes good sense in terms of historical developments, but in most other cases, the lists are alphabetical. This may create occasional peculiarities of juxtaposition, but nevertheless, an alphabetical list can be used by everyone who can understand the alphabet.

Many librarians will quote the rule of thumb that it costs as much to catalog a book as it does to buy one. The same cost of book cataloging applied to a slide which costs only a quarter obviously is out of scale. I think this is demonstrated by the fact that very few, if any, slide collections are fully cataloged. Because they are not, tremendous resources of very useful material have been lost in large collections. In many collections the only approach to the file is through the file itself. Our purpose was to create a call number that would in itself generate indexes, that would yield the cross-indexing and varied, multiple approaches that might be referred to as retrieval.

Our call number (fig. 1) consists of eigh-

Fig. 1. Configuration of the 18-digit call number

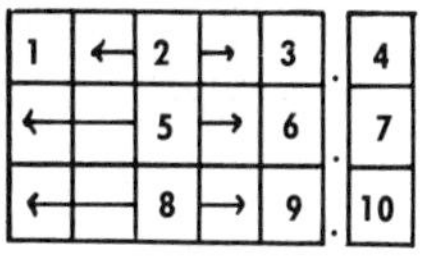

teen digits in three rows of six. Those eighteen digits are divided into ten sorting fields (fig. 2). Ten elements of the call number are identifiable and sortable on the IBM machine. A line of six digits approaches the maximum number of figures you can see and remember without having to recite it to yourself. We kept the line to six, and we have used letters, numbers, and letters in alternation, similar to the arrangement on an automobile license plate.

Fig. 2. Ten sorting fields

By systematically encoding specific types of information in specified sort fields, it is possible to machine sort on these fields, producing a variety of indexes. A typical art slide can be listed in these different contexts: chronological period, country, medium, style, artist or city of origin (for anonymous artists), subject content, technique, title, date of the work, city of present location, and source of the slide. All but the last three of these listings are direct products of the call number. A comparable variety of listings can be done for slides in history and science. The data-processing applications developed have purposely been kept simple.

The classification scheme will work effectively at three levels of automation. It can be used in a purely manual fashion where there is no access to computers or keypunch machinery. In a small collection you can use the system and get the advantage of manually identifying things as you thumb through.

At the second level, if keypunch and sorting machines are available, a small collection of a few thousand slides could be keypunched and the cards used as a retrieval device. By sorting on the various fields, you could pull out all the cards for temples, or all the cards for landscapes, for an artist's paintings, for a place name, or for a date. If a line printer is available, these cards can be used to print indexes or custom lists of what you have in any particular field in response to user requests. On this intermediate level, rudimentary data-processing techniques can be used if you have card-handling equipment available.

The third level is that of total mechanization, where you can transfer all this data from punch cards to magnetic tape or disc and then manipulate, print, and search by use of a computer. We do not know what the practical limits of this system are, how large a collection can be handled, but we are confident it can go into the hundreds of thousands of slides.

In the actual application of this system to a slide collection, there are three basic steps: the first, assigning the call number; second, labeling the slide; and third, if equipment is available, keypunching the information for data processing.

In assigning the classification, the first decision to be made in the process will often be the most difficult, the identification of the area of classification to which a slide belongs —history, art, or science. This is more difficult than you might imagine until you have attempted it. To help us arrive at the first basic choice, we have drawn up a flow chart series of questions against which to test each item. The list may appear formidable, but in actual usage it may take only a few seconds to reach a conclusion for most of the material. This list reflects the priorities that suit our purposes at Santa Cruz. Any library using this system should create a list of local priorities against which to make classification decisions. Our first priority is the archival history of our own institution.

**FIELDS 1·10:
CALL NUMBER**

J462R. K EXEKIAS
E962B. R ACHILLES &
AJAX
A178A. C AMPHORA 503
BC

ROME: VAT
B13.2.7 BUDEK

FIELD 11: The term that is coded
in Field 5 In effect, the main entry.

FIELD 12: The term that is coded
in Field 8

FIELD 13: Date of the work

FIELD 14: City of present location
and collection

FIELD 15: Source of slide

Fig. 3. A typical slide, fully labeled

1. Does the slide or picture illustrate any aspect of the history, the people, the environment of the local community or home institution? If not, proceed to next question. If yes, class in history using special geographical tables that must be created to suit local conditions. (These special tables are not included in the published classification.)

2. Is it a map of an identifiable locale on the earth? If not, proceed to next question. If yes, class in history. Extraterrestrial maps are treated as astronomy. Theoretical or unidentifiable maps of earth formations may be treated as earth sciences.

3. Is it a work of art? If not, proceed to next question. If yes, class in art. Some items may be physical works of art that are not produced by a camera but are deemed to have no artistic merit. In such cases the items may be considered in light of their historical or scientific content. On the other hand, a photograph may be classed as art if its subject content is indefinable or is clearly subordinate to its artistic qualities.

4. Does it illustrate the theoretical principles of science or the intellectual processes of scientific or technological research, not the end products of technology, since these are a part of the human environment? If yes, class in science.

5. Anything left over should illustrate some aspect of the history of man, his natural or artificial environment, his institutions, his activities; class in history.

History remains the miscellaneous catchall at the end of the list. Since the historical ap-

proach is the primary approach of the whole system, everything is classed as history that cannot be positively identified as an exception.

The typical 2-by-2-inch slide with an aperture of 1⅜ by ⅞ inch leaves room for two labels, and a microtypewriter will yield up to four rows of type on each label (fig. 3). The top label bears the call number, comprising ten sorting fields, as well as three fields containing natural-language information important to manual browsing. Field 11 is, in effect, the main entry or author entry. Each bit of information on the slide label can also be keypunched on a keypunch card (fig. 4).

The encoded information for the sample slide, a Greek vase painting, reveals the following about the slide:

Field 1. J places the work in the ancient period of art history from the beginning of historic dating to the 3rd century A.D.

Field 2. 462 is the geographical code for Greece.

Field 3. R identifies the art medium as ceramic or glassware, done by a known artist.

Field 4. K denotes the archaic style in Greek art, 600–480 B.C.

Field 5. E962 is the Cutter number for the artist's name, Exekias.

Field 6. B identifies the Greek vase shape as an Amphora.

Field 7. R identifies the subject matter depicted on the vase as mythological.

Field 8. A178 Cutter number for the first word in the title of the work, *Achilles and Ajax Amphora.*

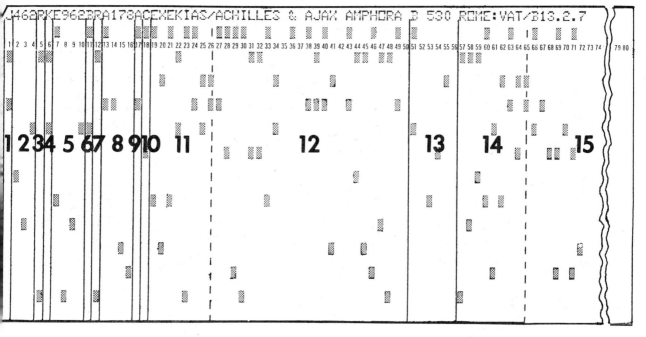

Fig. 4. Layout of the punched card showing the 15 sort fields

Field 9. A indicates that the picture is a view of the entire work.

Field 10. C indicates that this is the third slide in the file of this view.

Field 11. *Exekias* is the artist's name spelled out in full for visual scanning of the index. Field 5 provides the means for mechanical sorting and retrieval.

Field 12. *Achilles & Ajax Amphora* is the title in full for visual scanning of the index. Field 8 provides for mechanical sorting and retrieval.

Field 13. B530 is the date of the work, read as 530 B.C. Since no hyphen follows the date, it is understood to be a firm date and not an approximation.

Field 14. *Rome:Vat* indicates the present location of the work is Rome at the Vatican.

Field 15. B13.2.7 reveals the commercial source of the slide as Budek and gives the firm's catalog number.

Fields 9 and 10 are devices for arranging a multiplicity of slides of the same object in some meaningful order in the files. These two fields allow 27 times 26, or 676 views or versions of the same title in the file without running into classification troubles. Note that the total length for fields 11 and 12 is fixed, but the relative lengths of 11 and 12 are variable. If there is a very long artist's name, it leaves a short space for title. But if you have a short name, it means that more information can be put into the title field. This portion of our system could see a lot of expansion. We purposely forced this whole format onto a single keypunch card of eighty columns, and that is a terrific restriction. Our purpose was to create a system that would be very simple to input and operate. If you have more than one card per title, you have to assign serial numbers to keep the set together; that complicates card handling and inputting.

Field 13 is for date. Six columns are assigned, with room for four numbers in the center, a space to the left for *B*, indicating B.C., and a space to the right where we insert a hyphen if the date is an approximation. In the particular example shown, the work had been pinpointed to the year 530 B.C. If it had been *about* 530, or if the work had been done over a period of years, then the date entry would have been B530-.

Field 14 indicates the location of the work

of art. This can be important to a traveling researcher, who can identify works that are in the cities he plans to visit. The location of an historical event or of a fixed work of art, or the present location of a movable work of art, is entered in field 14. City name is preferred, though the next larger political or geographical subdivision may be used. Location names are spelled out in full on both the slide label and the keypunch card; they are not cuttered or other-

We can obtain a computer-oriented list in call number order or in other words, a shelf-list (fig. 5). The line of printing is identical to what is on the keypunch card. Spacing is inserted to make it easier to read, but otherwise the indexes are a direct card-by-card printout with no reformating or translation. With more sophisticated programming, nicer formating would be possible, producing a more readable page.

J462Q.M A061H.R M184A.	CLASSICAL	MAENAD & SATYR CHALICE	B 300-	LIPARI	813.5.7
J462Q.M A061P. P384A.	CLASSICAL	PELIKE,KERCH STYLE	B 300-	LONDON:BM	121.3.137A
J462Q.M A061P. P384A.B	CLASSICAL	PELIKE,KERCH STYLE	B 300-	LONDON:BM	813.5.5
J462Q.N A071Z. P295A.	HELLENISTIC	PATERA WITH RELIEF	B 200-	ATHENS:NM	121.3.138B
J462Q.P A0859.Z F981A.	SOUTH ITALIAN	FUNERAL CEREMONY	B 99-	CATANIA	813.5.10
J462R.K A486B.R D592A.	AMASIS	DIONYSOS & MAENADS NECK	B 530-	PARIS:BN	813.2.5
J462R.K C473W.H H432A.	CHARINOS	HEAD OF GIRL RHYTON	B 490-	TARQUINIA:MN	813.3.10
J462R.K E962B.R A178A.	EXEKIAS	ACHILLES & AJAX AMPHORA	B 530-	ROME:VAT	83.4.23
J462R.K E962B.R A178A.B	EXEKIAS	ACHILLES & AJAX AMPHORA	B 530-	ROME:VAT	5.24.17
J462R.K E962B.R A178A.C	EXEKIAS	ACHILLES & AJAX AMPHORA	B 530-	ROME:VAT	813.2.7
J462R.K E962B.R A179A.	EXEKIAS	ACHILLES & PENTHESILEA	B 525-	LONDON:BM	813.2.8
J462R.K E962B.R A179A.B	EXEKIAS	ACHILLES & PENTHESILEA	B 525-	LONDON:BM	M4.T25.30
J462R.K E962I.R D592A.B	EXEKIAS	DIONYSOS IN BOAT ATTIC	B 540-	MUNICH:ANTIQ	813.2.6
J462R.K N694B. A526A.	NIKOSTHENES	AMPHORA.BLACK-FIG.	B 500-	ROME:VAT	121.3.1350
J462R.K N694B.R S254A.	NIKOSTHENES	SATYRS & MAENADS	B 540-	-:PC	813.2.3
J462R.K N695E.M W872A.	NIKOXENOS	WOMEN AT WELL HYDRIA	B 530-	ROME:MNVG	813.3.3
J462R.K P974B.R H531A.	PSIAX	HERAKLES & NEMEAN LION:AMP	B 520-	BRESCIA:MCR	5.25.68
J462R.K P974B.R H531A.C	PSIAX	HERAKLES & NEMEAN LION:AMP	B 520-	BRESCIA:MCR	813.2.9
J462R.K P974B.R H531A.D	PSIAX	HERAKLES & NEMEAN LION:AMP	B 520-	BRESCIA:MCR	JK.5
J462R.K P974J.R H531A.D	PSIAX	HERAKLES & NEMEAN LION:AMP	B 520-	BRESCIA:MCR	5.26.20
J462R.K P974B.R H531A.E	PSIAX	HERAKLES & NEMEAN LION:AMP	B 520-	BRESCIA:MCR	813.2.10
J462R.K X522I.R H531A.B	XENOKLES	HERAKLES & TRITON KYLIX	B 570-	TARQUINIA:MN	813.2.4
J462R.L B515H.R A135A.	BERLIN PTR	ABDUCTION OF EUROPA	B 490-	TARQUINIA:MN	813.4.5
J462R.L B916Z.H D781A.	BRYGOS	DRINKER & HETAERA BOWL	B 490-	WURZBURG:AN	83.4.29
J462R.L K642B.R D592A.	KLEOPHRADES	DIONYSOS AMPHORA	B 500-	MUNICH:ANTIQ	U2.GR5.38
J462R.L K642B.R D592A.B	KLEOPHRADES	DIONYSOS AMPHORA	B 500-	MUNICH:ANTIQ	U2.GR6.41
J462R.L K642B.R D592A.C	KLEOPHRADES	DIONYSOS AMPHORA	B 500-	MUNICH:ANTIQ	813.4.1
J462R.L K642B.R D592A.O	KLEOPHRADES	DIONYSOS AMPHORA	B 500-	MUNICH:ANTIQ	813.4.2
J462R.L K652H.R T531A.	KLIO	THREE MUSES CHALICE KRATER	B 440-	ROME:VAT	813.5.1
J462R.L M499E.R P535A.B	MEIDIAS PTR	PHAON HYDRIA	B 410-	FLORENCE:MA	813.5.4
J462R.L N718H. A385A.	NIOBIO PTR	ATTIC CALYX KRATER	B 460-	FERRARA:MAN	121.3.135E
J462R.L P628H. C726A.	PIG PTR	COLUMN KRATER	C 480-	-	P11.SK19
J462R.L P782H. C169A.	POLYGNOTOS	CALYX KRATER	C 450-	-	P11.SK24
J462R.L S117K. L536A.	SABOUROFF PTR	LEKYTHOS	B 450-	-	P11.SK25

Fig. 5. Example of a computer-printed shelflist

wise coded. It is possible to sort these names mechanically, although the process is somewhat slower than sorting coded data. In addition to city name, the abbreviated name of a collection may be entered following the city when it is appropriate to a movable work of art.

Field 15 is used to record the source of the slide, with the expectation that this information will be useful in reordering or replacing a lost slide. A slide can generally be traced to one of three sources: a commercial catalog, a local cameraman who took an original picture or copied an illustration from a book, or another slide from which a duplicate was made. Simple codes have been devised for the sources of the Santa Cruz collection. Each library using the system can easily construct a code to meet its needs.

The same deck of cards can be sorted and resorted, keying on any element you wish, to produce a dozen more listings, each of which would place the slide in a different context. The Exekias vase might be found in an alphabetical list by artists' names, or *Achilles and Ajax* in an alphabetical list of titles, or a media list placing the Greek vase with other examples of pottery.

The single card format was developed to maintain a minimum effort of input. If we were to enlarge upon the rudimentary data-processing techniques, we would add more descriptors, more subject features, and longer titles. By using the technique of permuted printing, every significant word in the title could be picked out and used as a retrieval device. In a group portrait you may have two dozen people who can be identified by name. At most we can now code two of them and identify two of the names. If we expanded field 12 onto additional cards, we could include all of the names. Presently we can identify only one date in the file. For a work of art depicting a historical event, you should have both the date it was created for the artist and the date of the event pictured for the historian. We could expand our formats to make room for two dates or more. These are just programming problems.

The basic goal of this project was to create a classification system—first of all, a system of filing—that would also yield cataloging/indexing information that other classification systems have never produced. I think we have accomplished this goal. We have thirty to forty thousand slides fully cataloged by this system which has been in operation five years. However, we do not pretend to have done everything that could be done.

I want to give you some illustrations of some of the problems in making classification decisions. Assume we have a picture of an ant hill in the Congo. Where do you put that? A school of architecture might very well classify that as natural architecture. You might say it is a science slide because it illustrates the life and times of the ant. You might also say that it is historical, in the sense that it depicts the environment of a place. You have three choices, and this is the dilemma that any classifier faces. Here we go through the priority procedure I outlined earlier. Does the picture have to do with the local community or institution? No. Is it a map? No. Is it art? I would say no; it is not artificially created by man. Is it science? Does it illustrate any principle of science, such as Newton's law, or atomic principles, or does it show scientific research in process? My answer to that is no. This shows a part of the natural environment of the Congo. I feel it should be classed with twentieth-century history, with Congo the place name, and natural history and landscape the subject matter.

Question: Since slides can be duplicated rather cheaply, would it complicate your system if you had a slide like that in more than one place?

Comment: This is very dangerous unless you have the kind of control that would almost eliminate the problem in the first place. If you start duplicating information in this fashion, you increase the size of your file. This is why you have a classified order in the first place, to reduce this problem. The cheapness of duplicating slides makes it all the more tempting and all the more dangerous. A file with 40,000 items is a complicated file. If you adopt a policy which is going to turn it into a file of 120,000 items, it becomes even more complicated.

Question: Well, I will admit this, but how are you going to find this under *natural science?*

Mr. Simons: "Ant hill" would be assigned as a title, and it would be found together in a title listing with all the material from the science collection having to do with ants. Every collection is going to have a bias of its own that is perfectly legitimate; you make these decisions to fit whatever your local needs are. It is because of this kind of problem that we have attempted to gain the very important cross-indexing potential that most slide collections have never had.

Mr. Diamond: I think it is pretty obvious that the difference in sophistication between our two systems is rather marked. Simons has done a superb job. He has a far more sophisticated system in terms of the classification identifiers than the one we have developed at Fredonia. It is inclusive and it does an excellent job. It is critical to realize in discussing the two that there is a major operational logic and a structural difference between the two. At Santa Cruz there is a search and retrieval system, a basic system that is part of the shelving and classification system. At Fredonia the classification terms and the shelving terms do not have to be interrelated. This makes a critical difference in the operation of the system itself.

Now the prejudice that I have is that with the Fredonia system you can combine any variables in retrieving the slide. In Simons' lists of identifiers and in the structure, there are limits to the number of terms that can be applied to any one slide; in the Diamond system of random-access retrieval, any number of terms can be combined. In the case of the ant hill, any terms that might be meaningful to some user could be assigned to the slide and used by the person in retrieving the slide. There is a basic logical difference in the separation of shelving and retrieval and the flexibility or the limitations of terms that can be used in the retrieval system. The terms that Santa Cruz has are superb, and they should be transferred over into a retrieval system. Where I disagree is in the logic of retrieval and how you go about using these terms in locating a slide. This is where the two systems are markedly different.

Mr. Croghan: Mr. Simons, I am going to take a bit of time, I think, because I am not talking solely about this presentation. I have had a copy of this classification which I have studied with some very considerable interest. I will say that what you have done, you have done very well. It is highly sophisticated; you have used the technical devices remarkably well, and I think it is a very good classification. It is so good, in fact, that it goes into that very dangerous class, the works that you can examine using the very highest critical standards. In the case of most of the media classification retrieval devices I have looked at, if I were to use these standards, I would take one sharp, short look, give a merry laugh, and toss them over my left shoulder.

When you set out, your aims were to produce a universal classification scheme. Your argument for producing a separate one for slides, as distinct from the quite elaborate universal classification schemes that exist and that are of a far larger scale than yours in terms of content—Dewey, UDC [Universal Decimal Classification], or Library of Congress—was that there were large areas in these that were inherently not visual.

The example you were using was philosophy. Dr. Diamond told how, within his system, using his parameters, somebody had come up with a slide that was an illustration of existentialism. His system could not cope with it, just as yours could not cope with it, because you deliberately eliminated them. The Dewey Decimal Classification has got a place for existentialism; so has Library of Congress; so has the Universal Decimal Classification. They are there already. I am going to be fearfully British, and I am apologizing ahead of time. To put it bluntly, when you talk of using classification systems in this country for retrieval purposes, no one is using any of the major classifications to their full potential for retrieval in this country. *Dewey* would work, if it were used properly, more effectively within the scheme you have at the moment, using less digits than you have allowed yourself in your call number. You are not going to get as far in producing your scheme because you have not the time; *Dewey* has been going for ninety odd years; it is in its seventeenth edition.

One direction you could have taken was to apply the kind of thinking you have done to how *Dewey* could be used. The media librarian very much needs to look at these schemes that already have an enormous potential. *Dewey* has the potential, in terms of sheer volume of subject coverage—far more potential than yours.

The same thing applies to your mechanization. You have made very skillful use of the single punch card to produce what any librarian would recognize as a classified catalog and author catalog, though you did not actually use the word. Now we already have a considerable body of literature on the problems of cataloging and classified catalogs. How can this literature be related to the particular media? We need this very much.

I am interested in your order of priorities for slides. If you do not want to be bothered examining a scheme that has already got an inbuilt order such as Dewey, Library of Congress, or the others—fine, but I would rather have liked you to take the thinking you have already done and adapt it to the problem. We call them citation orders; these are your priorities orders. This is where you would meet Dr. Diamond, because, you see, he has his free-form descriptors; he has a search strategy. What he has not mentioned is, is there any standard search strategy—one that is going to be useful to the generality of librarians who simply want to pick up a good search strategy for slides without having the title worked out? This again is one of the things, surely, that we are here for, to do the thinking for all the librarians who have not the time to think about these media but also must start using them.

You are on the right line; I am criticizing you for not doing a good *enough* job. You have gotten near enough in one direction, but you were starting off to the other, and in between times you have run up, as well, a very useful, little mechanized system. I am tantalized by the fact that you could have taken the effort you put in all three of these on any one alone. We could really have started getting somewhere on this, but your basic assumption is that somehow slides are limited simply because they are pictures. They are not; they are conveying information, even in the art field. The whole field of iconography, even within art history itself, is devoted to symbolizing information and geometry. Slides *do* convey information. Any of these media convey information in a particular form.

Now books, I may say, are the most sophisticated medium of the lot. If you look at print on paper, there is nothing in any of the other media that comes anywhere near the sophistication of this particular one. It gives you highly structured information which can be called visual or audiovisual. It allows you instant access; it is easily duplicated. As a teaching machine a book is a very superb object. Even though we have had it around for four hundred years and are accustomed to using it, we should still look at it as an object in itself. The book is a remarkably sophisticated artifact. What we need, surely, in this institute—what I was hoping for when I came to this institute—was that we were going to be able to find out how far the media are special, are separate, and how far we can save time by using what has already been done.

I quote one concrete example from your own classification. You have quite an elaborate detail for the United States. Have you ever looked at the detail for the United States in the seventeenth edition of *Dewey*? It is much, much better than yours. It is far fuller, and if you spent time working this out, it is an awful waste of time, and I would much rather you had photocopied those ten pages.

Mr. Simons: Can I comment on the business of trying to use *Dewey* or LC for slide classification? I honestly think if you tried to do it, you would give up as we did. I will try to illustrate why. In LC art is represented by the letter *N,* with subdivisions *NA, NB, NC, ND, NE,* and *NK. N* is the most general, most all inclusive, and most encyclopedic in its treatment of art. It includes the encyclopedias of art and reference books that cover the whole scope from *A* to *Z,* from ancient to modern, all media, all places, everything. You cannot have a picture like that, so none of this is useful. *ND* is the classification of all paintings—still useless for single-frame pictures. Farther on will be a division for European painting, until finally we have a class that is meaningful to specific pictures, one that identifies the medium, time, and place of origin. We had to sift through many levels of generalities to get down to a specific usable class. In any book classification the preponderance of space is given over to generalities. Single pictures need to be described in specifics.

Question: The point we are trying to make here is that, in this wealth of terms in the *Dewey* schedules, the terms we need are there and they are organized. We select the terms that are applicable. It is not necessary that we end up with the same letter code in our process of transition. The important thing is that instead of starting work from scratch on the thesaurus of terms, we use this as a frame of reference.

Mr. Croghan: Just what I was saying about Mr. Simons' scheme, in fact. This is the fascinating thing about it; you isolated the three major areas in which one could do this. You could either improve the traditional classification scheme, which could be very useful; you could work on the application of positive principles, which would be very useful; or you could work on the mechanism. In any one of these you would have more than enough to do. When I think that you might have been sitting down, solemnly writing out long lists of the sciences or a list of the states of America when it is written down in *Dewey,* Library of Congress, and heaven only knows where else, it breaks my heart.

Mr. Simons: The geographical list comes right out of LC, simply for this reason. There was no need to invent a new list of words, but we did try to rearrange the terms to make browsing easier.

Mr. Diamond: I am concerned that we have all the identifiers that should be there and that the user can use these in any combination he needs, but we run into the fact in Simons' system that there are mutually exclusive terms. If you use one term, you cannot use other terms that happen to be in the same categorical list. We have devised a system that will allow users in different disciplines to identify an item and locate it. This is the key problem, utilizing the terms that exist.

Mr. Croghan: There are several possible solutions for an individual system. Before you design your system, isolate the problem. If somebody tells me, "I want browsing; I have a limited series of access points; I want open access; and I want to be able to do a multiple catalog," then use Simons' system. If somebody says, "I have a miscellaneous collection of wide subject range; I cannot predict how it is going to be used because we are a totally experimental college," I would say use Diamond's particular system. Those are different problems which require different solutions, and there is a whole spectrum of problems like this.

Mr. Simons: I would like one more chance to answer the complaint that *Dewey* or some other ready-made classification, could be used for slides. *Dewey* gives you ten equal blocks of classification. I am talking here about numbers, but you are correct; you should ignore the numbers and use the outline of information. Nevertheless, for ease of identity we can talk about the numbers. Even for book collections, some blocks are so full that you get very long Dewey numbers while others are loosely filled. I made the categorical statement that a collection of pictures is going to be heavily weighted by art. It may not be true in a medical library, but in the general academic setting, where a collection covers every subject taught on campus, it is inevitable that a collection of pictures will be strong in art.

Mr. Croghan: Then why do you call it a *universal* classification system?

Mr. Simons: It does include all the other subjects We took much out of *Dewey* and out of LC for art, but if we had used their structures, particularly their numbering systems, we would have been terribly unbalanced. LC is based on the letters of the alphabet. For our purpose, the

usable part of its art classification would be a tenth, perhaps, of N, so that one-260th of the possible notation available would be used for half or two-thirds of the collection.

Mr. Croghan: Two points, Mr. Simons, that I must make. If, in fact, you had said you were producing an art classification with other subjects, much of my comment this afternoon would not have been made. But you see, you label it a universal classification. You are publishing it with the indication that it is universal for everyone who wants to use it, and this puts it on a different basis. Secondly, you must not measure the amount of information in a classification scheme by the notation. You have literally to look at the list of terms on the page. You decide what you want to do from the materials you have, and the notational device will do it. I cannot understand why you fuss about the bits you do not need, because you have only to ignore the ones you do not use.

Comment: My doubts about this organization are that you have not really talked about the user and ideas, the user and content. As a user, I will come to a place of information, wanting a book, a slide, a film, a filmstrip, a tape, a recording. Are you going to send me to ten different systems in ten different ways? Bibliographers have studied and assessed these things we are talking about here for about a hundred years with a sophistication we do not know or understand, because we are generalists, not bibliographers. I wish you had used, as consultants to your project, people like Maurice Tauber, who has spent a lifetime in bibliography. This kind of person could help you look at organizing this system so that it would truly become a universal one. As it is now, it is not and cannot be universal in scope.

Mr. Simons: It is not universal in covering all media; it was not intended to be. It does purport to be universal in covering all subject matter in pictorial format.

Comment: In my own experiments I devoted my energies to trying to find common aspects to all media available and to work from that viewpoint. I think all our systems could have accomplished more if we had thought in less limiting terms, making effective experiments in trying to achieve the universality you are looking for.

Mr. Diamond: What you are saying makes a lot of sense. However, as you set up a collection, it has a particular frame of reference. The collection itself will state which terms are applicable to the collection. Whenever you add another element to a collection, you add a whole series of identifiers that may not have been there before. For example, if we set parameters for a new collection, within *Dewey* there is going to be a group of terms that are going to be applicable to the group of things. There are other terms in *Dewey* that are not going to be applicable because of the nature of the collection.

Mr. Simons: One last comment is in order. The goal of one system of organization and classification for all informational media, I am afraid, is unattainable. Existing classification systems, developed for books, will work very well for films, tapes, records, filmstrips, picture sets and slide sets. All these media have one very important element in common with books—the sequential development of ideas.

A single-frame picture cannot in itself develop a train of thought or a continuity of ideas. A picture may conjure up many ideas, but these are all in the eye of the beholder, subject to varying and even contradictory interpretations. Only a sequential medium can develop explicit ideas that can be described with objectivity and be classed in a system built on the verbalization of ideas. There is no chance of objectivity or consistency in classifying pictures unless the *visual image* is the basis of classification, not the presumed intellectual content. In our attempts to classify 40,000 images, we have proven to our satisfaction that book classifications are not usable. Perhaps someone else can prove otherwise.

Phonorecord Classification

Roger McFarland

Frequently we develop prototypes of equipment or systems and try them out with other libraries to see if there is a large enough market or interest to produce them. During the course of our travels and from feedback from our representatives, there appeared to be a rather serious problem in the area of records, particularly as it related to the recreational collection or public library. Not only was there general dissatisfaction with the classification systems that existed, but practically all libraries had unique systems for organizing their collections. It would be ideal if we could have achieved consensus on a total system, but we concluded that an interim step is probably better than the chaotic situation which prevailed.

If I have gained nothing else from this institute, I have learned that in order to discuss anything, I must first define the perimeters, the parameters, and the everything about it so that we shall all agree exactly on what we are talking about. We will be talking about the Alpha-Numeric System for Classification of Recordings, for which the acronym is ANSCR, pronounced *answer*. The alpha-numeric system for record classification is to be used as a class system for browser-oriented, recreational collections. It is not intended as a substitute for curriculum-based schemes, such as Dewey or Library of Congress, with particular applications in schools and in universities, for closed-stack arrangements, or for title selection, nor it is intended for media other than audiodiscs and audiotapes.

If one were to go into the record collections

Media Specialist, Bro-Dart Industries, City of Industry, California

of one hundred public libraries today, he would probably find ninety-five systems or schemes for classifying the browsing collections of recordings. Recognizing the lack of a satisfactory tool, librarians have formed their own particular systems to serve their own needs to the best of their ability and time available. Some of these have been adaptations of *Dewey,* whose proponents will readily admit is not very satisfactory. There are many similarities between schemes you know, those someone else has done, and the ANSCR scheme. We are not the initiators of all the *answers.* We took things from various sources, from other schemes that were being used, and developed a scheme we think is the most workable, comprehensive, and consistent type of classification scheme for this type of collection.

ANSCR is based on current need. There is no necessity to think in terms of a fifty-year period for the use of this classification scheme. It may not be relevant fifty years from now or even ten years from now, but it is relevant now. There is an established need right now, as evidenced by the confusion in the field; someone has called it classification chaos. We recognize our system as a "do it now" solution, one which will imediately have effect. While we want to see this system accepted, we have no plans to submit it to any professional organization for a seal of approval. It takes a long time for standards to become accepted unless there is consensus of opinion among those who are going to use it. We are not in competition with the Library of Congress. Bro-Dart is going to use this scheme in the production of catalog cards which we will sell to libraries. It is available to any and all who want to use it. All they have to do is purchase the book as a reference tool, and it becomes their right to use it as freely as they wish, as they do the Dewey classification or the LC schedules.

When we start talking about the particular problems and aspects of this scheme, it would be impossible, in this space, to verbalize all of the rules that are included in a 225-page book. We have devoted two years to the exploration of every situation we could think of in the development of ANSCR. There are undoubtedly some that we did not think of which would have to be included in a revision. The scheme has been developed with change in mind and contains built-in methods for altering—adding or deleting—that still will maintain continuity.

The recording industry is a volatile field where recordings come and go with the wind, and one must be able to adapt and change within a short span of years. Antony Croghan has defined classification as "a mental process of recognizing resemblances and grouping concepts by these like factors." I wanted to quote that because it is the underlying idea behind the formulation of this scheme, recognizing resemblances and grouping together these like factors. Our basic approach to the classification system was to look at the entire field of recordings which are available now, including music, spoken, and children's recordings. We tried to break the field into subject areas which were not only acceptable on their own as separate categories but which also bore some relationship to groupings by the various categories. For instance, if we look at recordings of operas (complete and also highlights), choral music, and vocal music, we find that there is definite relationship, in that all of these are some type of vocal music. Operas are broadest, perhaps, in the sense that they involve the most people in vocal reproduction of music. Choral music involves a lesser degree of participation; vocal music is the solo vocal category. If we visualize a browsing collection in which one is going to find a particular recording, all vocal music will generally be found together or in close proximity on the shelf or in the bin.

In orchestral music, instruments played are divided into several categories to represent the needs of the user. Chamber music involves fewer players, and there are also solo instrumentals. Band and electronic music are not so much types of music as methods of producing forms of music. A band can play a symphony or a concerto or a sonata or whatever, and an electronic synthesizer may play an adagio or fugue.

We also get into the areas which are a little less precise; for example, the distinction between classical music and popular music, such as musical shows and operettas or soundtrack music from motion pictures or television. In the popular music category we have such things as pop music, the Beatles, and two recognizable genres of popular music which we see here in the United States—country western and jazz. There is folk and ethnic music in the national sense of this country, or of Canada, or of Great Britain, or wherever this scheme is used. Holiday music will generally be composed of Christmas music, but there are recordings for specific holidays or events such as the Jewish and Christian holidays.

The scheme provides for spoken records, such as variety and humor, which may or may not involve some music. Categories also exist for plays, poetry, prose, and documentary recordings, either historical or commentary, and there is a category for instructional records. This does not mean educational records but instructional records, such as *How to Speak German* and *How to Practice Your Shorthand*. Specific sounds and specific effects, for which there is great demand in browsing or recreational collections, include those for silent home movies, sounds of doors slamming, railroad sounds, and sounds from the drag strip.

The last category we have provided for is children's recordings. It was placed last because in some collections this is an integral part of the whole recording collection, while in others it is placed in the children's department or in some other part of the building.

With this scheme, one has a classification system which treats not only music recordings, but all types of recordings. The patron needs only to become acquainted with one classification and he will find all records integrated in that one classification system. Many librarians catalog their music by some local scheme and their spoken records by *Dewey*. The user, confronted by this variation, finds it difficult to comprehend two systems.

ANSCR is an alpha-numeric scheme with designators composed of four terms. As subject categories were established, letters were assigned in sequence, leaving room in some cases for future expansion. There is no mnemonic intention, although LC happens to be choral music. To build the class number, we determine first that the recording is, for example, an opera recording and assign the letter *B*. The second element identifies the composer—*Pucc.* for Puccini, for example. When all of Puccini's operas are grouped together, the next term is an abbreviation of the title of the opera. Some classification systems stop here, but if they do, they are not able to identify the particular recording. Performance determines the uniqueness of a recording, and whether Schwarzkopf or Sutherland performs may be of vital importance to the user. We devised the fourth term to identify the performer. We take the performer's last initial and attach to it the other thing which uniquely identifies that recording, the last two digits of the manufacturer's commercial catalog number. B-Pucc-ML-S-41 is a class number which is unique to that recording and will never again appear on any other recording in that collection. We tested it by going through the complete 35,000 recordings in the *Schwann Catalog* and found a duplication in only two cases.

Question: You are perfectly right for 99 percent of the time, but what about all these artists who are now re-recording the Beethoven concertos that they did for the same companies on 33 rpm?

Mr. McFarland: I doubt that very many 78s would be included, since this scheme is intended for current long-playing (LP) recreational collections.

Question: Why did you decide on only two digits? Would you be more likely to avoid duplication if you used three digits?

Comment: True, although is it an unnecessary thing if your library has twenty-five re-cordings of one symphony? Also, even more likely, what rules have you developed for identifying the principal performer when a given singer sings in a London production and a hundred other productions of an opera?

Mr. McFarland: There are a number of pages which distinctly identify those. The rules are a guide to help you decide whether the instrumentalist is considered before the vocal performer or the soprano before the tenor. All rules do not apply in the same way in every category. In solo vocal music, the composer is not always as important to the user as the person doing the performing. If it is a collection of various songs from various composers, Joan Sutherland may be the unifying factor, which would be what you would want to know about a collection. In sounds and special effects there are very definite things the browser is interested in, such as railroad sounds; he is not interested in who produced them but in what kind of sounds they are. The user wants to know who is the author in plays and who is the performer in popular music.

Question: I would like to know if these things are arranged so that all of the Beatles' recordings or Frank Sinatra records are together.

Mr. McFarland: Yes, in most cases.

Question: Why did you choose your numbering system over the "cuttering" system?

Mr. McFarland: Because the cuttering system is contrived and bears no relationship to the actual piece that you are handling, the actual material. The cuttering system is derived from a table that may or may not reflect the actual performance and recording. The ANSCR notation ties it directly to the material that you are handling.

Question: Suppose we had a record by the Roling Stones of songs by the Beatles; it contains music written by the Beatles, and a Beatle enthusiast who is trying to find all the Beatle music he can find would not locate it.

Mr. McFarland: Have you cataloged this recording? Have you made an added entry for the Beatles? The class number cannot accomplish *everything* in terms of retrieval. You do not ask the Dewey numbers to give you editors' names and intricate subject matter.

Comment: A good index for this kind of

compilation would do this automatically.

Mr. McFarland: We should remember in conjunction with cataloging that what the class scheme does not do, the cataloging had better do.

Comment: This will be my final remark. I could do it better by Dewey and Cutter.

Mr. McFarland: If you go to the Long Beach Public Library, where Mary Pearson has used those for fifteen years, she will tell you that Dewey and Cutter are not adequate for a large collection. If you want to use Dewey, then I say, that is great. But, the greater percentage of those who work with these collections every day have said that they do not want Dewey.

Comment: This is the most useful thing I have ever seen. I have spent a fair amount of time trying to apply Dewey to phonograph records. In fact, if you can get that main information element into that much space, I am delighted.

Comment: You have produced a very neat example of a faceted classification which I think would work pretty well. Though I have not looked into the details of it, I think you have a very sound little scheme on the faceted principle, which in fact is a very good principle for computers.

Mr. McFarland: Anyone who would attempt to write a classification system has to be a little bit insane because of the problems one encounters. We really only took a very small part of a whole problem.

Comment: By your definition I am turning out forty lunatics a year, because my students of classification devise classification schemes from which they provide subject headings, a thesaurus, and subject description. Because they do this in the two hours we allocate in each of twenty weeks, they have no time for the detail that you have obviously spent your time on. Classification construction is a technique that can be taught quite easily.

Part 10

Statistics
and Terminology

Frank Schick, chairman of the American Library Association, Library Administration Division, Library Organization and Management Section Statistics Coordinating Committee, was invited to address the institute's Chicago session following considerable informal discussion of the requirements for the collection and dissemination of nonprint-media statistics in the Oklahoma session. After providing some background details about ALA and USOE statistics activities in general, he expressed his concern that "Nobody until now was willing or competent to assume this [nonprint] responsibility" and his desire "to set up a committee to solve the problem of how to define and how to count these items. . . ."

As a result of this discussion, an ALA LAD/LOMS Nonprint Media Statistics Committee was appointed with Pearce S. Grove, chairman. This committee has drafted a preliminary proposal to seek funds for a project to develop a handbook of terms and definitions for the statistical control of nonprint media.

In forming a terminology committee before the end of the first institute session, participants expressed their concern for the development of an accepted standard terminology as a basic prerequisite to all other areas of bibliographic control of nonprint media. At the third institute session in Detroit, Mary Cassata, a member of the institute committee and consultant to the ALA Glossary of Library Terms Subcommittee of the ALA Editorial Committee, described the subcommittee's considerations in the development of "a research proposal or project design that would describe the glossary revision project."

American Library Association and Nonprint-Media Statistics

Frank L. Schick

The area of nonprint-media statistics is the most significant subject of the unexplored sectors of the library data requirements in the United States and in the rest of the world. Regarding library statistics, this year promises to be a milestone because at long last, a century after the first official United States library statistics publication, a number of significant advances will occur. This first United States publication contains a table entitled "Principal Libraries in the United States," which is a two-page listing of 161 libraries, giving the name of the library, the geographic location, the date of funding, the number of volumes, and the library's annual increase in volumes.[1] Obviously, in 1870 there were no other media to be reported.

The Enabling Act of the Office of Education of 1867 charges the office with the direct responsibility "to collect statistics and facts showing the condition and progress of education for the several states; to compute such information that shall lead the people in the establishment and maintenance for an efficient school system and otherwise further the cause of education throughout the land." The data collection activities of the past century are not relevant to this presentation, and they have certainly been reported elsewhere.[2] But I should relate that the most significant change of recent years occurred in 1965, when the library statistics function was removed from the Library Services Division and transferred to the National Center for Educational Statistics (NCES), which was put in charge of all Office of Education statistical activities.

During the last two years many of the library statistics publications which were suspended have been revived. There are now some significant changes in the offing which add up to the fact that some surveys will be continued by National Center for Educational Statistics and others will be contracted outside and done through extramural channels. The overall direction within NCES is to coordinate the internal and extramural operations. This task would be more difficult had it not been for ALA, which took a hard look at the total library picture in 1964 when the conclusion was reached that there could not really be a meaningful United States library data collection unless there was a single source for definitions available and a coordinated method of accounting established.

With assistance of the Council on Library Resources, which spent about $70,000 on this project, the American Library Association

Chairman, LAD/LOMS Statistics Coordinating Committee; Director, School of Library and Information Science, University of Wisconsin, Milwaukee

[1] *The Report of the Commissioner of Education Made to the Secretary of Interior for the Year 1870* (Washington, D.C.: Govt. Print. Off., 1870).

[2] Frank L. Schick, "A Century of Library Statistics of National Scope," *1970 Bowker Annual,* (New York: Bowker, 1970), p.5–11.

published in 1966 *Library Statistics: A Handbook of Concepts, Definitions, and Terminology.* This publication included the activities of all the statistics committees of ALA and became the basic guide for data collection in the Office of Education. In addition, this publication served as a springboard for the drafting of the *U.S.A. Standard for Library Statistics* which has been published by the American National Standards Institute,[3] and the *International Library Statistics Standard,* which is to be adopted by United Nations Educational, Scientific and Cultural Organization in October of 1970. Almost without exception, the terms and definitions of the ALA statistics handbook were accepted by the United States Library Statistics Standard, and many of these concepts were adopted by the Interational Library Statistics Standard.

Another project which originated with the ALA Statistics Coordinating Committee is the *National Library Statistics Plan,* funded by NCES and handled for ALA by David Palmer, the former chairman of the Statistics Coordinating Committee. The National Statistics Plan will probably be published during 1970. This plan does not go into as much detail as you would prefer for nonprint media, but it gives valid guidelines for the national collection of items related to libraries, partly by NCES, partly by state agencies, and partly by professional associations.

The basic fact remains that none of these basic documents—the ALA statistics handbook, the United States standard, or the international library statistics standard—provide information on nonprint or audiovisual materials. The reason for this is simply that there was no group or committee of librarians within ALA, the Special Libraries Association (SLA), or the two international organizations (International Federation of Library Associations, and International Standards Organization Technical Committee 46) concerned with library statistics to do the job. Nobody until now was willing or competent to assume this responsibility to do a comparable job in this field. I am very glad that you are concerned

about this subject. As incoming chairman of the American Library Association, Library Administration Division (LAD) Statistics Coordinating Committee, I am very anxious to set up a committee to solve the problem of how to define and how to count these items which are being increasingly purchased, used, and stored in all types of libraries and information centers.

The structure in ALA is a bit complex, but there is a way to handle our statistical problems. For the last ten years we have found that LAD provides the means for a workable operation. We now have separate statistics committees for public libraries, school libraries, college and university libraries, and also for the various types of activities such as reference services and technical services. The statistics committees come together in the Statistics Coordinating Committee through their chairmen, who coordinate their efforts so that we move jointly towards the solution of some essential tasks.

Comment: I think the case has been put before us. Dr. Schick has said to members of his Statistics Coordinating Committee that the library statistics handbook and the *USA Standard for Library Statistics* require updating to include the newly developing areas of: (1) library automation, (2) library systems and information networks, and (3) audiovisual materials center development. Would you respond to the position statement for the Library Statistics Advisory Group about how we should plan to implement this procedure.

Mr. Schick: As I mentioned, the channel for these activities is the Statistics Coordinating Committee of ALA/LAD, and I will now proceed to request that a committee be created to handle this subject area. The first stage would be to delineate the problem. If money is needed for the next stage, I believe we know where to go.

Question: Dr. Schick, would it be appropriate for an ad hoc committee from this group to create a subcommittee, or perhaps an advisory committee?

Mr. Schick: Yes. If you come up with this recommendation, I can take it to the executive committee for LAD/LOMS, and I think

[3]USAS Z39.7-1968 (New York: U.S.A. Standards Institute, 1969).

it would have success. If you make some suggestions for members and a chairman, it could only speed up matters.

Question: What is LOMS?

Mr. Schick: There is the Library Administration Division (LAD), which has a number of sections such as the Library Organization and Management Section (LOMS), the roof under which all statistics committees in ALA operate. The way to start a committee is by requesting it be placed in this section. I am so concerned about nonprint-media statistics that I have written about the subject and have given it a great deal of thought. The committees now in existence stop when they come to this type of material.

Question: You said we need more definitions of terms, and we were working on that right now. We ought to deal with both terminology and statistics, because what is appropriate for one should be appropriate for the other.

Mr. Schick: Coordination would not be difficult. Basically, you have two problems: terminology and how to measure what you have defined.

Comment: I am almost certain that MARC will automatically be the basis of any kind of statistics. Your situation is rather like that in Great Britain, in that (1) the manufacturers do not know what they produce in statistical terms, (2) they do not care, and (3) the minute you ask for it, they assume there is some value in it and they promptly declare it a trade secret and would not tell you even if they knew. Even in the biggest and boldest media of all in Great Britain, the counting up of books is not done by the trade but is done by a trained bibliographer.

Mr. Schick: For some very odd reasons, which are not clear to most of us, what you do over there and what we do here are amazingly similar.

Comment: You might want to update and revise the Department of Audiovisual Instruction institutional handbook which came out in 1962. Next, you get the definitions standardized in all of the different handbooks at the same time. Some of this communication problem we have with definitions of terms would then be solved.

Question: Are you referring to the supplement to *AV Communication Review (AVCR)*?

Comment: Yes, it came out in *AVCR*. A revision committee has been named, but I do not believe it is in action.

Mr. Schick: Mr. Croghan made the point that there is no source to give you a listing of what is being produced now. There is no source in existence in the United States to do this, but this is not a great problem because we are only concerned with our collections in the various institutions across the country and not with industry production data. I think this is the basic point. We must develop a standardized way to account for the growth of these materials in our libraries.

The Terminology Crisis

Mary B. Cassata

Participants of this institute have become acutely aware of the importance of terminology. We recognize that communication begins with words but these words can bring understanding only when their connotations are the same for those who are trying to communicate. Although we are probably not as unfortunate as the people in the Tower of Babel, the words we have been using do not have the same meaning for all. A terminology committee has been formed to collect and define words. The list that has been developed includes media terms, library terms, and systems terms.

This initial effort got us involved in the *ALA Glossary* revision project. For a long time an American Library Association (ALA) subcommittee on terminology has been meeting and developing a strategy for revising the association's *Glossary*. It was inevitable that this institute's Terminology Committee would become concerned not only with defining our own words but also with defining words for the entire library profession which would reflect the impact of media and communications and information science and all the related terms indicating the new directions librarianship has been taking during the past several years.

ALA has asked us to develop a research proposal or project design that would describe the glossary revision project. The ALA subcommittee had hammered out certain guidelines. The audience, for example, for the new glossary was described as being a broad spectrum of practicing librarians, library science students at all levels—graduate, undergraduate, technician, and others who work in or use libraries, information centers, and related agencies, such as:

1. People in in-service training
2. Library staff without library science training
3. Other professionals and technicians working for the library, for example, information scientists
4. Nonlibrarians who need definitions.

At this point the subcommittee decided that the glossary should not attempt to serve the needs of the specialists, reasoning that although there are many specialists in our profession, their needs would be better met by other specialized glossaries and handbooks.

Regarding the scope of the glossary revision, the subcommittee decided on the following:

1. It should be a glossary, not an encyclopedia.
2. It should emphasize terms in the general field of librarianship and information science and general terms from special fields.
3. It should include technical terms used by librarians and information specialists.
4. It should include selected terms from the following fields:

   Audiovisual (includes media)
   Archives and manuscripts
   Automation
   Bibliography
   Microphotography

Head, Reference Department, University Library, State University of New York at Buffalo

Photoreproduction
Rare books
Special services
Education (those terms that are pertinent)
Information science
Printing
Bookbinding
Selected historical terms
Programmed instruction

However, it did *not* include:

1. General terms found in general dictionaries unless their definition in the field of librarianship has a different connotation
2. Foreign terms unless they are in general use in librarianship.

The purpose of the project is to provide an authoritative glossary of library, information science, and related terms in current usage to meet the needs of the audience as already defined.

Finally, although the subcommittee recognized that standardization of terms would be desirable, it recommends that standardization of terms in the field and exact meanings of terms not be attempted as part of the revision of the *Glossary*. The subcommittee does recommend that standardized definitions developed at the time the revision is being compiled be incorporated in the *Glossary* where feasible and appropriate but that compilation of the *Glossary* not be delayed at any point by awaiting the receipt of standardized definitions being planned or developed by any group. Terms would have more than one definition, as needed, to indicate varied and accepted meanings or usage.

Thus, a strategy was worked out. One method of attack was to contact editors of recently compiled glossaries for information and advice on procedures, problems, and pitfalls to avoid. Since it really did not matter what kinds of glossaries these editors had prepared, individuals were contacted who had put out glossaries, for instance, of microfilm terms, book terms, computer terms, communication terms, financial terms, education terms, political terms, nautical terms, space age terms,

and psychiatric terms. The advice was varied and sometimes even contradictory:

1. Work with a small group of knowledgeable people. Do not get tangled up with large numbers of people quibbling over pet phrases and all having slightly different ways of saying the same thing.
2. Consider the use of the computer for the preparation of the printing master. The computer will come in handy in updating the *Glossary*.
3. Do not use the computer. It is a waste of time.
4. Use some system of recording and manipulating terms, such as the McBee Keysort.
5. Become saturated with the literature. Make a massive search of all the literature—source books, periodicals, and pamphlets.
6. Make use of government-sponsored glossaries and glossaries developed by associations, professional groups, and independent manufacturers.
7. Extract definitions freely, after asking for permission, of course.
8. Put all terms on 3-by-5-inch cards and file them alphabetically.

It became evident that the project of constructing a glossary was no small task. One of the editors contacted, Donald Ely, who had constructed a glossary of audiovisual terms, advised it would be useful, if not indeed wise, to obtain endorsements for the library glossary project from recognized leaders in the field. Letters outlining the intent and scope of the project were written to outstanding librarians, educators, communicators, information scientists, and audiovisual specialists. Some of the persons contacted were Robert Downs, William Dix, Paul Wasserman, Eric Moon, Jesse Shera, Maurice Tauber, Paul Janaske, Robert Collison, Lester Asheim, Joseph Becker, Jerrold Orne, and Verner Clapp. Some of these experts suggested areas for terminology that had been disregarded. Robert Collison suggested the employment of representatives from all over the world in the project's advisory panel. He encouraged the issuing of small editions which would be frequently updated and cautioned against issuing supplements.

Collison even advocated printing the *Glossary* on paper that could be written on, with sufficient space in the margins or text for its critics to enter their comments.

Paul Wasserman felt that the descriptor *ALA* for the *Glossary* was inappropriate. He felt that including the name of one professional organization in the title effectively forecloses the prospect of others in the field using it as an authoritative source of information about definitions in their areas of subject interest. He stated that he arrived at this position after having conversations with persons in the more specialized fields of librarianship and information science and learning that they had "great sensitivity to the machinations of the American Library Association." He declared, however, that he was convinced of the need and value of an appropriate and timely glossary, but he expressed the hope that it be developed out of a mélange of interests, rather than simply those of the American Library Association, and that such a broadly conceived perspective would be reflected in its title.

Verner Clapp warned against the liberal use of jargon; Maurice Tauber urged the consideration of foreign terms that had come into popular American usage in dealer's catalogs and conferences.

In any event the message is clear: The publication of a glossary of library terms embodying the newer terminology from fields related to library science has been endorsed as a useful and important project.

Bibliography

Bibliographies

Ackermann, Jean Marie. *Guide to Films on International Development.* Beverly Hills, Calif.: Film Sense, 1967. 53p.

Allison, Mary L. *New Educational Materials 1968.* New York: Citation, 1968. 256p.

American Library Association. *Films for Libraries.* Chicago: The Association, 1962. 81p.

Approved Instructional Materials for Secondary Schools, 1968/69, Instructional Materials List. Rockville, Md.: Montgomery County Public Schools, Dept. of Instructional Materials, n.d.

Audio-Visual Equipment Directory. Evanston, Ill.: National Audio-Visual Assn., 1953– .

Audio Visual Source Directory for Services and Products. Tarrytown, N.Y.: Motion Picture Enterprises Publications, Inc.

AV Index: A Guide to Instructional Material Information in Selected Publications. Detroit. Audio-Visual Research Institute, 1961– .

Batcheller, David R., ed. *Films for Use in Teaching Drama and Theatre.* Washington, D.C.: American Educational Theatre Assn., Inc., 1967. 77p.

Blue Book of 16mm Films. Chicago: Educational Screen, Inc., 1925– .

British National Film Catalogue. London: British Industrial and Scientific Film Assn., 1963– .

Canadian Film Institute. *Catalogue of 16mm Films on Behavioral Sciences Available from the National Science Film Library.* Ottawa: The Institute, 1967.

Catalog of 16mm Films Available on Rental or Purchase in the United States. Ottawa: National Film Board of Canada, 1968. 64p.

Coppen, Helen E. *Survey of British Research in Audio-Visual Aids.* 2d ed. London: Educational Foundation for Visual Aids, 1968.

Dale, Edgar, and others. *Motion Pictures in Education; a Summary of the Literature.* New York: Wilson, 1938.

Dale, Edgar, and Trzebiatowski, Greg. "A Basic Reference Shelf on Audio-Visual Instruction." Stanford, Calif.: ERIC Clearinghouse, 1968. 17p.

Dove, Jack. *Music Libraries: Including a Comprehensive Bibliography of Music Literature and a Selected Bibliography of Music Scores Published Since 1957.* London: Andre Deutsch, 1965. 2v. 744p.

Drazniowaky, R. "Bibliographies as Tools for Map Acquisition and Map Collection," *Cartographer* 3: 138–44 (Dec. 1966).

Eason, Tracy. "A Selected Bibliography of A-V Media in Library," *Wilson Library Bulletin* 44: 312–19 (Nov. 1969).

Edling, Jack V. "A Basic Reference Shelf on Instructional Media Research." Stanford, Calif.: ERIC Clearinghouse, 1967. 10p.

Education Media Council. *Educational Media Index.* New York: McGraw-Hill, 1964.

Educational Film Guide. New York: Wilson, 1936–62.

Educational Film Library Association. *8mm Film Directory.* New York: Comprehensive Service Corp., 1968.

Educational Films and Filmstrips 1969. Whittier, Calif.: Moody Institute of Science, Educational Film Division, n.d.

Educational Films 1969. East Lansing: Michigan State University, 1969. 568p.

Educational Sound Filmstrip Directory. 4th ed, St. Charles, Ill.: DuKane Corp., Audio-Visual Division, n.d.

Educator's Guide to Free Films. Randolph, Wis.: Educator's Progress Service, 1949– .

Educator's Guide to Free Filmstrips. Randolph, Wis.: Educator's Progress Service, 1962– .

Educator's Guide to Free Tapes, Scripts and Transparencies. Randolph, Wis.: Educator's Progress Service, 1955– .

Feature Films on 8 and 16mm. 2d ed. New York: Continental 16, n.d.

Federal Advisory Council on Medical Training Aids. *1968 Film Reference Guide for Medicine and Allied Sciences.* Atlanta, Ga.: National Medical Audiovisual Center, 1968.

Film Canadiana. Ottawa: Canadian Film Institute, 1969– .

Films for Discussion (Adult). University Park: Pennsylvania State University, Audio-Visual Service, n.d. 34p.

Films for Safety and First Aid. 2d ed. University Park: Pennsylvania State University, Audio-Visual Services, n.d. 19p.

Films Incorporated. *Study Pak: Half Century of American Film; Dialogue with the World; Modern Approach to the Humanities.* Wilmette, Ill.: Films Inc., 1969.

Filmstrip Guide. New York: Wilson, 1948–62.

"Filmstrips and Motion Pictures Useful in Teaching Management" in M. H. Lowell, *Management of Libraries and Information Centers,* p.155–62. Metchuen, N.J.: Scarecrow, 1962.

Foster, Joanna. "Audio-visual Materials for Teaching Children's Literature," *Wilson Library Bulletin* 43: 154–59 (Oct. 1968).

Frankenberg, Celestine G. *Picture Sources.* 2d ed. New York: Special Libraries Assn., 1964. 203p.

Freidman, Florence B. *Classroom Teacher's Guide to Audio-Visual Material.* Rev. ed. Philadelphia: Chilton, 1961.

Glaser, Robert, and Marino, Mary Louise. "A Basic Reference Shelf on Programmed Instruction," Stanford, Calif.: ERIC Clearinghouse, 1968.

A Half Century of American Film: 500 Selected Features for Discriminating Viewers. Chicago: Films Inc., [1969]. 160p.

Harrison Catalog of Stereophonic Tapes. New York: M. and N. Harrison, Inc., 1955– .

Hartley, William H. *A Guide to Audio-Visual Materials for Elementary Social Studies.* Brooklyn, N.Y.: Rambler Press, 1950.

Herbert, Charles A. *Annotated Bibliography of Audio-Visual Aids for Management Development Programs.* New York: Research Service, 1958. 24p.

Hopkinson, Shirley L. *Instructional Materials for Teaching the Use of the Library.* San Jose, Calif.: The Author, 1966. 57p.

Humphrys, Alfred W. *Films on Art.* Washington: National Art Education Assn., 1965.

International Federation of Films on Art, Bulletin No. 4. Engl. ed. Ottawa: Canadian Center for Films on Art. May 1968.

Kone, Grace Ann. *8mm Film Directory: A Comprehensive Descriptive Index.* New York: Educational Film Library Assn., 1969. 532p.

Kula, Sam. *Bibliography of Film Librarianship.* London: Library Assn., 1967. 68p.

Landers, Bertha, ed. *A Foreign Language Audio-Visual Guide.* Los Angeles: Landers Associates, 1961.

Lane, David O. "Basic Collection of Records for a College Library," *College and Research Libraries* 23: 295–301 (July 1962).

Larson, L. C., and others. "Bibliography of Research in Audio-Visual Education and Mass-Media, 1930–1950. Mimeographed. Bloomington: Indiana University, 1950.

Lieberman, Irving. *A Working Bibliography of Commercially Available Audio-Visual Materials for the Teaching of Library Science.* Occasional Papers no. 94. Urbana: University of Illinois Graduate School of Library Science, 1968. 77p.

Limbacher, James L. *Feature Films on 8mm and 16mm: A Directory of 8mm and 16mm Feature Films Available for Rental, Sale and Lease in the United States.*

2d ed. New York: Educational Film Library Assn., 1968.

Lissner, John. "Pop/Folk/Jazz: Guideposts to a Basic Record Library," *Library Journal* 94: 158–61 (15 Jan. 1969).

McClusky, F. Dean. *The A-V Bibliography.* Revised. Dubuque, Iowa: Brown Book Co., 1955.

Marshall, June N., ed. *Sources of Free and Inexpensive Pictures. Pamphlets and Packets.* Washington, D.C.: National Aerospace Education Council, 1967.

Mental Retardation Film List. Atlanta, Ga.: National Medical Audiovisual Center, n.d.

Moldstad, John A. *Sources of Information on Educational Media.* Washington, D.C.: U.S. Dept. of Health, Education and Welfare, Office of Education, 1963.

National Art Education Association. *Slides and Filmstrips on Art.* Washington, D.C.: The Association, 1967. 40p.

National Audiovisual Center. *List of Government Medical and Dental 8mm Films for Sale by the National Audiovisual Center.* National Archive Publication 71–7. Washington, D.C.: The Center, 1970.

National Center for Audio Tapes 1970–72 Catalog. Boulder: University of Colorado, National Center for Audio Tapes, 1970. 123p.

National Information Center for Educational Media. *Index to 8mm Motion Cartridges.* New York: Bowker, 1969. 402p.

———. *Index to Overhead Transparencies.* New York: Bowker, 1969. 552p.

———. *Index to 16mm Educational Films.* 2d. ed. New York: Bowker, 1969. 1111p.

———. *Index to 35mm Educational Filmstrips.* 2d. ed. New York: Bowker, 1970. 872p.

National Medical Audio-Visual Center. *Dentistry. Selected List of Audiovisuals.* Atlanta, Ga.: The Center, 1968.

New York State Library Musical Recordings. Albany, N.Y.: University of the State of New York, State Education Dept., Division of Library Development, 1968. 28p.

1967–68 Tapes for Teaching, a Catalog of Audio Recording Tapes in the Library of the Pennsylvania Department of Public Instruction. Harrisburg, Pa.: Dept. of Public Instruction, Bureau of Educational Services, 1967. 333p.

Phonorecord Catalog of the New York State Library. Albany, N.Y.: University of the State of New York, State Education Dept., Division of Library Development, 1968. 28p.

Public Relations Society of American Information Center. *Films about Public Relations and Related Subjects.* New York: The Society, 1962.

Roach, Helen. *Spoken Records.* 2d. ed. New York: Scarecrow, 1966. 206p.

Rosengren, Harold J. *Three-Dimensional Teaching Aids for Trade and Industrial Instruction.* Washington, D.C.: U.S. Office of Education, 1961. 46p.

Rufsvold, Margaret I., and Guss, Carolyn. *Guides to Educational Media.* 3d. ed. Chicago: American Library Assn., 1971.

Schwann Long Playing Record Catalog. Boston: Schwann, 1948–

Selected Educational Motion Pictures: A Descriptive Encyclopedia. Washington, D.C.: American Council on Education, 1942.

Selected Films: Heart Disease, Cancer, and Stroke. Revised. Atlanta, Ga.: National Medical Audiovisual Center, 1968.

Selected List of Catalogs for Short Films and Filmstrips, 1963. New York: UNESCO, 1965.

Selected Mental Health Films. Washington, D.C.: National Clearinghouse for Mental Health Information, U.S. Public Health Service, 1967.

Selected References on Aging. Washington, D.C.: U.S. Department of Health, Education and Welfare, Administration on Aging, 1965.

Shetler, Donald. *Film Guide for Music Educators.* Washington, D.C.: Music Educators National Conference, National Education Assn., 1968.

Sources of Motion Pictures and Filmstrips. Rochester, N.Y.: Eastman Kodak Co., n.d.

Southeast Suburban Audio-Visual Library

Catalogue of Instructional Materials. Wayne, Pa.: Southeast Suburban Audio-Visual Library, 1968. 103p.

U.S. Department of Agriculture. Motion Picture Service. *Films of the U.S. Department of Agriculture.* Washington, D.C.: The Department, n.d.

Wabash Valley Education Center Media Catalog 1968. West Lafayette, Ind.: The Center, 1968. 149p.

Wade, Serena E. "A Basic Reference Shelf on Individualized Instruction." Stanford, Calif.: ERIC Clearinghouse, 1968. 8p.

———. "Media and Disadvantaged—A Review of the Literature." New York: ERIC Information Retrieval Center on the Disadvantaged at Teachers College, Columbia University, 1969. 24p.

Watanabe, Ruth. "Current Periodicals for Music Libraries," *Music Library Association Notes.* 23: 225–35 (Dec. 1966).

We Read. Selected Lists of Children's Books and Recordings. Prepared by the Children's Services Division of the American Library Association. Washington, D.C.: Office of Economic Opportunity, 1966.

Yonge, Ena L. *Catalogue of Early Globes, Made Prior to 1850 and Conserved in the United States: A Preliminary* Listing. New York: American Geographical Society, 1968. 118p.

Cataloging and Classification

Abbot, John E. "Cataloging and Filing of Motion Picture Films," *Library Journal* 63:93–5 (1 Feb. 1938).

Allen, Thelma E., and Hickman, Daryl Ann. *New Rules for an Old Game.* Vancouver: University of British Columbia, 1967.

Anderson, Sherman. "Cataloging the Contents of Certain Recordings," *Library Resources and Technical Services* 9:359–62 (Summer 1965).

Archer, Ellinor, and Gawith, Shirley. "Cataloging a Film Library," *Australian Library Journal* 11:121–4 (July 1962).

"Author Entry: Legion or There Abouts," *Dartmouth College Library Bulletin* 3:8–9 (Dec. 1938).

Badten, Jean, and Motomatzu, Nancy. "Commercial Media Cataloging—What's Holding Us Up?" *School Library Journal* 15:34–5 (Nov. 1968).

Barnes, Christopher. "Classification and Cataloging of Spoken Records in Academic Libraries," *College and Research Libraries* 28:49–52 (Jan. 1967).

Boaz, Martha Terosse. "Organization and Administration of Audio-Visual Aids in a College Library," A.M.L.S. thesis, University of Michigan, 1950. 53p.

Borduas, Jean-Rodolph. "Simplify Record Classification," *Library Journal* 85:4244 (1 Dec. 1960).

Bradley, John G., "Cataloging and Indexing Motion Picture Film," *American Archivist* 8:169–84 (July 1945).

Brahmo, S. "Processing of Maps; Including a Select Bibliography of Maps Pertaining to India Published During 1683–1853," *Library Herald* 9:117–28 (Oct. 1966).

Carson, Doris M. "Cataloging Nonbook Materials," *Wilson Library Bulletin* 39:562–64 (Mar. 1965).

"Catalog Cards for Film," *Library of Congress Information Bulletin* 10:14–15 (20 Aug. 1951).

"Cataloging Non-Book Materials," *Michigan Association of School Librarians* 18:24–26 (Fall 1968).

"Cataloging of Films and Filmstrips; Unesco Proposals," *UNESCO Bulletin for Libraries* 9:98–101 (May–June 1955).

"Cataloging of Materials Other Than Books; a Conference Discussion," *Library Association Record* 46:78–81 (May 1944).

Chibnall, Bernard. "British National Film Catalogue and Its Contribution to Information Work," *Aslib Proceedings* 15:141–45 (May 1963).

———. "National Film Library and Its Cataloging Rules," *Journal of Documentation* 11:79–82 (June 1955).

———, and Croghan, Antony. *A Feasibility Study of a Multi Media Catalogue.* Report to O.S.T.I. on Project S1/25/36. University of Sussex, 1969. 57p.

Clugston, Katharine W. "Anglo-American Cataloging Rules: Film Cataloging at the Library of Congress," *Library Resources and Technical Services* 13:35–41 (Winter 1969).

Cohen, Allen. "Classification of Four-Track Tapes," *Library Resources and Technical Services* 6:360–61 (Fall 1962).

Coover, James B. "Computers, Cataloging and Cooperation," *Music Library Association Notes* 35:437–46 (Mar. 1969).

Cox, Carl T. "The Cataloging of Records," *Library Journal* 85:4523–25 (15 Dec. 1960).

Cox, J. C. "Cataloging and Classification of Slides, Filmstrips, and Films," in *Catholic Library Association Conference Proceedings, 1960,* p.186–88. New York: Catholic Library Assn., 1960.

Crowther, G. "Cataloguing and Classification of Cine Film at the Royal Aircraft Establishment," *ASLIB Proceedings* 11:179–87 (July 1959).

Cunningham, Virginia. "From Schmidt-Phiseldeck to Zanetti," *Music Library Association Notes* 23:449–52 (Mar. 1967).

———. "The Library of Congress Classed Catalog for Music," *Library Resources and Technical Services* 8:285–88 July 1959).

Cunnion, T. "Cataloging and Classification of Phonograph Records," in *Catholic Library Association Conference Proceedings 1960,* p.180–85. New York: Catholic Library, 1960.

Darling, Richard. "Report on Preliminary Considerations of the Committee for the Use of Audiovisual Materials in Libraries," *Library Resources and Technical Services* 13:301 (Spring 1969).

Dean-Smith, Margaret. "Proposals towards the Cataloging of Gramophone Records in a Library of National Scope," *Journal of Documentation* 8:141–56 (Sept. 1952).

DeLerma, Dominique-René. "Philosophy and Practice of Phonorecord Classification at Indiana University," *Library Resources and Technical Services* 13:86–92 (Winter 1969).

Dome, John E. "Automation of Media Cataloging," *Audiovisual Instruction* 11:466 (June 1966).

Drake, Helen. "Cataloging Recordings," *Illinois Libraries* 46:145–52 (Fall 1964).

Fanning, David C. "The Cataloging of Film Material in the National Film Archive," *Library World* 62:280–82 (June 1961).

Fleischer, Eugene B. "Uniterm Your Audiovisual Library," *Audiovisual Instruction* 14:76–78 (Feb. 1969).

Gaunt, J. H. "Efficient Cataloging of Audio-Visual Innovations," *Audiovisual Instruction* 12:958–59 (Nov. 1967).

Geller, Evelyn. "Commercial Media Cataloging—What's Around?" *School Library Journal* 15:27–33 (Nov. 1968).

Grenfell, David. "The Cataloging of Films," *Librarian and Book World* 47:62–64 (April 1958).

———. "Standardization in Film Cataloging," *Journal of Documentaton* 15:81–92 (June 1959).

Hagen, Carlos B. "Information Retrieval System for Maps," *UNESCO Bulletin for Libraries* 20:30–35 (Jan. 1966).

———. "Proposed Information Retrieval System for Sound Recordings," *Special Libraries* 56:223–28 (Apr. 1965).

Hallowell, Jared R. "Some Information on the Cataloging of Phonograph Records," A.M.L.S. thesis, University of Michigan, 1960. 30p.

Hamman, Frances. "Bibliographic Control of Audiovisual Materials: Report of a Special Committee," *Library Resources and Technical Services* 1:180–89 (Fall 1957).

Hammond, Hilary. "A Punched Card Gramophone Record Catalogue at Luton [England] Central Library," *Library World* 68:168 (Dec. 1966).

Harvard-Williams, Peter, and Watson, S. A. "Slide Collection at Liverpool School of Architecture," *Journal of Documentation* 16:11–14 (Mar. 1960).

Haskell, Inez. "Cataloging of Records, Musical and Non-Musical for a General Library," *Pacific Northwest Library Association Quarterly* 8:150–55 (July 1945).

Holdridge, R. E. "Cataloging Non-Book Materials," *Audiovisual Instruction* 12:358–59 (Apr. 1967).

Kemp, Muriel Louise. "Worcester Free Public Library Gives Discs Full Treatment," *Library Journal* 73:406–8 (1 Mar. 1948).

Kenney, Brigitte L. "Psychiatric Videotape Indexing," *TV in Psychiatry Newsletter and Progress Report* p.8–21 (Dec. 1969).

Kuvshinoff, Boris W. "Graphic Graphics Card Catalog and Computer Index," *American Documentation* 18:3–9 (Jan. 1967).

Ladewig, Adelheid Gertrud. "Routine for Cataloging and Processing of Slides," *Journal of Cataloging and Classification* 6:67–68 (Summer 1950).

Ledoux, Jacques. *Study of the Establishment of National Centres for Cataloguing of Films and Television Programmes.* Paris: UNESCO, 1963. 34p.

Leon, J. L. "How to Catalog Magnetic Tapes," *Audiovisual Instruction* 13:311 (Apr. 1968).

Lincoln, Sister M. Edmund. "Techniques for Handling Phonograph Records," *Catholic Library World* 27:107–10 (Dec. 1955).

Line, Maurice. "A Classification for Music Scores on Historical Principles," *Libri* 12:352–63 (1963).

MacPherson, Beryl, and Berneking, Carolyn. "Phonorecord Cataloging—Methods and Policies," *Library Journal* 83:2623–24 (1 Oct. 1958).

Mary Alvin, Sister, and Michele, Sister M. "La Roche College Classification System for Phonorecords," *Library Resources and Technical Services* 9:443–45 (Fall 1965).

Mary Janet, Sister. "Cataloging of Non-Book Materials," *Catholic Library World* 24:153–55 (Fall 1953).

Mary Laurenta, Sister. "Classifying and Cataloging Filmstrips, Records, and Tapes," *Catholic Library World* 38:242–43 (Dec. 1966).

Maywhort, Helen Wooten. "All on the Card. Sullivan Memorial Library Has Record Cataloging Plan," *Library Journal* 11:806–8 (1 June 1946).

"Media Programs: Patterns of Organization," *Audiovisual Instruction* 10:111–14 (Feb. 1965).

Meikleham, Margaret H. C. "Cataloging the Record Collection in McMaster University Library," *Ontario Library Review* 29:154–57 (May 1945).

Miller, Philip L. "Cataloging and Filing of Phonograph Records," *Library Journal* 62:279–80 (1 Apr. 1937).

Moore, Norman B., and Flory, John, eds. *Proceedings of the First International Film Cataloging Conference 1951.* Evanston, Ill.: Film Council of America, Inc., 1952.

Morsch, Lucile M. "Printed Cards for Phonorecords: Cataloging," *Music Library Association Notes* 10:197–98 (Mar. 1953).

Nitecki, Joseph Z. "Simplified Classification and Cataloging of Microforms," *Library Resources and Technical Services* 13:79–85 (Winter 1969).

Noda, Octavio. "Film Catalog," *Film Library Quarterly* 1:55 (Summer 1968).

Ogi, Masaaki. "Pattern-Matching Technique Applied to Indexing and Retrieving Films for Television Use," in American Society for Information Science *Proceedings,* v.5, *Information Transfer.* p.89–93 Columbus: Greenwood, 1968.

Paine, L. F. "Cataloging Audio-Visual Materials," *Wilson Library Bulletin* 23:699–701 (May 1949).

Palmerlee, A. E. "Automation and Map Libraries: Thoughts on Cooperative Cataloging through Automation," *SLA Geography and Map Division Bulletin* 49:6–16 (Sept. 1967).

Peel, Ruth. "Changes in Cataloging and Computer Programming." Tulsa, Okla.: Oral Roberts University, 1969.

———. "The Development of Audio-Visual Cataloging in Oral Roberts University Library." Tulsa, Okla.: Oral Roberts University, 1969.

Perusse, Lyle F. "Classifying and Cataloging Lantern Slides for the Architecture Library," *Journal of Cataloging and Classification* 10:77–83 (Apr. 1954).

Pettingill, Ada D. "Film Subject Catalog," *Library Journal* 65:27 (1 Jan. 1940).

Redfern, Brian. "Arranging and Cataloging Gramophone Records," in his *Organizing Music in Libraries,* p.67–73. New York: Philosophical Library, 1966. 80p.

Robinson, S. A. "Cataloging of Music and Records." M.S.L.S. thesis, Western Reserve University, 1957. 36p.

Sample Catalog from the Automated Music and Score Catalog. Presented to the New York State Chapter of the Music Library Association, May 6, 1967. Binghamton,

N.Y.: State University of New York, Harper College Music Library, 1967.

Sanborn, William B. "San Francisco Audio Visual Materials Card Catalog," *School Library Association of California Bulletin* 28:5–6 (May 1957).

Sayers, W. C. Berwick. *A Manual of Classification for Librarians and Bibliographers* 3d rev. London: Andre Deutsch, 1959. 346p.

Scott, Edith. "Cataloging Non-book Materials." *Journal of Cataloging and Classification* 5:46–47 (Spring 1949).

Sherlock, M. "Cataloging Music and Records in the Douglas Library," *Ontario Library Review* 29:158–59 (May 1945).

Skoog, A. C., and Evans, G. "Slide Collection Classification," *Penn Library Association Bulletin* 24:15–22 (Jan. 1969).

Somerville, S. A. "Cataloging of Gramophone Records," *Librarian and Book World* 38:97–99 (July 1959).

Stevenson, Gordon. "Classification Chaos," *Library Journal* 88:3789–94 (15 Oct. 1963).

Stiles, Helen J. "Phonograph Record Classification at the United States Air Force Academy," *Library Resources and Technical Services* 9:446–48 (Fall 1965).

Stoops, Betty. "Cataloging and Classification Systems for Instructional Materials," *Audiovisual Instruction* 9:427–28 (Sept. 1964).

———. "Film Titles and Credits—Are They Adequate?" *Illinois Libraries* 48:83–89 (Feb. 1966).

Stow, Charles Edward. "Cataloging the Nonmusical Phonograph Record," *Library Journal* 70:20–21 (1 Jan. 1945).

Sunder, Mary Jane. "Organizing of Recorded Sound," *Library Resources and Technical Services* 13:93–98 (Winter 1969).

Taylor, K. I. "Cataloging Instructional Materials; Sample Catalog Cards from West Leyden's Center for Instruction Materials." Northlake, Ill.: The Center, 1963. 14p.

Tillin, Marian. "Treat Records like Books." *Library Journal* 85:4518–21 (15 Dec. 1960).

Von Oesen, Elaine. "Single Cataloging of Audio-Visual Materials," *Wilson Library Bulletin* 23:251–53 (Nov. 1948).

Wasserman, Morton N. "Computer-Prepared Book Catalog for Engineering Transparencies," *Special Libraries* 57:111–13 (Fall 1966).

Winston, Fred, and Winston, Mildred. "Indexing and Cataloging the 8mm," *The Instructor* 78:130,132 (Jan. 1969).

General

Adult Education Groups and Audio-Visual Techniques. Paris: UNESCO, 1958.

"Agreement for Facilitating the International Circulation of Visual and Auditory Materials of an Educational, Scientific, and Cultural Character." Beirut, 1948. 6p.

"Alphabetical Listing of Terminology," in *National Conference on the Implications of the New Media for the Teaching of Library Science,* p.208–26. Urbana: University of Illinois Graduate School of Library Science, 1963.

Amesbury, Dorothy. "Phonograph Records in the Library," *Library Journal* 62:453–54 (1 July 1937).

Arbaugh, Dorothy. "Motion Pictures and the Future Historian," *American Archivist* 2:106–15 (Apr. 1939).

"Audiovisual Practices among Colleges and Universities," *American School and University* 36:26–27 (July 1964).

A-V Task Force Survey: Final Report, special summary prepared for the Audio-Visual Committee, American Library Assn. University of Pittsburgh Libraries, 1969; reprinted in *American Libraries* 1, no.1:40–45 (Jan. 1970).

AV–USA 1969. Rochester, N.Y.: Hope Reports, 1969.

Balanoff, Neal. "James M. Wood Learning Center," *Audiovisual Instruction* 8:226–29 (Apr. 1963).

Barhydt, Gordon C., and Schmidt, Charles T. *Information Retrieval Thesaurus of Educational Terms.* Cleveland: Case Western Reserve University, 1968. 133p.

Barnes, E. A. "Learning Center Dramatizes Use of Latest Technical Developments," *College and University Business* 35:53–56 (Sept. 1963).

Bathorst, Leonard H., and Klein, Bruce. *A Visual Communications System*. Dubuque, Iowa: Brown Book Co., 1966.

Bennett, Fleming, and Culler, Jane L. *ACRL Audio-Visual Directory*. Chicago: American Library Assn., 1956.

Bergeson, Clarence O. "Relationship of Library Science and Audio-Visual Instruction," *Audiovisual Instruction* 12:100–3 (Feb. 1967).

Bertrand, John K. "Media Reference Center," *Audiovisual Instruction* 12:16–22 (Jan. 1967).

Bidwell, Charles M. "The Information Problem: Codes for Media," *Audiovisual Instruction* 12:325–28 (Apr. 1967).

Brahmo, S. "Role of Maps in Library Service," *Herald of Library Science* 5:203–9 (July 1966).

Brown, James W.; Lewis, Richard B.; and Harcleroad, Fred F. *A-V Instruction: Materials and Methods*. 2d ed. New York: McGraw-Hill, 1964. 592p.

———, and Norberg, Kenneth D. *Administering Educational Media*. New York: McGraw-Hill, 1965. 357p.

———, and Thornston, James W., eds. *New Media in Higher Education*. Washington, D.C.: Assn. for Higher Education, 1963. 183p.

Brunke, Elizabeth D. "National Film Board Library," *Ontario Library Review* 26:405–10 (Nov. 1942).

Burkett, J., and Morgan, T. S., eds. *Special Materials in the Library*. London: Library Assn., 1963. 179p.

Caldwell, Gladys. "The Los Angeles Public Library and the Motion Picture Studios," *ALA Bulletin* 19:270–72 (July 1925).

Chapman, Lousie. "Place of the Phonograph in the Library," *Library Journal* 63:765–68 (15 Oct. 1938).

Clarke, Virginia. "Now, Just One Place to Look," *Library Journal* 73:1233–36 (15 Sept. 1948).

Corey, Stephen M. *Audio-Visual Materials of Instruction*. Chicago: University of Chicago, 1949.

Cox, Robert A. "International Use of Computers for Media Control," *Audiovisual Instruction* 12:330 (Apr. 1967).

Cross, A. J., and Cypher, Irene F. *Audiovisual Education*. New York: Crowell, 1961. 415p.

Dale, Edgar. *Audio-Visual Methods in Teaching*. Rev. ed., New York: Dryden, 1954. 534p.

Dick, Grace Isabella. "New Opportunity for Librarians," *Library Journal* 58:772–73 (1 Oct. 1933).

Ducote, Richard L. *Program and Function Study*. Glen Ellyn, Ill.: College of Du Page, Instructional Resources Center, 1967. 62p.

———. *Recommendations to the American Library Association by the A.L.A. Audio-Visual Committee on the Implementation of the A-V Task Force Survey*. Chicago: American Library Assn., 1970.

Dupuy, Trevor Nevitt. *Ferment in College Libraries*. Washington, D.C.: Communication Service Corp., 1968. 158p.

———. *Modern Libraries for Modern Colleges*. Washington, D.C.: Communication Services Corp., 1968. 122p.

East, Marjorie, and Dale, Edgar. *Display for Learning*. New York: Dryden, 1952. 306p.

Eboch, Sidney C. "Computer Booking and Cataloging: Shadow and Substance," *Audiovisual Instruction* 12:322–24 (Apr. 1967).

Edinger, Lois. "Technology in Education," *Wilson Library Bulletin* 41:72–75 (Sept. 1966).

Educational Facilities with New Media, edited by Alan C. Green and others. Washington, D.C.: Dept. of Audiovisual Instruction, National Education Assn., 1966.

"Educational Films." *Wilson Library Bulletin* 14:778 (June 1940).

Educational Television: The Next Ten Years. Stanford, Calif.: Stanford University, Institute for Communication Research, 1962. 375p.

Ellsworth, Ralph Eugene. "Phonograph records in the Library," *Library Journal* 58:529–31 (15 June 1933).

Elton, Sir Arthur. "Film as Source Material for History," *Aslib Proceedings* 7:207–39 (Nov. 1955).

Erickson, Carlton W. *Fundamentals of Teach-*

ing with Audiovisual Technology. New York: Macmillan, 1965. 384p.

Fern, George H., and Robbins, Eldon. Teaching with Films. Milwaukee, Wis.: Bruce, 1946. 146p.

Fine, Benjamin. Teaching Machines. New York: Sterling Publishing Co., 1962. 176p.

Finn, James D. Teaching Machines and Programmed Learning, 1962: A Survey of the Industry. Washington, D.C.: U.S. Office of Education and National Education Assn., 1962. 85p.

Foltz, Charles. The World of Teaching Machines; Programmed Learning and Self-Instructional Devices. Washington, D.C.: Electronic Teaching Laboratories, 1961.

Ford, Harry J. "The Instructional Resources Center," Audiovisual Instruction 7:524–25 (Oct. 1962).

Fry, Edward B. Teaching Machines and Programmed Instruction. New York: McGraw-Hill, 1963.

Gee, Mable W. "Sink or Swim!" Wilson Library Bulletin 29:381–82 (Jan. 1955).

Geller, Evelyn. "The Marriage of the Media," Library Journal 93:2079–84 (15 May 1968).

Gerlach, Vernon S., and Fernbach, Irene. "How to Teach Library Skills without Really Being There," Library Journal 89:921–22 (15 Feb. 1964).

Gerletti, Robert C. "Digital Apoplexy: Certain Diagnosis, No Easy Cure," School Library Journal 15:36–37 (Nov. 1968).

Godfrey, Eleanor P. The State of Audiovisual Technology 1961–1966. Washington, D.C.: Dept. of Audiovisual Instruction, National Education Assn., 1967. 217p.

Goldstein, Harold. "Audio-Visual Services in Libraries: What One Course at Illinois Attempts to Do," Illinois Libraries 45:67–71 (Fall 1963).

———. "A/V Has It Any Future in Libraries?" Wilson Library Bulletin 36:670–73 (Apr. 1962).

Grady, Marion B. "Comparison of Motion Pictures and Books as Resource Materials," Ph.D. dissertation, Univ. of Chicago, 1951. 450p.

Gunther, Alfred. "Slides in Documentation,"

UNESCO Bulletin for Libraries 17:157–62 (May 1963).

Haas, Kenneth B., and Pacher, Harry Q. Preparation and Use of Audio-Visual Aids. 3rd ed. New York: Prentice-Hall, 1955.

Harrison, Kenneth C. "What English Libraries Are Doing," Library Journal 74:676–77 (15 Apr. 1949).

Harvey, John F. "Measuring Library Audio-Visual Activities," College and Research Libraries 18:193–98 (May 1957).

Horn, Andrew H., ed. "Special Materials and Services" Library Trends 4:119–212 (Oct. 1955).

Hudson, R. B. "New and Future Trends in the Use of Audio-Visual Materials," ALA Bulletin 63:39–42 (Jan. 1964).

Jones, Emil S. "Background and Philosophy of Film Library Service," Drexel Library Quarterly 2:102–10 (Apr. 1966).

Jones, G. P. "The Cinema, the School, and the Public Library," Library Assistant 15:6–12 (1921).

Kemp, Jerrold E. Planning and Producing Audiovisual Materials. San Francisco: Chandler, 1963.

Kindler, James S. Using Audio-Visual Materials in Education. New York: American Book Co., 1965.

Knirk, Frederick G., and Child, John, eds. Instructional Technology: A Book of Readings. New York: Holt, Rinehart and Winston, 1968.

Korte, D. A. de. Television in Education and Training: A Review of Developments and Applications of Television and Other Modern Audio-Visual Aids. Translated by G. du Cloux. London: Cleaver-Hume, 1967. 182p.

Kujoth, Jean Spealman. Readings in Nonbook Librarianship. Metuchen, N.J.: Scarecrow, 1968. 463p.

Layer, Harold A. "Ethnic Studies and Audiovisual Media: A Listing and Discussion." Stanford, Calif.: ERIC Clearinghouse, June 1969. 11p.

LeFeure, Mabel A. International Organizations and Associations with Audiovisual Activities: A Directory. Washington, D.C.:

Dept. of Audiovisual Instruction, National Education Assn., 1963.

Lembo, Diana. "A Stepchild Comes of Age," *Library Journal* 92:3122–23 (15 Sept. 1967).

Lemler, Ford L. "Descriptive Cataloging," *Audiovisual Instruction* 12:328–30 (Apr. 1967).

"Library and Documentation System Capabilities." Santa Monica: Systems Development Corp., 1969.

Lieberman, Irving. *Audio-Visual Instruction in Library Education.* New York: Columbia University School of Library Service, 1955. 213p.

——. "Use of Non-Print Media in Library School Instruction," in *Library Education: An International Survey,* p.247–72. Urbana: University of Illinois Graduate School of Library Science, 1968.

Lohrer, Alice. "Audio-Visual Library Plan," *Illinois Librarian* 22:8 (Dec. 1940).

Lumsdaine, Arthur A., and Glaser, Robert. *Teaching Machines and Programmed Learning, a Source Book.* Washington, D.C.: Dept. of Audio-Visual Instruction, National Education Assn., 1960.

Lyle, Guy R., and Krauskopf, R. "Phonograph Collections in Antioch College Library," *Library Journal* 59:266–67 (15 Mar. 1934).

McClusky, F. Dean. *Audio-Visual Teaching Techniques.* Dubuque, Iowa: Brown Co., 1949.

McDaniel, Irene H. "Stereo's Here to Stay," *Library Journal* 85:3381–83 (1 Oct. 1961).

McIntyre, C. J. "Impact on New Media on College Instruction," *Journal of Higher Education* 34:84–91 (Feb. 1963).

McKown, Harry C., and Roberts, Alvin B. *Audio-Visual Aids to Instruction.* 2d ed. New York: McGraw-Hill, 1949.

Margolin, Joseph, and Mahoney, James F. "Analysis of the Need for and Feasibility of More Effective Distribution of Government-Supported Non-Written Materials," *ERIC Research in Education* (Dec. 1968) EP 011 381.

"Modern Art Film Library Corporation," *School and Society* 42:15 (6 July 1935).

Moriarty, John H. "New Media Facilities," *Library Trends* 16:251–58 (Oct. 1967).

Motley, Drucilla. "Old Wine, New Bottles," *Library Journal* 93:3932–33 (15 Oct. 1968).

National Conference on the Implications of the New Media for the Teaching of Library Science. Urbana: University of Illinois Graduate School of Library Science, 1963. 233p.

National Education Association. Commission on Definition and Terminology. *The Changing Role of the Audiovisual Process in Education: A Definition and a Glossary of Related Terms.* Los Angeles: The Association, 1963.

——. Department of Audiovisual Instruction. *Highlights of Schools Using Educational Media.* Washington, D.C.: The Association, 1967.

"National Film Library," *School and Society* 42:237–38 (17 Aug. 1935).

The New Media: Memo to Educational Planners. Paris: UNESCO, International Institute for Educational Planning, 1967.

New Teaching Aids for the American Classroom. Stanford, Calif.: Symposium on the State of Research in Instructional Television and Tutorial Machines, 1960.

Noble, Lorraine. "This Film Publishing Business," *ALA Bulletin* 30:967–73 (Dec. 1936).

Nolan, John L. "Audio-Visual Materials," *Library Trends* 10:261–72 (Oct. 1961).

Norton, E. S. "Authors on Tape," *School Libraries* 15:35–37 (Mar. 1966).

Oppenheim, Helen L. "Audio-Visual Material in the Cape Provincial Library Service," *South African Libraries* 24:35–38 (Oct. 1956).

Pringle, Eugene A. "Audiovisual Materials and College Objectives," *Choice* 3:1107–9 (Feb. 1967).

——, ed. "Films in Public Libraries," *Drexel Library Quarterly* 2:93–198 (Apr. 1966).

Quilter, D. *Do's and Don't's of Audio Lingual Teaching.* Waltham, Mass.; Ginn, 1966.

Ranganathan, S. R. "On Audio-Visual Materials," *Granthalaya* 1:10 (Oct. 1955).

Reid, Seerley; Carpenter, Anita; and Daugherty, Annie Rose. *Directory of 3660 16mm Film Libraries*. Washington, D.C.: U.S. Dept. of Health, Education and Welfare, 1958.

Ress, Etta Schneider. *The Use of Pictures to Enrich School Resources*. Mankato, Minn.: Creative Educational Society, Inc. 1953.

Reuter, Wolfgang. "Erste Diathek in Berlin [First Slide Circulation Library in Berlin]," *Bucherei und Bildung* 18:548–49 (Oct. 1966).

Richey, James Ivory. "Survey of Audio-Visual Materials in State College and University Libraries in the Southern Association of Secondary Schools and Colleges," M.S.L.S. thesis, Atlanta University, 1955. 58p.

Ristow, Walter William. "Emergence of Maps in Libraries," *Special Libraries* 43:400–19 (July 1967).

Rossi, Peter H., and Biddle, Bruce J. eds. *The New Media and Education*. Chicago: Aldine, 1966.

Rothrock, Mary U. "Libraries and Educational Films," *ALA Bulletin* 34:169–73 (Mar. 1940).

Rufsvold, Margaret I., and Guss, Carolyn. "Proceedings of a Work Conference on Bibliographic Control of Newer Media." Mimeographed. Bloomington: Indiana University, 1960.

———. "A Proposed Method for Establishing Bibliographic Control of the Newer Educational Media for the Purpose of Informing Teachers Concerning Available Materials and Their Education Utility." Mimeographed. Bloomington: Indiana University, 1960. 12p.

———. "Some Sources of Information about Newer Educational Media for Elementary and Secondary Schools (1950–1960). Mimeographed. Bloomington: Indiana University, 1960. 152p.

Saettler, Paul. *A History of Instructional Technology*. New York: McGraw-Hill, 1968.

Sands, Lester B. *Audio-Visual Procedures in Teaching*. New York: Ronald, 1956.

Schmid, Calvin F. *Handbook of Graphic Presentation*. New York: Ronald, 1956.

Scuorzo, Herbert E. *Practical Audio-Visual Handbook for Teachers*. West Nyack, N.Y.: Prentice-Hall, 1967.

Shane, M. L. "Audio-Visual Aids and the Library," *College and Research Libraries* 1:143–46 (Mar. 1940).

Sharp, H. A. "Some Further Uses of Gramophones in Public Libraries," *Library World* 25:297–99 (1922).

Shores, Louis. "Audio-Visual Dimensions for an Academic Library." *College and Research Libraries* 15:393–97 (Oct. 1954).

Slesinger, Donald. "Educational Motion Pictures and the Library," *ALA Bulletin* 34: P222–23 (Aug. 1940).

Snaith, Stanley. "The Gramophone in Public Libraries," *Library World* 31:6–9 (1928).

———. "Music and Gramophones in Public Libraries," *Library Assistant* 18:60–65 (1925).

Stolurow, Lawrence. *Teaching by Machine*. Washington, D.C.: U.S. Dept. of Health, Education and Welfare, 1961.

Stone, C. Walter, "Development of Professional Tools for the Materials Center," in M. H. Mahar, ed., *School Library as a Materials Center,* p.7–11. Washington, D.C.: U.S. Office of Education, 1963.

———, ed. "Library Uses of the New Media of Communication," *Library Trends* 16:179–299 (Oct. 1967).

———. "Place of Newer Media in the Undergraduate Program," *Library Quarterly* 24:368–73 (Oct. 1954).

Strob, Thomas F. *The Uses of Video Tape in Training and Development*. New York: American Management Assn., 1969. 59p.

Strobecker, E. C., ed. *Allies of Books, a Report of the Workshop in Audiovisual Media, July 1–12, 1963*. Louisville: Catherine Spalding College, 1964.

Tauber, Maurice F., and Lilley, Oliver L. "Feasibility Study Regarding the Establishment of an Educational Media Research Information Service." Mimeographed. New York: Columbia University, 1960. 235p.

———, and Stephens, Irene Roemer. *Conference on the Use of Printed and Audio-Visual Materials for Instructional Purposes*. New York: Columbia University, School of Library Service, 1966. 241p.

Taylor, Calvin W., and Williams, F. W., eds. *Instructional Media and Creativity*. New York: Wiley, 1966.

Taylor, Kenneth I. "Instructional Materials Centers and Programs," *North Central Association Quarterly* 40:214–21 (Fall 1965).

Torkelson, Gerald. "What Research Says to the Teacher, No. 14," *Education Media*. Washington, D.C.: National Education Assn., 1968.

A Treasure Chest of Audio-Visual Ideas. Plainville, Conn.: Kalart Co., Inc., n.d. 32p.

United States. *Code of Federal Regulations*. Title 22, pt. 502, *World-Wide Free Flow (Export-Import) of Audiovisual Materials*.

Weaver, Gilbert G., and Bollinger, Elroy W. *Visual Aids: Their Construction and Use*. New York: Van Nostrand, 1949.

Webster, Jean. "Exploring the Visual," *Library World* 35:253–54 (May 1933).

Wendt, Paul R. *Audio-Visual Instruction*. Washington, D.C.: National Education Assn., 1966.

Wiman, Raymond V., and Mierhenry, Wesley C., eds. *Educational Media: Theory into Practice*. Columbus, Ohio: Charles E. Merrill, 1969.

Wittich, Walter Arno, and Fowlkes, John Guy. *Audio-Visual Paths to Learning*. New York: Harper, 1952.

———, and Schuller, Charles I. *Audio-Visual Materials: Their Nature and Use,* 4th ed. New York: Harper, 1966.

Wolf, G., ed. *Encyclopedia Cinematographica*. Gottingen: Institut fur den Wissenschaftlichen Film, 1964.

Wright, C. W. "At Central Washington State College: All Services Under One Roof," *Audiovisual Instruction* 8:222–25 (Apr. 1963).

Wrigley, M. J. "The Film in Its Relation to the Library: A Neglected Educational Agency," *Library World* 23:625–31 (1921).

Manuals

American Library Association. Division of Cataloging and Classification. *ALA Cataloging Rules for Author and Title Entries*. 2d ed. Chicago: The Association, 1949. 265p.

———. Public Library Association. Audiovisual Committee. *Guidelines for Audiovisual Materials and Services for Public Libraries*. Chicago: The Association, 1970. 33p.

Anglo-American Cataloging Rules. North American Text. Chicago: American Library Assn., 1967. 400p.

Aslib. Film Production Librarians Group. Cataloguing Committee. *Film Cataloguing Rules*. London: The Association, 1963. 71p.

Baker, Hazel. "Manual for an Audio-Visual Program for High School Librarians in Ohio." M.A. thesis, Kent State University, 1962. 38p.

Boehm, Eric H. *Cue System for Bibliography and Indexing*. Santa Barbara, Calif.: American Bibliographical Center, Clio Press, 1967. 45p.

Bradley, Carol June. *Manual of Music Librarianship*. Ann Arbor, Mich.: Music Library Assn., 1966. 140p.

British Film Institute. *Rules for Use in the Cataloguing Department of the National Film Archives*. 5th rev. ed. London: The Institute, 1960. 46p.

Canadian Library Association. Committee on Canadian Subject Heading. *A List of Canadian Subject Headings*. Ottawa: The Association, 1968.

Clarke, Virginia. *Non-Book Library Materials*. Denton: North Texas State College, 1953. 154p.

Classification for Motion Picture Books. New York: Museum of Modern Art Library, 1963. 16p.

Coates, E. J. *The British Catalogue of Music Classification*. London: Council of the British National Bibliography, 1960. 56p.

Colvin, Laura C. *Cataloguing Sample; A Comparative and Interpretive Guide*. Hamden, Conn.: Archon Books, 1963. 368p.

Croghan, Antony. *Faceted Classification for and an Essay on the Literature of the Performing Arts*. London: The Author, 1968. 120p.

Darrow, Dorothy. *Handbook for the Organiza-*

tion and Administration of Non-book Materials in the Dade County Public Schools. Library Bulletin no.15B. Dade City, Fla.: Dade City Public Schools and School of Education, University of Miami, 1955.

DeKieffer, Robert E., and Cochran, Lee W. *Manual of Audio-Visual Techniques.* Englewood Cliffs, N.J.: Prentice-Hall, 1962. 254p.

Design for Cataloging Non-book Materials Adaptable to Computer Use. Rochester, N.Y.: Genesee Valley School Development Assn., n.d.

Devigne, Roger. "Le Documentation Sonore et la Phonotèque du Musée de la Parole de l'Université de Paris," in *World Congress of Universal Documentation, 1937. Communications,* p.82–84. Paris: The Congress, 1937.

Dewey, Melvil. *Dewey Decimal Classification and Relative Index.* 17th ed. Essex Co., N.Y.: Forest Press, 1965. 2v. 2153p.

Eaton, Thelma. *Cataloging and Classification, an Introductory Manual.* 4th ed. Ann Arbor, Mich.: Edwards Bros., 1967. 231p.

Eboch, Sidney C. *Operating Audio-Visual Equipment.* 2d ed. San Francisco: Chandler, 1968. 76p.

Diamond, Robert M. *The Development of a Retrieval System for 35mm Slides Utilized in Art and Humanities Instruction.* Fredonia, N.Y.: State University College, Instructional Resources Center, 1969. 86p.

Florida. University. Gainesville. School of Library Training and Service. *Cataloging and Classifying Audio-visual Materials,* prepared by Bessie M. Daughtry. Mimeographed. 1950.

Foster, Donald Leroy. *Notes Used on Music and Phonorecord Catalog Cards.* Urbana: University of Illinois Graduate School of Library Science, 1962. 37p.

Gambee, Budd L. *Non-book Materials as Library Resources.* Chapel Hill: University of North Carolina, 1967.

Gladhill, M. B., and Christanson, F. M. *Classification Schemes for Motion Picture Collections.* Hollywood, Calif.: Academy of Motion Picture Arts and Sciences Library, 1941.

Harris, Evelyn J. *Instructional Materials Cataloging Guide.* Tucson: University of Arizona College of Education, 1968.

Havard-Williams, P., and Karling, S. A. *Rules for the Cataloguing of Slides in the Liverpool School of Architecture.* Liverpool: [The School], 1962. 8p.

Hawken, William R. *Copying Methods Manual.* Chicago: Library Technology Program, American Library Assn., 1966.

Hicks, Warren B. and Tillin, Alma M. *Developing Multi-Media Libraries.* New York: Bowker, 1970. 199p.

————. *The Organization of Nonbook Materials in School Libraries.* Sacramento, Calif.: California State Dept. of Education, 1967. 71p.

Joint Committee on Music Cataloging. *Code for Cataloging Music and Phonorecords.* Chicago: American Library Assn., 1958. 88p.

Jones, Emily S. *Manual on Film Evaluation.* New York: Educational Film Library Assn., 1967. 32p.

Keen, Eunice. *Manual for Use in the Cataloging and Classification of Audio-Visual Materials for a High School Library.* Lakeland, Fla.: The Author, 1955. 35p.

Lebrun, C. "Proposition de Regles Catalographiques Internationales Concernant le Film Educatif," International Institute for Documentation, *Quarterly Communications* 3, no.2 (1936).

————. "Un Instrument de Documentation: le Film Educatif," International Federation for Documentation, *Transactions* 14:158–59 (1938).

Lubetsky, Seymour. *Principles of Cataloging.* Los Angeles: Institute of Library Research, University of California, 1969.

McFarland, Roger B., and Saheb-Ettaba, Caroline. *ANSCR: Alpha Numeric Scheme for Classification of Recordings.* Newark, N.J.: Bro-Dart, 1968.

Mannino, Phillip. *ABC's of Visual Aids and Projectionists Manual.* Rev. ed. New York: Educational Film Library Assn., 1948.

Manual for Cataloging and Storage on Non-

Book Materials. Winnipeg, Man.: Winnipeg School Division no.1, Library Service Centre, 1967.

Manual for Organizing Audiovisual Media. Raleigh, N.C.: State Dept. of Public Instruction, Division of Educational Media, 1968.

Manual for Processing Non-Book Materials in Schools Libraries, for Use in Course 531: Technical Services. Kalamazoo, Mich.: Western Michigan University Dept. of Librarianship, 1966.

Manual for Processing Non-Print Media. Rockville, Md.: Montgomery County Public Schools, n.d.

Manual for Treatment of Non-Book Materials in School Libraries. Fremont, Neb.: Midland College Library, 1959. 17p.

Marshall, Ralph Thomas. "Organization and Cataloging of Films, Filmstrips and Recordings," M.S.L.S. thesis. Western Reserve University, 1952. 39p.

Murphy, Mabel A. "Staff Manual Classification and Cataloging Recordings." Carbondale, Ill.: University of Southern Illinois Library, 1966. Additions to 1968.

Music Library Association. *Code for Cataloging Music and Phonorecords* prepared by a Joint Committee of the MLA and the ALA Division of Cataloging and Classification. Chicago: American Library Assn., 1958.

Oral Roberts University Library. "Cataloging Handbook." Tulsa, Okla.: The Library, [1967].

Piercy, Esther J. *Commonsense Cataloging: A Manual for the Organization of Books and Other Materials in School and Small Public Libraries.* New York: Wilson, 1965. 223p.

"PLS Catalog Rules for Non-Book Material." Santa Ana, Calif.: Professional Library Service, n.d.

Processing Manual for Books and Non-Book Materials. Glen Ellyn, Ill.: College of DuPage, Instructional Resources Center, 1970.

Riddle, Jean; Lewis, Shirley; and Macdonald, Janet. *Non-Book Materials: The Organization of Integrated Collections.* Preliminary ed. Ottawa: Canadian Library Assn., 1970. 58p.

Rufsvold, Margaret Irene. *Audio-Visual School Library Service: A Handbook for Libraries.* Chicago: American Library Assn., 1949. 116p.

Sanderson, Jessie Mae. *Non-Book Library Materials, a Cataloging Guide.* Livonia, Mich.: Livonia Public Schools, Dept. of Instructional Materials Services, 1965.

Scholz, Dell DuBose. *A Manual for the Cataloging of Recordings in Public Libraries.* Baton Rouge, La.: The Author, 1963. 42p.

Scott, Margaret B., and others. *Cataloging for School Libraries.* Rev. ed. Toronto: Univeristy of Toronto College of Education, 1967.

Sears, Minnie Earl. *List of Subject Headings.* 9th ed. New York: Wilson, 1965. 641p.

Simons, Wendell W., and Tansey, Luraine C. *A Slide Classification System for the Organization and Automatic Indexing of Interdisciplinary Collections of Slides and Pictures.* Santa Cruz: University of California, 1969. 263p.

Slocum, Robert B., and Hacker, Lois. *Sample Cataloging Forms.* 2d rev. ed. Metuchen, N.J.: Scarecrow, 1968.

Snow, Kathleen M. *Manual for Cataloguing Non-Book Materials.* Calgary, Alta.: University of Calgary Bookstore, 1968.

Steele, Robert. *The Cataloging and Classification of Cinema Literature.* Metuchen, N.J.: Scarecrow, 1967. 133p.

Strauss, L. Harry, and Kidd, J. R. *Look, Listen and Learn: A Manual on the Use of Audio-Visual Materials in Informal Education.* New York: Association Press, 1948.

Trainor, Beatrice. *The Canadian Film Institute: The Cataloging and Classification in Its Library and Information Service.* Ottawa: Canadian Library Assn., 1960. 52p.

United Nations Educational, Scientific and Cultural Organization. Department of Mass Communications. *International Rules for the Cataloguing of Educational, Scientific and Cultural Films and Film-*

strips on 3" x 5" Cards. Preliminary ed. Paris: UNESCO, 1956. 53p.

U.S. Library of Congress. *Library of Congress Catalog—Motion Pictures and Filmstrips.* Washington, D.C.: The Library, 1967.

———. *Library of Congress Catalog—Music and Phonorecords.* Detroit: Gale, 1965.

———. *Rules for Descriptive Cataloging in the Library of Congress-Phonorecords.* Preliminary ed. Washington, D.C.: The Library, 1952. 11p.

———. Descriptive Cataloging Division. *Rules for Descriptive Cataloging in the Library of Congress: Motion Pictures and Filmstrips.* Washington, D.C.: The Library, 1965. 20p.

———. ———. *Motion Pictures, Filmstrips, and Other Projected Images; a MARC Format.* Washington, D.C.: The Library, 1970.

———. ———. *Rules for Descriptive Cataloging in the Library of Congress.* Washington, D.C.: The Library, 1949. 141p.

———. Subject Cataloging Division. *Music Subject Headings Used on Printed Catalog Cards of the Library of Congress.* Washington, D.C.: The Library, 1952.

Wegg, Mary Freeman. "Manual for the Descriptive Cataloging of Music in the Denver Public Library." A.M. thesis, University of Denver, 1951. 62p.

Wei, H. R. *Classification of Slide Films and Motion Pictures.* New York: Carnegie Endowment for International Peace and Educational Film Library Assn., 1951. 18p.

Westhius, Judith, and DeYoung, Julia M. *Cataloging Manual for Nonbook Materials in Learning Centers and School Libraries.* Ann Arbor, Mich.: University of Michigan, 1967. 35p.

Wetmore, Rosamond Bayne. "A Guide to the Organization of Library Materials in Schools and Small Public Libraries." Muncie, Ind.: Ball State University Dept. of Library Science, 1967.

Wynar, Bohdan S. *Introduction to Cataloging and Classification.* 3d ed. Rochester, N.Y.: Libraries Unlimited, 1967. 306p.

Organization and Administration

Alonzo, P. G. "Conservation and Circulation in Map Libraries: A Brief Review." *SLA Geography and Map Division Bulletin* 74:15–8 (Dec. 1968).

American Library Association. Information Science and Automation Division. "Specifications for Library Print Train Graphics." Chicago: The Association, n.d.

———. Library Technology Project. *Testing and Evaluation of Record Players for Libraries; Report Based on a Study Conducted for the Project by Consumer's Research, Inc.* LTP Publication no.5 Chicago: The Association, 1962.

"Audio Services and Facilities, a Panel Discussion," in *Library Environment: Aspects of Interior Planning,* p.41–50. Chicago: American Library Assn., 1965.

Babcock, Julia G. "How to Handle Slides and Records," *Public Libraries* 24:377 (1924).

Bachman, John W. *How to Use Audiovisual Materials.* New York: Association Press, 1956.

Bennett, Fleming. "Audio-Visual Service in Colleges and Universities in the United States," *College and Research Libraries* 16:11–19 (Jan. 1955).

Blair, Patricia O. "Treatment, Storage, and Handling of Motion Picture Film," *Library Journal* 71:333–36 (1 Mar. 1946).

Brainard, Edith M. "The Use and Administration of Audio-Visual Materials in Colleges in the Pacific Northwest: Report of a Survey," *College and Research Libraries* 14:317–19 (July 1953).

Bryant, Eric Thomas. *Music Librarianship: A Practical Guide.* London: James Clarke, 1959. 503p.

Calhoun, John M. "Preservation of Motion-Picture Film," *American Archivist* 30:517–25 (July 1953).

"Care and Storage of Computer Tape," *Ampex Magnetic Tape Trends.* Bulletin no.12 (Jan. 1967).

A Centralized Processing System for School Libraries in New York State. New York: Arthur D. Little, 1967.

Christen, Fred. "New Tools for Film Libraries." *Audiovisual Instruction* 12:312–13 (Apr. 1967).

Christensen, Ruth. "The Junior College Library as an Audiovisual Center," *College and Research Libraries* 26:121–28 (Mar. 1965).

Clark, Tommy A. "Instructional Materials Center." M.L.S. thesis, University of Mississippi, 1966. 58p.

Collings, Wayne R. "Processing of Audio-Visual Materials in a College or a University Library." *MLA Quarterly* 9:76–77 (Dec. 1948).

Collison, Robert L. *The Treatment of Special Material in Libraries.* London: Aslib, 1957.

Cowan, Jean C. "The Care and Treatment of Long Playing Records in Public Libraries," *Librarian and Book World* 47:76–79 (Apr. 1958).

Day, Dorothy L. "Films in the Library," *Library Trends* 4:174–81 (Oct. 1955).

Dearden, Amy. "Phonograph Records in Public Libraries: A Survey of Current Practice." M.S.L.S. thesis, Drexel Institute of Technology, 1950. 51p.

Dent, Ellsworth C., *The Audio-Visual Handbook.* Chicago: Society for Visual Education, 1949.

Duckles, Vincent, ed. "Music Libraries and Librarianship," *Library Trends* 8:495–617 (Apr. 1960).

Dudley, Dorothy H., and Wilkinson, Irma Bexold. *Museum Registration Methods.* Washington, D.C.: American Assn. of Museums and the Smithsonian Institution, 1968. 294p.

Ehrenberg, R. "Map Acquisition, Arrangement, and Description at the National Archives," *SLA Geography and Map Division Bulletin* 68:10–13 (June 1967).

Ellis, Shirley. "Thousand Words about the Slide." *ALA Bulletin* 53:529–32 (June 1959).

Erickson, Carlton W. H. *Administering Audiovisual Services.* New York: Macmillan, 1959.

Farber, E. I. "A-V Materials Are Here to Stay but Not Necessarily in th Library," *Alabama Librarian* 6:5–11 (Oct. 1955).

Faris, Gene, and Moldstad, John. *Improving the Learning Environment: A Study on the Local Preparation of Visual Instructional Materials.* Washington, D.C.: U.S. Office of Education, 1963.

Feo, Luciano de. "Les Archives Cinematographiques," in *World Congress of Universal Documentation, 1937. Communications,* p.101–4. Paris: The Congress, 1937.

Frary, Mildred P. "Library As a Materials Center," *School Libraries* 3:10–11 (May 1954).

Fulton, William R. "Criteria Relating to Educational Media Programs in Colleges and Universities." Washington, D.C.: Dept. of Audiovisual Instruction, National Education Assn., n.d. 10p.

———. "Evaluative Checklist, an Instrument for Self-Evaluating an Educational Media Program in Colleges and Universities." Washington, D.C.: Dept. of Audiovisual Instruction, National Education Assn., n.d. 9p.

Giannotta, K. M. "Suggested Plan for Organizing and Administering Audio-visual Services within a School Library Materials Center (Grades 7–12)." M.S. and L.S. thesis, Southern Connecticut State College, 1965.

Gould, Geraldine N., and Wolfe, Ithmer C. *How to Organize and Maintain the Picture/Pamphlet File* Dobbs Ferry, N.Y.: Oceana Publications, 1968. 146p.

Greer, Margaret Rutledge. "Library and Its Care and Use of Films," *Wilson Library Bulletin* 13:383–87 (Fall 1939).

Grove, Pearce S., and Totten, Herman L. "Bibliographic Control of Media: The Librarian's Excedrin Headache," *Wilson Library Bulletin* 44:299–311 (Nov. 1969).

Hensel, Evelyn Mildred. "Treatment of Nonbook Materials," *Library Trends* 2:187–98 (Oct. 1953).

Hickok, Beverly. "Handling Visual Aid Material," *Special Libraries* 46:358–60 (Oct. 1955).

International Association of Music Libraries. *Phonograph Record Libraries, Their Organisation and Practise,* ed. by H. F. J.

Currall. Hamden, Conn.: Shoe String, 1963.

Ireland, Norma Olin. *The Picture File in School, College, and Public Libraries.* Rev. ed. Boston: Faxton, 1952.

Irvine, Betty Jo. "Slide Collections in Art Libraries," *College and Research Libraries* 30:443–45 (Sept. 1969).

Joyce, Marlin F. "Administrative Problems of Music Librarianship." Master's project, University of Illinois, Library Science 405, Jan. 1958.

Klein, Margaret A. "A Filing System for Visual Aids," *Educational Screen* 12:103–4, 128–29, 161–62 (Apr., May, June 1933).

Lee, Anna Louise. "Organization and Administration of Audio-Visual Materials in a Selected Group of High School Libraries." M.S.L.S. thesis, Atlanta University, 1955. 57p.

Lee, R. E. "Library as the Center of the Audiovisual Program." M.A. thesis, Kent State University, 1951. 117p.

Lowrie, Jean E. "Organization and Operation of School Library Materials Centers," *Library Trends* 16:211–27 (Oct. 1967).

Lyman, E. L. "Arrangement and Care of Phonograph Records," *Library Journal* 62-544–46 (July 1951).

McDonald, Gerald Doan. *Education Motion Pictures and Libraries.* Chicago: American Library Assn., 1942. 183p.

McMurry, Glenn D. "Film Library Uses for the Computer," *Audiovisual Instruction* 12:314–20 (Apr. 1967).

March, Ivan. *Running a Record Library.* Blackpool, Eng.: Long Playing Record Library, 1965.

Marco, Guy A., and Roziewski, Walter M. "Shelving Plans for Long-Playing Records," *Library Journal* 84:1568–69 (15 May 1959).

Mitchell, Richard S. "Relationship of a College Audiovisual Center to the Library," *Minnesota Libraries* 17:175–77 (June 1953).

Mitra, D. K. "Maps in Libraries, Their Storage and Preservation," *Herald Library Science* 7:27–32 (Jan. 1968).

Morphet, Edgar, and Jessar, David L., eds. *Planning for Effective Utilization of Technology in Education.* New York: Citation, 1968.

Murphy, Mabel A. "Steps Leading to Decisions Concerning Policies, Organization, Procedures, Routines, and Service Related to Phono Discs and Listening Facilities at Southern Illinois University, Edwardsville." 1964.

Pearson, Mary D. *Recordings in the Public Library.* Chicago: American Library Assn., 1963. 153p.

Peskind, Ira J. "Organization of an Audio-Visual Unit in a Junior College Library," *College and Research Libraries.* 12:62–66 (Jan. 1951).

Pickett, A. G., and Lemcoe, M. M. *Preservation and Storage of Sound Recordings.* Washington, D.C.: U.S. Library of Congress, 1959. 74p.

Pressler, Joan. "Organizing Library-Based AV Materials," *School Libraries* 14:43–47 (Mar. 1965).

Rakestraw, Boyd B. "The Library as a Cooperating Unit in Film Distribution," *ALA Bulletin* 33:216–18 (15 Oct. 1939).

Redfern, Brian. *Organizing Music in Libraries.* New York: Philosophical Library, 1966. 80p.

Saunders, Helen E. *Modern School Library: Its Administration as a Materials Center.* Metuchen, N.J.: Scarecrow, 1968.

Smith, Nicholas N. "Film Care," *Bookmark* 27:231–32 (Mar. 1968).

Smith, Sidney B. "Simplified Procedures for Recordings," *Library Journal.* 69:211–12 (Mar. 1944).

"Springfield Lends Phonograph Records," *Library Journal* 58:86–87 (15 Jan. 1933).

Sragow, J. L. "Organization of the Recordings Collection of a Medium-sized County Public Library System," MS. in L.S. thesis, Catholic University, 1962. 77p.

Stevenson, Grace T. "Library Use of Films; the Film Today: A Basic Library Service." *ALA Bulletin* 50:211–24 (Apr. 1956).

Stone, C. Walter. "Listening Facilities in the Library," in *Library Environment: Aspects of Interior Planning,* p.34–40. Chicago: American Library Assn., 1965.

Stripling, E. M. "Technical Organization of Film and Visual Materials in College and

University Libraries," M.S. thesis, Columbia University, 1951. 115p.

Waygood, A. N. "Hints on Storing Non-print Materials," *Index: A Quarterly for School and Public Librarians* (Toronto) 1:24–25 (Spring 1968).

White, Brenda. *Slide Collections: A Survey of Their Organization in Libraries in the Field of Architecture, Building, and Planning.* London: Library Assn., 1967.

Yesner, Bernice L. *Administering Filmstrip and Record Collections.* New York: McGraw-Hill 1968.

Periodicals

American Record Guide. New York, 1934– .

Audio. Philadelphia: North American Publishing Co., 1917– .

Audio Cardalog. Larchmont, N.Y.: Max V. Bildersee, 1958– .

Audio Visual Communication Review. Washington, D.C.: Association for Educational Communications and Technology, 1953– .

Audio-Visual Communications. New York: United Business Publications, 1961– .

Audiovisual Instruction. Washington, D.C.: Association for Educational Communications and Technology, 1956– .

Audio-Visual Media/Moyens Audio-Visuals. Elmsford, N.Y.: International Council for the Advancement of Audio-Visual Media in Education, 1967– .

The Booklist. Chicago: American Library Assn., 1905– .

Cine World. Toronto: K. Godzinski, 1964– .

Dial-Access Information Retrieval and System for Education Newsletter. Westminster, Calif.: Slate Services, 1965– .

Education Summary. New London, Conn.: Croft Educational Services, 1947– .

Educational Broadcasting Review. Columbus, Ohio: National Assn. of Educational Broadcasters, 1941– .

Educational Development. Sheffield, Eng.: Educational Development Assn., 1946– .

Educational/Instructional Broadcasting. Los Angeles, 1968– .

Educational Media (Canada). Toronto: Educational Media Assn. of Canada, 1965–

Educational Product Report. New York: Educational Products Information Exchange, 1967.

Educational Screen and Audio-Visual Guide Magazine. Chicago: H. S. Gilette, 1922– .

Educational Technology. Englewood Cliffs, N.J.: Educational Technology Publications, 1961– .

Educational Television International. Elmsford, N.Y.: Pergamon, 1967– .

Educators Guide to Media and Methods. New York: Frank McLaughlin, 1966– .

Eight MM Magazine. London: Haymarket Press, 1962– .

ETV Newsletter. Ridgefield, Conn.: ETV Newsletter Co., 1967– .

Film Bild Ton; Zeitschrift fuer audio-visuelle Mittel in der Padagogik. Munich: Institut fuer Film and Bild in Wissenschaft und Unterricht Muenchen, 1951– .

Film Library Quarterly. Greenwich, Conn.: Film Library Information Council, 1967– .

Film News; the international review of AV materials and equipment. New York, 1939– .

Film World and A-V World News. Los Angeles: Sidale Publishing Co., 1945– .

High Fidelity/ Musical America. New York: Billboard Publishing, 1965– .

Illinois Libraries. (See audiovisual issues.) Springfield: Illinois State Library, 1919– .

Journal of Communication. Flint, Mich.: National Society for the Study of Communication, 1950– .

Journal of Educational Technology. London: National Council for Educational Technology, 1970– .

Journal of Programmed Instruction. West Nyack, N.Y., 1962– .

Library Resources and Technical Services. Chicago: American Library Assn., 1957– .

Music Library Association, Notes. Ann Arbor, Mich.: Music Library Assn., 1943– .

New University and New Education. London: New Education, Ltd., 1964– .

NSPI Journal. San Antonio, Tex.: National

Society for Programmed Instruction, 1962– .

Phonolog Tape Parade. Los Angeles: Phonolog Publishing Co., 1964–67.

Picture Scope. New York: Special Libraries Assn., Picture Division, 1953– .

Programmed Learning and Educational Technology. London: Sweet and Maxwell, 1964– .

Progressive Teacher. Morristown, Tenn., 1894– .

Screen Education News. Chelmsford, Mass., Filmboard, 1968– .

Sehen und Hoeren/See and Listen; Beitrage zur Paedagogik der audio-visuellen Bildungsmittel. Vienna: Hauptselle fuer Lichtbild und Bildungsfilm, 1962– .

Sight and Sound; a Review of Modern Aids to Learning. London: British Film Institute, 1932– .

Sightlines. New York: Educational Film Library Assn., 1967– .

SMPTE Journal. New York: Society of Motion Picture and Television Engineers, 1916– .

University Film Association Journal. Columbus, Ohio, 1949– .

Visual Education. London: National Committee for Audio-Visual Aids in Education, 1950– .

Selection and Acquisition

The Audio-Visual Equipment Directory. Evanston, Ill.: National Audio-Visual Assn., 1953– .

Audio Visual Market Place. New York: Bowker, 1969– .

"Audiovisual Selection Aids," *Wisconsin Library Bulletin* 62:180–81 (May 1966).

Billings, Jane Kelley. "Selecting for the Instructional Materials Center," *Wisconsin Library Bulletin* 64:9–12 (Jan. 1968).

Brubaker, Mildred J. "A & P of AV Materials," *Illinois Libraries* 49:129–40 (Fall 1967).

Clark, Joan E. "Selection and Presentation of Films and Film Programs for Adults; with List of Suggested Film Programs," *Bookmark* 27:159–63 (Jan. 1968).

Conference on the Use of Printed and Audiovisual Materials for Instructional Pur-

poses: Final Report. New York Columbia University School of Library Science, 1966. 241p.

Cox, Carl T. "Filmstrips: Selection, Evaluation, Cataloging, Processing," *Wilson Library Bulletin* 38:178–82 (Oct. 1963).

Daily, Jay E. "The Selection, Processing, and Storage of Non-print Materials: A Critique of the Anglo-American Cataloging Rules as They Relate to the Newer Media," *Library Trends* 16:283–89 (Oct. 1967).

Davis, Chester K. "Record Collections, 1960: *Library Journal* 85:3375–80 (1 Oct. 1960).

Dewey, Melvil. "Library Pictures," *Public Libraries* 11:10–11 (1906).

Dugan, James M., and others. *Guide to Audio-Visual Presentations.* New York: Wolf Business Publications (pub. for Battelle Memorial Institute), 1963. 149p.

Dunnetski, Stanley F. "Principles of Film Evaluation for Public Libraries," *Illinois Library* 49:89–92 (Feb. 1967).

Educational Film Library Association. *Film Evaluation Guide,* 1946–64. [NewYork]: The Association, [1965] 528p.

Educational Foundation for Visual Aids, London. Equipment Department. *Equipment for Audio-Visual Aids.* London: The Foundation, 1968. 27p.

The Elementary School Library Collection; Phases 1-2-3. General ed., Mary V. Gaver. 3rd ed. Newark, N.J.: Bro-Dart, 1967. 1210p.

"Film Mecca: Tenth Annual American Film Festival," *Library Journal* 93:3216–17 (15 Sept. 1968).

"Film Selection Policy of Special Service Film Library," *Bookmark* 25:203–6 (May 1966).

Golej, Peter. "Selection of Instructional Films for Schools," *Michigan Association of School Librarians* 13:1–5 (Winter 1964).

Hodges, E. D. "Selecting Materials to Support the Curriculum," *Childhood Education* 43:69–72 (Oct. 1966).

Jennings, P. M. *Audio-Visual Aids: A Classical Catalogue.* London: Centaur Books, 1966. 70p.

Lieberman, Irving. "Reference Service and

Audiovisual Materials: Recommended Books, Pamphlets and Periodicals for a Library and Audiovisual Materials Information Collections as Well as Tools for Selection of Material," in *National Conference on the Implications of the New Media for the Teaching of Library Science,* p.164–78. Urbana: University of Illinois Graduate School of Library Science, 1963.

Limbacher, James L. "Film Evaluation and Criticism," *Illinois Libraries* 46:121–25 (Feb. 1964).

Pula, Fred John. *Application and Operation of Audio-Visual Equipment in Education.* New York: Wiley, 1968. 360p.

Quinly, William J. "Selection, Processing, and Storage of Non-print Materials: Aids, Indexes, and Guidelines," *Library Trends* 16:274–82. (Oct. 1967).

Simons, Wendell W. "Choosing Audio-Visual Equipment." *Library Trends* 13:503–16 Apr. 1965).

Smith, Emily G., ed. *Records in Review.* New York: Taplinger, annual.

Supplement Film Evaluation Guide, 1968. New York: Educational Film Library Assn., 1968.

Thomas, Robert Murray, and Swartout, S. G. *Integrated Teaching Materials: How to Choose, Create, and Use Them.* Rev. and enl. New York: McKay, 1963. 559p.

Whitenack, Carolyn I. "New Resources for the School Library Materials Centers," in Illinois University Graduate School of Library Science, *School Library Materials Center; Its Resources and Their Utilization,* p.12–26. Urbana: Illini, 1964.

Wohlford, M. K. "Study of Record Collections in Public Libraries of the United States and Canada." M.A. thesis, Kent State University, 1951. 60p.

Standards

American Library Association. American Association of State Libraries. Survey and Standards Committee. *Standards for Library Functions at the State Level.* Chicago: The Association, 1963. 37p.

———. Association of College and Research Libraries. Audio-Visual Committee. *Guidelines for Audiovisual Services in Academic Libraries.* Chicago: The Association, 1968.

———. Association of Hospital and Institution Libraries. Hospital Library Standards Committee. *Standards for Library Services in Health Care Institutions.* Chicago: The Association, 1970.

———. Library Administration Division. *Standards for Library Services for the Blind and Visually Handicapped.* Chicago: The Association, 1967.

———. Public Library Association. Audio Visual Standards Committee. "Recommendations for Standards for Audio Visual Services in Public Library System." Mimeographed. Chicago: The Association, 1969.

———. ———. Audiovisual Committee. *Guidelines for Audiovisual Materials and Services for Public Libraries.* Chicago: The Association, 1970. 33p.

———. ———. Standards Committee. *Minimum Standards for Public Library Systems, 1966.* Chicago: The Association, 1967. 69p.

———. Resources and Technical Services Division. Copying Methods Section. *Microfilm Norms: Recommended Standards for Libraries.* Chicago: The Association, 1967. 48p.

American National Standards Institute. *Catalog 1970.* New York: The Institute, 1970.

ANSI Reporter. New York: American National Standards Institute, 1966– .

ANSI Standards Action. New York: American National Standards Institute, 1970– .

Borson, Robert. "Standardization," *Sweden Now* 3:39–40 (Mar. 1969).

International Federation of Library Associations. *The International Standardisation of Library Statistics:* A Progress Report. London: The Federation, 1968. 216p.

"ISO Recommendations," Publications of the International Organization for Standardization available from the Standard Institute. American National Standards Institute, *Catalog 1970.* New York: The Institute, 1970. 81p.

Joint Committee of the American Association of School Librarians and the Department of Audiovisual Instruction of the National Education Association. *Standards for School Media Programs.* Chicago: American Library Assn., 1969. 66p.

Meierhenry, Wesley C. "National Media Standards for Learning and Teaching," *ALA Bulletin* 63:238–41 (Feb. 1969).

Michigan Community and Junior College Library Administrators. Audiovisual Standards Committee. "Criteria Relating to Educational Media Programs in Junior Colleges." n.d. 12p.

National Education Association. Department of Audiovisual Instruction. *Quantitative Standards for Audiovisual Personnel, Equipment and Materials in Elementary, Secondary and Higher Education.* Washington: The Association, 1966.

———. ———. *Standards for Cataloging, Coding, and Scheduling Educational Media.* Washington, D.C.: The Association, 1968. 50p.

National Fire Protection Association. *Standard for the Storage and Handling of Cellulose Nitrate Motion Picture Film.*

Boston: The Association, 1967. 38p.

"The PH7 Committee," *Audiovisual Instruction* 15:70–71 (Jan. 1970).

Plunkett, Dalton G., and Quick, Allan D. *Cataloging Standards for Non-book Materials.* Tigard, Ore.: Northwest Library Service, 1968. 54p.

"Quantitative Standards for Audiovisual Programs," *Audiovisual Instruction* 10:462 (July 1965).

Sherman, Mendel, and Faris, Gene. "Standards and Evaluative Instruments for Audiovisual Programs," *School Libraries* 15:25–29 (May 1966).

Standards for Cataloging Nonprint Materials. Rev. ed. Washington, D.C.: Assn. for Educational Communications and Technology, 1971. 56p.

Troutman, Joan C. "Standards for Cataloging of Magnetic Tape Material," in *Final Report on Mechanized Information in the University Library Phase I—Planning,* p.1–34. Los Angeles: University of California, Institute of Library Research, 1967.

Index